# HUMAN RESOURCE MANAGEMENT

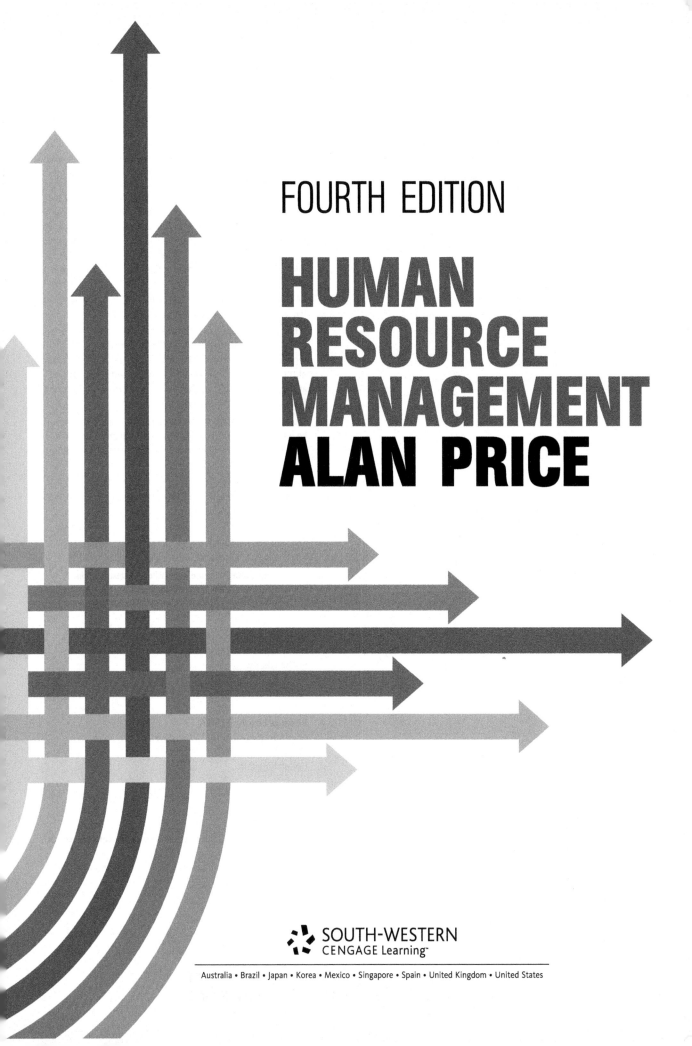

FOURTH EDITION

# HUMAN RESOURCE MANAGEMENT
# ALAN PRICE

SOUTH-WESTERN
CENGAGE Learning

Australia • Brazil • Japan • Korea • Mexico • Singapore • Spain • United Kingdom • United States

**SOUTH-WESTERN**
CENGAGE Learning™

**Human Resource Management**
**Fourth Edition**

Alan Price

For product information and technology assistance, contact **emea.info@cengage.com**.

For permission to use material from this text or product, and for permission queries, email **emea.permissions@cengage.com**.

*British Library Cataloguing-in-Publication Data*
A catalogue record for this book is available from the British Library.

ISBN: 978-1-4737-2835-6

**Cengage Learning EMEA**
Cheriton House, North Way, Andover,
Hampshire, SP10 5BE
United Kingdom

Cengage Learning products are represented in Canada by Nelson Education Ltd.

For your lifelong learning solutions, visit **www.cengage.co.uk**

Purchase your next print book, e-book or e-chapter at **www. cengagebrain.com**

Printed in the UK by Lightning Source
Print Number 01 Print Year 2015

# BRIEF CONTENTS

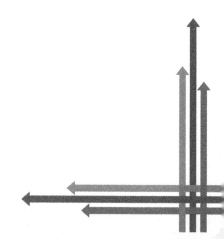

# CONTENTS

## PART ONE
## INTRODUCTION TO HRM 1

## PART TWO
## HRM AND THE BUSINESS ENVIRONMENT 75

# PART FOUR
## STRATEGIC HRM   261

# PART FIVE
## TALENT MANAGEMENT   343

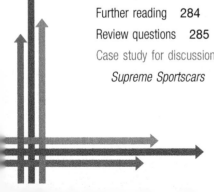

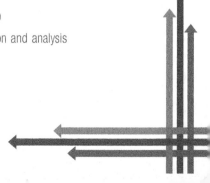

**PART SIX**
EMPLOYEE RELATIONS 483

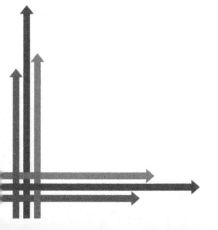

# LIST OF FIGURES

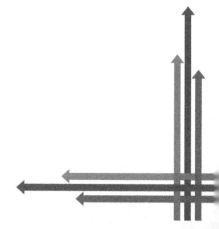

# LIST OF TABLES

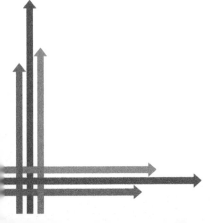

# LIST OF CASES STUDIES

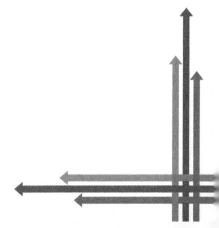

# ACKNOWLEDGEMENTS

My thanks are due to past colleagues, students and website contributors from many countries who helped me develop and test the contents of this book. I am indebted also to the many people at Cengage Learning, S4 Carlisle, India, Design Deluxe and others for their professionalism in producing the final book.

## REVIEWER ACKNOWLEDGEMENTS

Cengage Learning would like to thank the following academics for their valuable suggestions:

Amanda Shantz, Kingston University

Louise Preget, Bournemouth University

Nicolina Kamenou, Heriot-Watt University

Titus Oshagbemi, Queens University, Belfast

Vaughan Ellis, Glasgow Caledonian University

Pam Yeow, University of Kent

Chris Rowley, Cass Business School

The publisher also thanks the various copyright holders for granting permission to reproduce their material throughout the text. Every effort has been made to trace all copyright holders, but if any issues remain outstanding the publisher will be pleased to make the necessary arrangements at the first opportunity. Please contact the publisher directly.

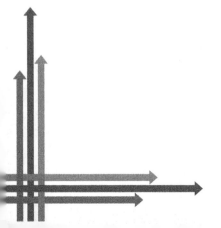

This book is intended to provide a comprehensive account of the critical issues in human resource management (HRM), taking the reader from an introductory level to a relatively sophisticated understanding of an increasingly important topic. The fourth edition of the book has been significantly streamlined and updated to take account of the recent recession in western economies, the significance of fast-developing countries such as China and India, and the increasing importance of HRM in the public, non-profit and voluntary sectors.

We will see that there is no universal agreement on the meaning of HRM. In fact, there are varying and contradictory models. Yet they embody common elements that distinguish them from previous approaches to managing people – specifically, personnel management.

The book takes a distinctive approach, locating the subject of human resource management and its various perspectives within a wider international context. We recognize that readers will come from a variety of backgrounds, that some will become HR specialists, but that many are interested in the relationship between human resource management and other organizational functions – business, public or voluntary sector. This is not a 'cookbook' of best practices: it is firmly focused on human resource management in the real world. Accordingly, we set out to understand the role and meaning of HRM from a number of practical and theoretical perspectives.

## FRAMEWORK FOR THE BOOK

The material in this text has a systematic framework with which we explore the complexities involved in managing people at work. There are four levels of discussion: environmental, organizational, strategic and operational. At the environmental level we see that the activities of people managers are constrained by a number of factors. For example:

→ Global and national economic activity, affecting organizational growth and funding and subsequently the balance between demand and availability of employees.

→ The actions of government and supranational structures such as the European Union (EU).

→ Legislation on a wide range of employment issues, including hours, diversity, working conditions, minimum pay, redundancy rights, consultation and so on.

→ Competing demands from stakeholders such as customers, service users, trade unions, shareholders, funding bodies, regulators and senior managers.

At the organizational level, the dimensions of size, structure and culture constrain and sometimes determine the way in which HRM takes place. Organizations range from one-person 'start-ups' to transnationals employing hundreds of thousands of people. As a consequence, HRM can vary from simply managing individuals at a very human level to the strategic and logistical issues involved in controlling vast numbers. Not surprisingly, HRM in small organizations tends to be commonsensical, with an emphasis on solving day-to-day problems. People management is a natural part of the owner or manager's role, along with finance, production, marketing, customer service and everything else.

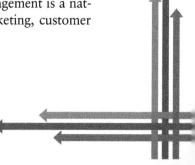

By contrast, large organizations require a more sophisticated and structured human resource function. Even where the notion of HRM as an integrated approach has been adopted as a strategy, with operational responsibility delegated to line managers, there is likely to be a major role for a specialist HR function. Such a function may be focused on coordination with operational activities such as resourcing, counselling, employee relations, communications and training/development provided on an in-house or external consultancy basis.

The next level – strategic decision making – is particularly relevant for this topic since HRM is often viewed as a strategic alternative to traditional personnel management. Employees are a major cost to organizations of any size. Hence decisions about employee requirements are strategic issues with important consequences for the profitability and growth of organizations.

The final (operational) level encompasses the activities of people managers, including recruitment and selection procedures, performance assessment, training and development, and employee relations. Increasingly, these aspects may be outsourced to external providers or delivered through modern web technologies. In this volume we see that they are individually important but also form part of a much wider approach to managing people.

## LEARNING FEATURES

The book includes a number of features to help students make the most of this text as a key element in their learning experience:

→ *Learning objectives* – the main learning outcomes that a student should aim to achieve from each chapter.

→ *Key concepts* – highlighted concepts of considerable significance in understanding HRM and related topics.

→ *HRM in reality* – boxed articles relating the topic under discussion to human resource management in the real world. This new edition includes over a hundred new articles, each with a discussion question.

→ *Tables and figures* – providing detailed information and graphical representation of major concepts.

→ *Chapter summaries* – brief outlines of the content and main points in each chapter.

→ *Further reading* – suggested articles and books providing greater depth and alternative perspectives on chapter topics.

→ *Review questions* – to check understanding of the principal issues raised in every chapter.

→ *Case studies for discussion and analysis* – provided at the end of each chapter, designed to stimulate critical analysis, discussion and reflection on the issues raised.

→ *Glossary* – alphabetical list of key terms used in the book with succinct explanations for easy reference.

## PLAN OF THE BOOK

The book is divided into six parts, each composed of a number of related chapters, and a conclusion. Part One addresses the development and scope of HRM as a philosophy of people management, critically examining the claim that it is a coherent and integrated approach to managing

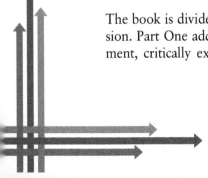

people. It also addresses the link between HRM and 'high-performance' or 'high-commitment' management, and the effects of new technology on its practice.

The chapters in Parts Two–Four take us through the environmental, organizational and strategic levels, also covering the employment market, human resource planning, organizational change and the nature of resourcing decisions in some detail. The remainder of the book, Parts Five and Six, addresses the key activity areas, including recruitment and selection, the management of diversity, performance management, reward management, human resource development and employee relations.

Each chapter includes a number of boxed articles designed to illustrate particular themes within a real-life context. The flavour of reality is emphasized throughout the book with references to contemporary issues in the media and debate in academic journals. HRM really happens out there – even if it is labelled as 'economics', 'labour' or 'industrial relations'.

## RELATED WEBSITES

This text benefits from companion websites:

→  www.cengagelearning.co.uk/price4 includes additional questions and case studies for students and PowerPoint™ slides and an instructor's manual for lecturers.

→  Sites in HRM Guide Network (http://www.hrmguide.net) – one of the largest and most comprehensive sources of human resource management information available on the Internet. HRM Guide is international in its scope with separate sections for a number of countries, including Australia, Canada, New Zealand, the United Kingdom and the United States of America. This is regularly updated with new articles and also provides direct links to human resource journals, societies, associations and business organizations throughout the world.

Alan Price, November 2010

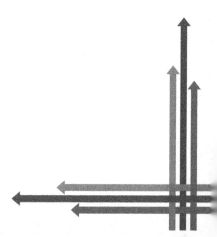

# WALK-THROUGH TOUR

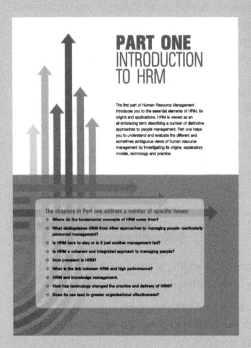

Part opener **Each part of the book has an opening section summarizing the content and structure of the following chapters, and also listing key issues addressed in the part.**

Chapter opener **Every chapter opens with a list of learning objectives that you should have acquired after studying the chapter, and also an outline of the chapter content.**

HRM in reality boxes **HRM concepts are brought to life in every chapter with real recent examples of HRM practice from all around the world.**

In-text boxes **Provide practical explanations of key ideas, issues and legislation.**

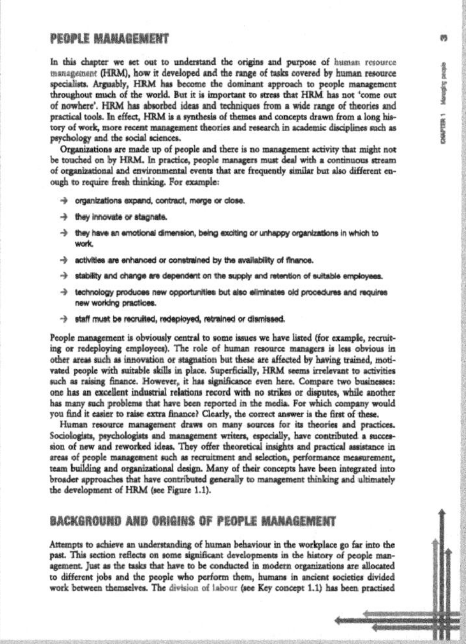

PEOPLE MANAGEMENT

In this chapter we set out to understand the origins and purpose of human resource management (HRM), how it developed and the range of tasks covered by human resource specialists. Arguably, HRM has become the dominant approach to people management throughout much of the world. But it is important to stress that HRM has not 'come out of nowhere'. HRM has absorbed ideas and techniques from a wide range of theories and practical tools. In effect, HRM is a synthesis of themes and concepts drawn from a long history of work, more recent management theories and research in academic disciplines such as psychology and the social sciences.

Organizations are made up of people and there is no management activity that might not be touched on by HRM. In practice, people managers must deal with a continuous stream of organizational and environmental events that are frequently similar but also different enough to require fresh thinking. For example:

- → organizations expand, contract, merge or close.
- → they innovate or stagnate.
- → they have an emotional dimension, being exciting or unhappy organizations in which to work.
- → activities are enhanced or constrained by the availability of finance.
- → stability and change are dependent on the supply and retention of suitable employees.
- → technology produces new opportunities but also eliminates old procedures and requires new working practices.
- → staff must be recruited, redeployed, retrained or dismissed.

People management is obviously central to some issues we have listed (for example, recruiting or redeploying employees). The role of human resource managers is less obvious in other areas such as innovation or stagnation but these are affected by having trained, motivated people with suitable skills in place. Superficially, HRM seems irrelevant to activities such as raising finance. However, it has significance even here. Compare two businesses: one has an excellent industrial relations record with no strikes or disputes, while another has many such problems that have been reported in the media. For which company would you find it easier to raise extra finance? Clearly, the correct answer is the first of these.

Human resource management draws on many sources for its theories and practices. Sociologists, psychologists and management writers, especially, have contributed a succession of new and reworked ideas. They offer theoretical insights and practical assistance in areas of people management such as recruitment and selection, performance measurement, team building and organizational design. Many of their concepts have been integrated into broader approaches that have contributed generally to management thinking and ultimately the development of HRM (see Figure 1.1).

BACKGROUND AND ORIGINS OF PEOPLE MANAGEMENT

Attempts to achieve an understanding of human behaviour in the workplace go far into the past. This section reflects on some significant developments in the history of people management. Just as the tasks that have to be conducted in modern organizations are allocated to different jobs and the people who perform them, humans in ancient societies divided work between themselves. The division of labour (see Key concept 1.1) has been practised

CHAPTER 1 Managing people 3

**Glossary terms** Key terms are highlighted where they first appear in the text and defined at the back of the book.

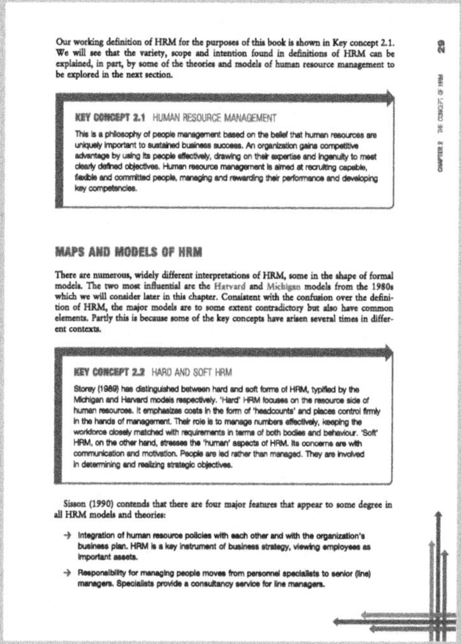

Our working definition of HRM for the purposes of this book is shown in Key concept 2.1. We will see that the variety, scope and intention found in definitions of HRM can be explained, in part, by some of the theories and models of human resource management to be explored in the next section.

KEY CONCEPT 2.1 HUMAN RESOURCE MANAGEMENT

This is a philosophy of people management based on the belief that human resources are uniquely important to sustained business success. An organization gains competitive advantage by using its people effectively, drawing on their expertise and ingenuity to meet clearly defined objectives. Human resource management is aimed at recruiting capable, flexible and committed people, managing and rewarding their performance and developing key competencies.

MAPS AND MODELS OF HRM

There are numerous, widely different interpretations of HRM, some in the shape of formal models. The two most influential are the Harvard and Michigan models from the 1980s which we will consider later in this chapter. Consistent with the confusion over the definition of HRM, the major models are to some extent contradictory but also have common elements. Partly this is because some of the key concepts have arisen several times in different contexts.

KEY CONCEPT 2.2 HARD AND SOFT HRM

Storey (1989) has distinguished between hard and soft forms of HRM, typified by the Michigan and Harvard models respectively. 'Hard' HRM focuses on the resource side of human resources. It emphasizes costs in the form of 'headcounts' and places control firmly in the hands of management. Their role is to manage numbers effectively, keeping the workforce closely matched with requirements in terms of both bodies and behaviour. 'Soft' HRM, on the other hand, stresses the 'human' aspects of HRM. Its concerns are with communication and motivation. People are led rather than managed. They are involved in determining and realizing strategic objectives.

Sisson (1990) contends that there are four major features that appear to some degree in all HRM models and theories:

- → Integration of human resource policies with each other and with the organization's business plan. HRM is a key instrument of business strategy, viewing employees as important assets.
- → Responsibility for managing people moves from personnel specialists to senior (line) managers. Specialists provide a consultancy service for line managers.

CHAPTER 2 THE CONCEPT OF HRM 29

**Key concepts** Essential HRM terminology is simply and concisely explained at relevant points in every chapter.

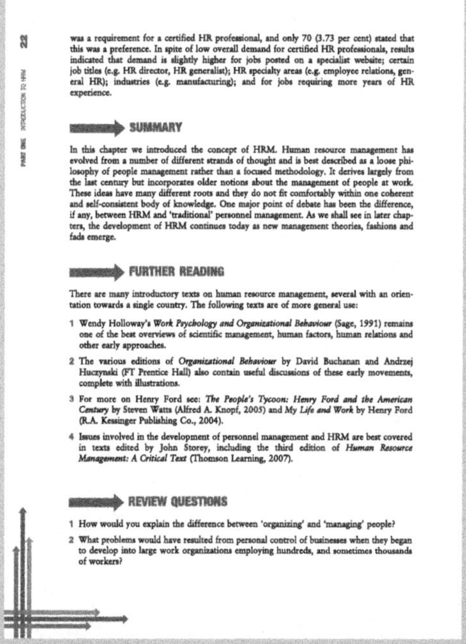

PART ONE INTRODUCTION TO HRM 22

was a requirement for a certified HR professional, and only 70 (3.73 per cent) stated that this was a preference. In spite of low overall demand for certified HR professionals, results indicated that demand is slightly higher for jobs posted on a specialist website; certain job titles (e.g. HR director, HR generalist); HR specialty areas (e.g. employee relations, general HR); industries (e.g. manufacturing); and for jobs requiring more years of HR experience.

SUMMARY

In this chapter we introduced the concept of HRM. Human resource management has evolved from a number of different strands of thought and is best described as a loose philosophy of people management rather than a focused methodology. It derives largely from the last century but incorporates older notions about the management of people at work. These ideas have many different roots and they do not fit comfortably within one coherent and self-consistent body of knowledge. One major point of debate has been the difference, if any, between HRM and 'traditional' personnel management. As we shall see in later chapters, the development of HRM continues today as new management theories, fashions and fads emerge.

FURTHER READING

There are many introductory texts on human resource management, several with an orientation towards a single country. The following texts are of more general use:

1 Wendy Holloway's *Work Psychology and Organizational Behaviour* (Sage, 1991) remains one of the best overviews of scientific management, human factors, human relations and other early approaches.
2 The various editions of *Organizational Behaviour* by David Buchanan and Andrzej Huczynski (FT Prentice Hall) also contain useful discussions of these early movements, complete with illustrations.
3 For more on Henry Ford see: *The People's Tycoon: Henry Ford and the American Century* by Steven Watts (Alfred A. Knopf, 2005) and *My Life and Work* by Henry Ford (R.A. Kessinger Publishing Co., 2004).
4 Issues involved in the development of personnel management and HRM are best covered in texts edited by John Storey, including the third edition of *Human Resource Management: A Critical Text* (Thomson Learning, 2007).

REVIEW QUESTIONS

1 How would you explain the difference between 'organizing' and 'managing' people?
2 What problems would have resulted from personal control of businesses when they began to develop into large work organizations employing hundreds, and sometimes thousands of workers?

**Summary, further reading and review questions** Each chapter concludes with a brief review of the chapter content, a list of related reading material, and a set of questions to test your understanding of the chapter.

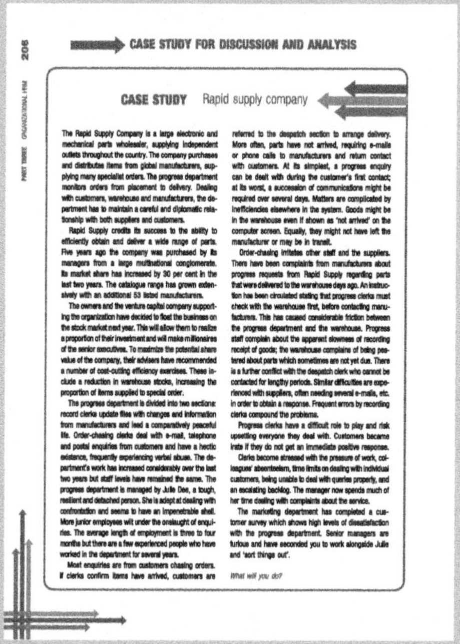

PART THREE ORGANIZATIONAL HRM 208

CASE STUDY FOR DISCUSSION AND ANALYSIS

CASE STUDY Rapid supply company

The Rapid Supply Company is a large electronic and mechanical parts wholesaler, supplying independent outlets throughout the country. The company purchases and distributes items from global manufacturers, supplying many specialist orders. The progress department monitors orders from placement to delivery. Dealing with customers, warehouse and manufacturers, the department has to maintain a careful and diplomatic relationship with both suppliers and customers.

Rapid Supply credits its success to the ability to efficiently obtain and deliver a wide range of parts. Five years ago the company was purchased by its managers from a large multinational conglomerate. Its market share has increased by 30 per cent in the last two years. The catalogue range has grown extensively with an additional 53 listed manufacturers.

The owners and the venture capital company supporting the organization have decided to float the business on the stock market next year. This will allow them to realize a proportion of their investment and will make millionaires of the senior executives. To maximize the potential share value of the company, their advisers have recommended a number of cost-cutting efficiency exercises. These include a reduction in warehouse stocks, increasing the proportion of items supplied to special order.

The progress department is divided into two sections: record clerks update files with changes and information from manufacturers and lead a comparatively peaceful life. Order-chasing clerks deal with e-mail, telephone and postal enquiries from customers and have a hectic existence, frequently experiencing verbal abuse. The department's work has increased considerably over the last two years but staff levels have remained the same. The progress department is managed by Julie Dee, a tough, resilient and detached person. She is adept at dealing with confrontation and seems to have an impenetrable shell. More junior employees wilt under the onslaught of enquiries. The average length of employment is three to four months but there are a few experienced people who have worked in the department for several years.

Most enquiries are from customers chasing orders. If clerks confirm items have arrived, customers are referred to the despatch section to arrange delivery. More often, parts have not arrived, requiring e-mails or phone calls to manufacturers and return contact with customers. At its simplest, a progress enquiry can be dealt with during the customer's first contact; at its worst, a succession of communications might be required over several days. Matters are complicated by inefficiencies elsewhere in the system. Goods might be in the warehouse even if shown as 'not arrived' on the computer screen. Equally, they might not have left the manufacturer or may be in transit.

Order-chasing irritates other staff and the suppliers. There have been complaints from manufacturers about progress requests from Rapid Supply regarding parts that were delivered to the warehouse days ago. An instruction has been circulated stating that progress clerks must check with the warehouse first, before contacting manufacturers. This has caused considerable friction between the progress department and the warehouse. Progress staff complain about the apparent slowness of recording receipt of goods; the warehouse complains of being pestered about parts which sometimes are not yet due. There is a further conflict with the despatch clerk who cannot be contacted for lengthy periods. Similar difficulties are experienced with suppliers, often needing several e-mails, etc. in order to obtain a response. Frequent errors by recording clerks compound the problems.

Progress clerks have a difficult role to play and risk upsetting everyone they deal with. Customers became irate if they do not get an immediate positive response.

Clerks become stressed with the pressure of work, colleagues' absenteeism, time limits on dealing with individual customers, being unable to deal with queries properly, and an escalating backlog. The manager now spends much of her time dealing with complaints about the service.

The marketing department has completed a customer survey which shows high levels of dissatisfaction with the progress department. Senior managers are furious and have seconded you to work alongside Julie and 'sort things out'.

*What will you do?*

**Case studies for discussion and analysis** Case studies situated at the end of each chapter present realistic challenging HRM scenarios inviting you to analyze the situation and discuss potential solutions.

# About the website

The fourth edition of *Human Resource Management* is accompanied by a range of exciting digital support resources, designed to support teaching and enhance the learning experience. Each resource is carefully tailored to the book and the needs of the reader. The website is structured for lecturers and students as follows:

→ A password protected area for instructors with, for example, a testbank, PowerPoint slides and an instructor's manual.

→ An area for students including, for example, multiple choice questions and weblinks.

To discover the dedicated digital support resources accompanying this textbook please go to: www.cengage.co.uk/hrm4e

## For students

→ Revision multiple choice questions

→ Weblinks

→ RSS feeds from the HRM Guide Network

## For lecturers

→ Instructor's manual

→ Case study notes

→ PowerPoint slides

→ ExamView testbank

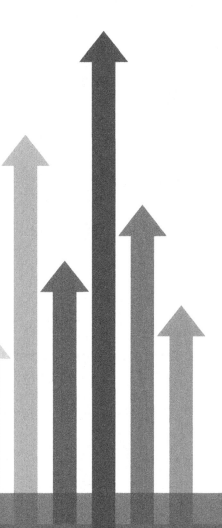

# PART ONE
## INTRODUCTION TO HRM

The first part of *Human Resource Management* introduces you to the essential elements of HRM, its origins and applications. HRM is viewed as an all-embracing term describing a number of distinctive approaches to people management. Part One helps you to understand and evaluate the different and sometimes ambiguous views of human resource management by investigating its origins, explanatory models, technology and practice.

### The chapters in Part One address a number of specific issues:

→ **Where do the fundamental concepts of HRM come from?**

→ **What distinguishes HRM from other approaches to managing people – particularly personnel management?**

→ **Is HRM here to stay or is it just another management fad?**

→ **Is HRM a coherent and integrated approach to managing people?**

→ **How prevalent is HRM?**

→ **What is the link between HRM and high performance?**

→ **HRM and knowledge management.**

→ **How has technology changed the practice and delivery of HRM?**

→ **Does its use lead to greater organizational effectiveness?**

# CHAPTER 1
## Managing people

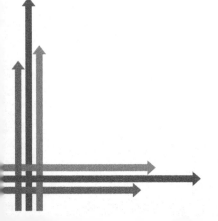

LEARNING OBJECTIVES

The purpose of this chapter is to:

→ Provide an overview of the history of people management.

→ Outline significant developments that led to modern human resource management (HRM).

→ Discuss the main differences between 'traditional' personnel management and HRM.

→ Introduce the key roles played by human resource specialists.

# PEOPLE MANAGEMENT

In this chapter we set out to understand the origins and purpose of human resource management (HRM), how it developed and the range of tasks covered by human resource specialists. Arguably, HRM has become the dominant approach to people management throughout much of the world. But it is important to stress that HRM has not 'come out of nowhere'. HRM has absorbed ideas and techniques from a wide range of theories and practical tools. In effect, HRM is a synthesis of themes and concepts drawn from a long history of work, more recent management theories and research in academic disciplines such as psychology and the social sciences.

Organizations are made up of people and there is no management activity that might not be touched on by HRM. In practice, people managers must deal with a continuous stream of organizational and environmental events that are frequently similar but also different enough to require fresh thinking. For example:

→ organizations expand, contract, merge or close.

→ they innovate or stagnate.

→ they have an emotional dimension, being exciting or unhappy organizations in which to work.

→ activities are enhanced or constrained by the availability of finance.

→ stability and change are dependent on the supply and retention of suitable employees.

→ technology produces new opportunities but also eliminates old procedures and requires new working practices.

→ staff must be recruited, redeployed, retrained or dismissed.

People management is obviously central to some issues we have listed (for example, recruiting or redeploying employees). The role of human resource managers is less obvious in other areas such as innovation or stagnation but these are affected by having trained, motivated people with suitable skills in place. Superficially, HRM seems irrelevant to activities such as raising finance. However, it has significance even here. Compare two businesses: one has an excellent industrial relations record with no strikes or disputes, while another has many such problems that have been reported in the media. For which company would you find it easier to raise extra finance? Clearly, the correct answer is the first of these.

Human resource management draws on many sources for its theories and practices. Sociologists, psychologists and management writers, especially, have contributed a succession of new and reworked ideas. They offer theoretical insights and practical assistance in areas of people management such as recruitment and selection, performance measurement, team building and organizational design. Many of their concepts have been integrated into broader approaches that have contributed generally to management thinking and ultimately the development of HRM (see Figure 1.1).

## BACKGROUND AND ORIGINS OF PEOPLE MANAGEMENT

Attempts to achieve an understanding of human behaviour in the workplace go far into the past. This section reflects on some significant developments in the history of people management. Just as the tasks that have to be conducted in modern organizations are allocated to different jobs and the people who perform them, humans in ancient societies divided work between themselves. The division of labour (see Key concept 1.1) has been practised

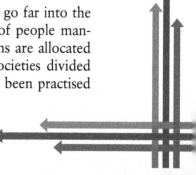

**FIGURE 1.1**

Influences on the development of HRM

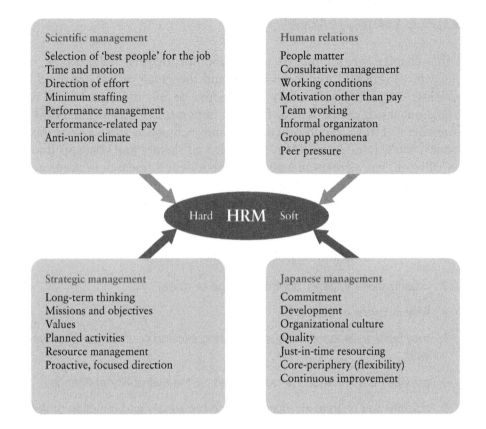

Scientific management
Selection of 'best people' for the job
Time and motion
Direction of effort
Minimum staffing
Performance management
Performance-related pay
Anti-union climate

Human relations
People matter
Consultative management
Working conditions
Motivation other than pay
Team working
Informal organizaton
Group phenomena
Peer pressure

Hard **HRM** Soft

Strategic management
Long-term thinking
Missions and objectives
Values
Planned activities
Resource management
Proactive, focused direction

Japanese management
Commitment
Development
Organizational culture
Quality
Just-in-time resourcing
Core-periphery (flexibility)
Continuous improvement

since prehistoric times: family groups shared the work of hunting and gathering; tasks were allocated according to skills such as ability to find food plants, track animals or cook; age, strength and health were taken into account and the oldest and youngest members were not expected to travel far from home or to be involved in the dangers of hunting. Division of labour required cooperation between members of social groups but their activities would not have been free of rivalry and competitiveness between individuals and neighbouring communities, anticipating some of the tensions of modern organizations. The issue of equality, embodied in modern diversity management, also has an important historical background as social customs in traditional societies determined separate roles and tasks for males and females. Anthropologists and social psychologists have provided insights into the dynamics of small groups and cooperative communities that have direct relevance to human resource management.

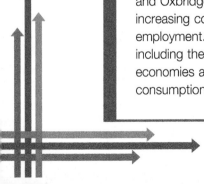

**KEY CONCEPT 1.1**   DIVISION OF LABOUR

This describes the subdivision of work so that specific tasks or jobs are allocated to individuals deemed most suitable on the basis of skill, experience or cultural tradition. All societies practise division of labour. Some cultures traditionally allocated tasks to particular social groups, such as the caste system in India. In others, higher status jobs have been reserved for the members of a power elite such as the products of the British public school and Oxbridge system or the French *grandes écoles*. Modern sociologists point to the increasing complexity of the division of labour through developments in global work and employment. There is an interplay between different forms of integration and differentiation, including the technical division and allocation of work, the interdependencies of work across economies and instituted processes of work in production, distribution, exchange and consumption (Glucksmann, 2009).

Self-sufficient communities, dependent on agriculture or fishing, rarely had more than 20–30 categories of labour, in contrast to modern industrial states that have thousands of different job types. Some functions, such as religious and political leadership or medicine, were restricted to individuals with inherited status or specialist knowledge. As civilization and technology evolved, however, specialization led to a proliferation of different forms of work as farmers and fishermen were joined by skilled craftworkers using metal, pottery and wood. Advances in technology were followed by the growth of relatively large social structures that faced many of the same problems as modern businesses and public organizations. In particular, it became necessary to identify or train people with the necessary competences to perform key tasks.

Every generation believes that its problems and achievements are greater than those of the past. Modern organizations are seen as being uniquely complex and on a larger scale than the enterprises of earlier times but, in the ancient world, large numbers of people were organized to build great pyramids, fortresses and irrigation systems; military leaders marshalled huge armies; slave owners operated massive plantations and mines. Consequently, leadership, power and organization have been matters of study and debate for thousands of years. We can instance the *Farmer's Almanac,* a 5000-year-old Sumerian text (modern Iraq) that included useful tips on the supervision of farm labourers – possibly making it the oldest known HRM textbook (Kramer, 1963: 105). The text advised the farmer to prepare a selection of whips and goads to keep men and beasts working hard. No idleness or interruptions were to be tolerated. Even planting barley seed had to be closely supervised as the unfortunate labourers were not trusted to do it properly.

This authoritarian approach has been prominent throughout most of recorded history and exemplifies the 'hard' form of human resource management that will be examined later in our discussion on models of HRM. It presents people management as the exercise of power by the powerful over those who work and places the greatest emphasis on the issue of control. In many respects this is a simple, unsophisticated and often effective method of people management with obvious attractions for those possessing power. To this day some managers favour this paternalistic approach (Pellegrini and Scandura, 2008) but it has significant negative implications for workers' motivation, self-respect and productivity (Coffey *et al.*, 2009). Consequently there has been a continuing and increasing search for less coercive ways of managing people. For example, it is now believed that the 4500 year-old pyramids of Egypt – the largest buildings on the planet until the 20th century – were not constructed by slaves under the lash but were put together by teams of peasants supervised by artisans with highly developed building skills (Shaw, 2003). The skilled personnel, at least, would have to have been selected, trained and managed effectively, possibly using 'softer' and more subtle methods of people management that took account of teamwork, individual motivation and reward for good performance.

So bullying and threatening behaviour would not have been the only methods of people management in the past. Indeed the military adventures of ancient leaders such as Alexander of Macedon were so dangerous and on such a massive and lengthy scale that considerable commitment was required from their followers. In renaissance Europe the Italian writer Niccolò Machiavelli detailed a wide range of strategies and tactics that continue to offer insights into the exercise of power. Anticipating some of today's management writers, Machiavelli considered that the ideal leader should have a degree of virtue and be regarded with both fear and love – although, if only one was possible, it was better to be feared than loved.

The division of labour required the most suitable people to perform skilled tasks, producing an early interest in the differences between individuals. Again in the 16th century John Huarte wrote about (in today's terminology) the practice of vocational guidance and

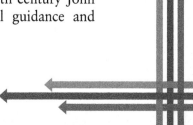

selection, maintaining that ability was innate. He classified people in the following way (cited in Smith 1948: 10-11):

1  Some have a disposition for the clear and easy parts, but cannot understand the obscure and difficult.

2  Some are pliant and easy, able to learn all the rules, but no good at argument.

3  Some need no teachers, they take no pleasure in the plains but seek dangerous and high places and walk alone, follow no beaten track; these must fare forthwith, unquiet, seeking to know and understand new matters.

By the 18th century, Adam Smith's *An Inquiry into the Nature and Causes of the Wealth of Nations* emphasized the importance of the division of labour in achieving increased productivity, signalling the Industrial Revolution that spread through the UK, western Europe and North America and continues to transform developing countries. 'Revolution' implies a rapid transition from craft to industrial methods but western industrialization was a relatively slow process in comparison with the recent development of economies in Asia. At the end of the 18th, and the beginning of the 19th centuries, workers were gradually concentrated in factories and work centres, more or less under their own free will. This concentration was linked to increasing mechanization and the consequent need for machine-operating skills. Developing from older craft-based industries, work was divided between employees according to the nature of their skills. One worker would no longer be totally responsible for all stages of production, such as making a piece of furniture. In the industrial system the task was subdivided into simpler, less skilful jobs. Different people would deal with parts of the process: one would turn chair legs, another would prepare seats, yet another would stain and polish and so on. However, Gospel (2009: 13) notes that the switch between artisan (or craft) and mass production has never been uniform:

> In practice, changes have been complex, with overlaps in types of production regimes over time and with older sectors adopting aspects of newer arrangements. Thus, skilled, small-batch production was never superseded in many areas often typified as mass production, such as metal-working and light assembly industries. Similarly, many aspects of work in modern retail stores, fast food restaurants and call centres are very much of a mass production kind.

By the late 19th century, the size and complexity of the new industries demanded more sophisticated methods of coordination and organization, eventually evolving into modern management. Until this time, workers were not directly employed by large capitalists: their employers were gang bosses, subcontracted to provide and organize labour. In the developed world, subcontractors of this kind continue to exist in the building sector and in fruit and vegetable picking. In developing countries their power is even greater. Under autocratic but loose control, skilled or unskilled workers largely organized their own efforts, forming autonomous teams. However, as factories grew larger and people were concentrated in greater numbers in specific locations, this indirect approach became increasingly unworkable. Individuals were needed to coordinate and control permanent workforces, which were directly employed by factory owners.

Initially they took the form of overseers, foremen or supervisors; exercising 'coercion by means of observation' (Foucault, 1977: 175). At first they were people promoted from the workforce: the concept of a distinct managerial class with separate recruitment paths evolved slowly. Jacques (1997) points out that 'the foreman was not in any sense a middle manager, but a key player in a form of control in the works radically different from and preceding *management*'. In a more general sense, the choice of supervisory or managerial staff (whatever the label) lay between the selection and development of existing workers

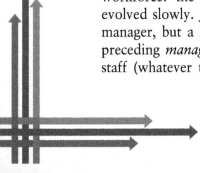

or the recruitment of individuals with specific qualities from some external source. This remains an important strategic choice for modern human resource managers (Bacon *et al.*, 2010).

Nineteenth century industry was dominated by individual owners, family businesses and partnerships. The principals of these companies managed their businesses in a direct, personal way, partly because the numbers of people involved were small enough to be within the span of control of a few individuals. Family-controlled businesses became a major economic force and many achieved considerable importance. Some of the most successful were happy to publicize their methods and were featured in the media of the time. Biographies of business leaders such as George Cadbury were written glorifying their achievements and presenting their ideas in largely uncritical terms. Along with explorers, scientists and colonial adventurers, business heroes were presented as role models for the masses. Such books met the demands of a reading population who preferred to perceive the world in terms of good and bad, heroes and villains, and required a presentation of success in simplistic terms. Examination of modern 'pop management' books suggest that little has changed (Fleming, 2009: 2).

Industrialization in the 19th century was accompanied by changes in political attitudes, emphasizing the conflict between left and right-wing beliefs. While right-wing thinkers focused on the benefits of technology and growth, left-wing theorists (particularly the Marxists) highlighted their negative aspects and the unfairness of power distribution. The debate about alienation (see Key concept 1.2), when workers did not feel committed to their employers (Edgell, 2006: 28), is an early manifestation of the issues surrounding employee engagement – a key element of HRM today.

### KEY CONCEPT 1.2   ALIENATION

This is a state of estrangement, or a feeling of being an outsider from society. Karl Marx observed that although work in a traditional, agricultural or craft-based society had been exhausting, workers had control over their own jobs. Their work required considerable knowledge and skill that had been removed from many factory jobs. Dull, boring and repetitive work induces a feeling of alienation. Assembly line workers are involved with a small part of the final product, have little control over the rhythm of their work and may have no idea of the significance of their contribution. Their work can appear to be alien with no relationship or meaning to their lives other than to produce income. As a consequence they may feel little enthusiasm and, often, active hostility towards what seems like forced labour.

## PROFESSIONAL MANAGERS

Much of the literature on management history is American in origin and, not surprisingly, attributes most of the credit for the development of management to US originators (Pearson, 2009: 79). Certainly, by 1900 the USA had undergone many decades of rapid, large-scale industrialization and pioneered new management techniques. Large American companies such as Heinz and Singer Sewing Machines had the characteristics of modern, highly structured organizations. They produced standardized consumer durables for the mass market. These organizations required a supply of trained managers. Notionally selected on the basis of ability and expertise – rather than family connections – they needed to know how to

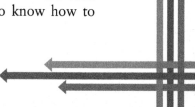

organize, reward and motivate their staff. In the USA, state and private universities were opened to cater for this new professional need.

The first companies of equivalent size and organization did not arise in Britain and the Commonwealth until the 1920s and management education was similarly late in developing. Like most European or Asian companies they still tended to employ relatives or to promote long-standing workers to management roles. Reliability and ability to impose discipline were held to be more important than technical knowledge. Increasingly, however, managers (especially those at a senior level) developed vested interests incompatible with those of the working-classes (labour) and shareholders (capital).

Jelinek (quoted in Mintzberg, 1994: 21) considers that F.W. Taylor and his ideas about scientific management, 'for the first time made possible the large-scale coordination of details-planning and policy-level thinking, above and beyond the details of the task itself'. This produced a new division of labour, splitting tasks and their coordination into different roles. So management had become 'abstracted' from day-to-day activities, allowing it to 'concentrate on exceptions'. An early form of the 'one best way' methodologies of dealing with people management, a distinctive form of scientific management was taken up in the new high-volume production industries. This came to be known as Fordism after the mass production methods used by Henry Ford for automobile manufacturing. Today, the just-in-time systems originally developed by Toyota in Japan bear a number of similarities to some aspects of scientific management.

## THE HUMAN FACTOR

The 'science' in scientific management was doubtful. At the same point in time, however, academic researchers had begun to take an interest in the practical aspects of work. Work psychology was pioneered by the German psychologist Hugo Munsterberg. Between 1900 and 1914, he applied the techniques of the young science of psychology to issues such as the selection of engineers to operate new machines, and the efficiency of various industrial practices (Thomson, 1968: 133). In Germany and the UK the demands of war boosted further research. In Britain, the Health of Munition Workers Committee (1915–17) was required to: 'consider and investigate the relation of hours of labour and other conditions of employment, including methods of work, to the production of fatigue, having regard both to industrial efficiency and to the preservation of health amongst the workers' (quoted in Thomson, 1968: 345).

In 1919, the researchers involved formed the UK National Institute of Industrial Psychology (NIIP), a body similar to the Australian Institute of Industrial Psychology founded in 1917. These organizations investigated and researched working conditions, and developed vocational guidance and selection techniques. In New Zealand, vocational guidance dates from 1913 where it was offered by the Christchurch branch of the YMCA. Initially the work of occupational psychologists bordered on physiology as they investigated fatigue and monotony. It had been believed that fatigue was caused by a build-up of toxins in the blood. It was even thought that an elixir could be found which would neutralize these chemicals; when injected into exhausted workers this could allow them to work indefinitely! The researchers proved conclusively that fatigue was not purely physiological – it was also psychological (Rose, 1975: 70).

Their work directly countered the myth that working longer hours produced greater output. In their research on monotony the NIIP psychologists took a deliberately anti-Taylorist perspective. They confirmed Taylor's views on the value of rest pauses but argued against the notion of 'one best way by a first-class man'. The simple truth was that individual tasks

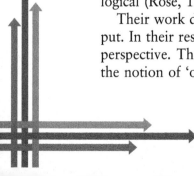

could be done equally effectively in a variety of ways by a diverse range of people. Different people had their own ways of performing effectively: they worked more efficiently when allowed to vary their own working methods. It became clear also that money was not the sole motivator for working people: the social relations between workers influenced their attitude to the job and their productivity. Workers were human beings and should be treated as such: the researchers had identified the importance of human factors.

In effect they had anticipated the conclusions of the more famous 'Hawthorne studies', but their reports – expressed in dry scientific language – made for dull reading, and were not accessible to a wide audience. Moreover, their income came from industrial commissions which were expected to be confidential. The most positive response came from the chocolate makers, Cadbury and Rowntree, which were Quaker-owned and humanitarian in attitude. They were receptive to ideas about training, vocational guidance, staff welfare and joint worker-management councils. Many, if not all, employers were not like-minded. The soft approach of the NIIP also had a hard centre, in the shape of efficiency measures such as selection tests to identify suitable workers for specific jobs.

Psychological tests for selection, or 'psychometric tests', were extensively developed in the USA and the UK from World War I through to World War II. Some two million Americans were tested during World War I alone. Their particular priority was the identification of 'subnormals' at one extreme and officer material at the other. After the war, testing became a lucrative commercial activity in the USA but introduced a worrying element of 'scientific' racism which has not been entirely eliminated.

## HUMAN RELATIONS

The US **human relations** movement dominated management thinking until the 1950s and was a significant influence on the development of modern HRM. The movement gained most of its inspiration from the famous Hawthorne studies at the Western Electric Company plant of that name in Chicago from the 1920s to the early 1940s. The plant employed 40 000 people and was regarded as progressive. The studies were organized by the company, with some assistance from the Harvard Business School. The intention was to find out how productivity might be affected if working conditions such as lighting, heating and rest pauses were varied. Elton Mayo, an Australian professor at Harvard, picked up these studies and publicized a new approach in American management philosophy which spread to many other countries.

## MANAGEMENT THEORY

The human relations and human factors approaches were absorbed into a broad behavioural science movement in the 1950s and 1960s. This period produced some influential theories on the motivation of human performance. For example, Maslow's hierarchy of needs provided an individual focus on the reasons why people work. He argued that people satisfied an ascending series of needs from survival, through security to eventual 'self-actualization'. In the same period, concepts of job design such as job enrichment and job enlargement were investigated. It was felt that people would give more to an organization if they gained satisfaction from their jobs. Jobs should be designed to be interesting and challenging to gain the commitment of workers – a central theme of HRM.

By the 1970s most managers participating in formal management training were aware of Theory X and Theory Y (McGregor, 1960); of Maslow and Herzberg's motivation theories;

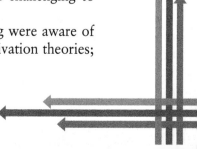

# KEY MANAGEMENT THEORIES

**Management by objectives** Based on work by Drucker in the 1950s, and further developed by McGregor, management by objectives (MBO) linked achievement to competence and job performance. MBO primarily focused on the individual, tying rewards and promotion opportunities to specific agreed objectives, measured by feedback from performance assessment. Individual managers were given the opportunity to clarify the purposes of their jobs and set their own targets. MBO developed into modern performance management schemes and performance-related pay.

**Contingency** Many researchers found difficulty in applying academic theories to real organizations. The socio-technical school developed models of behaviour and performance which took into account contingency variables, or 'it depends' circumstances, found in particular work situations (Burns and Stalker, 1961; Woodward, 1980). They argued that employees were part of a system that also included the equipment and other resources utilized by an organization. The system could not function optimally unless all its components – human and non-human – had been considered. The HRM concepts of coherence and integration derive, in part, from this line of thought.

**Organizational development** Also drawn from the long tradition of organizational theory, organizational development (OD) offered a pragmatic approach to change. Theory and practice were mixed in a tentative process called 'action research'. Organizational development familiarized managers with the idea that changes in processes, attitudes and behaviour were possible and that organizations should be thought of as whole entities.

**Strategic management** Directing people to achieve strategic objectives so that individual goals are tied to the business needs of the whole organization, strategic management has become a dominant framework for organizational thinking since World War II. It is based on concepts first used for large-scale military and space programmes in the USA. Frequently, it employs project and team-based methods for planning and implementation. Lately, internal (including human) resources and key competencies have been identified as crucial elements of long-term competitive success. Strategic management has become the major unifying theme of undergraduate and (especially) postgraduate business courses. The concern with strategy is said to distinguish HRM from personnel management.

**Leadership** Many writers have concluded that a visionary leader is essential, particularly in developing and inspiring teams. McGregor's (1960) *The Human Side of Enterprise* linked leadership and management style to motivation. McGregor expressed the contrast between authoritarian people management ('Theory X') and a modern form based on human relations ideas ('Theory Y'). His ideas parallel 'hard' and 'soft' HRM. Effective managers do not need to give orders and discipline staff, they draw the best from their people through encouragement, support and personal charisma. Later authors (such as Peters and Waterman, 1982) featured the leader's vision and mission as a quasi-religious means of galvanizing worker commitment and enthusiasm.

**Corporate culture** Deal and Kennedy (1982) popularized the belief that organizational effectiveness depends on a strong, positive corporate culture. They combined ideas from leadership theory and strategic management with prevailing beliefs about Japanese business success. Managers were exhorted to examine their existing organizational climates critically and work to change them into dynamic and creative cultures. The excellence movement inspired by Peters and Waterman (1982), and others, were particularly influential with practising managers, despite criticisms of the research on which it was based.

*Some people believe that managing people is just a matter of common sense. What benefits can human resource specialists gain from the concepts and theories described here?*

and knew where they should be in terms of the managerial grid (Blake and Mouton, 1964). These theorists advocated participative, 'soft' approaches to management. However, only a minority of managers in the USA received such training, with even fewer in other countries. Most operational managers concerned with production, engineering or distribution, had worked their way up from low-level jobs: they were probably closer in spirit to F.W. Taylor than the theorists of the 1950s and 1960s. This contrasted with personnel departments with a higher proportion of people who had received academic training; additionally, 'personnel' was an area where women were prevalent – as opposed to production which was male dominated. Were women naturally more open to human relations concepts than men?

In the UK, the influence of industrial psychology persisted in Alec Rodger's slogan 'fitting the man to the job and the job to the man'. Holloway (1991) quotes from a student handout issued by Rodger in the 1970s (which appears to ignore the concept of the working woman):

Fitting the man to the job:

→   through occupational guidance

→   personnel selection

→   training and development.

Fitting the job to the man:

→   through methods design

→   equipment design

→   design and negotiation of working conditions and

→   (physical and social) rewards.

## DEVELOPMENT OF THE PERSONNEL SPECIALISM

Personnel management has been a recognized function in the USA since NCR opened a personnel office in the 1890s. American personnel managers worked within a unitarist tradition, identifying closely with the objectives of their organization (Key concept 1.3). It was natural for HRM to emerge comparatively smoothly from this perspective.

### KEY CONCEPT 1.3   UNITARISM

This concept describes a managerialist stance which assumes that everyone in an organization is a member of a team with a common purpose. It embodies a central concern of HRM – that an organization's people, whether managers or lower-level employees, should share the same objectives and work together harmoniously. From this perspective, conflicting objectives are seen as negative and dysfunctional. By definition it is the opposite of pluralism: the acceptance of several alternative approaches, interests or goals within the same organization or society. Arguably, in the field of HRM, unitarism represents a US tradition, whereas pluralism is more typical of European attitudes towards people management.

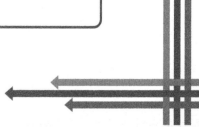

In other countries, the personnel management function arrived more slowly and came via a number of routes. Moreover, its orientation was not entirely managerial. In the UK, for example, its origins can be traced to the 'welfare officers' employed by Quaker-owned companies such as Cadbury. At an early stage it became evident that there was an inherent conflict between their activities and those of line managers. They were not seen to have a philosophy compatible with the world view of senior managers. The welfare officer orientation placed personnel management as a buffer between the business and its employees. In terms of 'organizational politics' this was not a politically viable position for individuals wishing to further their careers, increase their status and earn high salaries.

Tyson (1989) distinguished between three 'types' of personnel management jobs:

→   *'Clerk of works'*. The majority, involved in the routine of administration, record-keeping, letter-writing, setting up interviews and welfare matters. Reports to personnel or senior line manager.

→   *'Contracts manager'*. Likely to be found in large organizations with formal industrial relations structures. Involved in detailed short-term policy-making and resolving problems. A 'fixer' with some degree of influence on trade unions and senior management.

→   *'Architect'*. Probably highly qualified but not necessarily in 'personnel'. Broad portfolio with a significant strategic role. A business manager first and personnel manager second.

The second tradition – industrial relations – further compounded this distinction between personnel and other managers. In the acrimonious industrial relations climate prevailing in many developed countries throughout much of the 20th century, personnel/industrial relations managers played an intermediary role between unions and line management. Their function was legitimized by their role – or, at least, their own perception of that role – as 'honest brokers'.

But from the 1980s onwards governments with a neo-liberal or free market orientation, such as Margaret Thatcher's Conservative administration in the UK, reined in union freedom severely. Overall, there was a marked reduction in the importance of collective worker representation in many English-speaking countries. The perceived importance of collective bargaining reduced as managerial power increased. Trade union membership declined along with centralized pay bargaining and other forms of collective negotiation – and with them, the importance of the personnel manager with negotiating experience. The focus switched from the collective to the relationship between employer and individual employee. To support this change, a variety of essentially individualistic personnel techniques were applied to achieve business goals. These included performance measurement, objective setting and skills development related to personal reward.

As we can see from the list of functions in Table 1.1, personnel had become a well-defined but low status area of management by the 1980s. Practitioner Associations in industrialized countries recruited members in increasing numbers, developed qualification structures and attempted to define 'best practice'. Although they drew on psychology and sociology, the knowledge and practices they encouraged were largely pragmatic and commonsensical and did not present a particularly coherent approach to people management. Moreover, in some instances training and industrial relations were considered to be specialist fields outside mainstream personnel management. Traditional personnel managers were accused of having a narrow, functional outlook. For example, Storey (1989, p.5) commented that personnel management '... has long been dogged by problems of credibility, marginality, ambiguity and a "trash-can" labelling which has relegated it to a relatively disconnected set of duties – many of them tainted with a low-status "welfare" connotation'.

In practice, the background and training of many personnel managers left them speaking a different language from other managers and unable to comprehend wider business issues such as business strategy, market competition, labour economics and the roles of other

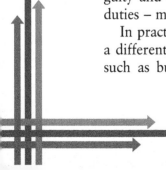

| Traditional personnel departments typically encompass functions such as: | |
|---|---|
| *Recruitment* | Advertising for new employees and liaising with employment agencies. |
| *Selection* | Determining the best candidates from those who apply, arranging interviews, tests, references and so on. |
| *Promotion* | Running similar selection procedures to determine progression within the organization. |
| *Pay* | A minor or major role in pay negotiation, determination and administration. |
| *Performance assessment* | Coordinating staff appraisal and counselling systems to evaluate individual employee performance. |
| *Grading structures* | Comparing the relative difficulty and importance of functions as a basis for pay or development. |
| *Training and development* | Coordinating or delivering programmes to fit people for the roles required by the organization now and in the future. |
| *Welfare* | Providing or liaising with specialists in a staff-care or counselling role for people with personal or domestic problems affecting their work. |
| *Communication* | Providing an internal information service, perhaps in the form of a staff newspaper or magazine, handouts, booklets and videos. |
| *Employee relations* | Handling disputes, grievances and industrial action, often dealing with unions or staff representatives. |
| *Dismissal* | On an individual basis as a result of failure to meet requirements or as part of a redundancy or closure exercise, perhaps involving large numbers of people. |
| *Personnel administration* | Record-keeping and monitoring legislative requirements, for example related to equal opportunities. |

**TABLE 1.1**
Specialist personnel functions

*Using Tyson's classification of personnel work into 'clerk of works', 'contracts manager' and 'architect', what role would each of these three types play in the functions listed in Table 1.1?*

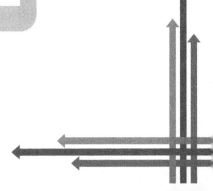

organizational functions – let alone balance sheets (Giles and Williams, 1991). The scene was set for a reintegration of personnel management with wider trends in management thinking.

## MANAGEMENT THINKING

Like fashions in hairstyle and clothing, management ideas come and go. One year's best-selling management concept is soon overtaken by the next 'big idea'. Significantly, however, a consistent theme has prevailed for more than two decades: the most successful organizations make the most effective use of their people – their human resources.

The emergence of HRM was part of a major shift in the nature and meaning of management towards the end of the 20th century. This happened for a number of reasons. Perhaps most significantly, as we will see in Part Two of this book, major developments in the structure and intensity of international competition forced companies to make radical changes in their working practices. From the 1970s onwards, managers in the industrialized countries felt themselves to be on a roller coaster of change, expected to deliver improved business performance by whatever means they could muster. Their own careers and rewards were increasingly tied to those improvements and many were dispatched to the ranks of the unemployed for not acting quickly and imaginatively enough. Caught between the need to manage decisively and fear of failure, managers sought credible new ideas as a potential route for survival.

The development of dynamic new economies in the Asia-Pacific region emphasized the weakness in traditional Western – specifically, American – management methods. To meet competition from East Asia, industries and organizations in older, developed countries were forced to restructure. The Japanese, in particular, provided both a threat and a role model that Eastern and Western companies tried to copy. Frequently, reorganized businesses in Australasia, Europe, North America and South Africa adopted Japanese techniques in an attempt to regain competitiveness. The term 'Japanization' came into vogue in the mid-1980s to describe attempts in other countries to make practical use of 'Japanese' ideas and practices, reinforced by the impact of Japanese subsidiaries overseas. Initially, the main interest lay in forms of technical innovation and manufacturing methods such as 'continuous improvement' and 'just-in-time'. And their ways of managing people also attracted attention.

## THE JAPANESE ROLE MODEL

Until 1868 Japan had been sealed-off from the outside world for 300 years. The sense of being 'different' remains. Kobayashi (1992: 18) comments that Japan has never set out to be integrated into the international community. Rather, the country adapted selective aspects of foreign cultures which seemed useful to its development. The Japanese borrowed freely from Western ideas, both at the turn of the century, and again during the period of reconstruction after World War II. However, Japanese industrialists did not simply copy American management methods; they revitalized Asian values (Chung, 1991).

A key to Japanese industrial progress was the development of 'Japan Incorporated': the close-knit cooperation between government and business. Specific industrial sectors were targeted for long-term market penetration and dominance. Supposedly competing businesses acted cooperatively at the expense of foreign firms, sacrificing immediate profits for later success.

Economic problems hit the West increasingly from the 1970s onwards and Japan's growing industrial dominance became obvious. This stimulated a flow of influential writing (for example, Ouchi, 1981; Pascale and Athos, 1981), leading to a continuing debate on the

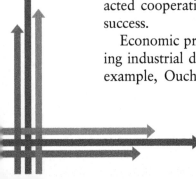

applicability of Japanese management methods to other countries. Ironically, Western managers have examined Japanese techniques just as intently as the Japanese studied the West half a century ago. Developing countries in East Asia took Japan rather than the USA as their model.

The term 'Japanization' came into vogue in the mid-1980s to describe attempts in other countries to make practical use of 'Japanese' ideas and practices as well as the impact of Japanese subsidiaries overseas. Japanese practice emphasized human resources as an organization's key asset. A key feature of Japanese businesses in the 1970s and 1980s was the emphasis on worker commitment, flexibility and development. Books such as Pascale and Athos' (1981) *The Art of Japanese Management,* highlighted the competitive advantage which the Japanese gained through effective people management. The message came through that 'essentially, it is the human resource among all the factors of production which really makes the difference' (Storey, 2001: 6).

Initially, the main interest lay in forms of technical innovation and manufacturing methods such as 'continuous improvement' and 'just-in-time'. More recently their ways of managing people have attracted attention. People management became a central strategic issue rather than a 'necessary inconvenience' (Goss 1994: 4). The early component ideas of HRM theory parallel elements of Japanese people management in that period. Whereas HRM is still a matter of rhetoric for most Western managers, however, the Japanese viewed it as a way of life: an instrumental approach to ever-increasing efficiency focused on employee commitment and skill. Traditionally, Japanese companies placed the interests of their employees first amongst their stakeholders (see Key concept 1.4), followed by customers and lastly the shareholders. This is virtually the opposite situation to that found in free market Western countries such as Australia, Canada, the UK or the USA. But the recessions of the last two decades forced a number of Japanese companies to adopt Western ways.

---

**KEY CONCEPT 1.4**  STAKEHOLDERS

Employees have rights and interests beyond pay. They are stakeholders along with members of other recognizably separate groups or institutions with a special interest in an organization. These include shareholders, managers, customers, suppliers, lenders and government. Each group has its own priorities and demands and fits into the power structure controlling the organization. Employees have limited importance in free market countries such as the USA, UK, Ireland, Australia or Canada, in comparison with most European and many Asian-Pacific countries. Notionally, shareholders are paramount in English-speaking countries. In reality, top managers normally have effective control and pursue their own interests – often at the expense of their staff. (This topic is dealt with at some length in Chapter 2.)

---

The Japanese role model is a mixture of racial stereotyping, myth and reality. It is difficult to tell when truth ends and myth begins. Foreign commentators encountering a radically different culture tend to emphasize the points of difference rather than the similarities. The Japanese were seen as workaholics, rarely taking holidays and eager to work every available hour. They were conformists with a distinctive form of decision-making based on consensus. They worked in teams and hated to be seen as individuals. They searched for continuous improvement and were proud to be identified with their employing organization. Large businesses offered slow but steady promotion paths and life-long careers in return for total commitment.

However, Japan is constantly changing. Most accounts of Japanese business practice refer to the behaviour and beliefs of a generation who had to work hard to restore the economy after World War II. The younger generation do not necessarily share their view of life and now live in very different economic circumstances. As recession deepened at the end of the 20th century, closures and retrenchments became a new feature of the Japanese industrial scene and the country entered into a lengthy period of stagnation. For a decade Japan was overshadowed by Asian competitors, especially China and India. Japanese companies first drew on their profits in lean times in order to keep their workforce. Companies in English-speaking countries would have been unable to withstand the wrath of shareholders demanding dividend payments. Responsibility for the security of their workforce was not simply a matter of goodwill or obligation but the necessary price for commitment from employees. This was difficult for companies operating in a global environment, exposed to fluctuations in the value of the yen or overseas economic demand. These companies made considerable use of peripheral workforces – primarily their suppliers' employees – who took the brunt whenever demand fell. These peripheral workers faced little or no income for prolonged periods while favoured employees in multinational organizations maintained their privileges. However, there is a general trend across Japanese industries away from a seniority-based reward system towards performance-related pay, a key element of western HRM practices (Conrad, 2010).

McCormick (2007) critiques the construction of 'the Japanese model' in western academic literature, demonstrating a considerable diversity across the different types of literature and concluding that this resulted from their different agendas. He notes that textbooks were focusing on the Japanese phenomenon in the 1990s – just when the media had decided that the Japanese model was on its way out in Japan. Moreover, they were basing their accounts on 1980s textbooks rather than using contemporary research for their sources. And lately they were moving away from the model despite research showing continued vitality of the Japanese model in large Japanese organizations. Keizer (2008) analyzed the rise in non-regular employment. He argued that a renewed duality in the job market is an important advantage of non-regular employment in terms of cost, and not just flexibility. But the significance of the cost advantage varies between industries and is particularly hard on the female workforce.

# FROM PERSONNEL TO HUMAN RESOURCE MANAGEMENT

Human resource management-type themes, including 'human capital theory' (discussed in Part Two) and 'human asset accounting' can be found in literature dating as far back as the 1970s. But the modern view of HRM first gained prominence in 1981 with its introduction on the prestigious MBA course at Harvard Business School. The Harvard MBA provided a blueprint for many other courses throughout North America and the rest of the world, making its interpretation of HRM particularly influential (Beer, Walton and Spector, 1984; Guest, 1987; Poole, 1990). Simultaneously, other interpretations were being developed in Michigan and New York.

These ideas spread to other countries in the 1980s and 1990s, particularly Australia, New Zealand, parts of northern Europe – especially the UK, Ireland and Scandinavia – and also South and Southeast Asia and South Africa. Today, the HRM approach is influential in many parts of the world. Typically, in this period HRM was presented in four distinct ways:

Firstly, it was as a radically new approach to managing people, demarcated sharply from traditional personnel management (Storey, 1989: 4). Personnel management was commonly

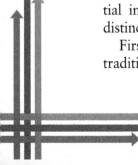

viewed as having an operational focus, emphasizing technical skills and day-to-day functions such as recruitment and selection, training, salary administration and employee relations. 'Personnel' was a detached and neutral approach to staff. By contrast, HRM was often portrayed as being proactive – looking at people in economic terms as either assets or costs to be actively managed. HRM was seen to be strategic, tying people management to business objectives. It was an attempt to manage people – not necessarily employees – in the long-term interests of the business.

Secondly, HRM was seen as an integrated approach which provided a coherent programme, linking all aspects of people management. Whereas personnel managers employed a piecemeal range of sophisticated techniques for assessment or selection, HRM integrated these within a meaningful and organized framework. Each element needed to fit into a pattern that ultimately met business needs. Additionally, HRM was seen to be holistic; in other words, it was concerned with the overall people requirements of an organization. It implied a significant shift towards more conceptual, higher-level concerns such as the structure and culture of the organization and the provision of necessary competences.

Thirdly, HRM represented a consistent view of people management in which employees were treated as valuable assets. An organization's reward systems, performance measures, promotion and learning opportunities were to be used to maximize the utilization of its human resources. In particular, they were focused on the attitudes, beliefs and commitment of employees to achieve behavioural consistency and a culture of commitment.

Finally, HRM was presented as a general management function. Personnel management was often viewed as the work of specialists, whereas HRM was the responsibility of all managers. In some organizations human resource experts provided an internal consultancy service to line managers. There was a particular stress on the role of top management and an overall increase in the status of people management. Traditional personnel managers had little power or prestige.

Why should HRM have attracted such attention, particularly from senior managers? From a strategic viewpoint, Lengnick-Hall and Lengnick-Hall (1988) identify a clear rationale for adopting the HRM approach:

→ HRM offers a broader range of solutions for complex organizational problems.

→ It ensures that an organization's people are considered as well as its financial and technological resources when objectives are set or capabilities assessed.

→ It forces the explicit consideration of the individuals who implement and comprise the strategy.

→ Two-way links are encouraged between the formulation of strategy and its human resource implications, avoiding problems which might arise from: (a) subordinating strategic considerations to HR preferences; and (b) neglecting an organization's people as a potential source of organizational competence and competitive advantage.

The renewed emphasis on the importance of human resources drew attention to the practice of people management. Conventionally, this had been divided between line and personnel managers, now frequently called human resource managers. For some, HRM was simply a matter of relabelling 'personnel' to redress the criticisms made about traditional personnel management and sceptics have argued that familiar personnel functions were repackaged and given a more upmarket image – 'old wine in new bottles' (Armstrong, 1987). Indeed, until the early 1990s, 'human resource management' textbooks tended to be slightly revised 'personnel management' texts covering familiar topics in a prescriptive manner.

Writing at that time, Torrington and Hall (1991: 15) concurred that the term was adopted in order to get away from the ineffectual image of previous eras: 'personnel managers seem constantly to suffer from paranoia about their lack of influence and are ready to snatch at anything – like a change in title – that might enhance their status'. It was also fuelled by longstanding criticisms from other managers. This includes a general prejudice that is often expressed within organizations and sometimes finds its way into print. Thus the following from an article entitled 'Support for an old-fashioned view', *The Independent*, 12 May, 1994):

> Many of us have long held the view that personnel management, or human resource management as companies sometimes insist on calling it, is a uniquely irrelevant executive function fulfilling no obvious purpose other than to stifle initiative, flair and creativity.

Similarly, Kellaway (2001) revisited an article about 'a piece of incomprehensible HR waffle that purported to lay out the future of HR', about which she had made 'a few averagely derogative remarks'. She cited 120 responses she had received of which 115 'referred to the HR profession with scepticism, sarcasm, rudeness or obscenity'. According to Kellaway, no one had a good word to say for HR; 'So demoralized are HR people that they churn out junk and when you attack it they do not even have the spirit to get angry'.

Where does this prejudice come from? Some critics have argued that personnel people should relinquish their ambiguous roles and adopt unashamedly managerialist positions. Others concluded that if human resources were fundamental to business success they were too important to be left to operational personnel managers. One of Lucy Kellaway's emailers stated: 'For HR to work it should (a) rename itself personnel and (b) stick to the basics, e.g. payroll, healthcare, training – of other people, not themselves – and pensions'.

But many commentators in the HR and management literature contend that major human resource decisions should be made by top managers and the consequences of those decisions should be carried through by line management. These considerations place HRM on a strategic rather an operational footing and therefore make HRM a concept of greater interest than personnel management to senior executives. However, in an article from the US business magazine *Fast Company* entitled 'Why We Hate HR', Hammonds (2005) repeats some familiar criticisms, stating:

> ...let's face it: After close to 20 years of hopeful rhetoric about becoming 'strategic partners' with a 'seat at the table' where the business decisions that matter are made, most human resources professionals aren't nearly there. They have no seat, and the table is locked inside a conference room to which they have no key. HR people are, for most practical purposes, neither strategic nor leaders.

Hammonds goes on to describe HR as 'at best, a necessary evil – and at worst, a dark bureaucratic force that blindly enforces nonsensical rules, resists creativity and impedes constructive change'. While conceding that HR is 'the corporate function with the greatest potential' and, theoretically, the key driver of business performance, he also considers it to be 'the one that most consistently underdelivers'.

Whatever the underlying level of hostility, or press disdain, it remains the case that, in larger organizations, there has been a reappraisal of the previously unfashionable and low-status personnel department. 'Personnel' cannot be regarded as peripheral if it controls an organization's people since the rhetoric states that they are its greatest resources. Many businesses have adopted some form of HRM in recognition of this importance. As Fowler (1987) famously stated, 'HRM represents the discovery of personnel management by chief executives'.

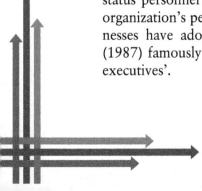

# HRM IN REALITY LAUGHING GURUS

The use of humour is one key to the success of management gurus. Researchers Dr Tim Clark and Dr David Greatbatch, authors of *Management Speak: Why We Listen to What Management Gurus Tell Us,* analyzed the techniques used by world-famous gurus such as Tom Peters, Rosabeth Moss Kanter and Gary Hamel. They found that successful gurus employ skilful communication techniques, especially humour, to promote their sometimes uncomfortable messages. Filling a lecture theatre or conference venue with laughter avoids alienating their audiences and brings people 'on-side'.

'Examining live and video-recorded performances of leading international gurus enabled us to analyze the presentational techniques they use to disseminate their ideas during live presentations', said Dr Greatbatch.

Gurus are faced with the problem of advocating unorthodox organizational practices that their audiences are probably not using, and disparaging the practices they are using. This is a delicate task with an inherent risk of alienating their audience members. So how do they do it? Dr Clark argues: 'These gurus remain highly regarded on the world-speaking stage and we wanted to discover their grammar of persuasion – in other words the communication techniques which underpin their frequently charismatic and persuasive public speaking performances'.

The study shows that gurus avoid offence by evoking laughter and telling stories. 'Basically, whenever the guru says anything potentially uncomfortable to audiences of managers they use humour and wrap it up as a joke', said Dr Greatbatch. The researchers found that gurus used a number of specific techniques to 'invite' laughter. 'Collective audience laughter is not simply a spontaneous reaction to humour or jokes', argued David Greatbatch. 'Rather, the gurus invite laughter by indicating when it is appropriate for the audience members to do so.'

Gurus used verbal and non-verbal actions to invite laughter, including:

→ laughing themselves

→ using exaggerated, ironic or comedic gestures

→ showing their teeth in a 'laughing' smile.

Having achieved laughter from the audience, the gurus played on this bonding to encourage the audience to feel part of an 'in group' sharing a common viewpoint with the gurus. The audience then began to turn against the management practices being criticized by the guru.

Storytelling seemed to be particularly important in the two processes of evoking laughter and deflecting criticism. The researchers found that more than two-thirds of audience laughter studied occurred within the context of stories. Stories make the gurus' messages more entertaining and memorable and also reinforce the authority of the gurus' knowledge. So their stories make constant references to famous and respected managers and organizations, personally known to the gurus. Audience research confirms that those speakers who use funny stories to develop their arguments are those who are most remembered.

'Our research clearly shows that gurus deploy humour at those points in their presentation where they face possible dissent', asserts Dr Greatbatch. 'Because they package their ideas in a non-offensive way, the world's leading gurus are never booed from the stage and typically generate very positive audience reaction and a high feel-good factor. Anyone can learn the techniques which they use and public speakers ranging from politicians to trainers could benefit from having a greater range of presentation techniques to deploy when necessary.'

*Management gurus have had a significant influence on the practice of management. Are their ideas brought into question by the use of the theatrical techniques described in this article?*

Source: Reprinted with permission from HRM Guide UK (http://www.hrmguide.co.uk).

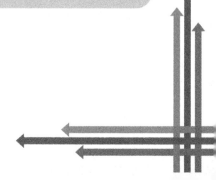

# THE NEW MANAGERIALISM

Schuler (1990) emphasized that the HR function had an opportunity to shift from being an 'employee advocate' (associated with personnel management) to a 'member of the management team'. Schuler's view was that this required HR professionals to be concerned with the bottom line, profits, organizational effectiveness and business survival. In other words, human resource issues should be addressed as business issues.

In fact, line and general managers have been instrumental in the adoption of HRM, often pushing changes through despite the resistance of personnel specialists (Storey, 2001: 7). Radical changes in business structures and supportive, largely right-wing, governments encouraged a renewed confidence in the power of managers to manage. The balance of power moved away from workers and their representatives with the collapse of traditional heavy industries in Western countries. High levels of unemployment allowed managers to pick

**TABLE 1.2**

Core roles in human resource management

Source: Plenary group of the Steering Committee for HRM Standards and Qualifications, South Africa, 1999.

| Function | Roles |
|---|---|
| **1** Planning and organizing for work, people and HRM | Strategic perspective |
| | Organization design |
| | Change management |
| | Corporate 'wellness' management |
| **2** People acquisition and development | Staffing the organization |
| | Training and development |
| | Career management |
| | Performance management |
| | Industrial relations |
| **3** Administration of policies, programmes and practices | Compensation management |
| | Information management |
| | Administrative management |
| | Financial management |

*Does this list of core HR roles differ in any significant way from the list of personnel functions given in Table 1.1?*

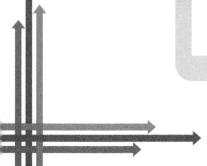

and choose new recruits. Existing employees felt pressurized to be more flexible under the threat of losing their jobs. As a result, managers were able to design more competitive organizations with new forms of employment relationships.

Encouraged by the writing of management gurus and, more recently, by the burgeoning legions of consultants (Legge, 2004: 2), managers eagerly adopted new management fads and fashions. Businesses moved away from multi-layered, rigid hierarchies and long-term career paths. Instead we saw an increase in flatter, project-oriented forms of organizations resourced in a flexible way – including short-term, part-time and contract workers. The stage was set for HRM, which was presented as a coherent and integrated philosophy by its originators, covering every aspect of people management (Beer *et al.*, 1984: 1). Yet, as we will discover in the next chapter, the adoption of specific HRM practices is still more dependent on management fashion than research and theory within the HR discipline, whether academic or practitioner (Rynes *et al.*, 2002).

## PROFESSIONALIZATION

Human resource specialists have found it difficult to achieve the same esteem and influence as their colleagues in other business functions such as finance and marketing, although their status is probably higher in the USA than most other countries. There have been some attempts at a professionalization of HR practice through certification programmes and encouragement of wider-ranging business knowledge within HR qualifications.

Sunoo (1999) argues that to be taken seriously, HR professionals need to understand the work of other business specialists, particularly in finance and strategy. The increasing need to quantify the costs of HR activities such as recruitment and the benefits from new initiatives require human resource practitioners to be comfortable with budgets and plans. Weiss (1999) agrees, concluding that human resource practitioners can only be taken seriously at a senior level (in other words, as 'strategic partners') if they have the following:

→ A broad understanding of the business.

→ A knowledge of how all the activities need to align.

→ A professionalism in investing in human capital and HR processes.

→ A unique perspective – one not provided by any other business specialist.

How do HR professionals obtain and demonstrate these qualities? A number of organizations provide certification with the aim of increasing credibility and career opportunities for newcomers and experienced HR practitioners. Certification is intended to demonstrate an understanding of human resource practices and their link to wider business issues. Observing that advertisements for human resource practitioner jobs increasingly require business qualifications and HR certification, Sunoo (1999) considers that:

> Clearly, today's business world demands a higher level of HR and business competency than ever before. Without advancing your career in HRM through certification and eventually even a master's degree in business administration, organizational development, human resources management or leadership, your chances of being taken seriously as a business partner are nil.

Other commentators are not so sure that certification is necessary. Aguinis, Michaelis and Jones (2005) analyzed 1873 HR job announcements available over a one-week period on four employment websites. Results showed that only nine (0.48 per cent) stated that there

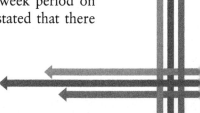

was a requirement for a certified HR professional, and only 70 (3.73 per cent) stated that this was a preference. In spite of low overall demand for certified HR professionals, results indicated that demand is slightly higher for jobs posted on a specialist website; certain job titles (e.g. HR director, HR generalist); HR specialty areas (e.g. employee relations, general HR); industries (e.g. manufacturing); and for jobs requiring more years of HR experience.

 **SUMMARY**

In this chapter we introduced the concept of HRM. Human resource management has evolved from a number of different strands of thought and is best described as a loose philosophy of people management rather than a focused methodology. It derives largely from the last century but incorporates older notions about the management of people at work. These ideas have many different roots and they do not fit comfortably within one coherent and self-consistent body of knowledge. One major point of debate has been the difference, if any, between HRM and 'traditional' personnel management. As we shall see in later chapters, the development of HRM continues today as new management theories, fashions and fads emerge.

 **FURTHER READING**

There are many introductory texts on human resource management, several with an orientation towards a single country. The following texts are of more general use:

1 Wendy Holloway's *Work Psychology and Organizational Behaviour* (Sage, 1991) remains one of the best overviews of scientific management, human factors, human relations and other early approaches.

2 The various editions of *Organizational Behaviour* by David Buchanan and Andrzej Huczynski (FT Prentice Hall) also contain useful discussions of these early movements, complete with illustrations.

3 For more on Henry Ford see: *The People's Tycoon: Henry Ford and the American Century* by Steven Watts (Alfred A. Knopf, 2005) and *My Life and Work* by Henry Ford (R.A. Kessinger Publishing Co., 2004).

4 Issues involved in the development of personnel management and HRM are best covered in texts edited by John Storey, including the third edition of *Human Resource Management: A Critical Text* (Cengage Learning, 2007).

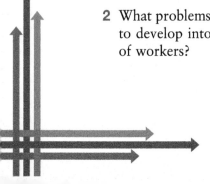 **REVIEW QUESTIONS**

1 How would you explain the difference between 'organizing' and 'managing' people?

2 What problems would have resulted from personal control of businesses when they began to develop into large work organizations employing hundreds, and sometimes thousands of workers?

3 How would you describe the main differences between the 'scientific management', 'human factors' and 'human relations' approaches?

4 What is HRM? Is it really different from personnel management? Summarize the main differences between personnel management and HRM as you see them.

5 Is 'relabeling' personnel as HRM anything more than a makeover or a cosmetic change?

6 How much does the concept of HRM owe to Japanese management practices?

7 Which theoretical developments do you consider to have contributed most to modern people management?

8 What is meant by 'management gurus'? What value can be placed on the ideas they have popularized?

 **CASE STUDY FOR DISCUSSION AND ANALYSIS**

Read the following case study and answer the question that follows

## Characteristics of engaging managers

Research by the Institute for Employment Studies indicates that engaging managers are made, not born – they learn from their own and other people's mistakes and modify their behaviour accordingly. The report is based on interviews with 25 'engaging managers' (identified as having high engagement scores of teams in their last employee survey), 22 'senior managers' (people managing the engaging managers) and focus groups with 25 teams managed by the engaging managers (a total of 154 people) (Robinson and Hayday, 2009). The seven organizations involved were:

→ The Association of Chartered Certified Accountants (ACCA)

→ Centrica

→ Corus

→ Her Majesty's Revenue and Customs (HMRC)

→ London Borough of Merton

→ Rolls-Royce

→ Sainsbury's.

The report concludes that great managers are focused on performance, taking the 'good bits' of other managers they have observed and avoiding the 'bad bits' of behaviour. They were effective communicators and showed improvement over time, according to senior managers. They were ready to show honesty and openness when breaking bad news and gave frequent individual feedback to staff. The features of engaging and non-engaging managers included the following:

*Characteristics of engaging managers*

→ high performers

→ communicators

→ visionary

→ empathizers

→ developers

→ enthusiasts

→ protectors

→ networkers

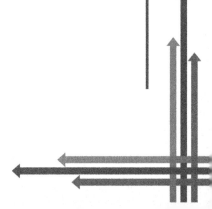

→  rocks

→  brave

→  jugglers

→  mavericks.

*Characteristics of disengaging and poor managers*

→  micro managers

→  muddlers

→  blamers

→  egoistical

→  pessimists.

According to Dilys Robinson, Principal Research Fellow at the Institute for Employment Studies:

> The excellent and engaging managers we spoke to have very varied jobs, different spans of control and seniority. But one thing they have in common is how very focused they are on performance. They all manage teams that are known to be high-performing within their organizations, which underlines how important engagement is in difficult times.
>
> We asked team members to draw pictures of how they see their managers. Interestingly, several people drew smiling devils, indicating that not all engaging managers toe the company line. The most popular picture of all was of a sun or a smiling face.
>
> The drawings gave us insight into engaging managers' characteristics. The teams value their managers' strategic vision, interest in them as individuals and fostering of positive team culture. Our engaging managers are challenging and approachable, and have good skills in communicating and listening. Their teams also expect them to be honest and development-focused. But engaging behaviours can be learnt and that's good news for aspiring managers.

Other key findings were:

→  Engaging managers, senior managers and teams all had clear views about disengaging behaviours to be avoided.

→  Disengaging behaviours included lack of empathy, poor communication and listening skills, being self-centred, failing to inspire, blaming others, aggression, poor delivery record, lack of approachability, lack of integrity and micro-managing.

→  Engaging managers were seen to be active internal networkers who did not necessarily feel a need to network externally.

→  Two-way communication was viewed as an essential feature of engaging management.

→  Engaging managers had in-depth knowledge of their organization, how their role fitted into the bigger picture and were able to communicate this effectively to their teams.

*What methods can managers use to gain the trust of their employees?*

*Source: Reprinted with permission from HRM Guide UK (http://www.hrmguide.co.uk.*

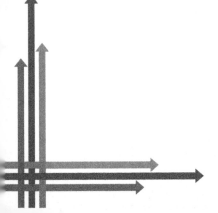

# CHAPTER 2
## The Concept of HRM

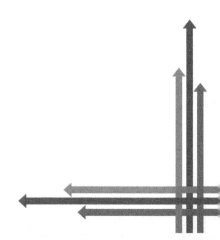

# DEFINING HUMAN RESOURCE MANAGEMENT

In the previous chapter we introduced the concept of human resource management and outlined the territory of people management covered by specialists in personnel or HRM. But what exactly is 'human resource management'? In Chapter 1 we discussed some of the theoretical and other developments which led to HRM being distinguished to some extent from 'traditional' personnel management. In this chapter we will examine the concept in greater detail.

Human resource management can seem to be a vague and elusive concept, not least because it has a variety of definitions (see Table 2.1). In fact, pinning down an acceptable definition can seem like trying to hit a moving target in a fog. Keenoy (1999) compares HRM with a hologram:

> As with a hologram, HRM changes its appearance as we move around its image. Each shift of stance reveals another facet, a darker depth, a different contour. As a fluid entity of apparently multiple identities and forms, it is not surprising that every time we look at it, it is slightly different. This is why, conceptually, HRMism appears to be a moving target, and why, empirically, it has no fixed (fixable) forms.

Keenoy's comparison is helpful in explaining why there are so many divergent definitions of HRM. This confusion reflects the different interpretations found in articles and books about human resource management. HRM is an elastic term (Storey, 1989: 8). It covers a range of applications that vary from book to book and organization to organization.

Simple reflection on the three words 'human resource management' does not provide much enlightenment. 'Human' implies it has something to do with people; 'management' places it in the domain of business and organization; but 'resource' is a highly ambiguous concept which many people find difficult to relate to. In fact, much of the academic literature suffers from forgetting the human element in HRM. Most of us would not take kindly to being classified as a 'resource', along with our desks and computers. It seems that there is a fundamental difficulty in considering a person's worth or value to an organization. This arises from that person's humanity. People are different from other resources and cannot be discussed in exactly the same way as equipment or finances. This difference lies at the heart of the antagonism and ambiguity that surrounds HRM in practice.

From an organizational perspective human resources encompass the people in an organization – its employees – and the human potential available to a business. The people in an organization offer different skills, abilities and knowledge that may or may not be appropriate to the needs of the business. Additionally, their commitment and motivation vary. Some people identify with an organization and are motivated to help achieve its objectives. Others regard their employing firm as a vehicle for their personal goals. Some may be overworked while others are underutilized. Invariably, there is a gap or mismatch between the actual performance of employees and the ideal requirements of a business. The thinking behind the models we discuss in this chapter is that human resource management should (somehow) close this gap to achieve greater organizational effectiveness.

The human potential available to a business includes the recognition and development of unrealized skills and knowledge. Ingenuity and creativity can be tapped to develop innovative services and products. This also extends to people outside an organization – contractors, consultants, freelancers, temporary and part-time workers – who can add expertise, deal with unusual problems and provide the flexibility to give a competitive advantage.

Despite the widespread use of the term 'human resource management' and the proliferation of books, journals, conferences, academic sub-groups, etc., the subject remains 'and always has been from its earliest inception, highly controversial' (Storey, 2001).

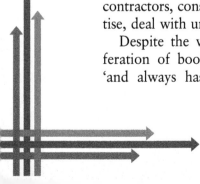

**TABLE 2.1**
Definitions of HRM

**27**

CHAPTER 2  The Concept of HRM

| Definition | Source |
|---|---|
| Human resource management involves all management decisions and actions that affect the relationship between the organization and employees – its human resources. | Beer *et al.*, 1984, p.1 |
| A method of maximizing economic return from labour resource by integrating HRM into business strategy. | Keenoy, 1990, p.3 |
| A strategic, coherent and comprehensive approach to the management and development of the organization's human resources in which every aspect of that process is wholly integrated within the overall management of the organization. HRM is essentially an ideology. | Armstrong, 1992, p.9 |
| Perhaps it is best to regard HRM as simply a notion of how people can best be managed *in the interests of the organization.* | Armstrong, 1994 |
| A diverse body of thought and practice, loosely unified by a concern to integrate the management of personnel more closely with the core management activity of organizations. | Goss, 1994, p.1 |
| HRM is a discourse and technology of power that aims to resolve the gap inherent in the contract of employment between the capacity to work and its exercise and, thereby, organize individual workers into a collective, productive power or force. | Townley, 1994, p.138 |
| Human resource management is a distinctive approach to employment management which seeks to achieve competitive advantage through the strategic development of a highly committed and capable workforce, using an integrated array of cultural, structural and personnel techniques. | Storey, 2001, p.6 |
| Human resource management is the attraction, selection, retention, development and use of human resources in order to achieve both individual and organizational objectives. | Cascio, 1998, p.2 |
| Human resources can be described as the organizational function accountable for obtaining and maintaining qualified employees. In today's complex environment, fulfilling that mission is a major contributor to an organization's success. | American Management Association, 2000, p.xvii |
| … The element of managerial work which is concerned with acquiring, developing and dispensing with the efforts, skills and capabilities of an organization's workforce and maintaining organizational relationships within which these human resources can be utilized to enable the organization to continue into the future within the social, political and economic context in which it exists. | Watson, 2003, p.1 |
| Designing management systems to ensure that human talent is used effectively and efficiently to accomplish organizational goals. | Mathis and Jackson, 2007, p.4 |

## HRM IN REALITY HUMAN RESOURCES

Sir, While visiting a patient in Edinburgh's Western General Hospital, I was shocked to see a six-foot-long board with large letters proclaiming: HUMAN RESOURCES. This distinguishes people who work in the hospital – doctors, nurses, porters, office workers, painters, managers – from other resources such as computers, laser beams, toilet rolls, refuse bins, beds, etc.

If these human resources are ill, are they labelled 'out of order' or 'broken down' and when being treated, are they being repaired? Are babies listed as 'in process of being manufactured' with an expected date when they will be 'operational'? Are old and dead people 'non-usable human resources' or can they be listed as 'replacement parts'?

When we define humans as resources, we are in danger of forgetting that we are dealing with people!

*Source: Cited in Price (1997).*

Storey describes HRM as 'an amalgam of description, prescription and logical deduction' and that it is an 'historically situated phenomenon'. Moreover, for Storey, HRM reflects the beliefs and assumptions of influential 'leading-edge' practitioners. There are grounds also to believe that it arose when confidence had been lost in more traditional approaches to people management because of new levels and types of competition.

Human resource management has often been presented as a proactive approach to managing people in contrast to the stereotypical view of personnel management (Ehnert, 2009: 88).

But some commentators see little difference between the two in their effects on the workforce, considering that historical and institutional changes are more significant (Godard, 2010). Proactive management emphasizes long-term thinking, anticipating changes and requirements before they become critical. But, in reality, HRM – like personnel management before it – is a mixture of anticipation and reaction as human resource managers may have to deal with unexpected problems and radical changes in employer policy such as site closures and redundancies because of market changes. To do so, they are expected to react quickly and competently within the bounds of employment law and contractual agreements. This requires that HRM should be both pragmatic and eclectic (Price, 2000): pragmatic because it aims to achieve practical solutions to real work problems; and eclectic because those solutions can be drawn from a variety of theoretical and managerial traditions as we saw in Chapter 1.

There remain questions about the nature of HRM, the domain it covers, the characteristics of HR practice, the reach of the subject and its antecedents, outcomes and impact. The controversy may have diminished somewhat since or become more focused on specific aspects of the subject (Bach, 2005: 15; Deckop, 2006: 9; Tyson, 2006: 62).

Table 2.1 gives a selection of definitions taken from various books and articles published over the past 30 years. Generally they come from an academic view of HRM. Arguably, the definitions may differ from the conceptual equivalent used by practitioners who are actively involved in human resource management. According to Hatcher (2006: 97):

Definitions of ... HRM are in many ways simple intellectual exercises. The extent that any of the many and varied definitions ... have been validated by practitioners or the extent they were developed with input from practice remains unclear, yet likely inadequate.

Our working definition of HRM for the purposes of this book is shown in Key concept 2.1. We will see that the variety, scope and intention found in definitions of HRM can be explained, in part, by some of the theories and models of human resource management to be explored in the next section.

---

**KEY CONCEPT 2.1**  HUMAN RESOURCE MANAGEMENT

This is a philosophy of people management based on the belief that human resources are uniquely important to sustained business success. An organization gains competitive advantage by using its people effectively, drawing on their expertise and ingenuity to meet clearly defined objectives. Human resource management is aimed at recruiting capable, flexible and committed people, managing and rewarding their performance and developing key competencies.

---

## MAPS AND MODELS OF HRM

There are numerous, widely different interpretations of HRM, some in the shape of formal models. The two most influential are the Harvard and Michigan models from the 1980s which we will consider later in this chapter. Consistent with the confusion over the definition of HRM, the major models are to some extent contradictory but also have common elements. Partly this is because some of the key concepts have arisen several times in different contexts.

---

**KEY CONCEPT 2.2**  HARD AND SOFT HRM

Storey (1989) has distinguished between hard and soft forms of HRM, typified by the Michigan and Harvard models respectively. 'Hard' HRM focuses on the resource side of human resources. It emphasizes costs in the form of 'headcounts' and places control firmly in the hands of management. Their role is to manage numbers effectively, keeping the workforce closely matched with requirements in terms of both bodies and behaviour. 'Soft' HRM, on the other hand, stresses the 'human' aspects of HRM. Its concerns are with communication and motivation. People are led rather than managed. They are involved in determining and realizing strategic objectives.

---

Sisson (1990) contends that there are four major features that appear to some degree in all HRM models and theories:

→ Integration of human resource policies with each other and with the organization's business plan. HRM is a key instrument of business strategy, viewing employees as important assets.

→ Responsibility for managing people moves from personnel specialists to senior (line) managers. Specialists provide a consultancy service for line managers.

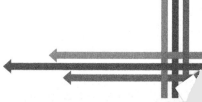

→ **Employee relations** shift away from **collective bargaining** – dialogue between management and unions. Instead, direct discussion between management and individual employees is encouraged.

→ A stress on commitment to the organization and personal initiative.

Softer models of HRM typically suggest that HR managers should become:

→ *Enablers* – structuring organizations to allow employees to achieve objectives.

→ *Empowerers* – devolving decision-making to the lowest level.

→ *Facilitators* – encouraging and assisting employees.

From this perspective, managers are no longer supervisors. The organizations move away from rigid hierarchies and power distinctions towards people taking responsibility for their own work. Guest (1987) provides a fusion of various HRM approaches into a theory of HRM which incorporates a number of policy goals:

→ Aim for a high level of commitment from employees, so that workers identify with the organization's goals and contribute actively to its improvement and success.

→ This enables the organization to obtain a high quality output from workers who want to continually improve standards.

→ An expectation of **flexibility** from workers – willingness to depart from fixed job definitions, working practices and conditions.

→ Strategic integration – all these strands link the organization's strategy. They are directed towards agreed objectives and interact with each other in a cohesive way.

These goals require support from top managers and integration of human resource strategy with business policy. The activities we outlined in Table 1.1 in the first chapter of this book are linked and overlaid by HR staff so as to improve communication and increase involvement, commitment and productivity. They are integrated and match the requirements of the organization's strategic plans. We cannot take a decision or make a change in one without having repercussions in at least some of the other areas.

The central aim of the HRM approach is to combine all personnel or human resource activities into an organized and integrated programme to meet the strategic objectives of an enterprise. It moves us away from commonsense solutions for day-to-day problems, such as 'get someone to fill that job', towards a conscious attempt to think through the consequences of hiring that 'someone'. Do we want a recruit who is perfect for that particular position right now, or an individual who might require considerable training but shows great adaptability? Do we hire someone for an overworked production department, knowing that the sales department are forecasting a drop in orders later in the year? The essential point of HRM is that the functions should be managed as a whole, and not as stand alone activities.

Legge (1989, 1995, 2001, 2004), for example, has been a steadfast critic of simplistic or evangelistic interpretations of HRM. The rhetoric of HRM claims that personnel and human resource management are distinctively different forms of people management. She demonstrates some flaws in this argument (Legge, 1989: 20; 1995: 36). Firstly, we have seen that 'hard' and 'soft' models of HRM themselves describe very different approaches. The 'soft' model can be identified readily with the welfarist tradition in personnel management

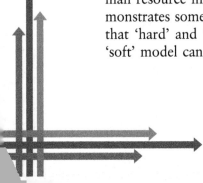

in countries such as the UK and Ireland, Australia, New Zealand and South Africa. Secondly, most texts do not actually compare like with like:

→ Accounts of HRM are normative – they are theoretical models of how human resource management could or should take place. That is to say, they express an 'ideal' or set of intentions for HRM. They do not tell us how human resource management actually happens in the real world. Moreover, the intentions of soft HRM are often pious and contradictory. We saw earlier that they are derived from much older concepts and techniques. What makes them 'HRM' is that their components are welded together into expressions of a particular, if divergent, philosophy of people management.

→ In contrast, accounts of personnel management are generally descriptive of personnel practice. Models of personnel are grounded in decades of activity whereas HRM is still comparatively new, and empirical evidence of its conduct is only beginning to emerge.

In short, we are comparing the stereotypical theories of a young form of people management (HRM) with the equally stereotyped practices of an old form (personnel management). If we seek out normative models of personnel management, Legge concludes that there is not much difference from normative models of HRM. We can do so by examining textbook accounts of personnel management in the 1980s which used the same terminology of 'integrating with organizational goals' and 'vesting control in the line' as newer HRM literature of the 'soft' variety. However, she finds differences in emphasis:

→ Personnel management focuses on the non-managerial workforce. HRM concentrates on managers and the 'core workforce'.

→ HRM is vested in line managers in their role as business managers not people managers. The focus is on managing all resources to maximize profit.

→ HRM models feature the role of senior managers in managing the culture of organizations.

Watson (2003) finds the use of 'hard' and 'soft' distinctions 'utterly unhelpful as an analytical tool', arguing that 'it confuses variations in intellectual or academic emphasis with variations in managerial practice'. More importantly, Watson considers that 'it ignores the political – economic context of managerial practices'. For Watson, the 'hard – soft' distinction is meaningless in a world where managers may choose either approach (or a mixture) on purely business grounds. Watson is equally unhappy with the use of the term 'rhetoric' (as opposed to reality) which he considers should be restricted to 'conceptualize the *linguistic techniques used by social actors to persuade others of the validity of their arguments*' (Watson's emphasis). Tellingly, he argues that:

To criticize managers for talking rhetorically is like criticizing birds for singing or dogs for barking. It is a manager's job to persuade people to think and work in particular ways.

From an entirely different perspective, Cakar and Bititci (2001) argue that whereas a number of authors, including Legge, have attempted to classify the various models of HRM using terms such as 'descriptive', 'normative' and 'prescriptive' (see Table 2.2), they do not offer precise definitions of these terms. Cakar and Bititci identify two sources of confusion: (a) confusion over the different types of classification, e.g. is there a difference between 'normative' (Legge, 1995) and 'prescriptive' (Storey, 1994a); and (b) a lack of clear definitions for each classification.

**TABLE 2.2**
Classifications of
HRM models

| Storey (1994a) | Legge (1995) | Tyson (1995) |
|---|---|---|
| Conceptual | Normative | Normative |
| Descriptive | Descriptive-functional | Descriptive |
| Prescriptive | Descriptive-behavioural | Analytical |
|  | Critical evaluative |  |

Cakar and Bititci (2001) state:

> HRM (people management) is a critical input enhancing the business results. ... HRM criteria cover planning, managing and improving the human resources; identifying, developing and sustaining people's knowledge and competencies; involving and empowering people. All these things have an effect on business results, because human resources are key assets. HRM has a significant impact on the performance of the manufacturing business.

Cakar and Bititci locate HRM within business process architecture, a classification of business processes into three groupings: manage processes, operate processes and support processes. They classify HRM as a support process together with finance and IT, arguing that HRM needs to be understood as a business process in order to improve manufacturing performance.

Boxall and Purcell (2003) point to two basic forms of normative HRM models or theories: best practice and best fit. Best practice approaches have been a feature of the debate since the 1990s, the best known of which are those presented by Jeffrey Pfeffer and David Ulrich. Pfeffer (1998) stresses, in a series of books, that the greatest competitive advantage is to be obtained from people rather than technology. He contends that investment in technology is not enough, because that technology is (or soon will be) available to competitors. And the more complex the technology, the more it requires people skills anyway. Instead we need that variant of HRM described as 'high-performance management' (US) or 'high-commitment management' (elsewhere). This topic will be discussed in Chapter 3. Ulrich (1997) argues:

> HR professionals must focus more on the deliverables of their work than on doing their work better. They must articulate their role in terms of value created. They must create mechanisms to deliver HR so that business results quickly follow. They must learn to measure results in terms of business competitiveness rather than employee comfort and lead cultural transformation rather than to consolidate, re-engineer or downsize when a company needs a turnaround.

Ulrich contends that modern HR professionals should have four roles: strategic partner, agent of change, administrative expert and employee champion. Each role furthers the goals of both the business and its employees. As strategic partner, the HR function must make sure that its practices, processes and policies complement the overall organizational strategy. It must also develop the capacity to execute that strategy in the minimum amount of time.

As we shall see in later sections of this book, organizational change has become a major issue due to speedier communication and global communication. The HR role as change agent, according to Ulrich, is that of a facilitator, involving modelling change to other departments, being a positive advocate of change across the entire organization, resolving

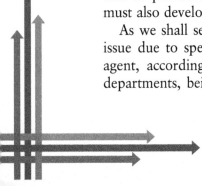

employee issues arising from change, and embedding change by implementing efficient and flexible processes.

The HR function spends most of its time as administrative expert, and rightfully so, according to Ulrich. This role covers the infrastructure of people management: recruiting, hiring, compensating, rewarding and disciplining, training, record keeping and terminating – and all of the other processes that involve people. HR's focus should be on ensuring that these processes are both efficient and optimized. The HR function must track, monitor and continuously improve on these basic processes to give credibility to its own existence.

The final role, 'employee champion', draws on the welfare manager roots of the personnel profession. This requires the HR function to know the concerns of employees and spend time talking to them and listening to their concerns. Moreover, according to Ulrich, the HR function should promote all possible methods of communication, including employee surveys, suggestion programmes, team meetings and any other means of sharing information and views. A key element of this role is ensuring that employees receive a fair hearing. We will discuss the concept of best practice further in later chapters on strategic HRM and change. We turn now to some of the most influential 'best fit' models of HRM.

## THE HARVARD MAP OF HUMAN RESOURCE MANAGEMENT

We noted earlier that the Harvard Business School generated one of the most influential models of HRM. The Harvard interpretation sees employees as resources. However, they are viewed as being fundamentally different from other resources – they cannot be managed in the same way. The stress is on people as *human* resources. The Harvard approach recognizes an element of mutuality in all businesses, a concept with parallels in Japanese people management, as we observed earlier. Employees are significant stakeholders in an organization. They have their own needs and concerns along with other groups such as shareholders and customers.

The Harvard view acknowledges that management has the greatest degree of power. Nevertheless there must be scope for accommodation of the interests of the various stakeholders in the form of trade-offs, particularly between owners, employees and different employee groups. The model also acknowledges the need for mechanisms to reconcile the inevitable tension between employee expectations and management objectives.

Beer *et al.* (1984) argue that when general managers determine the appropriate human resource policies and practices for their organizations, they require some method of assessing the appropriateness or effectiveness of those policies. Beer *et al.* devised the famous Harvard 'map' (sometimes referred to as the Harvard model) of HRM shown in Figure 2.1. This map is based on an analytical approach and provides a broad causal depiction of the 'determinants and consequences of HRM policies'. It shows human resource policies to be influenced by two significant considerations:

→ *Situational factors* in the outside business environment or within the firm such as laws and societal values, labour market conditions, unions, workforce characteristics, business strategies, management philosophy and task technology. According to Beer *et al.* these factors may constrain the formation of HRM policies but (to varying degrees) they may also be influenced by human resource policies.

→ *Stakeholder interests,* including those of shareholders, management employees, unions, community and government. Beer *et al.* argue that human resource policies should be influenced by all stakeholders. If not, 'the enterprise will fail to meet the needs of these stakeholders in the long run and it will fail as an institution'.

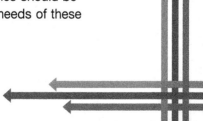

**FIGURE 2.1**

The Harvard interpretation of HRM

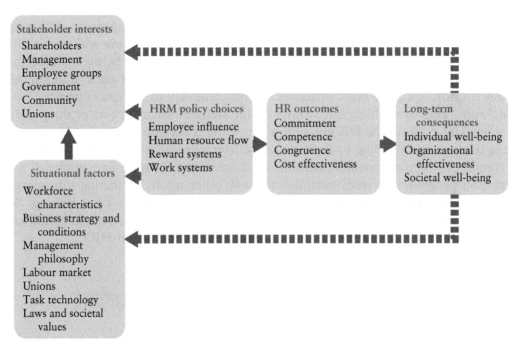

Source: Beer *et al.* (1984: p.16) Reproduced by permission of Professor M. Beer. Originally published in 1984 by The Free Press, a division of Simon & Schuster from *Managing Human Assets* by Beer, M., Spector, B., Lawrence, P.R., Mills, D.Q. and Walton, R.E. Copyright © 2003 M. Beer and B. Spector.

The emphasis is on psychological objectives: the 'human' side of human resource management, including:

→ motivating people by involving them in decision-making.

→ developing an organizational culture based on trust and teamwork.

Within the Harvard 'map' four strategic policy areas are addressed: human resource flows, reward systems, employee influence and work systems.

1 *Human resource flows:* managing the movement (flow) and performance of people:
   – into the organization, by means of effective recruitment programmes and selection techniques which result in the most suitable people;
   – through the organization, by placing them in the most appropriate jobs, appraising their performance and promoting the better employees;
   – out of the organization, terminating the employment of those no longer required, deemed unsuitable or achieving retirement age.
   Human resource policies must ensure the right mix and number of staff in the organization. This is achieved by the processes of resourcing and development of employee competences.

2 *Reward systems:* including pay and benefits designed to attract, motivate and keep employees.

3 *Employee influence:* controlling levels of authority, power and decision-making.

4 *Work systems:* defining and designing jobs, so that the arrangement of people, information and technology provide the most productive and efficient results.

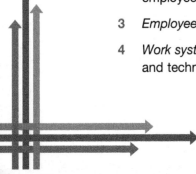

These policies result in the 'four Cs':

*Commitment* of employees to the organization's mission and values in a way thought to be typical of Japanese workers.

*Congruence*, linking human resource objectives with the organization's goals.

*Competence*, developing an appropriate mixture of skills, abilities and knowledge.

*Cost-effectiveness*, delivering performance in a competitive manner.

The Harvard model is strongly influenced by behavioural research and theory and stands in the tradition of 'human relations'. This is a humanistic and anti-authoritarian viewpoint which holds that employees will only adopt an organization's objectives if they wish to. They will not demonstrate enthusiasm and commitment if they are forced to comply. Accordingly, although strategic decision-making is channelled through top managers there is an emphasis on participation throughout the organization.

A further key point is that HRM is the responsibility of all managers – not just human resource specialists. Delivery of HRM initiatives is pushed down to line managers wherever possible. The Harvard model applies HRM to any manager with staff responsibilities. It should consider issues such as delegation, leadership, participation, team-building and organization from a non-specialist perspective. This will be further explored in Part Three in our discussion of organizational HRM. Taken to its extreme, it can be argued that if managers are sufficiently competent in handling people then personnel or human resource specialists are unnecessary.

Beer *et al.* (1984) argue:

> In the long run, striving to enhance all four Cs will lead to favourable consequences for individual well-being, societal well-being and organizational effectiveness [i.e. long-term consequences, the last box in Figure 2.1]. By organizational effectiveness we mean the capacity of the organization to be responsive and adaptive to its environment. We are suggesting, then, that human resource management has much broader consequences than simply last quarter's profits or last year's return on equity. Indeed, such short-term measures are relatively unaffected by HRM policies. Thus HRM policy formulation must incorporate this long-term perspective.

Beer *et al.* state that these 'four Cs' do not represent all the criteria that human resource policymakers can use to evaluate the effectiveness of human resource management, but consider them to be 'reasonably comprehensive' although they suggest that readers may add additional factors depending on circumstances.

## HRM POLICIES AND THEIR CONSEQUENCES

Beer *et al.* (1984) propose that long-term consequences (both benefits and costs) of human resource policies should be evaluated at three levels:

1 *Individual.* They argue that the well-being of employees must be considered separately and distinctly from that of the organization. Employees can be affected economically, physically or psychologically by HRM policies. But managers have different values and will weight those consequences differently according to those values. Some will focus on the organization at the expense of workers whereas others will regard employees as having legitimate claims to fair treatment.

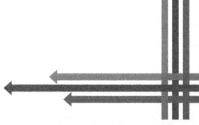

2   *Organizational*. Human resource policies have to be evaluated in terms of their contribution to business goals and organizational survival. Specifically, HRM policies can increase an organization's:
    – efficiency
    – adaptability
    – service performance
    – price performance
    – short-term results
    – long-term results.

3   *Societal*. HR practices can have wide consequences on society. For example, Beer *et al.* ask: 'What are the societal costs of a strike or a layoff?' They point out that 'alienated and laid-off workers may develop both psychological and physical health problems that make them burdens to community agencies funded by the local, state, or federal government. Today employers pass on many of the costs of their management practices to society'.

Beer *et al.* suggest that managers use their four Cs to analyze the questions raised above:

→   *Commitment:* do HRM policies enhance the **commitment** of employees to their work and their organization – and to what extent? Improved commitment may lead to more loyalty and better performance for the business. It can also benefit the individual through enhanced self-worth, dignity, psychological involvement and identity. And there is a societal spin-off because of these psychological benefits.

→   *Competence:* do HRM policies serve to attract, keep or develop employees who have valuable skills and knowledge – **competence** – both now and in the future? Again there are benefits at all three levels. If skills and knowledge are there when required, the organization benefits, and its employees experience an increased sense of self-worth and economic well-being.

→   *Cost-effectiveness:* the **cost-effectiveness** of particular HRM policies can be evaluated in terms of wages, benefits, turnover, absenteeism, strikes, etc. The costs can be judged for organizations, individuals and society as a whole.

→   *Congruence:* the question can be raised about the level of **congruence** in HRM policies between, for example:
    – management and employees
    – different employee groups
    – the organization and the community
    – employees and their families, and
    – within the individual.

## STAKEHOLDER THEORY

It is a fairly obvious truism that a wide range of people and interest groups have an involvement with any organization – including stock/shareholders, customers, suppliers, employees, the local community, government and others. They also have different and varying degrees of influence on the conduct and progress of the organization. There is a cultural context: the American stockholder approach contrasts strongly with the continental European or Japanese. The US approach (mirrored to some extent in countries like Australia, Canada,

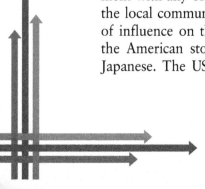

New Zealand, South Africa and the UK) places power (and reward) in the hands of the stockholder. According to Windsor (1998):

> Stakeholder theory is a critique of the strong stockholder doctrine in US corporation law and financial-economics theory positing that management's clear fiduciary responsibility is to maximize economic rents on behalf of the firm's legal owners (the residual claimants).
>
> Strong stockholder doctrine was articulated in *Dodge Brothers v. Ford* (1919), in which the Michigan Supreme Court ordered Ford Motor Co. to pay a special dividend.

In the stockholder model, other stakeholders – particularly employees – do not count. But Walker and Marr (2001) contend:

> It is always a mistake to operate as if employees are dispensable or easily interchangeable, because they are not. By definition, we cannot have an organization without the right employees – people who fit our cultures, who bring the right combination of talent, experience and personality to our organizations. These people are never easily replaced. Further, how humanely they are treated when they leave has a lasting impact on those who stay. It certainly sends a clear message about the company's commitment to workers.

You might think that stakeholder theory has its origins in HRM. Certainly the Harvard map of HRM of Beer *et al.* (1984) makes considerable use of the concept. But the main protagonist is regarded as being R. Edward Freeman, Olsson Professor of Applied Ethics at the University of Virginia's Darden School. He argued that managers should serve the interests of everyone with a 'stake' in (that is, affect or are affected by) the firm.

Stakeholders include shareholders, employees, suppliers, customers and the communities in which the firm operates – termed by Freeman the 'big five.' According to Freeman the purpose of the firm is to serve and coordinate the interests of its various stakeholders. The firm's managers are morally obliged to strike an appropriate balance among the big five interests when directing the firm's activities.

Shareholder theorists such as Milton Friedman argue that managers should serve the interests of a firm's owners – the shareholders. They contend that the social obligations of the firm are limited to:

→ making good on contracts

→ obeying the law

→ adhering to ordinary moral expectations.

Briefly, 'obligations to nonshareholders stand as sideconstraints in the pursuit of shareholder interests' (Marcoux, 2000: 1). Marcoux asks, in the Friedman vein:

> ...why firms are obligated to give something back to those to whom they routinely give so much already. Rather than enslave their employees, firms typically pay them wages and benefits in return for their labour. Rather than steal from their customers, firms typically deliver goods and services in return for the revenues that customers provide. Rather than free ride on public provisions, firms typically pay taxes and obey the law. Moreover, these compensations are ones to which the affected parties or (in the case of communities and unionized employees) their agents freely agree. For what reasons, then, is one to conclude that those compensations are inadequate or unjust, necessitating that firms give something more to those whom they have already compensated?

Even if one accepts the validity of stakeholder theory as a general approach, there remains a dispute over the meaning of 'stakeholder'. For example, Windsor (1998) considers that: 'who is

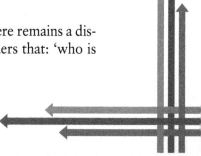

logically a stakeholder is in fact an unresolved matter in the literature' whereas Freeman's seminal conception was that the stakeholder community should include everyone who affected or was affected by an organization, a widely accepted definition. Samaras (2010) notes that stakeholders have different priorities (salience) and that measuring these is problematic, making it difficult to compare their relative importance.

Donaldson and Preston (1995: 86) distinguished between non-stakeholder *influencers* and 'true' stakeholders. They argued that stakeholdership as a concept is more than just a union of influence and impact. Windsor (1998) describes this restricted class of stakeholders as 'contributing beneficiaries'.

## A HARDER APPROACH: PEOPLE AS HUMAN RESOURCES

A different and more clearly 'best fit' view of HRM is associated with the Michigan Business School (Tichy *et al.*, 1982). There are many similarities with the Harvard 'map' but the Michigan model has a harder, less humanistic edge, holding that employees are resources in the same way as any other business resource. People have to be managed in a similar manner to equipment and raw materials. They must be:

→ obtained as cheaply as possibly

→ used sparingly

→ developed and exploited as much as possible.

Moreover, the same approach should be applied to all people who resource an organization – not just its employees. Human beings are 'matched' to business needs. They are recruited selectively and trained to perform required tasks. Whereas the Harvard approach was inspired by the behavioural sciences, the Michigan view was strongly influenced by strategic management literature. HRM is seen as a strategic process, making the most effective use of an organization's human resources. Hence there must be coherent human resource policies which 'fit' closely with overall business strategies.

In fact, HRM is seen as a secondary product of strategy and planning rather than a primary influence. Within this model, the purpose of human resource strategy is to assist in the achievement of an organization's goals. This requires an alignment of all HR systems with the formal organization. Since the nature of HRM is determined largely by the situation and the environmental context, there is little freedom of operation for human resource managers. At best, human resource managers can only choose from a menu of possible initiatives which fit business strategy. The Michigan School identified the following key areas for the development of appropriate HR policies and systems:

*Selection* of the most suitable people to meet business needs.

*Performance* in the pursuit of business objectives.

*Appraisal*, monitoring performance and providing feedback to the organization and its employees.

*Rewards* for appropriate performance.

*Development* of the skills and knowledge required to meet business objectives.

The Michigan model (see Figure 2.2) takes a top-down approach. In contrast with the Harvard viewpoint, control of human resources lies firmly in the hands of senior management. People are selected and trained to meet the performance needs of the organization.

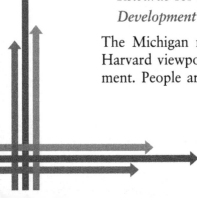

**FIGURE 2.2**

The Michigan model of HRM

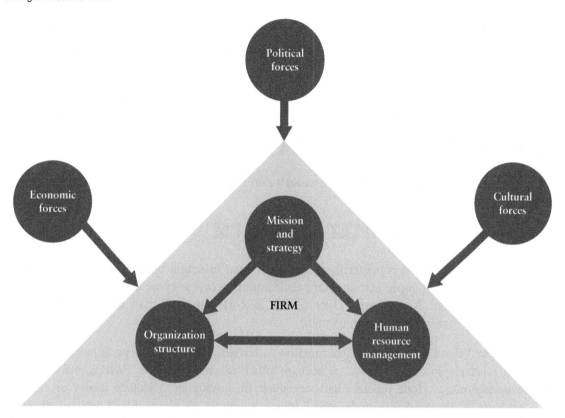

Source: Devanna *et al.* (1984) in Fombrun et al., *Strategic Human Resource Management* © 1984 John Wiley and Sons Inc. Reproduced by permission of John Wiley and Sons Inc.

However, this is not sufficient. Their attitudes and behaviour must also fit the strategic requirements of the business. The Michigan model advocates that HRM requires that employees show behavioural consistency with the ways of thinking and operating necessary to achieve business goals. For example, if strategy focuses on sales, employees will be expected to be extrovert, responsive and attentive to customer needs. On the other hand, an innovative strategy based on research and development will emphasise creativity, technical skill and long-term diligence. Behavioural consistency is an objective of change management, discussed in Chapter 12.

## ADOPTING HRM

So far, we have tried to establish a reasonably clear concept of HRM, despite the different emphases between the two major early models. At this point, however, we must inject a necessary element of caution. In the late 20th century human resource management was presented as a radical alternative to personnel management: so much so that it was regarded as a new paradigm (Kuhn, 1962) – a framework of thinking – consisting of exciting, modern ideas which would replace the stale and ineffective prescriptions of personnel management. Enthusiasts saw the transition from 'personnel' to 'human resources' as an inevitable and unstoppable process – a paradigm shift. In fact, the process has proven to be somewhat slow.

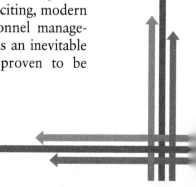

The HR function can be organized in a variety of ways. Adams (1991) identifies five main types of HR service, now commonly described as HR delivery models:

1  The traditional personnel department with a range of specialist human resource services.

2  In-house HR agencies which act as cost-centres, charging client departments for activities, e.g. recruitment.

3  Internal HR consultancies, selling their activities to the organization – possibly competing with outside agencies.

4  Business-within-business HR consultancy, selling services within and outside the company.

5  Outsourcing human resource services to an external provider.

## DIFFERENT INTERPRETATIONS OF HRM

As we have seen, HRM is primarily North American in origin but in the USA, far from causing a revolution in people management techniques, acceptance of the new interpretation has not been universal. Kochan and Dyer (2001: 272-3) comment that, despite an explosion of interest in human resource management:

> … we find that the human resource function within many American corporations remains weak and relatively low in influence, relative to other functions such as finance, marketing and manufacturing … little progress has been made in developing systematic theory or empirical evidence on the conditions under which human resources are elevated to a position where the firm sees and treats these issues as a source of competitive advantage. Nor is there much research that actually tests the effects of different strategies on the competitive position of the firm.

Why is this so? A number of explanations can be considered. First, there is the issue of perception: many US businesses fail to see the difference between HRM and earlier forms of people management. We observed at the beginning of this chapter that the term 'human resource management' had been used interchangeably with 'personnel management' in the USA. This continues to be the case. For example, many American 'HRM' texts are concerned with the functional activities of personnel specialists – their philosophy is little different from 1970s texts. In part, this is due to the managerialist and anti-union tradition of personnel management in the USA. For US practitioners, HRM was not such a radical departure from previous practice as it seemed to be for welfare-orientated personnel managers and industrial relations specialists in other countries. Legge (2004: 3) has changed her position or, perhaps more fairly, moved with the times, in concluding that the preoccupation with supposed differences between 'personnel management' and HRM is now a moribund, indeed meaningless, debate:

> There is little point in discussing the niceties of the differences between personnel management and HRM when, in the USA, HRM is just another term for personnel management. In any case it was a bit of a straw man debate. Whether HRM was considered to be different from personnel management – in the UK at least – largely depended on the point of comparison. Sharp distinctions and contrasts emerged if the normative aspirations of HRM were compared with the descriptive practices of personnel management, but otherwise faded into several different emphases, all of which, though, pointed to HRM, in theory at least, being an essentially more central, strategic task than personnel management.

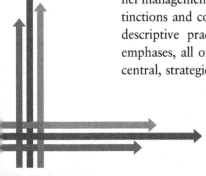

Kochan and Dyer (2001: 282) also point to the 'market failures' problem. HRM is generally portrayed as a long-term perspective. Within this context an organization's people are investments for the future. They are not to be hired and fired for short-term purposes. But this concept sits uneasily with the prevailing short-termist ideology of business in the English-speaking world. Long-term investment is expensive and requires the use of money which might otherwise be diverted to dividend payments. This draws unfavourable comment from shareholders. If all businesses in an industry were to take the same human resource initiatives there would be no problem. This is unlikely. Moreover, expensively developed staff can be creamed off by competitors unwilling to invest in training but prepared to pay a premium for competent recruits.

The difficulties associated with long-term, soft HRM are reflected in the history of IBM. As one of the world's major businesses, IBM was used as an example of excellence by Peters and Waterman (1982). It hit its high point in 1984 with profits of over US$6 billion – a sensational 25 per cent return on equity for shareholders. At that time it was the dominant force in world computing with 37 per cent of the total market. IBM was also featured by Beer and his colleagues as an example of a corporation which utilized the Harvard form of HRM. However, recent years have seen a significant shift towards a harder model as IBM encountered serious problems in the 1990s. Despite increases in overall revenues, the company was forced into major restructuring and job losses.

The IBM case emphasizes a number of difficulties associated with the adoption of 'soft' HRM. When business is good and continued growth seems probable, a company can afford to manage its people in a humane and considerate way. However, when the going gets tough and significant change is demanded, profitability becomes the prime consideration. The pressure for action from other stakeholders becomes overwhelming. It appears that, in such circumstances, managers have no alternative to adopting a 'hard' approach. The choice between hard and soft models is governed as much (if not more) by the prevailing market situation as it is by any question of managerial humanitarianism (Watson, 2003).

According to Weiss (1999: 3):

> In the past the HR department attempted to meet the company's needs without actively focusing on the company's direction and the return on investment. Today, however, the conditions under which HR needs to operate have changed. … Just as the finance department is responsible for overseeing the financial assets of the business, human resources' role is to oversee and be accountable for the investment in human capital (the money it takes to cultivate people and their talents). The company will maximize its return on this investment in human capital when HR maximizes the contribution people make to the company's strategic direction.

Weiss argues for the transformation of the human resource function in terms of its priorities, accountabilities, roles and organizational design. He emphasizes:

*Strategic value*, ensuring that HR focuses on transforming organizational processes and people management practices in order to achieve competitive advantage.

A *competitive mindset*, awareness that people management processes can be supplied by an outside specialist provider if the HR department is not efficient and proactive.

*Process outcomes*, achieving a balance between the need for measurable outcomes from HR initiatives and practices and 'excellence in process', i.e. doing it well. In the past human resource departments could have been accused of an obsession with the quality of practices, and showing little concern for the value of their outcomes.

Kochan and Dyer (2001) could find no evidence that American businesses (in general) had taken the value of HRM seriously. They argued that there was little in US management history – or in the behaviour of present-day American managers – 'to suggest that management

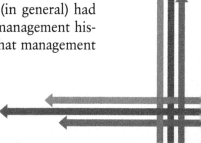

## HRM IN REALITY   THE FOURTH BEST JOB IN AMERICA

That's 'human resources manager', in case you're wondering, according to the *Money* magazine and Salary.com list of 50 Best Jobs in America.

The survey of about 250 of the best-paid jobs in 19 industries, mostly requiring higher education, found that software engineers have the best jobs in the USA, with college professors second and (the much better compensated) financial advisors placed third. Online surveys were completed by 26 000 people to rank the best jobs.

The HR profession is rated well on:

→   flexibility

→   overall compensation

→   opportunity for growth

→   level of stress.

Additionally, the survey highlights a trend toward outsourcing operational and administrative tasks, freeing HR to concentrate on a strategic role and adding to the challenge and interest in the profession.

'We're not surprised to see HR rank so highly. We couldn't agree more that HR is a great profession', said Susan R. Meisinger, SPHR, President and CEO of the Society for Human Resource Management (SHRM). 'The profession is rapidly evolving where HR executives are playing a much larger role in determining the overall direction of their organization. These developments add to the vibrancy of the profession as more organizations look to HR for strategies to align their workforce with the goals of the business.'

'HR is an exciting profession, and with the projected growth and competitive salaries, there will be many opportunities available for bright new HR professionals who want to play a critical role in shaping the success of organizations', added Meisinger.

Following HR came physician's assistant, market research analyst, computer/information technology analyst, real estate appraiser, pharmacist and psychologist.

*To what extent does this survey indicate that HR is a prestigious occupation?*

*Source: Reprinted with permission from HRM Guide USA (http://www.hrmguide.com).*

alone, left to its own devices, will produce the transformation in organizational principles needed to sustain and diffuse the delineated human resource principles'. Accepting that some senior executives may share general values such as those outlined by Weiss, Kochan and Dyer contend that other pressures tend to force them into short-term actions (such as firing people) in order to placate major shareholders. A study by Rynes *et al.* (2002) shows that only 1 per cent of a sample of HR managers, directors and vice-presidents said they usually read HR research literature and 75 per cent said they never read it at all. Not surprisingly, they made little use of the findings of HR research.

Dipboye (2007) cautions about taking HR research or 'HR science' too seriously. He produces a list of 'outrageous statements' and invites comment:

1   *Rigor in HR research is more façade than reality.* Researchers are using statistical and other mathematical techniques that are becoming too sophisticated for most of their readers to understand. But, Dipboye argues, the sophistication may be more a matter of appearance than reality and the formal models and theories they represent have never been tested empirically.

2   *HRM research is relevant only to academics.* Practitioners, as indicated in the study by Rynes *et al.*, do not read the literature, do not use the findings to improve their techniques,

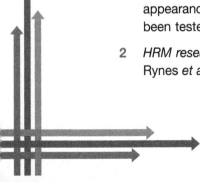

prefer management fads and fashions and have completely different frames of reference to those of academics.

3   *HR science has not advanced understanding or application.* He argues that research is not going much beyond the trivial and relying too much on existing literature to generate questions rather than to develop theory. He also points to the 'double-edged sword' implications of meta-analysis as an increasingly common technique.

4   *A scientific HR requires monogamy in research questions but promiscuity in methodology.* HR researchers need to widen their methodologies and try to answer 'big questions' rather than narrow fashionable questions.

5   *Recognize that HR is all OB.* Using OB (organizational behaviour) in a loose way he contends that all HR takes place in an organizational context and cannot be abstracted from organizational structures and processes.

6   *Simultaneously embrace the simplicity of science and the complexity of practice.* HR researchers need to recognize the narrowness of analytic approaches and the need to embody paradox and complexity in their theories.

7   *Take the M out of HRM.* Human resource researchers should look beyond the needs of managers to include the interests of all employees.

## THE SPREAD OF HRM

When HRM was imported into other countries, it arrived with many of the contradictions inherent in American practice. Further confusion was created as its principles were considered in the light of local people management traditions. As many commentators have been quick to point out, there is a 'central uncertainty' as to exactly what HRM is (Blyton and Turnbull, 1992: 2). The nature of HRM has been the focus of a particularly vigorous debate in the UK. Its meaning and distinctiveness from personnel management have been the topic of numerous articles, texts and conference papers. For example, Guest (1989, 1997) has developed a particularly influential model of HRM with six dimensions of analysis:

→   HRM strategy

→   HRM practices

→   HRM outcomes

→   Behaviour outcomes

→   Performance outcomes

→   Financial outcomes.

The model is prescriptive in the sense that it is based on the assumption that HRM is distinctively different from traditional personnel management (rooted in strategic management etc.). Additionally, it is idealistic, implicitly embodying the belief that fundamental elements of the HRM approach (essentially those of the Harvard map) such as commitment, have a direct relationship with valued business consequences. However, Guest has acknowledged that the concept of commitment is 'messy' and that the relationship between commitment and high performance is difficult to establish. It also employs a 'flow' approach, seeing strategy underpinning practice, leading to a variety of desired outcomes.

Like its American predecessors, this British model is unitarist (tying employee behaviour and commitment into the goals of strategic management) and lukewarm on the value of trade unions. Guest views the employee relationship as one between the individual and the organization.

Paradoxically, attempts to define HRM too precisely seemed to have resulted in confusion and contradiction rather than clarity. Already there are different variations on the terminology such as human capital management and *talent management* and jobs at the 'C' level occur with titles such as chief people officer as well as chief human resource officer. Nevertheless, personnel departments have refused to go away. A casual examination of job advertisements in the press will reveal that applications are sometimes still to be sent to 'personnel managers', 'personnel departments', and even 'staffing officers'. At the same time, advertisements for 'human resource' jobs are common – particularly at a senior level – even if applications are to be sent to the personnel office! Indeed, as we can see in the 'HRM in reality' box, the lead representative body in the UK continues to use the word 'Personnel' in its title, unlike its equivalents in the USA (SHRM – Society for Human Resource Management) and Australia (AHRI – Australian Human Resource Institute).

It is evident, therefore, that defining and accepting HRM comes down to a matter of opinion – or vested interest. Indeed, some interpretations have a strong constituency. It can be seen from Table 2.3 that each of these views has a natural audience able to identify their own interests with a particular interpretation. Hence it is possible to find accounts stressing one of the following:

→ *HRM is really personnel management.* Human resource management is a modernized form of 'personnel', repackaged to enhance the status of personnel managers. It has a hard edge, entitling HR managers to the same respect as finance professionals. HRM is based on integrated and coherent recruitment, assessment and development programmes. It is sophisticated, requiring rigorous training under the auspices of a professional body or university.

→ *HRM is a strategic model.* It employs the techniques of strategic management for the utilization of human resources. It focuses on senior managers' concern with achieving objectives and containing costs. HRM aims for a seamless link between business policy and recruitment, performance assessment, reward management, development and dismissal. HRM is a mechanism for control and the exercise of power by top management. It encourages employee attitudes and behaviour which are consistent with business goals. HRM is just one aspect of a senior manager's strategic repertoire. It requires a wide appreciation of the industry and the organization and fits resource-based theories which are familiar from business strategy literature. This interpretation owes its inspiration largely to the Michigan model.

→ *HRM is people management.* It covers all aspects of managing employees in its widest sense and emphasizes the role of line managers in overseeing their own staff. From this perspective, HRM is a new generic label for all the techniques and tactics available to manage people. It concentrates on translating organizational objectives into operational achievement by winning employee commitment and gaining high-quality performance. HRM is practical and pragmatic. This interpretation derives from the Harvard model. With some reservations, this is the approach taken in this book.

The value and popularity of HRM may derive from its openness to varied interpretations. It is possible to argue that the term is a useful, 'catch-all phrase, reflecting general intentions but devoid of specific meaning' (Guest, 1989). This allows it to be applied in a variety of circumstances. Individual authors and practitioners interpret HRM according to their own

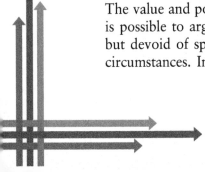

## HRM IN REALITY   THE MYTHS ABOUT HR CAREERS

A Chartered Institute of Personnel and Development (CIPD) survey published in 2005 found that most HR professionals are happy with their career choice and 81 per cent would make the same choice if they started all over again.

The CIPD report looks at the career experiences of over 1800 HR professionals and challenges many of the negative myths about human resource specialists. According to Jessica Jarvis, CIPD Learning, Training and Development Adviser and author of the report:

'It sometimes seems that it is fashionable for the HR profession to indulge in doom, gloom and self-loathing. But this survey turns some of the myths on their heads. A profession where the vast majority would pick the same career path if they could start over again is a confident one that is happy with itself.'

Main findings:

→ Contrary to the common belief that the most senior people in HR have little background in human resources and are parachuted into their jobs, the average HR director has 20 years' HR experience, has worked in four different organizations and taken five major career steps to their present jobs.

→ Human resource professionals are (mostly) not serial career changers. They average 15 years' service within the HR profession.

→ HR professionals do not lack experience elsewhere in the world of work. Just 26 per cent of those surveyed began their careers in human resources. Eighty-three per cent of respondents had worked outside HR at some point in their careers – typically, sales/marketing/retail, or possibly general business/management and finance.

→ Survey respondents rated the most important factors in a HR career as personal drive, business/ industry awareness and generalist experience.

→ Moving between organizations is seen as important to career progression. On average,

respondents had taken four major career steps and worked for an average of three organizations.

Staying in one organization, over-specializing and call centres/shared service centres were highlighted as significant barriers to career progression. Forty per cent of respondents felt outsourcing was having a negative impact on HR careers.

Apart from age, there were few reliable indicators of the chances of reaching senior levels in HR. These were: being a generalist rather than a specialist; having a degree; having worked for a number of different organizations and having had a number of significant career steps. But many other factors – including qualifications, experience and competencies – had an influential role in reaching senior ranks. Jessica Jarvis commented:

> It seems that this voicing of more positive beliefs about HR from those we surveyed signals a change in attitude within the profession, with people gaining more belief in the function's ability to become a more credible and respected business player. Certainly it seems that the time is now ripe for this to happen. Several factors are coming together to improve the standing of HR in the business community – the rise of business partnering is making HR more integral to the business, and prominent issues such as human capital reporting and corporate social responsibility are carrying HR up the corporate ladder. HR must step up to the challenge and demonstrate how their strategic activities can impact in business terms.

The CIPD report also highlighted some other myths and realities:

→ 'Nobody applies for top jobs any more – it's all done by head hunting'. Not true according to the survey. Job applications were the most likely way to senior HR positions. Only 26 per cent of directors and 17 per cent of senior/group executives were headhunted.

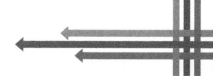

→ 'Consultants are too young to know much about HR'. Not according to the survey, the independent consultant group had an average age of 51. They had also, on average, been in HR for 22 years – longer than the average HR Director.

→ 'People in HR don't understand the business'. A mere 17 per cent of respondents had no experience of working outside the HR function. 'Business awareness/sense' was the second most

important factor in getting to the top in HR, and three-quarters agreed that 'Experience in another function (outside HR) furthers HR careers'.

*How would you explain the stereotypical views about human resource specialists given the findings in this report?*

*Source: Reprinted with permission from HRM Guide UK (http://www.hrmguide.co.uk).*

**TABLE 2.3**
Perceptions of HRM

| Perspective | Audience | Focus | Interest |
|---|---|---|---|
| HRM as people management | General/line managers | Managing people as a direct, inter-personal activity | Commitment<br>Performance<br>Leadership<br>Team-building |
| HRM as personnel management | Personnel specialists | Technical skills for assessment, selection, training, etc. | Appraisals<br>Recruitment<br>Selection methods<br>Development |
| HRM as strategic management | Senior managers | People as assets (and liabilities) | Strategic planning<br>Performance management<br>Development<br>Managing change |

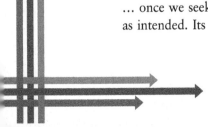

background, interests and intended audiences. Applying the principle from *Alice in Wonderland,* 'it is almost as if HRM is whatever you want it to be' (Armstrong, 1989: 60). Indeed, Keenoy and Anthony (1992: 238) consider that we should not look too closely:

… once we seek to explain HRM, to subject it to any analysis or criticism, it ceases to function as intended. Its purpose is to transform, to inspire, to motivate and, above all, to create a new

## HRM IN REALITY CHARTERED INSTITUTE OF PERSONNEL AND DEVELOPMENT

'HRM' has never been a favoured title amongst HR practitioners in the UK. In fact the HR community seems to have gone out of its way to avoid using the term. Currently the lead body in the UK calls itself the 'Chartered Institute of Personnel and Development' but this is just the latest in a long list of titles.

It originated as the 'Welfare Workers' Association' in 1913, changed to 'Industrial Welfare Workers' in 1924, changed again to the 'Institute of Labour Management' in 1931 and then the 'Institute of Personnel Management (IPM)' in 1946. The IPM label lasted for almost half a century.

Then in 1994 the 'Institute of Personnel Management' merged with the 'Institute of Training and Development' to become (very imaginatively) the 'Institute of Personnel and Development' (IPD). This was a time when management fashion dictated that basic human resource management should be conducted by line managers and it seemed that the old personnel profession might soon dwindle to a small number of recruitment, development and other specialists. Mike Bett, IPD president, argued that: 'There should be a professional personnel and development specialist on all top management teams: in the boardroom and on the executive committees.' The role of the IPD was to be 'the pre-eminent professional body influencing and improving the quality, thinking and practice of people management and development.' But there was little evidence that the influence and authority of personnel specialists

increased during the late 1990s. From 1 July 2000 the Chartered Institute of Personnel and Development replaced the IPD. Geoff Armstrong, Director-General of the CIPD said that: 'To all intents and purposes, the two organizations are the same.' In terms of staff, organization and mission that is. But he identified three benefits from proclaiming the chartership:

→ A recognition of professionalism, a body of knowledge and the practical competence of the membership.

→ It emphasizes the 'must belong' status of the organization for anyone involved in people management and development.

→ A recognition in the charter that this is a body that government and other influential bodies should consult.

Technology, globalization and competition are making renewed demands on the way people are managed. According to Geoff Armstrong: '…. we are the specialists, the experts in the field. As the knowledge economy gathers pace, our colleagues increasingly look to us to deliver the strategies that make the winning difference.'

Time will tell!

*Source: Reprinted with permission from HRM Guide UK (http://www.hrmguide.co.uk).*

'reality' which is freely available to those who choose or are persuaded to believe. To explain it is to destroy it.

## SUMMARY

The meaning and prevalence of HRM are topics that continue to attract debate and disagreement. As a consequence, practitioners and textbook authors use a diverse and sometimes contradictory range of interpretations. We found that HRM has a variety of

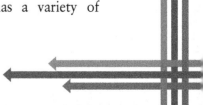

definitions but there is general agreement that it has a closer fit with business strategy than previous models, specifically personnel management. The early models of HRM take either a 'soft' or a 'hard' approach, but this may be a simplistic distinction as economic circumstances are more likely to drive the choice than any question of humanitarianism. The status of HRM is also problematic, with a range of views on the value and purpose of the profession.

 **FURTHER READING**

1 *Human Resource Management: A Critical Text* edited by John Storey (3rd edition, Cengage Learning, 2007) provides a wide-ranging and authoritative account of the origins and development of HRM.

2 David Ulrich's *Human Resource Champions* Harvard Business Press (1997), has been a best-seller among practitioners and outlines much of his thinking on the key roles of the HR function.

3 *The Future of Human Resource Management: 64 Thought Leaders Explore the Critical HR Issues of Today and Tomorrow,* edited by Michael R. Losey, Sue Meisinger and Dave Ulrich (2nd edition, Wiley, 2006) is a compilation of articles by an international panel of expert contributors who offer their views on the state of HR and what to expect in the future.

**REVIEW QUESTIONS**

1 Is HRM a fashion or is it here to stay? What is the probability that HRM will be the dominant framework for people management in the 21st century?

2 Compare and contrast the textbook and practitioner definitions of HRM. In what ways (if any) are they different?

3 Evaluate the following statement: 'HRM is in reality a symbolic label behind which lurk multifarious practices, many of which are not mutually dependent on one another' (Storey, 1992).

4 Is managing people just a matter of commonsense? If so, what value can we attach to theories and models?

5 What do you understand by the statement that 'functions should be managed as a whole, and not as stand-alone activities'?

6 Given Cakar and Bititci's criticism, how useful are 'typologies' of HRM such as Legge's?

7 Evaluate the contributions of Fitz-Enz, Pfeffer and Ulrich towards understanding the purpose of human resource management. Are they stating anything beyond the obvious?

8 Do you consider that the Harvard four Cs model can give us a complete evaluation of HRM in a particular organization?

9 What do you understand by the concept of 'stakeholder'?

10 The Harvard model of HRM is an idealistic representation of people management. In the real world it is bound to be displaced by harder models of HRM. Do you agree or disagree with these statements?

11 HRM theorists argue that employees are assets and not just costs. What does this mean in practice?

12 What are the main differences between the Harvard and Michigan models?

13 Compare and contrast the 'hard' and 'soft' forms of HRM. Is this a useful distinction?

 **CASE STUDY FOR DISCUSSION AND ANALYSIS**

Read the following case study. Is this a realistic or an idealistic portrayal of a senior HR job?

## The 21st century chief human resources officer

Senior HR leaders have a changing role to play with the rise in prominence of issues such as:

→ workforce demographics and global talent trends

→ corporate scandals and intensifying regulatory challenges

→ rising costs of health care and pensions

→ technology innovations enabling new ways of working

→ increasing globalization

→ endless pressures to boost workforce profitability and performance.

Meet a developing 21st century professional: the Chief Human Resources Officer (CHRO).

A 2006 report from Deloitte Consulting, 'Strategist & Steward: The Evolving Role of the Chief Human Resources Officer', outlines the challenges, processes and performance measures facing today's CHRO. According to the report, the modern CHRO is required increasingly to act as both strategist and steward. To quote Deloitte's media release, they are 'leaders who not only manage the HR function and operations team, but also collaborate directly with the CEO and board of directors on a range of critical business issues.'

Jeff Schwartz, principal and national co-leader of Deloitte Consulting's CHRO Services said:

'The requirements and perception of HR are changing dramatically as this function's leadership is now expected to play a central role in building and shaping – not just staffing – the enterprise strategy. This is an environment that HR leaders have longed for – where their executive peers would view HR as a business partner, rather than as a back-office administrator. Now CHROs must make sure that they are up to the task. The central challenge for CHROs is to view themselves as business leaders first, i.e., senior business executives responsible for the HR portfolio.'

Deloitte Consulting's framework categorizes the CHRO's roles and responsibilities in four major ways:

*Workforce strategist.* Integrating business strategy and overall performance are increasingly important tasks. As well as supporting and implementing overall workforce strategy, CHROs also have a significant role to perform in developing and informing HR strategy – helping the CEO and other senior managers design strategies that are consistent with global labour trends, available talent and next-generation leadership and employees.

*Organizational and performance conductor.* How do businesses get the best performance from their employees? Organizations are increasingly complex and

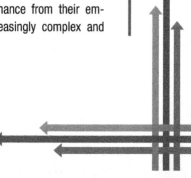

performance improvements can be required from departments involving:

→ operations across geographic boundaries

→ virtual teams

→ contingent workforces

→ telecommuting

→ job-sharing

→ flexible hours

→ workforce diversity.

Modern CHROs need to be able to navigate all such options, acting as change masters and architects of organizational structures and rewards programmes.

*HR service delivery owner.* Despite the increasing focus on wider business issues, CHROs must still provide cost-effective, day-to-day HR administration and operations. But they need to devote less time to overseeing their own HR systems and processes and spend more time managing a complex mix of in-house, self-service and external resources. Internal and external services must be blended into a cohesive and seamless working operation.

*Compliance and governance regulator.* CHROs must work directly with their boards on employee issues directly related to the critical areas of:

→ risk management

→ regulatory compliance

→ ethics

→ integrity.

Additionally, they are expected also to assist with a wide range of board-related issues, such as board member selection and orientation, executive compensation and succession planning.

William Chafetz, principal and national co-leader of Deloitte Consulting's CHRO Services said:

> The role of the CHRO as an enterprise business leader is still evolving – but this transformation has never been more timely or relevant. As human capital-related issues, such as baby boomer retirement, generational differences, skills gaps and workforce globalization continue to challenge a company's overall strategy and bottom line, the CHRO must become an increasingly familiar face and, in many companies, a potent force in the boardroom and executive suite, paving the way toward change, performance and new ways of working.

*Source: Reprinted with permission from HRM Guide USA (http://www.hrmguide.com).*

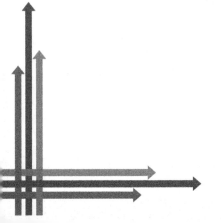

# CHAPTER 3
## HRM in practice

## LEARNING OBJECTIVES

The purpose of this chapter is to:

→ Introduce the concept of high commitment/performance work systems.

→ Provide an overview of human resource systems.

→ Evaluate the contribution of HRM and HR technology to business effectiveness.

→ Provide a checklist of HRM principles.

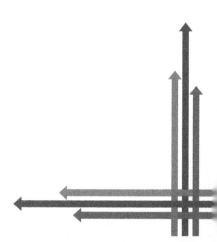

# HIGH PERFORMANCE WORK SYSTEMS

In all the debates about the meaning, significance and practice of HRM, nothing *seems* so certain as the link between HRM and performance. But is it? Legge (2001), one of the most respected and astute commentators on human resource management states:

> And what, might it be asked, are the present-day concerns of HRM researchers, who ... are of a modernist, positivist persuasion? In a word, their project is the search for the Holy Grail of establishing a causal relationship between HRM and performance. And in this search some success is claimed, in particular that the more the so-called 'high commitment/performance' HRM practices are adopted, the better the performance.

Legge argues that in order to examine the relationship between performance and HRM we need to address three fundamental questions:

1   How are we to conceptualize HRM?

2   How are we to conceptualize performance?

3   How are we to conceptualize the relationship between the two?

The theoretical meaning of HRM was addressed in the previous chapter. Here we will look at HRM operationalized (according to Legge's approach) in terms of high commitment or high performance work practices. In practice, unpicking the meaning of 'high performance management' from wider notions of management can be difficult. For example, the US Department of Labor (1998) defines high performance as: 'A comprehensive customer-driven system that aligns all of the activities in an organization with the common focus of customer satisfaction through continuous improvement in the quality of goods and services'.

You will probably have recognized that the roots of this definition lie in total quality management. In the past, the practice of TQM has often been procedural and bureaucratic but the high-performance approach has brought in elements of human relations or 'soft' HRM such as commitment and empowerment. The term was publicized by Nadler *et al.* (1992) within his 'organizational architecture' approach, focusing on 'autonomous work teams' and 'high performance work systems'. Lawler III (1991) used the term 'high performance involvement' as an alternative to empowerment, advocating the use of small teams of highly committed employees.

Is 'high performance management' just another management fad or fashion? Holbeche (2005: 10) ventures the opinion that 'while some guru-led management fashions may have come and gone over the last 20 years or so, the aspiration towards more sustainable high performance is a more enduring theme, underpinning much of what has gone before ...'.

The Institute of Work Psychology (2001) at the University of Sheffield states that high performance work systems usually involve three main sets of management practices designed to enhance employee involvement, commitment and competencies. They describe these as:

1   Changing the design and conduct of jobs through flexible working (especially functional flexibility – broadening the pool of 'who does what' through training), team work, quality circles, suggestion schemes.

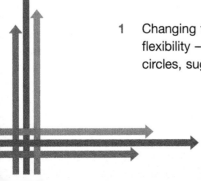

2   Ensuring that employees are given the knowledge and competences to handle high performance work through teamwork training, team briefings, interpersonal skills, appraisal, information sharing.

3   Resourcing and development practices designed to attract and keep the right people with the right motivation. These include some guarantee of job security, an emphasis on internal selection, sophisticated selection techniques and employee attitude surveys with feedback to the workers involved. Here there are further indications of an integration of 1970s and 1980s management techniques together with a certain amount of repackaging for the 21st century.

Pfeffer (1998) acknowledges that building a high-commitment organization is not easy and that CEOs are often too busy or distracted to focus on the people. However, he advocates the following as key elements of high-commitment management:

→ *Building trust* so that everyone in the organization can share knowledge.

→ *Encouraging change.*

→ *Measuring what matters,* arguing that financial data tends to be historical rather than what matters now. He advocates use of the '**balanced scorecard**', a technique that also weighs non-financial criteria in the equation.

---

**KEY CONCEPT 3.1**  BALANCED SCORECARD

A conceptual framework used to translate an organization's vision into a set of performance indicators, including measures of financial performance, customer satisfaction, internal business processes and learning and growth. Both current performance and efforts to learn and improve can be monitored using these measures.

---

Pfeffer (1998) presents his model of the high performance work system, including seven key factors:

1   *Employment security.* This is fundamental to gaining employee commitment. If employees are not in fear of working themselves out of their jobs, they will contribute freely to improved productivity. When employees are secure they are prepared to think and act with the long term in mind.

2   *Selective hiring.* Employment resourcing has to be disciplined to ensure that the right people are in the right places. Pfeffer advocates competency based selection aimed at identifying critical skills and job-related attributes. The quality of employees has a direct impact on organizational effectiveness and market success.

3   *Self-managed teams and decentralization of decision-making.* Traditional supervision should be replaced by peer control, allowing a large proportion of the workforce to accept accountability and responsibility for company performance. They are more likely to understand how their work affects the work of other employees. Ideas can be pooled and layers of unnecessary hierarchy disposed of.

4   *High compensation contingent on organizational performance.* Profits can still be made with higher pay rates if the right pay format is used, such as gain sharing, stock options

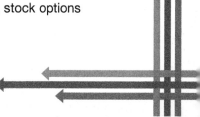

and pay for skill. When employees feel that they are fairly rewarded they are more likely to show commitment.

5 *Training.* Employees possessed of up-to-date skills and knowledge are more flexible and prepared to initiate change, predict and solve problems and take responsibility for product and service quality.

6 *Reduction of status differences.* Creating a more egalitarian workplace encourages open lines of communication. Employees have a greater sense of common purpose.

7 *Sharing information.* Making financial information available to employees encourages trust and commitment to the company. Employees can also prioritize multiple and conflicting goals.

In the public sector, the US Department of Labor (1998) sees high performance revolving around three main principles:

1 An organizational focus on achieving customer satisfaction.

2 A constant search for continuous, long-term improvement in all organizational processes and outputs.

3 Taking steps to ensure the full involvement of the entire workforce in achieving quality.

So what are the key operating practices of such a high performance system? According to the US Department of Labor they are:

*Leadership and support from top levels of management*: the most critical element of the process. Top managers must develop a climate of trust where risk-taking and innovation are encouraged and rewarded. This means that workers and managers must together develop a shared vision of where they want the organization to go. It also means that there must be tolerance shown towards the inevitable setbacks and mistakes along the way. And managers must be open to suggestions and requests from workers for the removal of barriers to good customer service. This implies a considerable change from the top-down 'I'm in charge and all mistakes will be punished' attitude prevalent among higher management.

*Strategic planning*: mapping out how the organization will achieve its strategic objectives. But such a plan must be constantly reviewed.

*Ongoing commitment to training and development for all employees*: not just top-middle ranking staff where organizations concentrate their funds too often. Neglecting the training and development of customer-facing staff is potentially damaging in terms of its consequences. Somehow, an organization must also withstand the pressure from budget-cutters to reduce training levels as an easy (and stupid) way of reducing costs.

*A focus on the customer*: not just meeting customer expectations but exceeding them, and devoting considerable energy into finding out the changing expectations of customers through surveys, feedback and other mechanisms. This applies to internal as well as external customers.

*A focus on quality*: advocating a TQM approach to dealing with problems as they occur and providing a perfect end product. This differs from the traditional 'inspect, reject or deal with complaint' approach.

*Empowering frontline employees and an emphasis on teamwork*: the buzzwords empowerment, employee involvement and teamwork come in here. Harness the intelligence and energies of your employees 'the potential for successful and quality results is virtually limitless'.

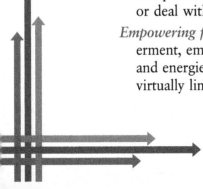

*Developing measures of progress*: data collection mechanisms to ensure that customers are receiving reliable and satisfactory service and that internal processes are functioning properly.

The US Department of Labor (1998) identified the following problems which also apply in most cases to all non-manufacturing sectors:

1   High performance is conceptually easier to understand in a manufacturing rather than a service context.

2   Competitiveness is a main motivating factor in the private sector, but scarcely a consideration in the public sector. 'Government is mission-driven rather than profit-driven'.

3   'Government is viewed by many as the archetypal, inflexible, hierarchical structure and therefore incapable of change.'

4   The traditional measurable outcomes of the manufacturing sector – reduced production costs, improved market share, increased profitability – are not so easy to measure in the service sector.

Some scepticism has been shown towards the apparent link between HRM and various interpretations of high performance. Gardner, Wright and Gerhart (2000) queried the nature of the evidence supporting the supposed value of HR initiatives in improving performance:

> While extremely promising, this research, with few exceptions, has relied on the survey responses from one knowledgeable informant per company to measure the quantity and quality of firms' human resource management systems. Reliance on just one informant makes the measurement of the human resource management construct susceptible to excessive random (i.e. unreliability) and systematic (i.e. bias) measurement error ...

As they point out, this threatens the validity of the construct that HR practices are directly related to high performance. Paradoxically, however, the two types of error may be having opposite effects. Citing earlier statistical work by Gerhart, they argue that random errors from single-informant surveys may be obscuring and therefore undervaluing the financial benefit of HR practices. Conversely, there is likely to be an over-estimate from systematic errors. Where do these systematic errors come from? Gardner *et al.* (2000) argue:

> This type of error will occur if respondents report HR practices based not on accurate valid estimates, but rather based on an implicit theory that high performing firms must be engaged in progressive HR practices while low performing firms must not be engaged in such practices.

They cite the example of a large diversified, perhaps multinational, company. If a senior HR person is asked to state the percentage of employees covered by a 'progressive' human resource practice, where does the HR person get the information from? Hopefully from a sophisticated human resource management system, but probably not. Instead, they contend, the respondent will provide an answer based on their own implicit theory (see Key concept 3.2) of what is happening in the firm.

## KEY CONCEPT 3.2   IMPLICIT THEORY

An internal or mental model of how and why a set of events or behaviours takes place. A belief system developed by individuals to explain part of their world or organization based on their own interpretations and experiences.

Discussing coverage of this issue in research literature they point out that surveys typically ask for the views of senior managers who, to paraphrase, are likely to believe in their own upbeat propaganda aimed at shareholders and employees. In more academic terms, they say that, surveying the literature, 'there is general consensus that executives' descriptions of past events suffer from low reliability'. They also point to studies which show that outsiders' judgements of a firm are based on financial performance and conclude that it is reasonable to assume that insiders are also likely to be influenced in the same way.

They formulated two hypotheses:

1   The estimated extent of the usage of human resource practices for high-performing firms will be greater than for low-performing firms.

2   The evaluation of the effectiveness of the HR function for high-performing firms will be higher than for low-performing firms.

These hypotheses were tested on line managers, HR executives, MBAs and HR masters students who were given scenarios of high- and low-performing companies and asked to rate a range of HR practices. The scenarios did not provide any information on HR practices, so their judgements were based entirely on implicit theories. The conclusion was that the hypotheses were confirmed to some extent in all four groups. This places a question mark on the supposed evidence from much of the survey research on the relationship between HR practices and high performance.

Wall and Wood (2005) critically evaluated 25 studies, including 'highly cited milestone studies of the mid- to late-1990s, and a selection of more recent ones (whose citation rate was yet to be determined)' and concluded that the evidence was 'promising but circumstantial'. They argue that consultants and researchers should temper the language they use, particularly the term 'high-performance' itself because it 'clearly presupposes the very effects researchers should be investigating, and should be avoided'. Also, they contend that terms such as 'impact', 'determinant' and 'effect' should be replaced by more modest terminology such as 'associated with' or 'related to', given the relatively weak relationships found.

Methodologically, Wall and Wood propose that researchers should aim to compare competing hypotheses rather than set out to prove or (notionally) disprove what is essentially a pet theory. Finally, they state that there is a need for research designs that counter the weaknesses of existing studies, specifically to overcome:

*Reliance on a single-source measure of HRM practices such as a CEO or HR manager*. These are often of unknown reliability, sensitivity and validity and typically are also the source of the measure of performance. Wall and Wood support the use of independent but suitably experienced auditors, external to the organization and unaware of its performance, drawing on multiple sources of information within the organization. Moreover, they should examine also other 'comparator practices' such as R&D or total quality to highlight the relative importance of HR practices.

*Use of small samples coupled with low response rates*. Larger sample sizes are essential to reveal the effects of complex interactions predicted from theory.

*Lack of sophisticated longitudinal studies*. In particular, studies to examine how changes in HR practices relate to subsequent changes in performance. These could be retrospective or prospective – in other words, looking backwards or forwards.

Recent work on the consequences of high performance systems show a positive relationship between high performance work system practices and employee attitudes, specifically on the attitudinal variables of job satisfaction, trust in management and organizational commitment (Macky and Boxall, 2007). However, the study showed complex negative interactions

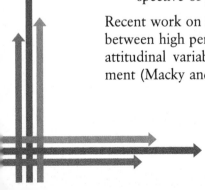

between specific practices that limit the positive outcomes of high performance systems for employees. Whereas Combs *et al.* (2006) found positive benefits of high performance work systems in a meta-analytic study, a longitudinal study by a Sheffield team (Birdi *et al.*, 2008) could not find a relationship with productivity. An Irish study (Guthrie *et al.*, 2009) found greater use of high performance work systems to be associated with positive HR and organizational outcomes with lower rates of absenteeism, higher employee retention rates and overall productivity benefits. Boxall and Macky (2009) conclude that the somewhat 'fuzzy' notion of high performance work systems should be grounded in the concept of 'high involvement' rather than 'contentious' selections of 'best practices'.

## HRM AND BUSINESS EFFECTIVENESS

One of the most significant issues faced by modern organizations is the use of technology to streamline activities, cut costs and increase business effectiveness. Perhaps later than many other business functions, technology has recently come into human resource management in a major way. There is still some debate on its cost effectiveness and ability to provide what is required. A decade ago, Walker (2001) stated that if HR technology was to be considered successful, it had to achieve the following objectives:

*Strategic alignment*: it must help users in a way that supports the users.

*Business intelligence*: it must provide the user with relevant information and data, answer questions and inspire new insights and learning.

*Efficiency and effectiveness*: it must change the work performed by HR personnel by dramatically improving their level of service, allowing more time for work of higher value and reducing their costs.

Despite extensive implementation of enterprise resource planning (ERP) projects, human resource information systems (HRIS), and HR service centres costing millions of dollars, Walker concluded that few organizations had been entirely happy with the results. Why was this? Many systems had been implemented by cutting HR staff, outsourcing and imposing technology on what was left. Arguably this approach should, at least, have cut costs. But Walker (2001) argued that survey results showed that overall HR departments had actually *increased* their staffing levels over the previous decade to do the same work. Moreover he considered that:

Most of the work that the HR staff does on a day-to-day basis, such as staffing, employee relations, compensation, training, employee development and benefits, unfortunately, remains relatively untouched and unimproved from a delivery standpoint.

Walker advocated business process re-engineering the HR function first, then re-engineering the HR work. He suggested the formation of re-engineering teams of providers, customers and HR systems users to examine the whole range of HR activities – including those which are not being done at present. The end product should be a set of processes organized into broad groupings such as resourcing, compensation or training and development. These processes should then be examined by the re-engineering team and redesigned to: (a) be better aligned with organizational goals; (b) streamlined so as to be cost-effective in comparison with the 'best in class'; and (c) have a better integration with other processes.

From this redesign comes the picture of a new HR function. What next? The organization could be restructured and the tasks handed out to existing or new staff. But Walker

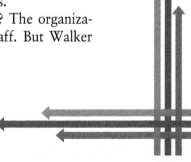

## HR SYSTEMS

Human resource systems can differ widely. They may be:

→ Intranets using web-type methods but operating purely within one organization or location.

→ Extranets encompassing two or more organizations.

→ Portals offering links to internal information and services but also accessing the worldwide web.

### Advantages

→ Familiarity (looking like web pages).

→ Attractiveness (colourful, clearly laid out, graphics).

→ Integration (linking different HR systems such as basic personnel records, employee handbooks, terms and conditions, contracts, various entitlements and payroll).

→ Allowing employees and managers to enter, check and amend controlled ranges of personal and other information.

→ Eliminating printing, enveloping and mailing of personnel and other employee Information.

→ Reducing need for telephone handling of routine enquiries by HR staff.

### Basic system requirements

1 Means of accessing and inputting information locally. Initially, they required desktop terminals using standard browsers such as Firefox or Internet Explorer to access information. Since then access means have proliferated to include laptops, netbooks, smart phones (e.g. BlackBerry, Apple iPhone) and other technologies.

2 In-house or outsourced means of serving and receiving information, ranging from an individual PC server to cloud-computing. Again, new technology and the widespread availability of Wi-Fi have liberated users from hardwired, office-limited systems. They can be accessed (almost) anywhere.

3 Appropriate software from specialist providers.

4 Security systems, including access control at various levels to prevent information being seen or manipulated by unauthorized users.

*Source: HRM Guide UK (http://www.hrmguide.co.uk).*

argues that the most effective approach is to introduce new technology to deal with the re-designed processes.

Walker also discusses a range of technologies available for re-engineered HR processes, contending that they are all capable of dealing with HR activities in a secure and confidential manner.

1 *Workflow.* Walker describes this as being like 'email with a database and built-in intelligence'. Essentially, a user accesses a range of employee records (perhaps their own) through a computer terminal, keys in data such as a change of address and submits the data electronically to the next person in the chain. The system is configured so that only certain individuals are authorized for a specific range of access or actions. The workflow chain is organized to ensure that the most suitable person approves an action. For example, a bonus payment would be authorized by a line manager's own manager. Also, the system can be structured so that bonuses over a certain level can be monitored

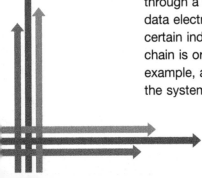

by a HR specialist. The paths and actions are all specified in accordance with company rules.

2   *Manager self-service.* Managers can have access to 'front-end' applications on their desk tops in the form of HR portals. Typically, they are able to view a range of personal details and aggregate information. They are also allowed to change and input certain details and model the consequences on their budgets of salary increases or bonus payments. More generally, policy manuals, plans and strategies can be made available. Walker highlights the facility to 'push' information requiring attention to managers – including those dreaded employee performance appraisals.

3   *Employee self-service.* Similarly, employees can view company information, change selected personal details, make benefit enquiries (pension plans, sick pay entitlement), book leave and apply for training programmes. Walker makes the point that 'portal technology will personalize this data further and "push" relevant data to them as well'.

4   *Interactive voice response (IVR).* A low-tech method, using the push-button control facility found in most modern telephones. Most of us are familiar with automatic responses such as: 'If your call is about vacancies in the accounts department, press 3 followed by #' when we dial large organizations. The system is restricted but easy to use and inexpensive in comparison to web-based methods. It is suitable for job openings and training course details where straightforward information can be recorded as simple scripts.

5   *HR service centres.* Walker notes that this has become one of the most widely used solutions to re-engineered HR in large organizations. Such centres centralize a number of HR processes and may deal with geographically widespread users. For example, he cites the Raleigh, North Carolina, service centre can deal with all of IBM's North American current and former staff. Operators or 'agents' take enquiries by phone, email or online that may already have been filtered through interactive voice response scripts or desktop HR systems. In effect, they deal with the relatively non-routine issues that cannot be handled by basic technology. However, they do use recognizable call centre techniques such as scripted protocols. The agent can enter keywords or a question into a knowledge database and bring up relevant information with which to answer the caller's query. If that query is not covered by information in the knowledge database it can be referred to a supervisor using workflow. HR service centres also have fax, email and postal facilities to send information, confirmations, follow-up queries and printed brochures to users. They are also monitored in the same way as conventional call centres and can generate useful statistics on types and frequency of enquiries. Walker contends that most reports show that organizations find HR service centres to be highly cost-effective and provider faster and more consistent answers than traditional HR departments.

6   *Human resource information systems (HRIS) and databases.* According to Walker (2001: 8–9): 'The HRIS system is the primary transaction processor, editor, record-keeper and functional application system which lies at the heart of all computerized HR work. It maintains employee, organizational and HR plan data sufficient to support most, if not all, of the HR functions depending on the modules installed'. It will also supply information to other systems and generate reports.

7   *Stand-alone HR systems.* A massive choice of applications are available from commercial vendors which can be linked to a HRIS. They include online application forms, tests, appraisal databases, 360-degree performance assessments and so on.

8   *Data-marts and data-warehouses.* Sources of information, usually held as relational databases which can be interrogated. Data-marts normally hold data from single sources, such as HR; data-warehouses amass information from multiple sources.

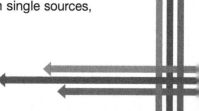

HR technologies have developed beyond payroll and staffing rotas to the point where they can now support workforce effectiveness in new and increasingly efficient ways. Most growth areas in HR technology fall under the umbrella of talent management. Organizations can expand applications that help attract and hire employees, for example:

→ recruiting

→ job posting and 'onboarding' solutions

→ employee retention

→ career development and online learning

→ rewarding staff via online performance management and reward portals

→ engagement with recognition programmes and online training opportunities.

### Employee self-service

Employee self-service (ESS) is a widely used and successful method of HR service delivery. Employees can amend personal details, view benefit plans and policies, access wellness information, view pension contributions, look at pay stubs and view job postings. Self-service removes the need for the HR function or administrative staff to copy information from paper sources for input or forwarding to employees and managers.

### Manager self-service

Manager self-service (MSS) did not take off as quickly as ESS but its application is increasing. Facilities include:

→ planning annual merit and base salary changes

→ viewing employee data history

→ initiating and approving job requisitions

→ posting jobs

→ viewing applicant CVs/resumés.

Managers' concerns with MSS have encompassed issues such as: level of data edits and validations required, usability of tools, improved processing time and the level of change management and communication at rollout. Those in charge of the design and implementation of HRIS have to consider how employees and managers will use the system. In particular, factors such as the additional information needed, the checks and balances to prevent misuse and the role of the HR function.

## HR PROFESSIONALS AND THE HR SYSTEM

The pressure is on for proactive HR innovations that contribute directly to the bottom-line or improve employee morale and efficiency. Ajuwon (2002) points out that the typical HR professional gets involved with one step in many different flows of work. Very often the involvement of HR has no purpose except to validate the process in some way and acts as an interruption to the flow of work. In other words, the HR function is a 'gatekeeper for information that's been deemed too highly classified for the data owner'.

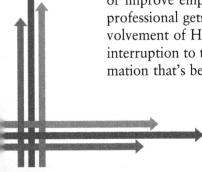

# HRM IN REALITY  HR EXECUTIVES MAKING MORE OF TECHNOLOGY

North American HR executives are increasing their commitment to talent management and the HR technology supporting it, according to Towers Watson, the global professional services company. Their 13th annual survey of HR service delivery trends and practices found that human resource departments are more confident than ever in the value and efficiency resulting from enhanced talent management systems.

Forty-two per cent of the 456 organizations surveyed listed 'talent/performance systems' among their top three HR service delivery issues for 2010. In fact, this was the most frequently selected issue identified by respondents and ranked highest as top issue by the greatest margin ever seen in the history of the survey. Fifty-one per cent of the organizations involved classified themselves as multinational/global companies and almost two-thirds (64 per cent) had more than 5000 employees.

The most critical HR service delivery issues for 2010 identified in the survey were:

→ Talent/performance management systems (42 per cent compared with 35 per cent in 2009)

→ Streamlining processes/systems (35 per cent – no change from 2009)

→ Increased involvement in strategic business-driven issues (27 per cent, up from 23 per cent in 2009)

→ Defining human capital metrics and dashboards (22 per cent compared with 17 per cent in 2009)

→ Recruiting/staffing services/systems (21 per cent, up from 12 per cent in 2009).

Tom Keebler, Global Practice Leader with Towers Watson's HR Service Delivery and Technology practice said:

Talent management technologies have unquestionably become one of the best ways for companies and HR departments to drive better employee performance and enterprise success following the recession.

In spite of the initial costs, organizations are increasingly deploying new or enhanced systems, recognizing that efficient and effective HR processes enable the flexibility and agility

employers need in an uncertain but growth-oriented business environment.

It is worth noting that the issue of 'cost' was not included in the list of top HR service delivery issues. Last year it was listed as one of the top three. Moreover, HR practitioners said many technology budgets escaped being cut during the recession with only 36 per cent of respondents having lower technology budgets in 2009 with 54 per cent having increased budgets for 2010 and 29 per cent maintaining last year's levels.

According to Tom Keebler:

HR's reliance on technology to achieve greater efficiency and cost savings during the recession allowed it to maintain and even grow HR technology budgets in a challenging business environment. As companies recover and budgets expand once again, leaders appear ready to make a forward-looking commitment to talent management systems that will reap substantial long-term rewards for the HR department, line managers and the broader organization.

In this environment, talent management technology has become a 'must have' competitive element, allowing managers and HR professionals to identify and develop talent through a more rigorous focus on performance and human capital metrics.

In our experience, companies are able to achieve greater satisfaction with the effectiveness and efficiency of their talent management systems when planned for holistically.

HR leaders who determine their integrated needs and clearly articulate their business strategy before making buying and implementation decisions are better equipped to differentiate among various options, make informed selections and align the HR function's needs with business objectives.

## Engaging employees through self-service

Manager self-service (MSS) and employee self-service (ESS) features are now common in the workplace. Seventy per cent of organizations believe that ESS and MSS lead to faster, more accurate transactions. Also, they

may encourage greater engagement and employee satisfaction among employees.

Tom Keebler commented:

> Past Towers Watson research, including the 2010 Global Workforce Study, has shown employees' and managers' desire for on-the-job empowerment. By implementing self-service options for critical career and rewards categories, organizations are simultaneously creating an environment of ownership and self-reliance that employees can build upon.

ESS and MSS have increased the efficiency of the HR function with 68 per cent of HR generalist/specialists and HR service centers/administrators reporting that ESS programmes resulted in less work. Only 15 per cent reported an increase in workload.

*What factors appear to be influencing the increasing use of human resource information systems?*

*Source: Reprinted with permission from HRM Guide USA (http://www.hrmguide.com).*

So HR is not actually making a measurable contribution – in fact, quite the opposite. HR involvement creates a queue or delay in the process. We should ask if the HR involvement is really necessary. Once upon a time the HR database had an 'all-or-nothing' quality – probably because it was paper-based. But now technology allows controlled access to various portions of the database. So an employee can safely amend his or her own address or bank account details, while the ability to change certain appraisal details might be confined to the line manager. In either case, there is no reason for HR to be involved. HR should move on from the role of intermediary.

Not surprisingly, the use of employee self-service systems for records, information, payroll and other functions is becoming increasingly common. Libraries of forms can be kept online to be downloaded as and when required. Wiki technology, similar to that used for the online Wikipedia encyclopaedia, allows in-house 'experts' to collectively build a HR knowledge database or employee manual on an incremental basis as procedures change. Systems can be enhanced to include streaming video, podcasts and other new software, providing wide access to corporate videos, training, etc. Email announcements, newsletters, corporate blogs and social media can be used to alert employees to new developments or urgent requests. Calls to HR service centres can be reduced by adding answers to common queries to wiki-based databases available online.

A study of 164 'enterprise level' Australian organizations at the end of 2009 found that 73 per cent had adopted a HRIS (Navigo, 2010). Enterprise level was defined as having 500 or more employees and the respondents to the survey were exclusively HR executives or managers/consultants responsible for HR technology. Adoption of HRIS was generally related to the size of the organizations with those having 5000–9999 employees all having HRIS, while only 67 per cent of organizations at the lower end (500–999 employees) had human resource information systems. Around 90 per cent of the very largest enterprises (100 000+employees) had HRIS, possibly because they had a high representation of retail companies, an industry that seems to have been relatively slow in adopting technology.

Defining a HRIS can be problematic as many payroll system vendors are incorporating limited elements of human resource data. Additionally, many organizations have a hybrid system, part manual and part automated. The top 'pure' HR systems in use among the organizations surveyed were: SAP HR (17.4 per cent), Frontier Chris21 (14.7 per cent), Peoplesoft (6.4 per cent), Oracle-e-Business (3.7 per cent) and Neller Preceda (3.7 per cent).

Forty-five per cent of those surveyed said they were satisfied or very satisfied compared with 28 per cent who were dissatisfied or very dissatisfied. However, only 10 per cent were very satisfied with their systems. In general, respondents with HRIS were 91 per cent more

satisfied than those without HRIS. Thirty-two per cent cited increasing efficiency as their main motivator for improving HR systems. Sixty-eight per cent of those with employee self-service and manager self-service were satisfied or very satisfied with their HRIS, compared with only 15 per cent among those who did not have ESS/MSS capability.

In a report for the Aberdeen Group, Saba (2010) benchmarked 160 organizations, comparing 'best-in-class' enterprises with those that were not on core HR activities, defined as:

→  payroll

→  benefits

→  health and safety

→  compliance

→  taxes

→  employee records/HR data

→  time and attendance, and scheduling.

The most commonly cited reasons to invest in core HR technology were 'inability of business leaders to leverage HR/workforce data to make better operational decisions' (48 per cent of those surveyed) and 'too much time spent on manual HR transactions' (41 per cent). Whereas cost had been a major concern in a corresponding 2009 study, growth was now a greater priority.

The 'best-in-class' organizations were typically:

1    Reacting to economic pressures to manage and control employees and their cost.

2    Increasingly automating human resource processes and empowering employees to reduce the burden on HR.

3    Communicating HR policies and procedures clearly, regularly reviewing employee handbooks, ensuring secure data, providing an escalation system for HR enquiries, integrating paid time off/leave with payroll and allowing employees to access their own data.

4    Using a range of automated payroll, HRIS, time and attendance, MSS and ESS.

The report notes that as HR is increasingly automated, the function becomes more centralized and there is less need for divisional or regional HR functions. A core or shared system provides increased data security and common metrics available across the organization.

During the 1990s the business process re-engineering approach resulted in many organizations taking a 'root and branch' look at HR and other processes. Subsequent reorganizations may have produced fresh, streamlined processes but often they became inappropriate or inefficient as circumstances changed. It is not enough to design a corporate human resource strategy or acquire a piece of technology. There has to be some way of ensuring effective operational delivery. A more fluid, constantly changing methodology is required. Ajuwon contends that we have the means:

It's more than innovating and/or streamlining your HR processes; or building an HR portal; or introducing a culture change programme. It's about weaving together all three in a way that sustains change, engages the entire organization and deploys the organization's knowledge assets to gain competitive advantage and deliver profitability, even in times of economic downturn.

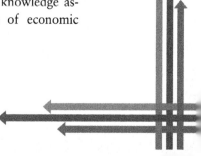

## HRM IN REALITY — HR POORLY SUPPORTED BY IT SYSTEMS

Results from 'The gap between IT and strategic HR in the UK', a study by talent management solutions company, Taleo in 2006 showed a significant disconnect between HR's strategic functions, including talent acquisition and workforce planning, and IT's ability to support these business initiatives.

The survey of 100 senior HR managers, all in organizations employing more than a thousand people, found that only a quarter thought that strategic functions such as workforce planning, leadership development and performance management were well supported by their IT systems. Only a third felt confident in systems support for recruitment and employee progression. Other findings included:

→ Current technology systems were out-of-date. Over half the respondents (55 per cent) felt that more sophisticated technology systems and processes were needed to support recruitment and development.

→ IT focused on lower-level, administrative functions. Respondents said that payroll and employee administration (68 per cent) and evaluation and management reporting (53 per cent) were adequately supported by IT. However, more strategic HR initiatives such as performance management (28 per cent), leadership development and planning (25 per cent) and strategic workforce planning (25 per cent) were not well supported.

→ Inadequate data and technology systems obstructed workforce management. Just 29 per cent of respondents felt that they had sufficient systems in place to gain a clear picture of existing employee skills.

→ The HR function was striving to become more strategic. 63 per cent of respondents cited talent management (including recruitment) as a significant priority in the year ahead.

Taleo research vice president, Alice Snell, said:

The gap between the support of administrative functions and strategic HR responsibilities needs to be addressed in order for HR directors to deliver results to the board. When HR directors can assess the workforce changes needed by the business, acquire and develop the talent needed to optimize the workforce and then measure the results, their true value can be realized.

Neil Hudspith, senior vice president, international operations, Taleo, added:

Findings of this study clearly show that HR is evolving to play a more strategic role in supporting fundamental business objectives, but the systems being used by HR functions are not keeping up. It's clear that talent management and other strategic initiatives are being recognized as essential functions by ambitious companies that want to retain and recruit the best people, but organizations need to arm their HR directors with the tools and technology needed to support this strategy. The right HR technology is a critical element of any HR strategy moving forward.

*What reasons can you suggest to explain the inadequacy of IT support for higher level and strategic HRM?*

*Source: Reprinted with permission from HRM Guide UK (http://www.hrmguide.co.uk).*

So-called 'Web 2.0' technologies such as wikis, blogs, social media and podcasts allow a degree of interaction so that anyone with expert knowledge, or even an opinion, can contribute to the HR function's evolving knowledge database.

As an example, in March 2010 the Manchester City soccer club commissioned Cascade, a HR software provider to provide a new human resource information system to streamline

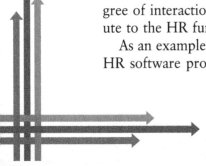

the club's HR processes. As one of the English Premier League's major clubs, Manchester City is a significant people business with 530 employees. It required a comprehensive HR software system to 'ensure the correct talent is recruited, trained and managed both on and off the pitch.' The Cascade software would replace the club's manual, paper-based processes and spreadsheets with an internet browser-based system. Data could be consolidated, paperwork reduced and efficiency improved.

## MEASURING THE IMPACT OF HRM

Human resource departments are often targeted by senior managers wanting to cut budget costs. So it makes sense for HR managers to know how to optimize their practices within tight financial constraints. A study by US benchmarking specialists, Best Practices, LLC, explored how businesses focus their limited HR assets into critical areas.

They found that most of the 'benchmark partners' they examined (companies identified as using best practices), outsourced a number of HR tasks in order to release staffing resources for more important functions. The most commonly outsourced functions were benefits and compensations.

Benchmark partners also tracked their HR metrics (measurements) carefully in order to determine return on investment and to evaluate performance. One company used a balanced scorecard, measuring a wide range of financial, quality, operational and strategic metrics to determine the HR department's performance and contribution to business profitability.

> ### KEY CONCEPT 3.3  BENCHMARKING
>
> Direct comparisons of different measures between an organization and 'best practice' competitors in the same business sector. This indicates the gap in performance, costs, morale, etc. between that organization and industry best practice.

## MAJOR FINDINGS

The following data analysis and best practice lessons were identified through quantitative surveys and executive interviews:

*Coordinate HR roles and responsibilities.* Most benchmark companies – whether centralized or decentralized – assigned corporate human resource functions the following responsibilities: managing benefits; compensation; leadership development/management; and human resource information systems and other HR technologies.

They also found that few business units had sole responsibility for any specific HR activity. In decentralized companies, business unit HR groups were also responsible for: staffing and recruiting; employee communications; and generalist functions.

*Centralize HR performance measurement.* Every benchmark company monitored their competitiveness for compensation/benefits, and over half tracked their overall headcount, employee turnover rates and safety incidents. But monitoring methods varied

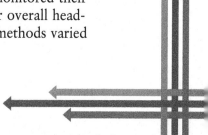

considerably Decentralized companies gave responsibility for HR performance measurement decisions to individual business units or locations, letting each decide which metrics to track and how to collect them.

*Maximize use of staffing and budgeting resources.* The ratio of employees to HR generalists among the companies surveyed ranged from 141:1 to 318:1. But the researchers pointed out that companies at the high end of this spectrum ran the risk of short-changing some of the tasks assigned to generalists.

*Self-service technologies.* Companies were increasingly creating HR call centres and incorporating self-service HR software programs within company websites in order to reduce administrative costs and time; increase information access to employees and managers; enable strategic HR; reduce overall HR headcount; improve information accuracy. In fact these companies regarded their HR call centres as valuable entry points and training grounds for future full-time HR employees. HR assistance offered through self-service software and call centres included clarifications on benefits plans; performance management worksheets and monitoring; questions about company policies; incentive compensation allocations; monitoring employee training administration.

Mahoney-Phillips and Adams (2010) comment that many HR initiatives are not taken seriously in the boardroom, largely because of the lack of quantifiable impact measurements. They describe how the HR corporate function in a global financial organization increased the impact of HR initiatives by developing an integrated and benchmarked metrics framework in partnership with divisional HR functions. Tootell *et al.* (2009) note that HR departments continue to be less prepared than other business functions, such as finance, to quantify the impact they have on business performance. In their study of New Zealand organizations they conclude that HR metrics remain elusive as the Holy Grail of HRM. Bourne and Haddon (2010), in a study of strategic change at the UK's Royal Mail, highlighted the value of appropriate metrics in evidence-based change. HR functions needed the analytical skills to combine 'hard' data relating to financial or operational performance measurements with 'soft' data from employee opinion surveys and assessment results.

## HRM IN REALITY   USING HR METRICS

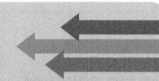

A report by The Conference Board in 2005 suggested that while few (12 per cent) of the surveyed organizations made significant use of HR measures to meet strategic targets, 84 per cent of 104 HR executives interviewed in the survey say that they would increase their use of people metrics over the next three years.

Stephen Gates, principal researcher at The Conference Board and report author, said:

> When determining how best to demonstrate achievement, human resource managers must choose from the hundreds of metrics that are currently available to track every aspect of an HR department's endeavours to recruit, develop and

retain employees. What's imperative for the health of their businesses, however, is that these HR professionals tie these people measures more closely into their efforts to meet their companies' overall strategic targets.

Lisa Hartley, director HCM Marketing, PeopleSoft, which supported the research said:

> Though widespread adoption has been slow, we all see that our best practice customers are beginning to use people metrics to understand and drive business decisions. We've had great people data for a long time. It's just that it hasn't been

presented in a relevant way. That is finally changing. We believe that the use of analytics is nothing less than transformational to making HR relevant to the strategic needs of the business.

## Is HR up to the task?

According to the survey, a mere 31 per cent of respondents felt that HR executives in their organizations had a strong understanding of strategic key performance indicators. Even fewer (25 per cent) surveyed considered their HR leaders capable of linking people measures to such indicators or (16 per cent) believed that HR professionals received extensive training to connect people measures to strategy.

Fifty-one per cent of participants in the survey said that HR professionals in their organizations were partially capable of identifying talent critical for implementing strategy but only 22 per cent said that those executives were fully able to identify strategic talent pools.

## Effective people metrics

HR professionals have tended to use metrics to study the time and cost of utilizing people, but they are more likely to:

→ provoke discussions with managers that lead to action plans;

→ serve as educational tools that help bring implicit ideas about the value of human capital to the surface; and

→ improve the HR decision-making process when they are used to evaluate the effectiveness and impact of people investments and HR activities.

Correlating popular individual measures with important perceived benefits can lead to a successful linking of certain people measures to specific strategies. The Conference Board report cites the following examples:

→ employee satisfaction and competencies/training metrics were found to match a policy of customer responsiveness;

→ leadership and competencies/training measures were found to have solid connections to innovation strategies;

→ remuneration and leadership measures can help boost revenue growth.

But most of the organizations surveyed only partially tied their people measures and targets to strategic plans (52 per cent) or annual budgets (46 per cent). Half of the survey participants reported that their people metrics were fully or partially linked to customer data.

## Making the case for people measures

Many respondents reported difficulties in implementing HR metrics with only 19 per cent rating their IT systems highly for HR data gathering. There is also an issue of organizational politics since HR metrics have implications on performance ratings, prestige, power and resource allocation. Many organizations were trying to build support for their HR metrics efforts through collaboration with colleagues from finance (54 per cent) and strategy (45 per cent) and employing business managers as champions for HR measures (43 per cent).

According to Stephen Gates:

> If people metrics highlight a problem that could be interpreted as critical of a business manager's performance, then the manager could be tempted to distort or suppress the negative data. When they point to a problem with HR's functional activities, then HR could also be motivated to hide negative data. In both instances, manipulating people data destroys the diagnostic power of the people metrics effort.

In 78 per cent of surveyed organizations, people measure reports are delivered to senior management. In a few companies, business managers – rather than HR representatives – present information back to business divisions directly, greatly enhancing the credibility of the process with those divisions.

'However, the finding that only 19 per cent of companies distribute briefings on people measurement to all of their business managers indicates that many companies do not view these reports as decision making tools for managers', said Gates.

*Summarize the main reasons for using HR metrics.*

*Source: Reprinted with permission from HRM Guide USA (http://www.hrmguide.com).*

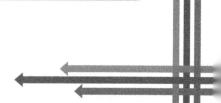

# A 10-C CHECKLIST FOR EFFECTIVE HRM

Conscious of the risk of 'destroying it' (HRM), we will conclude the first part of this book with a discussion of the principles which appear to be essential to understanding HRM. First, why do we need a concept such as HRM? Surely, people management is a matter of common sense. Certainly, some good people managers have – from many years of experience – developed an internal model which guides them well in the way they deal with their employees. However, there are many indifferent managers who appear to have learned little from their careers. In any case, students need to acquire a comprehensible and communicable framework without the benefit of years of experience. Second, if HRM has been in existence for at least two decades, has it not fulfilled its role? Unfortunately not. Comparing the early 1980s, the birth period of the subject, with the situation in the early 21st century, the need for a coherent approach to people management continues to be justified by some obvious deficiencies:

→ In the 1980s, personnel management had its own agenda: its priorities were not necessarily matched to those of the organization, and its professional training and structure focused on a narrow range of techniques at the practitioner level rather than emphasizing a global view of business needs. It is arguable that the 'personnel profession' has become aware of these criticisms and has gone some way towards addressing them. However, there is still room for improvement.

→ Other managers practised people management through a ragbag of often dubious and counter-productive methods, usually developed from intuition and experience. This continues to be largely the case.

→ In the 1980s, theories of strategic management concentrated on areas such as finance and marketing, tending to ignore human resources. Since then, theoretical accounts have become much more people-conscious, but there is still a gap between theory and practice.

As a consequence, the people in many organizations were, and are, dealt with in a largely inconsistent and parochial manner. The 'You are our most valuable asset and, by the way, you're fired' approach describes people management in so many workplaces. As we shall see in later chapters, the evidence shows that a meaningful form of HRM still does not prevail in many organizations. Little has changed.

So how should we practice meaningful HRM? At this point we introduce a systematic framework (Table 3.1) incorporating ten principles, each conveniently beginning with 'C' – in the best management guru style – for use as a checklist as we go through the various aspects of HRM discussed in this book. In fact, terms beginning with 'C' have a considerable track record in HRM and, therefore, the principles are not intended to be novel or surprising. The Harvard model has its central four Cs – commitment, congruence, competence, cost-effectiveness – three of which have been incorporated in our checklist. These and the other principles have been chosen because they are measurable in some way and are sufficiently broad in their totality to reveal the tension and balance that is the essential feature of effective HRM within the 'high commitment' or 'high performance' approach.

There is a risk of venturing into the 'prescriptive' but HRM is not simply a subject for academics who can afford to dissect ideas and argue over interpretations without worrying too much about their usefulness in real life. As with medicine and engineering, HRM is a practical subject with a foundation in theory, previous experience and forward thinking, based on a carefully assessed degree of risk. Real people managers have to deal with real situations, often with major cost implications. There is no time for sterile debate – they have to deliver – and it is not surprising that many and, perhaps most, pay little attention to academic theory.

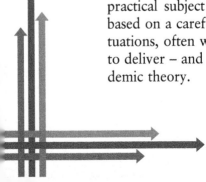

**TABLE 3.1**

10-C checklist
of HRM

69

CHAPTER 3 HRM in practice

| Principle | Purpose | Action |
|---|---|---|
| **1** Comprehensiveness | Includes all aspects of people management | People management must be organized, rather than left to ad-hoc decisions at local level |
| **2** Coherence | HR management activities and initiatives form a meaningful whole | Clear link between individual performance/ reward and business needs |
| **3** Control | Ensures performance is consistent with business objectives | Participative management, with delegation of *how* an objective is achieved |
| **4** Communication | Objectives understood and accepted by all employees; open culture with no barriers | Clear, simple and justified strategies; cascading process of communication with feedback to the top |
| **5** Credibility | Staff trust top management and believe in their strategies | Top managers are sincere, honest and consistent |
| **6** Commitment | Employees motivated to achieve organizational goals | Top managers are committed to their staff |
| **7** Change | Continuous improvement and development essential for survival | Flexible people and working systems; culture of innovation; skills training |
| **8** Competence | Organization competent to achieve its objectives – dependent on individual competencies | Resourcing strategies, selection techniques and human resource systems in place |
| **9** Creativity | Competitive advantage comes from unique strategies | System for encouraging and tapping employee ideas |
| **10** Cost-effectiveness | Competitive, fair reward and promotion systems | Top managers pay themselves on equivalent basis to staff |

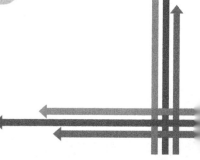

### Comprehensiveness

All people management activities should be part of a single, comprehensive system. This implies that the attitudes, behaviour and culture of every individual in an organization – especially those with people management responsibilities – should be integrated within a deliberate framework. This approach ensures that HRM is holistic and systematic, with every aspect – together with their interrelationships – brought into consideration. It reflects the perspective that business problems, especially those involving people management, are highly complex. The relevant variables are densely interconnected (Checkland, 1981). In other words, simple solutions are rarely possible.

### Coherence

The second principle of coherence addresses the internal balance and integration of the people management system. Strategies and actions must be consistent with each other. For example, if a business has a strategy of increasing sales of high-profit-margin products, rewards in the sales department should be focused on these products rather than less profitable items. Similarly, if the organization has chosen to take a team-based approach, recruitment and training should emphasize team skills rather than strong individualism.

### Control

As with any other form of management, HRM is aimed at directing and coordinating employees to meet an organization's objectives. As such, it cannot be anarchic nor totally democratic in its approach. However, the nature of control must be consistent with the remaining principles. Human resource literature mostly advocates a participative approach with a high degree of empowerment and delegation. An autocratic approach is unlikely to encourage good communication and employee commitment.

### Communication

Effective communication facilitates coherence. Serious attention must be given to communicating the organization's strategic objectives, together with the parameters – acceptable behaviour, cost and time – within which they can be achieved. Good communication is essential to the smooth running of the people management system. It must be a two-way process, made easier by new interactive technologies such as social networking. This can involve a cascaded flow of information from the top and also feedback from lower levels through surveys, performance measures, open meetings and web-based feedback. An open culture should be encouraged: employees need to feel confident that they can express their opinions and concerns without fear of retribution.

### Credibility

Many organizations spend a great deal of money and effort in their attempts to communicate with their employees. Often, however, employees dismiss glossy brochures and websites or time-consuming team briefings as so much management propaganda. A degree of healthy cynicism is unavoidable, but in today's down-sized workplaces this frequently extends into mistrust of and contempt for senior management. This feeling reflects the way many staff feel they are themselves regarded by management. Regaining trust depends on personal credibility which, in turn, can only come from honesty and sincerity.

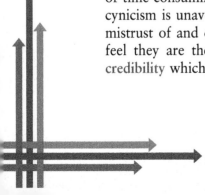

## Commitment

Earlier, we noted that the Harvard model of HRM places a strong emphasis on the notion of commitment. It embodies a 'can-do' approach, going further than is normally asked. Committed employees can give that competitive edge – the extra something which distinguishes a successful company from its lesser rivals. However, commitment is difficult to achieve. As we will find in our discussion in a later chapter, for employees to be actively engaged they need confidence in the organization, the people who lead it, the reward mechanism and the opportunity for staff to develop themselves. More than anything, it depends on the degree of commitment which managers show to their own people. Economic realities can jeopardize this commitment.

## Change

Businesses must change to survive. However, change is a difficult management task. Effective change requires sure-footed, considerate people managers who can take employees through the process with minimum anxiety and maximum enthusiasm. It requires the recognition that an organization's people should not be the pawns of strategy but active participants in change. Later in this book we will see that their detailed job knowledge, customer contact and ingenuity can be harnessed to provide ideas for improvement.

## Competence

Organizations must have the capability to meet changing needs. In current parlance this is often expressed in terms of competences – skills, knowledge and abilities. These are qualities possessed by the people who work for those organizations. Competences can be brought into businesses through the recruitment of skilled individuals. They can also be developed within existing people by investing in training, education and experiential programmes. The establishment and cultivation of a high level of relevant competences leads to a distinct competitive advantage.

## Creativity

Advantages can also come from the ingenuity of staff. Creativity is underemphasized in management training but it can lead to new products and services, novel applications and cost-savings. Competences such as detailed knowledge of products and procedures are required before innovation can occur. A creative environment develops from a trusting, open culture with good communication and a blame-free atmosphere. Conversely, creativity is inhibited by lack of trust or commitment and fear of the consequences of change.

## Cost-effectiveness

One of the original Harvard 'four Cs', it provides the hard kernel of an otherwise 'soft' model of HRM. Expressed in terms of profitability, it has been extensively used as the justification for large-scale job cuts. This aspect has attracted considerable criticism, primarily because of the obsessive way in which many senior managers have pursued 'down-sizing' at the expense of commitment to their staff. However, as a reflection of the value of its human assets, an organization has a duty to use its people wisely and cost-effectively. In itself, there is nothing wrong with an attention to cost – provided that it does not become the one and only management criterion.

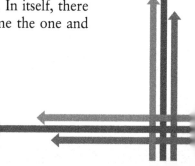

These checklist principles are developed further in later chapters. It can be seen that they are interlocked – failure to observe any one of them can lead to the breakdown of the people management system. Throughout the remainder of the book we will find illustrations of such failure, usually attributable to management belief that HRM initiatives and practices can be adopted on a 'pick and mix' basis.

## SUMMARY

In this chapter we discussed recent and ongoing ways in which the human resource management function is changing – perhaps more radically than ever before. The HR function and its activities are being examined in microscopic detail in many large organizations. Human resource processes, especially those involving the collection and dissemination of information, are being computerized and automated, potentially eliminating routine clerical activities. HR information and knowledge is being linked and integrated with other information systems, breaking down departmental barriers.

As HR processes become more easily measurable, the need for justification and the means to do so become more obvious. Many consultants have advocated the concepts of high performance organization and knowledge management, suggesting that they offer HR specialists the chance to push HRM to the fore. HR processes and their outcomes are central to these concepts and the introduction of technology allows more exact methods of determining whether or not human resource initiatives do affect the 'bottom line' and shareholder value.

Yet there are some cynical scepticism and contradictory research findings coming from HR practitioners and academics, some associated with dogged technophobia, together with justifiable questioning of the methodology, rationale and, not least, the capabilities of the systems and concepts we have discussed.

## FURTHER READING

1 Karen Legge provides a carefully reasoned critique of the high commitment/performance concept and its links to HRM in a chapter of Storey (ed.) *Human Resource Management: A Critical Text* (3rd edn, Cengage Learning, 2007).

2 Linda Holbeche's *High Performance Organisation* (Butterworth-Heinemann, 2005) sets out to provide information and practical tools for people engaged in leading organizational change.

3 *How to Measure Human Resource Management* (3rd edn, 2001) by Jac Fitz-Enz and Barbara Davison, published by McGraw-Hill, contains practical information on measuring elements of HR.

## REVIEW QUESTIONS

1 How would you define the following terms?

→ High performance work system

→ Human resource information system

→ Human resource service centre.

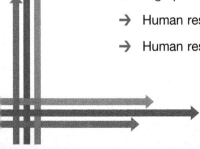

2 Is the concept of high performance management fundamentally different from HRM?

3 'High performance' and 'high commitment' are terms used to describe the same or a similar concept. What are the implications of the different terms on the management of staff?

4 What differences would you see in using the high performance approach for private and public sector employees?

5 Does current research show a clear link between HR procedures and high performance?

6 To what extent are HR processes and outcomes measurable?

7 What positive outcomes have been attributed to human resource systems? What are the disadvantages of such systems?

8 Distinguish between Manager Self-Service and Employee Self-Service capabilities.

9 In what circumstances would you *not* introduce HR technology into an organization?

 ## CASE STUDY FOR DISCUSSION AND ANALYSIS

Read the following case study. What is the likelihood of achieving a high-performance work system in the circumstances described?

Accenture

*HR and training not delivering skilled workforces*
Recent international research conducted for Accenture shows that most senior executives surveyed consider that their workforces lack the skills needed by their companies to achieve market leadership, and even critical functions are not performing as well as they should. Moreover, only 11 per cent of respondents said they were very satisfied with the performance of their human resource function with marginally fewer (10 per cent) rating their training function very highly.

Just 14 per cent of executives surveyed believed that the overall skill level of their organization's entire workforce was industry-leading. And only 20 per cent felt that the vast majority of their employees understood their companies' strategy and what was required to be successful in their industry.

Peter Cheese, global managing partner in Accenture's human performance practice, commented:

> The lack of essential skills is a vital issue for senior managers. As the competitive environment

grows more demanding and as markets become increasingly commoditized, the need to cultivate these skills – particularly in the critical functions – should be at the top of every corporate to-do list. Those companies that fail to develop their workforces risk losing their competitive edge.

Accenture attributes these shortcomings, in part, to a number of HR and training issues, including:
*Lack of connection to business drivers.* A mere 36 per cent of survey respondents said that their organizations tailored HR and training support to each function's needs and contributions to the business.
*Failure to measure the business impact of HR and training efforts.* Two-fifths (40 per cent) did not evaluate the impact of human resource and training efforts against profitability. Fifty per cent did not evaluate those efforts against revenues and sales.
*Inadequate knowledge capture and sharing capabilities.* Some 42 per cent of respondents said that the process of capturing and sharing knowledge was a

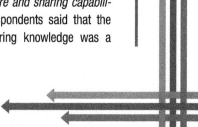

challenge or a severe challenge for their organizations. The following reasons were most commonly cited: lack of a common business culture across different locations (38 per cent); no knowledge support infrastructure with dedicated people (37 per cent); knowledge sharing typically not rewarded in the organization (32 per cent).

*The talent time bomb.* Sixty per cent of respondents expected to begin feeling the impact of the ageing workforce and impending retirement of baby boomers within the next five years. 28 per cent of these were already feeling the impact. Forty-three per cent of all survey participants said that talent sourcing was a challenge or a severe challenge, primarily because the talent pool was shrinking.

*Lack of functional leaders' involvement in people issues.* Few of the survey respondents said their heads of functions were highly involved in human capital management initiatives. Specific percentages were: customer service (29 per cent), finance (31 per cent), sales (34 per cent) and strategic planning (37 per cent).

### Human performance leaders

A number of companies were identified that Accenture refers to as 'human performance leaders'. These were defined as organizations in which the three functions their executives deemed to be most important performed at the highest levels. Compared to the 'laggards' in which none of the top three functions were high performers, performance leaders were more likely to succeed in addressing organizational issues that contributed to strong financial performance. The following were identified as high performing areas:

→ Acquiring new customers and increasing market share (43 per cent of 'human performance leaders' compared with 14 per cent of 'laggards').

→ Encouraging strong customer loyalty and retention (52 per cent against 17 per cent).

→ Responding to changing market conditions (52 per cent against 14 per cent).

→ Finding and developing talented leaders (39 per cent against 7 per cent).

→ Attracting and retaining skilled staff (30 per cent against 12 per cent).

→ Generating superior business value from technology investments (35 per cent against 15 per cent).

The findings show that 'human performance leaders' possess more effective HR and training support. The practices that help them excel include:

→ Formal measures to measure the impact of all HR and training support activities on their top functions.

→ Tailored HR and training support to match the contribution of specific functions.

→ A more strategic approach to HR and training, including viewing the HR function leader as a strategic business partner to the executive suite.

'A company's ability to manage its workforce strategically and develop its capabilities will set it apart from its competitors', said Peter Cheese. 'Some companies focus well on one or two aspects of human capital management, such as learning or internal communications, but the best take a broad view of managing their workforce. These are the companies that vastly increase their chances of being industry leaders.'

The study was conducted by GfK NOP Limited on behalf of Accenture between February and April 2006. It included telephone surveys with 251 senior executives – chief executive officers, chief operating officers, chief financial officers and chief information officers, human resource leaders, chief learning officers – in the United States of America, United Kingdom, Australia, France, Germany and Spain. Respondents' companies came from seven broad industry sectors: retail, travel and transportation, financial services, electronics and high tech, communications, energy and utilities.

*Source: Reprinted by permission from HRM Guide USA (http://www.hrmguide.com).*

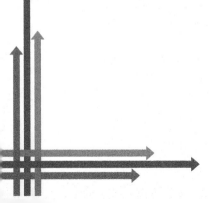

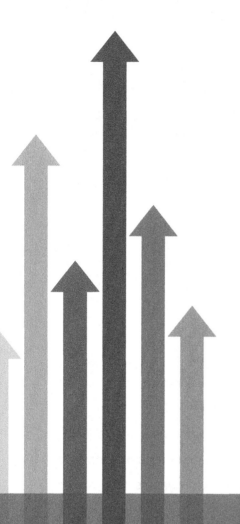

# PART TWO
# HRM AND THE BUSINESS ENVIRONMENT

People management within individual organizations cannot take place in isolation from the rest of the world. The chapters in the second part of the book investigate the relationship between HRM and the global business environment. They provide a wide or 'macro' perspective and introduce a number of fundamental issues which are developed further in later chapters in the book.

**For example:**

→ **Is there a clear link between human capital and national success?**

→ **What is the effect of globalization on the practice of HRM?**

→ **How do multinational companies manage their people?**

→ **Do governments determine the effectiveness of HRM?**

→ **What is the employment market?**

→ **Have traditional nine-to-five jobs been replaced by more flexible work patterns?**

# CHAPTER 4
## HRM and the global economy

## LEARNING OBJECTIVES

The purpose of this chapter is to:

→ Outline positive and negative aspects of the globalization of trade and production that affect human resource management.

→ Provide an overview of the HR implications of economic growth and stagnation.

→ Critically evaluate the importance of regional trading blocs and multinational companies in the process of globalization.

→ Highlight human resource issues pertaining to international outsourcing and offshoring.

→ Introduce the roles of supranational organizations such as the International Labour Organization and the World Trade Organization regarding the management of people.

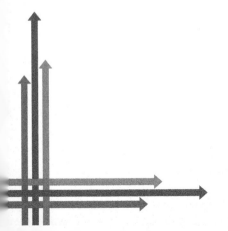

# GLOBALIZATION

'The modern business has no place to hide. It has no place to go but everywhere' (Lane, Distefano and Maznevski, 1997).

We concluded the previous chapter by considering HRM as a people management system, acknowledging its intricate and interdependent principles. However, HRM is a system within other systems. The most complex of these is the international business environment (see Key concept 4.1). The forces that act on people management are not purely internal to an organization. They encompass innumerable active players in the world economy, including international agencies, governments, competitors, unions, speculators and consumers – each pursuing their own goals.

## KEY CONCEPT 4.1 THE BUSINESS ENVIRONMENT

'All factors which exist outside the business enterprise, but which interact with it' (Needle,1994: 26). Traditionally, human resource managers have been closely involved with employment legislation, industrial tribunals and trade unions at a functional level. HRM's strategic emphasis requires a focus on other environmental variables. Government economic, social security, education and training policies affect the supply, cost and quality of available employees. International competition, strategic alliances and supranational organizations such as the European Union are exercising increasing influence on people management.

Changes in the business environment such as the financial crisis of 2007/2008 have major consequences for people managers. These forces may be so powerful that an individual organization loses the discretion to pursue its own strategies (Kochan and Dyer, 2001: 282). In essence this means that factors outside a company's control will affect its requirements for human resources and the way they are managed. For example, unexpected changes in competitor technology or currency exchange rates may compel a business to abandon long-term human resource plans and shed staff in order to survive. Globalization is frequently cited as the most significant factor affecting the deployment of human resources worldwide.

## KEY CONCEPT 4.2 GLOBALIZATION

A systematic trend towards integration of production and marketing with brand-named goods and virtually identical 'badge-engineered' products such as cars being made available throughout the world. This process has been fostered by 'transnational' or 'multinational' companies operating in more than one country. Such companies are relatively free to switch resources and production from one country to another. Typically this is done in order to maximize the benefit (to the corporation) of greater skills availability and lower employee costs. This has been described as the new international division of labour.

Why is globalization (Key concept 4.2) important to our understanding of human resource management? Examine the business pages of any national newspaper and you are

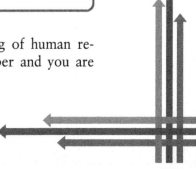

almost certain to find examples of businesses engaged in cross-border mergers, takeovers or expansion overseas. Moreover, domestic mergers of banks, airline companies and even retailers are often explained as defensive moves by national organizations attempting to build sufficient critical mass to withstand competition from giant multinationals. Businesses simply cannot ignore the global dimension, and neither can human resource managers.

Scholte (2000) argues that globalization involves 'the growth of "supraterritorial relations" among people'. Physical location is becoming steadily less relevant as new technology and increasingly complex international supply links are developed. This has a considerable impact on culture, language and working practices throughout the world. Globalization is driven by marketing to a considerable extent. Large corporations are attempting to achieve global recognition in their particular market sectors. Brands such as Coca-Cola, McDonald's, BP and Shell are internationally recognized and have become drivers for growth and market dominance. The implications for the nature and availability of work and its management are profound.

Branded products are becoming less diverse. Consequently employees in one country increasingly use the same manufacturing processes as any other and are expected to achieve equivalent standards of productivity. As a result, the costs and skills of human resources have become a matter of competition between countries. And giant corporations can take advantage of this competition. The car industry is a clear example in which a few major players, especially Ford, Toyota and General Motors, manufacture specific models (or basic 'platforms') in a number of global locations with parts coming from competing sources. The investment that drives such activities criss-crosses between developing and developed countries with investment going from the poorer to the richer countries as much as it does in the opposite direction (Mattoo and Subramanian, 2009).

Will standardized products and production techniques lead to virtually identical human resource practices throughout the world? We will see later in this book that significant cultural and linguistic differences between and within countries provide major obstacles to a 'homogenized' global HRM. But some degree of standardization is inevitable. This issue has been the subject of debate for some time. In the 1980s it was discussed under the heading of the 'internationalization of labour'. Some commentators considered that different regions or countries should specialize in specific industries depending on the factors that gave them a competitive advantage (Legge, 1995). Two main types of economy were envisaged:

1   Countries that had cheap, low-skilled labour focusing on assembling low-cost, high-volume products or producing agricultural or mineral commodities. This was typical of 'third-world' countries in an early stage of development with China as a prime example in the early 21st century.

2   Countries with well-paid, skilled 'knowledge workers' who concentrated on the provision of goods and services with a high value-added component.

In reality, economies are more complex and most countries demonstrate characteristics that are between these two extremes (Dicken, 1998; Fishlow and Parker, 1999). But this kind of analysis led some economists in developed countries into discounting the importance of mass production. Instead they advocated that advanced countries should concentrate on high-value sectors such as financial services and information technology. Similar ideas today are addressed in the concept of the 'knowledge economy'.

The International Labour Organization (2000) concluded that globalization intensified in the latter years of the 20th century, especially in terms of trade, investment, financial liberalization and technological change. Despite some fluctuations, growth in world trade has continued into the 21st Century. In 2005, for example, the value of world merchandise exports increased by 13 per cent to US$10.1 trillion, while the value of world commercial services exports rose by 11 per cent to US$2.4 trillion (WTO, 2006).

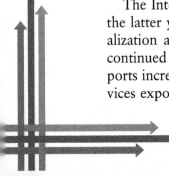

The ILO states (International Labour Organization, 2000: vii):

> The benefits of globalization have been very unevenly distributed both between and within nations. At the same time a host of social problems have emerged or intensified, creating increased hardship, insecurity and anxiety for many across the world, fuelling a strong backlash. As a result, the present form of globalization is facing a crisis of legitimacy resulting from the erosion of popular support.

Some of the main factors identified as being at the root of widespread public disquiet are:

→ Reduction in job security because work (and therefore jobs) can be moved from one country to another.

→ Undercutting of one country's wages by another, leading to erosion of wage rates.

→ Exceeding generally accepted working hours and exposure to health and safety risks in order to cut costs.

In some developing countries globalization has widened inequality. For example 70 per cent of India's workforce remain in subsistence agriculture. India has more indigenous billionaires than any other country with the exception of the USA, but one in three of its 1.1 billion population are living on less than $1 per day (Thornton and Thornton, 2009).

Weisbrot (2002: 10–12) makes the following observation:

> Consider this: In Latin America and the Caribbean, where gross domestic product grew by 75 per cent per person from 1960 to 1980, it grew by only 7 per cent per person from 1980 to 2000. The collapse of the African economies is more well known, although still ignored: GDP in sub-Saharan Africa grew by about 34 per cent per person from 1960 to 1980; in the past two decades, per capita income actually fell by about 15 per cent. Even if we include the fast-growing economies of East Asia and South Asia, the past two decades fare miserably. For the entire set of low- and middle-income countries, per capita GDP growth was less than half of its average for the previous 20 years. Also, as might be expected in a time of bad economic performance, the past two decades have brought significantly reduced progress according to such major social indicators as life expectancy, infant and child mortality, literacy and education – again, for the vast majority of low- and middle-income countries.

In total contrast, Kostas Karamanlis (2006), Prime Minister of Greece and Chair of the 2006 OECD Ministerial Council held a strongly positive view of globalization:

> … fostering trade can lead to a new era of prosperity for the world. Trade and globalization should not be seen as a threat to job security but rather as a challenge for a more prosperous world. Maintaining living standards in our societies cannot be achieved by protecting jobs in uncompetitive industries, but by investing in knowledge, innovation and well-targeted social welfare systems. Also, training, re-training and life-long learning systems have a crucial role to play. There are several examples of countries demonstrating that open, competitive economies can achieve prosperity, without sacrificing social cohesion, especially when assistance for adjustment during transition facilitates the introduction of reforms.

Fofack (2009) shows that despite the deepening integration and interdependency of countries and regions, those that focus on knowledge creation and the production of high-tech and manufactured goods, dependent on leading-edge technology, are those that benefit the most from globalization. Most of sub-Saharan Africa has been relegated to the role of end-users and the income gap with the globalizers has widened even more.

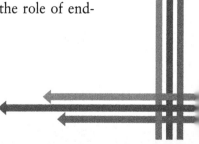

**HRM IN REALITY** REACTING TO THE GLOBAL CRISIS

A survey by Booz & Company of 828 senior managers from 65 countries published in 2009 explored corporate responses to the global economic crisis and the impact on social responsibility agendas. Respondents came from a variety of major industries. Over one-third (37 per cent) were CEOs or reported directly to CEOs; an additional 24 per cent were two layers below CEO. Managers from Western Europe predominated (38 per cent) followed by North America (30 per cent) and emerging markets (28 per cent).

Respondents were asked to assess their company's financial strength (ability to function without immediate external financial support) and competitive strength (relationship to competition in respect of costs, product/brand positioning, technology/capabilities, leadership/management and ability to influence or collaborate with regulatory authorities). Companies were categorized as strong (both financially and competitively), stable (strong financially but weak competitively), struggling (weak financially but strong competitively) or failing (weak in both areas).

The survey found that irrespective of their designation, companies were finding it difficult to identify effective responses to the current economic downturn (40 per cent questioned whether their leadership had a credible plan in place). Many respondents (46 per cent) doubted their leader's ability to implement a crisis strategy even if apparently credible. One-third of CEO and CXO-level respondents were not confident about their own plans.

The survey also found that 65 per cent of struggling companies had responded insufficiently to ensure their own survival (such as increased attention to asset disposal or pursuit of external funding). One-quarter of companies that considered themselves financially secure were not taking advantage of opportunities to improve their position. More than half (54 per cent) of respondents expected their organizations to emerge from the crisis stronger but the survey did not support this optimism, finding discrepancies between many companies' financial and competitive position and their strategic response.

Bill Jackson, Booz & Company senior partner explained:

> Companies have focused on the near term, some at the expense of the long-term opportunities. The strong need to go long. They need to create a view of new industry structure. Many strong and stable companies are playing things too short-term oriented for the moment. The really struggling and failing companies have reacted dramatically and some have already moved into bankruptcy.

The survey found that, in many cases, companies were not following the most appropriate course. It concluded:

→ While struggling and failing companies would be expected to accelerate efforts to improve working capital positions, slash overheads, drive process improvements and renegotiate deals with suppliers, surprisingly many are not. Between a quarter and a third of respondents say their companies are pursuing such strategies no more aggressively than they were before the crisis.

→ Stable and strong companies are more focused on cutting costs across the board and conserving cash than on opportunities to strengthen their competitive positions.

→ While stable companies would be expected to capitalize on the crisis by buying companies with compelling products or brands but weak finances, or pursuing other growth initiatives, 21 per cent are pulling back on mergers and acquisitions, as are the same per centage of strong companies. One in five stable companies is also investing less in new products or slowing moves into emerging markets.

Bill Jackson added:

> A real issue is with the 'tweeners' – companies holding on by their fingernails. They have reacted to the near term cash issues; they are working on renegotiating their bank covenants, but one wrong move and they are done. Their boards are worried,

since this crisis is new and different to most executives' experiences.

Additional survey findings include:

→ Forty per cent of respondents expected 'green' and other corporate social responsibility initiatives to be significantly delayed as a result of the recession. This was especially pronounced in transportation (51 per cent) and energy (47 per cent).

→ Despite the depth of the challenges faced, 54 per cent of respondents overall believed that the crisis would ultimately have a positive impact on their companies' competitive position (59 per cent of managers in emerging markets compared with 53 per cent in North America and 52 per cent in Western Europe). Seventy-five per cent of managers expressed a positive view of their companies' current financial strength; only 13 per cent said they worked for financially weak companies.

→ Among managers below CEO and CXO levels, 51 per cent thought senior leadership lacked the capabilities to carry out crisis plans. Researchers suggest this is apparently at odds with the optimism expressed in other responses.

→ Forty-three per cent of respondents from the financial sector believed that stakeholders from business, government and unions were collaborating effectively to stabilize their industry. Less positive responses came from those in healthcare and pharmaceuticals (56 per cent critical); telecommunications and media (42 per

cent); and transportation and commercial services (41 per cent).

The survey identifies three steps to restructuring in the current economic crisis:

1 Get an accurate read on the environment and the company's position in it. An accurate self-diagnosis is critical to end the cycle of inappropriate strategic actions.

2 Design a good plan that does enough, but not too much, when time is short and resources may be diminished in a crisis. Identify a limited set of straightforward initiatives that have the potential to make a difference quickly.

3 Communicate and execute, which is vital to regaining the confidence of all stakeholders, from sceptical managers to risk-averse shareholders.

Bill Jackson concluded:

Many top executives are still reacting and are not ahead of the curve yet. They are still operating with their cumbersome processes and lines of communications. This is slowing them down. They are not getting the right homework fast enough, nor are they able to enact decisions quick enough or to the extent they expect. This crisis calls for a new, more direct leadership approach.

*What factors distinguish companies that survive and do well after a financial crisis from those that do not?*

Source: Reprinted with permission from HRM Guide International (http://www.hrmguide.net/).

Sen (2002) tries to balance positive and negative views of globalization. He notes that proponents and opponents of globalization tend to perceive it as global westernization. Those who have a positive view of globalization consider it to be a 'marvellous contribution of Western civilization to the world'. Many see a stylized sequence of history in which everything important happened in Europe: the Renaissance, the Enlightenment and the Industrial Revolution. These led to improved living standards in the West that are now being spread to the rest of the world. From this perspective, 'globalization is not only good, it is also a gift from the West to the world'.

But those with the opposite point of view see globalization as an extension of Western imperialism. They see contemporary capitalism as being 'driven and led by greedy and grabby Western countries in Europe and North America' using 'rules of trade and business relations that do not serve the interests of the poorer people in the world'.

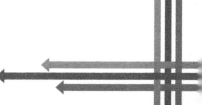

On the other hand, Jackson (1998) argues that the concept of globalization has been demonized by opponents of the free market, contending that 'they have shamelessly used it to exploit fear and ignorance'. He considers that claims that globalization leads to lowered real wages and 'destroys jobs, causes financial crises, creates social tension and undermines national sovereignty' are false. Jackson refutes such claims despite a prevailing but naive public belief in their status as 'self-evident truths'. He considers that globalization is not a new phenomenon. On the contrary, it is just an alternative name for 'free trade' and an ongoing process of the internationalization of trade and capital, concluding: 'What many fear today was commonplace a hundred years ago. Globalization is no more damaging or destabilizing now than it was in the 1890s'.

Preble (2010) contends that a more careful balance of the key issues surrounding globalization, namely jobs, inequality and poverty; national sovereignty and cultural diversity, and the natural environment can make the process sustainable.

The degree of perceived job insecurity is highlighted in the OECD survey shown in Table 4.1.

**KEY CONCEPT 4.3** THE INSECURITY THESIS

Heery and Salmon (2000) identify a connection between globalization and the 'insecurity thesis', a belief that: 'Employment in the developed economies has become more insecure or unstable in the sense that both continued employment and the level of remuneration have become less predictable and contingent on factors which lie beyond the employee's control'.

Perception of the effects of globalization is coloured by such views. One consequence is that the media take a keen interest in human resource practices throughout the world – no matter how remote the location. The coverage inevitably increases public awareness and hostility towards practices that may be viewed as unfair or exploitative. This creates pressures to bring such practices within the remit of international bodies.

## TRADING BLOCS

Partly due to the activities of multinational firms, international trade has grown to colossal proportions in recent decades. The bulk of this trade is concentrated in three major trading blocs:

1  The North American Free Trade Area (NAFTA) – essentially Canada, Mexico and the USA.

2  The European Union (EU) with 27 member states at the time of writing and a number of additional applicant countries.

3  The Asian-Pacific region with various trading arrangements and including Australia, Japan, New Zealand, Singapore and many developing states.

Other trading arrangements include the Andean Community, the Caribbean Community and Common Market (CARICOM), LAIA, formerly the Latin American Free Trade Area, MERCOSUR, the Economic Community of West African States (ECOWAS) and the Arab Common Market (United Nations, 2005: 63–64).

Individual countries may belong to a number of trading blocs. The 25 OECD countries (plus Lichtenstein) average 11 trading arrangements per country; Latin American and

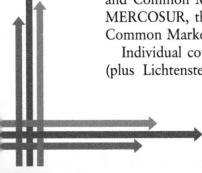

| Country | Unsure of a job even if they perform well (per cent) |
| --- | --- |
| Korea | 46 |
| UK | 41 |
| Japan | 38 |
| United States | 37 |
| Australia | 37 |
| France | 37 |
| Sweden | 36 |
| Czech Republic | 35 |
| New Zealand | 34 |
| Germany | 34 |
| Italy | 32 |
| Finland | 31 |
| **Unweighted average** | **30** |
| Greece | 29 |
| Spain | 27 |
| Canada | 27 |
| Hungary | 26 |
| Switzerland | 26 |
| Belgium | 26 |
| Austria | 23 |
| Ireland | 23 |
| Netherlands | 22 |
| Denmark | 20 |
| Portugal | 21 |
| Norway | 17 |

**TABLE 4.1**

Job insecurity across the OECD in 2000

Source: Arnal, E., W. Ok and R. Torres (2001), "Knowledge, Work Organisation and Economic Growth", p.26, *OECD Labour Market and Social Policy Occational Papers*, No. 50. http://dx.doi.org/10.1787/302147528625 Reproduced with permission of OECD.

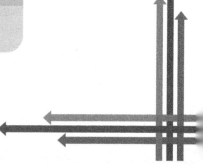

**HRM IN REALITY** EMPLOYEES VALUE COMPANY STABILITY

Employees of all ages are placing greater emphasis on company stability when making career decisions but four out of ten of those surveyed for specialized staffing firm Robert Half International in 2010 said they are more likely to consider moving to new organizations as a result of the recession.

Kathryn Bolt, president of Canadian operations said:

> Our research reveals that there are several parallels across generations, which may be partly attributed to recent economic challenges. As the job market rebounds, understanding what motivates employees can help companies augment their recruitment and retention efforts.

The conclusions are based on a survey of more than 1400 professionals from Canada and the United States in full-time employment who have, or are studying for, university degrees. This included 502 hiring managers. Respondents came from across the age range: baby boomers (approximately 46–64 years old); Generation X (approximately 32–45 years old) and those from Generation Y (approximately 21–31 years old) meeting the academic criteria for the study.

Other significant findings include:

→ Pay is not keeping up with performance – 37 per cent of respondents felt they were not being fairly compensated for greater workloads associated with the recession.

→ Work is more engaging – 28 per cent agreed they were more involved in their work as a result of the recession.

→ Generational views on post-recession career progression differ – among the youngest employees, the most popular plan was to look for a new job as the economy recovers. Those from Generation X were more inclined to update their skills. Baby boomers most commonly responded that they intend staying with their current employers.

→ Cross-generational teams bring challenges and rewards – while 72 per cent of hiring managers agreed that managing multi-generational teams poses a challenge, more than one-third of

employees felt that teams incorporating different levels of experience increase productivity.

→ Retirement plans are being put on hold – 46 per cent of respondents believe they will work beyond the traditional retirement age, more than one-third said the recent recession has had a very significant impact on their retirement plans.

Researchers identified a number of similar responses across the generations surveyed. Working for a stable company and job security were identified as two of the most important aspects of the work environment, valued more than a short commute or working for a socially responsible company. Salary, company stability and benefits were considered the most important factors when evaluating offers of employment. The most valued benefits were extended healthcare coverage, dental coverage, vacation time and Registered Retirement Savings Plan matching. Among those planning to work past the traditional retirement age, the great majority cited the recession as an important factor in their decision, regardless of their current age. The most commonly cited benefit associated with being part of multi-generational teams was the concentration of different experience providing specialist knowledge.

The survey also identified some significant generational differences, especially with regard to post-recession career progression:

→ Thirty-six per cent of respondents from Generation Y planned to look for new job opportunities compared to 30 per cent from Generation X and 24 per cent of the baby boomers;

→ Respondents from Generation X were more inclined to enhance their skills sets (38 per cent) and build tenure with their existing companies (33 per cent) than other generations;

→ More than half of baby boomers surveyed (54 per cent) said they would work past the traditional retirement age compared to 46 per cent of Generation X and 39 per cent of Generation Y;

→ More from Genereation X had increased their retirement savings since the recession (34 per cent compared with 27 per cent of baby boomers);

→ Over half of baby boomers (54 per cent) felt the greatest challenge working with multiple generations was 'differing work ethics and approaches to work/life balance' (compared with 45 per cent from Generation X and 35 per cent from Generation Y). Respondents from Generation Y were more likely to identify 'differing communication styles' (29 per cent compared with 16 per cent for both Generation X respondents and baby boomers).

Kathryn Bolt commented:

With the job market stabilizing, many employees, particularly Gen Y professionals, may start to consider other employment opportunities. Developing a sound retention strategy, including the review of top performers' career paths and compensation levels should be a priority for companies looking to maximize emerging growth opportunities.

*How would you explain the variation in attitudes towards job security in different age groups?*

*Source: Reprinted with permission from HRM Guide Canada (http://www.hrmguide.net/canada/).*

---

## HRM IN REALITY  NEW 'WAR FOR TALENT' IN ASIA

A survey of Asian reward professionals by Thomsons Online Benefits shows expectation of a return to the 'war for talent' amongst employers in the region.

The *Asia Employee Rewards Watch 2010* found that the greatest HR challenges reported by survey respondents in Asia are:

→ employee retention (61.19 per cent)

→ maintaining/improving morale and employee engagement (54.23 per cent)

→ controlling employee costs (39.80 per cent).

This survey of 201 organizations – the third *Asia Employee Rewards Watch* – indicates a positive attitude towards the future in Asia with far fewer consequences from the economic crisis than those experienced by western counterparts. In fact, 63.68 per cent of respondents said that they are preparing for a period of growth, with a mere 13.43 per cent believing that their business is heading for a period of contraction.

Other major findings include:

*Reward strategy*

→ The recession has put 85.88 per cent of respondents under increased pressure to minimize costs and improve return-on-investment in 2010. But 44.72 per cent said their reward costs are escalating most significantly on salaries. Not surprisingly, 60.59 per cent of reward professionals were having difficulties in defending the amounts they were spending on employee rewards.

→ Over a half of respondents (50.25 per cent) – far more than in 2008 – stated they have a documented reward strategy in place. This suggests that the economic crisis has led to a more robust governance approach to reward management. However, two in ten businesses still do not have a robust reward framework.

→ 33.53 per cent of respondents said they could not report return-on-investment of reward spend very well with 27.06 per cent saying they could not do so at all.

*Employee benefits*

→ 26.47 per cent said that their biggest issue in relation to their benefits package administration is the burden on internal resources; and 23.53

per cent complained about their benefit providers' administrative efficiency.

→ 18.82 per cent of respondents did not know how much they spent on employee benefits. Amongst those who did know, the most common estimate (21.18 per cent) was 15–25 per cent of salary.

→ 37.43 per cent of respondents continue to use traditional paper-based processes for benefits administration.

→ Changes most likely to be introduced into this year's benefits package are:

→ reviewing health and well-being offerings (49.12 per cent)

→ considering implementing flexible benefits (32.75 per cent)

→ introducing total reward statements (21.05 per cent)

### Flexible benefits

→ 19.41 per cent already have flexible benefits and 21.76 per cent are considering their implementation. Just 2.7 per cent are currently in the process of implementing them.

→ 57.46 per cent of those planning to implement flexible benefits intend to do so within six months to two years. Costs were the major factor in the implementation decision.

### Health and well-being

→ 61.39 per cent of respondents source their benefits externally through an insurance broker. 34.81 per cent approach the provider directly.

→ 48.73 per cent actively measure and report on sickness absence levels.

Marcus Underhill, Global Reward Director for Thomsons Online Benefits said:

> The current and future economic climate looks promising for Asia, while uncertainty persists for western economies. Companies in Asia are now in acquisition and expansion mode, credit flows are returning to normal levels (in some places asset bubbles have formed), and (if not already) Asia will return to robust employment norms. Employees will need to be engaged all over again and the war for talent will become a familiar dilemma.
>
> Forward thinking companies are looking for ways to improve employee engagement and how they communicate reward programs. According to our research, nearly a quarter of respondents with traditional benefit plans (21.76 per cent) are considering implementing flexible benefit programs.

*What factors might be responsible for the positive outlook in Asia?*

*Source: Reprinted with permission from HRM Guide International (http://www.hrmguide.net).*

Caribbean countries average eight schemes; East Asia, two schemes; and the Pacific, seven arrangements (*ibid*). Globalization and the consolidation of trade within such regional trading blocs are leading to a shift from trade between countries with distinct economic boundaries, to a world economy where national boundaries are not so significant. Instead cross-border manufacturing and trade in goods, services and financial products are now commonplace (ILO, 2000).

The boundaries of the trading blocs are shifting and generally expanding. The most obvious example is the European Union, which has absorbed countries in central and eastern Europe that were formerly beyond the Iron Curtain. Integration of former communist countries into the free world brings different philosophies and practices of management into focus and possible conflict. Currently the central and eastern European countries have a much lower standard of living than most of the EU's long-standing members. The Czech Republic is closest to the western European norm with tourism booming and exports to the EU replacing business lost in the former communist countries. It seems reasonable to assume that inequalities between eastern and western Europe will gradually even out as businesses move to the regions with lower costs. However, the evidence of recent economic history

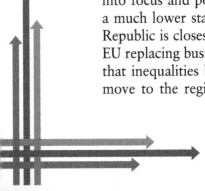

# HRM IN REALITY   UK BUSINESS VULNERABLE TO GLOBALIZATION

A TUC report acknowledges that UK employees undoubtedly benefit from cheap goods and greater prosperity resulting from globalization, but are more vulnerable to its negative effects than others in Europe. In a submission to the government's 2007 comprehensive spending review, the TUC says that priorities for funding should include support for workers who are adversely affected and for British companies to increase their competitiveness on the global market.

The TUC report says that UK employees are more vulnerable to negative effects of globalization than their European counterparts for three main reasons:

→ Britain buys more than it sells on the global market.

→ The UK is home to more multinational companies who can easily relocate overseas.

→ UK business strategy typically keeps down costs in areas such as wages and investment in skills and training, which risks work being outsourced to countries where it can be done more cheaply.

TUC general secretary Brendan Barber said:

Globalization has made a real difference to the quality of life of working people in the UK and across the world but there are victims as well as winners. Too many British workers are losing their jobs when companies move abroad or fail to compete. Cheap DVD players and clothes are scant compensation if you are being downgraded to poor quality, insecure, low-paid work.

Of course we can't say 'stop the world I want to get off' and turn back the tide of globalization by erecting barriers to try and protect industries and jobs. But that does not mean we are powerless in shaping its impact. The government must provide support to older and unskilled individuals to help them adapt to the opening up of world markets and ensure that all UK workers benefit.

But the UK also has a responsibility, mainly through international trade agreements, to make sure that workers in developing countries have access to decent work.

The TUC report highlights economic trends that may adversely affect UK workers. While the EU as a whole has a trade balance, Britain imports 25 per cent more than it exports. Germany accounts for 27 per cent of EU exports compared with 12 per cent from the UK. UK trade in services as a percentage of gross domestic product (GDP) has grown in line with EU figures. However, trade in goods has fallen in the UK while increasing across the EU, reflecting the decline in UK manufacturing and growth in GDP. UK companies are more vulnerable to international variations such as price changes, and are failing to capitalize on growing world markets. Only the USA is more popular for foreign direct investment than the UK. Such investment is good for jobs and economic growth, but multinational companies can easily move jobs overseas.

The TUC argues that fewer UK jobs are at risk from globalization than is often assumed, but 'displaced' employees earn less in future work – if they can find it. They are also more affected if they are older, have been in their jobs a long time or have had to change industries. Eight months after being laid off, only half the former MG Rover workers were in full-time work and on average were earning £3523 less a year.

Reducing taxation, regulation and public spending are not the most important factors in managing the effects of globalization. Only Germany and some Canadian provinces have lower business taxes than the UK and the UK labour market is one of the least regulated. The biggest global traders among OECD nations have large public sectors and high government spending.

The TUC argues that government could balance costs and benefits of globalization if they prioritized:

→ increasing skills levels to raise productivity

→ developing a modern industrial strategy for the global market

→ securing UK energy supply and investing in environmental technology

→ improving transport links in growth areas of the country

→ promoting lifelong health to increase employment chances for older workers.

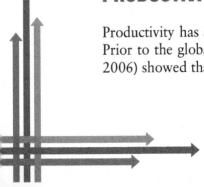

The TUC makes the following specific proposals:

→ Establish a UK fund to provide training and job search support administered at regional level, to partner the EU Globalization Adjustment Fund set up in 2005.

→ Develop a 'responsible restructuring' model that would require companies moving jobs abroad to insure redundant UK workers for 70 per cent of any fall in earnings for up to two years. It would include consultation with trade unions and help employees find work or set up their own business.

→ Invest in the employability of workers in industries threatened by global competition. This would include various measures to improve UK skills levels across the workforce and to keep older and disabled workers in employment.

→ Promote industrial and service sectors that employ high-skilled, well-paid workers to improve international competitiveness.

→ Extend government support for science and industry.

*How realistic were the TUC's proposals?*

Source: Reprinted with permission from HRM Guide UK (http://www.hrmguide.co.uk).

indicates that this may not happen quickly – if at all. The reality has been that whereas poorer areas have cut employee costs to maintain their competitiveness, more affluent regions have been unwilling to consider this tactic and have turned to more upmarket quality products instead.

Countries such as South Korea, Taiwan and Singapore and, particularly, China and India have shown much faster rates of economic growth than those of the West. Competitive labour costs and strong adherence to the work ethic have appeared highly attractive to foreign investors. Chung's (1991: 419) remarks remain true:

Business people from and in the Asian-Pacific area have become more self-confident, and they are demanding respect for Asian culture if European or American business people want to cooperate with them. The one-way street is a thing of the past, and what is needed now is the ability to engage in culture-specific dialogue. The ability to communicate interculturally has become a crucial factor for success in the global business of the future.

Within the trading blocs, there is increasing scope for integration and rationalization. This is exemplified by the defence and aerospace industries in the EU. Cuts in defence expenditure following the end of the Cold War, together with ever-escalating costs for the development of new planes and other equipment, have encouraged a consolidation between the former national defence specialists. Closer working arrangements such as those employed by Airbus Industrie will replace joint development and marketing agreements. The consequences on employment will probably include overall staff reductions within the sector, increased specialization and a demand for higher language and technology skills.

## PRODUCTIVITY COMPARISONS

Productivity has a direct relationship with the wealth of any country (see Key concept 4.4). Prior to the global financial crisis of 2007/2008 a study by the Conference Board (Van Ark, 2006) showed that US productivity had outpaced most developed countries in recent decades and that information and communication technologies have been the major drivers of US productivity growth. For example, in 2005, although sharply reduced from the previous year's 3.0 per cent, the USA's productivity growth of 1.8 per cent compared with Japan at 1.9 per cent and markedly outperformed an average of 0.5 per cent in the 15 older members of the EU. Productivity growth in the EU-15 ranged from 1.5 per cent in Ireland to -1.3 per cent in Spain. After the 2007/2008 financial crisis, most western countries experienced negative growth and consequent reductions in productivity while China, India and other parts of Asia – excluding the moribund economy in Japan – seemed virtually unaffected.

---

**KEY CONCEPT 4.4** PRODUCTIVITY

Productivity may be defined as the amount of output (what is produced) per unit of input used. Labour is one input amongst many. Total productivity is dependent upon a variety of diverse and hard to measure inputs. One simple measure of productivity is the gross domestic product (GDP) per person-hour worked. But it is also a simplistic measure of productivity because it neglects a number of factors such as capital investment.

---

China has had remarkable rates of productivity growth in recent years, averaging 8.7 per cent a year since 2000. India has achieved more modest rates, averaging 4.1 per cent in that period, but this reflects around double the increase in employment levels compared with China.

# ECONOMIC GROWTH AND EMPLOYMENT

The growth of the economy is the most significant overriding variable for people management because it determines overall demand for products and services and hence employment. The British economy has the longest industrial history but UK growth has been consistently slow, rarely exceeding 3 per cent per annum. There is a tendency for countries that are lower in the GDP league to have higher rates of growth in a 'catching-up' process. Consequently, high rates of growth in the People's Republic of China and India have accompanied medium growth in the developed countries. However, this is not universal – there has been consistently low growth in Africa, for example. A research report from the Economist Intelligence Unit published in 2006 predicted that more than half the growth in the world's GDP over the period to 2020 will come from China (27 per cent), the US (16 per cent) and India (12 per cent).

The reasons for differing rates of growth have been endlessly debated but the effective exploitation of human resources appears to be a crucial factor. The nature of the link between human resources and economic success is not simple. This is illustrated by attempts to provide an index of international competitiveness.

For some years the World Economic Forum (WEF), an international business organization, and the Institute for International Management Development (IMD), a Swiss business school, cooperated in the production of such an index. Since 1996, however, they have produced independent league tables. Table 4.2 shows the WEF comparisons for 2005 and 2010.

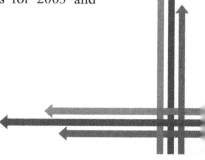

**TABLE 4.2**
Relative competitiveness

Source: Adapted from International Institute for Management Development, World Economic Forum.

| 1995 | | WEF 2005 | | WEF 2010 | |
|---|---|---|---|---|---|
| 1 | USA | 1 | USA | 1 | Switzerland |
| 2 | Singapore | 2 | Singapore | 2 | Sweden |
| 3 | Hong Kong | 3 | Denmark | 3 | Singapore |
| 4 | Japan | 4 | Iceland | 4 | USA |
| 5 | Switzerland | 5 | Finland | 5 | Germany |
| 6 | Germany | 6 | Canada | 6 | Japan |
| 7 | Denmark | 7 | Taiwan | 7 | Finland |
| 8 | Netherlands | 8 | Sweden | 8 | Netherlands |
| 9 | New Zealand | 9 | Switzerland | 9 | Denmark |
| 10 | Norway | 10 | UK | 10 | Canada |
| 11 | Austria | 11 | Canada | 11 | Hong Kong SAR |
| 12 | Sweden | 12 | France | 12 | UK |
| 13 | Canada | 13 | Austria | 13 | Taiwan |
| 14 | Taiwan | 14 | Belgium | 14 | Norway |
| 15 | UK | 15 | Japan | 15 | France |
| 16 | Australia | 16 | Iceland | 16 | Australia |
| 17 | Luxembourg | 17 | Israel | 17 | Qatar |
| 18 | Finland | 18 | Hong Kong | 18 | Austria |
| 19 | France | 19 | Norway | 19 | Belgium |
| 20 | Chile | 20 | New Zealand | 20 | Qatar |

Competitiveness indices are calculated by combining hundreds of different measures. These range from GDP per head to estimates of the competence of a country's managers. The WEF regards government regulation and welfare provision as negative factors for national growth, whereas openness to international trade and investment are viewed favourably. Hence, for example, the UK's comparatively low pension burdens and flexible employment market are seen as strengths. These ratings reflect two important perspectives of the role of human resources in the competitiveness debate. We can regard them as the 'hard' and 'soft' versions of macro HRM.

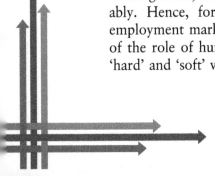

# MULTINATIONALS AND GLOBAL COMPETITION

Businesses are not entirely passive or helpless. They are also active players in their environment. They can influence and, sometimes, control their markets. Effectively, major industrial sectors such as petroleum, information technology, aerospace and automobile manufacture are dominated by a small number of multinational corporations. At a local level, strategic alliances between small companies can have the same effect: establishing a degree of control and predictability on the market.

It has been estimated that some large corporations operating internationally, described as multinationals, are responsible for a greater proportion of international trade than most independent states. At one time, companies such as IBM in the USA, ICI in the UK, Volkswagen in western Germany and Toyota in Japan were viewed as national champions. They were key players in those countries' economic activities. Their senior managers influenced governments. As long as profits flowed, shareholders, banks and employees were relatively content. In recent decades, however, industrial competition has become global. National champions have become multinational corporations moving functions around the world without loyalty to any nation. Research and development takes place in one country, manufacturing in a second, with sales in different continents.

This importance has given them the power to play one country against another and to take actions that would be unacceptable for companies operating within single states. Their ability to switch investment from one country to another has been a significant cause for concern. Multinationals are major determiners of action on the world scene, able to move their operations from country to country in defiance of government attempts to maintain minimum wages or workers' consultation. Private capital is being moved around the world in search of profit from flexible and open economies. Complex factors attract this capital: it is not simply a case of the cheapest employees. Japanese manufacturers have opened factories in the UK and other parts of Europe where employee costs are high in comparison with developing countries. They have done so in order to avoid EU import restrictions and cut transport costs. But they have also created jobs in developed rather than developing countries in order to make use of better skills and education.

Uncontrolled globalization has not gone unquestioned. The possibility of social dumping puts societies and national economies under intense pressure and is generally destabilizing (see Key concept 4.5).

## KEY CONCEPT 4.5   SOCIAL DUMPING

The concept of social dumping describes the practice of switching production from countries with relatively high employee costs to those with cheap labour. It is an accusation made against large multinational corporations. Social dumping has led to long-term structural changes including the closure of older, heavy manufacturing industries such as steel and shipbuilding in established industrial countries.

Initially, corporations such as Ford adopted a policy of dual-sourcing, in which two or more plants in a regional trading bloc such as Europe or North America had the same function, for example building engines. If there were engineering or industrial relations problems in one plant, the other could supply the required components. This insurance policy became less necessary as quality control improved but afforded the opportunity of shifting

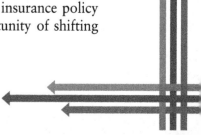

production, and hence employment, from the country with the greater labour costs to the cheaper. Potentially, this had the effect of driving down employee costs. Deliberate government policy has made dismissal cheaper and easier in the UK than in other European countries, thereby encouraging manufacturers in volatile industries to consider the UK for inward investment. However, this policy has its drawbacks. Short-term expediency induced corporations to close UK plants because this was effectively easier than tackling less competitive European plants protected by social legislation.

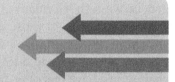

**HRM IN REALITY**  OUTSOURCING MAY BE COUNTER-PRODUCTIVE

Increased use of business practices such as outsourcing, hiring temporary workers and reliance on project-based teams is having a detrimental effect on employees and may pose long-term problems for employers, according to research led by North Carolina State University published in *Social Problems* in 2010. The researchers point out that job satisfaction affects employee loyalty, workplace efficiency and quality of life.

Lead author Dr Martha Crowley, an assistant professor of sociology said:

> We spend a great deal of our time at work, so it is an important part of our lives. If our work experience is unpleasant, it affects every aspect of our lives and ultimately it affects our ability to do our jobs.

The researchers analyzed data on working conditions, workplace relationships and behaviour of professional employees over the last eighty years. They found increasing use of strategies designed to improve productivity and profits including layoffs, outsourcing jobs, replacing salaried employees with contract staff and assigning workers to short-term teams for individual projects.

Martha Crowley commented:

> We found that, while these measures have succeeded in increasing performance pressure, there have also been unintended consequences.

The impact on employees is often negative and immediate. Professional workers may experience increased stress. Projects and co-workers may change frequently,

resulting in a greater sense of chaos at work. Other consequences include increased fears about job security and a distrust of management.

The researchers identified other significant short-term and long-term implications for employers:

→ Professionals are less likely to help co-workers because they are primarily concerned to protect their own jobs.

→ Conflict between workers is detrimental to efficiency and quality and contributes to high levels of stress.

→ Implementation of these business practices has resulted in less loyal employees, no longer so committed to company goals and more likely to seek new opportunities as the economy recovers.

→ Retention will require additional incentives.

Martha Crowley concluded:

> Some firms have had a lot of success by handling their employees differently. Treating your employees well can be a way to boost your profits and productivity simultaneously without generating the unintended consequences of tactics based on fear.

*How close is the association between job insecurity and initiatives such as outsourcing?*

*Source: reprinted with permission from HRM Guide USA (http://www.hrmguide.com).*

Another feature of multinational activity has been the sourcing of components of manufactured products in different countries. Low skill items were the first affected, but more sophisticated items have followed. Wage levels and required skills are not constant factors and it can be argued that this form of sourcing is a natural and progressive feature of industrial growth. Alternatively, it could be described in terms of unscrupulous corporations chasing low wages around the world with the connivance of desperate and sometimes corrupt politicians. A number of countries have tried to attract foreign direct investment by creating special economic zones, free of the usual taxation arrangements. The most famous of these – maquiladoras – are concentrated on the Mexico–US border.

## The maquiladoras programme

Maquilas or maquiladoras are assembly plants that import parts and export the finished products. Initially developed under the auspices of the Mexican Government in the 1960s, they have mushroomed in Mexico and other Latin American countries. They produce manufacturing exports geared to the US market. The Mexican government copied similar plants in the 'tiger' economies of South-East Asia, almost all owned by US multinationals. The term has its derivation in '*maquila*' – the fee collected by a miller for processing grain in Mexico's colonial period (Teagarden, Butler and Von Glinow, 1992).

In Mexico, the programme is restricted to Mexican-registered companies formed with the purpose of manufacturing, assembling, repairing or other processing of goods destined mainly for the export market – but they can be wholly owned by partner operations in other countries. They were introduced as part of a Mexican government human resource strategy described as the 'Border Industrialization Programme'. According to Teagarden, Butler and Von Glinow (1992), the aims of this programme were to:

→ increase the level of industrial activity in Mexico, particularly in the border area.

→ create new jobs.

→ increase the domestic income level.

→ facilitate technology transfer into Mexico and encourage absorption of relevant skills.

→ attract foreign exchange.

Foreign multinationals benefited from significantly lower costs than similar operations in the USA – especially wages, energy and rent. Creating jobs is a key part of maquiladora operations. According to Mexican law, maquiladora companies must create a minimum of 25 jobs. But the Ministry of Commerce and Industrial Development can authorize an operation to begin with fewer than 25 jobs – as long as the number increases from year to year.

According to Mexican employment law, nine out of ten workers taken on by an employer must be Mexican nationals. But this rule has been enforced flexibly for management and technical personnel in the case of maquiladora companies. Moreover, the rule does not apply to foreign workers who are not employed by the Mexican maquiladora company but rather by a foreign partner company.

Maquiladora employment reached 1.3 million in October 2000, and then fell to 1.1 million, with about 400 of the 3700 maquiladoras closing during 2001. By 2004, however, maquiladora employment had begun to rise again and the number of plants rose to 4700. The emphasis switched to a more balanced workforce making technologically advanced parts for major US companies in the automobile, electronics and textile industries. The companies that have made use of maquiladoras include General Motors, Ford, General Electric, Honeywell, Fisher Price, Mattell, Sony, Sanyo, Matsushita, Hitachi and Lucky Goldstar.

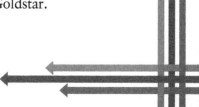

## HRM IN REALITY    OUTSOURCING MEDICAL RECORDS THREATENS LIVES

Thousands of lives are being threatened because of the 'dangerous practice' of sending medical notes overseas for typing, according to speakers at the UNISON annual conference in 2006.

Speaking anonymously, one medical secretary said that mistakes had 'undoubtedly increased' since notes dictated by NHS doctors were transcribed in South Africa, the Philippines and India. The transcribers do not have medical records, prescriptions or letters to compare for accuracy.

Condemning the practice as dangerous, UNISON general secretary Dave Prentis said:

> It's beyond belief. It does not improve the service and the health and welfare of patients is being put at risk. Look what happened to hospital cleaning when it was privatized – a 50 per cent increase in infections. The government needs to rethink this off-the-wall idea.

The union also says that outsourcing is risking patient confidentiality and leading to job losses among local staff. For example, they cite East and North Herts NHS Trust which has issued redundancy notices to 160 medical secretaries and asked for 58 volunteers.

According to Dave Prentis: 'Medical secretaries in the NHS work to 99.8 per cent accuracy targets and once "phased out" their knowledge and expertise will be lost forever'.

Some of the mistakes collected by UNISON include confusing:

→ 'hypertension' (high blood pressure) with 'hypotension' (low blood pressure)

→ 'a septic' (infected) with 'aseptic' (not infected)

→ '15 mg' and '50 mg' drug dosages.

'With more staff and an unknown technology there is greater scope for error', said UNISON head of health Karen Jennings. 'All the government is doing is looking for a cheaper workforce – yet it's doctors and medical students in these other countries that are being used to do the transcriptions.'

*Are UNISON's criticisms of offshoring valid or blown out of proportion?*

*Source: Reprinted with permission from HRM Guide UK (http://www.hrmguide.co.uk).*

Working and living conditions in the maquiladora regions have been heavily criticized. Employers have resisted unionization, frequently ignored Mexican employment legislation and paid low wages to employees living in squalid shanty towns. US labour activists have been particularly critical as up to 800 000 relatively well paid manufacturing jobs have disappeared across the border. But average rates of pay have moved upwards in recent years and the Mexican government has indicated its intention to follow the path of countries such as Malaysia into higher-skilled jobs. Higher wage rates have already led to the departure of many sweatshop textile manufacturers for more vulnerable countries in Central America such as Guatemala and Honduras.

## INTERNATIONAL OUTSOURCING AND SUBCONTRACTING

The marriage of global telecommunications and advanced information technology has resulted in a phenomenon known as 'teletrading'. Initially, teletrading focused on low-skill work being handled by low-wage workers, but the trend is towards transferring more skilled programming and query handling.

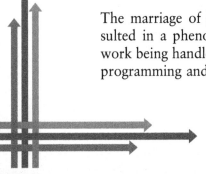

Heeks (1996) identified five main factors to explain the massive growth in software subcontracting to Indian suppliers:

1   Indian software programmers were paid substantially less than their counterparts in the West. According to Heeks this meant that Indian subcontractors were typically charging about 70 per cent of western contract rates and 40 per cent for work carried out offshore.

2   The Indian education system was producing a huge pool of software workers who were highly educated and fluent in English. Conversely, most Western countries had skill shortages in this sector.

3   The Indian software market was itself growing so that use of Indian subcontractors laid the ground for future strategic penetration of Indian markets.

4   Indian companies were enthusiastic about cooperating with foreign high-tech organizations in order to gain access to new markets and technology.

5   The Indian government had become more open towards inward foreign investment and collaboration.

Despite the criticisms of multinationals, many governments – including those of developed countries such as the UK and those of underdeveloped economies – have devoted much energy and money into attracting overseas investment. In the 1980s and 1990s, the British focused on American and Japanese manufacturers of computers and electronic equipment, many of which left for the attractions of cheaper workforces in eastern Europe and South America in the 21st Century.

Lasserre and Schutte (1999) argue that outside investment depends upon the level of economic development. Looking at east Asia, for example, they identify five levels:

1   *Platform countries*, such as Singapore and Hong Kong, which can be used for regional coordination, initiating new contacts and gathering intelligence.

2   *Emerging countries*, for example Vietnam.

3   *Growth countries*, particularly China.

4   *Maturing economies*, as in South Korea and Taiwan.

5   *Established economies*, such as Japan.

Multinationals have ruthlessly played one country or region against another, accepting the highest subsidies and lowest controls over pollution and workers' welfare. Environmental and employee legislation in their 'home' countries has been cynically avoided by transferring production overseas. Trade unions have been slow and largely ineffective in providing employee protection to match global managers.

Admittedly, however, despite the bad press multinationals also produce clearly positive benefits. Multinationals have introduced innovative human resource practices including: mobility packages; cross-cultural and language training; greater sensitivity to national management practices; recruitment and development of local employees; and some exciting international careers.

Even in such quasi-monopolistic sectors, however, management is constrained by a range of environmental factors. Western economies have experienced alternating periods of global recession and recovery. Spurts of growth have been followed by cuts in both production and employment. In a dynamic economy, businesses expect growth in sales, production and ultimately in employee numbers. Conversely, companies experiencing recession or intense competition may have to retrench – 'downsize' in modern management speak. For

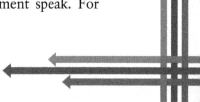

**HRM IN REALITY**   OFFSHORING WORRIES BUT DOES NOT DEMOTIVATE EMPLOYEES

A fifth of employees in the UK worry about their jobs because of the risk of 'offshoring' to low-cost countries such as India or China, according to research from consultants Watson Wyatt published in 2006.

'Offshoring jobs can reduce costs and enhance service. But it can also unnerve and demotivate home country employees', said Jonathan Gardner, an economist at Watson Wyatt. 'We wanted to know how much of a concern to employers this should be.'

Watson Wyatt researched employees' feelings about job security in UK-based companies that have offshored work, compared with their counterparts in organizations that had not shifted jobs overseas. Five thousand people were sampled:

→   Thirty-seven per cent worked for companies that offshored work for the UK market, either directly or had suppliers that had done so

→   Fifty-two per cent had not had this experience

→   'Don't knows' – 11 per cent were unable to answer.

Thirty-six per cent of those with experience of offshoring said they felt less secure in their job as a result of the trend to offshoring, compared with 11 per cent of employees in the second group; and 1 per cent of the first group felt that there was a large risk of their own job being offshored within the next 12 months, compared with 2 per cent in the second group. In fact, 13 per cent of the first group were prepared to admit that their job could be done equally as well offshore as in the UK, compared with 5 per cent of those with no experience of offshoring.

Differences between the two groups were less pronounced when motivation was considered:

→   Around 30 per cent of those with experience of offshoring said they were less motivated at work, compared with 19 per cent in the group without such experiences.

→   Twenty-one per cent of the first group said they were less willing to take risks and share new ideas at work. This compared with 15 per cent in the second group.

→   Fifty-eight per cent of those with offshoring experience thought that perceived stress at work was manageable, compared with 66 per cent of the second group.

'The impact on motivation seems to be fairly small', said Jonathan Gardner. 'Perhaps most telling is the result of the question as to whether or not they were considering finding a new job in the next year.'

Thirty-six per cent of people who had already experienced offshoring said they would be looking for a new job in the next 12 months. But this was little different to the 37 per cent of those who had not had the experience. Employees may feel less secure and a little less motivated because of offshoring but this does not increase the likelihood that they will start hunting for a new job. Watson Wyatt argue that this may be because they are working in industry sectors where competing employers are also engaged in offshoring.

'While the majority of employers may consider the short-term demotivational – and consequent productivity – impact of offshoring acceptable, they cannot afford to be complacent', said Jonathan Gardner. 'It should be of great concern if otherwise committed and high performing employees for whose roles their employer has no plans to shift overseas are being demotivated by fears of offshoring.'

*Are employees in developed countries such as the UK right to be worried by the consequences of offshoring?*

*Source: Reprinted with permission from HRM Guide UK (http://www.hrmguide.co.uk).*

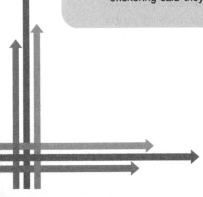

instance, in the mid-1990s air travel recovered slowly from recession. Airlines struggled to meet competition and cut costs to remain in existence. Orders for new aeroplanes were deferred or cancelled. The consequences for aeroplane manufacturers were severe. The world's largest aircraft manufacturer, Boeing, was forced to cut production, leading to thousands of job losses. Similarly, losses at the Dutch company Fokker, leading producer of medium-sized aircraft, impacted heavily on its major German shareholder Daimler-Benz. By the year 2000 production of aircraft was brisk once more.

Then, on 11 September 2001 the sudden impact of terrorism at the World Trade Center in New York brought airlines to their knees and returned the aircraft production industry to the doldrums. Employment in tourism, airlines and aircraft production was dramatically affected throughout the world by the events of one day. No human resource strategist could have forecast such sudden changes in employment needs.

# SUPRANATIONAL ORGANIZATIONS

## *The International Labour Organization*

The International Labour Organization (ILO) is the highest international authority responsible for the conduct and development of human resources. It has a global programme on decent work (ILO, 2000) with the overall goal for the global economy of providing 'opportunities for all men and women to obtain decent and productive work in conditions of freedom, equity, security and human dignity'. It outlines four objectives:

→ *Creation of employment.* Developing a positive environment in which investment and enterprise creation can take place both nationally and internationally with due regard to good practice. Specifically, the ILO considers that there should be worldwide recognition of 'the interdependence between respect for freedom of enterprise for investors and freedom of association for workers'. It calls for a particular focus on stimulating creativity, innovation and entrepreneurship and promoting small enterprises.

→ *Promotion of human rights at work.* With a special focus on the rights of women, the ILO highlights freedom of association, collective bargaining, non-discrimination, forced labour and child labour. The ILO measures annual progress in these areas.

→ *Improvements in social protection.* These include legislation governing dismissal and redundancies.

→ *Promotion of strong institutions* to improve social dialogue between business and labour. Such institutions may include works councils, arbitration systems, joint consultative committees and a variety of other institutions.

## *World Trade Organization*

According to the World Trade Organization website:

> The World Trade Organization (WTO) is the only international organization dealing with the global rules of trade between nations. Its main function is to ensure that trade flows as smoothly, predictably and freely as possible.

The WTO came into existence in 1995 as successor to the General Agreement on Tariffs and Trade (GATT) established after World War II. It began as a result of the tariff reduction

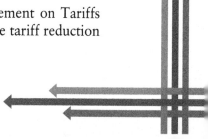

negotiations known as the Uruguay Round. It is not designed to deal with employment regulation but, by its actions, it has a major influence on human resources around the world. Its member states account for 97 per cent of world trade.

It has been severely criticized by environmentalists, union activists and others. For example, the International Forum on Globalization (IFG) describes the WTO as follows (see http://ifg.org/wto.htlm):

> … among the most powerful, and one of the most secretive international bodies on earth. It is rapidly assuming the role of global government, as 134 nation-states, including the US, have ceded to its vast authority and powers. The WTO represents the rules-based regime of the policy of economic globalization. The central operating principal of the WTO is that commercial interests should supersede all others. Any obstacles in the path of operations and expansion of global business enterprise must be subordinated. In practice these 'obstacles' are usually policies or democratic processes that act on behalf of working people, labour rights, environmental protection, human rights, consumer rights, social justice, local culture and national sovereignty.

The WTO has also been accused of not addressing the impact of unfettered free trade on employment rights, although countries that enforce employment rights are at a disadvantage compared with countries that consistently violate employment conventions promulgated by the International Labour Organization.

 ## SUMMARY

Human resource management takes place within a business environment that is increasingly global in its reach. Globalization is a hotly debated subject with many implications for the practice of HRM, both within and between countries. The allocation of human resources depends on comparative issues such as international competitiveness and productivity, factors that are themselves dependent upon a wide range of variables. Foreign inward investment and subcontracting can bring benefits in terms of increased employment opportunities, earnings and economic development but this may be at the expense of comparatively low pay, poor working conditions and denial of employment rights. However, along with a trend towards reduction of trading barriers and encouragement of international trade, there is an increasing call for worldwide regulation of labour issues.

## FURTHER READING

There are numerous books on globalization, many with a markedly political agenda.

1 *The Silent Takeover: Global Capitalism and the Death of Democracy* by Noreena Hertz (published under the Heinemann, Arrow and Free Press imprints, 2001, 2002) takes a highly critical view of the uncontrolled behaviour of multinationals in the globalization process.

2 *Globalization and Its Discontents* by Joseph E. Stiglitz (W.W. Norton, 2002) adopts an all-round view of the process of globalization.

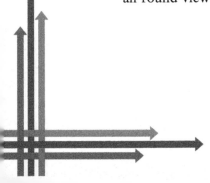

3 For a positive view see *In Defense of Globalization* by Jagdish Bhagwati (Oxford University Press, 2004).

4 *The Maquiladora Reader: Cross-Border Organizing Since NAFTA* edited by Rachael Kamel and Anya Hoffman (American Friends Service Committee, 1999) is a union-minded text.

5 *Smart Sourcing: International Best Practice* by Andrew Kakabadse and Nada Kakabadse (St. Martin's Press, 2002) takes a managerial perspective on wider subcontracting issues.

6 *What's This India Business? Offshoring, Outsourcing and the Global Services Revolution* by Paul Davies (Nicholas Brealey, 2004) is a practical guide on offshoring.

## REVIEW QUESTIONS

1 What is globalization? Why should globalization concern human resource managers?

2 Outline the positive and negative attributes of globalization for:

   a. employees in the developed world

   b. employees in the developing world.

3 Given the evidence provided, are you for or against globalization?

4 What is the relationship between a country's international competitiveness rating and employment prospects in that country?

5 What do you understand by 'labour productivity'? How is it measured?

6 Summarize the relationship between labour productivity and the economic well-being of a country. What other factors are involved?

7 What are the job creation strategies open to developing countries that need to provide employment for growing populations?

8 As an international HR consultant you have been asked to consider the merits of introducing a 'maquiladora' programme for a Caribbean country. What would you advise?

9 Outline the factors to be evaluated before a major computer supplier outsources software development to a developing country.

10 What is the role of the International Labour Organization in the growth of global employment?

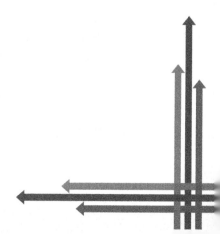

# CASE STUDY FOR DISCUSSION AND ANALYSIS

Read the following case study and answer the questions that follow.

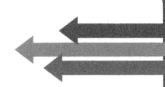

## Change in Japan

The recession of the 1990s and early 2000s seemed to be of a different order from those of the past. In just one year – from October 2000 to October 2001 – the number of people with jobs fell to 64.05 million, a drop of 1.03 million. The Labour ministry estimated that for every 100 people seeking work, only 55 jobs were available. At the end of October 2001, 49.3 per cent of high school students who had graduated in June and looking for jobs were still unemployed – the worst level ever recorded. Overall, unemployment reached 5.4 per cent in May 2002, the highest for 50 years.

Smaller Japanese companies without financial muscle suffered badly. In October 2001, 1804 businesses employing 19 550 workers went bankrupt. This was the 32nd consecutive month in which more than 10 000 people lost their jobs due to bankruptcy.

At the start of the recession in the 1990s, the larger companies tried to avoid compulsory redundancies through redistributing human resources, freezing recruitment and early retirement. Major companies also laid off 'temporary' workers, typically comprising 10 per cent of the staff. This was followed by reduction in overtime – possibly 20 per cent of an average worker's pay packet. Then came the first announcements of redundancies in core workforces.

Nissan, the country's second-largest car maker, announced heavy losses and began a restructuring involving 5000 fewer staff (9 per cent of its employees). The most dramatic part of the announcement was the closure of the Zama plant employing 2500 workers. This was a showcase factory capable of making 260 000 cars a year, using the most advanced technology, including extensive employment of robots. However, Nissan did not anticipate any job losses at all from this move, offering transfers to other Nissan plants. Then Nissan received an injection of cash and an equity investment from Renault on condition that Western management techniques were introduced.

By 2002 profitability was soaring – at the expense of traditional Japanese employment practices and job levels.

During much of the recession the rising value of the yen made overseas production cheaper than domestic manufacturing for Japanese multinationals. This had the effect of exporting jobs. After a period of huge investment in Japan and overseas, much of the domestic production capacity was standing idle. Initially the over-capacity was not tackled by sacking workers. Redundant executives were left within organizations as *Madogiwazoku,* the 'window-gazing tribe' with nothing to do but stare out of their windows. Western managers would not have hesitated to close surplus factories and make large numbers of workers redundant. Japanese businesses had to overturn their basic philosophy in order to come to terms with firing their people.

At first, many Japanese companies exerted pressure on higher salary earners to leave of their own accord. Managers over 45 earning 10 million yen or more were the main target. Ironically, this generation had been accustomed to doing what their employers asked them to do. Now they were asked to leave and found it difficult to say no. Companies exerted psychological pressures on them, for example appealing to their sense of duty by leaving and helping the company's financial situation.

In general, Japanese manufacturing companies employed large numbers of people they did not need. More critically, overstaffing in the Japanese retail and distribution system was remarkably high in comparison with manufacturing and with retailers in the West. One estimate put the surplus at 1.5 million people in manufacturing alone, with around 4 million overall. If these workers were dismissed, the true level of unemployment would be 11–12 per cent.

Japanese attitudes towards workers in overseas operations were less sympathetic. American employees of Japanese subsidiaries falsely assumed that, if not

having a job for life, their employment was virtually secure. Instead, American employees were shed quickly when orders fell. Americans were not the only people to lose their jobs: hundreds of Japanese executives were sent home to lower-status positions.

Underlying the reaction to the recession is a change in Japanese beliefs. The attitudes of the workaholic senior executives of the post-war era are not shared by their middle-aged successors and even less by young graduates. They have different values and are prepared to take on some of the risks of the Western way of business. Whether or not the recession is quickly overcome, a falling birth rate and increasing independence for young people require long-term changes. Excellence in manufacturing has disguised organizational inefficiency. The commitment expected from employees can no longer be guaranteed. Younger men and women with career aspirations are not prepared to work 'long hours for little money while waiting to fill dead men's shoes'. For the first time, there is a debate about fast-track career paths, appointment on merit and performance pay.

By 2002 a survey of companies listed on Section 1 of the Tokyo Stock Exchange showed that the lifetime employment and seniority systems considered typical of Japanese companies were being severely questioned. Just 19.5 per cent of the companies that responded said that they would continue the lifetime employment systems into the future – 53.9 per cent said that they were considering re-examining them. However, Rebick (2005) argues that, although there has been an increase in 'involuntary separations', Japanese firms have continued to engage in labour hoarding and the increase in unemployment has come mostly from a slowdown in hiring. In practice, he contends, job guarantees for 'regular' employees have not gone away. The poorly educated have suffered the most as the opportunities for regular employment have diminished. Rebick (*ibid*) agrees that graduates have also turned to less traditional forms of work as the restrictions of regular employment have become less attractive.

*Why were Japanese people management practices questioned during the recession of the 1990s and early years of this century?*

*Should Japanese multinationals treat Japanese and foreign employees in different ways?*

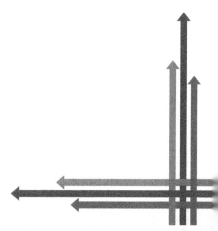

# CHAPTER 5
## HRM and the job market

## LEARNING OBJECTIVES

The purpose of this chapter is to:

→ Outline some of the major theories about why people work.

→ Develop an understanding of the conditions and salaries for which people work and the expectations they have of employers.

→ Explore the relationship between human capital and national employment levels.

→ Determine some of the effects of competitor activities on employee availability.

→ Investigate the patterns of work that are replacing 'nine-to-five' jobs.

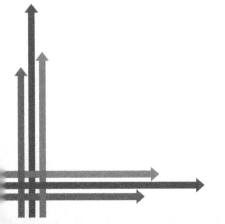

The employment or job market (see Key concept 5.1) is the ultimate source of all new recruits. The dynamics of this market affect human resource managers directly when they deal with employee resourcing or set competitive reward packages. To do so effectively, they need to understand the expectations of prospective employees and have an insight into their decision making process when applying for, or accepting jobs.

We begin this chapter by exploring the reasons why people seek employment. These are evaluated first from an economic perspective, introducing competitive market and institutional theories, and from social and individual viewpoints. The chapter moves on to consider the issue of unemployment. Finally, the characteristics of the flexible job market are debated, including new forms of part-time working and the effects of greater female participation in the working economy.

---

**KEY CONCEPT 5.1**   THE EMPLOYMENT MARKET

The employment market comprises all those people who are available for work. Neo-classical economics views this potential workforce as forming a labour market. The market is affected by national or regional supply and demand for appropriately skilled employees. It is constrained by demographic factors such as the number of young people leaving schools and universities and by cultural norms such as expectations for mothers to stay at home looking after children.

---

## WHY DO PEOPLE WORK?

The simple answer in most cases is that they have to. Few of us have the private resources needed to maintain a satisfactory lifestyle without an income from employment. This seems obvious but the issue becomes much more complex on examination. For example, many wealthy people (or lottery winners) continue to work even though they do not 'need' to. Moreover, unless they are in a desperate financial state, people pick and choose the type of work they are prepared to do. Professions such as nursing and social work attract large numbers of people despite relatively low rates of pay in many countries. Clearly, there are many other factors, other than money, that have to be taken into account in understanding people's motives in the employment market.

The issue has been made all the more complicated because economists have provided several different and contradictory theories in this area. They can be divided broadly into two main approaches: competitive and institutional.

### Competitive market theories

These are derived from the neo-classical economic concepts of rational choice and maximization of utility. The assumption here is that individuals choose jobs that offer them maximum benefits. The utility or value of these benefits – money, vacation time, pension entitlement and so on – varies for different individuals according to their personal preferences. People move from one organization to another if improved benefits are available. At the same time, employing organizations attempt to get the most from their employees for the lowest possible cost. It can be argued that pure competitive theories of the employment

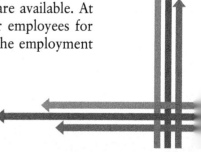

market have little to do with HRM since they are not 'concerned with what goes on inside organizations' (Claydon, 2001: 70). It can also be argued that employment markets are never truly competitive because of various 'rigidities' such as union intervention, minimum-wage laws or social protection rights that are not found in other markets.

In the purest form of competitive employment market (remembering that this is likely to be more theoretical than real) the outcome is a dynamic and shifting equilibrium in which both employees and organizations compete to maximize benefits for themselves. Within a specific region or industry there is a balance between supply and demand for human resources. Pay and conditions for employees – the theory goes – are determined by the relative scarcity or abundance of their skills and abilities in the employment market. Competitive forces push wages up when demand for products – and hence employees – increases, and downwards when the economy is in recession. In the latter case a 'market clearing wage' is arrived at eventually which is sufficiently low to encourage employers to increase recruitment and eliminate unemployment. This discourse reinforces the view that employees are objects to be traded like any other commodities in the market – human resources in the hardest possible sense. Supposedly, they offer themselves – their skills and human qualities – for sale to the highest bidders. Within this mindset they could just as well be vegetables on a market stall.

In reality, it is obvious that the job market does not work in such a simple fashion: people do not move readily between organizations in search of higher wages; most firms do not cut benefits when unemployment levels are high and cheaper workers are available. Indeed, in the 1980s wages soared for those in work at the same time as unemployment levels increased. Such contradictions are partly explained by the omission of HR development issues such as training and career structures in competition theories. More generally, they assume that employment markets are purely external when, in fact, large organizations have internal job markets operating through promotion and transfer of existing employees.

Competition theories assume that job-seekers have perfect knowledge of available jobs and benefits. Job-searching is an expensive and time-consuming business. The unemployed do not have money and those in work do not have time. The result is that few people conduct the extensive searches required to find jobs that meet their preferences perfectly. In practice, most individuals settle for employment which is quickly obtained and which exceeds the 'reserve minimum wage' they have in mind. There is a considerable element of luck involved. Moreover, the job-seeker does not make the choice: in most cases the decision is in the hands of the employer.

In a test of competitive labour market theory, Machin and Manning (2004) selected a situation that would come within most economists' definition of a competitive labour market (elder care assistants working for competing firms in the South of England) and found that the distribution of wage rates deviated markedly from that predicted by competitive market theories. They concluded (p. 383):

> ... it is hard to avoid the conclusion that there are very serious limitations to the usefulness of the competitive model in explaining the data. In particular, we feel that the competitive model cannot explain one of the most striking patterns our evidence reveals – the presence of very little wage dispersion within firms, and of high wage dispersion between firms. Moreover, what wage dispersion there is does not seem to be closely related to the characteristics of workers that seem to be associated with high productivity.

Entry barriers to job sectors provide a further constraint on the competitive job market. Many jobs are restricted to people possessing key skills – often specific to a particular firm or industrial sector, or fitting a particular demographic background. In fact, the external job market is made up of many sub-markets with widely different circumstances and constraints.

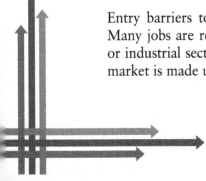

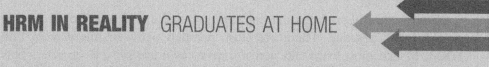

# HRM IN REALITY GRADUATES AT HOME

In 2006 Experience, Inc. announced the findings of its Life After College online survey of recent American graduates on the growing 'boomerang kids' trend towards returning to live in the family home, career paths and the overall reality of life after college.

The majority of respondents (58 per cent) returned to live with parents after college, three-quarters did so immediately on graduating and one-third stayed more than 12 months. About half (48 per cent) of those who returned home did so to save money; 37 per cent were unemployed. Returning home was financially advantageous with no contributions paid towards utilities (92 per cent), rent (85 per cent) or groceries (74 per cent). Attitudes to returning to the family home varied: 59 per cent reported feeling 'indifferent or neutral'; 31 per cent 'embarrassed'; and 10 per cent 'proud and happy'.

Job-hopping has become customary for today's graduates; the average tenure at a first full-time job is 1.6 years. Three-quarters had changed jobs in the five years following graduation:

→   up to one year (36 per cent)

→   one to two years (51 per cent)

→   three to five years (77 per cent)

Only 23 per cent had remained with the same employer since graduating. Seventy-five per cent chose to stay within their home state when changing jobs. Respondents cited various reasons for changing jobs, the most common being:

→   salary increase (18 per cent)

→   unhappy with existing employer (17 per cent)

→   to try a new profession, department or company (13 per cent)

→   move home (9 per cent)

→   promotion (3 per cent)

*Why are graduates keener to change jobs than they are to leave the parental home?*

Reprinted with permission from HRM Guide USA (http://www.hrmguide.com).

Wills *et al.* (2009) found that London employers in the cleaning sector were increasingly dependent on a diverse pool of overseas-born workers. Here the migrant division of labour (MDL) is seen as a product of semi-autonomous actions taken by employers, workers and government in a specific London context. This particular division of labour can only be explained by a complex interaction of employer demand and a preference for immigrants over UK-born workers, migrants' 'dual frame of reference' and limited access to state benefits and government control of immigration, benefits and employment legislation.

## Institutional theories

An alternative approach places its main focus within the firm rather than the external job market. Institutionalists do not accept the principle of individual maximization of utility, arguing that both individuals and organizations cooperate to some extent and take account of the preferences of others in similar situations. Individual workers are less concerned with maximum benefits than achieving a fair rate compared with their peers. But this comparison may be restricted to employees within the same organization: most people appear indifferent (much of the time, at least) to benefits offered by other employers and large variations occur between firms in the same sector. Employers set wages for a variety of reasons ranging from profitability to tradition – competition with other firms is a relatively minor consideration. As a result, remuneration levels within many firms are relatively rigid. Wage

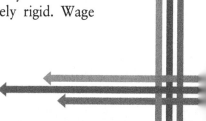

rates are more likely to go up than down and are largely immune to influence from the external job market.

Competition theories assume that hiring and firing in reaction to changing market conditions is good practice. There are close parallels between this way of thinking and 'hard' HRM. In fact, most firms take active steps to avoid employee turnover. This is because turnover is disruptive and costs money. Recruitment advertising and redundancy payments are expensive and training new employees represents a considerable investment in time and effort. Organizations may encourage workers to remain with them by means of HR policies that increase benefits such as annual leave and pensions in line with length of service.

---

### KEY CONCEPT 5.2  INSIDERS AND OUTSIDERS

Employers know that replacing existing workers with others from the outside world has inherent costs. This inhibits recruitment from the external employment market. Also, to some extent, there are costs or risks that inhibit employees from looking for work outside the organization. Consequently, there is rarely a free flow of workers in and out of a business. This disconnection is reflected in the pay and conditions of established employees ('insiders') which may deviate considerably from the 'market rate' in the wider world. Insiders will tend to push for a premium rate of pay, regardless of more competitive rates acceptable to outsiders, because of their perceived power to retain their jobs.

---

Reflecting on our discussion in Part One, we can conclude that institutional approaches to the job market have a greater affinity with 'soft' HRM. They recognize that group effects underlie notions of fairness and loyalty, fundamental to the notion of employee commitment. They are consistent with the stakeholder concept, recognizing the important roles played by government and trade unions. For example, the 'insider–outsider' model offers an explanation for simultaneously high wages and high levels of unemployment (Lindbeck and Snower, 1988). Insiders have stakeholder status whereas outsiders do not (see Key concept 5.2). Outsider status particularly affects immigrants. Frijters, Shields and Price (2005) found that immigrants to the UK do not compete effectively for employment. Job search methods are less successful; they are as likely to gain employment through informal routes; and the probability of success increases with years since immigration. This may partially explain why immigration has little impact on the job market.

At the organizational level, human resource managers also affect the nature of the market as a result of their recruitment and redundancy strategies. When business is optimistic recruitment numbers increase; if conditions are bad, employees may be shed. Technological change is a further complicating factor, leading to fewer but more highly skilled employees.

Figure 5.1 demonstrates some of the forces that shape the employment market, including elements discussed in Chapter 6, such as the major role played by government, particularly in the shape of legislation. The interactions between organizations and the job market are debated again later in the book when we consider human resource strategy. At this stage it is appropriate to note some omissions from most accounts of this subject such as the influence of social class, age, status, gender and ethnic origin in the job expectations of employees and the attitudes of employers towards these characteristics. As we shall see in later discussions on equal opportunities, suitable people can appear invisible to managers who associate competence for high-level jobs with a particular age, accent, sex or colour.

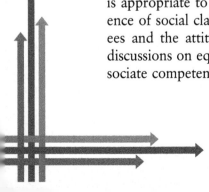

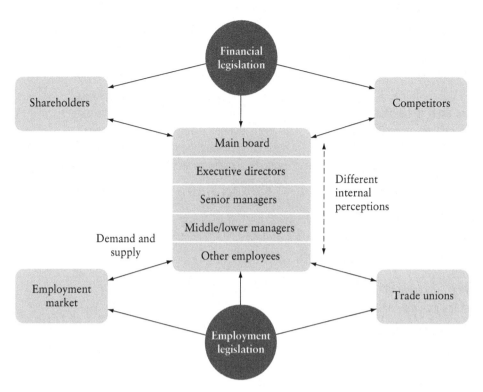

## HRM IN REALITY  JOB SATISFACTION IN THE UK

Results from a survey of over 1000 workers for The Work Foundation conducted in 2006 reveals positive attitudes towards work but also confirms that work remains simply a way of making a living for many people. Commissioned as part of The Work Foundation's campaign for 'good work' the study found most people feel their work has got better since the beginning of their working lives.

The survey found:

→ Sixty per cent said their satisfaction with work had increased, 31 per cent felt it had gone down, and 8 per cent said it had stayed the same.

→ Seventy-eight per cent said they found their work 'stimulating and challenging' (55 per cent agreeing strongly with this statement) and 69 per cent said their work was a 'source of personal fulfilment'.

→ Eight-six per cent did not agree with the statement 'I regard my work as meaningless' with only nine per cent saying they agreed (the remainder did not express a view).

→ Just over half (51 per cent) said their work was 'a means to an end'. People with lower pay and lower skills tended to be less satisfied with their jobs.

→ Over three-quarters of respondents describe themselves as 'very satisfied' (35 per cent) or 'quite satisfied' (43 per cent) with their current jobs; 10 per cent were neither satisfied nor dissatisfied; 6 per cent were 'quite dissatisfied'; and 5 per cent very dissatisfied.

Will Hutton, chief executive of The Work Foundation, said:

Traditionally, work has been seen as purely a grim economic necessity, which there is no getting out of, and little more to be said about. Our survey indicates that that view is no longer a fair reflection of how people feel. Today, work is increasingly thought of as a source of fulfilment, an important aspect of life that matters to people in a very personal way.

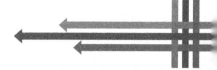

Other key findings in the survey included:

→ Women are slightly more likely to be satisfied with their job than men.

→ The over-55s are more likely to be satisfied with their job than younger workers, especially those aged 16–34 years.

→ Managers and professionals are more likely to be satisfied than other occupational groups.

→ People earning over £50000 per year are more likely to be satisfied than those who earn less.

Will Hutton said:

Employers and organizations are going to have to think much harder about the jobs they offer. The wage packet still matters, but there are crucially important psychological, social, and personal dividends from work, too – it is about money and meaning. Well over two thirds of workers regard work as a source of personal fulfilment to them, but only a very few employers ever succeed in making the most of this huge personal appetite for work that more and more people have.

*How would you explain the concept of work having 'meaning'?*

Source: Reprinted with permission from HRM Guide UK (http://www.hrmguide.co.uk).

## SOCIAL PREFERENCES

Participating in employment is not an 'all-or-nothing' decision: individuals also determine the amount of time they are prepared to devote to paid work. The allocation of time is affected by 'expected market earnings', taking travel, clothing and taxation into account. Traditionally, time given to 'market work' is distinguished from that devoted to any other activity – described as 'leisure'. However, it is recognized that time outside paid work is not necessarily devoted to pleasure. Far from lying on a beach, sipping a cool drink, people spend much of their 'leisure' time on some form of work without pay. This could be housework, maintenance, looking after children, cooking or providing a voluntary service.

Deciding to take a job, or not, involves a trade-off between family members. If an additional member works, there should be a reduction or reallocation of that person's unpaid activities. Employment may change lifestyle significantly. In developed countries this can result in the purchase of labour-saving devices such as a dishwasher, changing from fresh to ready-prepared food and hiring a cleaner or child-minder.

The decision to seek employment can be complex and is likely to be taken in conjunction with other members of the household. The household is viewed as the 'decision-making unit' that chooses how to allocate its members' time, evaluating the comparative advantages of working as against not working. Where the possibility of choice exists, the emphasis can be on working for money in order to buy the largest possible house, a brand new car, expensive holidays and consumer goods such as convenience foods. Alternatively, the household can minimize working time and maximize leisure, making do with a more modest home and car, spending effort on home-grown and prepared food. Golden (2009) argues that research on the interrelationship between work and family life is skewed towards the organization – employee relationship, with the role of the family seen as emotional and material support for the employee and adapting to organizational needs. Taking a systems approach shows that the family has a greater significance.

In a fluid and global economy there are decisions to be made also about relocation. For example, in two French studies Challiol and Mignonac (2005) found strong evidence for decision-making based on compromise when dual-earning couples were faced with career opportunities that required one partner to change geographical location.

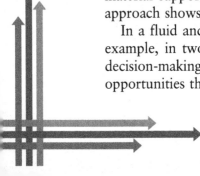

Doing without paid work in order to maximize free time is an opportunity cost. In other words, if paid work is available, not working has a cost for the household. There may be preferences for particular family members to stay at home typically mothers – whereas others (fathers) are expected to earn a wage. As we will see later in this chapter, this pattern has changed radically in most industrialized countries in recent years.

Recognition of household preferences is important to people managers because there are strong cultural differences between one region and another. There are considerable pressures on potential and actual workers to behave in the way perceived as normal for their particular society. However, most organizations pay little attention to the domestic influences on an employee's motivation and performance. Employees are recruited and their

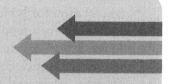

## HRM IN REALITY  MOST SENIOR EMPLOYEES NEVER STOP WORKING

A poll of executives and professionals conducted in 2008 by MRINetwork, a major international search and recruitment organization found that the majority rarely stop working. Typically, they worked evenings, weekends and during their commute. Many believed that their employers were responsible for creating the situations that lead to overwork.

Seventy per cent of 500+ people surveyed said the organizations they worked for did not do a good job at fostering a work/life balance. Sixty-five per cent of participants in the poll were frequently still working after normal office hours, a further 19 per cent worked 'sometimes', 9 per cent occasionally. Only 5 per cent said they never did so.

Michael Jalbert, president of MRINetwork, commented:

> They often feel they have no choice but to work as much as it takes to meet management's expectations. More enlightened managers, however, are beginning to realize that the X and Y generations are much more committed to forging a balanced life than the retiring baby boomers. This will inevitably lead to a reevaluation of the performance requirements of individual positions within many companies, especially as the younger generation moves into higher management levels.

A number of factors influence the rising number of people whose work day extends far beyond the traditional hours. Obviously technology that makes staying connected almost anywhere in the world effortless is a significant contributor. And for many people that's led to an almost compulsive need for 24/7 interaction.

He noted that many organizations were understaffed.

> Most people simply have more work to do than they can accomplish in eight or even ten-hour days. In some cases, working overtime has masked the need to hire more mid-to-upper-level employees. If the work is getting done satisfactorily, senior management may not be aware of gaps in their workforce.

But many employees love what they do.

> The greater their interest and commitment to the work they do, the more they seem to work – even when it's not required of them. To these people, the ability to stay connected to their work via a variety of technological devices is an asset rather than a liability.

Michael Jalbert notes that, especially for telecommuters, there is a blurring of the distinction between being 'at work' and 'off work'. 'As much as employees value flexible work schedules, this arrangement can also encourage working more and playing less.'

*Why do executives and professionals tend to work excessively hours?*

*Source: Reprinted with permission from HRM Guide USA (http://www.hrmguide.com).*

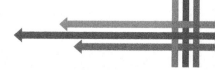

performance assessed as if they were entirely free agents with no domestic responsibilities or interests outside work.

When is it worthwhile going to work? The total available resources of the household unit may be weighed up in the equation, including the time available for all its members, other income and total wealth. The financial benefit of work can only be gauged when tax, social security deductions, travelling, child-minding costs and so on have been calculated. This benefit may prove insignificant.

Mathematical models have been developed to predict the hours that people are prepared to work. They take into account factors such as the availability of overtime work, the effects of taxation, opportunities for self-employment and payment by results (Sapsford and Tzannatos, 1993: 27). Empirical studies do not necessarily support this approach – unemployment is an experience that can arrive like a tidal wave. There may be no opportunity to make a free decision on whether or not to work. During a recession, for example, it can be common for both partners in a relationship to lose their jobs in quick succession (Morris, 1987). Women tend to be in highly vulnerable part-time jobs.

Morris argues that his research contradicts the notion of the household decision-making model. He concludes that such models take no account of the local social network that influences beliefs and expectations of employment. Neither do they accommodate local differences in employment opportunities and cultural ideas of gender behaviour. Job choices also reflect individual career plans and preferences. In the UK, in a study of males in the job market, Kaplanis (2010) found that the availability of people with high skill levels in a locality impacts strongly in a positive manner on the local employment chances of men who have no qualifications. The impact on employment on other educational groups proves to be either insignificant or significantly negative. Kapanlis' findings are consistent with the consumer demand hypothesis which holds that the demand for local low skill services is increased by the presence of highly educated, high income people in a locality.

## INDIVIDUAL PREFERENCES

We have seen that people do not behave as mere commodities. Human behaviour involves deep complexities that bring unpredictability and apparent contrariness into the employment market. Most people's motives and ambitions involve much more than seeking the highest salary. Money is important but to a degree that varies between individuals. People will remain in comparatively low-paid jobs such as nursing because the satisfaction that comes from helping other people can be valued above a high salary. There has been much criticism of the quality of work offered by the fast-food industry, a major area of youth employment. However, Allan *et al.* (2006) concluded that employee attitudes towards 'McJobs' were not entirely negative after studying students' perceptions of work in the fast-food sector in Australia. Fast-food workers were generally dissatisfied with industrial relations and work organization, and much more satisfied with human resource management and social relations aspects of their jobs.

An economic model based purely on income will go some way to explain employment behaviour on the large scale but it will not explain *individual* human behaviour. Other motivations come into play in determining people's approach to work. As we can see from Table 5.1, psychologists have attempted to provide explanations at the individual level.

Ardichvili and Kuchinke (2009: 155) argue that 'work as a process and an institution ... transcends individual frames of reference and links the person to the social, economic and political realms'. The significance of understanding the 'meaning of work' or the 'meaning of working' – some theorists differentiate between the two – is that it underlies one of the

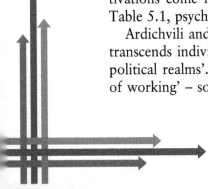

TABLE 5.1
Psychological
benefits of work

Source: Adapted from
Warr (1987).

111

CHAPTER 5    HRM and the job market

| Factor | Characteristics |
| --- | --- |
| **Opportunities for control** | Limited control over work, or no job at all, leads to higher levels of anxiety, depression, tiredness and psychosomatic symptoms. Also lower general life-satisfaction and self-esteem. |
| **Opportunities for skill use** | People benefit from stretching jobs. Morale, self-esteem, sociability and life satisfaction are reduced when a worker's job is de-skilled or lost. Some people can compensate through hobbies or voluntary work, but many are unable to fill the gap. |
| **Goal and task demands** | Jobs set demands on our lives in general. Many unemployed people find it hard to fill their time, often spending a high proportion sleeping, sitting around or watching TV, further contributing to lowered morale. |
| **Variety** | Work can increase variety, providing a contrast with home life. It also provides the income to pay for experiences such as cinema, music, sporting activities and holidays. |
| **Environmental clarity** | Work helps us understand and predict the world around us. Mental health is better if we are clear about our roles and purpose in life. Conversely, uncertainty is detrimental, especially over a lengthy period. |
| **Availability of money** | The unemployed have a lower income level (40–60 per cent on average) than those in work. This can make it difficult to repay credit and keeping up mortgage payments, adding further stress. Expensive activities are curtailed, contributing to feelings of isolation and boredom. |
| **Physical security** | In western cultures people are brought up to value personal and private space. To provide feelings of personal security, self-worth and well-being they need a home to call their own. This requires an income. |
| **Opportunity for interpersonal contact** | Interaction with other people reduces feelings of loneliness and provides emotional support. |
| **Valued social position** | Work provides a self-identity and a feeling of worth. |

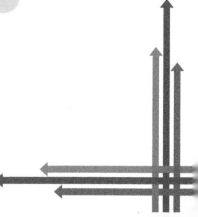

most fashionable concerns of HRM or talent management: employee engagement or commitment (Flesher, 2009: 255). It is common to ask the question: 'What do you do?' For many of us, self-identity is provided by a job. Comparing South Korea, Germany and the United States, Kuchinke (2009) contends that the meaning of work varies across the three countries and has changed in different degrees since industrialization. He argues that work is more central to self-identity in the United States than in Germany, where life outside work is equally important.

The psychological benefits obtained from work include the fulfilment of social needs such as companionship, group cohesion and a sense of belonging. Kidder (2006) points to the limitations of an economic model to explain employment behaviour using bike messengers as an example. Bike messengers work in a dirty and dangerous occupation with low pay and no benefits. Nevertheless, many messengers consider their occupation to be their primary source of identity. The creativity and spontaneity of courier work allows messengers to become emotionally attached to their job. It brings the thrill seeking of leisure pursuits into the workplace, which creates an authentic self intimately tied to the occupation, a rare achievement in an increasingly rationalized employment system. Sweet and Meiksins (2008) compared relatively low-paid and poorly qualified infant school teachers and senior care centre nursing support staff in the United States with equivalents in Scandinavian countries, where higher professional qualifications are required and higher salaries are paid. They found much greater self-esteem and career satisfaction among the Scandinavian employees.

Twenge *et al.* (2010) looked at the work values of a nationally representative sample of US high school seniors in 1976 (Baby Boomers), 1991 (GenerationX or GenX) and 2006 (Generation Me or GenY). They found that leisure values increased steadily over the generations while work centrality declined. Status and earnings were most highly valued by GenX and least by Baby Boomers. Altruistic work values such as helping and societal worth were the same across the generations. However, social values (for example, friendship) and intrinsic values (such as having an interesting, results-oriented job) were regarded as less important by GenY than by Baby Boomers.

## PARTICIPATING IN THE EMPLOYMENT MARKET

Who is involved in the job market? We have seen that the resourcing of organizations is affected by national or regional availability (supply) and demand for appropriately skilled employees. On the supply side of this balance, people can be divided into three groups, the first two of which are described as 'economically active' (Key concept 5.3). Rates of economically active participants fluctuate, with a trend towards increasing participation from the 1960s to the early 21st century. For example, the participation rate in Australia increased from 57.4 per cent of over-15-year olds in 1961 to 65.2 per cent in 2008. The bulk of the increase took place among women of whom only 28.9 per cent were economically active in 1961 compared to 58.3 per cent in 2008. In the 15–64 age group of both sexes, the OECD average was 70 per cent in 2007 with rates such as 75 per cent in the USA, 76 per cent in Australia and the UK, 78 per cent in Canada and New Zealand, 80 per cent in Sweden and 81 per cent in Switzerland.

**KEY CONCEPT 5.3** ECONOMICALLY ACTIVE

The economically active comprise two groups: (a) *the employed* – those in paid work; and (b) *the unemployed* – those who are looking for paid work but are unable to find it.

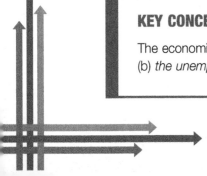

| Country | Unemployment %2010 | Unemployment %2006 |
| --- | --- | --- |
| Australia | 5.8 | 5.2 |
| Belgium | 8.6 | 8.2 |
| Canada | 8.7 | 5.7 |
| Denmark | 7.8 | 4.4 |
| Finland | 9.3 | 8.1 |
| France | 9.8 | 9.4 |
| Germany | 8.0 | 9.1 |
| Ireland | 12.9 | 4.2 |
| Italy | 9.1 | 7.7 (Dec 2005) |
| Japan | 5.1 | 4.2 |
| Netherlands | 5.9 | 4.2 |
| New Zealand | 6.6 | 3.9 (March) |
| Norway | 3.7 | 3.9 |
| Poland | 10.6 | 16.9 |
| Portugal | 10.6 | 7.7 |
| Spain | 20.1 | 8.2 |
| Sweden | 9.3 | 5.3 |
| UK | 7.9 | 5.2 |
| USA | 10.4 | 4.8 |

**TABLE 5.2**
Comparative levels of unemployment (Quarter 1, 2010)

Source: Labour Force Statistics (MEI), under labour from OECD.Stat Extracts, http://stats.oecd.org, accessed October 2010. Reproduced with permission for OECD.

Economically inactive people are neither in paid work nor seeking jobs, including people in education, with medical conditions, looking after dependents and the retired. Proportions of these categories vary from country to country, depending on economic conditions and custom. Accurate figures for each group are not easily calculated. In particular, it is difficult to estimate true unemployment because the unemployed are identified on the basis of registration with state agencies. As an illustration, Table 5.2 shows official figures for a number of OECD countries in 2006 and 2010. Usually the registration of individuals as unemployed is linked to the payment of unemployment relief or other social security benefit. If the benefit system is generous, people are more likely to register. Conversely, if benefits are restricted the registered unemployment figure decreases.

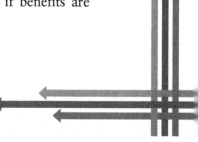

Developed countries have experienced considerable variations in unemployment levels. This is reflected in changes in public expectations and concern over the level of unemployment. It can be argued that more people would work if jobs were easy to find – but they do not search when work is scarce. This has been called the 'discouraged worker hypothesis' (see Key concept 5.4). Workers calculate the probability of finding a job in relation to the wage they are likely to get and conclude that the effort is not worthwhile. This hypothesis suggests that the number of active job-seekers decreases in times of high unemployment, leaving an unmeasurable hidden unemployment rate behind the official statistics. As with many other western countries, the 2007–2009 recession seriously affected the UK's economic output – more so than any other recession since the Second World War. However, the unemployment level did not increase to the degree experienced in previous recessions despite being at its lowest level for thirty years. Gregg and Wadsworth (2010) conclude that this difference can be attributed to:

→ High levels of profitability for firms going into the recession.

→ Supportive government monetary and fiscal policies during the period of recession.

→ Reductions in real producer wages.

→ Comparatively stable real consumer wages.

**KEY CONCEPT 5.4** DISCOURAGED WORKER HYPOTHESIS

Workers calculate the probability of finding a job in relation to the wage they are likely to get and conclude that the effort is not worthwhile.

Organizations in free market countries focus on the external employment market, seeking new staff from outside the business. This is compatible with a competitive market approach in which employees are recruited when needed and dispensed with when no longer required. This view also provides a clear rationale for the 'hard' HRM form of employee planning that we will discuss in a later chapter. In the first part of this book we observed that the softer Harvard model of HRM emphasizes commitment between organizations and their employees. The latter approach is more consistent with social market and East Asian capitalist models. In Germany and Japan – together with the ideal organizations of 'soft' HRM rhetoric – the traditional focus has been on the internal employment market with:

→ Recruitment taking place almost entirely at the lower levels from the pool of available school-leavers and graduates.

→ Organizations offering a structured career on a lifetime basis.

→ Little movement, or labour turnover, between organizations.

You will remember from earlier discussions on Japan that, until recently, major Japanese companies offered life-long employment and career development. German organizations emphasize the recruitment of apprentices who will eventually fill middle and senior posts, whereas in free-market countries companies advertise vacancies externally at all levels. This has implications on the average job tenure in different countries. An ILO Report (ILO, 2004), using data from a variety of sources between 1998 and 2004, found that people

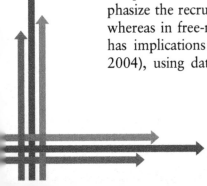

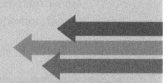

## HRM IN REALITY
### IMMIGRATION AND ITS EFFECTS ON THE JOB MARKET IN THE UK

→ The rate of immigration to the UK rose from 1995 to the recession of 2007–2009 when the stock of immigrants fell back.

→ The level of overseas-born people in the UK's working age population rose from 8 per cent in 1995 to 14 per cent or 5.3 million in late 2009.

→ But the UK still has a smaller share of immigrants in the total population (10.2 per cent) than many other developed countries, for example Australia (25 per cent), the United States (13.6 per cent) and even Germany (12.9 per cent).

→ The highest proportion of immigrants to the UK in recent years came from Poland, India, Pakistan, South Africa and the United States.

→ Immigrants are generally younger and better educated than UK-born individuals with most recent immigrants being even more educated.

→ There is a considerable disparity in regional levels of immigrants with an overwhelming concentration in London. For example, about 60 per cent of the working age population in the London Borough of Brent are immigrants while less than 3 per cent of the working age population of Knowsley are overseas-born.

→ There is a strict 'points' system controlling access to work of non-EU immigrants.

→ Overall, immigration has been positive for the UK as both low- and high-skill gaps in the job market where there are shortages of workers have been filled, with little effect on wage or employment levels.

*Why does hostility towards immigration prevail despite the evidence for positive benefits?*

*Source: Adapted from Wadsworth (2010).*

stayed with one employer for an average of 12.2 years in Japan, 11.2 years in France and 10.6 years in Germany. This compared with 8.2 years in the UK and 6.6 years in the USA.

Trends and levels vary significantly between public and private sectors. At the end of the 20th century, public sector tenure levels were over twice those of the private sector. This may be partly explained by the tendency of government workers to be older than their counterparts in private industry. Also, there is a lesser likelihood of public sector employees being laid off or being affected by cyclical factors to the degree experienced by private sector workers – for example those in construction or wholesale and retail trade. However, after the recession of 2007–2009 public sector workers have been targeted in cost-cutting measures in countries such as the UK.

Intriguingly, the archetypal East Asian economy, Singapore, has seen high rates of employee turnover to match its remarkable growth rate due to competition for scarce skills. Similarly, Japanese companies have changed their traditional practices to attract electronics experts with premium technological skills.

Projections of the future size of the employment market are critical to planned economic development. On a local basis, individual companies need to anticipate the availability of suitable recruits to meet business planning needs. These are normally calculated from:

→ **Demographic trends** (Key concept 5.5), including the birth rate at least 16 years previously.

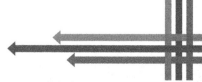

→ Retirement rates (in the last few decades there has been a pronounced trend towards earlier retirement in developed countries, which is likely to be reversed as people live longer and age discrimination is banned.

→ Numbers of people in higher education.

---

**KEY CONCEPT 5.5** DEMOGRAPHIC TRENDS

Long-term changes in the overall population level and age distribution in countries, regions and localities due to variations in birth, death and migration. These changes affect the availability of employable people.

---

Reductions in demand for manual work have seen many unskilled workers leaving the employment market. Ranzijn *et al.* (2006) studied the impact of mature-aged unemployment on individuals in Adelaide, South Australia and suggest that their quality of life is substantially impaired. Frustration at being unable to contribute to society, support adult children and use skills can lead to the 'peg-down' phenomenon, described as an intermediate step between becoming unemployed and premature exit from the workforce.

**HRM IN REALITY** LIVING LONGER, WORKING LONGER

People in developed countries are living longer and many are working well past traditional retirement age. Some are even returning to work after 'retiring' or opting for 'portfolios' of paid and volunteer positions, according a MetLife Mature Market Institute® study, *Living Longer, Working Longer: The Changing Landscape of the Aging Workforce*, conducted by David DeLong & Associates, Inc. and Zogby International in 2006.

'Today, older workers view retirement as a desirable state, not a particular date', said Dr David DeLong, author of *Lost Knowledge: Confronting the Threat of an Aging Workforce* and a research fellow at the MIT AgeLab. 'When we conducted the study, we found that mature workers are struggling to balance the conflicting pressures of income security, post-retirement-age employment and, often, age discrimination – perceived or real – as they look for a sense of security and meaning during their "retirement" years.'

This study is unusual in that it examines the actual work experiences of 2719 employees aged 55–70 whereas most other studies offer predictions of aging Baby Boomers' retirement expectations. The MetLife study shows that the following percentages of respondents are working or looking for work:

→ Seventy-eight per cent of respondents aged 55–59

→ Sixty per cent of 60–65 year-olds, and

→ Thirty-seven per cent of 66–70 year-olds.

Around 15 per cent of employees across all three age groups, have accepted retirement benefits from previous employers, but have chosen to return to work (or are looking for work). These 'working retired', represent:

→ Eleven per cent of 55–59 year-olds

→ Sixteen per cent of 60–65 year-olds

→ Nineteen per cent of 66–70 year-olds.

*Motivations to work*

There are significant differences between age groups when it comes to the motivation to work. Employees aged 55–59 cited economic incentives as the major motive, with 72 per cent of this group saying that 'need income to live on' was their primary reason for working. Sixty per cent of 60–65-year-olds also cited this as their main motivation, followed by a desire to 'stay active and engaged' (54 per cent) and 'do meaningful work' (43 per cent). However, 72 per cent of 66–70 year-olds cited the desire to 'stay active and engaged' as their primary reason to work, followed by 'the opportunity to do meaningful work' (47 per cent) and 'social interaction with colleagues' (42 per cent).

### What does 'retirement' mean?

Respondents in the MetLife study cited the following definitions of retirement:

→ 'freedom from the demands of work' (26 per cent)

→ 'more control over one's personal time' (24 per cent)

→ 'limited financial concerns' (21 per cent)

→ 'the ability to pursue other opportunities.'

'As organizations seek to attract and retain older workers, they must be careful not to lump all "older workers" into the same category – it's important to differentiate the work experiences and motivations of these employees. While some may be working for financial reasons, others place a special premium on feeling engaged and doing work that means something', says Sandra Timmermann, Ed.D., gerontologist and director of the MetLife Mature Market Institute. 'Recruiting and retaining older workers requires careful consideration of job design, work environment and creating new and challenging opportunities.'

### What motivates the 'working retired'

Twenty per cent of working retireds age 60–65 said they 'wanted to try something new and different'. However, this option was cited by only 12 per cent of 55–59-year-olds and 7 per cent of 66–70 year-olds. Nineteen per cent of 66–70-year-olds cited 'becoming self-employed or starting a business' compared with 7 per cent of 60–65-year-olds and 8 per cent of 55–59-year-olds.

28 per cent of respondents aged 55–59 said they were 'self-employed or business owner'. This increased to 36 per cent of 60–65-year-olds and 42 per cent of 66–70-year-olds.

'Clearly, these findings suggest there are conditions in the job market and in older workers' desire for autonomy and flexibility that make self-employment an attractive option for those in their late sixties', said Dr DeLong. 'As the oldest Boomers turn 60 in 2006, their desire for autonomy and trying new things could portend a significant wave of departures in the next five years. Employers will need to identify ways to retain the valuable knowledge of these workers.'

### Financial reality

Financial necessity underlies the need to work for many older employees. Eighteen per cent of Baby Boom workers aged 55–59 said that they expected to have no access to retirement benefits (e.g. pension, 401(k), SEP) and are likely to feel compelled to work beyond traditional retirement age. Fourteen per cent of those aged 60–65 and 10 per cent aged 66–70 expected to receive nothing but Social Security when they finally cease working.

'Retirement experts have been predicting for years the serious repercussions that will arise as Baby Boomers' lack of retirement assets collides with their increased longevity to create widespread economic hardship. The rational solution – to continue working full-time beyond traditional retirement age – is at odds with many Boomers' interests, values and priorities for their retirement', notes Dr Timmermann.

### Some other survey findings

**Age discrimination.** Older workers frequently cited 'age bias' as a reason for unsuccessful job searches, including:

→ Thirty-nine per cent of 55–59-year-olds

→ Forty-two per cent of 60–65-year-olds

→ Sixty per cent of 66–70-year-olds.

**Preference for part-time work.** Of those still in employment, 76 per cent of 55–59 year-olds worked more than 35 hours a week, compared with only 39 per cent of 66–70 year-olds.

**Portfolio work.** Interviews were also conducted for the study, in which some older employees said their lives had taken on a 'portfolio quality' – mixing part-time paid work, volunteer work and travel, together with more time for hobbies and family. In fact, 25 per cent of survey respondents across all age groups had more than one paid job with about 20 per cent of those working having two jobs, and another 4 per cent having three jobs.

*Why are some older people keen to work while others are not?*

Source: Reprinted with permission from HRM Guide USA (http://www.hrmguide.com).

# EMPLOYEE SUPPLY AND DEMAND

Individuals determine how much time they will devote to paid work for a variety of reasons. The proportion of people of working age in work, or seeking jobs, is described as the labour force participation rate. The flow of young people into the workforce is fundamental to the employment market. The underlying demographic pattern is changing throughout the world. Whereas most developing countries have seen an explosion of growth in the youngest age groups, the developed world is experiencing a reduction in birth rate. This follows a baby boom after World War II which produced a wave of people who will mostly retire in the first quarter of the 21st century. In Western Europe and North America, numbers of people entering the employment market have been falling. This will reduce the overall size of their workforces, shifting the age balance towards older employees. This has been compensated by a massive increase in working women, especially in part-time jobs.

Key demographic trends include the following:

→ Populations in developed countries are stabilizing or declining. Birth rates are tending to fall below replenishment rates.

→ Ageing populations in 'first world' countries may be counter-balanced by immigration.

## HRM IN REALITY    TEMPORARY MIGRANTS BOOST INVENTION

Research from Harvard Business School and the University of Michigan published in the *Journal of Labor Economics* in 2010 found that highly skilled temporary immigrants to the US contribute to technological innovation without detriment to native-born workers.

The study compared immigration to the US from 1995 to 2008 under the H-1B visa program (applicable to highly skilled workers) with the number of US patent applications filed over the same period. Reflecting government restrictions on immigration levels, the number of visas varied from 65000 to 195000 a year.

The researchers explain that as patent applicants' nationalities are not recorded, they used their names as an indication of birthplace. The study found that in periods when more H-1B visas are granted, the number of patent applications filed by people with Chinese and Indian names increased significantly in locations where organizations depended on the program. The number of applications filed by people with names they categorized as 'Anglo-Saxon' did not fluctuate in the same way.

The study concludes that much of the increase can be attributed to highly skilled temporary immigrants.

Authors William R. Kerr and William F. Lincoln explained:

> We conclude that total invention increased with higher [H-1B] admissions primarily through the direct contributions of immigrant inventors. We are also able to rule out displacement [of native workers].

They continued:

> This study quantifies the impact of changes in H-1B admission levels on the pace and character of US invention. We hope that this assessment aids policy makers in their current decisions about appropriate admission rates in the future.

*Why would skilled temporary immigrants be particularly beneficial?*

*Source: Reprinted with permission from HRM Guide USA (http://www.hrmguide.com).*

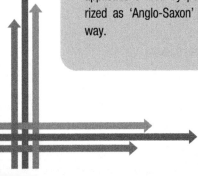

→ Developing countries experience a period of rapid population growth as infant mortality rates are reduced – well in advance of birth control measures being adopted.

→ Most developing countries experience population pressure for decades until stability is achieved.

→ The population balance will change markedly between the developed and developing world. Eventually the developed world will decline in importance, in line with their reduced working population.

### Employee demand

Demand for workers is linked to the economic cycle, increasing in boom times and decreasing in recession. Other factors include the adoption of new technology, productivity improvements and changing skill requirements. Superficially, calculating employment supply and demand seems easy. In practice, the combination of variable consumer demand, development of new products and technology and economic turbulence make it extremely problematic. In recent decades, for example, commentators have confidently predicted both permanently high levels of unemployment *and* shortages of labour.

As we observed in the last chapter, the role of the state is important in this respect: through fiscal or monetary policy, governments can directly increase or diminish consumption and economic activity. Such actions lead quickly to changes in demand for human resources as firms relate their requirements to production or provision of services. Activity in service and manufacturing services may follow different patterns. The decline in manufacturing in the UK, for example, has been dismissed as unimportant by some commentators who believed that production jobs would be replaced by new work in financial and other services. The reality is that these sectors have proven incapable of generating enough employment to compensate for the loss of full-time jobs in manufacturing. As we shall see shortly, there has been a widespread trend for well-paid jobs to be replaced with low-paid, part-time work.

## ACTIVE LABOUR MARKET PROGRAMMES

Active labour market programmes (ALMPs) are government initiatives to reduce unemployment and increase participation in the employment market. They include public works, training and retraining, job search assistance, support for self-employment or new enterprises and wage subsidies (Dar and Tzannatos, 1999). Such programmes are justified in a variety of ways. For example, the provision of public works is a demand side intervention, whereas training is intended to have an effect on supply side skills availability. However, all such interventions are based on the assumption that the employment market is failing in some way or that the social outcomes (particularly unemployment) are unacceptable.

Dar and Tzannatos (1999) review 100 evaluations of such programmes undertaken in OECD and developing countries (including Turkey, Hungary, Poland, the Czech Republic and Mexico) and draw some general conclusions:

→ Public works may help the most disadvantaged groups such as older workers, the long-term unemployed and people in distressed regions by acting as a poverty/safety net. However, they are ineffective in providing a channel into permanent employment.

→ Job search assistance programmes have a greater positive impact and are more cost-effective than other ALMPs. They are most effective when the general economic climate is

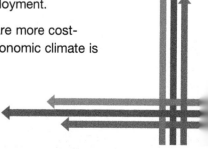

favourable. However, they do not appear to significantly improve either the employment prospects or wages of young job-seekers.

→ Training for the long-term unemployed is useful when the economy is improving. The best returns are offered by small-scale, tightly targeted on-the-job training programs, especially those aimed at women and older groups. In general, however, they are rarely cost-effective and no more successful than job search assistance programmes in terms of post-programme placement and wages.

→ Mass retraining for redundant workers is usually ineffective and, as in the case of the long-term unemployed, is also more expensive and no more effective than job-search assistance.

→ Training for young people has no positive impact on either their employment prospects or post-training earnings. Such programmes generally offer a negative return on the investment.

→ Start-up assistance for small business is usually taken up by a small proportion of the unemployed and the failure rate of these businesses is high. Targeting at women and older individuals increases the likelihood of success.

→ Wage subsidy programmes are unlikely to be effective and may be exploited by unscrupulous employers.

## PART-TIME AND TEMPORARY WORKING

Part-time employees contract to work for anything less than normal full-time basic hours. Advantages to employers can include: more intensive work with less time used for breaks; lower absenteeism; enthusiasm and commitment can be higher (less opportunity for boredom); and less unionization among part-time staff.

The main forms of part-time work include:

→ *Classical.* Work that does not require full-time cover, typically restricted to a few hours each day. For example, cleaning offices, or staffing a canteen.

→ *Supplementary.* Where a part-time worker replaces overtime and for example, performs an evening shift, or works short days to cover peak periods.

→ *Substitution.* In which part-timers replace full-timers through job-splitting. It is common for older workers to be retained as part-timers before full retirement.

More recent types of part-time work include key working and job sharing. Key working is typically found in service industries such as retailing. Service work differs from 'traditional' work. Peak activity occurs on days and at times when other workers are at leisure. Peak times may be so short that it is impossible for an employer to use full-time workers effectively. In these circumstances few 'core' full-timers are required. Correspondingly, a large number of 'peripheral' part-timers work at busy periods. Peripheral numbers can be shrunk or expanded as required. This allows greater flexibility than would be possible for a completely full-time workforce.

Job sharing is where two people are responsible for one full-time job, dividing pay and benefits in proportion to the hours worked. Days or weeks may be split or alternate weeks worked. An advantage for some employees, job sharing can also benefit employers. For example:

→ Sharers can overlap hours so that busy periods receive double cover.

→ Jobs are at least partly covered when one person is away through illness or annual leave.

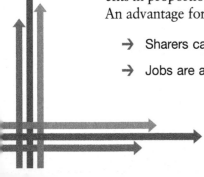

→ Two individuals can bring greater experience and a broader range of views to a job than a single employee.

Job sharing allows skilled people to be retained if they give up full-time employment. However, there are some disadvantages such as:

→ Training, induction and administration overheads for two people.

→ Finding a suitable partner with matching skills and availability if one sharer leaves.

→ Communication on tasks that cannot be dealt with quickly ('hand-over' problems).

→ Responsibility for staff can be problematic; people may find difficulty in working for two supervisors.

→ Fair allocation of work.

Part-time workers come especially from specific groups, including:

1   *Female parents with children.* The largest group, typically working when children are at school.

2   *Retired or semi-retired.* Supplementing pensions, filling time and using their skills. Again, they tend to work during the day.

3   *Moonlighters.* With full-time jobs elsewhere, supplementing income in the evening or at weekends. For instance, driving mini-cabs, delivering free newspapers or bar work.

4   *Students.* Supplementing grants or servicing loans by delivering papers, pizzas, serving in fast-food outlets. They may also work in vacation periods or undertake seasonal work, for example, in the tourist industry.

Paradoxically, many managers question part-timers' commitment, seeing them as being primarily home-oriented. They are often excluded from interesting and senior positions. Part-time workers tend to get fewer training and promotion opportunities. Some managers have contradictory beliefs about women part-timers. On the one hand they believe them to be reliable, loyal and flexible. At the same time, they consider that they take time off to be

## HRM IN REALITY  INVOLUNTARY PART-TIMERS

A report from the School of Social Service Administration at the University of Chicago published in 2010 found that a record number of US employees are involuntarily working part-time as a result of a reduction in their hours or being unable to find a full-time job. This effect of the recession is in addition to unemployment currently affecting nearly 10 per cent of the workforce. Susan Lambert, associate professor, commented:

> Certainly the current recession is contributing to underemployment, as evidenced by the proportion

of American workers classified as 'involuntary part-time'.

Researchers explain that the US Census Bureau applies the term 'involuntary part-time' to those working less than 35 hours a week because they could not find a full-time job or because of 'slack demand'. There were 9.2 million workers in this category in November 2009. Although the largest recorded figure, it reflects trends seen in earlier recessions. The labour market added 1.5 million involuntary part-time workers between

1981 and 1982 (for a total of 6.8 million workers) and 2.3 million between 1992 and 1993 (for a total of 6.7 million workers).

The current study investigated management and employee aspects of scheduling practices in a national retail apparel firm. Researchers explain that the majority of waged and salaried employees are hourly or part-time workers who are particularly vulnerable to imposed changes. They receive limited formal employee benefits, and many are ineligible for public benefits (such as unemployment insurance, cash assistance, or family and medical leave). Their work schedules are typically arranged with little prior notice and are often unpredictable. The researchers call for changes in public policy as well as company practices to address these issues.

Susan Lambert said:

I think it is important to underscore that employment has become increasingly precarious over the past 30 years, not just during recessionary periods, due to structural changes in the economy, reductions in labour protections and evolving employer practices that pass risk from the market onto workers. The current recession highlights these insecurities, bringing much-needed attention to the plight of disadvantaged workers who are struggling to keep their jobs as well as maintain sufficient hours to make ends meet. The problems faced by hourly, low-level workers are unlikely to go away when the economy fully recovers.

Whatever the economic conditions, employers frequently use 'just-in-time' practices to maintain control over costs and demand. Hourly workers' schedules are used to accommodate fluctuations often with limited notice. This disadvantages workers trying to manage their finances, childcare arrangements and other aspects of family life.

Julia Henly, associate professor, said:

Unpredictable work schedules can translate into instability in family routines and practices, placing additional burdens on already strapped and busy families, their caregivers and extended family members. We find that hourly retail employees with more predictable work schedules report lower levels of stress, less work-to-family conflict and fewer work interferences with non-work activities such as scheduling doctor's appointments, socializing with friends and eating meals together as a family.

Among other significant findings:

→ Hours vary substantially for both part-time and full-time hourly workers, with full-time employees working more hours but also experiencing the greatest fluctuations in hours from week to week.

→ The more hours employees work and the less their hours fluctuate, the longer they remain at the firm, even after accounting for factors such as age, race and job status.

→ Job turnover is high, particularly for part-time sales associates, younger workers, African Americans and recently hired workers.

→ Management practices contribute to job turnover irrespective of individual worker characteristics. Managers who strategically limit staff numbers with the goal of providing each sales associate with sufficient hours have lower turnover and higher retention rates.

The researchers acknowledge the importance of workplace flexibility in public policy debates as more parents try to reconcile competing demands of work and family life. Common flexibility options include allowing workers to work reduced hours, work at home or vary the start and end times of the working day. These may make sense for managerial and professional roles but are less applicable to many low-level hourly workers. This issue will be addressed in four government-sponsored regional conferences scheduled for the next twelve months.

The authors comment:

Fortunately, policy makers, advocacy groups and researchers are becoming increasingly interested in developing and promoting flexibility options for US workers in hourly jobs. As these initiatives proceed, it will be important that they reflect the range of work conditions found in hourly jobs, including low-wage jobs in service industries.

The third author is Anna Haley-Lock, an assistant professor of social work at the University of Wisconsin.

Question:

*How would you evaluate the consequences on motivation and employee turnover of voluntary and involuntary part-time working?*

*Source: Reprinted with permission from HRM Guide USA (http://www.hrmguide.com).*

with children and give precedence to partners' careers. Webber and Williams (2008) contend that working mothers at both the top and bottom ends of the employment hierarchy are uniquely disadvantages by their part-time jobs and respond in different ways. However, in general they take responsibility for the 'choices' they have made, thereby absolving their employers of any blame for the exploitation and discrimination against part-time workers.

## Temporary workers

It is frequently assumed that temporary job contracts are increasing but this statement 'needs to be heavily qualified' (Martin and Stancanelli, 2002). An analysis of 1985–2000 data from 13 OECD countries shows that the proportion of temporary employment in total salaried employment has risen (on average) by less than three per cent. France, Italy, the Netherlands and Spain are responsible for much of this less than massive increase. In five other countries, the proportion actually decreased. Countries in this category include the USA. Martin and Stancanelli (2002) suggest, 'one reason for the low recourse to temporary work in the United States may be that US permanent positions are less rigidly protected than in Europe, for instance, so there is less incentive for employers to offer temporary contracts'. On the other side of the Atlantic, Biggs (2006) analyzed data from the employment agency industry plus Labour Force Surveys from 1997–2004 to reveal a reduction of over a quarter of a million temporary workers in the UK over a six-year period. Regional variations were apparent, with increases in Northern Ireland and Wales. This was thought to reflect the impact of new legislation and a stable economy.

The largest temporary staff agency, Manpower Inc. places 2 million people in a year, over 40 per cent of whom go on to permanent employment. More than 10 per cent of workers in the EU have temporary jobs, with the highest level (30 per cent) in Spain. A UK Labour Force Survey found that 1.6 million British workers were employed on a temporary basis.

Forde and Slater (2006) examined Labour Force Survey data on agency workers in the UK and found no evidence of a relationship between the use of agency workers and the growth of the 'knowledge economy'. Instead, their use seems to be governed by short-term issues and the need to keep labour costs down – although the long-term costs may be higher than using permanent staff. Forde and Slater's analysis of occupations found that people in managerial occupations were significantly less likely to be in agency employment and there was only an insignificant positive relationship between professional and associate professional occupations with agency employment. This contrasted with data for clerical, personal and protective, operative and other occupations where there was a significant relationship with agency working suggesting that agency work was most closely related to low-paying entry-jobs in the service sector.

Additionally, there are commitment issues to consider: 50 per cent of agency workers were found to be involuntary, i.e. they could not find a permanent job. Only 30 per cent were agency workers because they did not want permanent employment. Druker and Stanworth (2004) found that employers expected agency workers to show loyalty, commitment and high levels of motivation but the employers gave little in return. Autor and Houseman (2010) did not find any benefits in obtaining consequent long-term employment from temporary work through a scheme in Detroit but an article in *Human Resource Management International Digest* (Anon, 2010) describes a learning programme at the Clinton Cards Group in the UK that is designed to turn temporary staff into long-term employees. Forde and Slater's (*ibid*) data indicate agency workers' comparatively high levels of dissatisfaction about the content of their work and opportunities for using their initiative. Longer term contracts and the possibility of permanent jobs might improve levels of commitment, they conclude. Hall (2006) comes to similar conclusions in a study of agency workers in Australia. Comparing attitudes and preferences of agency workers with permanent

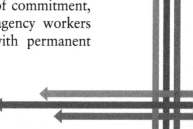

employees, he found agency workers to be no more satisfied with their level of flexibility than direct workers. Moreover, agency workers were less satisfied with their pay, job security, use and development of skills, autonomy and influence at work. Hall concludes that, in fact, the use of agency workers may be incompatible with human resource strategies based on high performance work practices.

Apart from the familiar 'temps' obtained from specialist agencies, two other groups of temporary workers can be highlighted:

→ *Contingent employees.* In the UK there are 500000 professional and highly-skilled people working on temporary contracts. For example, 'interim managers'. These are generally freelance executives aged over 40. Most assignments last for 40–80 days, allowing for short-term problems to be handled without long-term commitment to expensive staff. Specialist expertise can be bought in for specific tasks or projects. Contingent managers have been rated highly in functions such as human resources, finance, information technology, marketing, operations and property.

→ *Seasonal employment.* Seasonal workers are hired to cope with fluctuations in demand – to keep down stock volumes, and hence cost. For example, the chocolate industry has especially high periods of demand at times when gifts are commonly given, such as Christmas.

From the employee's point of view, part-time or temporary work may be both convenient and attractive to many people. McDonald, Bradley and Guthrie (2006) studied a group of 275 working mothers and found that nearly two-thirds of those working full time would prefer to work part time. The major reasons for not acting on this preference were the nature of the job and lack of available career opportunities for part-time employees.

For most people, however, part-time jobs are no substitute for the loss of full-time jobs but the 20th century concept of the nine-to-five job and a lifetime career may be disintegrating in favour of much more flexible arrangements. Levels of insecurity and stress are rising as people have increasingly uncertain working lives. It has become a truism that most people will experience at least two or three careers in their lifetime. Handy (1989: 46) sees work becoming part of a portfolio of activities. At any one time, individuals may have a number of part-time jobs, together with leisure or study periods.

## ▶ SUMMARY

In this chapter we discussed some important features of the employment market. We considered factors which lead to people seeking work and joining that market. We examined key economic and psychological concepts and identified a number of links with fundamental elements of HRM. Participation in the job market was investigated, comparing rates in different countries. Different working patterns were described as a prelude for later discussion of flexibility.

## ▶ FURTHER READING

The range of books on the employment market is vast but tends towards political or economic analysis. The following books are of particular interest:

1 *Global Employment Trends Report*, published by the International Labour Organization each year takes an overview of recent key developments.

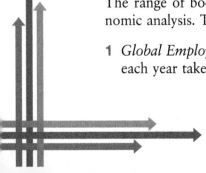

2 *Unemployment: Past and Present* edited by Philip Arestis and John McCombie (Palgrave Macmillan) takes a broad view of unemployment and looks at the lessons of experience and theory.

3 *Employment and the Family: The Reconfiguration of Work and Family Life in Contemporary Societies* by Rosemary Crompton (Cambridge University Press, 2006) takes a gender and comparative perspective on the way employment has changed in recent years.

 **REVIEW QUESTIONS**

1 How is it possible to regard jobs as being in a market? Discuss the usefulness of the competitive market model in describing the ways in which the employment market functions in the real world.

2 Summarize the main differences between competitive market and institutional models of the employment market. How do competitive and institutional models of the job market relate to 'hard' and 'soft' versions of HRM?

3 Describe in your own words what is meant by the 'labour force participation rate'.

4 To what extent do people behave as individuals – as opposed to households – when they seek work? Consider your family, relatives or friends as examples.

5 Is full employment a practical goal for every country?

6 What is the relationship between levels of welfare payment or unemployment benefit and the level of employment?

7 How will demographic trends affect employment in your country in the 21st century?

8 Outline the advantages and disadvantages of part-time jobs for employers and employees.

9 Why has the introduction of new technology not led to a 'leisure revolution'?

10 Summarize the advantages and disadvantages of 'active labour market programmes'.

 **CASE STUDY FOR DISCUSSION AND ANALYSIS**

## Rob's career/Jefford Trading

1   Rob is a student on placement with a thriving media marketing company. As an intern, he enjoys the challenges of dealing with customers and other staff. He prefers work to university where, academically, he is an average performer. Rob enjoys some parts of his course but dreads other aspects – particularly the end of semester assessments. He was pushed into higher education by an ambitious father whose own career

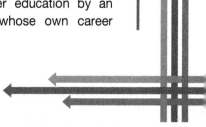

was limited by his lack of qualifications. Personally, Rob cannot wait to complete the course and get on with his career.

Rob's placement company has lost a number of key staff to a competitor. Senior managers have looked at the younger staff and highlighted Rob as a potential high-flyer. He has the energy and the enthusiasm to cope with the long hours and the considerable travelling required. They have offered Rob a higher level position which is now vacant. The rewards are high and the prospects for the next few years are excellent. However, Rob has been told that he cannot accept this position and return to full-time education to complete his final year.

Rob has to make a choice quickly. What factors should he take into account in making his decision?

2   Jefford Trading is a medium-sized business selling high quality designer furnishings. Originally started 20 years ago from one small shop, Jan and Keith Jefford have built the company into a multi-shop retailer with ventures around the country. In the last three years business has become a struggle: other firms have entered the same market and rental and other costs have risen sharply. The company continues to make a profit but further expansion will be hard work.

There are 57 employees. Apart from the founders there is one other director, Paul Stevens the company secretary (49), who looks after major contracts and personnel. He is competent but not ambitious. There are five middle managers, all graduates under 35 picked by Paul, with responsibilities for buying, logistics, finance, marketing and retailing respectively. The logistics and retail managers are responsible for most of the staff. Junior managers run the shops, all without higher education qualifications but keen. The other head office staff are of mixed ages with little potential for advancement.

The Jeffords have worked long hours developing the company, taking few holidays and little money out of the company. Keith is 48, looks much older and has some health problems. Jan is 43, more determined but worried about her husband. The managers have suggested that they take over the running of the company, allowing the owners to sit back and enjoy life.

The Jeffords' accountants have little faith in the managers: they believe them to be too young and inexperienced. The accountants have advised the sale of the company and investment of the proceeds. The Jeffords accept this is sensible advice but would prefer to keep the company going.

**You have been brought in as a consultant to advise them. What would you do?**

*How would you conduct your investigation?*

*What are the options?*

*What do you anticipate your recommendations to be?*

*How are the Jeffords likely to react?*

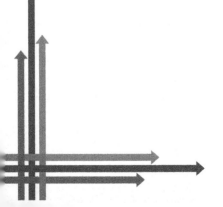

# CHAPTER 6
## International perspectives: culture, the state, human capital and ethics

## LEARNING OBJECTIVES

The purpose of this chapter is to:

→ Outline the impact of diverse global cultures on business behaviour.

→ Provide an overview of the role played by governments in creating the context for human resource management.

→ Outline the concept of human capital and its implications for development.

→ Explore ethical dimensions to human resource management.

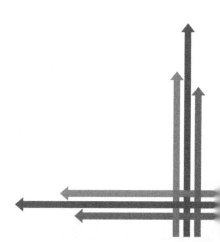

No single approach to people management can ever be guaranteed to be more effective than any other. Different business environments generate different forms of managerial structures that can be equally successful in world markets. Organizations reflect the social, political and financial institutions of the countries in which they operate. Growth in international business has led to massive interest in differing global approaches to people management.

## NATIONAL CULTURES AND BUSINESS BEHAVIOUR

Management practices vary throughout the world. Culture, history, language and beliefs underlie much of this variation. More than any other business function, the practice of people management has been closely linked to national culture (see Key concept 6.1).

---

### KEY CONCEPT 6.1 CULTURE

The anthropologist Edward Taylor (1871) defined culture as 'knowledge, belief, art, morals, law, custom and any other capabilities and habits' acquired through membership of society. In a narrower sense the term is used to describe the differences between one society and another. In this context, a culture is an all-pervasive system of beliefs and behaviours transmitted socially. Specifically it consists of the set of values – abstract ideals – and norms or rules held by a society, together with its material expressions (Giddens, 1989: 30).

---

Comparing one country with another we find components of people management are accorded different degrees of importance and are carried out differently. The activities undertaken by HR managers vary as a consequence. However, there has also been recent consideration of the extent to which globalization, the internationalization of business and consolidation of legal systems dilute the impact of national identity. It is increasingly possible to distinguish practices that are universally applicable from those based on a particular national culture.

Globalization has been driven largely by issues of marketing, cost and competition. Consequently, people management on the international scale has often lagged behind other management functions (such as production and finance) at both practical and theoretical levels.

## ETHNOCENTRISM AND CULTURAL DIFFERENCES

According to Taylor (2006: 12):

> Ethnocentric people tend to form pre-conceived judgements of different cultures based on one experience, or based on limited evidence. Therefore, despite the fact that a person from a different culture may have many unique personal qualities, the ethnocentric person cannot see beyond their own fixed ideas even when those ideas are wrong, so their mind remains closed.

There is a misleading assumption that the social, class and cultural values underlying management ideas are – or should be – 'normal' for every country. Perceptions of normality

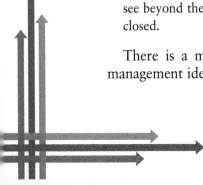

vary widely and tend to be based on stereotypes (Chakkarath, 2010). The following list (based on the work of Campbell and associates, cited in Triandis, 1990: 35) highlights key conclusions from studies of ethnocentrism. Characteristics of the 'in-group' are that everyone tends to:

→ Define their own culture as 'natural' and 'correct' and other cultures as 'unnatural' and 'incorrect'.

→ Perceive in-group customs as universally valid – 'what is good for us is good for everybody'.

→ Think that in-group norms, rules and values are obviously correct.

→ Consider it natural to help and cooperate with members of one's in-group.

→ Act in ways which favour the in-group.

→ Feel proud of the in-group.

→ Feel hostility towards out-groups.

Scientifically based management methods are regarded as culturally neutral and universal (Chung, 1991). In fact, they are mostly North American and based on that particular culture. English is the major business language, consolidating the spread of largely American business concepts (Brewster and Tyson, 1991). These methodologies were accepted as 'received wisdom' in large areas of the world. However, eastern countries can be just as ethnocentric. Lee (2006), for example, states that the Chinese are '... a very nationalistic race, they have continued to preserve ethnic practices and traditional customs and characteristics in modern business negotiations'.

Shih, Chiang and Kim (2005) interviewed expatriate employees and human resource managers of five multinational enterprise subsidiaries in the information technology industry. All used standardized performance forms set by headquarters and not tailored to local operating environments. Lack of on-the-job training for expatriates was found to be prevalent. Divergent practices in goal setting, performance appraisal and performance-related pay were largely attributed to the parent company's culture.

Brewster (2002: 14–17) highlights the complexity of integration and differentiation that international HRM encompasses and tensions between global and local practices. He considers that the pat phrase 'think global, act local' used by many consultants is meaningless in practice. Many organizations are divisionalized, one part operating 'globally', another 'locally'.

Walton (1999) distinguishes between a global mindset and an international mindset. Managers in an internationally minded company are 'more one-directional, ethnocentric, outward-looking from the country in which they are based'. Whereas a true global organization will feature highly adaptable managers, and an organizational value structure that allows managers to detach themselves from their original national roots and thereby shed their ethno-centric outlook (Rhinesmith, 1996).

This global-oriented mindset suggests that multinationals should take into account a balance of factors including:

→ Differing national employment legislation, ways of doing business, customs, national investment policies, fiscal incentives, attitudes to foreign investment and other competitors.

→ Issues related to physical location, including local market potential, geographical and cultural distance from the company's base, transport logistics and communications.

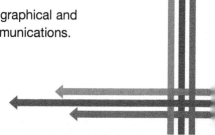

→ Employee costs including wages, training needs, skills availability, social and industrial infrastructure.

→ Fit of new locations with existing customers, management and production.

→ The organizational structure of the firm.

## CULTURES AND STANDARDS

Cultures are subjective and we take our own for granted. Each culture has a 'world view' – a set of values and beliefs. This is meaningful to its members but alien to others. It is normal to 'use our own culture as the standard and judge other cultures by the extent they meet the standard' (Triandis, 1990: 34). As we have seen, this ethnocentrism can be related to the concept of the 'in-group' – those people we identify with. It can be argued that the export of Western (American) management methods by multinationals and business schools – including HRM – is an example of ethnocentrism on a massive scale.

American business school models commonly have been assumed to represent 'best practice', with universal applicability regardless of local tradition, culture or business history. But there have been occasions when the universality of these methods has been questioned. For example, Brewster (2002: 5) observes that '… in Europe HRM is less dependent, companies have less autonomy and freedom of action, trade unionism is more important, the social partners have more influence, legal regulations are more important and there is a stronger tradition of employee involvement'.

Trompenaars and Hampden-Turner (1997) point out that international HR (and other) managers have a particularly difficult task. They have to operate in three different cultures at the same time: their culture of origin; the culture within which they are currently working; and the corporate culture of the organization. The training they are offered does not necessarily help. For example, Shen and Darby (2006) examined international training and development policies and practices in ten Chinese multinational enterprises (MNEs). They found that they provided limited training to expatriates and other nationals and lacked any systematic international management development system. They describe the MNEs as having an essentially ethnocentric approach to international training and development, providing different levels of training and development for host-country nationals and others.

Culture is important also when employees in different countries operate as a 'virtual team'. Horwitz, Bravington and Silvis (2006) identified cross-cultural communication improvement, managerial and leadership communication, goal and role clarification and relationship building as the most important factors leading to effective virtual team performance.

### Cultural variety

Cultures should not be confused with countries or so-called 'nation states'. There is a danger in examining cultures as 'wholes': there are not only differences between cultures but also within cultures (Brewster and Tyson, 1991). Hofstede (1994 [1991]: 10) argues that an individual's culture has several levels:

→ National – according to country (or countries for migrants).

→ Regional and/or ethnic and/or religious and/or linguistic.

→ Gender – different assumptions and expectations of females and males.

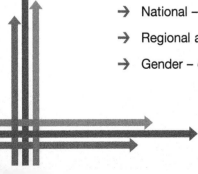

→ Generation – differences between age groups.

→ Social class – linked to educational opportunities and occupations.

→ Organizational – different organizations have their individual cultures.

We can see that this presents a complex mixture for a selector to attempt to disentangle; for a performance assessor to misunderstand; a management developer to 'correct'. There is massive scope for a clash of cultures – and prejudices. As we shall see in our later chapter on the management of diversity, there is a major issue about the real meaning of 'equal opportunities' in this context.

## The perception of time

Managing people depends a great deal on our perceptions and expectations of others. We assess, we select, we reward according to our own criteria. Triandis (1990) identifies a number of dimensions of difference that people managers can be taught to recognize and respect. One example is 'cultural complexity', which particularly affects the perception of time. How do we feel about people who do not turn up to an interview on time, or fail to complete a task within the agreed period? If we live in an industrial culture we will regard them unfavourably.

Another significant time characteristic is that of short or long-term orientation (Hofstede and Bond, 1988). In Part One we identified HRM as a philosophy of people management that is long term in its intent. The root of this orientation lies in comparisons of US and Japanese management.

The short-term attitudes of senior American executives have been much criticized. Managers with financial or legal backgrounds have gravitated to the top at the expense of those with technical or scientific expertise. This has led to a prevailing management style emphasizing cash management with fast measurable returns. Mergers and takeovers, disposals and closures fit neatly into this mindset whereas long-term research, product development and people management have been neglected. Senior managers – and governments – elsewhere in the English-speaking world have followed the US lead.

In Part 1 of this book we saw that Japan served as a role model for Western businesses in the 1980s. HRM owes much of its inspiration to the long-term and people-orientation of Japanese business. It was believed that the Japanese had 'magic answers' for people management that could be identified and translated into Western contexts. However, in the 1990s the Japanese role model lost some of its mystique when its industrial dominance appeared to have peaked. Ironically, major Japanese companies began to introduce Western methods of people management.

## Confucianism

Hofstede and Bond (*ibid.*) attribute the long-term orientation in East Asians to 'Confucian Dynamism' embodying values from the teaching of Confucius such as perseverance, a need to order relationships by status, a sense of shame and a habit of thrifty saving. Yang (2005) points to the different emphases between various Confucian cultures. In Korea, for example, there is an emphasis on emotion and feelings ('jeong') related to the Western concept of emotional intelligence.

More generally, Tan and Chee (2005) found several factors unique to a Confucian context that facilitated the development of trust: diligence, perseverance, filial piety, thriftiness, respect for authority, a shared value of collective effort, harmonious relationship in the office, humbleness and magnanimous behaviour.

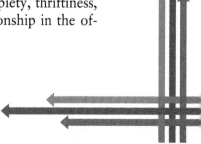

**TABLE 6.1**
Ways of thinking

Source: Adapted from
Chung (1991).

|  | European | Asian |
|---|---|---|
| *Thinking styles* | Causal, clear-cut, single-track thinking – one thing follows another | Network, whole vision, complex, taking in different perspectives |
| *Decision styles* | To suit controls<br>Individual, free<br>To suit the majority | Based on trust<br>Group solidarity<br>Reaching consensus |
| *Behaviour* | True to principles.<br>Based on legal principles<br>Dynamic, facing conflict<br>Open, direct, self-confident, extrovert | To suit a situation<br>To suit a community<br>Harmonious, conservative.<br>Restrained, indirect, with self-assurance, introvert |

## *Roles*

Triandis (1990) relates cultural complexity to the way we define our working and other roles. In complex societies roles become increasingly specific and compartmentalized. We can behave differently in each role. In less complex societies, roles are diffuse, affecting every aspect of people's lives. Religion, politics and matters of taste are important in diffuse cultures. They are less important in role-specific cultures. Developed countries tend to be role-specific, avoiding role confusion. Theory and best practice in key HRM areas such as selection, performance measurement and development assume an equal opportunities approach in which people are dealt with without favour or prejudice. However, this notion is alien to diffuse-role cultures in which it is natural to favour members of one's own family or community.

Diffuse-role cultures value politeness and courtesy – even towards people who are disliked – something that would be regarded as hypocrisy in specific cultures. Again human resource texts assume that outright, if tactful, honesty is required in rejecting job applicants, counselling for performance weaknesses and dismissal. This approach can appear arrogant and aggressive to people from diffuse societies.

## PSYCHOLOGY AND CULTURE

Cultural differences are deeply imbedded. Chung (1991), for example, draws on the psychology of thinking styles to explain differences between business cultures (see Table 6.1). This model provides a cultural explanation of the different forms of people management: contract-based in the West; commitment-based in the East.

## CULTURAL TRAINING

Human resource managers have a considerable role to play in preparing staff for work away from their country of origin. Given the range and sensitivity of cultural differences, it is clear that people working in an international context can benefit from tuition in the business customs and social manners of the countries they will work in. Training can encompass language, social behaviour, local business structure and practice. Argyle (1991) details a number of key behavioural features that differ between cultures.

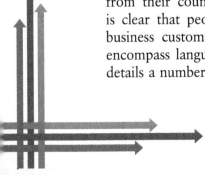

## Non-verbal behaviour

*Proximity, touch and gaze.* Cultures can be classified as contact or non-contact. For example, Arabs and Latin Americans stand much closer to each other than East Asians and Northern Europeans. In Greece, staring is regarded as an expression of interest and politeness, even at a complete stranger in the street. Conversely, a Caribbean employee may avoid eye-to-eye contact with a manager during a conversation, having been taught to regard this as discourteous.

*Expressiveness.* The Japanese are reluctant to be too expressive for fear of causing offence. Many Northern Europeans are also reticent in showing emotion. By contrast, African-Caribbean people are more likely to be open about expressing opinions, including negative emotions and attitudes.

*Gestures.* It is dangerous to make use of one's own familiar gestures in another country.

*Accompaniments of speech.* People often expect listeners to show obvious attention while they are talking. Failure to do so can be interpreted as lack of interest or boredom. This feedback is not expected in all cultures.

*Symbolic self-presentation.* Appearance, dress, badges and uniforms have significance for individuals in a particular culture but may mean nothing to outsiders.

*Rituals.* Seating positions at a dining or conference table may be highly significant to one culture and virtually irrelevant to another.

## Customs or rules

*Bribery.* A bribe in one culture is a gift in another. In many cultures it is normal to pay a commission to people involved in a transaction. People such as civil servants, managers and sales representatives expect a percentage of the contract value. Western European and North American tradition regards this as unethical if not illegal.

*Nepotism.* Cultures that feature personal obligations to large extended families expect powerful individuals to look after relatives; for example, by giving jobs or contracts. This 'social welfare' system is normally governed by codes of conduct that regulate its abuse.

*Gifts.* Every culture expects its members to give presents in certain circumstances such as weddings or birthdays. Some cultures extend gift-giving to everyday business meetings.

*Buying and selling.* The importance of bargaining varies from 'fixed price' cultures where haggling is regarded with distaste, to others where negotiation is expected in any transaction.

*Eating and drinking.* Every culture has taboos about food and drink, and norms relating to consumption.

*Rules about time.* Being on time is regarded as polite and a demonstration of business efficiency in Western countries. Conversely, lateness is taken as normal in other cultures.

## Language

The use of language has critical implications. For example, in any interpersonal context, people managers must be aware of cultural differences covering areas such as: directness, politeness, acknowledgment of status, use of humour and forms of address.

Some customs are illustrative of differences in underlying attitudes (see Key concept 6.2) and what is regarded as ethical practice (see Key concept 6.3). This has much wider implications for people management. Ethical dilemmas have many cross cultural dimensions. The position of working children is but one example.

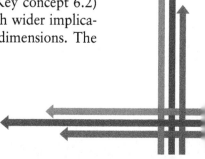

## KEY CONCEPT 6.2   ATTITUDES

Attitudes are dispositions held by people, towards or against people, things and ideas. They have individual components based on factors such as personality and understanding, and social elements derived from shared experiences and cultural history. Attitudes are complex systems of belief, evaluation, emotion and behaviour (Eiser, 1994; McKenna, 1994: 251).

## KEY CONCEPT 6.3   ETHICS

Standards of personal, professional and corporate behaviour – principles of conduct – that result in the just and fair treatment of others. Some make a distinction between this and moral behaviour that takes into account prevailing social custom and culture in the definition of what is right and wrong.

## RESPONDING TO EXPLOITATION

The UK government set up the Gangmasters Licensing Authority (GLA) in 2006 to protect vulnerable employees in the fresh produce supply chain from exploitation. By licensing workforce providers (often known as gangmasters), it seeks to ensure that businesses supplying and using largely seasonal staff are complying with employment legislation. This relates to terms and conditions such as wages, hours of work, sick pay, time off and health and safety. A number of industrial sectors are covered including agriculture, fish processing, horticulture and food/drink packaging.

The immediate precipitating tragedy was the deaths in 2004 of 21 Chinese immigrants working as shellfish collectors in Morecambe Bay in the north-west of England who were left to drown by their employers as notoriously dangerous tides came in.

In October 2010, UK media reported the case of seven Romanian children aged between nine and 16 who had been discovered, along with a group of adults that included their parents, picking vegetables on a farm in central England. Temperatures were close to freezing; the workers were in unsuitable clothing and lacked proper facilities. The gangmaster involved was said not to be licensed by the Authority.

Paul Whitehouse, chair of the GLA told the BBC:

> We discovered the children working, some of them with their parents but others without and in conditions which, for the adults alone, were appalling. No proper clothing, no water, no appropriate lavatory facilities and so on. This was a very clear case of exploitation.

The child protection charity ECPAT UK reported that 215 children had been identified as having been trafficked into the UK in the 12 months up to June 2010, the vast majority (97 per cent) for work purposes.

# NATIONAL AND ORGANIZATIONAL CULTURES

In this section we examine some specific contributions to cross-cultural understanding, including the classic research conducted by Hofstede (1980). Cultural stereotypes are composed of a few accurate notions mixed with generalizations, misconceptions and prejudice.

Organizations are microcosms of national cultures, reflecting crucial differences. Hofstede (1980: 1994) compared several thousand IBM employees in over 50 countries using attitude questionnaires. He found significant differences between employees in different countries, despite similar jobs and membership of an organization with a strong corporate culture.

Using sophisticated factor analysis, Hofstede attributed the variation to four main dimensions: power distance; collectivism versus individualism; masculinity versus femininity; and uncertainty avoidance (see Table 6.2).

## Power distance

How marked are the status differences between people with high and low degrees of power? Questions tested whether:

→ people were afraid of expressing disagreement with their managers.

→ management style was perceived as paternalistic, autocratic, participative and so on.

→ employees preferred a particular management style.

Individuals in countries with autocratic management styles preferred their own bosses to have that style. In a culture where respect for authority is a valued quality, participative management can make people feel uncomfortable. Individuals in countries with low power distance scores preferred consultation.

## Collectivism versus individualism

Is a culture focused on individuals or groups? Hofstede describes most societies as 'collectivist' in a non-political sense. In these cultures people obtain their identity from an extended family or a work organization. This is particularly relevant to people management since most of its concepts come from the USA – a strongly individualistic country. Individualistic cultures are characterized by:

→ An emphasis on care for self and immediate family – if necessary, at the expense of others.

→ 'I' consciousness – heightened awareness of the distinction between oneself and other people.

→ Self-orientation – looking for advantage and career progression for the individual.

→ Keen defence of the right to a private life and personal opinions.

→ Emphasis on decisions being made individually.

→ Emotional independence from the work organization.

→ Autonomy and individual financial security.

High power distance and collectivism usually go together. In collective cultures socially respected jobs are valued highly. In contrast, individualistic cultures value personal success, responsibility and self-respect. Triandis (1995: 33) points to key differences leading to reward and promotion: 'People in individualistic countries have the tendency to emphasize

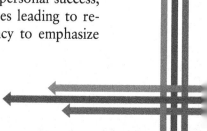

**TABLE 6.2**
Cultural dimensions

(after Hofstede, 1980, and others)

| Dimension | High | Medium | Low |
|---|---|---|---|
| Individualism (versus collectivism) | Argentina, Australia, Belgium, Brazil, Canada, France, Ireland, New Zealand, Spain, UK, USA | Austria, Germany, Israel, Italy, Japan, Netherlands, Scandinavia, Switzerland, South Africa | Chile, Greece, Hong Kong, India, Iran, Mexico, Pakistan, Peru, Portugal, Taiwan, Singapore, Turkey |
| Power distance (inequality between levels in organizations) | Belgium, France, Iran, Hong Kong, Nigeria, Philippines, Singapore, South America, Spain, Taiwan, Thailand | Japan | Australia, Germany, Italy, UK, USA |
| Uncertainty avoidance (intolerance of ambiguity) | Austria, Argentina, Belgium, France, Germany, Greece, Iran, Israel, Italy, Japan, Spain, Turkey, South Africa, Switzerland | | Australia, Canada, Ireland, Netherlands, New Zealand, Scandinavia, UK, USA. |
| Masculinity (competitiveness) | Japan, Austria, Venezuela, Italy, Switzerland | Canada, Jamaica, Greece, India, Hong Kong, Pakistan, South Africa, UK, USA | Chile Netherlands, Scandinavia, Costa Rica |
| Work centrality | Japan | Belgium, Israel, USA | Germany, Netherlands, UK |
| Job satisfaction | Canada, UK, Germany, Netherlands, Scandinavia | | Greece, Spain, Italy, Portugal, Japan |

*ability* more than is necessary, and to underemphasize *effort*. In collectivist cultures, the reverse is true.'

Hui (1990: 193) argues that Hofstede's notion of the collective is too vague: people in collective cultures relate to particular in-groups, not to everybody. Collectivist cultures emphasize harmony, and avoidance of shame or loss of face. These are social elements of culture emphasizing obligations to others within the in-group.

Further contradictory evidence was provided by Ramamoorthy *et al.* (2005) who analyzed 180 MBA students from the USA, Ireland and India on their individualism/collectivism

(IC) orientations and preferences for HRM practices. Contrary to expectations, the Indian sample tended to be the most individualistic.

## Masculinity versus femininity

Hofstede rates the aggressiveness of a culture as masculinity – its level of individual assertiveness and competition. Positive responses to questions relating to high earnings, recognition, advancement and challenging work rated highly on masculinity. Good working relationships, cooperation, living in a desirable area and employment security were scored at the 'feminine' end of the dimension.

> *Recruitment.* Applications in 'masculine' cultures are expected to be couched in positive, achievement-orientated language. Interviews are searching and sometimes aggressive. In contrast, applicants from 'feminine' cultures are expected to be modest about their achievements, giving the opportunity for interviewers to 'discover' undeclared talents.

> *Meetings.* In 'feminine cultures' meetings are held to achieve cooperation, exchange ideas and solve problems. The intention is positive and participative. In masculine cultures meetings are more competitive and are used for displays of power, posturing and political point-making.

The masculine–feminine dimension helps to explain the different forms of market found in Part Two, and the styles of management and employee relations prevalent in those markets.

## Uncertainty avoidance

How do people deal with conflict, particularly aggression and the expression of feelings? Uncertainty avoidance measures people's reactions to unusual situations. High uncertainty avoidance favours precise rules and superiors to be obeyed without question. Low uncertainty avoidance leads to flexibility. Arguing with superiors is acceptable.

## Dimension mix

The characteristics of national business cultures are further defined by the particular mix of these four dimensions. Hofstede argues that the choice of organization structure is strongly influenced by the prevalent culture. A culture with high power distance and strong uncertainty avoidance prefers a functional 'pyramid of people' hierarchy. Lower power distance but high uncertainty avoidance encourages organizations with a clear structure, rules and procedures. Low power distance and uncertainty avoidance favours a flexible structure focused on human relations. Large power distance and low uncertainty avoidance features a strong paternalistic boss and an organizational model based on the family.

Hofstede's statistics have been questioned but the thesis remains popular. A study by Pheng and Yuquan (2002) compared construction workers in Singapore and two cities in China, demonstrating some interesting variations:

> *Power distance.* Singapore workers showed a higher power distance than their Chinese counterparts. In Singapore, superiors and subordinates were more likely to consider each other as unequal. Chinese employees were likely to regard the hierarchical system as an inequality of roles, established for convenience, which could change in different circumstances. This attitude leads to more decentralized organizations with flatter hierarchies and fewer supervisors.

> *Uncertainty avoidance.* Singapore respondents had a low index value for uncertainty; Chinese respondents had a high index value. According to Pheng and Yuquan: 'In Singapore, people

CHAPTER 6  International perspectives: culture, the state, human capital and ethics

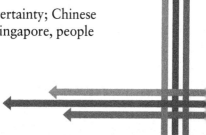

## HRM IN REALITY   CROSS-CULTURAL PERSPECTIVES

A study by Cristina B. Gibson of the University of Western Australia and Dana M. McDaniel of the University of California, published in *Perspectives on Psychological Science* in 2010 highlights variable attitudes to work among different cultures. Cautioning against a 'one size fits all' approach to business and management styles, the authors suggest a cross-cultural perspective can facilitate co-working in an era of globalization.

The way in which employees conceptualize teams is one indication of cultural difference. Use of sports-related metaphors in the United States was found to be less common elsewhere. In Latin America, the work team tended to be compared to the family.

Cristina B. Gibson, Winthrop professor in the school of business commented:

> If you just use those two contrasts and think about what you might expect from your family versus what you might expect from your sports team, you start to see the differences. Families are involved in all parts of your life, and are expected to celebrate with you socially. Your involvement in your sports team is more limited. Less caretaking, more competitive.

The authors also cite varying attitudes to desirable characteristics in a leader. Not every culture admires charisma, when a strong personality is used to inspire loyalty.

Cristina B. Gibson said:

> The very same behaviours that are deemed desirable from a leader in one culture might be viewed as interference or micromanagement in other settings.

The authors argue that there are implications both for employers and those conducting research. Organizations, teams and individuals may have different values and preferences; cultural variability is likely to become more apparent with the expansion of globalization.

*Why are leadership characteristics viewed differently in various cultures?*

*Source: Reprinted with permission from HRM Guide USA (http://www.hrmguide.com).*

feel less threatened by ambiguous situations. Emotions are shown less in public. Younger people are trustworthy. People are willing to take risks in life. The authorities are there to serve the citizens. Conflicts and competition can be contained on the level of fair play and are used constructively'. In China, on the other hand, 'people tend to establish more formal rules, reject deviant ideas and behaviour, accept the possibility of absolute truths and the attainment of unchallengeable expertise. Younger people are looked upon suspiciously. People are concerned with security in life. Ordinary citizens are incompetent, unlike the authorities. Conflict and competition can unleash aggression and should therefore be avoided'.

*Individualism/collectivism.* Singapore workers are more individualistic than their counterparts in China, tending to think of themselves as 'I' and also tending to classify people by individual characteristics, rather than by group membership. Employees in China are less inclined to differentiate an individual from the group and put a lower emphasis on self-actualization.

*Masculinity/femininity.* The masculinity score in the Singapore construction industry is lower than that for respondents in China, meaning that Chinese employees tend to place a greater emphasis on work goals such as earnings and advancement and also on assertiveness.

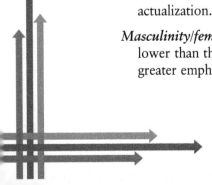

In Singapore, by contrast, respondents showed a greater concern with personal goals, a friendly atmosphere, getting along well with the boss and others, etc.

### Converging cultures?

The accelerating trend towards the internationalization of business is eroding these cultural differences. Throughout the world, younger and more travelled managers are more alike in attitudes and practices than colleagues less open to foreign influences. They prefer to associate with people who have similar ideologies and personalities – even if they come from different cultures. Additionally, technological development is leading to an increasing convergence of business methods.

## THE STATE AND INTERVENTION

National and regional governments have a powerful influence on the practice of HRM because they set the legislative, regulatory and economic contexts in which people work. Economists typically describe such government initiatives as 'labour market policies'. Abrahart and Verme (2001) distinguish three broad types adopted around the world: the Japanese, European and American models.

The Japanese model relied (at least until the early 1990s) on full employment as one basic principle of a stable society. The emphasis was on the 'internal labour market' rather than the external job market. Firms were hierarchical, protecting their workers from the consequences of economic fluctuations. Workers were expected to be fully committed to their employers. Government supported business through skills upgrading and training or identifying production alternatives for changing markets. Labour market policies were part of economic and industrial strategies managed by relevant government departments. Abrahart and Verme describe this as an 'enterprise-centred and industry-driven form of labour market management'. The Japanese model was the main frame of reference for many Asian governments until relatively recently.

Abrahart and Verme perceive the European model as one that accepts market laws and the existence of unemployment – but only as a 'necessary temporary condition to facilitate and maximize the allocation of labour'. There is limited government intervention in support of firms. The unemployed are supported by maintaining their income and providing training schemes to help them find jobs. The European model accepts that the market periodically fails to protect the public interest and that governments need to step in to mitigate the short-term economic and social consequences. Unemployment support tends to be generous and is meant to provide a basic standard of living. Responsibility for labour market policies lies with ministries of employment. Abrahart and Verme describe this as a 'mediating, public-interest driven labour market management style'.

The American model places considerable limitations on government intervention. Firms can dispense with employees to match economic fluctuations. The role of government is to 'maximize mobility of workers and minimize labour market rigidities such as hiring costs and mismatching of the supply and demand of labour'. Short-term unemployment benefits are provided but the unemployed are expected to very actively seek work. Abrahart and Verme perceive this as an individualistic model. For example, in the area of employee relations:

→ Employment conflicts have been rare in Japan as workers expected to be protected by their enterprises and the government.

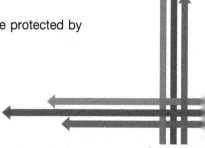

→ In the European model the government is seen as a mediator that can protect the interests of both employees and enterprises.

→ In the American model, however, labour disputes are viewed as civil disputes between individuals for lawyers and the courts to settle.

Abrahart and Verme describe the American model as a 'liberal market-driven labour management system'.

Changes in economic or political circumstances also can lead to decline in employment opportunities and living standards. Before the economic collapse dating from 2008, the USA generated more new jobs than other developed countries through flexible job markets, minimal welfare benefits and comparatively low wages for unskilled work. However, the cost has been considerable social inequality and a high crime rate. In most other developed countries the employment market is subject to a greater level of governmental control. Governments attempt to influence the quantity and quality of workers in their job markets by means of economic, social and employment legislation, and investment in human capital through education and training programmes.

Underlying beliefs regarding the degree of employment protection, unemployment benefits, and acceptable wages have become tougher throughout developed countries indicating a general swing towards 'the American model'. Parties supposedly at opposite ends of the political spectrum have adopted policies advocating:

→ restrained and affordable public sector spending (fiscal prudence).

→ control of inflation.

→ encouragement of inward investment.

→ tax rates that compare favourably with those of international competitors.

→ employment protection that does not cause rigidity or inflexibility in the job market.

→ maintenance of government legislation restricting the scope of trade union activities.

→ partnership between public and private sectors to revitalize investment-starved infrastructure.

→ the reform of education to boost the nation's skill base.

In the European Union, the pursuit of a single market has led increasingly to measures allowing free circulation of employees and freedom of residence in any EU country. Other barriers to job mobility are being removed with recognition of different educational qualifications and further social and economic cohesion. There are increasing moves towards standardization of employment regulation and protection measures to further promote a single European job market with the goal of full employment. The result is an apparent hybrid between a US-style, 'free for all' employment market and the former rigid, social protectionism of mainland western Europe.

The European Union created a new dimension for people management in its member states with initiatives aimed at improving economic conditions in less privileged regions. The differences in income between the EU's richest and poorest regions are dramatic, ranging between 30 per cent and 209 per cent of the average.

Pressure for the EU to adopt a unified, interventionist approach to the unemployment problem resulted in conflict between the majority social market (Key concept 6.4) position and those supporting the free market. Countries such as the UK held that the 'market' would take care of the problem if employment laws were relaxed and 'flexibility' encouraged. However, a pool of unskilled people in rundown industrial or mining areas is not

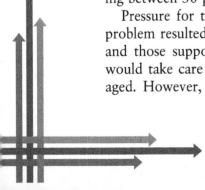

sufficient to attract industry. Companies need to be able to draw on an infrastructure of transport facilities, service companies and highly trained potential employees.

---

### KEY CONCEPT 6.4  SOCIAL MARKET

Alfred Müller-Armack, Secretary of State at the Economics Ministry in Bonn, Federal Republic of Germany (1958–1963), defined the social market as an economic system that combines market freedom with social equilibrium. The government plays a regulating role and creates the framework for market processes, going beyond securing competition to ensure social equity.

---

During the first decade of the 21st century, the EU aimed to 'become the most competitive and dynamic knowledge-based economy in the world, capable of sustainable economic growth, with more and better jobs and greater social cohesion' (Bolkestein, 2000). However, these goals were based on the assumption that it could achieve average annual economic growth of around 3 per cent and a labour participation rate rising from 61 per cent in 2000 to 70 per cent in 2010.

Further pressure on EU member states comes via three routes (Leibfried and Pearson, 2000):

*Direct positive pressures of integration.* Actions taken directly by the European Commission to create a social dimension.

*Direct negative pressures of integration.* Through the market-building process that encourages labour mobility and freedom of provision of services.

*Indirect pressures of integration.* Stemming from factors such as tax harmonization, common European currency (with implications for setting a unified interest policy) and other economic initiatives.

Less affluent governments have an uphill battle to achieve high growth and reduced unemployment in the face of rapidly increasing populations and low levels of industrialization. In the Middle East and North Africa, for example, the International Labour Organization estimates the need for at least 5 million new jobs each year from 2000, rising to 6.18 million in 2015. But, according to World Bank estimates, these countries already have among the highest unemployment rates in the world.

Dicken (1998) concludes that successfully developing economies have one thing in common:

Despite many popular misconceptions, none of today's NIEs (newly industrializing economies) is a free-wheeling market economy in which market forces have been allowed to run their unfettered course. They are, virtually without exception, *developmental* states: market economies in which the state performs a highly interventionist role.

The Economic Research Forum (2000) also argues that most governments in the region still perceive their role as employers and producers of public goods. They contrast this with the growth model of the newly industrialized countries (NICs) which they see as 'a deliberately selective approach to intervention by the state to provide an optimal institutional environment'. This approach is made up of a number of elements:

→ Maximizing the flow of knowledge to all market players (market information, technology, quality education and training) through establishment of a modern information infrastructure connecting them with knowledge networks.

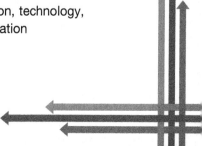

→ Transforming government bureaucracy from being a passive or even obstructive element in the economy into an active agent of development. This requires creation of an elite technocracy recruited on merit and operating in a transparent environment with clear objectives, rewards and penalties; grounded in an effective system of monitoring and performance evaluation.

→ Aiming for rapid insertion into the global market and opting for openness and flexibility in political and economic institutions to realize the potential productivity gains of the second economic revolution.

## LEGISLATIVE FRAMEWORKS

One of the most important environmental constraints on the job market and the activities of people managers comes from the law. Employment law changes continuously and varies extensively in different parts of the world. Much of the legislation relating to business derives from custom or precedent. Within the Anglo-Celtic countries these have been systematized into a common law framework. Many of these countries also have a written constitution which provides a further code. Most European countries employ an entirely code-based system called civil law. A further element is that of 'equity', which is discretionary and has relevance to cases involving non-monetary actions or injunctions, for example against an illegal strike.

In the 21st century, national governments have become law-making machines, creating a complex legal environment for businesses. Governments implement statutes for strategic reasons, ensuring, for example, that employees who are disciplined or dismissed are dealt with in a particular manner. Organizations that fail to meet their legal obligations must compensate aggrieved individuals appropriately. Not only does this apply to current employees but also ex-employees and job applicants. One of the major complications for human resource managers is that relevant laws differ from country to country, and also between different states within countries with a devolved or federal structure.

### The emphasis of anti-discrimination legislation

Countries with legal systems based on common law, including Australia, Canada, Ireland, New Zealand, the UK and the USA, have used civil rather than criminal law as the main method of counteracting discrimination. Government bodies may assist but, in essence, it is up to individuals to pursue their case. Possible costs are a negative aspect of this approach but there is a benefit in the lower burden of proof required (Lappalainen, 2001). There is also room for compromise and conciliation.

Legislation can take a number of forms:

*Positive action.* Measures to prevent discrimination and remove inequalities by insisting, for example, on non-discriminatory recruitment procedures, training programmes and pay rates. Positive action does not include any preferential treatment for disadvantaged groups.

*Affirmative action* or positive discrimination. Designed to redress the disadvantage experienced by particular groups including women, members of ethnic minority communities and the disabled. Criticized by some white, middle-class males who argued that laws intended to encourage equality were unfair to them.

*Targeting.* Quotas for the employment of particular groups.

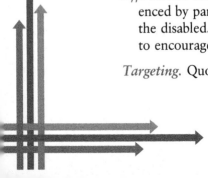

**HRM IN REALITY** RECESSION IMPACTS ON JOBS, INCOMES AND EMPLOYEE ENGAGEMENT

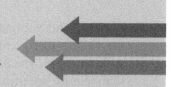

Most European businesses are finding it difficult to attract and motivate the skilled individuals needed to recover from the economic crisis, according to research from global professional services company Towers Watson. Cost-cutting has also had a negative impact on existing employees and organizations are looking afresh at how they attract, motivate and engage their workforces.

In fact, the Towers Watson Global Talent Management and Rewards Survey 2010, prepared in conjunction with WorldatWork, the international association of HR professionals, shows that businesses worldwide are finding that attracting critical-skill employees is a major issue. Sixty-five per cent of organizations surveyed around the globe reported problems attracting critical-skill employees. In Europe, 58 per cent of respondents were experiencing these problems to a great or moderate extent and 61 per cent also said they had similar difficulties attracting top performers.

Globally, the economic crisis had forced businesses to cut costs. In Europe the top three actions were:

→ hiring freezes (75 per cent)

→ salary freezes (63 per cent)

→ layoffs/redundancies (57 per cent).

Respondents acknowledged that these cost-cutting measures have been tough on employees.

→ Sixty-one per cent of European respondents said that employees' workload had increased as a result

→ Forty-seven per cent felt they had adversely impacted on employees' ability to manage workplace stress

→ Forty-four per cent said the measures had a negative effect on employees' healthy work-life balance

→ Fifty-one per cent believed that there had been an adverse impact on overall employee engagement.

Carole Hathaway, senior consultant at Towers Watson, said:

Employers need to address the adverse issues amongst employees caused by cost-cutting. It is

critical that companies re-motivate and re-engage their employees as there is a clear link between increased employee engagement and improved business performance. Business leaders therefore need to show their employees how they intend to build trust and demonstrate interest in their employees' well-being – whilst also doing so in as cost-effective ways as possible.

Many companies are re-evaluating reward and talent management programmes because of the impact of cost-cutting on employee:

→ Fifty-eight per cent of businesses surveyed are ensuring readiness of skilled people for critical roles

→ Fifty-six per cent are creating more movement, rotation and development opportunities for skilled people

→ Fifty-three per cent are investing more in building internal pipelines of talent.

Carole Hathaway added:

The business climate has clearly affected companies' ability to attract and re-motivate top-performing employees. At least in part because these key people simply are in no rush to seek employment elsewhere given the uncertainty over economic recovery and the future of their current pay and benefits package. But these are the very people most likely to leave should a better offer come along. Many employers have also underestimated the impact of pensions, job security and flexible working arrangements on employees' decisions whether or not to leave their organization.

*What are the most significant factors constraining the recruitment of critical skill employees?*

*Source: Reprinted with permission from HRM Guide (http://www.hrmguide.net).*

# HUMAN CAPITAL

Personal and national success is increasingly correlated with the possession of skills. Skilled individuals can command a premium salary in periods of high economic activity. Worldwide, unemployment levels remain high, while organizations have difficulty filling vacancies that require specific expertise. A shortage of skilled people can act as a limiting factor on individual organizations and on the economy as a whole. For example, in Canada and the UK small businesses report an inability to expand because of the difficulty in finding people with the right skills. Small firms are also vulnerable because their owners may lack basic marketing and finance skills. It is in the interest of any country to maximize its human resources by investing in the skills of its workforce: its human capital (see Key concept 6.5). Human capital is a crucial component of a country's overall competitiveness.

---

**KEY CONCEPT 6.5**  HUMAN CAPITAL

It can be argued that economic growth, employment levels and the availability of a skilled workforce are interrelated. Economic growth creates employment but partly depends on skilled human resources – a country's human capital. The concept encompasses investment in the skills of the labour force, including education and vocational training to develop specific skills.

---

**HRM IN REALITY**  EUROPEAN SKILLS IN DEMAND

According to CEDEFOP (The European Centre for the Development of Vocational Training) most of the projected 8.5 new jobs created in Europe over the next ten years will be in knowledge- and skill-intensive occupations, including high level management and technical jobs.

Despite the economic crisis, which CEDEFOP estimates has cost the EU some 10 million jobs, slow recovery over the next ten years will bring the total number of jobs close to the 2008 peak of 235 million. Around 80 million job opportunities will become available by 2020, including jobs vacated through retirement or job-changing.

The demand for skilled non-manual workers will grow significantly, but the types of job will be different with marked reductions in conventional office jobs and increases in service work, including security, catering and caring. Many manual jobs will disappear

as technology changes the nature of work. The net result is projected as a rise from 29 per cent of jobs requiring high-level skills in 2010 to 39 per cent in 2020. Correspondingly, the percentage of jobs requiring low levels of skill will drop from 20 per cent to 15 per cent.

*Balancing high-level skills and suitable job openings*
In the long run, there is a need for more people with high-level skills, but the balance between people with available skills and suitable jobs will vary. This is particularly evident at the moment as recruitment of young people has been taking place at a low level because of the recession.

A recent CIPD survey of 700 graduates in employment in the UK conducted by YouGov found that 59 per cent of employees who graduated in the last two years were not working in a field or profession related to their

degree subject. Additionally, among graduates not working in a field related to their subject:

→ Fifty-eight per cent said this was because they were unable to find a suitable job

→ Twenty-eight per cent said that their degree did not equip them with the skills needed for the workplace

→ Twenty-one per cent said that they chose a new career path after finishing their degree

→ Twenty-four per cent had since decided to postpone the start of the careers entirely.

The CIPD has queried the British Government's continued expansion of enrolment on university degrees, and the new 75 per cent target for young people to be educated up to degree level, given the results of this study and the contraction of the UK job market.

According to Tom Richmond, Skills Adviser at the CIPD:

Our survey findings suggest the Government's target of 75 per cent of young people achieving a degree or equivalent level qualification is counter-productive and should be urgently reviewed. As rising youth unemployment threatens to create a 'lost generation' of jobless young people, the rising number of students unable to work in jobs related to the subjects they studied at university threatens to create a 'disillusioned generation' of graduates, unable to find graduate-level employment but still saddled with thousands of pounds worth of debt.

If this is the situation today when our graduation rate is 39 per cent then the consequences for future graduate job prospects look bleak indeed if there really is an attempt to nearly double the numbers of graduates in the UK. To compound this, the recent announcement of an extra 20 000 university places in this year's Budget makes the creation of a 'disillusioned generation' even more likely.

Government should focus on understanding the needs of learners and employers, as well as providing young people with better information about the realistic employment prospects and salaries typically available for holders of degrees in different subjects. This will help ensure there is a better link between demand for, and supply of, graduate jobs.

The Government also needs to spend more time and effort developing and promoting the new

vocationally-based diplomas for 14–19-year-olds to ensure that more young people have the key skills to enter the workforce at age 16 or 18, rather than encouraging such a high proportion of them to study for degrees. Our survey suggests this over promotion of university or equivalent level study could leave many without the knowledge and skills that will genuinely help them find graduate-level work and apply it in the workplace.

According to CEDEFOP, their research 'suggests that formal overqualification is not a problem *per se*. But underutilization of skills and competences is certainly a potential problem for individuals, employers and society as a whole.'

### Employer training across Europe

According to another of CEDEFOP's recent reports, *Employer-provided vocational training in Europe: Evaluation and interpretation of the third continuing vocational training survey*, training investment by companies had actually dropped by 27 per cent per employee in 2005 compared with 1999. Also, almost two-fifths (39 per cent) of EU enterprises in the EU did not provide any continuing training for their employees, either in 1999 or 2005. CEDEFOP consider that the situation may have worsened during the recent economic crisis.

Some countries are doing better than others with Eastern Europe gaining ground but Western Europe worsening. Slovenia has showed the greatest improvement, rising from a low level of performance to a borderline high performance. France retained its high level of performance, but the other high performers in 1999 (the Netherlands, Sweden and Finland) had worsened significantly by 2005. The Czech Republic had joined the ranks of the high performers by 2005. Belgium and Germany, both medium performers had slipped a little.

Amongst the low performers, Romania, lowest of all in 1999, had improved in all dimensions, and Spain and Portugal had also improved. But Greece had gone backwards between 1999 and 2005, placing it last in the EU-27.

*How critical is it to have employees educated to degree level in modern organizations?*

*Source: Reprinted with permission from HRM Guide UK (http://www.hrmguide.co.uk/).*

## HRM IN REALITY  AUSSIE BOSSES SUPPORT LEARNING

Australian employers show up well in a global comparison of support for employees' further education and training, according to a Robert Half Finance and Accounting Workplace survey in 2006.

Eighty-four per cent of Australian finance and HR managers in the survey stated that their organization paid all (or part of) the cost of additional education programmes for their employees. This compares with a global average of 77 per cent. Six per cent of respondents also said that their organization supported employees who were engaged in further training with flexible working hours.

According to Nigel Barcham, managing director of Robert Half Finance and Accounting, supporting employees through continued education is becoming a very important part of Australian companies' employment and HR policies:

It is the offer of benefits such as payment or reimbursement for additional education programmes that can make or break an employee's decision to work for a company. Over the past decade, Australia has truly become a global player, attracting workers from all over the globe. Training on intercultural behaviour should be incorporated into every workplace to ensure staff coming into the organization are able to integrate seamlessly with those already working there.

Sixty-five per cent of Australian survey respondents, and 50 per cent globally, said that with increasing globalization of business, training on intercultural behaviour would help employees understand cultural differences.

When hiring new managers, 60 per cent of Australian and UK respondents, and 57 per cent of New Zealand finance and HR managers in the survey, believed that a higher level of work experience was equally important to outstanding graduation results.

However, 36 per cent of Australians surveyed thought that work experience was more important than academic results while an additional 3 per cent believed that outstanding graduation results should be mandatory for management recruits.

Nigel Barcham considers that employers should not discount the benefits of a candidate's experience in the workplace.

Outstanding academic results may show a candidate satisfies the role technically. However, work experience will often provide those higher level skills important to managers, such as problem-solving skills, the ability to adapt to difficult situations and most importantly, people skills.

Those invaluable qualities make for a more 'rounded' manager, something a candidate with a degree alone will not necessarily possess.

*Do you agree that work experience is more important than qualifications?*

*Source: Reprinted with permission from HRM Guide Australia (http://www.hrmguide.net/australia/).*

Human capital development in the form of education and skills training can be an effective response to constraints imposed on the employment market. Specific skills may be in short supply – even during periods of high unemployment – and technological developments require new competencies.

There is considerable variation between education and training levels in different countries. For example, technology and production have long been regarded as high-status activities in Germany. As a consequence, German businesses are much more committed to

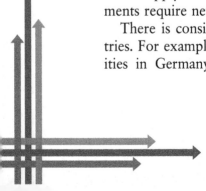

technical training than their UK equivalents. Ironically, training systems in the two countries are similar, depending on a mixture of academic education and vocational courses – unlike France, Japan and the USA where there is a greater concentration on full-time education. Countries that have shown some of the highest rates of growth, for example Singapore and Malaysia, have invested heavily in the education and technical skills of their population.

Whereas the British apprentice system had been more or less dismantled by the 1980s, it remained intact in Germany. Clarke (2006b) compares attitudes to construction industry labour in the UK and other leading European countries. The UK industry is characterized by casual self-employment, output-based pay, rigid trade divisions, low levels of training and a sharp division between operative and professional/technical skills. Skill shortages beset the industry and the solution focuses not on employment regulation and a comprehensive industry-wide training scheme, but on importing the necessary skilled labour. Other leading European countries rely on higher skill levels, based on knowledge gained through the training process and on a more stable and collectively negotiated structure of training provision and employment.

Reluctance to train apprentices is not confined to the UK. Wolter, Mühlemann and Schweri (2006) looked at why so many Swiss firms choose not to train apprentices when cost-benefit studies of apprenticeship have shown that training costs are offset by the productive work most apprentices contribute during the course of their apprenticeship. Using maximum-likelihood selection models, they estimated the net cost of training for firms without an apprenticeship programme. They showed that switching to a training policy would lead to a significantly higher net cost during the apprenticeship period. This less favourable cost-benefit ratio was determined not so much by cost than by insufficient benefit.

Skill requirements are particularly critical at the managerial level. For example, the arrival of multinational corporations in China has led to an increased demand for professional managers. In the past, Chinese colleges have produced large numbers of technicians but few accountants, lawyers or marketing specialists.

Competition is not restricted to marketing and product development. It also entails competition for staff. Availability of skilled employees in the external job market may constrain growth. Additional expensive advertising may be required, together with the offer of enhanced salaries to attract suitable applicants. We saw in Part One that businesses are inhibited from investing in training by the non-activity of other businesses in the same sector. Companies that promote training and development risk staff being poached for higher wages by organizations that have not made a similar investment (Kochan and Dyer, 2001: 282).

The reluctance of many employers to engage in training can probably be pinned down to two issues: (a) the short-term, cost-based approach to all management activities (in this case, demand for a quick and obvious benefit from training expenditure); and (b) the difficulty of proving the connection between training and improved efficiency.

Human capital theory also deals with personal investment in self-development, such as enrolling on a degree course. It presupposes that individuals balance the cost of education and training (time, loss of income, fees) against the benefits of a higher income in the future. As such it predicts that the young are more likely to invest in training because their losses are relatively less – and the potential gains greater – than for older people. In general, the income of employees with degrees and other higher education qualifications is significantly higher than that of people who ceased education at an earlier stage.

It has been suggested that the value of education may lie not in any real investment in skills but in its 'screening' power (Sapsford and Tzannatos, 1993: 89). Recruiters assume that individuals with 'pieces of paper' are better candidates than those without. Qualifications are used as a cheap and easy selection filter.

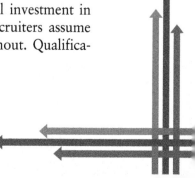

## HRM IN REALITY    MORE EFFORT NEEDED FOR APPRENTICE TRAINING

The shortage of university places has led students to look for apprenticeships as an alternative but they are likely to be disappointed according to the TUC, which says that employers are failing to provide enough places on schemes that provide on-the-job training.

BT is an exception. With 24 000 applications for 221 places, the telecommunications company decided to extend its apprenticeship scheme. Scarlet Harris, TUC apprenticeships policy and campaign officer, welcomed the news and expressed support for schemes such as BT's which have a solid qualifications framework and lead on to degree-level courses and good training in the workplace.

Scarlet Harris said:

> More large employers should follow BT's example and consider expanding their apprenticeship schemes. Companies employing 500-plus employees provide 16 per cent of the total employment, yet offer only 5 per cent of apprenticeship places overall. Large employers are providing only three apprenticeship places for every 1000 16–24-year-olds they employ. The Government has said that it is putting an extra £150 million into apprentices, but the apprenticeships system will only be a success if employers are willing to take them on.

Apprenticeships are not a second-best route for those who have failed to achieve in the academic world – or have failed to get a university place. What we are pushing for – and I think the Government is as well – is that they are seen as a valued route in themselves.

The TUC advises students to apply for credible schemes that offer:

→ a fair wage.

→ sufficient time for training.

→ real opportunities for employment and career progression.

Scarlet Harris added, 'The drive to increase the quantity of apprenticeships on offer must not come at the expense of quality.'

The TUC's own learning and skills organization Unionlearn can provide advice in the workplace about apprenticeships. It also negotiates fair wages and conditions for apprentices. Union learning reps act as mentor for young people on apprenticeship programmes.

*Source: Reprinted with permission from HRM Guide UK (http://www.hrmguide.co.uk).*

We can see from Figure 6.1 that human capital is a significant unifying concept in HRM. It links four major people management activities – resourcing, assessment, development and reward - with an environmental variable which is a key to both organizational and national success. Each of these areas is further explored in later chapters in this book. Table 6.3 locates macro HRM in the context of a changing world and a background of economic uncertainty.

Education plays a key role in causing and, potentially, curing institutionalized discrimination in advanced countries. As early as the 19th century, the sociologist Weber held that people should be promoted solely on the basis of relevant qualifications. He proposed this condition in order to overcome the nepotism and patronage that prevailed in the public and private sectors at that time. Since then qualifications have become significant, if not essential, requirements for a successful career.

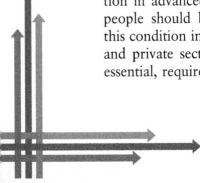

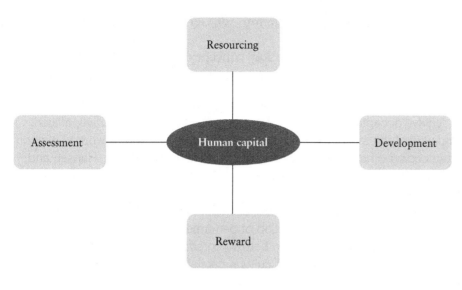

**FIGURE 6.1**

Human capital and major HR activities

| Levels of analysis | | | | |
|---|---|---|---|---|
| | **Environment** | **Organization** | **Strategy** | **Activities** |
| *HRM type* | Macro HRM | Organizational HRM | Strategic HRM | Operational HRM |
| *Features* | Economy Labour market Culture Political climate | Structure Culture Power Functions | Mission Objectives Policy Planning | Recruitment Development Reward Dismissal |
| *Traditional responsibility* | State | Senior management | Senior management | Personnel |
| *Modern responsibility* | Supranational National Multinationals | Managers Employees | Senior-middle management | Line managers HR specialists |

**TABLE 6.3**

Macro HRM in context

The importance of education for personal advancement is best illustrated in France, where a simple equation traditionally existed between management success and intellect. Intellect was taken to be the possession of the right qualifications from the right educational institutions. In France, not only was admission to one's first job dependent on educational attainment but attendance at a *grande école* eased (and still eases) the path to promotion.

French education was highly selective, emphasizing the production of 'high-fliers' who would be given early responsibility in their business careers. They produced managers with an analytical perspective in which every business issue was seen as an intellectual problem. People rejected by this process had poor prospects compared to those in countries like the

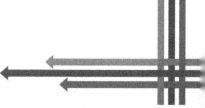

USA – where theoretically anyone could get to the top - or Germany, where training is seen as the key to effective performance.

Education fails to deliver true meritocracy (see Key concept 6.6) for a number of reasons, for example:

→ Life chances are not taken into account. People from privileged backgrounds have more opportunity to achieve acceptable qualifications. They tend to have supportive, affluent parents who understand the system. It is much harder for those having to work to support themselves, often coping other care responsibilities. In a Norwegian study, Hansen and Mastekaasa (2006) looked at how social class origin affects academic performance at university. They argue that selection procedures for higher education are strong enough to make it unlikely that lower-class students are less talented than students from higher-class backgrounds. However, in an examination of performance at Norwegian universities they found that there was a clear association between grades and class with students from classes that scored highly in respect of cultural capital doing best. This distinction was true for first-year and higher-level studies across a majority of the 36 fields they studied.

→ Second chances are discouraged or have reduced effectiveness. Educators, particularly university academics, have achieved their position by passing exams and acquiring degrees. Their personal status and function is legitimized by the belief that clearing these hurdles is indicative of underlying intellect. They tend to demonstrate limited empathy for people who fail examinations unless there are easily identifiable reasons such as major illness or bereavement. In fact, a whole range of non-intellectual factors can be responsible: domestic, financial or motivational. The critical traditional timespan for education (14–21) coincides with the transition to adulthood – a traumatic maturational period for many. However, those attempting to recover the situation at a later (more stable) age encounter many obstacles.

→ Snobbery. Possession of a 'good' degree from a 'good' university is viewed generally as evidence of intrinsic virtue, allowing entry to a range of powerful in-groups. However, in-groups are associated with prejudice against outsiders. For example, the development of mass higher education in the UK has produced a considerable disquiet among some.

**KEY CONCEPT 6.6** MERITOCRACY

Meritocratic procedures aim to make judgements on the basis of evidence of competence such as examination results or the achievement of targets. A meritocratic but socially fair system should:

→ Take aggregate outcomes into account. In other words, if the process does not produce a balanced proportion of gender, ethnic origin and so on, then it is unfair.

→ Take life chances into account.

→ Require organizations to institutionalize the representation of specific groups within their key decision processes – including selection and promotion.

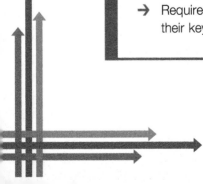

# HRM IN REALITY  PSYCHOPATHIC ORGANIZATIONS

Corporate responsibility researchers have found that many large organizations display the criteria psychiatrists use to classify people as psychopaths. Research from the Turku School of Economics in Finland (Ketola, 2006) suggests that organizations showing evidence of psychopathic behaviour would benefit from a 'prince of virtues' approach to awake them from a '100-year sleep'.

### Psychopathic characteristics in organizations

The article matches the personality characteristics of psychopaths (shown in bold) with some examples of organizational behaviour:

→ **Unconcern for others' feelings**: harsh treatment of employees, customers and partners – sudden terminations of employment contracts and business contracts.

→ **Inability to maintain human relations**: transferring business operations from country to country in order to minimize production expenses – constant change of employees and partners.

→ **Disregard for others' safety**: products and production methods endangering human health and the environment – dangerous working conditions.

→ **Dishonesty and lying to one's own advantage**: keeping silent about the risks of hazardous products and production methods, covering them up and denying their existence – deceiving employees, customers and partners.

→ **Inability to feel guilt**: when exposed for wrongdoing, asserting innocence (denial), blaming others (projection) and justifying one's action (rationalization).

→ **Inability to observe the laws and norms of society**: breaking human rights, labour, contract and environmental laws and agreements when it is economically more beneficial than observing them.

The author of the report, Dr Tarja Ketola, considers that managers and employees working in large companies that employ psychopathic practices which breach people's basic values carry a huge mental burden. However, she argues a solution can come from using ethical principles employed by individuals in their personal lives.

'According to the natural law (*lex naturae*) people all over the world share the same sense of morality, irrespective of their religion and background,' says Dr. Ketola. 'Why then, should people keep their personal values separate from their work values? If key individuals or the majority of personnel within psychopathic companies realize that the same ethical principles they use in their personal life also apply in business life, the "spell" will be broken and they will overcome organizational resistance to genuine corporate responsibility.'

She believes that these results suggest that 'psychopathic' organizations can move towards ideal responsibility by developing their economic, social and ecological responsibilities in harmony on the basis of virtue ethical values.

Dr Tarja Ketola notes: 'If these companies can stop schizophrenically separating their staff's personal values from their professional values, allowing people in organizations to integrate them into a natural harmonic unity, the corporate responsibility "100-year sleep" could be over'.

*Should people keep their personal values separate from their work values?*

*Source: Reprinted with permission from HRM Guide UK (http://www.hrmguide.co.uk).*

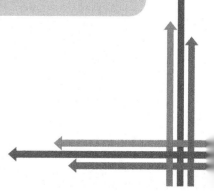

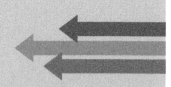

**HRM IN REALITY**  ANONYMOUS WHISTLE-BLOWING ALLEGATIONS OFTEN IGNORED

Research from the University of New Hampshire published in the *Journal of Management Studies* in 2010 found that corporate directors responsible for internal whistle-blowing systems often take no action regarding anonymous allegations, even when they involve grave accounting breaches. However, in the case of otherwise identical non-anonymous allegations, audit committees trend to act promptly with significant resources allocated to the investigation. This study is the first to investigate this issue with practising audit committee members.

The researchers explain that public corporations in the US are required to provide anonymous whistle-blowing channels to their employees. The intention is to increase reporting without fear of retaliation from management, thereby protecting shareholders from the consequences of fraudulent accounting and auditing. This study explores the operation and success of these whistle-blowing channels.

Analysis was based on responses from over eighty audit committee members from US publicly-traded companies asked to assess and respond to whistle-blowing allegations from a variety of sources. Researchers found that anonymous allegations received very different treatment from non-anonymous reports. The former were largely ignored, particularly when the allegation threatened a senior manager's reputation. Researchers conclude that this failure in a potentially important strategy for addressing financial fraud highlights contraindications to directors serving on multiple corporate boards and suggests the need for an independent body to investigate whistle-blowing allegations.

Co-author and associate professor, Jake Rose, Ph.D. commented:

> We found that when an allegation poses a threat to a director's professional reputation, a form of distortion of information occurs. An audit committee has an incentive to not investigate the allegation when it creates a reputation threat, and this causes the committee member to believe the allegation is less credible. Our presumption is that most corporate managers, auditors and corporate

directors are honest and ethical people. However, under certain circumstances, 'good' people can engage in 'bad' behaviour.

*Whistle-blowers and personal values*

Research from the University of Illinois published in *Business Ethics Quarterly* found that connecting with employees' emotions and personal value systems could encourage whistle-blowing in relation to a range of work-related crimes and misconduct. Researchers point out that fraud alone is estimated to cost US businesses US$ 652 billion annually.

Graduate student Abhijeet Vadera said: 'It's very difficult to encourage people to blow the whistle if you ignore the role of emotions and personal identity, which most company policies do at this point.'

Researchers comment that previous studies have proved inconclusive about the motivations of whistle-blowers and found no consistency in characteristics such as age, gender and length of employment. The current study surveyed employees of a large cement-manufacturing plant in India, of whom 40 per cent said they had witnessed wrongdoing in the workplace. Half failed to report it, citing reasons such as lack of confidence that management would act or fears of retaliation, including losing their jobs. However, emotional reactions were a strong factor for those who did speak out.

Abhijeet Vadera explained: 'When I interviewed whistle-blowers, almost all of them cried during the interview. The survey showed that people mostly blow the whistle because they are absolutely angry over something that they feel is unfair or unjust.'

Researchers conclude that organizations can encourage an active moral response to wrongdoing through regular training sessions examining a range of right and wrong behaviours and their consequences for individuals and the company itself.

Ruth Aguilera, professor of business, commented: 'Employers need to explain that wrongdoing can cause an Enron-type scandal that could sink the company, or eat into the revenue that covers payroll and raises.

Knowing the implications can bring their moral identity and emotions to the forefront, making them more likely to blow the whistle.'

This approach can also facilitate identification with the organization and employee loyalty, especially in the economic downturn.

Ruth Aguilera continued: 'If I care deeply about my company, I'm more inclined to defend it and blow the whistle on wrongdoing. If my job is just a paycheck, I'm more inclined to just say 'whatever' if I see something wrong.'

The researchers argue that this approach should be adopted in conjunction with a company ethics policy that incorporates guidelines for whistle-blowers and commits the organization to acting on the information received. They suggest that the majority of current policies are designed merely to comply with US Federal law. Those adopted by Fortune 500 firms tend to confirm to a pattern and fail to reflect the distinctive qualities of the different organizations.

Abhijeet Vadera concluded: 'Training programs and capitalizing on emotions are only effective if you have a good system in place. If you don't have a good system, what's the use of encouraging people to report wrongdoing?'

*Is whistle-blowing ethical?*

Source: Reprinted with permission from HRM Guide USA (http://www.hrmguide.com).

 ## SUMMARY

This chapter considered a number of issues from an international perspective including national and business cultures, the role of the state, legislative frameworks and human capital. The significance of cultural differences has been heavily influenced by Hofstede's pioneering work on IBM. Government intervention in matters affecting HRM has a cultural basis and national and international legislative frameworks are increasingly important in determining the conduct of people management. The development of human capital through national educational and vocational policies also affects the ability of organizations to compete effectively on a global stage.

 ## FURTHER READING

Most books about human capital are focused on the firm, but more generally:

1 *Cultures and Organizations: Software for the Mind, Third Edition: Intercultural Cooperation and Its Importance for Survival* by Geert Hofstede (McGraw-Hill Professional, 2010) is a revised and updated account of Hofstede's work.

2 *Human Capital Management: Achieving Added Value Through People* by Angela Baron and Michael Armstrong (Kogan Page, 2008) cuts through a lot of the mystique.

3 *International Management: Culture and Beyond* by Richard Mead and Tim G. Andrews (Wiley-Blackwell, 4th edition, 2009) covers the ground in its title. There is a huge selection of books available on employment policies in the European Union.

4 Michael Gold's *Employment Policy in the European Union: Origins, Themes and Prospects* (Palgrave Macmillan, 2009) looks at the EU's social dimension.

5 *Human Resource Management: Ethics and Employment* (OUP Oxford, 2007) edited by Ashly Pinnington, Rob Macklin and Tom Campbell covers a wide range of issues.

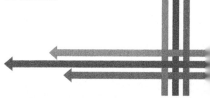

# REVIEW QUESTIONS

1  Summarize the main benefits from gaining an understanding of international HRM. What are the arguments against employing the same human resource practices throughout the world?

2  What is 'culture'? Do attempts to classify cultures into groups or types enhance our understanding of international HRM?

3  To what extent do national cultures determine corporate cultures? How many different cultures can you identify in your own country? What are the implications of the differences between these cultures for human resource managers?

4  How can the concept of 'in-groups' help to explain the inadequacies of equal opportunities policies?

5  Is it possible to describe national business cultures without resorting to stereotypes? Does the analysis provided by Argyle go beyond cultural stereotyping?

6  Explain the following terms in your own words: power distance; avoidance; role specificity.

7  How does the notion of time vary around the world?

8  Define the concept of human capital in your own words.

9  What are the most effective measures open to a government for improving a country's human capital? Is it possible to quantify a nation/company's human capital?

10  What are the benefits of apprenticeship systems to a country's human capital base? Should apprenticeship schemes be restricted to practical skills learning?

11  In what ways do approaches to people management differ between 'social market' and 'free market' countries. Relate these differences to hard and soft models of HRM. Define 'ethics'. What does ethical HRM entail?

# CASE STUDY FOR DISCUSSION AND ANALYSIS:

### Location choice/ Graduate development

1  You have been appointed general manager at a new European subsidiary of a Japanese manufacturer. The subsidiary is controlled by three senior Japanese managers who have been seconded from the parent company for a five-year period. Your first task is to identify and shortlist suitable locations for production and then participate in choosing suppliers and staff.

**What elements of employment legislation, government support and industrial relations would encourage you to locate in a particular country? Describe the likely decision processes and contrast with the way a**

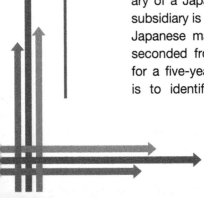

**typical local company would have dealt with the same problem.**

2   Leyanne has recently graduated with a degree in business studies, specializing in finance. She has been recruited as a trainee by a large conglomerate involved in airport management and cargo distribution. The company operates in Australia, Singapore, Europe and the Caribbean. Corporate headquarters are in Sydney, Australia but the largest operational units are in Singapore and Germany. The organization prefers to develop its own management and expects a broad range of experience and grasp of different cultural traditions. Leyanne is ambitious and wants to become a senior manager in the company.

**Outline a possible career plan for Leyanne, including aspects that the company should take responsibility for and issues for her own self-development.**

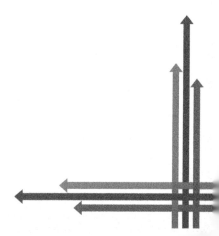

# CHAPTER 7
## Flexibility, work-life balance and wellness

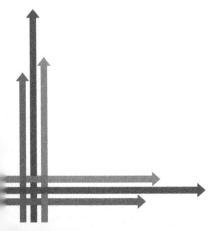

## LEARNING OBJECTIVES

The purpose of this chapter is to:

→ Debate the concept of flexible working.

→ Evaluate the feasibility of a work–life balance.

→ Discuss the role of HR practitioners in work–life balance and workplace health.

→ Investigate the personal, organizational and HR implications of stress.

# FLEXIBILITY

We have already observed that one of the most pronounced trends in recent years has been the replacement of full-time, long-term jobs with other types of positions. These include part-timers, 'temps', consultants, franchisees and so on. Business strategies have focused increasingly on flexible working in order to reduce employee costs of products and services (see Key concept 7.1).

> ### KEY CONCEPT 7.1   FLEXIBILITY
>
> The concept covers a combination of practices that enable organizations to react quickly and cheaply to environmental changes. In essence, flexibility is demanded from the workforce in terms of pay, contractual rights, hours and conditions and working practices. This extends to the employment market, requiring jobseekers to show a willingness to move location, change occupation and accept radically different terms of employment.

Flexibility has become a much-quoted term. Neo-liberal commentators argue that, at the environmental level, competitiveness comes from the reduction of perceived 'rigidities' in the employment market. Rigidities in the job market have been pinpointed as causes of industrial decline and flexibility has become an unquestioned 'good'. Rigidity includes lack of mobility, refusal to accept new conditions, unorthodox working hours and so on. By scrapping minimum pay rates, removing legislation which limits employers' rights to hire and fire, and generally deregulating the job market, they believe that businesses will achieve the maximum degree of competitiveness (Zemanek, 2010).

Simplistically, it can be argued that the terms have an implicit political agenda: rigidity equates with worker protection and therefore left-wing, socialist attitudes; flexibility matches with 'hard' HRM, exploitation of workers and hence a right-wing, capitalist approach. In practice, flexible working can take a variety of forms that are differentially attractive to employees depending on their personal circumstances (Nadler *et al.*, 2010). For example, in an Irish study Russell *et al.* (2009) found that part-time work and flexitime tended to reduce work pressure and the conflict between work and non-work life, working from home seemed to increase levels of work pressure and work–life conflict. Blake-Beard *et al.* (2010) argue that, in order to maintain a socially sustainable workforce, organizations should make flexibility a norm, gaining an understanding of workers' lives outside the organization and allowing access to flexible working arrangements across the dimensions of gender, race and class.

We can classify the common forms of flexibility as:

*Numerical flexibility.* Matching employee numbers to fluctuating work levels. This is difficult to achieve with 'regular' workers on full-time, long-term contracts.

*Functional flexibility.* Abolishing demarcation rules and skill barriers so that workers can take on a variety of jobs.

*Pay flexibility.* Offering different rates of pay for the same work – depending on geographical location and skills availability.

A further requirement is 'flexible specialization'. Consumer demand increasingly reflects individual tastes. Purchasers want an ever-wider choice of goods, making it difficult, if not impossible, for mass production techniques to satisfy the market. The Fordist assembly-line

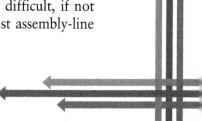

## HRM IN REALITY  GIVE US A 6.00AM START

Many British workers would welcome the introduction of a 6.00am start, if they could go home earlier in exchange, according to research by business communications firm Your Communications.

The survey of over 2000 employees carried out in 2005 found that a majority believed they work most efficiently between 6.00am and 3.00pm.

A mere one in 20 said they were most productive between 3.00pm and 6.00pm and almost half the respondents said they could do their job as effectively from home.

Your Communications argued that this could spell the death of the traditional 9 to 5 working day. In particular, allowing employees to work flexibly from home at times best-suited to them meant that businesses could dramatically boost their productivity.

The report also concluded that employers should consider the 'obvious benefits' that flexible working schemes bring, including: strengthening staff loyalty, and improving employees' work–life balance.

'Most workers believe they work more effectively at different times of the day', said Paul Lawton, from Your Communications. 'Flexible work arrangements, which allow them to work from home, at their clients' offices, or for that matter at airport lounges, may help them to work more productively and vary their working hours.'

*What is your ideal pattern of working hours?*

*Source: Reprinted with permission from HRM Guide UK (http://www.hrmguide.co.uk).*

is outmoded – even if it does offer cars in colours other than black. Producers must switch equipment and employees from one product to another in a flexible but economic way. Staff must have versatile skills. Proponents of flexible specialization hold that mass production, the dominant industrial force of the 20th century, is obsolete, along with Taylorism and Fordism. Organizations in developed countries will only survive by employing a multi-skilled, highly flexible core workforce able to turn their hands to a wide variety of tasks.

Atkinson's (1984) 'flexible firm' model combines flexibility with Japanese concepts of 'core' and 'peripheral' workforces (see Figure 7.1). Core workers are employed on standard contracts. Peripheral workers are employed by subcontractors, or on short-term contracts. However, Atkinson's model does without mutual obligations essential to the Japanese system: core workers provide functional flexibility – but without lifelong employment; peripheral workers and subcontractors are not rewarded with close, long-term relationships.

**FIGURE 7.1**

Core and peripheral workers

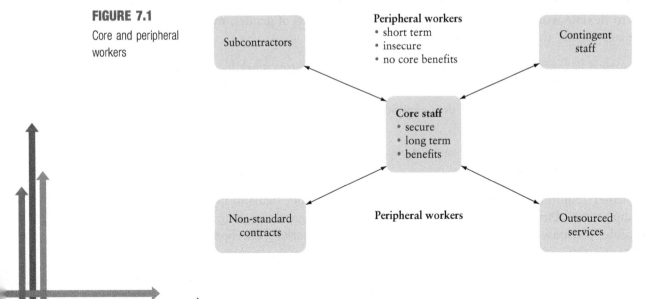

## HRM IN REALITY  FLEXIBLE WORKING MAY HAMPER CAREERS

A 2006 study by business communications provider Inter-Tel questioned over 100 office-based workers about attitudes to flexible working. This identified positive reasons for applying to work flexibly but significant doubts about the likely response of employers. Significant findings included:

→ Ninety per cent of respondents agreed that all employees should have the same right to request more flexible work patterns, irrespective of domestic circumstances.

→ Thirty per cent felt their organization did not respond equitably to such requests and 54 per cent were unsure about this issue.

→ Sixty per cent believed requesting greater flexibility could have a negative impact on the careers of people without children.

→ Eighty-two per cent considered flexible working a privilege; only 18 per cent felt it should be a right.

→ Forty per cent felt their employer would not trust them to work from home.

Duncan Miller of Inter-Tel EMEA said:

> The trend for home working continues to grow. Data from the UK Office of National Statistics confirms that there are now more than two million people working from home and a further eight million opting to spend at least part of their working week outside the office. Clearly, there are still issues to be overcome and an education process needs to take place so that everyone knows what their rights are and ways in which they can improve their work/life–balance.

Over two-thirds of respondents identified 'a better quality of life' as the most important reason for applying to work flexibly. Other factors centred on more time for family (22 per cent), non-work activities such as courses (6 per cent), and travel (3 per cent).

Duncan Miller concluded:

> We are now at a stage of technological development where people can work as effectively from their home or on the move, as they can at a desk in their company's office. Of course, flexible or home working is not feasible or suitable for all organizations, but employers should be looking at ways to address the work/life balance of their staff and be very clear on their policy in this area. A happier, healthier workforce can lead to greater productivity in the long term and increase staff retention.

New rights to flexibility may be leading to a reversal of the trend seen over the last decade. A 2001 Industrial Society (now the Work Foundation) survey of 516 human resource specialists found that 91 per cent of respondents' organizations used some form of flexible working. This compared with 84 per cent in 1998. Seventy-five per cent of respondents said that flexible working made good business sense for the organization, with almost two-thirds (63 per cent) saying that it built trust, loyalty and commitment.

*Summarize the advantages and disadvantages of flexibility to employees and employing organizations?*

*Source: Reprinted with permission from HRM Guide UK (http://www.hrmguide.co.uk).*

Against a background of globalization, workers have been forced to accept a reduction in employment rights, unsociable working hours, short-term contracts and lower pay rates. This development has occurred throughout the industrialized world. It has been driven by competition, primarily from Asia. It is also a development that has attracted a considerable degree of theoretical and ideological debate. Flexibility enables organizations to react quickly and cheaply to environmental changes. In free market countries there is a trend towards replacing full-time, long-term jobs with other employment relationships.

Nevertheless, this is still a minority situation. For example, 70 per cent of workers in the UK have been employed by the same organization for over 20 years.

The idea of flexibility has definitely taken root but its theoretical basis has weaknesses. On the one hand, it is consistent with the concept of the 'virtual organization' to be discussed in Chapter 8, forming and re-forming to meet particular demands. Conversely, it is doubtful that we are really moving to a 'world of quasi-bespoke production concerned with gratifying fleeting market whims' (Hyman, 1988). Rather, niche marketing is concerned with defined 'varieties' of mass produced products. Consumers are not purchasing unique cars made to their specific requirements, but red 2.3 litre high-specification models, or white 1.0 litre basic models from a controlled choice – built in factories that Henry Ford would find recognizable. The availability of such varieties has more to do with computer-controlled robots, switchable from one program to another, than with a flexible, multi-skilled workforce.

While much of the discussion on flexibility has focused on manufacturing, other industries have made long use of flexible arrangements. Thiel (2009) modelled the complex flexible schedules used in the French fresh food industry which required rapid staffing decisions on the number of employees, their hours and the source of labour: permanent, temporary, contract and subcontracted.

---

## HRM IN REALITY    CORRECTING MYTHS ABOUT TEMPORARY WORK

A 2010 report from Canadian staffing firm Accountemps corrects common misconceptions about temporary work and its role in the current job market.

Myths include:

1 Temporary assignments are mainly clerical or lower skilled – in fact the fastest growth is in professional and technical occupations, as the advantages of flexibility become increasingly apparent. Companies now hire temporary staff for positions at all levels from accounting clerk to chief financial officer.

2 Temporary work can't be included on a resume – in fact all temporary assignments should be included. The report recommends listing the staffing firm as the employer and describing the duties undertaken on various placements.

3 Temporary work will interfere with a search for permanent employment – in fact experience of temporary work can actually enhance the chance of securing full-time employment. Many organizations view interim engagements as an effective way of assessing potential employees and go on to hire on a permanent basis. Temporary workers have an opportunity to expand their skills and experience while earning an income.

4 Temporary work doesn't pay well – in fact temporary and contract positions typically pay the same as salaried ones; individuals with the most sought-after skills can often command a premium.

5 Job seekers will have to pay to work with a staffing firm – professional staffing firms never charge job seekers for their services; all fees are met by client companies.

Kathryn Bolt, president of Accountemps' Canadian operations said:

> As companies determine their staffing levels in response to increased business activity, many are turning to temporary employees at all levels. Temporary work has resulted in full-time employment offers for many job seekers and is a valuable career option for professionals to consider.

*What are the disadvantages experienced by temporary workers?*

*Source: Reprinted with permission from HRM Guide Canada (http://www.hrmguide.net/canada/).*

Further problems arise in practice. Where are the necessary skilled people supposed to come from? A true transition to total flexibility requires a system for training non-permanent workers. Most employers are not equipped to provide this. Companies in countries such as Australia and the UK have been heavily criticized for under-investing in training their permanent employees. Ironically, the same countries have a weak record of providing such training on a national basis as well. In a Canadian study, Fang (2009) found that organizations relied extensively on flexible hours and extra overtime as short-term solutions to meet skill shortages.

Employees have their own views on flexibility. Hall and Atkinson (2006) investigated employee perceptions of flexibility utilized or available to them in an NHS Trust. They found that informal rather than formal flexibility was more widely used and valued, generating an increased sense of employee responsibility. Staff needed to be proactive to access formal flexibility but some did not see it as relevant to themselves. The significance of gender in the flexibility debate has been understated as the issue of family-friendly working arrangements is particularly significant to women (Atkinson and Hall, 2009). Hornung *et al.* (2009) investigated informal ('idiosyncratic') flexible working arrangements made between individual telecommuting workers and supervisors in German public administration and discovered that such deals were typically initiated by employees and were justified in terms of performance, motivation and work-life benefits.

Anderson and Kelliher (2009) argue that flexible working arrangements impact on employee engagement (discussed in Chapter 10) through a positive relationship with organizational commitment, job satisfaction and employee discretionary behaviour. Arguably, flexibility can provide a win-win solution to family and business needs, benefiting both (Thomson, 2008).

## HRM IN REALITY BLURRING THE BOUNDARIES OF WORK AND HOME

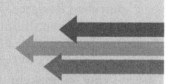

Employees with flexible schedules tend to experience greater blurring of boundaries between work and other parts of their lives, especially family-related roles, according to research from the University of Toronto published in the *Journal of Family Issues* in 2010. Sociology professor Scott Schieman and PhD student Marisa Young drew on data from a national survey of more than 1200 North American workers to measure the extent of schedule control and its impact on work-family processes.

Scott Schieman explained:

Most people probably would identify schedule control as a good thing – an indicator of flexibility that helps them balance their work and home lives.

We wondered about the potential stress of schedule control for the work–family interface. What happens if schedule control blurs the boundaries between these key social roles?

Participants were asked: 'Who usually decides when you start and finish work each day at your main job? Is it someone else, or can you decide within certain limits, or are you entirely free to decide when you start and finish work?'

The study found that those with more flexibility are also more likely to work at home, attempting simultaneous work – family multitasking. Those reporting more blurring of work-family boundaries also tend to experience more conflict between roles and a consequent

increase in stress. Researchers point to substantial evidence linking work–family conflict to poorer physical and mental health outcomes.

The study assessed work–family conflict by responses to questions such as:

→ 'How often have you not had enough time for your family or other important people in your life because of your job?'

→ 'How often have you not had the energy to do things with your family or other important people in your life because of your job?'

→ 'How often has your job kept you from concentrating on important things in your family and personal life?'

However, the researchers also identified benefits to flexible working.

Scott Schieman said:

People who had partial or full schedule control were able to engage in work–family multitasking activities with fewer negative consequences in terms of conflict between their work and family roles. Overall, our findings contribute to an ongoing – and complicated – debate about the costs and benefits of different forms of flexibility for workers.

*Why might flexible working arrangements reduce absenteeism?*

*Source: Reprinted with permission from HRM Guide Canada (http://www.hrmguide.net/canada/).*

## WORK–LIFE BALANCE

On a common-sense level it is widely accepted that well being is enhanced by a balance between all aspects of daily life. Work is a critical area of everyday occupation but it is just one of a number of associated domains, including family life, leisure, education and self-care that also have goal-directed activities (Anaby *et al.*, 2010).

A baseline study ('Work–life Balance 2000') conducted jointly by the Institute for Employment Research, University of Warwick and IFF Research concludes that there is a widespread demand from employees for the right to balance work and home life. It also reveals that businesses prefer to offer stress counselling for the personal consequences of long working hours (49 per cent) rather than provide assistance for childcare (9 per cent).

One in nine of full-time employees (including men with children) work more than 60 hours every week. Two-thirds of male employees believe that part-time working would damage their career prospects. At the same time there is a clear demand for greater flexibility – especially from fathers. In general, men seem to have a greater enthusiasm for working from home than do women. Virtually all the respondents to both surveys – employees and employers alike – agreed with the concept of work–life balance. But one in eight of employees still worked Saturdays and Sundays and around 20 per cent of employees worked for 24-hour/seven-day-week businesses.

Other conclusions of the study were:

→ Eighty per cent of workplaces had employees who worked more than their standard hours with 39 per cent doing so without extra pay.

→ Just 20 per cent of employers were fully aware of increased maternity leave rights and 24 per cent fully aware of new paternal leave rights.

→ Twenty-five per cent of entitled female employees took less than 18 weeks maternity leave.

→ Fifty-five per cent of employers consider it acceptable to allow staff to move from full-time to part-time work in some cases.

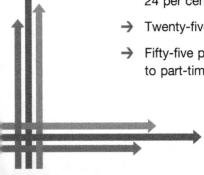

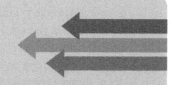

# HRM IN REALITY  LONG HOURS BAD FOR THE HEART

Research led by University College, London and published in the *European Heart Journal* found that working overtime is bad for the heart. The study forms part of the long-term follow-up of more than 10000 London office-based civil servants (the Whitehall II study). Researchers compared people working a normal seven-hour day with those working a minimum of three hours extra. They found that this level of overtime is associated with a 60 per cent increased risk of heart-related problems (including death due to heart disease, non-fatal heart attacks and angina).

Dr Marianna Virtanen, epidemiologist at the Finnish Institute of Occupational Health said:

> The association between long hours and coronary heart disease was independent of a range of risk factors that we measured at the start of the study, such as smoking, being overweight, or having high cholesterol.
>
> Our findings suggest a link between working long hours and increased CHD [coronary heart disease] risk, but more research is needed before we can be confident that overtime work would cause CHD. In addition, we need more research on other health outcomes, such as depression and type 2 diabetes.

The Whitehall II study recruited 10308 volunteers aged 35–55 from 20 civil service departments in 1985. The third phase (1991–1994) introduced a question on working hours. Based on an average of 11.2 years follow-up, the current research analyzes results from 4262 men and 1752 women aged between 39 and 61, up to the most recent period for which clinical data are available (2002–2004). Researchers caution that while the cohort includes several occupational grades it inevitably has no blue-collar or private sector workers.

Researchers identified 369 cases of fatal CHD, non-fatal heart attacks (myocardial infarctions) or angina. After adjusting for socio-demographic characteristics (such as age, sex, marital status and occupational grade) and 21 risk factors they found that working three to four hours overtime (but not one to two hours) was associated with a 60 per cent higher rate of CHD compared with no overtime.

Considering possible explanations, results indicate that working overtime is associated with type A behaviour pattern (a tendency towards aggressive, competitive, tense, time-conscious and hostile behaviour), psychological distress (depression and anxiety) and poor sleep patterns. In addition, researchers highlight undiagnosed high blood pressure associated with work-related stress; and 'sickness presenteeism' (employees who habitually work overtime also tend to work when ill, may ignore symptoms and not seek medical advice). Researchers also suggest that people working overtime, but in jobs where they have more freedom over work-related decisions, may have a lower risk of CHD. However, the current findings were independent of all of these factors.

Marianna Virtanen explained:

> We did not measure whether subsequent changes in these factors during the follow-up period altered the association. One plausible explanation for the increased risk could be that adverse lifestyle or risk factor changes are more common among those who work excessive hours compared with those working normal hours. Another possibility is that the chronic experience of stress (often associated with working long hours) adversely affects metabolic processes. It is important that these hypotheses should be examined in detail in the future.

Lead author Mika Kivimäki, professor of social epidemiology, concluded:

> At the moment there is no research on whether reduction in overtime work reduces CHD risk. Further research on this topic is therefore needed. Our own future research will include analyzing data over periods of time to examine whether working long hours predicts changes in life style, mental health and traditional risk factors, such as blood pressure, blood glucose and cholesterol. We hope that this research will increase understanding of the mechanisms underlying the association

between long working hours and coronary heart disease. We will also examine whether overtime work increases the risk of depression, as recent research suggests that depression increases the risk of coronary heart disease.

An accompanying editorial is provided by Gordon McInnes, professor of clinical pharmacology at the Western Infirmary, University of Glasgow. While echoing researchers' caution about the specific characteristics of the study's subjects, he nevertheless concludes that the findings may have far-reaching implications for cardiovascular risk assessment.

Gordon McInnes said:

These data from a large occupational cohort reinforce the notion that work stress attributable to overtime is associated, apparently independently, with an increased risk of coronary heart disease. A trend for risk to be related to hours of overtime worked supports this conclusion. If the effect is truly causal, the importance is much greater than commonly recognized. Overtime-induced work stress might contribute to a substantial proportion of cardiovascular disease. Physicians should be aware of the risks of overtime and take seriously symptoms such as chest pain, monitor and treat recognized cardiovascular risk factors, particularly blood pressure, and advise an appropriate lifestyle modification.

Quoting British philosopher Bertrand Russell, Gordon McInnes concluded:

'If I were a medical man, I should prescribe a holiday to any patient who considers work important'.

*Source: Reprinted with permission from HRM Guide UK (http://www.hrmguide.co.uk).*

→ Twenty-four per cent of employees now work flexitime with 12 per cent working only during school terms.

→ Fifty-six per cent of women preferred flexible working after a pregnancy – for example, part-time or home-based – to having a longer maternity leave period.

A report from The Work Foundation, commissioned by UNISON, the public service union, concludes that public sector employers may 'talk the talk' on work–life balance, but in practice have limited commitment to changing standard working patterns (Visser and Williams, 2007). The survey found that three-quarters of public sector employers have initiatives and policies in place addressing work-life balance issues for at least some staff. This is considerably higher than average and includes flexible working, job sharing, home working, term-time contracts, career breaks, childcare provision and time off to care for sick children.

However, only half of respondents felt they had real choice about their working arrangements and only just over half were aware of available work-life options. Some 53 per cent said their workplace offered flexitime; 52 per cent job sharing; 19 per cent working from home; and 32 per cent term-time working. These figures were much lower than the stated availability in all workplaces.

A third of respondents believed their employers were not committed to helping them achieve work-life balance. Some reported their managers tried to restrict uptake of flexible working by failing to communicate available options, or by dissuading people from requesting them.

The survey identified examples of the difficulties of working flexibly. For example, one respondent said that there was an unwritten policy that employees who worked 12 hour shifts were eligible for career progression, while those who did 8 hour shifts to fit around family commitments were not.

A common complaint was being made to feel like a troublemaker if the possibility of work-life balance arrangements was raised with employers. One respondent said their manager had told them 'I don't do part-time'. In several organizations, flexibility was only available to selected staff.

Respondents also reported that available work-life balance options were often inappropriate. For example, nearly three-quarters of respondents (71 per cent) expressed a strong preference for time off to care for adult dependents but fewer than half of workplaces offer this option. By contrast, 80 per cent of employers offer job sharing, but only 37 per cent of respondents say this is of use to them.

Other key survey findings include:

→ One in four said that work was too demanding.

→ A total of 30 per cent said their career had been damaged by caring responsibilities.

→ Two-thirds (66 per cent) said their job was stressful compared with 34 per cent who said home life was stressful.

→ A total of 68 per cent called for greater flexibility in working arrangements.

→ Some 66 per cent said extending work-life balance options to workers without children would be worthwhile.

The researchers suggest that respondents may be struggling to see the benefit of work-life balance policies but remain committed both to the principle and to their jobs. Some 70 per cent said they are satisfied with their job and share the values of the organization they are working for. A total of 77 per cent said they have a high degree of control over how they work. Some 99 per cent agreed that people work best when they can balance work and other aspects of their lives.

## HRM IN REALITY   TELECOMMUTING BETTER THAN OFFICE WORKING

Research from Brigham Young University published in the *Journal of Family Psychology* in 2010 found that telecommuters experience a better work–life balance than office-based employees even when working significantly longer hours. The study analyzed data from 24 436 IBM employees in 75 countries to identify the number of hours that had to be worked before 25 per cent reported interference with personal and family life.

Office workers with relatively inflexible schedules reached this point when their hours exceeded 38 hours per week. Those who had the possibility of telecommuting were able achieve 57 hours per week with their time typically divided between office and home depending on the nature of the task being undertaken. Both male and female workers appreciated the advantages of flexible working arrangements.

Lead author E. Jeffrey Hill, a professor in the school of family life noted: 'Telecommuting is really only beneficial for reducing work–life conflict when it is accompanied by flextime'.

Formerly one of IBM's first telecommuters starting in 1990, Jeffrey Hill commented: 'Managers were initially sceptical about the wisdom of working at home and said things like, "If we can't see them, how can we know they are working?"'.

The study found that more than 80 per cent of IBM managers currently agree that productivity increases when flexible working arrangements are made available. In the current economic situation, financial constraints are encouraging more widespread introduction of such schemes.

Jeffrey Hill commented: 'A down economy may actually give impetus to flexibility because most options save money or are cost-neutral. Flexible work options are associated with higher job satisfaction, boosting morale when it may be suffering in a down economy'.

*Younger workers keener on web commuting*

A telecommuting study from 2008, *Web Commuting & the American Workforce* commissioned by Citrix Online,

a division of Citrix Systems, Inc. has found younger workers are particularly keen on flexible working. The study showed that employees aged 18–34 are twice as likely to prefer flexible working conditions than older employees. In fact, 70 per cent of survey respondents agreed that working remotely would be a welcome opportunity.

Termed 'web commuters' in the study, a growing number of employees performed at least some of their work away from their office, at non-standard hours, using web-based technology. The study, conducted by *the polling company, inc.* and sponsored by Citrix Online, which claims to provide easy-to-use, secure and affordable web-based services for remote computer access and online collaboration, found that:

→ Twenty-three per cent of US employees regularly worked offsite using web technology and 62 per cent of those who do not would like to do so.

→ Employees aged 18–34 were most likely to look forward to controlling their own schedules, while respondents aged 35–44 indicated that they would value more time with family.

→ In general, the younger the worker, the more likely they were to see the value of online tools and services that allowed them to work remotely, reflecting their greater familiarity with the Internet.

Kellyanne Conway, CEO and president of *the polling company, inc.* said: 'As Baby Boomers retire, employers will be forced to compete for younger workers, for whom technology is a native tongue. Offering the ability to web commute is an easy way to provide a valued benefit to this age group'.

'Anyone of any age can benefit from new, low-cost technologies that are as easy to use and as indispensable as email and cell phones', commented Bernardo de Albergaria, vice president and general manager, global marketing and eCommerce for Citrix Online. 'Younger workers expect freedom and flexibility, and online remote access and collaboration services enable people to work on their own terms. When employers provide these tools for connecting employees with their PCs, customers, prospects and co-workers across town or halfway around the world, everyone benefits.'

*Why should organizations involve themselves with non-work issues?*

Source: Reprinted with permission from HRM Guide USA (http://www.hrmguide.com).

## WORKPLACE HEALTH

According to Naidoo and Wills (2000: 270):

> The relationship between work and health may appear substantial but it is viewed in different ways by different groups of people. One of the defining characteristics of the workplace setting is that it brings together a variety of groups who have different agendas with regard to work and health. The key parties are workers or employees and their trade unions or staff associations, employers and managers, occupational health staff, health and safety officers, environmental health officers and specialist health promoters.

The Chartered Institute of Personnel and Development's 2010 report on sickness absenteeism in the UK shows that absence in the National Health Service (NHS) averages 11 days per employee per year. This is significantly higher than the public sector average of 9.7 days, which, in turn is much higher than the average absence levels in the private sector of 6.4 days and 8.3 days in the non-profit sector.

The report shows that monitoring of absence is increasing but half of employers do not measure the cost of absence. It identifies the most effective techniques as:

→ return-to-work interviews

→ trigger mechanisms to review attendance

→ disciplinary measures for unacceptable absence.

# HRM IN REALITY   ABSENCE MANAGEMENT IN IRELAND

A 2009 article in the *Irish Times* highlighted a campaign to control excessive absenteeism by the Health Service Executive (HSE). Under the Health Act, 2004, the HSE has assumed responsibility for Health and Personal Social Services for everyone living in the Republic of Ireland. It replaced ten regional health boards and a variety of other organizations and is now Ireland's largest employer with over 130000 employees.

The HSE's 2009 Service Plan featured increases in service provisions and reductions in costs, including savings in staffing areas such as:

→ work practice reform (redeployment of staff, more flexible working arrangements)

→ sick leave

→ absenteeism

→ overtime

→ use of agency workers

→ allowances,

→ a 3 per cent reduction in management/ administration staff through planned redundancies.

According to the *Irish Times*, HSE has been auditing absenteeism levels for several months. Unpublished figures from October indicate an average level of 5 per cent lost hours due to absenteeism in the main teaching hospitals. However, the level in some hospital sections is much higher: for example, running at 12 per cent among general support staff at the Midwest Regional Hospital in Limerick.

The newspaper cites the intention of HSE's national HR director to eliminate 'double-digit absenteeism or inappropriately high sickness levels where they occur'.

## Monitoring absenteeism

A survey by Mercer Human Resource Consulting in 2006 found that almost two-thirds (65 per cent) of Irish businesses made no attempt to calculate the annual cost of absenteeism to their companies. Moreover, the survey of top Irish businesses found that most had no idea about the impact of employee absences on their direct or indirect costs.

According to Kevin Kinsella, a consultant at Mercer Human Resource Consulting:

> Our experience in this area and indeed our research demonstrates that reporting and measurement of absence plays a very effective role in reducing absence levels. However, many companies take a casual and sporadic approach to absence management and fail to actively manage a major cost driver.

The survey also found that:

→ Twenty-six per cent of those surveyed estimated the cost of absenteeism to be more than 500000 euros a year.

→ Minor illnesses were the most frequently cited causes for absence, amounting to 33.2 per cent of days lost.

→ Almost 20 per cent of absences were due to musculoskeletal illnesses and back pain.

→ Ninety per cent of surveyed organizations said that 'recording' of absence was their number one tool in combating absence levels.

→ Twenty per cent of surveyed organizations reported absence levels in excess of 6 per cent per annum.

→ Sixty-five per cent did not calculate the cost of absence to their business.

→ Forty-five per cent of managers whose responsibilities included dealing with employee absence had not received relevant training.

→ Forty-one per cent of managers with responsibilities in this area had no formal targets.

The Mercer Human Resource Consulting survey shows that senior managers are highly aware that 'absence management' is an issue for their business, but very few companies are taking an appropriate, strategic approach to reducing absenteeism in their businesses. Kevin Kinsella said:

> There will always be short-term absence in organizations. Mercer's experience and research

suggests that there is no one 'magic cure' to manage sickness absence. The introduction of a range of simple measures such as absence reporting, early interventions on health issues, the provision of health insurance and the provision of support and training for line managers, can however, dramatically reduce absenteeism levels.

**The Mercer view is that the cost of employee sick days can have an impact on overall competitiveness so it is** important that organizations review and manage their absence procedures. Mercer believes that effective reporting and measurement can drive behavioural change particularly when supported by senior management.

*Why are absence levels high in health services?*

Source: Reprinted with permission from HRM Guide UK (http://www.hrmguide.co.uk).

## HRM IN REALITY    HEALTH AND SAFETY NOT OVERREGULATED

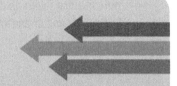

Recent research from the University of Liverpool and Liverpool John Moores University in 2010 found that safety in the workplace has been adversely affected by policy changes relating to health and safety over the last ten years, with reduced levels of enforcement by the Health and Safety Executive (HSE). These findings challenge the perception that health and safety is overregulated.

The report entitled *Regulatory Surrender: death, injury and the non-enforcement of law* found that inspections of business premises fell by 69 per cent and investigations of health and safety-related incidents by 68 per cent. The study also identified a 48 per cent reduction in prosecutions of organizations for breaching HSE regulations.

Dr David Whyte, reader in sociology at the University of Liverpool, said:

> The idea that health and safety has 'gone mad' does not seem to hold true. The collapse in inspection, investigation and enforcement has dramatically reduced the chances of businesses being detected and prosecuted for committing safety offences. Most serious injuries now are not even investigated. For example, only a third of

amputations are now investigated by the Health and Safety Executive.

Researchers explain that the new UK government elected in May 2010 announced a wide-ranging review of health and safety regulations in response to claims that industry had been 'saturated' by legislation passed by the outgoing administration. The Liverpool study concluded that the HSE's inspection and enforcement powers had been reduced, resulting in increased numbers of employees at risk of suffering work-related accidents or injuries.

Professor Steve Tombs, of Liverpool John Moores University, commented:

> HSE's senior management have effectively surrendered to the Government's lighter touch regulatory agenda. Not only is the agency now more vulnerable to further 'reviews' of regulation, but workers too are increasingly vulnerable – as managements are far less likely to respond to workers' demands to comply with the law in the absence of a credible enforcement threat.

Source: Reprinted with permission from HRM Guide UK (http://www.hrmguide.co.uk/).

## HRM IN REALITY    HR CHANGES CAN INCREASE STRESS

Research funded by the Economic and Social Research Council as part of its Future of Work programme has found that teamworking and other contemporary employment practices can put as much strain on a woman's family relationships as working an extra 120 hours a year.

The study by Patrick McGovern, Stephen Hill, Colin Mills and Michael White entitled *Market, Class, and Employment* found significant changes in British job prospects and conditions over the period 1984–2004. Despite competitive market pressures employers have maintained long-term career relationships with their employees. However, introduction of practices such as team-based forms of work organization, individual performance-related pay, and an emphasis on development of individual potential has demanded greater effort and higher performance.

Researchers found that while these human resource management practices are thought to improve staff morale and to form an essential element in successful business performance, the resulting stress has an adverse impact on employees' family relationships. Women are generally more affected than men and are less likely to get support from male partners also in pressurized jobs. Both are more likely to experience anxiety about childcare.

Researchers highlight ICT surveillance as a significant new source of strain at work. They found that 52 per cent of all employees (20 per cent of workplaces) have their work monitored by computerized systems. This has led to a sharp increase in work-related stress reflected in feelings of exhaustion and anxiety. The study found an overall 7.5 per cent increase among employees subject to ICT surveillance compared with those in similar jobs supervised in more traditional ways. Administrative and white-collar staff in settings such as call centres reported a 10 per cent increase.

Michael White commented: 'Computers and IT systems are bringing surveillance to most workplaces. Now for the first time we can see how this development is damaging employees' well-being'.

Researchers found that recent US employment practices have not been replicated in Britain. It might have been assumed that highly competitive market condi-

tions would result in both private and public sector employers resorting to hire and fire practices, temporary jobs and a decline in training and career planning. While British employers continue to use redundancy to adjust employee numbers, in general they remain committed to retention and long-term development.

The study found that the proportion in permanent employment remains above 90 per cent and increased during the 1990s. Fixed-term or casual employment grew in the 1980s but declined in the subsequent decade. Researchers argue that increased use of communication techniques, employee participation, team organization, training and development and performance rewards are indicative of efforts to maintain a long-term workforce.

Researchers suggest that the decline in trade union recognition and membership could increase the chances of unfair treatment but found that this has been mitigated in part by a growth in alternative forms of employee engagement such as meetings with management and consultation. The study found that by 2000 about one third of employees were participating in individual pay bargaining. Researchers note that this is more likely to occur in non-unionized workplaces and is leading to increasing inequality. Managers and professionals are more likely to negotiate personal pay deals; women are less likely to bargain over pay when recruited or to be represented by a union. Thus the ability of women to challenge the gender pay gap is doubly limited.

The research concluded that class differences in job rewards have increased since the early 1990s. Pay inequality increased between 1992 and 2000, reflecting substantial increases in average earnings for senior managers and significant though lower gains for other managers. Pay for individuals in semi-routine and routine occupations either saw no real increase or declined.

Other benefits such as occupational pensions, sickness pay and paid holidays also showed a marked class difference in favour of higher managerial and professional groups which tended to increase over time. There was a similar gap in job desirability, reflecting both pay and other factors such as flexibility and autonomy.

Researchers conclude that inequality in pay and bene-fits will probably continue to grow. Managers and pro-fessionals are more able than other groups to benefit from increasing opportunities for personal pay bargain-ing and performance deals.

Patrick McGovern commented:

The major story about work in Britain is not that it has become more precarious or fragmented, rather it has become more demanding while the returns have become more unequal. The major winners in the so-called new economy are professional and managerial employees who have actually moved further ahead of the rest of the labour force.

*Why might HR practices increase stress?*

*Source: Reprinted with permission from* HRM Guide UK *(http://www.hrmguide.co.uk/).*

Ironically, public sector employers are much less likely to use disciplinary measures than private sector or non-profit employers, and have the most generous sick pay arrangements.

Health and safety are workplace issues with considerable organizational and legal implications for HR and other managers. Naidoo and Wills (2000) identify a number of benefits to organizations from the promotion of health in the workplace as (a) 'hard' benefits, such as improvements in productivity as a result of reduced sickness, absence and staff turnover; and (b) 'soft' benefits, including enhanced corporate image.

Organizations may introduce specialist occupational health staff tasked with the following (Naidoo and Wills, *ibid.*):

→  surveillance of the work environment, such as monitoring the effects of new technology.

→  introducing initiatives and providing advice on the control of hazards.

→  surveillance of employee health including assessing fitness to work and analyzing sickness/absence reports.

→  organizing first aid and emergency responses.

→  involvement with adaptation of work and working environment to the worker.

Changes away from large, labour-intensive manufacturing organizations towards more fragmented, technology-based industries have dramatically altered the nature of occupational health over the last few decades – in developed countries, at least. Boyd (2001) argues that health and safety (as a topic) occupies a somewhat rhetorical role in HRM literature. Boyd looked at HRM and the management of health and safety in the airline industry and found that airlines have adopted a short-term cost-cutting approach to both in response to increasingly competitive trading conditions. The focus has been on reducing operating costs, achieving immediate productivity gains and prioritizing profit over employee health and safety.

## STRESS

Stress is a commonly used word. It has been taken from physics where mechanical stress has been a long-standing concept. In its physical context it describes a strain leading to distortion of an object. For example, a steel girder may bend as the result of temporary forces such as strong winds acting against a bridge. Eventually, however, if the strain is long-lasting or excessive, the girder breaks. Psychological stress draws on the physical analogy but the strain on human beings is seen as coming from life's pressures, boredom, overwork,

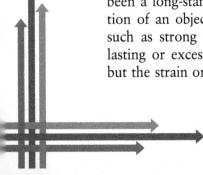

threat and ambiguity. In essence, pressure overcomes the ability to cope. The social readjustment rating scale shown in Table 7.1 gives an indication of the life events that individuals find most stressful.

Stress is a subjective experience: it is not necessarily easy to identify stress in another person. Neither is it clear that the experience is the same for different people. Indeed, it is apparent that similar situations will produce entirely different reactions in different

| Rank | Life event | Mean value |
|------|-----------|-----------|
| 1 | Death of partner | 100 |
| 2 | Divorce | 73 |
| 3 | Marital separation | 65 |
| 4 | Jail term | 63 |
| 5 | Death of close family member | 63 |
| 6 | Personal injury/illness | 53 |
| 7 | Marriage | 50 |
| 8 | Fired at work | 47 |
| 9 | Marital reconciliation | 45 |
| 10 | Retirement | 45 |
| 11 | Illness of family member | 44 |
| 12 | Pregnancy | 40 |
| 13 | Sex difficulties | 39 |
| 14 | Gain new family member | 39 |
| 15 | Business readjustment | 39 |
| 16 | Change in financial state | 38 |
| 17 | Death of close friend | 37 |
| 21 | Foreclosure of mortgage | 30 |
| 27 | Begin/end school | 26 |
| 32 | Change in residence | 20 |
| 41 | Holiday | 13 |

**TABLE 7.1**
Social readjustment rating scale (excerpt items)

Source: Adapted from Holmes and Rahe (1967).

**TABLE 7.2**
Symptoms of stress

Source: Adapted from
Arnold, Robertson and
Cooper (1991).

| Physical | Mental | Illnesses |
|---|---|---|
| *Appetite loss* | Irritability | Hypertension |
| *Craving under pressure* | Lack of interest in life | Coronary thrombosis |
| *Indigestion* | Unable to cope | Hay fever |
| *Fatigue* | Feeling a failure | Migraine |
| *Insomnia* | Self-dislike | Asthma |
| *Sweating* | Decisions hard | Colitis |
| *Headaches* | Hiding feelings | Dyspepsia |
| *Cramps* | Loss of humour | Skin disorders |
| *Nausea* | Dread of future | Diabetes |
| *Fainting* | Feeling ugly | Tuberculosis |
| *Frequent crying/ wanting to cry* | Unable to finish one task before going on to next | Menstrual difficulties |
| *Impotence* | Fear of open or enclosed spaces | Hyperthyroidism |
| *High blood pressure* | | Depression |

individuals. Table 7.2 shows the wide range of symptoms that have been linked with stress. Burnout is a related concept (see Key concept 7.2).

**KEY CONCEPT 7.2**  BURNOUT

This refers to a condition in which individuals are completely negative about themselves and their lives. It is associated with physical and mental fatigue. Sufferers feel worthless, disregarded, pessimistic about the future and lacking in control of their lives. This state has been described particularly in professionals such as nurses

Stressors include a long list of factors. Too much or too little work may both be stressful. De-layering, downsizing, rightsizing: changes in organization and job structure are rife in modern industry and are perceived as stressful by those who are made to change.

Where job numbers are slashed, the remaining workforce may be pressurized and also be concerned about the future of their own jobs. The 2:3:2 formula – half the people doing three times the work for twice the money – brings its own pressures.

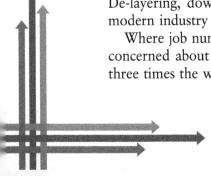

# HRM IN REALITY
## HEALTH EFFECTS OF WORK-RELATED STRESS AND SHIFT WORK

Research from the University of Michigan Medical School published in 2010 in the *American Journal of Gastroenterology* found that nurses working shift patterns, especially those rotating between day and night, had a significantly higher risk of developing irritable bowel syndrome (IBS) and abdominal pain than those permanently on daytime rotas.

Lead author Sandra Hoogerwerf, assistant professor of internal medicine said: 'We know that people participating in shift work often complain of gastrointestinal symptoms such as abdominal pain, constipation and diarrhea. These are the same symptoms as IBS.'

The researchers explain that IBS is the most common functional bowel disorder. It is not amenable to diagnostic testing but is identified by clinical symptoms such as recurrent episodes of abdominal pain or cramping associated with altered bowel habits.

The study recruited 399 nurses working three shift patterns: 214 on permanent day duty; 110 on permanent nights and 75 rotating between the two. More than 85 per cent were women. Researchers identified a higher prevalence of IBS and abdominal pain in participants working shifts, particularly those rotating between day and night. This finding was independent of reported sleep disturbances.

Sandra Hoogerwerf explained:

'We know the colon has its own biological clock and that's what increases the likelihood of having a bowel movement in the first six hours of the day. Shift work can cause chronic disruption of that biological rhythm, resulting in that clock to constantly be thrown off and needing to adjust, creating symptoms of diarrhea, bloating, constipation and abdominal pain and discomfort.'

The researchers suggest that patients with IBS should be alerted to the possible impact of their work schedule on their condition.

### Stress and coronary heart disease

Research from Université Laval's Faculty of Medicine published in the *Journal of the American Medical Association* in 2007 has demonstrated that chronic job strain after a first heart attack may double the risk of suffering a second one.

The researchers explain that previous studies had confirmed a relationship between work-related stress and a first coronary heart disease (CHD) event, but the few studies conducted on the association with recurrent CHD were limited in scope and inconsistent in their findings.

Researchers led by Chantal Brisson followed a group of 972 people aged 35 to 59 who had suffered a heart attack. They were interviewed at six weeks, two and six years after returning to work concerning their health, lifestyle, socio-demographic status, and degree of work stress. A job was defined as stressful 'if it combined high psychological demands (heavy workload, intense intellectual activity and important time constraints) and little control over decision-making (lack of autonomy, creativity and opportunities to use or develop skills)'.

The study found that 124 participants suffered a second heart attack and 82 experienced unstable angina. People reporting high levels of work stress at six weeks and two years were twice as likely to suffer another CHD event. Researchers found that the risk remained the same after allowing for variables such as severity of the first heart attack, other health conditions, family history, lifestyle, socio-demographic status, personality and other work-environment factors. They also found that job strain did not increase the probability of experiencing a second CHD event during the first two years.

Chantal Brisson commented: 'It makes sense on a biomedical level, since the pathological process at the source of the CHD requires some time before it can manifest itself.'

The researchers conclude that these findings should alert employers to the need to protect people from potentially harmful situations when they return to work after a heart attack.

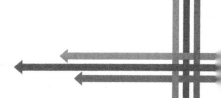

**Chantal Brisson said:**

Employers and occupational health service professionals must find ways to modify the psychological demands of a job or the level of control over decision-making for people returning to work after a heart attack. It can be done, and encouraging autonomy, creativity and the development of professional abilities in the workplace is not incompatible with a company's productivity.

*Source: Reprinted with permission from HRM Guide USA (http://www.hrmguide.com).*

The UK Health and Safety Executive (HSE) has published research showing that occupational groups reporting highest levels of work-related stress were teaching, nursing, management, professionals, other education and welfare (including social workers), road transport and security (including police and prison officers). In each of these groups at least one in five reported high stress (two in five among teachers). Full-time workers were more likely to report high stress than part-time employees.

High levels of stress were reported most frequently by people in managerial and technical occupations, those educated to degree level and those earning more than £20000. Non-white employees reported comparatively higher levels of stress than white workers but it is pointed out that the numbers involved were small. Little difference was reported in stress levels between male and female workers.

Alker and McHugh (2000) looked at the rationale used for introducing employee assistance or advisory programmes (EAPs) in UK organizations. They found that support was more likely to be given for organizational change than for more humanistic reasons. They offer the explanation that this is consistent with managers' work roles.

 ## SUMMARY

This chapter has focused on the relationship between forms of flexible working, the consequences on work-life balance and employee health and well-being in the workplace. Competitive pressure has placed extra burdens on employees, especially those with career aspirations. These burdens can cause health problems, particularly those that are stress-related. HR practitioners have at least a moral responsibility to deal with such matters and encourage the setting up of supportive mechanisms such as employee assistance programmes.

## FURTHER READING

1 *Flexible Working* by John Stredwick and Steve Ellis (CIPD, 2nd edition, 2005) covers the subject from policy to practice.

2 *How to Reduce Workplace Conflict and Stress: How Leaders and Their Employees Can Protect Their Sanity and Productivity from Tension and Turf Wars* by Anna Maravelas (Career Press, 2005) takes a practical but unconventional approach to workplace conflict.

3 *Work–life Balance For Dummies* by Jeni Mumford and Katherine Lockett (John Wiley and Sons, 2009) is a 'how-to' book.

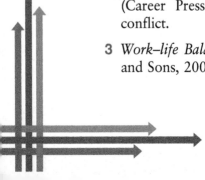

4 *Tolley's Health and Safety at Work Handbook*, (Tolley Publishing, 2011) discusses health and safety in the UK legal context.

 **REVIEW QUESTIONS**

1 What do you understand by 'flexibility'? Is total flexibility possible?

2 Distinguish between numerical and functional flexibility. How would demands for flexibility differ between organizations in the following sectors: (a) public service, e.g. local government; (b) production; (c) retailing; and (d) the hotel industry?

3 What is 'work–life balance' and how can it be achieved? Is total work–life balance an impossible goal?

4 Should human resource practitioners be involved with health and safety at work?

5 What is stress?

6 What can HR practitioners do to support stressed employees?

 **CASE STUDY FOR DISCUSSION AND ANALYSIS**

Read the following article. What roles should HR and line managers take in dealing with physical and verbal abuse?

## Almost a third of nurses experience abuse

Almost one-third of nurses who took part in a large-scale Tasmanian study reported that they had been subjected to both physical and verbal abuse in the previous four working weeks and a quarter had considered resigning as a result, according to research published in the UK-based *Journal of Advanced Nursing* (Farrell, Bobrowski and Bobrowski, 2006).

The survey was conducted by researchers from the University of Tasmania and was supported by the Australian Nursing Federation. Questionnaires were sent to the 6326 nurses registered with the Nursing Board of Tasmania in late 2002. Some 38 per cent completed the survey, but when this was adjusted for the number of registered nurses actually working during this period, the figure was nearer 55 per cent.

Some form of abuse in the previous four working weeks was reported by two-thirds of the 2407 nurses who took part. This ranged from being sworn at, slapped and spat upon, to being bitten, choked and stabbed. The abused nurses described an average of four verbal incidents and between two to three physical incidents during the period covered. Of nurses who had been physically abused, 69 per cent had been struck with a hand, fist or elbow and 34 per cent had been bitten. A further 49 per cent said they had been pushed or shoved, 48 per cent had been scratched and 38 per cent spat at. In addition, 6 per cent reported that they had been choked and just less than 1 per cent stabbed.

Verbal abuse was most likely to take the form of rudeness, shouting, sarcasm and swearing. However, 2 per cent said that their home or family had also been threatened. Patients and visitors were the most likely people to abuse nurses, but 4 per cent who reported physical abuse said that it was carried out by

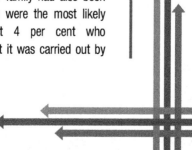

another nurse and 3 per cent by a doctor. Of those reporting verbal abuse, 29 per cent said that the perpetrator was a nurse colleague and 27 per cent a doctor.

Lead author Professor Gerald Farrell, now based at La Trobe University School of Nursing and Midwifery in Victoria, Australia said:

> The present findings point to a work environment that is both distressing and dangerous for staff. Eleven per cent of nurses told us that they had left a post because of aggression and 2 per cent had left nursing completely. Two-thirds of those who experienced aggression said that it affected their productivity or led to errors in their work. Ten per cent said it was the most distressing aspect of their work, after the 51 per cent who cited workload as the biggest problem.

Another key finding of this research was that although verbal and physical abuse spreads across every branch of healthcare from paediatrics to psychiatry and community services to critical care few staff made their complaints official.

The researchers believe that the restricted time frame of the study and the fact that aggression was carefully defined, with clear distinctions between verbal and physical abuse, may have captured a greater range of incidents than previous studies. The study concludes that workplace aggression is a worldwide problem and further research is needed to discover why levels are so high in modern healthcare settings.

Gerald Farrell continued:

> Our research shows that many nurses are working in environments in which they cannot provide the care that they think is best for patients. At the same time they have to contend with high levels of verbal and physical abuse. It's not surprising that some nurses have left the profession altogether and many more are thinking about it.
>
> "We live in an era when employers are constantly being told that they have a duty of care for employees. It's a sad reality that nurses who spend their lives caring for others and providing such a valuable service continue to feel so vulnerable in the workplace.

*Source: Reprinted with permission from HRM Guide Australia (http://www.hrmguide.net/australia/).*

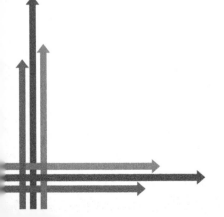

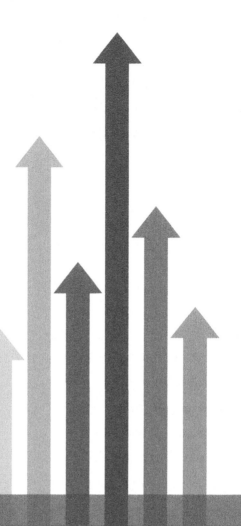

# PART THREE
# ORGANIZATIONAL HRM

This part of the book examines HRM within the organization. Human resource practices are enabled and constrained by a variety of organizational factors, including organizational size, structure, culture and employee commitment.

**The chapters in Part Three address a number of specific issues:**

→ **What are the different structures found within organizations and what effect do they have on human resource management practices?**

→ **Are there any significant differences between people management practices in small and large organizations?**

→ **What are entrepreneurs like as people managers?**

→ **How do organizations grow and what are the implications on HRM?**

→ **What is the relationship between corporate culture and human resource management?**

→ **What is employee engagement and how is commitment achieved?**

→ **Is employee branding a road to commitment or a method of brainwashing employees?**

→ **How do we manage professionals without losing their trust and commitment?**

# CHAPTER 8
## HRM and organizational structure

## LEARNING OBJECTIVES

The purpose of this chapter is to:

→ Investigate why organizations structure their people management systems in different ways.

→ Discuss research findings on human resource management in small and medium-sized businesses.

→ Determine the influence of organizational goals on the management of human resources.

→ Outline the advantages and disadvantages of alternative organizational structures.

→ Compare and contrast the work of human resource specialists in different forms of organization.

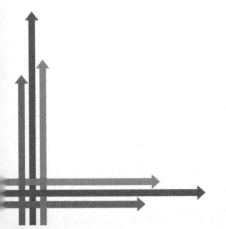

# INTRODUCTION

This is a world of organizations: more and more elements of life that were once matters of personal action are now integrated into organizational frameworks. Modern society depends on people working together effectively to solve problems and achieve objectives that are beyond the scope of individuals. It is a truism to say, therefore, that all people management takes place within organizations. But what are they? We talk about familiar corporations such as Google, the BBC and Apple as if they were objects. Yet we cannot see them in their totality. We recognize them as entities but they are also intangible: 'Although organizations are real in their consequences, both for their participants and for their environments, they are essentially abstractions. They cannot be picked up and dropped, felt, or fulfil any of the other tests that we apply to physical things' (Butler, 1991: 1).

The very idea of something, which everyone is aware of but no-one can fully grasp, is fascinating in itself. It has spawned an entire field of academic enquiry – organization theory. Whitley (2003: 483) states:

> From being a collection of rather uncoordinated research areas within sociology, psychology and other academic disciplines, the study of organizations became a distinct intellectual endeavour with its own journals, training programmes and teaching positions in major US universities in the 1960s and 1970s.

Initially it focused on formal structures, developing early work by Weber and others on the notion of 'bureaucracy', but the field has since diversified considerably. Where books on organization used to focus inwardly on structured – almost mechanical – management systems, seemingly ignoring environmental pressures, modern approaches are more likely to consider social networking, telecommunications and outsourcing as major features of business organization. Key concept 8.1 outlines some of the main characteristics identified by organization theorists. In this chapter we focus on how they can be understood in terms that have meaning for people managers.

---

### KEY CONCEPT 8.1  ORGANIZATIONS

Organizations are the means by which human and other resources are deployed so that work gets done. They can be defined by a number of characteristics:

→ They are social entities created by humans.

→ They have purpose expressed in the form of common goals.

→ They are unrestricted in range – from corner shops to multinational corporations.

→ Each organization has a boundary – but not necessarily a geographical or physical boundary – that leads to inclusion of some people and exclusion of others.

→ Within this boundary, people are patterned into a structure composed of formal and informal relationships.

---

First, we must recognize that the term 'organization' is wide-ranging: it can be used to describe bodies as disparate as Toyota and scout troops. For our purposes, the concept has to be defined more narrowly. The key lies with the nature of control within organizations

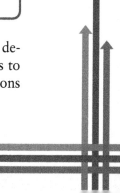

functioning on business lines, exercised through the employment relationship between staff and management and integration with internal and external parties. Business organizations such as Microsoft or News International are set apart from 'social arrangements' – for example lunch clubs or photographic societies – by a preoccupation with controlled performance (Huczynski and Buchanan, 2000: 10). They are set financial, service or production targets that determine the activities of their employees and external providers. People managers have a critical role in monitoring and controlling performance in order to achieve these targets. In the first part of this book we stressed that HRM is a 'holistic' approach to people management. To make the best use of an organization's human resources, it is necessary to manage not only its people but also its corporate structure and culture.

Organizations are highly complex, and not amenable to simple analysis, but managers must attempt to predict and control their activities in order to conduct business. Stewart (1993: 3) explains the value of theoretical understanding to practising managers:

> ... even the most practical managers can think about a problem more easily if they have some frame of reference that will help them to decide what kind of problem it is. ... Organizations are highly complex. We do not understand enough about how they work to have developed comprehensive theories. Instead we have a number of partial explanations which have been put forward by writers from different backgrounds. Each represents a different way of looking at organizations. An understanding of these different viewpoints can help managers to identify what kind of problem they are worrying about.

The formal allocation of people management responsibilities is fundamental to the process. Businesses vary considerably in this respect: small firms tend to incorporate people management within line or general management; larger organizations are likely to have specialist functional roles. We noted that these roles might have titles such as 'human resource manager', 'chief talent officer' or 'people manager'. These titles do not give much indication of the activities undertaken or the power vested in the jobs. In fact, they differ significantly from one firm to another. This chapter explains some of the major reasons for these variations. We begin by placing organizations in their environmental context: the competitive business world. We go on to discuss how and why organizations are formed and their implications for the nature of the people function.

## ORGANIZATIONS AND THE BUSINESS ENVIRONMENT

Competitive pressures on businesses and national economies have increased markedly in recent decades. As a consequence, the organizations that impact on our lives are constantly changing. Powerful entities have arisen at the international level – the European Union being a prime example – and multinational corporations increasingly dominate particular sectors such as cars and aerospace. New competitors are emerging and forcing older organizations to adapt and reform themselves in order to survive.

Like Russian dolls, most organizations are parts of larger entities with one business unit fitting within another, larger structure or network. They are the complex products of a world subject to the international division of labour, geographic rationalization, product differentiation and the revolution in business and personal communications brought about by the humble microchip. There is nothing unusual in a business section in Cork reporting to a Dublin-based department within the Irish operating division of the European subsidiary of a US multinational. Theoretically, this reporting may be instantaneous and seamless – it does not matter where in the world it takes place. For marketing purposes some firms deliberately obscure these relationships. Walking through a typical high street or shopping mall in

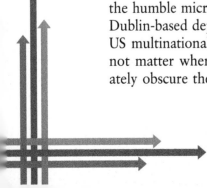

a developed country, we find an apparent diversity of retail traders. In fact, many are brand names controlled by just a few conglomerates.

In Part Two we saw that organizations also interact with their environment through the regulatory, economic and cultural framework in which they operate. Different levels and types of organization supervise, support and impede each other's operations with contradictory demands. External stakeholders such as governments, financiers, customers and shareholders exercise their influence through legislation, tax benefits, interest rates, consumer demand and the purchase and sale of shares.

Organizations reflect the values and norms of society, supplying products and services that meet the needs of the culture in which they function. They structure and manage themselves in ways that are acceptable to those societies. Inevitably, therefore, there are differences in the nature of organizations between one country and another with some more likely to adopt bureaucratic, hierarchical organizations while others tend towards flatter, less rigidly differentiated structures.

Different structures affect the way people are managed. HRM is intimately bound up with the way firms are organized. Businesses throughout the world require the same basic human resource activities: they recruit new employees; they develop and train their staff; they have reward systems; they have control and feedback mechanisms; and people must interrelate and make decisions (Brewster and Tyson, 1991: 9). But these issues are handled in different ways, reflecting the expectations and acceptable behaviour patterns within national business cultures. Similarly, employee values and attitudes are shaped to a considerable extent by people's native culture. Since national cultures are so pervasive they also strongly influence the cultures within organizations.

This chapter focuses on organizational structure but we must be aware that structures are partly determined by culture. People have strong feelings towards the organization in which they work. Tata, HSBC and Qantas are psychological entities to which employees react positively or negatively, a perspective that underpins the concept of employer branding. Internal stakeholders – employees, managers and owners – expect organizations to operate in an acceptable manner but the notion of acceptability is culturally determined and varies from one country to another. For example, Korean employees expect and accept more authoritarian management than their Japanese neighbours. Expectation and acceptability are important factors in determining the range of possible organizational structures that can operate successfully in a particular country.

To a considerable extent, therefore, environmental factors constrain the operations of commercial enterprises; but, conversely, businesses must control elements of the environment to ensure their own survival. Organizations are not passive – they can take a number of actions that increase their freedom in meeting environmental demands. Managers do so by devising strategies for survival and growth that can prove to be beneficial or counterproductive. They can influence public perception through advertising, or achieve competitive advantage by developing new products.

Equally, an organization's prospects can be improved by deploying its human resources in a novel and effective way, drawing on their competences and creativity. Throughout the world, the use of human resources is moving away from the employment of inflexible, full-time workers with expectations of lifelong careers in a single organization. Businesses can make strategic choices between a range of alternatives: part-timers, contingent workers, outsourcing, franchises and so on, as we shall see in our discussion of flexibility later in this chapter.

Some organizational strategies have been misguided. In the last few decades most large corporations have engaged in tumultuous restructurings, variously described as 'downsizing', 'rightsizing', 'de-layering' and 'focusing on core areas'. These dramatic disruptions were

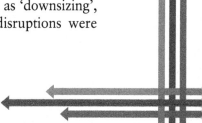

justified largely on financial grounds and were reactions to major changes in the economy. Often the consequences for employees – including those remaining – were negative. Older redundant workers had to accept early retirement. Others faced long periods of unemployment. Morale then slumped and stress increased amongst surviving employees who were expected to work harder in a climate of uncertainty.

In many organizations blind pursuit of cost-effectiveness destroyed the credibility of senior managers in the eyes of their staff, leading to a marked reduction in employee engagement and commitment. In this chapter we seek to pinpoint more positive approaches in the organization of people management.

## DIMENSIONS OF ORGANIZATION

How can we differentiate one organization from another? Large companies spend considerable amounts of money on developing strong images for themselves. Corporate logos, decoration schemes, uniforms, marketing literature and advertisements are all designed to create a favourable impression with customers and share analysts. But public image tells us little about an organization as an employer. In fact, it obscures the nature of people management.

From our perspective the first question to ask in any organization is: who manages the people? In Part One we noted that early HRM models placed the responsibility for people management with line managers. This is a debate in itself: should the management of people be part of the function of every manager in an organization; or does it demand an expertise which can be expected only from trained specialists? Opinions have changed markedly, due sometimes to fickle fashion and sometimes to the idiosyncratic opinions of senior managers. One view is that managing people is what business is all about and, therefore, every manager and supervisor should deal with the individuals within their area of responsibility. Conversely, it can be argued that the detailed aspects of people management such as resourcing and reward management are too complex for the average sales manager, accountant or engineer – untrained in the behavioural sciences – to handle satisfactorily.

In reality examples are found along the entire length of the dimension from specialist to non-specialist. The decision to manage people in a particular way depends on a number of factors, including the basic organizational dimensions we shall consider next: goals, size and structure.

### Organizational goals

According to Simon (1955: 30):

> Organizations are formed with the intention and design of accomplishing goals; and the people who work in organizations believe, at least part of the time, that they are striving towards these same goals. We must not lose sight of the fact that, however far organizations may depart from the traditional description … most behaviour in organizations is *intendedly rational behaviour.*

As we have seen, the rhetoric of HRM attaches great importance to strategy and the linking of employee performance to organizational goals (Key concept 8.2). What are these goals? They are expressions of a company's purpose and long-term objectives. Often written in the form of a mission or values statement, they give purpose or direction to an organization. They are intended to influence the behaviour of employees but few small companies have a written statement and many larger companies provide woolly verbiage without clear meaning. We will discuss mission statements in more detail later in this book when we consider HR strategy.

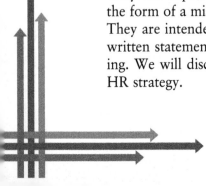

## KEY CONCEPT 8.2 ORGANIZATIONAL GOALS

The logical starting point for human resource management lies in an organization's goals – the reasons for its existence. Most modern businesses express these goals in the form of a mission statement. The allocation and control of human resources serves to assist or constrain the achievement of these objectives.

Taken at face value, mission statements appear to show that businesses have clear objectives. Traditionally, competitive market models portray the firm as a single decision unit engaged in maximizing profits. This approach ignores the possibility of conflict between owners, managers and employees. Organizations are political structures – usually surface unity is purely cosmetic. Organizations do not themselves have goals – their public objectives are those of some dominant person or group. Hidden behind the published goals of a business we find a series of conflicting agendas held by various individuals or work units. So, for example, the human resources section may have its own priorities, inconsistent with those of senior management. The HR department may be concerned with being 'professional', using the best selection techniques and careful job evaluation, whereas senior executives may be more concerned with short-term employee costs.

### Size

Organizations can range from single-person businesses to multinational corporations employing hundreds of thousands of people. Generally, the sophistication and importance of people management is greater in larger organizations. However, sophistication does not lead necessarily to effective people management. In small companies all management functions – including human resources – are dealt with by the owners. By 'professional' standards these activities – especially selection and training – often are inadequately handled, yet the quality of the employment relationship can be high. Owners and employees work on a down-to-earth, personal level. Some are genuine friends and there may be mutual trust and confidence. Conversely, larger organizations employ highly trained human resource practitioners using advanced selection, assessment and reward techniques. But size also brings problems in meeting the need for comprehensiveness, coherence, control and communication, resulting in the possibility of remote and conflict-ridden relationships between people at the top and bottom of the firm. Analysis of data from the UK 1998 Workplace Employee Relations Survey (WERS) shows that large workplaces (over 500 employees) are

**HRM IN REALITY** IMPRESSIVE TITLES ARE MORE THAN CHEAP REWARDS

More and more organizations are doling out impressive-sounding job titles, many including superlatives such as 'chief'. One reason is to stop key executives from leaving, according to Michael Jalbert, president of MRINetwork, a major search and recruitment organization. But titles such as chief marketing officer, chief innovation officer and chief risk officer also mark the extra responsibilities that CEOs are delegating to senior staff.

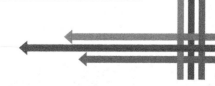

Michael Jalbert said:

> CEOs and presidents of companies realize that running a successful business requires an effective leadership team. Many top executives have more autonomy in the running of their departments than ever before. This results in a greater sense of ownership and fosters loyalty.

Jalbert considers that 'chief' titles are best used to signal strategically important issues in the organization. For example, banks often have a chief risk officer now to make sure that they are in compliance with laws governing accountability. And many businesses have a chief marketing officer to show the importance of customer acquisition. But organizations expect results in return for these titles.

'If the CMO can't deliver results fast enough – such as increase market share and improve brand awareness – they don't last long', said Jalbert.

Retaining top talent is a particular problem in organizations with flat structures. Inventing posts with prestige titles is one of the few options to keep employees happy in their careers. 'Some of the more creative "chief" titles cater to the desire of up-and-coming managers to possess titles that reflect what they do. This generation of workers is unimpressed with traditional titles and impatient to get ahead. They're also willing to change jobs to get what they want', he said.

But 'title creep' can be counterproductive. Jobs that do not deliver on impressive titles repel rather than retain talent. 'People can easily see through new titles that offer prestige in name only. If the job doesn't also bring added responsibility and recognition, employees can feel that they are being manipulated', said Jalbert, observing that the title 'vice president' has become so common that it is almost meaningless.

'Meaningful recognition within the organization is critical', said Jalbert. 'Mere titles won't suffice in the long term.'

### Celebrity CEOs

Executive titles, rewards and personal self-belief are intertwined. Mathew Hayward of the University of Colorado at Boulder and co-authors Violina Rindova and Timothy Pollock of the R.H. Smith School of Business at the University of Maryland at College Park published an intriguing paper 'Believing One's Own Press: The Causes and Consequences of CEO Celebrity', in the July 2004 issue of *Strategic Management Journal*. In this paper they pointed to the unhealthy relationship between CEOs' belief in themselves and the way they were written up in the media. They argued that executives should not believe their own press because it tended to become bad news for their organizations.

According to Mathew Hayward, who has since written a book on the same theme (*Ego Check: Why Executive Hubris is Wrecking Companies and Careers and How to Avoid the Trap*), journalists often create an inflated image of CEOs by attributing their organizations' positive performances solely to their CEOs' strategic actions.

The trouble begins, said Hayward, when they start to believe the hype.

'What you have is journalists affecting the outcome of how businesses are run by affecting the CEO', Hayward said. 'Once CEO celebrities are created, they tend to believe the hype and see themselves as invincible. I think this has greatly contributed to the CEO excesses we have seen over the past few years.'

The public are fascinated by celebrities and perhaps the media is just giving the public what it wants – more celebrities.

But Hayward says there's more to it than that:

> The public wants to believe that individuals are in control, so they happily accept these accounts as being true. When CEOs display idiosyncratic personal behaviour in public, it becomes easier for journalists to provide accounts that bolster attributions of the firm's action to its CEO. By and large this is very dysfunctional for the company, because when CEOs buy into their own celebrity, they will tend to want to have the company revolve around them. Most notably they will want to continue the behaviour and actions that got them on the magazine cover, which isn't necessarily good for the company.

*Why are job titles so important in an organization?*

*Source: Reprinted with permission from HRM Guide USA (http://www.hrmguide.com).*

five times more likely to have a HR specialist than workplaces with 25–49 employees (Cully *et al.*, 1999: 50). Similarly, titles including the words 'human resource' were more likely to be used in larger workplaces, although a greater proportion of personnel specialists in workplaces with fewer than 50 employees (40 per cent) were using such titles than in any other size group (Sisson, 2001). Also, the HR practices identified as 'high commitment or high performance' were more common in larger workplaces.

To make sense of size differentials, it is useful to divide business enterprises into three categories (Curran and Stanworth, 1988):

1 Small-to-medium enterprises (SMEs), further subdivided by the European Commission into: micro-enterprises, with less than ten employees; small enterprises, with 10–99 employees; and medium enterprises, employing 100–499 people.

2 Large commercial enterprises with over 500 people.

3 Organizations within the public or state sector. These continue to have distinctive characteristics despite government attempts to place them on a business-like footing.

## Cooperatives

The origins of this form of organization are lost in history. The first successful cooperative in North America was initiated by Benjamin Franklin in 1752. The Philadelphia Contributionship for the Insurance of Houses from Loss by Fire provided fire insurance for its members in Pennsylvania – and has continued to do so into the 21st century. In fact, the 'Contributionship' was the first mutual in the USA and is now the third oldest corporation in the country. But Benjamin Franklin probably copied a model of fire insurance pioneered in Britain in the 17th century.

Other ventures in the UK included a corn cooperative formed by workers in the Chatham and Woolwich areas of south London in the 18th century. Most significantly, the 19th century development of retail and wholesale cooperative societies pioneered in Rochdale in the north of England brought fair-priced groceries to the working classes. By the 1970s, however, the number of cooperatives in the UK had dwindled to around 20. Elsewhere, however, the concept took root throughout the world. According to the International Cooperative Alliance (http://www.coop.org) 800 million people are involved with cooperatives globally with 100 million being employed by them – 20 per cent more than multinational enterprises.

The work team became a fashionable obsession amongst human resource theorists and consultants in the 1990s. In the small cooperative the work team *is* the organization. This offers us an opportunity to examine the supposed benefits of teamworking in a relatively pure form. According to the International Cooperative Alliance, cooperative relationships are based on seven principles:

1 Voluntary and open membership.

2 Democratic member control, usually based on 'one-member, one-vote'.

3 Member economic participation, with 'surpluses' allocated to further investment or dividends.

4 Autonomy and independence.

5 Education, training and information for all participants and the general public.

6 Cooperation among cooperatives.

7 Concern for community.

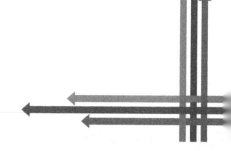

Cooperatives arise in three ways:

→ as new business start-ups, deliberately created in this fashion.

→ as buy-outs of existing factories or companies by the workforce.

→ as conversion of existing enterprises into cooperatives.

Of these, the first has been the most common. They tend to be providers of services, usually benefiting from the different skills of the participants, rather than manufacturers, although farming cooperatives have become common. Most start-ups of this nature have been established with groups of fewer than five people who feel that the cooperative relationship fits their social values and need to structure their own work. But some are larger – 30 cooperative organizations in the United States of America have an annual turnover of over 1 billion US dollars. However, there are many instances of cooperatives failing. An examination of such organizations can tell us a great deal about the advantages and disadvantages of the 'softer' aspects of HRM such as participative management, commitment and the functioning of self-organized teams. Table 8.1 summarizes the nature of people management in smaller cooperatives, using our familiar 10-C checklist for HRM.

Larger cooperatives such as mutuals and agricultural cooperatives may employ managers but ultimate power lies in the democratic voting system. Similar structures are found in legal and medical practices, where specialists are independent but obtain administrative support and accommodation from the practice in which they operate. Success in such a system requires much tolerance and goodwill. Many cooperatives have failed because of a lack of clear strategy and leadership; often the maintenance of a harmonious relationship has obscured the need for financial viability. However, some have expanded to a considerable size; for instance the John Lewis Partnership is a major retailing force in the UK and over 100 million Americans invest with mutuals and other cooperatives. But even large cooperatives face structural problems that impact on people management because of their size.

## Managerial structures

As organizations grow larger and technology becomes more complex, it becomes increasingly difficult to coordinate the people involved in an enterprise (see Key concept 8.3). Beyond a certain size it is impossible for one person to know what people are doing or even what their names are. It is necessary to introduce some form of managerial structure as a framework for control and coordination. Large businesses – including sizeable cooperatives – have to be organized in a deliberate, formal way, probably with groups of workers reporting to individual managers or supervisors.

**KEY CONCEPT 8.3** COORDINATION

Tasks divided among a group of individuals must be synchronized and integrated in some way so as to achieve the overall objectives of the group. Jobs must fit into a coherent flow of work. Coordination involves the distribution of decision-making. This can be formal, with rigid rules and regulations, or informal, giving freedom for local decisions. Coordination may be routine, because of structure and control mechanisms, including a performance management system or direct, by management action.

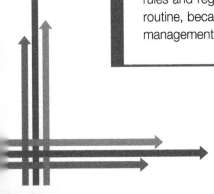

TABLE 8.1
HRM in cooperative
businesses

187

HRM and organizational structure

CHAPTER 8

| Principle | Range | Comment |
| --- | --- | --- |
| 1 *Comprehensiveness* | Cooperatives are uniquely focused on their working members | People systems such as resourcing and training are not necessarily sophisticated |
| 2 *Coherence* | Medium–good, depending on mutual understanding between members | Where specific aspects have not been discussed and agreed, members may 'do their own thing' |
| 3 *Control* | Generally decentralized | Assertive members can have undue influence |
| 4 *Communication* | Tends to be fairly good with shared and well-understood objectives | Generally open with intermittent conflict and possible political factions |
| 5 *Credibility* | Strategies have to be discussed and agreed (or accepted) by all | Management and staff are the same in smaller cooperatives |
| 6 *Commitment* | Belonging implies commitment | People vary and there are committed activists and less committed 'passengers' |
| 7 *Change* | May be slow because of the need for consensus agreement | A sensitive and highly political subject and may be the major cause of conflict |
| 8 *Competence* | Competent initially but needing to bring new partners in as requirements change | What happens to the partners whose skills are no longer appropriate? |
| 9 *Creativity* | Can be high | Where members are free to deal with own areas of work |
| 10 *Cost-effectiveness* | Depends on realism of the partners | Transparent and equitable as pay is agreed among members |

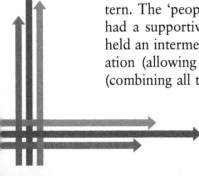

Along with a formal structure there is likely to be a clearer division between specialist functions, including that designated to look after aspects of people. Someone, at least, has to keep basic records. Typically HR managers are closely involved in the effective distribution of people and the development of management structures. The focus is on matching human resources to strategic objectives. Larger organizations display some degree of specialization, centralization and hierarchy (see Key concepts 8.4, 8.5 and 8.6). This applies to people management as much as to any other activity.

---

**KEY CONCEPT 8.4**  SPECIALIZATION

The division of work between individuals or departments, allocating responsibilities for specific activities or functions to people who can achieve a high standard of work in a relatively narrow range of activities. They may require specific training or expertise. For example, HR managers are concerned with organization of the HR function and resourcing of all other functions.

---

**KEY CONCEPT 8.5**  CENTRALIZATION–DECENTRALIZATION

This depends on where decisions are taken. The human resource function may be held within a separate headquarters department or devolved to local sections. Alternatively, it may be allocated to line managers, with an in-house 'consultancy' provided by specialists for procedures such as selection, development and performance measurement.

---

**KEY CONCEPT 8.6**  HIERARCHY

The structure by which individual responsibility and authority is divided in an organization, usually represented by a tree and branch chart and reflecting the perception of senior managers. 'Vertical complexity' is indicated by a tall or flat hierarchy. 'Taller' organizations tend to be bureaucratic but have clear lines of command. Each individual has one boss. 'Flatter' organizations are increasingly common. They demand more responsibility and self-control from staff, but decision-making and authority are less clear.

---

For a long time, large organizations were bureaucratic – typified by precise job titles, grading structures and segregated departmental activities. Status and responsibility were matched accordingly. We noted earlier that French organizations have continued to follow this pattern. The 'people function' was identified with the personnel department, which primarily had a supportive, maintenance role in a comparatively rigid framework. This department held an intermediate position – part of the 'glue' which held the balance between differentiation (allowing specialist tasks to be fulfilled by relatively expert people) and integration (combining all those tasks into a coordinated whole).

Nowadays organizations are structured more diversely and the people function has taken on a variety of forms. The diffusion of HRM ideas on the one hand and simple cost-cutting on the other have led to a move away from 'all-embracing' personnel departments in many companies, particularly in Scandinavia and the UK. Line managers have become more involved in activities such as selection, recruitment and performance appraisal. Typically, there is a division of work between various aspects of people management. Senior management may take responsibility for human resource strategy; line managers assume operational responsibility for their people; human resource specialists provide specific services ranging from administration to selection programmes and counselling.

In line with the fundamental HRM principles of comprehensiveness and coherence, the basic elements of people management must be interdependent. Supervision, recruitment and selection, training and development, reward systems and performance management cannot be considered in isolation. Each activity has implications for a number of other functions and subtly influences many more. Interactions throughout an organization's systems have to be assessed before making changes in any one function. The move away from permanent, nine-to-five jobs towards short-term contracts, part-timers and subcontracting offers a particular opportunity for human resource specialists with expertise in training, contracting and controlling workers in these categories.

Large organizations cannot be discussed as a homogeneous group. Their human resource and other management functions are dependent on the nature of their structures.

# ORGANIZATIONAL STRUCTURES

Organizations can be regarded as people management systems. They range from simple hierarchies along traditional lines to complex networks dependent on computer systems and telecommunications. Structures may be relatively formal, following strict reporting lines; alternatively, they may be based on informal working relationships. Structures are power and control systems which constrain or facilitate the freedom of employees to act and make decisions.

Chandler (1962) argued that structure follows on from strategy. Human resource managers can encourage strategies that foster both cost-effectiveness and employee commitment. Whether as line managers or specialist practitioners, they are able to use employee information and assessments to gauge the effectiveness of a particular structure. As managers they can influence or determine changes leading to improved employee performance and productivity. Organizational structures can be classified into a number of types, including functional, divisional, federations, matrix and networks.

## Functional structures

Early organizational design divided enterprises into relatively simple parts, splitting them into defined activities such as production, marketing or personnel. This is still a common structure in medium-sized companies but it has become unusual in large (particularly multinational) organizations. Such a design normally divides human resource management between specialized activities dealt with by a designated department (Figure 8.1) and day-to-day aspects handled by the operational functions.

As we can see from Table 8.2, there are both advantages and disadvantages to such an arrangement. On the one hand, functional organizations are simple to understand with clear lines of command, specified tasks and responsibilities. Staff can specialize in a particular business area such as production or marketing and follow well-defined career paths. This is equally true of human resource specialists who can develop expertise in specific areas such

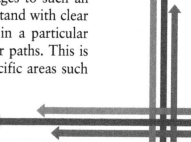

**FIGURE 8.1**
Functional
structures in HR

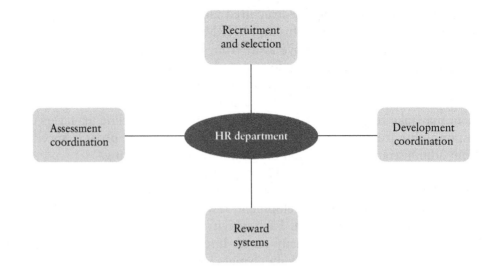

as employee relations or reward management. Table 8.3 details a number of specialist roles performed by human resource specialists in functional and other large organizations.

However, there are also major disadvantages to functional structures. People managers have to tread carefully because this form of organization is prone to interdepartmental conflict, often degenerating into 'them and us' tribal warfare. Coherence and good communication are particularly hard to achieve between virtually independent functions. Moreover, HR development is complicated as it is difficult for individuals to gain a broad range of experience and an overview of the organization as a whole. Additionally, functional organizations have a tendency towards rigidity and ever-increasing layers of management. Since the late 20th century, however, larger organizations of this type with tall and bureaucratic hierarchies have suffered the brunt of reorganization and de-layering. Restructuring is further considered in Chapter 12.

## Divisional structures

Divisions may be based on specific products or product ranges, as in the pharmaceutical industry, or alternatively on a territorial basis. Divisions encourage team spirit and identification with a product or region. Managers can develop broad skills as they have control of all basic functions. Performance of business units and their employees can be readily monitored because costs and productivity are tied to product or territory. This allows organizations to:

→  increase investment with certainty.

→  introduce new divisions for additional products.

→  dispose of ineffective or unwanted divisions without repercussions on the remainder.

Each division is likely to have a devolved human resource function. There is a risk, however, of duplicating activities between head office and divisional human resource departments and of conflict between staff in successful and unsuccessful divisions. The divisional level may be intermediate between corporate headquarters and individual business units. Consequently, the division plays a coordinating role, reconciling decisions taken at the corporate and business unit levels. This results in a complex picture of people management, outlined in Table 8.4.

The key issue for people managers is the relationship between division and corporate head office. A few large organizations do without HR specialists at this level but most assign

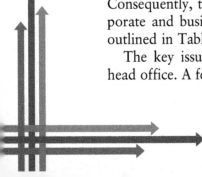

TABLE 8.2
HRM in functionally
structured
organizations

191

CHAPTER 8  HRM and organizational structure

| Role | Activity | |
|------|----------|---|
| 1 *Comprehensiveness* | Different functions are likely to be treated differently | Specific people systems such as resourcing and training may be sophisticated |
| 2 *Coherence* | Low–medium, as functional managers block or value different aspects, e.g. performance-related pay | Organization is divided into separate camps |
| 3 *Control* | Split between functions | Some functions are more powerful than others |
| 4 *Communication* | Good vertically within a function but dreadful horizontally between functions | Prone to 'us and them' misunderstanding and warfare between departments |
| 5 *Credibility* | Promotion and reward policies not understood if they do not fit functional needs | Parochial view restricts comprehension of overall business objectives |
| 6 *Commitment* | Focused on functional department, not whole organization | People march in different directions |
| 7 *Change* | Structural change regarded as threatening | Managers fight to preserve departmental power |
| 8 *Competence* | High at functional and individual levels | Limitations on developing generalists with all-round abilities |
| 9 *Creativity* | Limited | Little cross-fertilization between functions |
| 10 *Cost-effectiveness* | Can be good if management kept to minimal levels | Specialist managers expect professional rates: jealousy between functions. |

**TABLE 8.3**
Specialist HR roles in large organizations

| Role | Activity |
|------|----------|
| *Chief human resource officer* | Human resource director/manager. Head of specialist people management function |
| *Personnel administrator* | Formerly a clerical function concerned with maintaining paper records. Latterly requires expertise in creating and developing computer databases of human resource information |
| *Employee relations manager* | A long-standing specialist role with responsibility for collective bargaining and liaison with trade union officials. Now extends to employee involvement and communication |
| *Recruitment specialist* | Less common than previously. Trained in interviewing techniques and psychometric testing. May be occupational psychologist in larger organizations. This activity is often outsourced to specialist firms |
| *Training and development specialist* | Previously concerned with direct training. Now becoming an internal consultancy role. Often possessing a psychology qualification |
| *Human resource planner* | Statistical and planning expert providing projections of human resource requirements for strategists |
| *Employee counsellor* | Comparatively new but increasingly common role. May be part-time or outsourced. Requires counselling qualification and knowledge of stress reduction techniques. Typically replaces the welfare role of personnel management |
| *Health and safety officer* | Ensures that legislation on workplace health and safety is complied with. Liaises with local authority and other enforcement officials |

a role, usually of a policy nature, to the centre. Hence central HR departments in companies such as Ford, Barclays and Sainsbury are comparatively large. This makes sense where the activities in different locations or divisions are closely related. In practice, the more diversified and unrelated the divisions, the more likely it becomes that HRM is fully devolved to divisional level. In very diverse conglomerates, even senior managers are recruited and developed locally.

## Federations

One variant of the divisional form, which has a particular relevance because of its human resource implications, is the 'federation', a loosely connected arrangement of businesses with a single holding company or separate firms in alliance. For example, a decade ago the

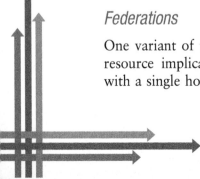

| Principle | Range | Comment |
|---|---|---|
| 1 *Comprehensiveness* | Successful and unsuccessful divisions are likely to be treated differently | Centrally provided people systems such as performance management may be sophisticated |
| 2 *Coherence* | Corporate HR strategies may be neutralized at divisional level | Divisional people managers behave independently |
| 3 *Control* | Divided between divisions and head office | Scope for conflict and confusion |
| 4 *Communication* | Can be good within divisions but more problematic between divisions and head office, and poor between divisions | Prone to resentments and misunderstandings between head office and divisions |
| 5 *Credibility* | Corporate HR strategies not understood if they do not fit divisional needs | Parochial view restricts comprehension of overall business objectives |
| 6 *Commitment* | Focused on division – not whole organization | Divisions quasi-independent |
| 7 *Change* | Emphasis on acquisition and de-merger | Managers fight to preserve integrity of division |
| 8 *Competence* | High at functional and individual levels | Limitations on developing generalists with all-round abilities |
| 9 *Creativity* | Scope for considerable creativity in suitable divisions | Small firm climate encourages cooperation between functions |
| 10 *Cost-effectiveness* | Tendency for managerial/administrative jobs to be duplicated | Little consistency between divisions |

Cable & Wireless group functioned as a worldwide federation of equals with a small corporate centre. HRM operated on a partly formal, partly informal basis. The central human resource function offered an extensive support facility for international managers. This form of organization attracted criticism from stock market analysts who found difficulty in comprehending its subtle informality.

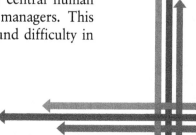

## Matrix structures

As we have seen, both functional and divisional forms suffer from the 'them and us' problem between different parts of the organization. A number of large businesses have experimented with matrix structures to try and overcome these difficulties. Matrix structures focus on project teams, bringing skilled individuals together from different parts of the organization. Individuals are responsible to their line manager and to the project manager for different aspects of their jobs.

Their effectiveness is dependent not only on the provision of skilled people but also clear information on location and activities. This is difficult to achieve and many matrix experiments have resulted in failure, largely due to the 'matrix muddle': a general confusion of roles and responsibilities. Some activities may be duplicated because no-one understands the structure, and others may be neglected because it is assumed that someone else is responsible. Some of these difficulties have been overcome in more recent 'network' structures.

## New structures

Older accounts of people management within organizations propose a highly structured, directive role for managers. This kind of management style and the rigid organizational context which it requires are inconsistent with the 'tight–loose' frameworks advocated by gurus such as Peters and Kanter. They propose new relationships which offer the flexibility to respond quickly to changing market demands but also allow retention of effective managerial control. Such organizations require a fine balance between centralization and decentralization. The key lies in organization design (see Key concept 8.7).

### KEY CONCEPT 8.7  ORGANIZATION DESIGN

The design of an organization patterns its formal structure and culture. It allocates purpose and power to departments and individuals. It lays down guidelines for authoritarian or participative management by its rigidity or flexibility, its hierarchical or non-hierarchical structure. Appropriate design is crucial to effective use of resources and long-term success and survival.

In recent years the emphasis has been towards differentiated but integrated organizations. This paradoxical view stresses that individuals work for the business rather than for specific departments which might compete rather than cooperate with each other. Communication and information distribution systems in earlier days were based on paper memos and reports. Paper-based systems could only work if functional activities were broken down into defined, quasi-independent sections.

Today, developments in telecommunications and computing allow raw or analyzed data to be collected electronically and distributed to any point in the organization. This makes it easier for an organization to be managed as a whole. As we have seen, such an organization is likely to be slimmed-down, de-layered and focused on core activities. Non-core functions, including HR activities such as recruitment and training, can be outsourced. Integrated information technology allows previously unimagined control mechanisms and organizational forms. The boundaries between organizations become increasingly blurred and the nature of

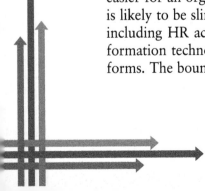

people management takes on a new and complex level of intricacy. For example, we can ask how we manage 'employees' who have no employment contract with our own organization?

Managers, including human resource specialists and others, must play a new role. They cease to be checkers and order-givers. Instead they are more likely to become:

→ enablers, structuring organizations to allow employees to achieve objectives.

→ empowerers, devolving decision-making to the lowest level.

→ facilitators encouraging and assisting employees.

In such a context, people managers are no longer supervisors. Their organizations move from rigid hierarchies and power distinctions towards an environment where people take responsibility for their own work. Various forms of integrated structure are technically and ideologically feasible within relatively loose arrangements that encompass different organizations, agencies and specialist contractors.

## Networks

In the context of organizational design, networks extend firms beyond their own boundaries. Focused organizations concentrate on core activities – those areas in which they believe they have particular strengths. Other functions are provided by subcontractors, which may be different business units within the firm or entirely independent providers. For example, one organization manufactures and sells its products but purchases its research, design and computing functions from other firms within the network. Snow, Miles and Coleman (1992) distinguish a number of network types:

*Internal networks.* Composed of business units, mostly owned by the parent organization, each specializing in one function. These units network with other internal units and also interact with external suppliers and customers. This is a development of the divisional system.

*Stable networks.* Basically working to the core-periphery model of flexibility which we will consider later in this chapter. A small core of professional and managerial staff subcontracts most of its activities to external providers. Television stations frequently work on this basis.

*Dynamic networks.* A further extension where the core acts as a broker for independent suppliers, producers and distributors.

In general, networking takes some familiar producer–wholesaler–distributor concepts, extends them into new industrial sectors and binds them into a seamless structure with no visible boundaries between individual parts of the network.

Human resource management takes on issues in networked structures that are outside the familiar boundaries of the employee–employer relationship. Traditional personnel management is replaced by operational managers with strengths in people management – true 'human resource managers'. People managers in networked structures are diplomats, encouragers and resource-allocators. Table 8.5 outlines the main characteristics of HRM in network structures.

## Virtual organizations

Advancing technology allows firms to extend the network concept to form enterprises with no permanent structures. These **virtual organizations** bring people together for specific

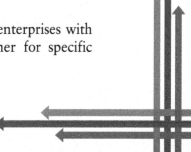

## HRM IN REALITY WORKING REMOTELY ALLEVIATES MORE STRESS THAN IT CREATES

Employees who spend most of their working week as telecommuters have greater job satisfaction than people who are primarily office workers, according to a study from the University of Wisconsin-Milwaukee (UWM).

Kathryn Fonner compared the advantages and disadvantages of the two work arrangements and found the main benefit of teleworking for at least three days a week to be decreased work–life conflict. While poor workplace communication is often cited as the biggest disadvantage of telework, respondents reported this as being of minimal importance and, although they exchanged information with others less frequently than office-based workers, they reported similar timely access to important work-related information.

According to Kathryn Fonner the results of the study suggest multiple reasons why high job satisfaction and teleworking are linked. Specifically, remote working tends to shield employees from distracting and stressful aspects of the workplace, including office politics, interruptions, endless meetings and information overload.

'Our findings emphasize the advantages of restricted face-to-face interaction, and also highlight the need for organizations to identify and address the problematic and unsatisfying issues inherent in collocated work environments', said Fonner. 'With lower stress and fewer distractions, employees can prevent work from seeping into their personal lives.'

Kathryn Fonner added that, as well as introducing teleworking, organizations can consider a number of other strategies to increase job satisfaction including:

→ Limiting meetings and mass emails.

→ Streamlining communication by creating an accessible repository of information.

→ Designating times and spaces for office-based employees to work uninterrupted.

→ Creating a supportive climate where employees can register concerns without fear of retaliation

→ Encouraging employees to disconnect themselves from work communication when their day is finished.

*The study is reported in the November 2010 issue of the Journal of Applied Communication Research.*

### Who telecommutes?

Rising oil prices have resulted in many professionals considering telecommuting as an economical work option, but spending too much time working from home can mean saying goodbye to promotion prospects.

Surveys developed by OfficeTeam, a leading staffing service specializing in placement of administrative professionals, were conducted by an independent research firm in 2006 and included responses from 100 senior executives in Canada and 150 in the USA.

They found 32 per cent of Canadian respondents and 43 per cent of US respondents said telecommuting was best suited for staff-level employees, compared with 28 per cent and 18 per cent respectively who felt telecommuting was most beneficial for managers.

In addition, more than half of Canadian respondents and more than two-thirds of US respondents said senior executives at their firms rarely or never telecommute.

When asked, 'At which level do you think telecommuting programmes are most beneficial?' participants responded:

| Level | Canada (%) | USA (%) |
|---|---|---|
| Staff | 32 | 43 |
| Manager | 28 | 18 |
| Executive | 16 | 14 |
| Administrative support | 15 | 11 |
| Don't know/no answer | 9 | 14 |

When asked, 'Overall, how frequently do senior executives at your firm telecommute?' participants responded:

| Frequency | Canada (%) | USA (%) |
|---|---|---|
| Very frequently | 18 | 5 |
| Somewhat frequently | 21 | 23 |
| Rarely | 38 | 55 |
| Never | 20 | 12 |
| Don't know/no answer | 3 | 5 |

According to Diane Domeyer, executive director of OfficeTeam, it is often easier for staff-level employees to telecommute because their work can be performed autonomously. However, even those people who work from home need to spend time in the office. Diane Domeyer added:

> Effective management requires plenty of 'face time' with employees. Supervisors should have an open-door policy, and that means being available to staff who need guidance with projects. Employees who work from home must ensure that being out of sight doesn't also mean being out of mind for promotions, team projects and plum assignments.

*What jobs are unsuitable for teleworking?*

*Source: Reprinted with permission from HRM Guide USA (http://www.hrmguide.com/).*

projects. Teams dissolve on completion, to reappear in new combinations for other tasks. The network is composed of expert nodes. These are people who add value through their knowledge. Traditional hierarchical structures have no role in this model. Departments, divisions and offices disappear leaving an amorphous mass of people connected electronically and meeting only when required. Through web-based technology and teleworking, there is scope for considerable change in the nature of work.

## ORGANIZATIONAL STRATEGIES

If the purpose of organizations is to coordinate people's activities to achieve certain objectives, why do they go about it in such different ways and why are some organizations spectacularly poor at achieving their goals? A partial explanation comes from organizational design. This may be strategic or unplanned. Some organizations have come into being almost through accidents of history. Perhaps they started as small enterprises with individuals taking on regular or specialist roles, looking after stock, keeping financial records, going out to meet customers and so on. As the business expanded individual jobs grew into departments, following the same division of work; eventually, the original job-holders moved on but their functions remained to be done by other people. A mature organization is still shaped according to the skills and personalities of people who are no longer there.

Other organizations are designed in a particular way from their inception. Government departments may be set up to achieve a particular social purpose. Their objectives, form and operation will be determined by conscious thought. To some degree, organizing (patterning) of all enterprises is deliberate. Even the 'accidental organization' will be remodelled and reshaped at some time.

Some enterprises contain the remnants of a succession of reorganizations. Most large organizations are diversified. They operate in different product areas. In the free market model prevalent in English-speaking countries, this has happened mainly by acquisition of

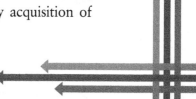

**TABLE 8.5**
HRM in networked
organizations

| Principle | Range | Comment |
|---|---|---|
| 1 *Comprehensiveness* | Dependent on design of organizational structure – is it formalized or *ad hoc*? | Flexibility of the organization allows expertise to be bought in for any need |
| 2 *Coherence* | Amorphous nature of organization can lead to incoherence | Reward, performance and development systems apply to some, but not to others |
| 3 *Control* | Project or customer-driven | Dependent on software systems |
| 4 *Communication* | Tends to consist of informal connections forged to solve problems and achieve task goals | Self-managed and problem-solving approach leads to direct communication |
| 5 *Credibility* | Evident that organization is there to meet project or customer needs | Emphasis on performance gives high credibility to the network |
| 6 *Commitment* | Focused on project, not whole organization | No long-term commitment to the organization required |
| 7 *Change* | Organization changes continuously | Structure and processes driven by customer needs |
| 8 *Competence* | Focus on skilled knowledge workers | Dependent on identification and availability of most suitable people |
| 9 *Creativity* | Emphasis on people devising their own approach to work | Freedom for creativity comes from self-management |
| 10 *Cost-effectiveness* | Theoretically, human resources are perfectly matched to work | Minimal supervision requirement |

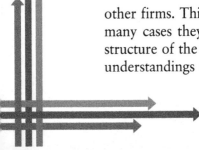

other firms. This has a number of implications for the overall organization of such firms. In many cases they will display 'hybrid' characteristics, preserving much of the character and structure of the original businesses. Such organizations are prone to inconsistencies and misunderstandings on people management issues (Table 8.6).

TABLE 8.6
Summary of
organizational
structures

199

CHAPTER 8   HRM and organizational structure

| Type | Focus | Benefits | Disadvantages |
|------|-------|----------|---------------|
| *Functional* | Department, e.g. sales, accounts, personnel | Simple to understand. Clear lines of command Specialist expertise Career structures | Slow to react. 'Us and them' Hierarchies tend to grow into vast pyramids Managers have difficulty in gaining organization-wide perspective |
| *Divisional* | Product or market, e.g. pharmaceuticals | Self-contained units Can be evaluated separately | Conflict between divisional and organizational objectives |
| | Geographical territory, e.g. brewing region | Can be added to, closed or sold as wholes Team-based, loyalty to division and product Managers obtain overall experience | Morale difficulties in unsuccessful divisions Duplication of functional activities, e.g. marketing, human resources |
| *Federations* | Loose relationship | Informal, flexible | Disliked by stock exchange commentators |
| *Matrix* | Project or team | Strong focus on project, client objectives | Complex. Conflict between reporting lines. Conflict over allocation of resources |
| *Networks* | Nodes. Individuals as resources | Talents focused on task. Seamless organization – no departmental boundaries. Open to external contributors | No job security. Potentially anarchic |

# HRM PRACTICES IN THE SMALL BUSINESS

Defining the role of HRM in small organizations is problematic because of the limited research findings available. Serious appreciation of HRM in small to medium-sized enterprises

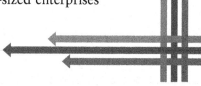

(SMEs) is a comparatively recent phenomenon. HRM researchers have largely ignored the SME sector, preferring to concentrate on large organizations with recognizable HR systems. The complexity and wide-ranging sizes and structures of SMEs is ignored and 'management training and advice to SMEs is based largely on textbook prescriptions that require the adoption of formal management procedures more suited to large firms' (Kotey and Slade, 2005: 16). Yet the SME sector is an important aspect of any country's economy, already employing large numbers of people and embodying future growth potential. The information available on people management in these organizations, however, is sparse. Researchers attempting to investigate the topic have found access difficult, largely because small business owners are often busy entrepreneurs and perhaps regard academics with some suspicion. Smaller companies should be fruitful subjects for study because many conduct people management in the direct fashion advocated by HRM models (Table 8.7) and are typified by:

*Centralized control.* A spider's web, with the owner at the centre. Limited financial and organizational resources ensure that people management is a non-specialist activity. The small business tends to be direct and informal. The character of the principal determines the climate, the morale of the workforce and whether it is a friendly or unfriendly place to work. Employees have poorly defined responsibilities and little authority. The principal normally controls all major functions. Job tasks, pay rates and benefits are negotiated with the owner. The boss hires and fires, determines pay and conditions and requires considerable flexibility from the workers (see Figure 8.2).

*Strategy.* There is little forward planning. Decisions are taken when problems are encountered. Staff development and training are often neglected. Succession and career planning are rare. Performance assessment is rudimentary and arbitrary.

*Fire-fighting or crisis management.* Employees are expected to be totally flexible, prepared to work long or irregular hours. They must perform a variety of tasks without necessarily having appropriate skills or training.

*People function.* Companies with fewer than 50 employees are unlikely to have an identified human resource function.

Wilkinson (2000) provides an analysis of responses to questions about the practice of HRM in the 1997 CBR survey of 2520 small and medium-sized, independent, manufacturing and business service firms. This revealed that: 35 per cent of respondents used job rotation/multi-skilling; 31.9 per cent used performance-related pay; 29.6 per cent used total quality management; and 13.1 per cent used quality circles. Grouping the last two procedures together as 'quality management', 39 per cent of firms used none of these categories, 30 per cent used one only, 23 per cent used two and just 9 per cent used all three.

Firms that used HRM-type procedures were more growth-oriented than those that did not. But these companies also saw the greatest obstacles to growth, identifying shortages of skilled labour and marketing, sales and management skills as significant constraints. HRM-users rated these limitations 10 per cent higher in significance than non-users. The most marked difference was between firms that used performance-related pay and those that did not.

According to Wilkinson (2000: 9):

The positive associations between the growth and related business objectives, and HRM, and between HRM and non-price competitive strategies, are not difficult to explain. Firms looking to grow, expand their market share and increase the return on assets in highly competitive conditions, can be expected to adopt non-price competitive policies, and to support these by HRM strategies geared to: involving employees more in reducing costs, improving quality and productive performance; increasing their skill and flexibility to make this possible; and linking their pay to performance to reward their effort. In this sense, product market and HRM strategies are complementary and proactive means of securing the firms' objectives in a hard competitive environment.

| Principle | Range | Comment |
|-----------|-------|---------|
| 1 *Comprehensiveness* | All people management handled by owner/small executive team | Tends to the extreme: comprehensively good, or totally ineffective |
| 2 *Coherence* | Dependent on owner's personality | May be haphazard and idiosyncratic |
| 3 *Control* | Often completely centralized | Can be either autocratic or 'clubby' |
| 4 *Communication* | Highly variable: objectives may be a mystery to staff | Dependent on owner: often an open culture with direct communication |
| 5 *Credibility* | Highly variable: employees tend to develop a fixed opinion of the owner | Owner's personality is visible to all |
| 6 *Commitment* | Can be exciting and challenging for people of the right type | People who relate to the owner will stay – others will quickly leave |
| 7 *Change* | Varies between static and growth businesses | Change usually reactive rather than strategic |
| 8 *Competence* | Dangerously dependent on the abilities and knowledge of the owner and core staff | Often erratic and personalised resourcing: 'development' unsystematic and restricted to the chosen few |
| 9 *Creativity* | Most SMEs do the same as their competitors: the few exceptions are destined for success | Creative owners generally make use of their own ideas |
| 10 *Cost-effectiveness* | Often run on a shoe-string: minimal staffing and low pay | Most owners do not reward themselves and their staff on the same criteria |

HRM-using firms were found to be dedicating a greater proportion of total employee costs to formal training than non-HRM-using firms. In fact, roughly twice as many firms using quality management procedures had formal training than did companies not using quality management. HRM-using companies were also more innovative than non-users, citing an

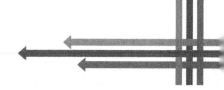

**FIGURE 8.2**

HRM in the
small firm

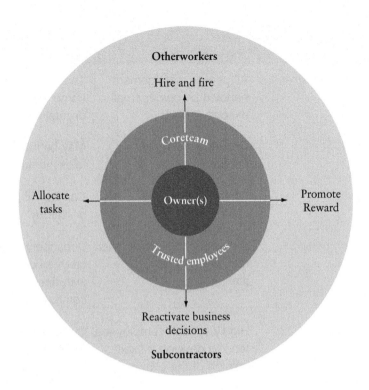

extension of their product range, improving product quality and gaining market share as the main reasons for innovation.

A further means of improving performance is to network with other companies. A third of the firms surveyed had some form of formal, informal or partnership arrangements with other businesses. Most commonly these were suppliers, customers or other companies in the same business sector. A few SMEs had developed links with colleges or universities. The reasons given by firms involved in some form of external collaboration were to: expand the range of expertise (75 per cent); assist in development of specialist services or services required by customers (70 per cent); provide access to UK markets (54 per cent); and provide access to overseas markets (45 per cent).

HRM-using businesses were significantly more like to collaborate with other firms than non-users. HRM-using firms were also more likely to use services or advice from outside agencies, contractors and consultants. Another striking finding was that companies that used 'bundles' of HRM practices fared better than those using a more restricted range. Firms that used all three HRM practices did better than those that used none by the following percentages: innovation (+80 per cent), exporting (+124 per cent) and increased employment (77 per cent).

Kotey and Slade (2005) reported on a survey of 371 micro, small and medium-sized firms on the Sunshine Coast of Queensland, Australia. They found that the adoption of formal HR practices increased with organizational size but there was a substantial move towards formal HRM quite early in the growth process. Some of the major trends that occurred with growth were:

→ Use of a greater range of recruitment sources such as newspapers and government agencies and a wider range of selection techniques. However, these were used more extensively at the operational level in micro and small firms, with the recruitment process

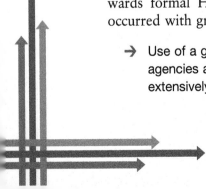

for managers lagging behind in terms of sophistication. This tended to be corrected in medium-sized firms. Word-of-mouth recommendations prevailed in the smaller firms but this approach did not produce applicants with the levels of skill required by medium-sized firms.

→ On-the-job training prevails in all SMEs but other training methods were used as firms grew in size. Delegation of training to supervisors and middle-managers increased in larger SMEs but, even there, more on-the-job training came from owner-managers than delegated staff. External training for operational staff decreased as firms grew, presumably because of better in-house training capabilities, but external training for managers increased. Medium-sized firms became more formal in their training procedures. For example, orientation was check-listed in half the firms of that size surveyed.

→ While micro firms could monitor employee performance on an observational basis, increasing size required some degree of formal appraisal. Small and medium-sized firms did this extensively for operational staff but formal appraisal of managers tended to be restricted to medium-sized businesses. Rating scales were the most common method for operational staff.

→ HR policies and documentation appeared very early in the growth process, reflecting legislative requirements, for example on health and safety, and the need for individual records and control as the number of staff grew beyond the point where the owner-manager knew all the employees. While application forms were extensively used, job descriptions were not always provided in small and medium-sized firms, reflecting the inherent flexibility of employment in SMEs.

## THE HR ROLE IN LARGE ORGANIZATIONS

People management functions are themselves affected by organizational strategies. Moves to restructure large organizations and reduce the number of managers have affected HR specialists as much as anyone else. The activities of the HR function have been 'balkanized' or parcelled-up into discrete areas (Sisson, 1995: 96), mirroring 'developments in management more generally' (Sisson, 2001: 78).

HRM may be organized in a number of ways (Adams, 1991):

→ Traditional 'personnel'-type departments providing a full range of HR services.

→ In-house agencies, or cost centres, performing one or more activities such as recruitment. Their costs are automatically charged to client divisions or departments.

→ Internal consultancies that 'sell' their activities to other parts of the organization, perhaps in competition with external services.

→ Business-within-a-business arrangements that provide both internal and external services to clients inside and outside the organization.

→ Outsourcing, sub-contracting HR activities to external agencies.

By the late 1990s, based on the UK 1998 WERS data, Millward, Forth and Bryson (2000: 80) could state: 'One of the most significant changes is that the people responsible for managing employee relations in 1998 were quite different from those who were managing it at the beginning of the 1980s.' Specifically, responsibility for HRM had shifted away from general managers to HR specialists and line managers and HR specialists were better qualified.

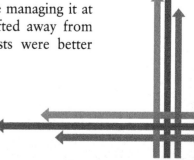

Turning the developments of recent decades on their head, Coggburn (2005) examined views on the possible merits of centralizing HR in Texas, a US state where public HR functions had always been decentralized. Traditional justifications for centralized HR included:

→ Employees were afforded better protection from political coercion.

→ Standardization of HR processes led to more equitable conditions (such as equal pay for equal work).

→ Consistency of HR service delivery.

→ Efficiency gains because of economy of scale.

→ More professional HR service leading to better employee selection and assessment.

In practice, however, a centralized HR function can be perceived as being:

→ Too rigid, more interested in enforcing rules than in responding to individual HR needs.

→ Slow, with time-consuming procedures, losing some of the best applicants because of the time taken to process the paperwork.

→ Complex, with labyrinthine grievance procedures that make it impossible to sack poorly performing employees.

Conversely, Coggburn argues, today's orthodox thinking is that decentralized HR has the benefit of speed, local discretion and autonomy, and, therefore is more efficient, effective and responsive. Moreover, it is more appropriate for modern, flexible working arrangements. Coggburn asserts that, ironically, efforts to outsource the HR function to a single outside provider will lead to a new version of centralization.

 **SUMMARY**

Organizations are taking increasingly divergent forms but the key dimensions of size and structure still constrain the people function. HRM is conducted in a variety of ways, partly due to these constraints but also because of strategic decisions taken to meet organizational goals. Businesses can choose to vary their structures and their people management systems for a number of reasons. Increasingly, flexibility is required from employees and managers to meet new circumstances. Centralized personnel departments have been largely replaced with more specialized units, some of which may be outsourced. Nevertheless there are opportunities for human resource specialists dealing with complex issues arising from new organizational structures and flexible working patterns. These include contract arrangements, selection, control, assessment and training.

 **FURTHER READING**

The literature on large organizations is vast.

1 *Organization Theory and Design* by Richard L. Daft, Jonathan Murphy and Hugh Willmott (Cengage Learning, 2010) is a leader in its field.

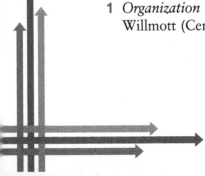

2 *Organization Theory: Modern, Symbolic, and Postmodern Perspectives* by Mary Jo Hatch (Oxford University Press, 2006) provides a good overview of organizational theory.

3 *Organizational Theory, Design and Change* 6th edition by Gareth R. Jones (Pearson, 2009) takes organizational change as its centrepiece.

4 *Understanding Organizations* by Charles Handy, Oxford University Press, 4th edition (1993) remains the most user-friendly introduction.

 **REVIEW QUESTIONS**

1 What are the principal dimensions by which organizations vary? What are the implications for the management of their human resources?

2 How would the management of people differ between small and large organizations?

3 How does the size of a small business limit the practice of human resource management? What difficulties are human resource specialists likely to experience in dealing with a founding entrepreneur as a business grows?

4 Few small companies become major corporations. In terms of people management, why do you think this is so?

5 What is 'micro-management' and what is its significance to a growing business?

6 How can knowledge about effective people management aboard a ship be regarded as relevant to small business management?

7 Is it the case that: (a) firms using HRM procedures benefit because of those procedures? Or (b) firms that are forward-looking and growing are more likely to use HRM procedures because they are forward-looking and growing?

8 What are the major differences between the following types of organization: (a) functional structures; (b) divisional structures; and (c) networked organizations? How is people management likely to be organized in each of these? What priorities and constraints will human resource specialists experience within each type of structure?

9 What HRM issues might be problematic for larger cooperatives?

10 Discuss the consequences of advances in information technology on business organization and the work of employees. In what ways would the activities of human resource specialists differ between networked or virtual organizations and more traditional organizational structures?

11 How would you implement a major reorganization in a large company involving a change from a tall, hierarchical structure to a flatter organization based on self-managing teams?

12 How has the organization of the human resource function changed over the last few decades? What opportunities are there for human resource specialists in diversified, flexible organizations?

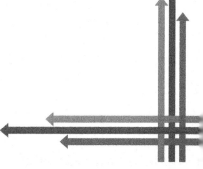

## Rapid Supply Company

The Rapid Supply Company is a large electronic and mechanical parts wholesaler, supplying independent outlets throughout the country. The company purchases and distributes items from global manufacturers, supplying many specialist orders. The progress department monitors orders from placement to delivery. Dealing with customers, warehouse and manufacturers, the department has to maintain a careful and diplomatic relationship with both suppliers and customers.

Rapid Supply credits its success to the ability to efficiently obtain and deliver a wide range of parts. Five years ago the company was purchased by its managers from a large multinational conglomerate. Its market share has increased by 30 per cent in the last two years. The catalogue range has grown extensively with an additional 53 listed manufacturers.

The owners and the venture capital company supporting the organization have decided to float the business on the stock market next year. This will allow them to realize a proportion of their investment and will make millionaires of the senior executives. To maximize the potential share value of the company, their advisers have recommended a number of cost-cutting efficiency exercises. These include a reduction in warehouse stocks, increasing the proportion of items supplied to special order.

The progress department is divided into two sections: record clerks update files with changes and information from manufacturers and lead a comparatively peaceful life. Order-chasing clerks deal with email, telephone and postal enquiries from customers and have a hectic existence, frequently experiencing verbal abuse. The department's work has increased considerably over the last two years but staff levels have remained the same. The progress department is managed by Julie Dee, a tough, resilient and detached person. She is adept at dealing with confrontation and seems to have an impenetrable shell. More junior employees wilt under the onslaught of enquiries. The average length of employment is three to four months but there are a few experienced people who have worked in the department for several years.

Most enquiries are from customers chasing orders. If clerks confirm items have arrived, customers are referred to the despatch section to arrange delivery. More often, parts have not arrived, requiring emails or phone calls to manufacturers and return contact with customers. At its simplest, a progress enquiry can be dealt with during the customer's first contact; at its worst, a succession of communications might be required over several days. Matters are complicated by inefficiencies elsewhere in the system. Goods might be in the warehouse even if shown as 'not arrived' on the computer screen. Equally, they might not have left the manufacturer or may be in transit.

Order-chasing irritates other staff and the suppliers. There have been complaints from manufacturers about progress requests from Rapid Supply regarding parts that were delivered to the warehouse days ago. An instruction has been circulated stating that progress clerks must check with the warehouse first, before contacting manufacturers. This has caused considerable friction between the progress department and the warehouse. Progress staff complain about the apparent slowness of recording receipt of goods; the warehouse complains of being pestered about parts which sometimes are not yet due. There is a further conflict with the despatch clerk who cannot be contacted for lengthy periods. Similar difficulties are experienced with suppliers, often needing several emails, etc. in order to obtain a response. Frequent errors by recording clerks compound the problems.

Progress clerks have a difficult role to play and risk upsetting everyone they deal with. Customers became irate if they do not get an immediate positive response.

Clerks become stressed with the pressure of work, colleagues' absenteeism, time limits on dealing with individual customers, being unable to deal with queries properly and an escalating backlog. The manager now spends much of her time dealing with complaints about the service.

The marketing department has completed a customer survey which shows high levels of dissatisfaction with the progress department. Senior managers are furious and have seconded you to work alongside Julie and 'sort things out'.

*What will you do?*

# CHAPTER 9
# Growth, culture and knowledge

## LEARNING OBJECTIVES

The purpose of this chapter is to:

→ Outline the nature of entrepreneurship.

→ Evaluate the consequences of business growth on human resource practice.

→ Discuss research findings on human resource management in small and medium-sized businesses.

→ Introduce the concept of culture at the organizational level.

→ Evaluate the contribution of Deal and Kennedy to the debate on corporate culture.

→ Discuss how cultures may be managed.

→ Investigate the usefulness of knowledge management.

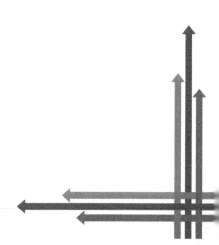

This chapter discusses three critical areas of organizational HRM: growth, culture and knowledge.

# BUSINESS START-UPS AND ENTREPRENEURSHIP

Until the late 1970s and early 1980s it was assumed that small businesses were a thing of the past: 'big is beautiful' was the prevailing view. Since then it has become clear in countries such as Hong Kong, Singapore and latterly the UK and the USA, that small firms are the basic seeds of a successful economy. They are a dynamic force for growth in comparison with the relatively slow movement of large and bureaucratic organizations.

Why do people start businesses and what does entrepreneurship involve? (see Key concept 9.1). The opportunity, motivation and cultural support for starting new businesses varies widely around the world. Eight per cent of adults in the USA were in the early stage of entrepreneurial activities (TEA) in 2009 according to the *Global Entrepreneurship Monitor, 2009*. This compares with 18.8 per cent in China, 15.3 per cent in Brazil and a remarkable 33.6 per cent in Uganda. Rates are much lower in established industrial countries: for example, Germany (4.1 per cent), the UK (5.7 per cent), France (4.3 per cent), Netherlands (7.2 per cent) and Japan (3.3 per cent). The explanation for these differences is complex and includes national cultural differences and the social capital (networks of relationships) possessed by individual entrepreneurs (Tata and Prasad, 2010). For example, in a number of East Asian countries the Chinese family-owned business is a key economic unit. Few of these businesses are large as younger members tend to spin off their own enterprises.

> **KEY CONCEPT 9.1** ENTREPRENEURSHIP
>
> A classic definition of entrepreneurship is provided by Timmons (1994: 7): 'Entrepreneurship is the process of creating or seizing an opportunity and pursuing it regardless of the resources currently controlled.'

Catlin and Matthews (2001: 6) list the following classic entrepreneurial strengths:

→ vision and a pioneering spirit.

→ being able to see possibilities where others do not.

→ always searching for new opportunities and challenges.

→ possessing energy and passion.

→ having a drive to succeed and achieve results with high standards of excellence.

→ being creative – idea generators, able to 'think out of the box'.

→ constantly striving to do things better.

→ proactive and focused on the future.

→ intelligent, capable and decisive.

→ having a strong sense of urgency.

→ confident about taking risks.

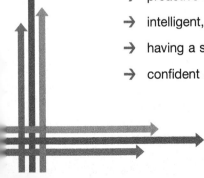

## HRM IN REALITY   SMALL BUSINESSES CREATE MOST JOBS

Research from the Globalization and Economic Policy Centre (GEP) at the University of Nottingham in 2010 found that small businesses employing fewer than 100 workers account for 65 per cent of new British jobs created in an average year.

Co-author Dr Peter Wright, associate professor of economics, said:

> There has always been a discussion about whether small entrepreneurial firms or large firms are more important in terms of job creation. It's clear from this research that small companies employ a significant proportion of the workforce and account for most new jobs.
>
> Although their failure rates are higher, they certainly have more of a role to play than many economists have previously recognized. Therefore if the government could identify why so many of these firms fail then it could have a significant impact on net job creation.

Previous research from GEP found that Britons who become unemployed as a result of company failure experience an average income reduction of about 50 per cent in the first year. The effect remains detectable five years years later, with incomes significantly lower than those earned by individuals who have remained in employment.

In the study, researchers analyzed data from the Office for National Statistics' Inter-Departmental Business Register for the period 1997–2008 and found that an average of 53 000 jobs a week were created in the private sector compared to 47 000 lost (2.6 million compared to 2.35 million annually).

Researchers found that small firms employed between 38 and 52 per cent of all workers. They accounted for 65 per cent of jobs created and 45 per cent of those lost. In the service sector the comparable figures were 15.6 per cent of jobs created and 13.6 per cent lost. The manufacturing sector declined over the period (10 per cent created and 13.7 per cent lost).

Peter Wright commented:

> These relative rates reflect the continuing decline in manufacturing, which was shrinking every year. The difference in the growth rates of the two sectors is largely because of differences in the creation rate rather than destruction.

The researchers found manufacturing suffered the most rapid contraction in English regions (the North East, West Midlands and London). The North West, Scotland, the East of England, Yorkshire and Northern Ireland experienced the fastest expansion in the service sector.

Peter Wright concluded:

> People might be surprised by our overall figures, but they show how dynamic the UK employment market really is. It's not necessarily a bad thing for the economy, but it does mean there are likely to be many people changing jobs involuntarily.
>
> That may involve considerable adjustment costs and also has important implications in terms of training provisions. Many workers will need to change or update their skills regularly to stay in work and maintain income levels in such a dynamic market.

*Why are small businesses better at creating jobs than their larger counterparts?*

*Source: Reprinted with permission from HRM Guide UK (http://www.hrmguide.co.uk).*

→ problem solvers seeking new challenges and believing that nothing is impossible.

→ a determination to succeed, be wealthy or 'make a difference'.

Stolze (1999: 16) divides the reasons why entrepreneurs start businesses into two categories: reactive and active. Reactive reasons are negatives that push people out of working for other

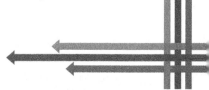

people; active reasons are the positives that pull people towards the idea of working for themselves.

Reactive reasons include:

1   *Inequity between contribution and reward.* People who are high achievers tend not to enjoy working in large organizations. According to Stolze: 'They want rewards based on accomplishment – not on seniority, conforming to the corporate culture, or political clout.'

2   *Promotion and salary policy.* Large organizations tend to categorize people and mavericks do not fit the conventional promotional paths and salary bands.

3   *Adversity.* One of the commonest reasons – basically, job insecurity. When the job is not safe, people tend to think about alternatives. According to Stolze: 'I get very upset when a young college graduate seems unduly concerned about a retirement plan, fringe benefits and so forth. Long ago, I concluded that there is only one kind of job security that means anything – your ability to get another job fast'. Redundancies may also mean severance packages, allowing people to fund their own businesses.

4   *Red tape and politics.* Stolze says they are 'shortcomings of all large organizations that drive the entrepreneurial type bananas. Politicians and bureaucrats are rarely entrepreneurs'.

5   *Champion of orphan products.* Those of us who have cared about products or services outside the mainstream can understand how negative a large organization can be about 'orphan products'. This can be a first step towards the entrepreneurial leap.

Active reasons include:

1   *Wanting to be one's own boss.* According to Stolze: 'Many entrepreneurs have personality traits that make it difficult (if not impossible) for them to work for others'. Running their own business is the only solution. But also, there is the opportunity of professional satisfaction, seeing a job through, using time more flexibly and so on.

2   *Fame and recognition.* Stolze does not consider this to be a common reason for starting a business, considering that there are 'more extrovert egotists' in established large organizations. In fact, he believes that starting one's own business is often a lesson in humility.

3   *Participation in all aspects of a business.* The all-round experience is elating and challenging. Being able to see the whole picture is more interesting than being one 'cog in the wheel'.

4   *Personal financial gain.* This can be important for some people, but not all. Potentially, the gains are much greater than normal wages.

Entrepreneurship offers a way through employment barriers for certain groups, such as immigrants (Thandi and Dini, 2009). Using data from the German Socioeconomic Panel, Constant and Shachmurove (2006) examined entrepreneurial differences between different groups in Germany: West Germans, East Germans, guestworkers and other immigrants. They found that while the probability of self-employment increased significantly with age for all these groups, greater levels of education and having a self-employed father were important influences on the choice of self-employment for West Germans only. Immigrants were pushed into self-employment to avoid being unemployed but this often proved to be a way of achieving considerable economic success. Apart from East Germans, self-employed people in all groups earned more than those on a salary with immigrants having

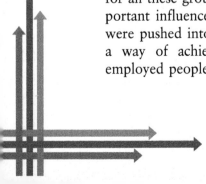

the highest earnings of all. By contrast, in Argentina Montes Rojas and Siga (2009) found that the groups most likely to start a micro-enterprise were the native young, poorly educated and the middle-age, highly educated.

Lesonsky (2001) considers that, according to surveys and research, entrepreneurs share some common personality traits – confidence being the most important. They have confidence in themselves, in their ability to sell their ideas, set up their own businesses, and trust in their intuition. Confidence is essential in the fiercely competitive world of small business. The value of confidence is shown in a commonly held belief that the critical determinant of entrepreneurship is the ability to raise significant amounts of money from investors: 'If you can make people believe in your dreams and share your goals so that they are willing to invest hard-earned cash in your venture, chances are you have what it takes' (Lesonsky, 2001: 14). Greenbank (2006) examined the decision making process leading to small business start-ups and classified potential owners as 'dissatisfiers' or 'motivators'. Uncertainty arises because the motivation to become self-employed is often based on beliefs rather than actual experience. This increases the perceived level of risk attached to self-employment as a career option.

## COLLABORATIVE ENTREPRENEURSHIP

There has been extensive research on collaboration between enterprises (to be considered later) but little on the relationship between entrepreneurs within an organization. This is despite the fact that it has been well known for decades that 40–60 per cent of small businesses have been collaboratively funded or acquired (see Key concept 9.2).

**KEY CONCEPT 9.2**  COLLABORATIVE ENTREPRENEURSHIP

Cooperation between two or more individuals in order to found or acquire a business. The degree and nature of collaboration may vary from one company to another in terms of financial input, time devoted, skills and knowledge.

Quince (2001: 5) identifies three types of relationship within collaborative entrepreneurship:

1   The enterprise is an economic entity, having economic relations with other organizations and individuals. Moreover, there is an economic relationship between the co-founders or acquirers. Co-owners both provide and *are* resources: their own human capital in terms of skill, knowledge and experience, labour and often finance. In return, they are entitled to a share in the profits of the firm.

2   The co-owners or co-founders have an organizational relationship in which roles, responsibilities and accountability have been allocated.

3   An interpersonal relationship exists, typically embedded in a pre-existing social or personal friendship with friends, work colleagues, family or life partners.

How do SMEs fit into the knowledge economy? Nunes *et al.* (2006) investigated knowledge management understanding and usage in small and medium knowledge-intensive

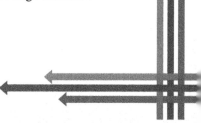

enterprises. Organizations studied acknowledged that adequately capturing, storing, sharing and disseminating knowledge can lead to greater innovation and productivity, but managers were not prepared to invest the relatively high effort on long-term knowledge management goals for which they had difficulty establishing added value. Knowledge management activities within SMEs tend to happen in an informal way, rarely supported by purposely designed ICT systems.

Most of the research into small businesses has focused on the economic dimension. But there are also issues of self-identity and notions of possession. As Quince points out, the 'I am the business' and 'My baby' elements of possession are 'common, if potentially psychologically damaging, entrepreneurial perspectives'. The business is perceived as an extension of the self.

Many new business ventures are family-based and, even with solo ventures, many entrepreneurs are reluctant to move away from family and friends (Dahl and Sorenson, 2009). Quince (2001: 7) reports on a study of almost 500 East Anglian businesses in the manufacturing and business services sectors, each employing between 15 and 250 workers. A high incidence of collaborative entrepreneurship was found with 238 (60 per cent) of the 395 first generation independent firms having been founded or acquired collaboratively. Of these, 50 were family firms. Intriguingly, of the other 188 (non-family) firms that had been founded or acquired collaboratively, almost a half (43 per cent) were now owned by just one of the collaborators. According to Quince:

> Follow up telephone conversations with 47 remaining owners suggested that in 60 per cent of these cases the break-up of the team had been acrimonious. These conversations indicated the level of personal trauma associated with such conflict, including one case of attempted murder, several cases of serious assault and fraud, attempted suicides, depressions and mental or family break-ups.

## SMALL FIRM GROWTH

Most small businesses never become large, and many are unsuccessful. Some of the reasons for this can be traced back to the start-up. Goltz (1998) describes a number of the common-sense elements of starting a business, for example:

1   Going into business for yourself is more responsibility than you can possibly imagine. You may start off thinking that when you go into business for yourself, you do not have to answer to anyone. In fact, the list is endless: your bank, your customers, your spouse, the Revenue people and so on.

2   Behind every failed business are a dozen friends who said it was a great idea. And they did – enthusiastically – along with your life partner. It is always best to get an expert opinion and not to rely on people who want to be supportive and not hurt your feelings.

3   If you've got it, use it. Even if it's a great smile. Hard work is not enough – you need to leverage the assets you have. And assets could be just about anything.

4   It is easier to steal a share of the market than create a market. Remember that Bill Gates was not the first in the computer software market. You might believe that a totally original idea is the key to success but if you have no competition you cannot be sure that there is a market out there.

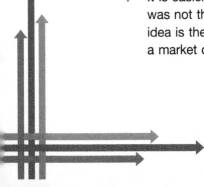

# HRM IN REALITY   PRESSURES ON SMALL BUSINESS OWNERS

A mere 21 per cent of small business owners employing the fewest staff (between two and ten) are earning more than they hoped for when starting their companies – despite working an average of 58 hours per week. This finding comes from an online survey of small business owners conducted by IPSOS Public Affairs in 2010 on behalf of hourly job website SnagAJob.com.

However, almost two-thirds (63 per cent) of owners employing up to 100 people said that starting their own business has been more satisfying than anticipated. This rose to 71 per cent among those planning to recruit within the next 12 months.

The survey included 511 small business owners of whom 255 had between two and ten employees and 256 between 11 and 100. The great majority (91 per cent) cited 'being their own boss' as one of their top three reasons for starting a business, with 44 per cent saying it was the most important motivation. Nearly three-quarters (72 per cent) cited 'achieving a higher income' among their top three reasons. The frustrations associated with small business ownership included:

→ bookkeeping (cited by 38 per cent)

→ HR issues (31 per cent), and

→ recruiting (18 per cent).

The survey found that 61 per cent of respondents intended to recruit in the next year to increase headcount (35 per cent) or because of turnover (26 per cent). When recruiting, 58 per cent said that 'identifying qualified applicants' was their biggest challenge. They were most likely to use free methods, the best results coming from:

→ referrals (60 per cent)

→ newspaper classified advertisements (13 per cent)

→ walk-in enquiries (8 per cent)

→ online job boards (8 per cent).

Other significant findings included:

Among small business owners that had grown their companies to employ 11 to 100 workers, 40 per cent said that it had been more financially rewarding than anticipated (compared to 21 per cent with two to ten employees). However, they spent an average of 69 hours a week working towards their business (compared to 58 hours a week at smaller firms).

On average, small business owners spent 63 hours a week working (including time spent at the business, time at other locations and an average of 16 hours 'multi-tasking' when at least some attention was being given to the business).

Small business owners may underestimate the difficulty of the enterprise. On a scale of one to ten, ranging from 'not at all difficult' to 'more difficult than imagined' the average response rated the difficulty as 6.6. Four out of ten (39 per cent) rated it an eight or higher compared to just 13 per cent who rated the difficulty as three or less.

Shawn Boyer, CEO of SnagAJob.com said:

> Small businesses – much like the hourly workers we serve – are the backbone of America's economy. Small businesses employ just over half of private-sector employees, and more than half of the US workforce is employed by the hour. Therefore, we're in a unique position to help match these large segments of the workforce.

*What reasons can you suggest for the high level of entrepreneurship in the USA?*

*Source: Reprinted with permission from HRM Guide USA (http://www.hrmguide.com/).*

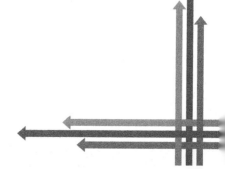

Flamholtz and Randle (2000, p.9) state:

> The first challenge entrepreneurs face is that of establishing a successful new venture. If they have the ability to recognize a market need and to develop (or to hire other people to develop) a product or service appropriate to satisfy that need, their fledgling enterprise is likely to experience rapid growth. It is at this point, whether the entrepreneur recognizes it or not, that the game begins to change. The firm's success creates its next set of problems and challenges to survival.

Entrepreneurs such as Richard Branson of Virgin, Bill Gates of Microsoft and Michael Dell are unusual. Rarely do the founders of start-up businesses remain in charge as their businesses become large organizations. Catlin and Matthews (2001: 4) point out: 'The irony of entrepreneurial leaders is that the very behaviours and habit patterns that lead to success at one stage of growth can contribute to failure at the next stage. It seems that just when you get good at something, you discover it's the wrong thing to be doing!' In a study of high-growth firms in Finland, Littunen and Niittykangas (2010) found that they could be differentiated from low-growth organizations by factors such as the entrepreneurs know-how and the use of external networks in the first four years and the development of internal networks in years five to eight.

There are several models of business growth ranging from three to ten stages (Rutherford, Buller and McMullen, 2003). For example, Flamholtz and Randle (2000) identify the following stages of successful business growth:

1   new venture

2   expansion

3   professionalization

4   consolidation

5   diversification

6   integration

7   decline and revitalization.

Catlin and Matthews consider that entrepreneurs begin with an intuitive leadership style. In the start-up phase they can make decisions 'on the fly', improvise when required and manage everything on a day-to-day basis. As the business expands, this approach results in more and more frenzied activity, less time to think and a gradual feeling of being overwhelmed. Flamholtz and Randle point to characteristic organizational growing pains such as:

→   feeling that there are not enough hours in the day.

→   spending too much time 'fire-fighting'.

→   not knowing what other staff are doing.

→   a failure to understand the organization's goals.

→   not enough good managers.

→   an attitude of 'I have to do it myself if I want it done properly'.

→   meetings are generally felt to be a waste of time.

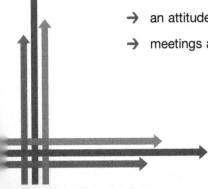

→ plans are rarely made and where they exist they are seldom followed, so that things are often not done.

→ some people do not feel secure about their positions.

→ sales may be increasing, but profits are not.

These problems are symptomatic of a lack of organizational and managerial infrastructure that can support a larger and more complex operation. The original leadership style has become inappropriate and inadequate. Now there is a need for leadership to be more deliberate and for growth to be designed rather than accidental. Nevertheless, a successful owner needs to combine this approach with the best of their entrepreneurial characteristics to achieve consistent growth. The various types of business owner have different motives and entrepreneurial characteristics (see Table 9.1).

Flamholtz and Randle consider that the firm (and therefore the entrepreneur) has to go through 'a fundamental transformation or metamorphosis from the spontaneous *ad hoc*, free-spirited enterprise that it has been to a more formally planned, organized and disciplined entity'. Catlin and Matthews contend that if the founder is to remain in charge of the expanding business, he or she has to:

→ Develop strategies, products/services, customers and markets.

→ Develop organizational processes for planning, management and work flow – and also the infrastructure to accommodate growth and expansion.

→ Recruit new people and develop teams to handle growth. Kirkwood (2009) highlights the inability to recruit skilled employees as a significant reason for failure to grow in a study of New Zealand service firms.

| Type | Characteristics |
|------|-----------------|
| 1 *Craftsmen* | Self-employed in order to spend as much time as possible expressing their creativity. This freedom would not be possible in a large organization. They would prefer to make the product or provide the service personally and are reluctant employers. They probably experience difficulties in marketing or sales, and resent spending time on paperwork and administration. Many are 'hobbyists' and fail to create a viable business. |
| 2 *Promoters (opportunists)* | With the ambition of creating personal wealth through 'deals'. Many have a succession of different businesses with varying degrees of success. They are not committed to a specific product or service. Proactive individuals, they are focused on marketing and finance and capable of rapid rates of growth in the right circumstances. |
| 3 *Professional managers* | Aim to develop businesses with the hierarchical characteristics of larger organizations. They aim for controlled and sustained growth and take a long-term view of their businesses. |

**TABLE 9.1**
Types of business owner

Source: Based on Hornaday (1990, p.29).

→ Create a business culture to align people and teams so that they work together effectively.

→ Monitor the evolution of the business and adapt their own leadership style as the business expands and changes.

But what if the owner-entrepreneur is unable to meet these requirements? Flamholtz and Randle contend that there are four alternatives:

1   Resign and let someone else be brought in to run the organization.

2   Move up to chairperson, allowing a new manager to run day-to-day operations.

3   Carry on as before and hope the problems will go away.

4   Sell out and start a new entrepreneurial venture.

In general, they conclude: 'Founder-entrepreneurs typically experience great difficulty in relinquishing control of their businesses. Some try to change their skills and behaviour but fail. Others merely give the illusion of turning the organization over to professional managers.'

Few researchers have considered the value of learning in helping business growth. Friedrich *et al.* (2006) designed a three-day action learning programme to improve the skills of entrepreneurs in South Africa in relation to personal initiative, planning, goal setting and innovation. They divided a sample of 84 entrepreneurs into an experimental group who took the training course, and a control group who did not. They compared the two groups after six months. The training group showed much greater progress in their business performance than the control group.

## Working in small businesses

Entrepreneurs start small businesses in order to obtain freedom, challenge and personal income. Starting one's own business offers a way around the lack of equal opportunities. Women are strongly represented in the SME sector although Kariv (2010) found little difference between male and female entrepreneurial techniques apart from in the ways they encouraged creativity and innovation. Immigrants often overcome prejudice, language difficulties and barriers in the employment market by starting their own businesses. The picture is different for employees, however. Staff in small businesses can feel insecure because of the lack of structure and planning. Career aspirations are frustrated as most owners either do not wish the business to expand beyond their personal span of control or do not have the management skills necessary for effective delegation. Few corner shop owners have the skills or inclination to develop large businesses and many of their children are disinclined to carry on with the family firm. In contrast, the best entrepreneurs have a range of general business skills – including people management – and even passion and intuitive foreknowledge (Bradley, 2010) or have the good sense to obtain specialist assistance from:

→ *Consultants.* Providing advice on recruitment, pay and benefits, management structures and organizational change associated with growth.

→ *Training agencies.* Providing skills training on a local or regional basis.

→ *Networks.* Small businesses can link together to pay for resourcing and development assistance, possibly through chambers of commerce and business clubs.

Entrepreneurial structures can only function up to a certain size. When they become too large for personal relationships they must evolve into a more clearly defined organization.

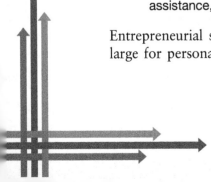

The nature of people management must change fundamentally when this occurs. However, it is possible to preserve some of the informal and non-hierarchical characteristics of the small business by forming a formal cooperative or, informally, a team-based organization.

## CORPORATE CULTURE

As Deal and Kennedy (1982: 15) propose: '... people are a company's greatest resource, and the way to manage them is not directly by computer reports, but by the subtle cues of a culture'. In this section we turn to the cultures that distinguish one organization from another, whether or not they are in different countries. It has been long recognized that the organization cannot simply be described in terms of its formal structure (Bakke, 1950). Often this is no more than window dressing: the illusion of order that senior management believe they have created.

Formal organization design is concerned with only certain activities that are felt important to the organization. All other aspects of working life, from gossip on the line to complaining about management, are the territory of the informal organization (see Key concept 9.3). Real action depends on this informal structure of opinion leaders and power-brokers (Brunsson, 1989: 7). The formal organization is there for 'demonstration and display to the outside world ... defined as rituals'. Management literature earlier in the 20th century frequently regarded informal behaviour as undesirable: 'Basing their actions on the logic of formal organization, they try to neutralize or do away with the informal behaviour through directive leadership, management controls and pseudo human relations programmes' (Argyris, 1957: 231).

> **KEY CONCEPT 9.3** THE INFORMAL ORGANIZATION
>
> An organization is both a formal and informal entity. The formal aspect of an organization is its official structure and public image visible in organization charts and annual reports. Behind and in parallel with the 'official' system there is the reality of action and power commonly described as the 'informal' organization: 'those patterns of coordination that arise among members of a formal organization which are not called for by the blueprint' (Schein, 1988: 16). The informal organization is an elusive concept, describing the complex network of psychological and social relationships between its people. It is an unrecognized world of cliques and politics, friendships and enmities, gossip and affairs.

This was typical of the North American business schools that tended to view organization structure as a prescriptive matter of 'one best way' with scant regard for functional purpose or cultural location. This form of management served to increase feelings of dependence, submissiveness and subordination amongst employees. Ironically, workers coped by increasing the scope of the informal organization, using it as a mechanism to counter management initiatives.

By the 1980s, however, the informal organization was regarded in a new and more favourable light. From being perceived as something to be ignored or bludgeoned out of existence, it was realized that features of the informal organization could be harnessed

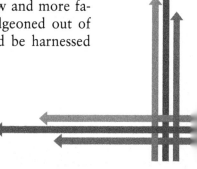

for competitive advantage (Truss, 2001). The informal organization could help counter the 'silo mentality' that works against sharing of knowledge between sections or departments, especially if people who spanned boundaries can be identified (Chakravarthy, 2010). The key roles in an informal organization include: opinion leaders, central connectors, bottlenecks, experts, consultants, helpful people and 'pilus prior' (first lancer) – a person who has problem solving, expertise and accessibility characteristics (Toni and Nonino, 2010).

The notion of the informal organization developed along with the concept of corporate culture – a central theme of the 'excellence' literature (Peters and Waterman, 1982) as well as HRM and total quality management (see Key concept 9.4). Its major exponents presented a 'strong' corporate culture as a key factor in enhancing competitive performance through greater employee commitment and flexibility (Deal and Kennedy, 1982). From this perspective employees in strong cultures are thought to know what is expected of them while conversely, staff in weak cultures waste time trying to discover what is required. The view here is that employees identify with a strong culture and take pride in their organization.

### KEY CONCEPT 9.4  CORPORATE CULTURE

The simplest – and probably most often – quoted definition is Bower's (1966) 'the way we do things around here'. Trice and Beyer (1984) elaborated this as: 'the system of ... publicly and collectively accepted meanings operating for a given group at a given time'. Hofstede (1994 [1991]) describes corporate culture as 'the psychological assets of an organization, which can be used to predict what will happen to its financial assets in five years time'.

The creation – or even the definition – of such a culture is not easy. In managing people to achieve organizational goals, organizations prefer clarity, certainty and perfection (Pascale and Athos, 1981: 105). However, those same organizations have people as their basic building bricks. Their human relationships involve ambiguity, uncertainty and imperfection. The trick of good management is to honour, balance and integrate these. One way to do so is somehow to use the information channels of the informal organization to transmit and reinforce messages of commitment to management goals. Jones (2006) undertook a cultural analysis of organizational energy and commitment in a family business in the American south and found a 'mutual confirmation' between southern cultural values and those in the organizational history of the firm. The company, Omega Coffee and Tea, provides its employees with a powerful affirmation of cultural identity, which is then transformed into commitment, energy and effectiveness. Rask *et al.* (2010) investigated possible tensions between the need to observe diversity legislation across a number of countries and IKEA's corporate culture. They concluded that the company managed the task of preserving a strong corporate culture and making local adaptations very well.

Unlike many other 'new' management ideas, corporate culture has endured and appears to have had a 'material effect upon the politics of work' (Willmott, 1993: 515). We will see in Chapter 12 that a whole industry has arisen to supply management of change programmes, much of it devoted to changing and strengthening corporate cultures, for example developing a service orientation (Gebauer *et al.*, 2010). However, it is worth noting that although a wealth of literature exists publicizing the importance of culture change, most of this is relatively uncritical.

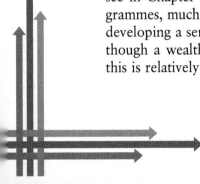

# HRM IN REALITY MEETINGS, MEETINGS

*Meetings are depressing for most people – but not everyone*

Meetings, don't we hate them? Apparently, there was a doubling (at least) of meetings at work in the second half of the 20th century. The implications have been little studied but recent research on the link between the experience of meetings and the effects on worker well-being has shown some surprising findings.

Written by a team of psychologists, led by Steven G. Rogelberg from the University of North Carolina at Charlotte, the research (Rogelberg *et al.*, 2006) is claimed to be the first international scientific study ever conducted on the effects of meeting time on employee well-being and is based on responses from 980 employees to two work surveys.

One significant finding is that more people actually believe that meetings are a positive part of the workday than they will admit publicly. 'When speaking publicly, people generally claim that they hate meetings', said Rogelberg, 'but in the surveys you see a different story – some people's private sentiments are much more positive.

'It's an interesting finding because it really helps to explain why we have all these meetings. And, though they are typically publicly negative, overwhelmingly people say that they want the day to have at least one meeting. They have to feel like they are accomplishing something positive in their meetings to produce this response', he said.

The two surveys tested the impact of meetings on employees in two different contexts – at the end of a specific day and in general, by examining the number of meetings employees had in a typical week.

It appears that some individuals see meetings as interruptions while others regard them as welcome events. The study finds that the effects of meetings on worker well-being is 'moderated' by three different factors:

1 by whether jobs specifically require group work

2 by whether the meetings were efficiently run; and perhaps most importantly,

3 by where the worker falls on the personality scale of her/his 'accomplishment striving'.

'People differ on this accomplishment striving personality scale', Rogelberg explained. 'In general, you can think of people who are high in accomplishment striving as those individuals who are very task-focused, who are very goal-focused, who have goals and objectives for the day that they want to get accomplished. People who have low accomplishment striving are not slackers, though – they are just individuals with a much more flexible orientation to work and like to allow the agenda for the day to emerge much more naturally'.

According to this research, individuals high in accomplishment striving are predictably and negatively affected by meetings – particularly if they are frequent. A large number of short meetings affect their well-being more than a few long meetings – even if they take the same overall amount of time.

But meetings had a positive impact on respondents with low scores on accomplishment striving. They seemed to welcome meetings and the more time they spent in meetings, the greater their sense of well-being.

'People who are high in accomplishment striving look at meetings more from the perspective of seeing them as barriers to getting real work done', Rogelberg said. 'But the others may view meetings as a way to structure their day or a way to network and socialize. As a result, these people see meetings as a good thing.'

Steven Rogelberg observes that there are some intriguing social paradigms operating that disguise the dynamic. 'It is socially unacceptable to talk about liking meetings, unless someone else starts talking about it', he said, explaining why the low accomplishment striving folks do not go public with their preference for meetings. 'And it is also interesting that the people who are high on accomplishment striving are not complaining more than the others. The toll that meetings take seems to be much more subtle. If you ask these individuals if they are more dissatisfied with the meetings, they don't report anything different from those who enjoy meetings', he said.

*How do meetings contribute to the development and maintenance of a company culture?*

*Source: Reprinted with permission from HRM Guide USA (http://www.hrmguide.com).*

# THE DEAL AND KENNEDY MODEL OF CORPORATE CULTURE

We have noted that, together with Peters and Waterman's *In Search of Excellence* (1982), Deal and Kennedy's *Corporate Cultures* (1982) was inspirational in this area. As a prelude to discussion of the role of corporate culture in people management, it is appropriate to outline Deal and Kennedy's model. It incorporates five critical elements: the business environment; values; heroes; rites and rituals; and the cultural network.

In line with our discussion in Part Two, Deal and Kennedy argued that the activities of governments and competitors, changes in technology, customer demand and general economic conditions are instrumental in shaping the cultures of organizations with survival potential. The orientation of organizations within this environment – for example a focus on sales or concentration on research and development – develops specific cultural styles.

## Values

Values are at the heart of corporate culture. They are made up of the key beliefs and concepts shared by an organization's employees. Successful companies are clear about these values and their managers publicly reinforce them. Often values are unwritten and operate at a subconscious level.

## Heroes

Personifications of the organization's values: achievers who provide role models for success within the company. Heroism is an element of leadership that has been virtually forgotten by modern managers: 'Since the 1920s, the corporate world has been powered by managers who are rationalists, who do strategic planning, write memos and devise flow charts' (Deal and Kennedy, 1982: 37). Heroes, on the other hand, create rather than run organizations; are intuitive rather than decisive; have all the time in the world because they make time; are experimenters rather than routinizers; are playful; get things 'just right'. Heroes have vision and break the existing order if necessary in order to achieve that vision. Deal and Kennedy describe this process in terms of 'making success attainable and human'. A figurehead such as Sir Richard Branson, is presented as being the Virgin group, serving the purpose of 'symbolizing the company to the outside world' (Deal and Kennedy, 1982: 40).

## Rites and rituals

Ceremonies and routine behavioural rituals reinforce the culture. Examples include product launches, sales conferences, away days or the Friday afternoon 'beer-bust'.

## The cultural network

This is the carrier of stories and gossip that spreads information about valued behaviour and 'heroic myths' around the organization. Marshall and Adamic (2010) identify four characteristics in effective corporate storytelling: purpose, allusion, people and appeal. They contend that stories that meet the following criteria are likely to have a greater impact on corporate culture and employee behaviour:

→ are told for a particular reason.

→ refer to an organization's history and role in its sector.

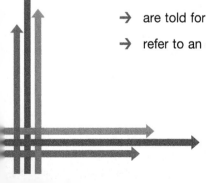

→   are told by the right person to the proper audience.

→   contain an inspiring emotional appeal.

The degree of factual accuracy in the content of corporate stories can be questioned. Michelson and Mouly (2000: 339) attempt to draw a distinction between rumour and gossip:

> While the basis of rumour is information that is unsubstantiated, gossip may or may not be a known fact. ... This distinction is more a matter of degree than substance and the issue becomes problematic in the context of celebrity or political gossip. In such cases the 'facts' or 'truth' are likely to be highly elusive. It is also conceivable that the initiation of rumour may be underpinned by some element of 'truth', no matter how obscure or circumstantial the evidence. The extent of factuality or truth is hard to determine any way, and one can never know if something is a 'white lie' or 'half truth'.

Table 9.2 outlines an anthropological classification of the elements of corporate cultures.

---

**KEY CONCEPT 9.5**  RUMOUR AND GOSSIP

Rumour is typically regarded as unsubstantiated talk that is not supported by evidence or authority. Gossip is commonly held to have a factual basis of some kind.

---

Deal and Kennedy produced a framework with two key dimensions: the 'risk' attached to the company's activities and the speed of 'feedback' to employees. Taking the extreme combinations of these two dimensions they described four types of culture:

1   *Tough guy culture:* characterized by entrepreneurial, high-risk-taking individuals, receiving quick feedback, but with a low level of teamwork. Such companies tend to follow a cycle of boom and bust, with the possibility of high earnings during the successful period.

2   *Work hard, play hard:* where work is fun and there is plenty of action with low risk and quick feedback on success. A high volume sales company is a typical example. The individual works alone but has a supportive team.

3   *Bet-your-company:* high-risk, long-term industries usually requiring significant technical expertise, such as the oil and aerospace businesses.

4   *Process culture:* low-risk, low-feedback organizations, typical of traditional models of public institutions, banks, civil service, etc., where the focus is on the actual conduct of the work. In this kind of culture, status issues such as the right to sign-off memos and use of graded titles are of paramount importance.

Different kinds of people have varying degrees of success in these cultures. Someone who reacts well to a high-pressure, fast-moving 'work-hard, play-hard' culture will be unhappy and unsuccessful in a process culture. With the wrong cultural style an individual can lose self-esteem and confidence. Deal and Kennedy (1982: 17) reasoned, 'culture shock may be one of the major reasons why people supposedly "fail" when they leave one organization for another'. Cultural fit is often ignored in selection procedures, leading to unhappy and nonproductive experiences for some.

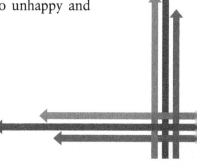

**TABLE 9.2**
Elements of corporate culture

| Element | Ingredients |
|---|---|
| *Company practices* | *Rites:* planned, dramatic events in the life of the organization.<br><br>*Ceremonial:* a series of rites such as the launch of a product, a graduation ceremony, the annual shareholders' meeting.<br><br>*Ritual:* standardized, unimportant activities such as the Friday afternoon pub session that used to be a common place. |
| *Company communication* | *Stories:* based on true events.<br><br>*Myths:* untrue stories, old-timers stories.<br><br>*Sagas:* heroic company histories.<br><br>*Legends:* involving heroes and heroines in the organization's history.<br><br>*Folk tales:* fiction with a message indicating successful behaviours that led to promotion or reward.<br><br>*Symbols and slogans:* powerful components of a corporate identity, serving to create a recognizable image for people inside and outside the organization. They include colour schemes, letterheads, logos and uniforms. |
| *Physical cultural forms* | *Artefacts:* tools, furniture styles, appliances and other equipment used in a factory or office. Some companies collect these in a haphazard way over time, others have central purchasing policies which ensure harmonization.<br><br>*Physical layout:* offices, production areas and canteens may be laid out in an ad hoc manner or planned to follow an organizational theme. |
| *Common language* | *Organizations* develop their own terminology and ways of expression. In Disneyland theme parks, staff are not employees but 'cast members' who wear 'costumes' (uniforms) 'onstage' (at work). 'Guests' (customers) use the 'attractions' (rides). Use of such terminology helps employees slip into role. At Land Rover, employees were called 'associates' and all wore company overalls (including the managing director). |

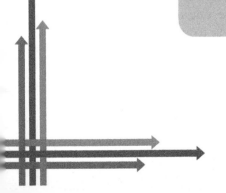

# CORPORATE CULTURE AND PEOPLE MANAGEMENT

The concept of corporate culture continues the tradition of human relations and 'Theory Y' (McGregor, 1960). It fuses the two and moves further away from the logic of scientific management and Fordism towards a view of self-motivated employees who have internalized the values of the business (Willmott, 1993: 524).

For example, Hartmann (2006) identified a culture of innovation and creativity in a Swiss construction company fostered by immediate feedback, the existence of communication channels for implicit knowledge, the capacity for employees to be granted autonomous work and task identity, specifically identified innovation projects and a comprehensive reward and incentive system. If the culture is strong, people do not need orders or directives. Social norms constrain individual discretion so that employee values are those of the organization. In HRM terms the focus on values and norms is important to achieve behavioural consistency and commitment to the objectives of the business. The key point is that corporate culturalism requires the management of culture so that the 'correct' values are acquired. In effect 'normal', rational techniques of management are applied to the affective (emotional) domain (Willmott, 1993: 532). In other words, culture management is a 'hard' approach in thoroughly 'soft' territory. As an example, Thomson (2010) describes the use of an arts-based approach to achieve cultural change in an assessment business.

## HRM IN REALITY LONGER HOURS

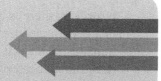

A survey conducted for the Ordre des conseillers en resources humaines agréés (CRHA) in 2010 found that most Quebec employees do not envy their bosses and over half (53 per cent) would not trade places if given the opportunity. Only 27 per cent would do so immediately, 19 per cent after some hesitation. The survey found 62 per cent of women would not want their boss's job, compared to 46 per cent of their male counterparts.

Florent Francoeur, CRHA president said:

These findings sound the alarm for managers. Succession problems are tricky and often neglected in many organizations. Management needs to come up with sound strategies to prepare the next generation. This is a crucial issue for organizations' survival and their future.

The survey also found that long work hours are a deterrent to accepting promotion. Nearly half of respondents (42 per cent) gave this as the main reason they would refuse, followed by a heavier workload (14 per cent) and having to manage a team or human resources (13 per cent).

Florent Francoeur concluded:

Obviously, not every employee is interested in or has the ability to hold a management position. But the survey shows that it's time for some companies to change their culture of long work hours. Employees don't necessarily perform better just because they spend more time at the office. Performance is measured by outcomes.

*Is a 'long hours' culture necessarily a bad idea?*

Source: Reprinted with permission from HRM Guide Canada (http://www.hrmguide.net/canada/).

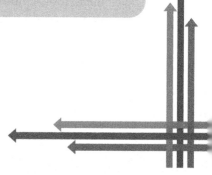

Based on Handy (1993), corporate culture and organization types can be classified as follows:

1   *The club culture.* Typical of a small company; a personal, informal culture focused on the owner. The leader is all. This form of culture is suitable for new ventures needing strong personalities and fast responses.

2   *Role culture.* Hierarchical with an organizational chart portraying an orderly set of job boxes (roles). Individuals are less important than the roles they fill. A role culture is managed not led, with a formal communication system. Such a culture is best for stable, unchanging organizations with routine tasks. There is a strong tendency to adopt the role culture with increasing size, leading to a mechanistic, bureaucratic organization.

3   *Task culture.* The main focus is on groups such as project teams. Organization is based on trust and respect and geared to plans not procedures. This is a problem-solving environment – exciting and challenging but expensive to run. Work is based on projects. There is little job security: staff leave when tasks are finished.

4   *The person culture.* This is radically different and suited to professionals who are self-managing and require minimal structure or supervision. The focus is on talent and professional expertise – management has low status. This is reflected in non-managerial titles such as 'Dean'. Such a culture is best suited for professional practices and educational establishments.

However, there is an underlying tension between the 'humanizing' and the 'control' aspects of people management that is evident in this process. Whereas Theory Y was unashamedly humanistic, delegating discretion and freedom of choice to individual workers, corporate culturalism advocates: 'a *systematic* approach to creating and strengthening core organizational values in a way that *excludes* (through attention to recruitment) *and eliminates* (through training) *all other values*' (Willmott, 1993: 524, original emphases). Appelbaum and Shapiro (2006) argue that remodelling an organization's norms, attitudes and social values in order to achieve a culture based on core ethical values is a worthy objective. Zablow (2006) also supports the notion of creating an ethical workplace by remodelling corporate culture.

People are promoted, appraised and rewarded according to management perception of their acceptance of core values. Hence the view in the Deal and Kennedy approach and much other corporate culture literature is that culture can be created and managed from the top. In this respect it is a departure from older ideas about informal organizations which are more closely aligned to the view that an organizational culture emerges from social interaction (Meek, 1988: 293). In fact, the literature appears to transfer culture from the informal to the formal organization. As such it becomes the property of management and open to manipulation on their part. This has become the underlying logic for major change initiatives in many large organizations.

Furthermore, there is a common assumption that a unified culture – a 'monoculture' – exists to which all members of the organization belong. Earlier, we saw that narrow, simplified stereotypes of national cultures are misleading: most countries are pluralities with different regional, ethnic and class cultures. In the same way every organization has different cliques and minority groups with varying perspectives of culture. Far from being a management tool, culture can be regarded as a form of collective consciousness, reflecting the diversity of opinion, politics and ambition to be found in any organization. Indeed, as a product of the great mass of employees interacting with each other, it is often anti-managerial.

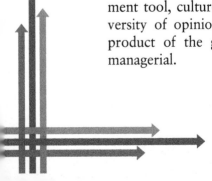

Legge (1995: 185) asks 'If senior managers seek to manage "organizational culture", what exactly is it they are seeking to manage?' We can distinguish, therefore, between corporate culture as it is presented in most of the literature, and organizational culture. The former reflects the view that culture is something which an organization 'has', the latter that an organization 'is' (Smircich, 1983). Corporate culture is portrayed as something created by management that employees must accept. If we choose the organization culture view, however, we must acknowledge its long-term interactionist basis. From this perspective, it is difficult to see how senior management can control the culture of a firm – it is too diffuse, embedded and ever-changing. Indeed Legge (1995: 186) suggests:

> Corporate culture – that shared by senior management and presented as the 'official' culture
> of the organization – may be only one of several sub-cultures within any organization, and may
> be actively resisted by groups who do not share or empathize with its values. If the corporate
> culture makes no sense of the organizational realities experienced by the employees other than
> senior management, it will not become internalized outside that small sub-group.

This idea of a small 'official' corporate culture floating on top of a multicultural informal organization is mirrored earlier in Handy's classification of cultures. Senior managers typically form a dynamic club culture that they believe to be universal in the organization whereas, in reality, it sits uncomfortably on top of a depressed and antipathetic role culture. From the managerial point of view, therefore, culture is a major variable to be influenced rather than a creation to be managed.

The concept of organizational climate, the prevailing 'atmosphere' in an organization, has been highlighted as an important mediating element in the transmission of culture. For example, Aarons and Sawitzky (2006) found that organizational climate partially mediated the effect of culture in mental health services where staff retention is an ongoing problem. Both elements impacted on job satisfaction and commitment and work attitudes significantly predicted one-year staff turnover rates.

## KNOWLEDGE MANAGEMENT

The concept of knowledge management (Key concept 9.6) seems to give fresh insights into the theory of the firm and it is also the subject of claims about a completely new kind of economy – the 'knowledge economy'. Knowledge is scarcely as novel a concept as many protagonists of knowledge management claim and a large number of organizations have attempted knowledge management projects – not always successfully.

O'Dell and Essaides (1998) argue that knowledge management is more than a managerial fashion because:

→ The power of learning will never be obsolete.

→ Some people may treat knowledge management as a religion but real knowledge management is practical rather than theoretical and should have bottom-line results.

→ Technology is not relied upon to make processes efficient, instead, technology is used to facilitate the sharing of knowledge in people's heads.

→ It is consistent with modern team- and process-based approaches to management.

We will see later that there are criticisms of the way that information technology has come to dominate conferences and publications on knowledge management and, in doing so, often lost the point. In fact, knowledge is more than technology.

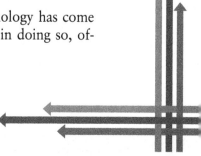

### WHAT KNOWLEDGE MANAGEMENT IS NOT

→ Knowledge management (KM) is *not* a new religion or spiritual calling.

→ It is *not* an attempt to rally disgruntled employees around an appealing physical concept.

→ It is *not* an existential search for the truth. (Actually, it's about the entirely worldly task of making money.)

→ It is *not* a science or a discipline – yet.

→ It is *not* the latest management fad.

*Source: O'Dell and Essaides, (1998).*
*Note: Authors' emphases.*

---

**KEY CONCEPT 9.6**   KNOWLEDGE MANAGEMENT

'Knowledge management caters to the critical issues of organizational adaption, survival and competence in face of increasingly discontinuous environmental change. ... Essentially, it embodies organizational processes that seek synergistic combination of data and information processing capacity of information technologies, and the creative and innovative capacity of human beings.' (Malhotra, 1998: 59)

---

Stewart (2001) identifies three significant ideas in changing the ways in which organizations are run:

*Total quality management.* An approach that unified targeting, performance and teamwork.

*Business process re-engineering.* Produced a new attitude towards processes that can be made explicit and the knowledge that makes them work can be transferred between individuals.

*Intellectual capital.* Stewart divides intellectual capital or knowledge assets into two main forms: 'hard' assets such as patents, copyrights, software and databases; and, most importantly, 'soft' employee-focused assets including skills, capabilities, expertise, culture and loyalty.

Wolff (2005: 38) calculates that the percentage of employees in the USA who could be described as information workers increased from 37 per cent of the workforce in 1950 to 59 per cent in 2000. These include employees who produce knowledge as well as those who handle data. Wolff (2005: 42) concludes that much of the increase in the 1990s was driven by investment in computers and that the 21st century may not see the same rate of growth as data jobs are outsourced overseas.

Knowledge management has been approached from a number of perspectives, with information management and organizational approaches being two of the most important. In fact, within organizations and especially in conferences and journals, information technology and human resources have competed for the lead role. Information technology has tended to be the dominant force but not always beneficially (Storey and Quintas, 2001).

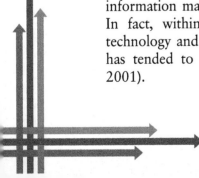

# TACIT AND EXPLICIT KNOWLEDGE

Knowledge management owes its inspiration to the work of the philosopher Michael Polanyi and the Japanese organization learning 'guru' Ikijuro Nonaka. Both of these theorists argued that knowledge has two forms: explicit and tacit, which has some similarity to Stewart's hard and soft knowledge assets (Key concept 9.7).

---

**KEY CONCEPT 9.7**   EXPLICIT VERSUS IMPLICIT KNOWLEDGE

*Explicit knowledge* is the obvious knowledge found in manuals, documentation, files and other accessible sources.

*Implicit, or tacit knowledge* is found in the heads of an organization's employees and are more difficult to access and use, for obvious reasons. Typically, an organization does not even know what this knowledge is. Worse, the knee-jerk reaction of top managers who fire employees at the first sign of any downturn means that the knowledge is often lost.

---

Grant (1997) argues that HRM can improve an organization's competitiveness through its impact on the 'knowledge base' of a business: the skills and expertise of its employees. Management of human resources can provide a competitive advantage through a knowledge management perspective. One strategy is to encourage replication of tacit knowledge within an organization without allowing it to replicate outside. From this perspective, organizations should:

1   Accept that knowledge is a vital source for value to be added to business products and services and a key to gaining competitive advantage.

2   Distinguish clearly between explicit and tacit knowledge.

3   Accept that tacit knowledge rests inside individuals and is learned in an unstructured and informal way.

4   Identify and tap this tacit knowledge and make it part of the 'structural capital' of the business, so that it can be made available to others.

Drucker (1998) contends that knowledge management will have a major impact on the structure of future organizations. He predicts that knowledge-based organizations will have half the number of management layers found in businesses today – and the number of managers will be cut by two-thirds. Drucker considers that the organizational structures featured in current textbooks are still those of 1950s manufacturing industries. In the future, businesses will come to resemble organizations that today's managers and students would not pay any attention to: hospitals, universities and symphony orchestras; in other words, knowledge-based organizations 'composed largely of specialists who direct and discipline their own performance through organized feedback from colleagues, customers and headquarters'.

In the 20th century information was collected in order to monitor and control workers. 'Knowledge' was held at the top of the organization where strategies were determined and decisions made. But this Tayloristic view of the organizations ignored the wealth of knowledge held by ordinary workers. In Drucker's opinion, specialist knowledge workers will resist the primitive 'command and control' model of people management in the same way as professionals such as doctors and university teachers do already. Moreover, 21st century employees have a greater understanding of information technology than their predecessors, having grown up with social networking, smartphones and the online world

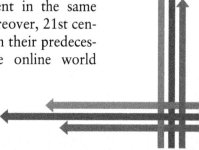

(Calabrese, 2010). Velde (2010) observes that expatriate employees build up a considerable bank of knowledge. When they are repatriated they often leave the organization – taking their knowledge with them. She argues that managing international human resources needs to incorporate strategies for transferring that knowledge to other employees.

Oliver and Kandadi (2006) identified ten major factors affecting knowledge management practices and associated organizational culture. These include leadership, organizational structure, evangelization, communities of practice, reward systems, time allocation, business processes, recruitment, infrastructure and physical attributes.

Davenport and Prusak, in *Working Knowledge* (2000) say that knowledge, data and information are not identical concepts. They point out that confusion between the three has resulted in many organizations investing large amounts of money in the technology of knowledge management without achieving any useful results. They consider that understanding the difference between the three concepts is crucial:

> Organizational success and failure can often depend on which one of them you need, which you have, and what you can and can't do with each. Understanding what these three things are and how you get from one to another is essential to doing knowledge work successfully.
>
> *Data* is hard, factual information often in numerical form – it can tell you when, and how often something happened, how much it cost and so on, but it does not say why it happened. Organizations love accumulating vast quantities of data – the sheer bulk of which serves to confuse and obscure any value.

*Information* for Davenport and Prusak comes in the form of a message – and it is the receiver rather than the sender of the message who determines that it is information – through some communication channel whether voice, email, letter, etc. It is different from data in that it has meaning or shape. In fact, data can be transformed into information with the addition of meaning and they list a number of ways, each beginning with C:

> *Contextualized:* the purpose of the data is known.
>
> *Categorized:* the unit of analysis or key component is known.
>
> *Calculated:* perhaps through a statistical or mathematical analysis.
>
> *Corrected:* through the removal of errors.
>
> *Condensed:* by being summarized or tabulated.

*Knowledge* transcends both data and information in a number of ways. Davenport and Prusak define it as follows:

> Knowledge is a fluid mix of framed expertise, values, contextual information and expert insight that provides a framework for evaluating and incorporating new experiences and information. It originates from and is applied in the minds of knowers. In organizations it often becomes embedded not only in documents or repositories but also in organizational routines, processes, practices and norms.

## KNOWLEDGE MANAGEMENT PRACTICE

Proponents of knowledge management argue that long-term competitive advantage can come from mapping and tapping tacit knowledge. But simply agreeing with this principle on the grounds of commonsense does not tell us how to do it. And many accounts of

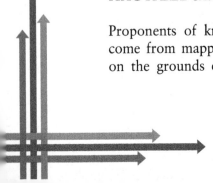

knowledge management fall down on this issue. One notable exception is Tiwana (1999) who points out:

> In the technology industry, companies that have prospered are not the companies that have invented new technology, but those that have applied it. Microsoft is perhaps a good example of a company that had first relied on good marketing, then on its market share and now on its innovative knowledge – mostly external.

Tiwana considers that Microsoft has also learned a great deal from its past failures, describing its founder Bill Gates as 'the richest man in the world: a fierce, tireless competitor who hires people with the same qualities'. Microsoft uses knowledge management without a specific knowledge management agenda and gains by applying knowledge rather than creating it. In fact, according to Tiwana, tangible business assets such as technology, patents or market share can only provide a business with a temporary advantage. Eventually, a particular market-leading technology, for example, becomes the staple of every business in the same industry.

Often organizations do not know what they know. And if they do know what they *did* know:

→ That knowledge can be out of date.

→ The person(s) who possessed it may have gone – perhaps to a competitor.

→ The knowledge has been replaced or updated.

→ The location or possessor of the new knowledge is not known.

Schack (2004: 2) highlights the confusion about knowledge, even for people who can be described as 'experts':

> Performance seems to accompany knowledge, and experts clearly know more about the fields in which they are active. However, closer inspection … reveals a frequent failure to distinguish between knowledge that is functionally relevant for the control and organization of actions, and knowledge that merely accompanies actions or justifies them in retrospect. As a result, we cannot assume that the knowledge high performers (experts) report is the same as the knowledge responsible for their performance.

Corrall (1999) gives examples of how knowledge can be stored and accessed:

*Knowledge databases and repositories (explicit knowledge):* Storing information and documents that can be shared and re-used, for example, client presentations, competitor intelligence, customer data, marketing materials, meeting minutes, policy documents, price lists, product specifications, project proposals, research reports, training packs.

*Knowledge route maps and directories (tacit and explicit knowledge):* Pointing to people, document collections and datasets that can be consulted, for example, 'yellow pages'/'expert locators' containing CVs, competency profiles, research interests.

*Knowledge networks and discussions (tacit knowledge):* Providing opportunities for face-to-face contacts and electronic interaction, for example, establishing chat facilities/'talk rooms', fostering learning groups and holding 'best practice' sessions.

## KNOWLEDGE MANAGEMENT, KNOWLEDGE SHARING – OR SHEER BUNKUM?

In a scathing attack on the concept of knowledge management, Wilson (2002) concludes that the 'knowledge management idea' is '… in large part, a management fad, promulgated

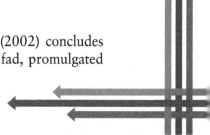

mainly by certain consultancy companies, and the probability is that it will fade away like previous fads.' In his opinion, the concept rests on two foundations:

*The management of information:* Wilson finds much of the topic to be no more than the re-labeling of 'information management'.

*The effective management of work practices:* Based on a Utopian vision of business organization where everyone benefits from information exchange, individuals are free to develop their own expertise and organizational 'communities' determine how that expertise is used.

According to Wilson, we are some distance from that Utopia: 'Whatever businesses claim about people being their most important resource, they are never reluctant to rid themselves of that resource (and the knowledge it possesses) when market conditions decline'. He instances British Airways, which dispensed with 7000 of its 'knowledge resources' after the 9/11 terrorist attack in 2001, and Barclays Bank, which reduced its worldwide workforce by 10 per cent in the same year despite profits of £2 billion. Wilson passes judgement on these actions: 'No imagination appears to have been used by either of these companies to determine ways in which their "most important resource" might be more effectively employed to increase turnover and profits'. He asks: 'If getting promotion, or holding your job, or finding a new one, is based on the knowledge you possess – what incentive is there to reveal that knowledge and share it?'

**HRM IN REALITY** HOARDING KNOWLEDGE

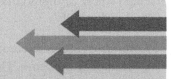

*Forget knowledge sharing – colleagues hide their best ideas*

Has a colleague ever ignored you when you asked for information? Did you have the feeling that they were deliberately avoiding you or were only pretending to be ignorant? Recent research suggests that you may have been right.

Catherine Connelly, assistant professor of HR and management at McMaster University's De-Groote School of Business, has found that workers often protect their knowledge, even taking steps to hide it from colleagues. Catherine Connelly and colleagues David Zweig of the University of Toronto and Jane Webster of Queen's University presented their findings at the annual conference of The Society for Industrial and Organizational Psychology in 2006.

She considers that companies regard knowledge acquired on the job as proprietary and implement expensive knowledge management systems to ensure those in the know share with others and says that this behaviour is bad for business.

Catherine Connelly says that the reluctance to share produces a contagious tendency to hide important knowledge and as a result productivity suffers.

Connelly's research indicates that employees are more likely to share with people they trust and treat them fairly. 'When organizations emphasize positive relationships and trust among employees, knowledge sharing will become part of the culture', she explained.

Clues you've been a victim of knowledge hiding:
You ask a colleague for help, and they say:

→ 'I'm sorry. My boss doesn't want this to be public right now.'

→ Nothing. They ignore your request.

→ 'I don't know. Maybe someone else can help you out.'

Why people engage in knowledge hiding:

→ they feel that an injustice has been done to them

→ they are distrustful of co-workers or management

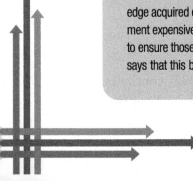

→ they are retaliating against someone else's behaviour toward them

→ the organizational climate encourages secrecy, not sharing

→ they can get away with it.

How to encourage knowledge sharing:

→ emphasize positive relationships and trust among employees

→ explain the mutual benefits of having colleagues share their knowledge

→ treat all workers fairly and respectfully

→ make knowledge sharing part of the culture.

*How important is the nature of organizational culture in knowledge management?*

*Source: Reprinted with permission from HRM Guide Canada (http://www.hrmguide.net/canada/).*

 ## SUMMARY

We commenced this chapter with an examination of entrepreneurship and the growth (or not) of small enterprises into large organizations. The early years of an organization sets a pattern for the culture it will have in later years. Corporate culture involves the informal organization, including myths, rumour and gossip mediated by power relations and channels of communication that are not prescribed by management. Establishing or changing a corporate culture is difficult. Knowledge has become an increasingly important element of competitive performance. The management of that knowledge requires an understanding of formal processes as well as the informal channels that transmit information within and between sections of an organization.

 ## FURTHER READING

1 *Entrepreneurship* by David Stokes, Nicholas Wilson, and Martha Mador (Cengage Learning, 2010).

2 *Entrepreneurship: Successfully Launching New Ventures* by Bruce R. Barringer and Duane Ireland (Pearson Education, 3rd edition, 2009).
The above are both student-oriented and cover a wide range of issues.

3 Terrence E. Deal and Allen A. Kennedy's (Perseus, 1984) *Corporate Cultures: Rites and Rituals of Corporate Life* is a classic text on culture within organizations, appearing in a number of editions.

4 *The Corporate Culture Survival Guide* by Edgar H. Schein, published in a revised edition by Jossey-Bass in 2009, is an interesting book by one of the recognized experts on the field.
There is a vast selection of books about knowledge management, few questioning the entire concept and many having an IT orientation.

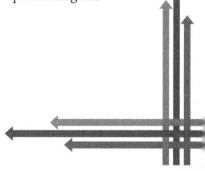

5 *The New Edge in Knowledge: How Knowledge Management Is Changing the Way We Do Business* by Carla S. O'Dell and Cindy Hubert (John Wiley and Sons, 2011) takes a view of knowledge management in the era of social media.

6 *Knowledge Management in Organizations: A Critical Introduction* by Donald Hislop (OUP Oxford, 2$^{nd}$ edition, 2009) is one of the few that include a human resource perspective.

 **REVIEW QUESTIONS**

1 Outline some of the ways in which people management skills could be made available to entrepreneurs.

2 Are entrepreneurs special people? How would you explain the difference between a 'nascent entrepreneur' and an entrepreneur who succeeds in starting a business?

3 Why does the level of entrepreneurship vary between countries?

4 How does the size of a small business limit the practice of human resource management? What difficulties are human resource specialists likely to experience in dealing with a founding entrepreneur as a business grows?

5 What do you consider to be the main advantages and disadvantages of collaborative entrepreneurship? Why do collaborative ventures often end as single-owner companies?

6 To what extent do national cultures determine corporate cultures? How many different cultures can you identify in your own country? What are the implications of the differences between these cultures for human resource managers?

7 How can the concept of 'in-groups' help to explain the inadequacies of equal opportunities policies?

8 Explain the difference between organizational 'culture' and 'structure'. Is there a difference between the two concepts?

9 In what ways are the informal organization and the corporate culture of that organization (a) the same; (b) different?

10 What insights have Deal and Kennedy provided to further our understanding of corporate culture?

11 Is it the case that: (a) firms using HRM procedures benefit because of those procedures or (b) firms that are forward-looking and growing are more likely to use HRM procedures because they are forward-looking and growing?

12 How would you define the following terms?

    (a) High performance work system

    (b) Knowledge

    (c) Knowledge management.

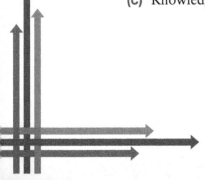

## The craft partnership/ royal ocean

1   The Craft Partnership is a cooperative of 20 independent producers. They are based at an old factory site on the outskirts of town that is divided into small workshops. HR, marketing and finance services are provided by an office manager and two staff. The cooperative has grown successfully over the last five years. Now they have the opportunity of taking on a much larger site adjacent to the tourist centre.

Opinion is divided among the partners on the way forward. Some are content to stay as they are. A few have said that they will leave and set up on their own if the cooperative gets much larger. Others are excited by the prospect of better facilities, room for growth, and space for new members in the cooperative. They also see big advantages in being accessible to tourists.

The office manager sees this as the opportunity to make more radical changes. She is concerned that the partnership is unwieldy and makes external finance difficult. She spends much of her time sorting out squabbles between partners and trying to get them to share resources sensibly. Some partners are overworked and others do not have enough to do. She can see many ways of increasing efficiency if the partnership becomes a conventional business. This could be done by creating a holding company, making the existing partners both shareholders and employees. A local venture company is prepared to make a substantial investment for a 50 per cent share in the new organization. However, they would require a formal structure with defined management roles. They feel that the office manager would make a suitable managing director.

***She has arranged a meeting with the partners and the venture company. (a) How should she proceed? (b) What is the reaction likely to be? (c) What is the way forward?***

2   The Royal Ocean is a well-established resort hotel. Its clients are in the middle to upper income bracket and many return year after year. It has developed a reputation for attentive service and is regarded as expensive but good value. In recent years, however, a new marina development further down the coast has provided extra competition. The new hotels are larger and more modern, boasting a choice of restaurants, bars and leisure facilities. They have seriously affected the Royal Ocean's profitability.

The hotel is on a restricted site and the owners, a small regional chain, cannot afford substantial capital investment. Like most hotels it has a highly seasonal pattern of business. Despite the competition, the Royal Ocean has no difficulty in filling rooms during peak periods. Occupancy rates have been mainly affected during quieter periods. The company has decided to encourage more business out of season through selective promotions to group travel organizers. During the low season, the country has a national holiday when, traditionally, the hotel has allowed most of its staff to take two days off. The small number of remaining employees has been sufficient to cater for the few guests. In the past, visitors at this time of year have tended to be middle-aged people seeking quiet relaxation. They have been happy to

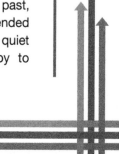

tolerate restricted service in the restaurant, bar and pool area.

This year, the hotel has achieved 80 per cent occupancy over the holiday period. The regular clients have been vastly outnumbered by families with young children.

Rooms have been sold cheaply to low-income groups who are not expected to spend heavily on the more profitable services. Accordingly, the hotel general manager decided not to increase staffing to normal weekly levels. He felt that the low return would not justify upsetting employee morale.

However, the consequences have proven to be unfortunate. The regular clients have been angered by the inability of the hotel to provide even the basic service experienced in previous years.

Most shops, restaurants and visitor facilities in the area are closed because of the holiday. The clients are forced to remain within the hotel. The restaurant has been besieged by noisy family groups. The pool area has become a playground. Clients are waiting for up to 20 minutes for an elevator because children are continuously going up and down in them. The quiet middle-aged regulars are complaining vociferously to any member of staff they can find. It seems that they are largely affluent professionals who are accustomed to having their way. They are becoming increasingly demanding and are threatening never to come back.

*What can be done (a) now and (b) in the future?*

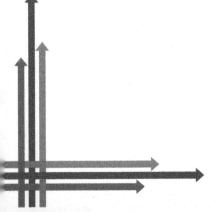

# CHAPTER 10
# Employee engagement

## LEARNING OBJECTIVES

The purpose of this chapter is to:

→ Introduce the concept of employee engagement.

→ Evaluate the true nature of commitment.

→ Relate commitment to culture.

→ Examine the practice of employer branding as a form of commitment management.

→ Debate the concept of employee involvement.

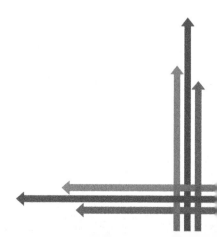

# EMPLOYEE ENGAGEMENT AND COMMITMENT

Organizational commitment is a central concept in HRM (see Key concept 10.1). It is one of the 4 'Cs' featured in the seminal Harvard model discussed in Chapter 1 and one of the measurable criteria in our 10-Cs checklist of HRM effectiveness (see Part 1). More recently there has been a tendency to subsume the concept within the topic of employee engagement.

> **KEY CONCEPT 10.1**  COMMITMENT
>
> Commitment is defined as the degree of identification and involvement that individuals have with their organization's mission, values and goals (Mowday, Steers and Porter, 1979). This translates into: their desire to stay with the organization; belief in its objectives and values; and the strength of employee effort in the pursuit of business objectives (Griffin and Bateman, 1986).

Rhetorical accounts of human resource management have claimed that organizations that adopt the philosophy of HRM gain integration and coherence in their people management processes and systems. Integration is dependent on a strong and binding link between employee behaviour and the goals of the organization. According to this viewpoint, commitment to the mission and values of the organization is a fundamental principle. As a concept it is clearly related to that of 'strong' corporate culture, and accounts of strategies to counter low employee engagement emphasize the need to build cultures that strengthen commitment as in the case of Kia motors (Tomlinson, 2010). Employee engagement goes further than simple compliance or surface behaviour: it is an emotional attachment to the organization. For example, Osborne and Cowen (2002: 227) make the claim:

> A 'true believer' mentality pervades high-performing organizations. Everyone believes in the vision of the business and that it will bring certain success. People believe that they are involved in something bigger than simply their own self-interest. They have a strong sense of identity with the organization and act as if they were owners.

In particular, the Harvard approach views employee commitment as the key determiner of competitive performance. In Chapter 3 we observed that people working within a culture of commitment are prepared to work longer, apply greater ingenuity to resolve a problem and try that much harder to win an order. In effect they are in a high-commitment culture.

From this perspective, employee engagement comes within a climate of trust. It requires a shared understanding between employees at all levels as mutual stakeholders in the future of an enterprise. It emphasizes the employment relationship between worker and employer and raises questions about the mutual obligations of both parties. Is it reasonable, for example, to expect employees to volunteer suggestions that could produce reductions in the time and effort required to perform a task if there is a risk of job losses as a result?

It is easy to see how engagement can arise in a high-trust culture such as that which prevailed in Japan until the 1990s. It can be understood also within the context of the consensus social market in parts of Europe where jobs have a considerable degree of protection, employees are consulted through works councils and there is generous social security provision for people without jobs. But how can commitment arise in businesses operating in the free markets of most English-speaking countries where there is an imbalance of power between different stakeholders?

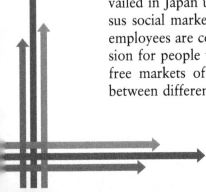

Commitment has also been the subject of research for some time because of its strong psychological connotations. Initially, attention was paid to commitment as behaviour. For example, Salancik (1977) identified four behavioural elements:

→ *Explicitness.* Is it clear that an act of commitment took place? Can it be denied? Was it consciously determined?

→ *Revocability.* Can we change our minds? Can the act be undone?

→ *Volition.* Is an act performed under our own volition or under the control of someone else?

→ *Publicity.* Has an expression or act of commitment been made in public?

Commitment arises as individuals perform acts such as joining a firm, working long hours and speaking well of the organization to customers or friends. Employees reflect on their own behaviour and conclude that because they have done something which is favourable towards their own organization, and done so in front of others, apparently of their own free will, they must have a commitment to that organization. In other words, free choice and public behaviour reinforce a feeling of commitment.

In recent years the emphasis has shifted towards a significant framework in social psychology that revolves around the concept of 'attitudes'. Attitudes are seen to have three components (McKenna, 2000: 248). These are: belief (cognitive), feeling (affective) and action (behavioural or conative). Each can be positive or negative. The emotional (affective) component seems to be of greatest significance, able to influence or override the other two. From this viewpoint, commitment is seen as having three key elements (Allen and Meyer, 1990):

→ *Affective:* the individual's emotional attachment to an organization.

→ *Continuance:* an individual's perception of the costs and risks associated with leaving the organization (equivalent to the behavioural component).

→ *Normative:* the obligation and responsibility a person feels towards the organization (equating to the cognitive component).

Research on attitudes indicates that these components usually show a considerable degree of consistency with each other. But this is not always the case. For instance, employees can feel proud of a company and believe that they owe an obligation for past good treatment, training or promotion. However, they may be aware that pay is relatively low and other organizations offer more attractive prospects. Lee and Gao (2005) studied organizational commitment among Korean retail employees by analyzing relationships among two facets of commitment (affective and continuance), three facets of job satisfaction (pay, co-worker, and supervisor) and two work outcomes (effort and propensity to leave). In the Korean retail setting they found:

1  satisfaction with pay and satisfaction with supervisor significantly increase both affective and continuance commitment;

2  satisfaction with co-workers positively influences affective commitment but has no significant effect on continuance commitment; and

3  affective commitment increases job effort but decreases the employees' propensity to leave the firm, while continuance commitment reduces propensity to leave but does not increase job effort.

It is clear, therefore, that employee engagement and its central notion of commitment are not as simple as some HR theorists maintain (Agrawal and Sadhana, 2010). In practice,

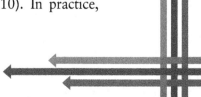

## HRM IN REALITY  EMPLOYERS IN FANTASY LAND

Eighty per cent of Australian businesses believe they are seen as great employers offering positive and rewarding workplace environments. But 63 per cent of jobseekers say that employers are 'not delivering' on expectations.

Staff are likely to leave in droves from employers who do not deliver on original employment promises, according to a 2005 Hudson Report. The Hudson national survey of over 8000 Australian employers, found a significant disconnect between how Australian businesses think they are viewed as a workplace, by current and prospective employees, and reality. Hudson conclude that this could be costing Australian businesses millions in staff turnover at a time when they cannot afford to lose people.

The report found that 80 per cent of Australian managers believe that their company's workplace reputation is clearly understood, proactively managed and aligned with what employees expect of them. But only half of these employers actually have a system in place to measure this so-called 'great' reputation! Moreover, a Hudson survey of more than 2500 jobseekers has revealed that 63 per cent of them believe their current employer is not delivering the employment experience that was promised to them.

Matt Dale, Hudson's National Practice Manager for Talent Management, said, 'These results sound a clear-warning to Australian businesses who believe they are getting it right and living up to their employees' expectations.

In many cases, companies are operating under a misguided impression and believe their workers are happy in the workplace, when the truth is that they're not. Their employment promise may be working extremely well in luring employees into the company, but fails miserably when it comes to retaining them in the long-term.

Disillusioned employees will simply leave if they feel the organization has not delivered on the employment experience that was originally promised to them. In a market where skills shortages are rife and candidates are in the driving seat, employers simply cannot afford to let this happen.

Matt Dale also commented that unfortunately, many businesses invest heavily in communicating an employment brand promise but fail to align this with actual employment experience.

'In order to get an employment brand right, it means understanding what current and prospective employees want and defining a clear and compelling value proposition. Most critically, all of the organization's current human resources programmes, policies and practices must be aligned with the brand so that it has substance and integrity with employees across the whole organization', he concluded.

Hudson recommends the following for businesses wishing to develop their employer branding:

→ Focus the employment brand on retention not just attraction.

→ Systematically measure workplace reputation.

→ Develop a clear and sustainable brand promise and align it with the employment experience.

→ Leverage the power of the company's existing market brand.

→ Ensure close interaction between the HR function and the company's marketing team.

*Why do businesses appear to have a distorted view of the way they are perceived by their employees?*

*Source: Reprinted with permission from HRM Guide Australia (http://www.hrmguide.net/australia/).*

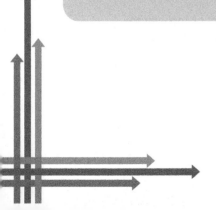

many of us hold ambivalent attitudes towards our employing organizations, perhaps enjoying our own jobs and the company of our fellow employees but wary of the intentions of senior executives. Nevertheless, according to the rhetoric, engaged employees are crucial to high performance, not least because (Gotsi and Wilson, 2001: 102):

> ... staff and their behaviour represent the reality of the organization to the customers and therefore, if their behaviour does not live up to the expectations created through the organization's external communication campaigns, the organization's overall reputation will be damaged.

## COMMITMENT AND CULTURE

A culture of engagement or commitment is frequently cited as a goal for organizational change (Tomlinson, 2010). Paradoxically, however, change programmes designed to instill modern business methods and 'lean-mean' management structures can rebound, leading to a reduction in employee engagement. Osborne and Cowen (2002) see a culture of commitment as a crucial basis for high-performance and identify a number of characteristics of such a culture:

*Emotion-packed vision.* A simple, compelling vision for the future that resonates with employees. It must be easy to understand and visualize and go 'beyond simply making money'.

*'True believer' mentality.* Every employee having a belief in the vision of the business and convinced that it will bring certain success. The key is a strong sense of identity with the organization so that ordinary employees act as if they are owners.

*Plain vanilla values.* Three or four essential and basic values that may be formally expressed or implicit in the way the business is conducted. They need to be simple and have some emotional appeal. For instance, Jack Welch, formerly of General Electric, who highlighted self-confidence as the core of employee success, and also added speed and simplicity as basic values. Fair treatment is another typical 'high commitment' value.

*Pride and dissatisfaction.* An apparently contradictory mix of intense employee pride in the company combined with a dissatisfaction with their current performance. According to Osborne and Cowen (*ibid.*): 'Edgy ideas and attitudes are pervasive. High performers have a commitment to learning from every mistake and every success.'

*Peer respect.* From Osborne and Cowen's observations, high-performing organizations rarely rely on fear to motivate employees. Instead, an urge to earn and maintain mutual respect appears to govern the behaviour of senior managers. Respect for oneself comes as a result of respect from others. According to Osborne and Cowen: 'Cynicism is regarded as weakness, an excuse for not getting the job done.'

*Long-term relationships.* Instead of switching jobs frequently, from one company to another, long-term relationships are seen as the path to personal success. Employees expect to work for their company and with each other for a long time. This is related to peer respect since short-term 'one-upmanship' is not seen as a positive way forward in a high-performance organization.

*Fun.* Success is celebrated publicly and loudly.

O'Malley (2000:7) considers that commitment is not easy to obtain:

> Companies that are able to create commitment realize that commitment ultimately is personal. This is the hard part of commitment that has profound implications for corporate conduct.

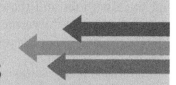

## HRM IN REALITY EMPLOYEE WORK PERCEPTIONS PREDICT ORGANIZATIONAL SUCCESS

Employees' perceptions of work conditions have a significant impact on the performance of their organizations, according to research from Gallup, Inc. published in *Perspectives on Psychological Science* in 2010.

Lead author James K. Harter explains that numerous studies have linked attitudes to employment to mood outside work and health outcomes such as coronary heart disease. The current study was based on more than 2000 business units of ten companies (including retail stores, factories and sales offices). Researchers analyzed employee satisfaction surveys and retention rates, customer loyalty and company financial performance to identify relationships between employee job satisfaction and outcome measures.

Results indicate that employee work perceptions predict organizational success. Where employees have positive perceptions of their jobs, their organizations benefit from higher retention, increased customer loyalty and improved financial outcomes. The study found that employees' perceptions of their jobs have a greater effect on organizational outcomes than the reverse.

Researchers suggest that an important role for managers seeking to improve employee satisfaction and company success would be to 'clarify expectations for employees by helping employees see the ultimate outcomes the organization is working to achieve and how they play a role in achieving those outcomes'.

The authors commented:

> One implication is that changes in management practices that improve employee perceptions of specific work situation variables will increase business-unit outcomes, including financial outcomes.

*How would you explain the link between employee expectations and organizational outcomes?*

Source: Reprinted with permission from HRM Guide USA (http://www.hrmguide.com).

---

It requires being consistent in what one does even though there may be short-term costs attached; it requires being flexible and making exceptions; and it requires making choices about what employees are prepared and unprepared to do – and providing reasons. Commitment is not created through a grab bag of trendy corporate goodies. It requires the patient and concerted attention of the whole organization.

O'Malley lists a number of reasons why companies feel they cannot create a culture of commitment:

*Too hard.* The process is perceived as being too difficult. In essence, the company has decided that its management is not good enough to obtain commitment.

*Too costly.* When changes are considered to improve conditions for employees, the immediate focus is on the costs involved rather than the ultimate benefits: 'If it costs money and is not related to physical or financial capital, the answer is *no*' (O'Malley, 2000: 7).

*Too different.* Business is supposed to be hard-nosed whereas treating employees in a way that will foster their commitment is seen as 'soft'. HR professionals worry about their soft image in the company, especially if a commitment programme fails.

*Too hopeless.* Companies may assume that they are in a competitive industry where staff are constantly being poached from other organizations. They conclude that there is nothing that can be done – unaware that other businesses *are* doing something.

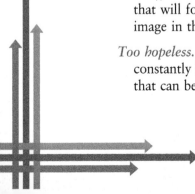

From a positive perspective, Medlin and Green (2009) argue that higher levels of engagement can come from formal, structured goal setting processes. In turn, higher levels of employee engagement lead to greater optimism among the workforce and that improved optimism then produces higher levels of individual performance. Engagement is seen to integrated with the emotional mood of a workforce.

## ENGAGEMENT STRATEGIES

According to Smither (1994) there are five barriers that are commonly encountered in changing organizations: disruption of personal relationships; the perceived threat to status; a preference for the status quo; economic factors; and problems arising from the use of consultants. If there is a risk that engagement may be a casualty of change initiatives, how is it best protected and developed? The answer seems to be that it must be regarded as a specific strategic objective in itself. In addition, it must be remembered that 'hearts and minds' commitment cannot be gained by top-down imposition of changes that run counter to the beliefs of employees.

Total quality management (TQM) programmes have been shown to be particularly effective in obtaining commitment. This may be due to their systematic and apparent objectivity, employing project management and other documentation to verify quality standards. These standards are externally justified: they are required to satisfy customers and are not seen as a local management invention. Commitment is reinforced by inbuilt feedback mechanisms that inform staff and management of quality levels.

On a positive level, an engagement programme should involve a thought-through package of measures that addresses:

*Communication.* Outlining the direction that the organization's strategy is taking and the purpose of any changes. Staff need to understand why decisions have been taken before they will cooperate in their implementation. Additionally, they must be encouraged to contribute to the process from their experience and ideas.

*Education.* Where change involves new technology, systems or procedures there must be a suitable training package available to provide confidence in their use. Training also builds commitment and respect through direct contact with managers involved in planning developments.

*Ownership.* Commitment is encouraged by involving people in decisions and making them responsible for implementing specific actions.

*Emotional identification* is more likely in an atmosphere of enthusiasm. This can be created by acknowledging and encouraging responsibility and recognizing hard work and results.

*Performance* assessment and reward structures should be focused on commitment.

*Rewards* in the form of pay, bonuses and prizes can be linked to visible commitment behaviour. The introduction of performance-related pay has been extensive in recent years. Normally this has been justified as a method of increasing commitment. However, as we shall see in Chapter 17, evidence shows that performance-related pay can encourage a small proportion of good performers at the expense of demotivating the majority. In practice it reduces morale and leads to accusations of unfairness.

*Employment contracts* can include clauses to prevent employees from publicizing information or opinions that might disadvantage the organization. Regrettably, such 'gagging' clauses have been used by management in public sector organizations,

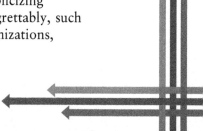

# HRM IN REALITY    EMPLOYEE ENGAGEMENT

Kansas State University research has found support for the view that employees who are engaged in their work, including higher levels of vigour, dedication and absorption in daily activities, also have better moods and are more satisfied at home.

The research was presented by Clive Fullagar, professor of psychology, Satoris Culbertson, assistant professor of psychology, and Maura Mills, graduate student in psychology, Manhattan, at the 2009 Society for Industrial and Organizational Psychology annual conference in New Orleans. Satoris Culbertson said:

> Our research indicated that individuals who were engaged in positive experiences at work and who shared those experiences with significant others perceived themselves as better able to deal with issues at home, became better companions and became more effective overall in the home environment.

The study followed 67 extension agents over two weeks to determine the relationship between daily work engagement and work-to-family facilitation. The participants completed two surveys each day – one at the end of the working day and the other before going to bed for the night. They also undertook a separate survey at the start of the two-week period and another at the end. According to Satoris Culbertson, stress at work and stress at home interact in both directions. The results suggest that engagement is significantly related to daily mood, and that mood also positively correlates with work-family facilitation. Both work engagement and work-to-family facilitation vary considerably from one day to the next.

'Just because an employee might not be invigorated or dedicated to his or her work on a Monday doesn't mean he or she won't be engaged on Tuesday or vice versa', said Culbertson. 'Additionally, one's work can facilitate things at home to a different extent depending on the day and what has happened on that particular day.'

Stressing that engagement refers to positive work involvement rather than more negative forms of job involvement like workaholism and work addiction, which have different effects on home lives, Culbertson said:

> Work addicts, or workaholics, have been shown to experience higher levels of work-family conflict. On the contrary, our study showed that higher levels of engagement were related to higher levels of work-family facilitation rather than conflict.

She believes that organizations can build on these findings and intervene in the workplace arguing that it is important for organizations to help employees balance work and personal lives.

'Practically, our results indicate that engagement is controlled by situational factors that are manageable by the organization', Culbertson added. 'Generating high levels of engagement among workers has a positive impact on the work–family interface.'

*Suggest reasons why so many US workers are actively disengaged.*

Source: Reprinted with permission from HRM Guide USA (http://www.hrmguide.net/usa/).

where staff feel themselves committed to public service rather than a particular hospital trust, for example.

Whittington and Galpin (2010) identify seven key elements:

→ an integrated HR value chain – a set of organizational practices that set a 'macro' context for:

→ full-range leader behaviours incorporating contingent reward and transformational behaviours.

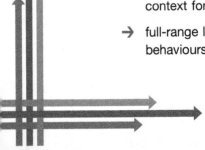

→   job enrichment through variety, significance, and task identity.

→   challenging and specific performance goals.

→   in-role job performance.

→   extra-role performance behaviours.

→   employee trust in a leader.


## JUSTIFYING COMMITMENT

Western managers have often imported the concept of engagement without a supporting framework. Some have appealed to the good sense of employees – a management rhetoric that presents commitment as voluntary. Supposedly, people are won over by the sound sense of strategic objectives and the 'obvious' view that commitment produces positive benefits for both staff and management. What are these benefits? First, management is made easier. A committed workforce consists of self-motivated staff who can function without the need for orders or managerial control. Left to themselves, they will work in a manner consistent with business objectives. Secondly, employees gain from management trust. They are empowered to make decisions and are rewarded through achievement. But what if the rhetoric is not matched by reality?

There are a number of contradictions inherent in the notion of commitment. Earlier, we discussed commitment in terms of three elements: emotion, belief and behaviour. As a combination of these, commitment can range between 'affective identification' and mere 'behavioural compliance' (see Key concepts 10.2 and 10.3) (Legge, 1995: 44). For instance, it can be confused with the phenomenon of 'presentism' – the idea that putting in long, and perhaps ineffectual, hours is a demonstration of engagement with the organization.

**KEY CONCEPT 10.2**  AFFECTIVE IDENTIFICATION

A real intellectual and emotional identification with the organization.

**KEY CONCEPT 10.3**  BEHAVIOURAL COMPLIANCE

Appearing to have attitudes and behaviours expected by senior managers without any real commitment.

Kunda (1991, cited in Willmott, 1993: 538) found evidence of 'distancing' in a study of middle managers in a company where the rhetoric of commitment and corporate culturism was strong. Managers deftly played the game of appearing to be committed to the organization's culture while, in reality, maintaining a sense of detachment from the process. In fact,

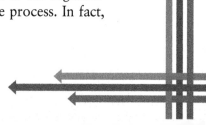

## HRM IN REALITY   EMPLOYEE ENGAGEMENT AND MANAGER BEHAVIOUR

A telephone survey conducted for Lynn Taylor Consulting has shown that – rather than helping to create the conditions for employee engagement – manager behaviour is seriously worrying employees across the country. When bosses stay behind closed office doors, workers begin to fear for their jobs. No fewer than 76 per cent of respondents to the survey said that the 'closed door scenario' triggers thoughts of being laid off.

According to Lynn Taylor, author of, *Tame Your Terrible Office Tyrant™ (TOT): How to Manage Childish Boss behaviour and Thrive in Your Job* (John Wiley and Sons, July 2009):

> In today's economic environment, employees are searching for every clue to determine their job fate. Too often, not enough direct input is given to employees, and so non-verbal cues are heavily relied upon. Managers working behind closed doors may be shutting out more than noise – they may be shutting down productivity.

The US telephone survey of 1000 respondents, 18 years of age or older, was conducted by a national independent research firm. The study concluded that employees averaged 2.8 hours (168.8 minutes) a day worrying about personal job concerns, such as mass lay-offs or losing their own jobs. Respondents were deeply suspicious of boss behaviours such as keeping office doors closed. When asked how often they think a boss's closed door was a signal of lay offs, the respondents said:

| | |
|---|---|
| Always | 11 per cent |
| Often | 32 per cent |
| Sometimes | 33 per cent |
| Rarely | 15 per cent |
| Never/Don't Know | 9 per cent |

'Changes in manager behaviour, such as a closed door, more private conferences or less direct communication all represent potential "exit signs" to many employees', said Lynn Taylor, adding that while managers have to deal with more sensitive personnel issues today than in previous decades, they can counter employee concerns at a critical time with more proactive communication.

'Acknowledging the astounding impact a small gesture can have on corporate productivity in tense times is a good first step. Providing your team with reassurances whenever possible will mitigate unnecessary panic and help them stay focused', she said.

'Many employees may also avoid speaking up to their bosses for fear of being shown the door, when, in fact, their ideas might boost a company's bottom line at a time when that is sorely needed. Opening your door literally and figuratively might not only mean greater profitability. In some cases, it might also help keep the doors of your business open', Lynn Taylor concluded.

*How can managers be encouraged to show greater openness?*

*Source: Reprinted with permission from HRM Guide USA (http://www.hrmguide.com).*

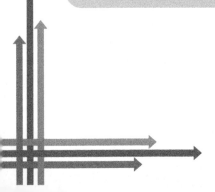

# HRM IN REALITY    AUSTRALIANS MOST LIKELY TO LEAVE

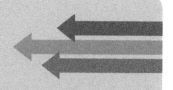

Australian workers are more likely to change employers over the next 12 months than staff in 16 other countries, according to 2010 research by employee engagement consultants Infogroup/ORC.

Based on responses from 9300 employees worldwide, the study found that 57 per cent are engaged with their current organizations, with Australia placed seventh, narrowly behind the United States and Germany.

The report by Phil Pringle of Infogroup/ORC found that Australian organizations were more affected by a lack of employee commitment to stay in the medium to long-term than by a current unwillingness to contribute or perceptions of their organization as a bad place to work.

For responses to the statement 'I intend to be working for my organization in 12 months time', Australia scored 8 percentage points below the global norm and 16 percentage points below Germany, 14 percentage points below Russia, and 10 percentage points below Switzerland. For responses to the statement 'It would take a lot to get me to leave my organization', Australia scored 6 percentage points below the global norm.

The study found that lack of commitment to stay with their current organization did not reflect poor HR practice and that Australia compared favourably in this respect with nations such as China, the UK, Spain, Singapore, Italy, Hong Kong and Japan. Responses to four statements scored at least 10 percentage points above the global norm:

→ 'I believe my organization is an equal opportunity employer.'

→ 'There are policies/practices in place to support me if I experience stress or pressure.'

→ 'Health and safety is taken seriously in my organization.'

→ 'I am satisfied with the training I receive for my present job.'

The study concluded that lack of commitment to stay was associated with interlinked themes of line manager capability and career progression. Over a third of Australian respondents were neutral when asked whether their line manager inspired them to work more effectively. A quarter actively disagreed with the statement 'I receive regular and constructive feedback on my performance'. In addition, 60 per cent responded neutrally or negatively to the statement 'Opportunities for career advancement at my organization are based on merit'. One third were neutral, and nearly a quarter (23 per cent) were negative towards the statement 'I am satisfied with the opportunities I have to get a better job in this organization'. The report suggests that as global competition for talent continues to increase, the onus is on line manager capability to recognize potential and engage employees in the long-term to enhance organizational success.

Wendy McInnes, director of employee research for Asia Pacific, commented:

> The story the data is telling is not surprising. Time and again we hear staff leave their managers, rather than their organization. Infogroup Perspectives has identified that Australian employees want to deliver value for their employers. However if managers can't nurture, develop and recognize their employees' talent, they will look elsewhere; no matter what positive feeling they have towards the organization.

*What factors contribute to lack of commitment to stay?*

*Source: Reprinted with permission from HRM Guide Australia (http://www.hrmguide.net/australia/).*

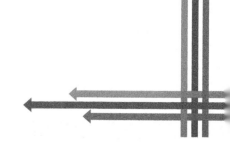

## HRM IN REALITY EMPLOYEES AND EMPLOYERS: 'A MARRIAGE BREAKDOWN IN PROGRESS?'

A survey of 2000 UK employees commissioned by the Chartered Institute of Personnel and Development (CIPD) has found that relationships between employers and employees in many workplaces are characterized by poor communication and low levels of trust resulting in underperformance, low productivity and high staff turnover.

'Working Life: Employee Attitudes and Engagement 2006' is written by Catherine Truss, Emma Soane and Christine Edwards from the School of Human Resource Management at Kingston University and Karen Wisdom, Andrew Croll and Jamie Burnett from Ipsos MORI.

Comparing the situation to a marriage under stress, the authors highlight some of the survey findings relating to communication and trust:

→ *We just don't talk anymore:* Around one-third of employees (30 per cent) say they rarely or never get performance feedback; 42 per cent feel they are not kept well informed about organizational developments; only 37 per cent are satisfied with opportunities to communicate views and opinions to management.

→ *You just take me for granted:* One-quarter (25 per cent) of employees rarely or never feel their work counts; only 38 per cent feel they are treated with respect by directors and senior managers.

→ *You really get me down:* Some 44 per cent of employees feel under excessive pressure at least once or twice a week; 22 per cent overall and 32 per cent of managers experience high levels of stress.

→ *The magic is gone:* Almost half of employees (43 per cent) are dissatisfied with their relationship with their manager; 26 per cent rarely or never look forward to going to work.

→ *I just can't trust you:* One-third of employees (32 per cent) are dissatisfied with the management of their organization; only 37 per cent have confidence in their senior management team and 34 per cent trust their senior managers.

→ *I want out:* About one-quarter of employees (26 per cent) are dissatisfied in their job; 47 per cent are looking for another job or in the process of leaving their current job.

Mike Emmott, CIPD employee relations adviser, said:

As in any marriage, good relationships need work and commitment. But with only three in ten employees engaged, the findings suggest many managers just aren't doing enough to keep their staff interested. Lack of communication means many employees feel unsupported and don't feel their hard work is recognized.

Catherine Truss said:

There is so much that managers can do to make their staff feel valued and improve levels of engagement that will benefit both employers and employees. We found that people who are engaged with their work perform better, are more likely to act as advocates for their employer and experience more job satisfaction. So it is in the interests of everyone to find ways of addressing low levels of engagement in the workplace.

*Why are employers often reluctant to communicate honestly with their employees?*

*Source: Reprinted with permission from HRM Guide UK (http://www.hrmguide.co.uk).*

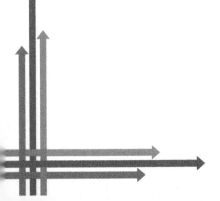

many Western organizations have a prevailing climate of cynicism, with employees and managers alike acting out their roles with little faith in the outcome of their actions. Watson (1994: 74), questioned managers in one organization and obtained the following response from one participant: 'We are a pretty committed bunch but I don't think ZTC knows what to do with that commitment'.

Yaniv and Farkas (2005) show that person–organization fit (POF) – the fit between organizational values and the individual values of employees – can play a significant role in closing the gap between corporate brand values as perceived by customers and those declared by management. If companies transfer corporate brand values to customers that appear to differ from reality, employees may perceive this as a lie resulting in a lack of identification with the corporate brand and an unwillingness to support it adequately. As a consequence customers feel mistrust towards the corporate brand. Person–organization fit has usually been studied in relation to internal organizational aspects such as commitment, identification, job satisfaction, intention to leave and willingness to do extra work. Yaniv and Farkas argue that HR managers should also regard the POF as a means of improving the organization's external performance. They caution that a strong corporate culture associated with a high POF might lead to inflexibility and inability to see the need for change.

## EMPLOYEE ENGAGEMENT EXAMINED

The term 'employee engagement' is increasingly popular among HR consultants and the notion has attracted academic interest although there is debate about its meaning, some concluding that it is too wedded to commitment to the exclusion of other issues such as well-being (Robertson and Cooper, 2010). Macey and Schneider (2008) consider that employee engagement refers to positive feelings held by employees about their jobs and also the motivation and effort they put into work. Engagement leads to positive employee behaviours that lead to organizational success.

According to Macey and Schneider, engagement should not be confused with satisfaction or commitment. They identify two components of employee engagement:

→ feelings of engagement (focus and enthusiasm), and

→ engagement behaviour (proactivity and persistence).

So, they distinguish between engagement and satisfaction:

→ engagement connotes energy and not satiation

→ satisfaction connotes satiation and contentment but not energy.

They argue that employees come to work ready to be engaged but organizations need to create the conditions that will release that energy. They believe that employees will feel and act engaged when managers create the right conditions that allow them to do so. The essential condition for feeling engaged, they contended, is fair treatment leading to a feeling of trust which, in turn, allows them to feel safe to be engaged.

According to Macey and Schneider:

Our framework places an emphasis on the management of human resources in ways that respect the energy people bring to the work place, and it puts the responsibility on management to create the conditions for employee engagement. Management is responsible for creating the conditions at work that will facilitate employee engagement.

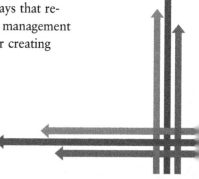

Craig and Silverstone (2010) contend that collective engagement is the key to high performance and that organizations which focus exclusively on individual engagement miss out on this. From a study of large US companies they found that fostering collective engagement begins by engaging one team, one workgroup and one workforce at a time.

## EMPLOYER BRANDING

> Your employer brand can be a magical combination of what your business values, offers and rewards – marrying what your brand promises outside with what your experience demands inside; what your business believes in and how you fundamentally respect the people who deliver your brand (Sartain and Schumann, 2006, p. 24).

Many commercial organizations are well experienced at promoting and cultivating a relationship between themselves and their clients through their brand image. Coca-Cola, BMW, McDonalds, Sony and BP are just some of the organizations whose brands are recognized throughout the world. Brands are not simply logos or names: by their existence they encourage people to develop a faith in the products or services provided by an organization and a belief in the integrity and reliability of its staff. Well regarded brands are valuable in themselves and companies work hard at maintaining their brand images. Recently, the concept of branding has been extended from the organization as supplier of goods and services to the organization as an employer (see Key concept 10.4).

### KEY CONCEPT 10.4 EMPLOYER BRANDING

The practice of developing, differentiating and leveraging an organization's brand message to its current and future workforce in a manner meaningful to them. Using the methodology of a corporate brand-building strategy to attract and keep quality employees. Employer branding is aimed at motivating and securing employees' alignment with the vision and values of the company. From a HR perspective, the concept has subsumed the older term 'internal branding' that was essentially the process of communicating an organization's brand values to its employees.

The basis of employer branding is the application of the same marketing and branding practices to a company's human resource activities (specifically, recruitment and retention) as it uses for consumer-targeted marketing and branding efforts. In other words, the business markets its brand image to its staff. And just as customers will cease buying a company's products or services when a promise is unfulfilled, its employees will also leave if the company fails to live up to its employer brand promises. Sartain and Schuman (2006: 22) believe that 'your employer brand is shorthand for the emotional connection with employees. It frames how you motivate employees to deliver what your business promises to customers and how you nurture an environment that prospective employees will want to join.'

The concept of employer branding draws on the notion that employees who fully understand and embrace an organization's culture, values and business objectives are more likely to share common goals with the organization, work for those goals and share information

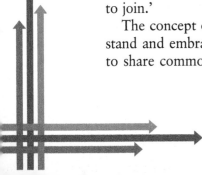

## HRM IN REALITY   MOST SENIOR MANAGERS LIVE THE BRAND

The 2008 CIPD Recruitment, Retention and Turnover Survey found that 71 per cent of organizations surveyed were already using the employer brand as a recruitment tool. However, employer branding is more than a recruitment tool. It can make a significant difference to the bottom line through its effect on employee retention and engagement.

According to Rebecca Clake, Adviser, Organization and Resourcing for CIPD:

> The importance of a strong employer brand in today's business environment cannot be exaggerated. Talented candidates aren't just looking for a healthy pay package, their expectations go far beyond that.
>
> An organization's attractiveness is strongly linked to its brand in the employment market place – what it is seen to stand for and how that matches up with the values of individuals. For the employer brand to be successful this external brand needs to be more than rhetoric, but to reflect the real experience of working for the organization.

A survey by Mercer Human Resource Consulting in 2006 showed that employees understand their role in the delivery of a high standard of customer service more clearly when their senior managers 'live' their organization's brand.

According to the survey, 85 per cent of senior managers claimed that they demonstrated their company's brand values in their own behaviour. Of these, 87 per cent believe all or most of their employees are fully aware of their role in providing a positive experience to clients. However, this figure drops to 58 per cent where the senior person does not live the company's brand.

Jim Matthewman, Worldwide Partner at Mercer, said:

> Employees play a crucial role in creating customer satisfaction and need to understand their role in delivering their organization's brand values to clients. Senior people should lead by example to influence the behaviour of their staff.

The survey results highlighted the importance of ensuring HR processes, including:

→   training

→   development and

→   reward.

These processes reinforce the brand philosophy. Ninety-three per cent of businesses that align their HR processes with brand values believe that most employees understand their role in the provision of a positive experience to clients.

According to Jim Matthewman:

> Companies need to link job performance criteria and measurement to behaviours that support brand principles to encourage employees to live their company's brand. The key aim is to develop employees into knowledgeable brand ambassadors, so they can improve their service to clients and, ultimately, enhance business performance.

The survey shows that internal communication is important; 90 per cent of businesses making the effort to promote their external brand internally believe that all or most of their staff are fully aware of their role in delivering a positive customer experience. But this percentage drops to 65 per cent for companies that do not use internal communication to support the external brand.

'By promoting brand values internally, companies can help ensure all employees understand brand objectives. Regular engagement with staff is required to make sure employee behaviour changes in a way that supports stated business goals', Jim Matthewman said. 'Employers who encourage their staff to exhibit brand values when dealing with clients can create differentiation and advantage that competitors will be unable to copy.'

*How would you distinguish between corporate branding and employer branding?*

*Source: Reprinted with permission from HRM Guide UK (http://www.hrmguide.co.uk).*

with other people. Employer branding reinforces perception of the organization's culture (as top managers perceive it) through a variety of messages, behaviours and other forms of communication. The employer brand is linked to the internal brand and the corporate brand (Foster *et al.*, 2010). Edwards (2010) identifies useful connections between employer branding and aspects of organizational research and theory, including: organizational attractiveness to job candidates, the psychological contract, organizational identity, organizational identification and organizational personality characteristics

Employer branding begins with the recruitment process because this offers a number of tools that can be used to create perceptions of an employing organization, including:

→ job advertisements and descriptions

→ the interview process

→ offer letters

→ information packs for new recruits

→ employee handbooks

→ induction and training.

Effectively managed, and this should be comparatively simple for professional marketers, the recruitment process can be used to create a positive relationship between candidates and the organization. It depends on relatively simple, thought-through procedures that consistently project a company's image and values in order to create strong, positive views of the organization. This can even extend to unsuccessful candidates. Beyond recruitment, Maxwell and Knox (2009) found that although specific characteristics of the employer brand varied between organizations, they fell into similar categories: employment, organizational successes, construed external image and product or service characteristics.

Gotsi and Wilson (2001) found that PR consultants considered it essential to have an alignment between employee behaviour and the values that an organization's brand stands for. They quote one consultant who stated that: 'aligning brand actions with brand promises is a critical test for managers'. The consultants they investigated highlighted the need to ensure that there was no gap between what an organization was saying in the outside world and what people believed inside that business. Employees were perceived as 'brand ambassadors' and brand marketing would only be successful if they 'lived the brand'. From this perspective, organizations have to (a) encourage employees to 'buy in' to the business vision and values; and (b) ensure that everyone within the organization clearly understands the purpose of the common set of values.

Within their line of thinking it is necessary for such conditions to be realized for employees to be able to reflect them through their own behaviour. There has to be an understanding of the brand, if staff are to 'live the brand' and its values (see Key concept 10.5). One of their interviewees observed that for this to happen 'reputation has to be based on reality in order to be credible'.

## KEY CONCEPT 10.5 LIVING THE BRAND

Identifying with an organization's brand values to such an extent that employees' behaviours fit exactly with the image that the business is trying to portray to its customers.

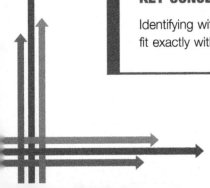

It is worth observing that, while it may be comparatively easy to convince a new recruit of the positive nature of a company's culture, employer branding can be quickly undone if the organization turns out to be rather different from the recruit's initial perceptions (Moroko and Uncles, 2008). In fact, an employer brand that departs considerably from reality can be counter-productive, leading to rapid disillusionment rather than sustained commitment.

Gotsi and Wilson (*ibid.*) indicate that the twin tasks of aligning staff behaviour with brand values and getting employees to 'live the brand' are very difficult – far more difficult than other aspects of conventional brand marketing such as creating a visual identity for an organization. They quote a consultant as saying: 'it's much harder to get people's behaviour and culture aligned with a brand, because people are much more unpredictable than graphics. People talk, walk, think, do things; graphics just stay there'.

To achieve these goals it is necessary to treat employees as an audience for corporate communications to ensure that all stakeholders receive the same message. The aim of internal communications, according to Gotsi and Wilson's respondents, is to encourage employees to believe that they can live up to projected brand values. This is done by talking and listening to staff and being aware of their need to believe in the organization's vision and values. But, whereas most consultants proposed a top-down communication exercise from senior managers to lower levels of employees, Gotsi and Wilson are more impressed by a minority view that communication should be two-way. They argue that communication should be a learning exercise in which ideas are shared and feedback obtained from the 'front line'.

Specifically, they contend that for employees' behaviour to reflect brand values organizations must align human resource management practices with their brand values. Recruitment policies, performance appraisal, training and reward systems must fit with brand values, otherwise conflicting messages will be sent about the behaviours that are really important for the business. Recruitment policies must be aimed at attracting the type of people who can fit the desired culture; performance management must identify and encourage behaviours that relate to brand values; reward systems should benefit people who live the brand.

Blumenthal (2001: 37), using the term 'internal branding' (IB), concludes:

> While searching for meaning is uncomfortable and putting power in the hands of frontline employees is risky, it may also be the only way to actually find the kind of meaning that transforms employees' lives. If employees 'can live with it or without it', then the brand is not living up to its potential. As Bergstrom points out, people are looking to be a part of something special, something connected, something that they can be proud of building. Brand, and its particular application internally, has the potential to be wielded in that way. Although at its worst, IB can prove a cynical exercise, at its best there is potential for more than just profit. IB can provide a basis for mutual respect, community, and honest win-win relationships that profit the organization precisely because it improves the quality of people's lives.

# EMPLOYEE INVOLVEMENT

Employee involvement is a wide-ranging topic that hinges on the notion that managers may have a prerogative to manage but this prerogative should not be exercised without considering the opinions of their employees (see Key concept 10.6). The concept of employee involvement has a moral, practical and legal basis. The moral dimension is difficult to resolve since it involves an ethical debate on the 'right' of managers to manage and the 'right' of employees to have a say in the way the organization is managed. Fundamentally, it is a

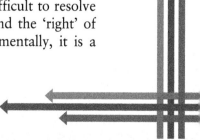

matter of personal opinion. The practical and legal aspects are more easily explained and justified.

---

### KEY CONCEPT 10.6  EMPLOYEE INVOLVEMENT

An umbrella term that is inconsistently and imprecisely used to embrace a diverse range of management processes involving participation, communication, decision making, industrial democracy and employee motivation.

---

There are sound practical reasons for taking account of employee views before making significant decisions. They include an acknowledgement of the greater and more detailed knowledge that experienced employees may have of specific processes when compared with a manager who may be relatively new or who has never been involved at a working level with those processes. Changes may seem perfectly reasonable and desirable to the manager, operating at a distance from the activity to be changed. But skilled workers may be aware of implications that are invisible to the manager. In fact, the concept of knowledge management is based on the value of individual expertise and experience that need to be harnessed and used for the benefit of the organization – rather than being ignored by over-confident and unwise managers.

The authority of managers may be constrained by an organization's own rules in the form of company handbooks, job definitions, reporting paths and consultation procedures so that the involvement of employees in decision making cannot be avoided. We noted in previous chapters that legislation can also impose requirements for consultation, for example in the form of works councils required under European legislation. In practice, most countries have employment legislation in place that sets the rights of employees within a legal context. Their rights are usually prescribed both individually and collectively so that (theoretically, at least) it is impossible for an organization and its managers to have total discretion over consultation and, to a lesser extent, involvement.

According to Holden (2001):

> There is an enormous range of employee involvement schemes, varying from those which are informational mechanisms to full-blown democratic systems where employees have as much say in the decision making as does management. This makes an all-encompassing definition problematic. In addition, different labels have been attached to these processes, such as employee or worker participation, industrial democracy, organizational communications, co-determination, employee influence, etc., each of which have their own definitions.

Marchington (2001) considers that employee involvement became prominent in the 1980s as an attempt by employers to find participative ways in which to manage staff. The trend in recent decades towards individual rather than collective employee relations may have encouraged interest in employee involvement. The UK 1998 Workplace Employee Relations Survey (Cully *et al.*, 1999) showed that even in firms that recognized trade unions, managers consulted individual employees (57 per cent) in preference to union representatives (36 per cent). In fact, 41 per cent of the companies surveyed did not have any union involvement but a mere 8 per cent stated that they never involved individual employees.

The nature of the relationship between employer and employee is described as the 'psychological contract' (see Key concept 10.7). Townley (1994) sees an inevitable gap between

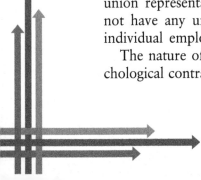

what is promised and what is realized: 'the naturally occurring space between expectation and deliverance of work'. The psychological contract implies some kind of exchange within the employment relationship but this is obscured by the power of the economic relationship between employer and employee.

253

> ### KEY CONCEPT 10.7  THE PSYCHOLOGICAL CONTRACT
>
> An informal understanding between the employer and employee. Unlike the formal employment contract, this has no physical existence. It is a set of expectations held by both employers and employees in terms of what they wish to give and receive from their working relationship (Rousseau and Parks, 1993).

Perhaps anticipating employer branding and its implications, Monks (1996) suggests that management of the psychological contract could be a suitable job for the human resource manager. In order for this to be possible, Townley (1994) points to three areas where knowledge is required:

*Knowledge of the workforce as a population:* where human resource information systems, employee surveys and staff feedback are as important as traditional personnel records.

*Knowledge of the activity or work to be performed:* detailed information obtainable through job analyses, quality circles and, more recently, the techniques elaborated for knowledge management.

*Knowledge of individual workers:* through performance assessments and feedback interviews.

She sees the employment relationship becoming a 'calculable arena' – a transformation of 'soft' HR based on indeterminate and sometimes unspecified understanding into a 'harder' form based on detailed information. In her view human resource practices are technologies through which 'activities and individuals become knowable and governable'. From this perspective, HRM becomes a powerful methodology that can turn the apparently imprecise and subjective topic that was once 'personnel' into a technology of people.

In an Australian study, Winter and Jackson (2006) examined perceptions of the state of the psychological contract between managers and employees (including work environment and factors such as salary, recognition and rewards, trust and fairness, open/honest communication). Assessments of the state of the contract were similar. However, managers tended to construct rational explanations and emphasize resource constraints and financial considerations, while employees constructed emotional explanations and attributed the situation to unfair, uncaring or distant management. Winter and Jackson's findings suggest that managers need more effective communication strategies placing them in a better position to explain to employees how the organization can meet (or not) specific contract expectations and obligations. Hess and Jepsen (2009) found more similarities than differences in the attitudes of different generational groups towards psychological contracts.

## EMPLOYEE INVOLVEMENT IN PRACTICE

Unlike Townley, Marchington (2001) sees employee involvement as a feature of 'soft' rather than 'hard' HRM. In firms with a hard orientation, Marchington considers that the

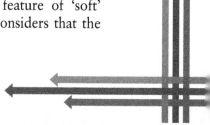

'numbers-driven', cost-cutting mentality reduces involvement to a one-way communication channel aimed at transmitting management decisions and propaganda to staff. This contrasts with organizations that are true believers in employees as their 'greatest asset' where there is a strategic commitment to sharing information and opinions and achieving a workplace culture that meets business needs. Bennett (2010) describes employee involvement as a form of employee voice initiative which may be seen differently by HR practitioners and unions.

Peccei and Rosenthal (2001) examined attempts to engender desirable customer-oriented behaviours among employees in the context of a major change initiative in a retail company. The change programme followed (by now) orthodox management theory which assumed that management behaviour, job design and values-based training would produce a feeling of empowerment among employees, and that this sense of empowerment would lead to pro-social customer-oriented behaviour. A large-scale employee survey showed that staff who took a positive view of management behaviour and who had also participated in values-based training were more likely to feel empowered. In turn, Peccei and Rosenthal found a positive relationship between psychological empowerment and customer-oriented behaviour (see Key concept 10.8). Similarly, health service staff who felt involved showed less cynicism towards change (Albrecht, 2010).

## KEY CONCEPT 10.8  EMPOWERMENT AND EMPOWERING

Murrell and Meredith (2000: 1) define empowering as: '... mutual influence; it is the creation of power; it is shared responsibility; it is vital and energetic, and it is inclusive, democratic and long-lasting'. They argue that 'empowerment' implies a finished process, a state of constancy. Whereas: 'Empowering ... suggests action – enabling the growth of individuals and organizations as they add value to the products or services the organization delivers to its customers, and the promotion of continuous discovery and learning'.

Marchington (2001) identifies the following characteristics in employee involvement schemes:

1  Employee involvement is a process primarily instigated by management.

2  Employees are assumed to want greater involvement, regardless of its form.

3  A unity of purpose is thought to be achievable between employees and their managers.

4  There is an expectation that employee involvement will lead to greater commitment and productivity.

Marchington (*ibid.*) also states:

> For many observers, notions of employee involvement (EI) and participation are central to any consideration of human resource management. Terms such as 'empowerment', 'team working', 'autonomy' and 'communications' are peppered throughout the management literature which publicizes and celebrates the latest initiatives in HRM. Similarly, the concepts of involvement form part of many academic discussions of HRM. Either as explicit elements of its policy and practice, or implicitly as a potential contributor to the achievement of higher levels of employee commitment.

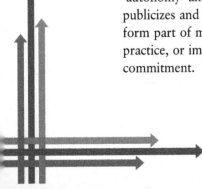

He notes that belief in the link between direct employee involvement and high levels of commitment and performance is based on some questionable assumptions:

1   That line managers will be committed to employee involvement and will ensure that it happens in the workplace.

2   That employee involvement positively influences staff attitudes, causing them to change their working behaviour which, in turn, leads to greater effectiveness and productivity.

3   That trade union officials and other employee representatives will allow themselves to be marginalized or led into acceptance of the management agenda.

Schuster (1998) asks why managers were so slow in adopting employee-centred management. He postulates five main reasons:

1   Complacency and inertia. He argues that, until recently, many executives had never questioned or considered changing the fairly comfortable status quo.

2   The short-term focus of 'management systems in general, and reward systems in particular'. Executive performance bonuses and incentive plans are tied to one year – and certainly not aimed at building a committed workforce over the long term.

3   Inability to measure the impact of HR practices. Schuster contends that: 'Until recently, little attention has been paid to executive performance regarding effective utilization of human resources, in part because standards for comparison did not exist. Our lack of *control* [original emphasis] over the efficient utilization of the most expensive single cost of operation in many organizations is indeed remarkable.'

4   Reluctance to give up their special status, executive privileges and managerial power.

5   Perhaps the most significant explanation of all - that many managers would like to introduce high-involvement practices 'but are unsure how to begin or exactly how to proceed'.

Pun, Chin and Gill (2001) investigated the characteristics of successful employee involvement initiatives in Hong Kong. They found the most critical factors to be: management commitment; rewards and motivation with a clear corporate mission; continuous improvement; and both extrinsic and intrinsic rewards. Contrary to the view that line managers are obstacles to employee involvement, Fenton-O'Creevy (2001) found that middle managers' attitudes were no more negative than those of senior managers. But there was a complex relationship between perceptions of their own degree of empowerment and attitudes towards employee involvement. Managers with experience of employee involvement were more likely to be supportive, but not if they had recently lost a job. Intriguingly, however, managers who had been through de-layering were more likely to support the involvement of employees. In a UK study, Cox, Zagelmeyer and Marchington (2006) concluded that involvement is not simply there or not: there are degrees of 'embeddedness', a combination of depth and breadth of involvement. The greater the breadth and depth, the higher the resulting commitment and job satisfaction.

According to Fisher (1999: 3):

Empowerment has clearly become the latest in a long litany of vogue practices that have ebbed and flowed over corporations like the changing of the tide. Today it is estimated that virtually every corporation in North America and Western Europe is using various forms of empowerment somewhere in their organization. Many even utilize an advanced form of empowerment called *self-directed work teams* (SDWTs) – now more commonly called *high-performance work systems*.

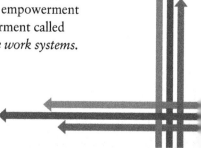

In fact, SDWTs are in a direct line of descent from the 'socio-technical systems' of the 1950s. Fisher argues that companies that take the concept seriously consider empowerment to be more than a passing fad. He also sees the team leader as a key role in the empowerment process. In the past the equivalent would have been supervisor, 'foreman', or manager. Now their titles may include terms such as 'facilitator' or 'adviser' and 'lead', 'coach' or 'train' rather than 'plan', 'organize', 'direct' or 'control'. Under the traditional form of management, supervisors would control subordinates by telling them what to do. In other words, the supervisor was the boss. Fisher contends that all traditional managers are supervisors but, for empowerment to take effect, they must become team leaders. Fisher *(ibid.,* p.11) justifies this by saying that: 'Competitive advantage comes from fully utilizing the *discretionary* effort of the workforce, not from buying the latest gadget or using the latest management fad. Voluntary effort comes from employee commitment, and commitment comes from empowerment.'

On the face of it, power-sharing which resulted in workers taking responsibility for shop-floor decisions on quality, safety, productivity and material seemed attractive to both managers and employees. But trade unions might choose to obstruct or subvert the process. Gill and Krieger (1999) surveyed workplaces in ten European Union countries and found a considerable gap between the rhetoric and reality of direct participation. Different forms of direct participation were widespread in the ten countries but the scope was relatively limited. The survey also showed that works councils and union representatives were more likely to be 'agents of change' rather than barriers to achieving employee involvement. This will be discussed further in Chapter 20.

For Murrell and Meredith (2000) managers in an empowering organization:

→ Believe that leadership belongs to all employees – and not just a few.

→ Know that the company is most likely to succeed when employees have the tools, training and authority to do their best work.

→ Understand that information is power – and share it with all employees.

→ Value employees enough to build a culture that values and supports individuals.

→ Create opportunities for finding solutions and for designing what-can-be, not searching for problems and what-should-have-been.

→ Understand that fostering empowerment is a continuous effort – not an end-point to be checked off a list of objectives.

Lee and Koh (2001) argue that although empowerment has been actively practised, the exact meaning of the terms 'empowerment' and 'psychological empowerment' have not been thought through. They contend that empowerment is quite distinct from related concepts such as authority delegation, motivation, self-efficacy, job enrichment, employee ownership, autonomy, self-determination, self-management, self-control, self-influence, self-leadership, high-involvement and participative management. They conclude that empowerment is not just a fad, but a unique concept reflecting a new managerial approach. Conversely, Harley (1999), using data from the 1995 Australian Workplace Industrial Relations Survey could find no meaningful relationship between empowerment and employee autonomy.

Ichniowski *et al.* (2000) review a number of theories as to why high skill, high-involvement workplaces are believed to be more effective than traditional 'top-down' management regimes. They divide these theories into two basic groups:

1   Those that focus on the effort and motivation of workers and work groups and suggest that people work harder.

2   Those that focus on changes in the structure of organizations that produce improvements in efficiency.

In the first group, the emphasis may be on 'working harder' and 'working smarter'. People may work harder if they find elements of a job to be interesting or enjoyable, and this may come from rewards or feedback. They are also less likely to resent aspects of the job if they have contributed to its design. Myrna (2009) advocates giving employees more responsibility for their own performance assessments as a means increasing involvement through empowerment.

As regards working smarter, innovative work practices can lead to improved efficiency. Workers can suggest improved work practices because they have a more intimate knowledge of the job than managers or external consultants. Moreover, open discussion allows employees to modify their own work processes to fit more effectively with others as they become aware of the 'bigger picture'. Ichniowski *et al.* point to the need to change work culture from 'rate-busting' – discouraging high levels of performance – to one that values greater efficiency. This process can be encouraged by specifically rewarding high performance through collective bonuses. Helper, Levine and Bendoly (2002) surveyed the benefits of employee involvement practices for blue-collar workers in the auto-supply industry and found wages to be 3–5 per cent higher than would otherwise be the case. They attribute the cause to improved efficiency.

Theories in the second group may emphasize innovative work practices that can also lead to improvements in organizational structure that are independent of motivational effects. Ichniowski *et al.* (2000) give the following as examples:

→  Cross-training and flexible job assignment may reduce the costs of absenteeism.

→  Delegating decision making to self-directed teams can reduce the number of supervisors or middle managers and improve communication.

→  Training in problem-solving, statistical process control and computer skills may enhance the benefits of information technology.

→  Involving workers and unions in decision making can reduce grievances and other sources of conflict.

It is clear that such changes associated with employee involvement are complex and make it 'difficult to isolate any single causal mechanism that produces their effects on economic performance'. Nevertheless, Ichniowski *et al.* conclude that the companies which adopt such practices 'should enjoy higher productivity and quality ... leading to lower costs and higher product demand, all else equal'. But this comes at a cost because employee involvement programmes can be expensive due to extra meetings and related activities. In a study of 4000 employees in 29 manufacturing companies Park *et al.* (2010) found that employee involvement was more effective in capital-intensive than labour-intensive organizations.

Silvestro (2002) reports empirical findings from one of the UK's largest supermarket companies that seem to challenge the notion that employee satisfaction and loyalty are key drivers of productivity, efficiency and profit. The study shows an inverse correlation between employee satisfaction and the measures of productivity, efficiency and profitability. In fact, the most profitable stores were those in which employees were least satisfied and length of service tended to be lowest. One possible explanation is that managers at ground level were being pressurized to maximize store efficiency, leading to 'dysfunctional managerial behaviour at store level'. Jones *et al.* (2010), on the other hand, found that productivity increased even for simple tasks in a retail environment.

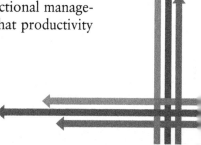

**SUMMARY**

In this chapter we examined the concept of employee engagement particularly in relation to the concept of commitment. Commitment has been a particular feature of human resource literature since the 1980s as a result of its inclusion in the influential Harvard map of HRM and the apparent advantage it gave Japanese firms over their Western counterparts. In recent years, internal brand management has been subsumed by the process of 'employer branding' – an attempt to build organizations that embody brand values by attracting, keeping and developing employees who 'live the brand' through the alignment of marketing communications and HR practices. We reconsidered the link between commitment and culture questioning its true justification and meaning and addressed the issue of commitment in the management of professionals. Finally we examined ways of involving employees as an aspect of employee engagement.

 **FURTHER READING**

1  *The Essential Guide to Employee Engagement: Better Business Performance through Staff Satisfaction* by Sarah Cook (2008), published by Kogan Page provides a wide range of international case studies.

2  *Employee Engagement: Tools for Analysis, Practice, and Competitive Advantage* (Wiley-Blackwell 2009) by William H. Macey, Benjamin Schneider, Karen M. Barbera, and Scott A. Young attempts a scientific approach at identifying the drivers of engagement.

3  *Brand From the Inside: Eight Essentials to Emotionally Connect Your Employees to Your Business,* by Libby Sartain and Mark Schumann (2006), published by Jossey-Bass, takes an enthusiastic practitioner approach to the subject.

**REVIEW QUESTIONS**

1  What do you understand by 'employee engagement'? To what extent are you committed to the organization in which you work or study?

2  Why is commitment significant in human resource literature?

3  What is the relationship between brand management, employer branding and employee engagement?

4  Take a well-known brand name as an example. What are its values and how should HR practices be aligned to fit?

5  Is employer branding an ethical form of 'internal marketing' or an attempt at brainwashing staff? How can individuals retain their individuality and freedom of expression in an organization that emphasizes employer branding?

6  Would you classify Osborne and Cowen's description of a high-commitment organization as idealistic or realistic? How would you design an employee involvement programme for an organization you know well?

7  To what extent is employee empowerment attainable? Is it just an example of management rhetoric?

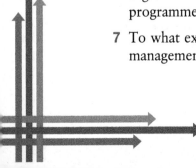

8 Outline some of the principal drivers and barriers to effective employee involvement.

9 What is the relationship between the concepts of 'strong culture' and 'employee engagement'?

10 Is it possible to obtain commitment in a situation where redundancies are inevitable?

 **CASE STUDY FOR DISCUSSION AND ANALYSIS**

## Ark Nurseries

Ark Nurseries is a specialist wholesaler of fresh and freeze-dried herbs and vegetables. These are grown within the country or brought in from other parts of the world and packaged in a small, chaotic factory. Most of the sales are to small retailers and restaurants in middle-class areas. The company was founded ten years ago and has prospered as its products have become familiar and customers have been increasingly interested in a more varied range of foods.

The managing director founded the company with her late husband and has taken complete control since his death three years ago. She was always accustomed to working hard and now spends virtually all her waking hours on company business. Her main interest is selecting and marketing new products and she is happy to spend a lot of her time travelling to meet growers and attending trade fairs and exhibitions. She is frequently away from the office for weeks at a time.

Employee numbers have gradually increased and most of the more senior managers have been with her for several years. She deals directly with her managers, usually on a one-to-one basis as problems come up, and dislikes committee-type meetings. An outgoing and energetic person, she takes decisions quickly, based on intuition and her experience of the market. She takes advice from her staff but does not feel obliged to follow it. Generally, she is a talker rather than a listener and is accustomed to having her way. She insists on vetting all staff recruitment, promotion and pay increases and takes all equipment-purchasing decisions herself. There is no one specifi-

cally in charge of human resources, each functional manager being responsible for their own staff. Pay is good for the area and employees are generally pleased to work for the company. The factory has a five-day week and is open for ten hours a day. There is no appraisal or performance management system, with senior staff being paid salaries and factory workers receiving wages based on a piece-rate system.

The sales manager has just clinched a deal with a major supermarket group which has agreed to take Ark produce for its 60 stores. The managing director was surprised by his success but is delighted that it has finally been achieved. The contract was announced last week but reactions within the company have been mixed. The managing director has spent years trying to break into this market and is astonished by the attitude of most of her senior staff. They have been accustomed to steady but undramatic growth and are now faced with tripling sales over the next three years. They argue that their regular growers could not meet the demand at the right level of quality, especially as the supermarket group will expect stringent standards and exact financial penalties for late delivery.

Over the last few days, fierce arguments have broken out between the managing director and her staff and there have been threats of resignation. However, she is convinced that the contract is feasible and that resignations will not happen because of the unemployment situation.

*As a human resources consultant how would you analyze the situation and how could you help?*

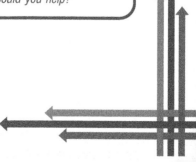

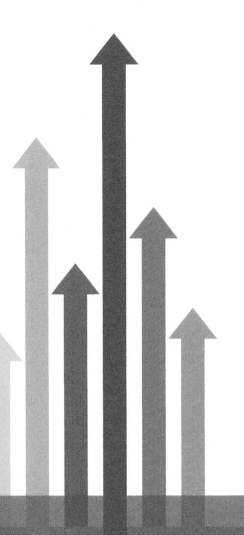

# PART FOUR
## STRATEGIC HRM

This part of the book discusses the basis, preparation and implementation of strategic HRM. Human resource management is closely identified with business strategy by many authors. In fact, HRM is typically distinguished from traditional personnel management by its concern with meeting business objectives in a strategic fashion.

**The chapters in Part Four address a number of specific issues:**

→ **What is strategy?**

→ **What is the role of HRM in the strategic process?**

→ **How are human resource strategies prepared and implemented?**

→ **What is the relationship between strategic HRM and human resource planning?**

→ **How does HRM impact on the process of organizational change?**

→ **What is the role of HR practitioners in outsourcing, mergers and acquisitions?**

→ **How can behavioural change be achieved?**

→ **What strategies are available for recruitment and retention?**

→ **How are resourcing strategies prepared?**

# CHAPTER 11
## People strategies

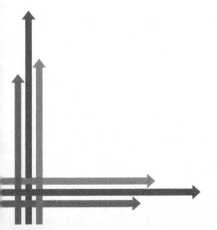

## LEARNING OBJECTIVES

The purpose of this chapter is to:

→ Determine the nature and prevalence of strategic HRM.

→ Evaluate the influence and involvement of people managers in high-level decision-making.

→ Identify different approaches to strategic HRM, and outline their strengths and weaknesses.

→ Consider how people strategies and practices can be adapted to meet perceived threats and opportunities in a changing business environment.

# STRATEGY AND HRM

In Part One we saw that many theorists consider a strong link with strategy to be the key difference between HRM and earlier philosophies of people management. Exponents of HRM emphasize the importance of an organization's people in achieving its overall business objectives. Typically, it is claimed that human resource strategies combine all people management activities into an organized and integrated programme to meet the strategic objectives of an enterprise. For example, HR leaders are seen as being in a unique position 'at the intersection of strategy, communication and talent' (McLaughlin and Mott, 2010). It is claimed also that HRM is different from personnel management primarily because of its supposed emphasis on the link between people policies and overall business strategy. For example, Guest (1993: 213) distinguishes traditional personnel management from HRM 'by virtue of the way in which the former ignored, but the latter embraces strategy'. This contrasts with the 'technical-piecemeal' approach of personnel management.

Purcell (2001: 59) concludes that 'the integration with strategy is central to all models of HRM and virtually all authors are agreed that this is *the* distinctive feature of HRM, compared with personnel'. Personnel management, we are told, is essentially reactive whereas HRM, exemplified by HR strategy, is proactive. The personnel model focused on short-term, largely operational matters of little interest to strategists. HRM, by contrast, takes a longer perspective and is closer to the heart of the organization. It takes a proactive stance towards the competitiveness and efficiency of the organization, unlike the mundane and reactive, day-to-day orientation of personnel management, with a particular emphasis on measuring significant workforce elements through HR metrics (Gates and Langevin, 2010). However, this distinction is not accepted unanimously: 'HRM's claim to take a strategic approach to employment touches a particularly raw nerve among personnel managers. "*Of course*" personnel management has "*always*" advocated a strategic approach' (Hendry, 1995: 12).

Moreover, human resource strategies are not easy to identify with both academics and practitioners finding it difficult to understand what HR strategy means in practice. Research in recent years has looked at the detail of HR strategy linking, for example, measures such as technological know-how and entrepreneurial experience with more conventional people management concepts such as workforce skills, pay structures and employee development in even the smallest firms to find evidence of effectiveness (Georgiadis and Pitelis, 2010). HR practitioners also find difficulties in reconciling some of the requirements of being a strategic business partner with 'personnel manager'-type concerns such as promoting the well-being of employees (Brown *et al.*, 2009).

Sceptical or cautionary comments from the UK and Australia where (as in India, Ireland, Malaysia, New Zealand, Singapore and South Africa) there is a perceived dichotomy between 'personnel management' and HRM, contrasts with the situation in North America where Rothwell, Prescott and Taylor (1998: 5) compare 'traditional HR' and its more modern (and dynamic) form, 'strategic HR':

1   Traditional HR practitioners do not have enough 'working knowledge of what business is all about or of the strategic goals of the organizations they serve'. Instead they present what appears to be a social (i.e. dangerously liberal) agenda without explaining the organizational benefits. As a result the impression is created that they have little concern for business results.

2   They lack leadership ability, especially if they have no line management experience and are viewed as having less interest in helping line managers solve their problems than they have in meeting HR objectives, such as complying with employment legislation.

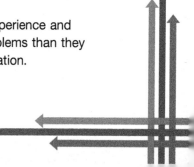

3   HR practitioners are viewed as reactive. For example, insisting on individual pay scales when the organization has otherwise decided on a team-based approach. 'They appear unresponsive – and even resistant – to line management needs, interests and business pressures.'

4   They sometimes seem unable to take on 'the lead in establishing a vision for change and garnering the support necessary to lead the change'. The result is that they lose credibility and respect.

5   They are seen as 'fad-chasers' who try to use solutions for problems in other workplaces and 'drop them in place without taking into account the unique business objectives, corporate culture, organization-specific politics and individual personalities of key decisionmakers found in their own organizational settings'.

Such criticisms of 'personnel management' or old-school HR are common and strategic HRM is seen as a possible solution.

## HR AND THAT ELUSIVE STRATEGIC ROLE

Recently, Maxxim Consulting interviewed 20 CEOs of FTSE350 companies in the UK and found that only four knew exactly how many people worked in their respective head offices. Also, just four CEOs knew how much their head offices cost to run each year.

According to Claire Arnold, a Partner at Maxxim Consulting:

> Our study shows that at most UK corporate headquarters, unnecessary layers of complexity and bureaucracy often accumulate over time. This is an area that many of the FTSE350 are set to review in 2008 with a view to finding cost-savings. The fact that so few of the Chief Execs we interviewed for our study were sure exactly how many people worked at head office is a clear indication that there's some serious housekeeping to be done.

Granted this was an extremely small study and it must be regarded as illustrative rather than definitive. But, nevertheless, what part should HR managers play in such 'housekeeping' exercises?

It seems that finally senior managers – some of them, at least – are willing to give HR managers a significant role in strategic decisions. But how many human resource managers know how to fulfill that role? Paul Kearns (2003: 4) tells the tale of a workshop exercise for senior human resource managers when participants were given a military scenario. Briefly, they were asked to envisage that they, and a thousand soldiers under their command, had been dropped behind enemy lines – with no information about their opposition. What would they do? The first response he received was 'I'd retreat'. Kearns comments: 'Why does this response from an HR person not surprise me?' It doesn't surprise me either because so many HR managers are used to operating someone else's strategy, rather than participating vigorously in their organizations' strategic decisions.

Noting that 'business partner' and 'strategic thinker' have featured as the most important roles in some recent surveys of human resource management, Jamroq and Overhot (2004) observe that 'there's something elusive and ambiguous about this widely touted goal of becoming a strategic business partner'. They cite a recent conference on the future of HR where a panel of human resource experts came out with the statement that 'I can't define it, but I know it when I see it' when asked to define the term 'strategic business partner'.

### Measuring the effectiveness of HRM

Is measurement at the root of the problem? Are HR managers measuring the wrong things? One common approach is to use a 'Balanced Scorecard' which includes a range of HR measures as well as the more traditional financial and other metrics. Gubman (2004) feels that 'Too many HR

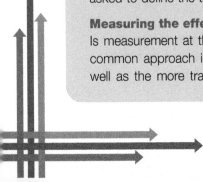

scorecards focused on operational metrics: Time to hire, cost per hire, percentage of appraisals completed, etc. While important to track, these kinds of measures will not get HR to the strategic partner role. They only reinforce the view of HR as an administrative function. Key HR measures needed to be central to business success.'

More beneficially, according to Gubman, HR managers should focus instead on the same two major issues as their financial colleagues: return and growth. 'HR-things' can only create economic value from three sources:

→ Employee turnover and retention

→ Productivity – revenue against employee costs

→ Expenditure on the HR function and related activities.

Providing measures for these three elements does not require any 'rocket science' because they relate to three familiar HR goals:

1 Attracting, developing and retaining staff

2 Aligning, engaging, measuring and rewarding performance

3 Controlling or reducing HR costs.

HR-relevant measures for growth are trickier and need to be tailored to the organizations' individual situation. Grubman believes that HR measures can be devised that, like market share, can indicate trends and forecasts for improved revenue in the future. He argues that the following are the most significant growth-related human resource measures at present:

→ Leadership development, to be measured in terms of unique candidates ready to assume executive and other major roles.

→ Engagement – levels of employees' intellectual and emotional commitment to their work.

→ Diversity, particularly the number of women and ethnic minority employees coming through the system or 'talent pipeline'.

Tamkin *et al.* (2008) used a set of criteria described as the '4A model' (Access, Ability, Attitudes, Application) in their study of almost 3000 British organizations and found that the use of 'bundles' of HR practices produced improved performance and profitability. They suggest a number of issues that HR managers should focus on:

→ **Access**. The quality of the recruitment process: putting serious effort into attracting high quality applicants; using policies and practices that 'ensure the ongoing movement of the best people through the organization'.

→ **Ability**. Effective, long-term development plans focused on the needs of employees and the business. These plans should be constantly monitored to ensure their effectiveness. The researchers also highlight the need for a high workforce quality, e.g. possession of degrees.

→ **Attitudes**. Aligning employees to the objectives of the organization – 'vital in terms of capturing discretionary effort'. They emphasize one-to-ones, appraisals and reward strategies related to organizational performance.

→ **Application**. Encouraging autonomy, empowerment and generation of ideas.

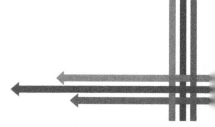

**Behaving proactively**

Weiss (1999) argues that HR managers must demonstrate the ability to provide stimulating ideas and challenge decisions that do not have business value. To do this, they need to perform at the same intellectual level as their colleagues in an executive meeting. Most importantly, they need to wear a 'business hat' rather than a 'HR hat' otherwise they will be relegated to the traditional administrative or tactical (second-level) role that has bedevilled the human resource function for decades. Weiss considers that HR managers need to demonstrate the following to show their ability to add value:

→ Broad understanding of the business, thus helping the human resource function to contribute to the overall direction of the company.

→ Knowledge of how all activities need to align, enabling the company to maximize the success of its strategic initiatives.

→ Professionalism in investing in human capital and HR processes, allowing HR to help guide employees and the organization's decision-making.

→ A unique perspective, allowing the HR function to become an 'ideas merchant' so that people and the outcomes of organizational processes can be made into strategic advantages.

Finally, we can consider Gubman's belief:

HR needs to keep moving itself forward, toward the strategic partner role, by becoming better profit-and-loss business leaders. Be the ones to lead companies back into thinking externally, about customers and markets and how to create unique value for them. What a surprising and powerful role that would be for HR leaders! Start measuring HR impacts on real business results, not HR activities. Instead of measuring time to hire, measure the people aspects of opening up a new market and the returns they generate.

*Source: Reprinted with permission from HRM Guide UK (http://www.hrmguide.co.uk).*

# STRATEGIC MANAGEMENT

Strategy is about choice. The underlying assumption is that firms can make deliberate decisions about their markets, the products or services they provide, prices, quality standards and the deployment of human and other resources. According to most discussions of the subject, strategic thinking is based on rational decision-making, taking into account the competitive and financial pressures on an organization and the resources available to it, including its people. It imposes orderly, logical thinking on a messy real world, modelling the present situation and predicting the consequences of specific actions (see Key concept 11.1). In order to evaluate these outcomes there is an emphasis on quantitative statements – such as the number of people needed – based on an explicit set of objectives and an ever-evolving (and, hopefully, improving) set of managerial measures (Bloom and Van Reenen, 2010). But we will see that this approach has been questioned and alternative approaches have been proposed for strategic human resource management.

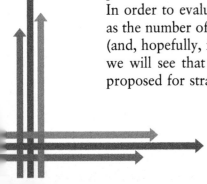

> ### KEY CONCEPT 11.1 STRATEGY
>
> A strategy is the means by which an organization seeks to meet its objectives. It is a deliberate choice, a decision to take a course of action rather than reacting to circumstances. It focuses on significant, long-term goals rather than day-to-day operating matters.
>
> As we observed in Part One, rhetorical accounts paint a picture of HRM as being focused and managerial, unified and holistic and driven by strategy.

Under the influence of the Harvard MBA, business strategy has become an influential and integrative discipline at the organizational level. The emphasis on a planned approach to development and growth brings together the functional elements of operations management, marketing, finance and human resource management into a cohesive whole. Strategic management is a process by which organizations determine their objectives, decide on actions and suitable timescales, implement those actions and then assess progress and results. Fundamentally, it is the task of senior managers, although more junior employees contribute to the process and the implementation of strategy.

But there is a considerable debate about what 'strategic human resource management' (SHRM) actually means (Key concept 11.2). There are many definitions, including:

→ 'A human resource system that is tailored to the demands of the business strategy' (Miles and Snow, 1984).

→ 'The pattern of planned human resource activities intended to enable an organization to achieve its goals' (Wright and McMahan, 1992).

→ 'By *strategic* we mean that HR activities should be systematically designed and intentionally linked to an analysis of the business and its context' (Schuler, Jackson and Storey, 2001, p.127).

Such definitions range from a portrayal of SHRM as a 'reactive' management field where human resource management is a tool with which to implement strategy, to a more proactive function in which HR activities can actually create and shape the business strategy (Sanz-Valle, Sabatar-Sanchez and Aragon-Sanchez, 1998) and have a decisive role in organizational crisis management (Wang *et al.*, 2009).

> ### KEY CONCEPT 11.2 STRATEGIC HRM
>
> Strategic HRM takes a long-term perspective and is concerned with issues such as corporate culture and individual career development as well as the availability of people with the right skills. It incorporates redundancy and recruitment planning and is increasingly focused on decisions about maintaining the internal capability of an organization's workforce to perform specific functions or to contract out (outsource) an activity to an external provider.

The range of activities and themes encompassed by SHRM is complex and goes beyond the responsibilities of personnel or HR managers into all aspects of managing people. It

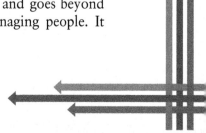

focuses on 'management decisions and behaviours used, consciously or unconsciously, to control, influence and motivate those who work for the organizations – the human resources' (Purcell, 2001: 64). For example, Mabey, Salaman and Storey (1998) look at the subject from four perspectives:

1   The social and economic context of SHRM – including the internal (corporate) and external environments that influence the development and implementation of HR strategies.

2   The relationship between SHRM and business performance, emphasizing the measurement of performance.

3   Management style and the development of new forms of organization.

4   The relationship between SHRM and the development of organizational capability, including knowledge management.

Other authors have attempted to provide more analytical frameworks for SHRM. Delery and Doty (1996), for example, make distinctions between three different theoretical frameworks:

1   *Universalistic:* where some HR practices are believed to be universally effective.

2   *Contingent:* the effectiveness of HR practices are supposed to be dependent on an organization's strategy.

3   *Configurational:* where there are believed to be synergistic effects between HR practices and strategy crucial for enhanced performance.

Wright and Snell's (1998) model of SHRM aims to achieve both fit and flexibility. They emphasize a distinction between HRM practices, skills and behaviour in their relation to strategy on the one hand, and the issue of tight and loose coupling of HR practices and strategy on the other.

## STRATEGIC HRM: THEORY AND PRACTICE

Why do management theorists stress the importance of strategy? A number of reasons are apparent:

→   Strategic literature largely emphasizes the internal resources of a business as the source of competitive advantage. This 'resource-based' perspective (Boxall, 1996) views a firm as a bundle of resources. Such resources must possess four qualities for advantage to be maintained:
    — *Value.* They must add value to the organization's activities.
    — *Rarity.* They must be rare and (preferably) unique.
    — *Inimitability.* Competitors should have difficulty in copying them.
    — *Non-substitutability.* They cannot be replaced by technology.

Although the resource-based view originally came from economics, commentators such as Boxall have argued that it is particularly applicable in the case of human resources. The resources embodied in an organization's people are found in the form of skills, expertise and experience (Storey, 1995: 4). Knowledge management can be viewed as a development of the resource-based view of the firm but focused on one particular aspect – tacit knowledge.

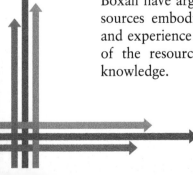

→ HRM models focus strongly on strategy. Certainly, this is the case. However, models of human resource management largely derive from American business schools. The prevailing philosophy in these schools has been analytic, and strategic. This line of reasoning offers an explanation but not a justification. In fact, it is circular because if one asks why they devised strategic models for HRM, the answer might simply be that 'they would, wouldn't they'.

→ Strategy is intellectual and, therefore, interesting – to management theorists. It is analytical and can be conceptualized in terms of models, abstractions and even numbers. In other words, it deals with a business subject within an orthodox academic framework. This contrasts with forms of operational management that deal with 'boring admin'. Day-to-day management tends to be commonsensical, uses ragbags of techniques that – from experience – have been found to work, and deals with messy problems. It is unteachable and difficult to intellectualize. Students without business experience find discussion of real-life people management hard to relate to. It does not have the tidiness and coherence of a proper subject with 'right' answers. Far easier to regard it with contempt!

→ Degree courses major on strategy. Since the advent of the Harvard MBA, there has been a steady trend towards a final year focus on 'business policy' for undergraduate business studies degrees. The underlying rationale is the provision of an integrative subject that prepares students for high-level business jobs. It is taught by looking backwards – retrospective examination of case studies that are prepared within recognized frameworks. Essentially, it is a case of 'where did they go wrong' and, occasionally, right. Intriguingly, however, employers consistently ask for practical business skills such as presentation and teamwork – not strategic thinking. Essentially, strategy is for senior managers. In a time of mass higher education few students will ever become senior managers, and those who do will not achieve such jobs for at least a decade.

→ Strategy is important. It deals with high-level decisions, concerning itself with the 'big agenda'.

## Strategy and planning

If strategy is deemed so important by theorists, how much impact has strategic thinking had on practitioners? First, the emphasis given to strategy by HRM theorists has led to significant interest from senior managers. For example, there is a stress on the importance of maximizing the performance and potential of an organization's people. This does not come necessarily from an altruistic and soft-hearted interest in their welfare. More likely, it derives from a hard-headed appreciation of the long-term contribution they can provide to the business. 'Soft' HRM focuses on an organization's people as assets so that time spent on training and development is an investment in human capital (see Part Two). But the organization's strategy for HRM may not see the HR function as a core part of the business, resulting in an outsourcing contract.

Hence strategic HRM can fit the interests of senior executives and there is evidence, for example from Australia (Sheehan, Holland and Cieri, 2006), of increasing involvement of senior human resource managers in strategic decision-making and implementation. On the other hand, Rasmussen *et al.* (2010) looked for evidence of growing strategic influence and higher managerial status in data from the 2004 New Zealand Cranet Survey. They found indications of higher awareness of 'people issues', greater influence of HRM practitioners on the process of strategic decision-making and improved professional status. However, formalized HRM strategies were not as prevalent as expected – with many organizations not having a HR department. Moreover, in numerical terms there was no increase in the

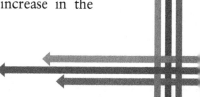

presence of senior HR managers among the senior executives of a typical New Zealand organization.

There are some major difficulties for HR practitioners brought up in the personnel tradition. First, as we have noted, knowledge of wider business functions has not been a strength of the personnel profession. There is a gulf in personality between those attracted to strategy and the people actually dealing with human resources at company level. Differing interests and outlooks on life can lead to a serious failure of communication. Wright (2008) draws attention to the conflict between HR practitioners as they attempt to reconcile the new roles of 'business partner' and 'internal consultant' with the more day-to-day non-strategic functions that many practitioners continue to perform. He concludes that while some have gained improved self-esteem and organizational status, the broad identity of the HR 'profession' has been undermined. There are now different sub-groupings in the profession: those with routine transactional and those with strategic transformational activities. Also, entry barriers to the profession have been reduced as people with backgrounds in other managerial specialisms are attracted to the higher status strategic roles.

---

**HRM IN REALITY**  ONGOING COMPETITION FOR TALENT

A survey of 167 Canadian human resources leaders in 2010 found that organizations are facing an increased 'flight risk' with employees considering new opportunities as the economy recovers. The Conference Board of Canada's second such report, *Valuing Your Talent: Human Resources Trends and Metrics* argues that employers need to develop workforce strategies to attract and retain employees in the current climate.

Ruth Wright, associate director of leadership and human resources research said:

> The recession gave employers only a brief reprieve from looming workforce shortages and an ongoing competition for talent. A growing economy and an aging workforce mean that it is just a matter of time before pressure in labour markets begins to build again.
>
> The demand for skilled people never went away during the downturn, and concerns about skills and talent shortages are evident even at the highest level of organizations.
>
> Management and leadership development, and succession planning, are high priorities for HR leaders. Many organizations – particularly in the private sector – are identifying key leadership positions for the purpose of succession planning.

Respondents are aware that their workforce is aging, with nearly half over the age of 45. Among their most significant current challenges are attraction, recruitment and retention of workers and building leadership capacity.

Management and leadership development and strategic workforce planning are seen as priorities both in the short and medium term. The importance attributed to succession management and especially knowledge transfer and management has significantly increased since the first survey in 2005, overtaking employee engagement as priorities.

*Global context*

A recent survey by Ernst & Young (Canada) found that organizations are responding to challenges posed by the current economic climate by adopting more sophisticated approaches to talent management. The report *Managing Today's Global Workforce* is based on responses from more than 340 senior executives from Fortune 1000 companies around the world, including Canada. Examining successful programs and differing practices across regions and sectors, it found that leading companies are increasing competitiveness by integrating talent management with overall business strategy and human resources initiatives focusing on employee engagement and enhanced flexibility.

Respondents identified the most important planned talent management initiative as 'building their internal talent pipeline to fill critical future needs' (64 per cent), followed by 'understanding and coordinating global talent resources to fill key positions' (33 per cent); and 'offering flexible work strategies such as job sharing, telecommuting, flex hours and phased-in retirement' (31 per cent). Concern over future gaps in talent among technical and middle management positions was expressed by 28 per cent and 26 per cent respectively. More than half of respondents (63 per cent) report aligning their current talent management programs to their business strategy, and pro-actively modifying them to reflect changes in company direction.

Ronny Aoun, executive director, human capital practice, said:

> Companies need to align business strategies with talent management programs that will engage and develop the right individuals, because having the right competencies, skills and experiences are the key to competitive differentiation and success as a market leader. And as Canadian organizations continue to grow their operations across the globe, it's vital that a company's internationally mobile employees are also kept top-of-mind.

The survey addressed issues raised by global organizations offering international assignments (60 per cent of respondents). Over one-third have no talent management program in place for mobile employees. Only 32 per cent of respondents say all the components of their talent management programs are integrated across the entire organization, while 24 per cent do not integrate their programs at all.

The report argues that it is critical for companies to respond to specific needs of mobile employees, while maintaining awareness of labour legislation and demographics relevant to each setting. Knowledge held by these employees should be retained and managed. Many respondents state that repatriation or retention after repatriation is not a priority for their organizations, resulting in loss of international experience. Successful companies require well-executed talent management programs, globally integrated and customized to the characteristics of their workforce.

**Ronny Aoun commented:**

> Now, more than ever, Canadian organizations need to provide opportunities that appeal to the diversity of their employees. By understanding the needs and motivations of employees, organizations will be better able to retain the necessary skills and competencies to emerge stronger in the future.

*What benefits can be expected from having thought-through talent management strategies?*

Source: Reprinted with permission from HRM Guide Canada (http://www.hrmguide.net/canada/).

---

On the one hand, business school strategists have tended to minimize human resource considerations because of the ambiguity and uncertainty attached to human behaviour. Humans are the most unpredictable of strategic resources. Michael Porter, the doyen of strategic management, virtually discounted the HR aspects of strategy. On the other hand, personnel departments generally employed practitioners who viewed themselves as pragmatists dealing with practical issues such as recruitment, pay and discipline 'on the ground', remote from the grand theories of strategists.

The second difficulty comes from their historic role of independent arbitrators between staff and management. As conciliators and apologists personnel managers depended on the ability to find compromises and reconcile the two sides rather than developing a clear agenda of their own. As a result, they make uncomfortable stakeholders, unable to fight their corner. Instead they are forced to react to the decisions of more powerful stakeholders. In practice then (Giles and Williams, 1991: 31):

> ... personnel specialists find strategy difficult. Personnel specialists have not developed the strategic skills needed to contribute to their organization's effectiveness. Current education and training programmes give them little insight into how to link business, technical and human

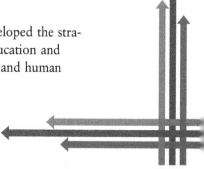

resource management skills in times of great uncertainty. Personnel specialists do not speak the language of top management in marketing and manufacturing and often seem to clam up when confronted with all the noughts on a company balance sheet.

Herein lies the source of difficulty between the planning mentality and human resource management. Good people managers, through intuition or experience, are profoundly aware of their lack of control over people. In a high proportion of situations, the most carefully constructed and devious tactics will fail to get people to behave in a desired way. Experienced managers will regard this as normal and inescapable. People are not puppets and it is not surprising that they do not behave as such. Coming to terms with this is very much a matter of personality. Managers with a high tolerance of ambiguity, able to operate in fluid, uncertain situations, gravitate towards jobs with a considerable people element.

In contrast, human quirkiness and unpredictability do not fit the planning mindset that demands ordered, rational and entirely predictable behaviour. Communication between dedicated planners and people managers can be a painful business. To the HR manager a plan can seem to be a statement of intentions, an attempt to forecast an ideal world – but not to be stuck to rigidly. If circumstances change, surely the plan can be bent to accommodate this? To the planner, human resource thinking seems woolly and vague. HR managers do not convey a feeling of confidence: they are far too tolerant of deviant behaviour and seem incapable of *making* employees toe the line. They are incorrigible 'firefighters' and hence likely to be perceived as unsuitable for senior, strategic roles. Not surprisingly, HR managers with a background or experience in other business functions are more likely to be accepted as authoritative by strategists.

## FORMING HR STRATEGIES

Identifying the relationship between HRM and strategy, it seems, is simpler in theory than it is in practice. Frequently, strategic HRM is a matter of rhetoric. Organizations can usefully be grouped into five alternative categories on the basis of their approach towards human resource strategy (Torrington and Hall, 1995: 47):

1   Businesses in which there is no consideration whatsoever of human resource issues in the preparation of organizational strategy. Typical of firms 20 years ago and still found in many small companies.

2   Organizations in which there is a growing understanding of the role of human resources in implementing corporate strategy. Human resource strategy cascades on from organizational strategy, very much along the lines of the Michigan model described in Chapter 2. The purpose of HR strategy is to match the requirements of organizational strategy, ensuring the closest possible fit in terms of employee numbers, skills and so on.

3   Businesses in which the relationship becomes two-way with some ideas initiated by HR managers. There is an element of debate about the people management consequences of particular strategies before they are implemented.

4   Organizations in which the HRM concept has been accepted and people are seen as the key to competitive advantage. Corporate and human resource strategies are developed simultaneously. They are coherent and comprehensive.

5   Companies where human resources become the driving force in the development of strategy. There is an overriding emphasis on developing their skills and capitalizing on their competences.

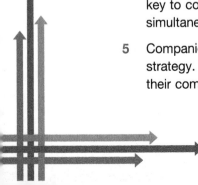

In practice, organizations may adopt any of these approaches.

Strategies can encompass many issues. Whether or not a business gives prominence to its human resource strategies, when the organization takes decisions on its intended market and product or service range, it also determines the types of job and skills required (Purcell, 1995: 63). Where organizations are genuinely concerned with their people, HRM normally focuses on certain strategic sub-goals, or second-order strategies in Purcell's terminology, as shown in Table 11.1. For example:

→ Resourcing an organization with the most suitable people at the right time, in the right place. We will consider this issue in depth later in the book but for the moment we will note that, from a strategic viewpoint, there are two important elements:

   (a) knowledge of and participation in the formulation of 'official' strategy; and

   (b) awareness of underlying developments that will produce 'surprises' that lead to about-turns in the official policy, typically with little or no notice.

→ Planning the redeployment or dismissal of staff who are no longer required for specific tasks. The emphasis varies between free market and social market companies with the former taking a hard-HRM line and the latter being committed to a softer approach.

→ Determining the cultural characteristics appropriate to an organization's business objectives. Implementation requires us to plan the socialization, performance assessment, development and change programmes needed to realize that culture.

→ Developing key skills for new products or equipment. This includes consideration of external and internal resourcing, training programmes, formal education and job rotation.

Examining HR strategy within our 10-Cs checklist of HRM we can see in Table 11.2 how each element, or combination of elements, can be made the focus of strategy. Guest (1987), for instance, identifies a circular relationship between a number of strategic goals:

→ As we have seen, HRM aims for a high level of commitment from employees, so that they identify with the organization's goals and contribute actively to its improvement and success.

| Level | Organizational focus | Environmental constraints |
|---|---|---|
| *First-order strategies* | Long-term objectives<br>Range of activities, markets, locations | Supranational authorities<br>Government<br>Culture and tradition |
| *Second-order strategies* | Internal operating procedures, organizational structure | Capital market<br>Product market<br>Consumers |
| *Third-order strategies* | Strategic choice in HRM | Job market<br>Workforce Law |
| *Outcomes* | Style, structure, conduct of HRM | |

**TABLE 11.1**
Levels of strategy affecting HRM

Source: Adapted from Purcell (1989).

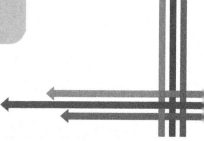

**TABLE 11.2**
Checklist for
strategic HRM

| Principle | Definition | Action |
|---|---|---|
| 1 Control | Effective organizations require a control system for cohesion and direction | Clear, unambiguous mission statement supported by strategies and organization able to meet objectives |
| 2 Contiguity | Human resource management should be closely matched to business objectives | HR strategies developed at board level and integrated with all other strategies |
| 3 Coherence | Allocation and activities of human resources integrated into a meaningful whole | People management must be organized, rather than left to ad hoc decisions at local level |
| 4 Communication | Strategies understood and accepted by all employees. Open culture with no barriers | Clear, simple and justified strategies: cascading process of communication with feedback to the top |
| 5 Credibility | Staff trust top management and believe in their strategies | Top managers are sincere, honest and consistent |
| 6 Commitment | Employees motivated to achieve organizational goals | Top managers show the same commitment to staff |
| 7 Competence | Organization competent to achieve its objectives – dependent on individual competences | Resourcing strategies, selection techniques and human resource development systems in place |
| 8 Compensation | Competitive, fair reward and promotion systems. | Top managers pay themselves on equivalent basis to staff |
| 9 Creativity | Competitive advantage comes from unique strategies | System for encouraging and tapping employee ideas |
| 10 Change | Continuous improvement and development essential for survival | Flexible people and working systems; culture of innovation; skills training |

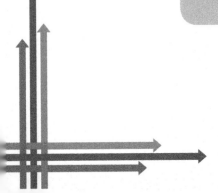

→ In turn, this enables the organization to obtain a high-quality output from workers who want to continually improve standards.

→ Within this environment, there is an expectation of flexibility from workers: a willingness to depart from fixed job definitions, working practices and conditions.

→ Strategic integration – all these strands link the organization's strategy. They are directed towards agreed objectives and interact with each other in a cohesive way.

# BUSINESS GOALS

Organizations are formed to achieve certain goals. Strategic thinking focuses on these long-term objectives. Thompson and Strickland (1998) provide a framework for strategic management based on five major activities that incorporate objective-setting:

→ Deciding the type of business in which the business will operate, developing a strategic vision and producing a set of values together with a general strategy.

→ Identifying the strategic issues for the business and setting strategic objectives.

→ Developing strategic action plans.

→ Creating and implementing strategic action plans for units within the business.

→ Evaluating, revising and refocusing strategy for the future.

Human resource strategies are derived from overall business objectives in the same way as investment or marketing strategies. We noted also in Chapter 10 that employee engagement and commitment is seen to be particularly crucial for competitive advantage. For true commitment to occur, conventional management wisdom sees the need for employees to accept and believe in an organization's goals.

A mission statement communicates these goals to everyone in a company (Key concept 11.3). Mission statements have a particular significance in large companies where communication can be difficult and, as we have seen, departments and 'political' groups frequently focus on their own sectional interests. A small business may not need such a statement since its employees and owners have a clear understanding of its reasons for existence.

---

**KEY CONCEPT 11.3**  MISSION STATEMENT

A mission statement should convey the essence of what an organization is about: why it exists, what kind of business it intends to be, and who its intended customers are. The mission is translated into objectives or goals within the strategic management process.

---

What prevents such a statement from being no more than a set of banal platitudes? It can be tied to some form of performance measure, perhaps in the form of detailed objectives. The mission statement is locked into the company's first-order strategies (see Table 11.2). These are major decisions on its long-term aims and the scope of its activities (Purcell, 1995: 67).

As we can see in the 'HRM in reality' article, outsourcing has been claimed to achieve major cost savings but the truth is more complex. Elliott (2006) views outsourcing as the

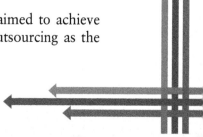

latest in a series of cost-cutting approaches after downsizing and de-layering. Gospel and Sako (2010) consider outsourcing as a form of corporate restructuring, the nature of which depends on the existing organization structure and the paths open to the firm in supplier markets. They compared HR outsourcing in two comparable consumer products companies, Procter & Gamble (P&G) and Unilever. They found that P&G's relatively high level of centralization caused it to create an internal shared services centre before outsourcing. Unilever, on the other hand, was more decentralized and used outsourcing as an opportunity to standardize its systems and processes across the world.

It has to be conceded that many organizations have a mission statement simply because it is the done thing to have one on the corporate website. Often they serve no clear purpose, tending to use competitors' mission statements as a frame of reference and adding little to the employer brand (Ingenhoff and Fuhrer, 2010). As Whitehill (1991: 123) points out, this has not been the case in large Japanese firms:

> A statement of mission, or overall philosophy, is particularly significant within the Japanese management system. It is this broad policy declaration which establishes the corporate culture within which regular employees will spend their working lives. Becoming 'socialized' within the corporate culture, and internalizing the company spirit (*shafu*), are important foundations for building the Japanese employee's remarkable loyalty and dedication to the company.

Hence the mission statement plays a crucial role in developing the uniquely Japanese forms of organizational culture and commitment discussed in Part Three. Hirota *et al.* (2010) found in a study of 128 Japanese organizations that, in addition to financial benefits, those firms that had a strong sense of mission – expressed through their mission statements – were more likely to retain employees and promote managers from within, suggesting relatively high levels of engagement. More widely, there is some evidence for a link between firm performance and mission statements in SMEs (Alavi and Karavi, 2009).

## HRM IN REALITY   OUTSOURCING TO LATIN AMERICA

A survey by Harris Interactive in 2010 on behalf of Capgemini, a leading provider of consulting, technology and outsourcing services, found that Latin America is a significant emerging outsourcing destination for US companies. India remains the most popular, chosen by 60 per cent of respondents, followed by China (27 per cent) with Latin America selected by 25 per cent.

The survey was conducted online among 300 senior executives at Fortune 1000 companies. The top reasons for selecting Latin America as part of outsourcing strategies are:

→ labour costs (69 per cent)

→ technology and infrastructure capabilities (49 per cent)

→ availability of skilled labour (48 per cent)

→ economic stability (44 per cent) and

→ language proficiency (41 per cent).

This reflects a general pattern in outsourcing decision-making, suggesting that the role of Latin America will continue to expand. Other reasons cited are unique to the region, such as proximity to the US, time zone alignment and accent neutrality.

The survey also found that 45 per cent of respondents who currently do not outsource to Latin America expressed interest in considering the region for future development. The great majority (89 per cent) believe that Latin America is an emerging market that will become increasingly important to US businesses; 83 per cent agree that there are advantages to doing business in this region and 56 per cent that it is becoming easier to operate in Latin America compared to other locations.

David Poole, vice president and head of Americas business process outsourcing, commented:

As the economy rebounds, companies are looking to use outsourcing more strategically as a tool to increase efficiency, yield significant cost savings and drive growth; this includes considering locations beyond India. The expansion of Capgemini's outsourcing services in Latin America,

and our work with Unilever, Coca-Cola Enterprises and other clients in the region underscores our understanding of our clients' needs and ability to provide the right global delivery model for multinational businesses.

*What are the consequences of outsourcing on globalized companies?*

*Source: Reprinted with permission from* HRM Guide International *(http://www.hrmguide.net/).*

# STRATEGY FORMATION

Strategic management takes into account all the complexities of the business environment, the pressures that prevail upon an organization, and the resources available to it. Despite a concentration on objective planning, it remains essentially an art rather than a science and draws on a range of theories, models and practical techniques. There is no single approach that guarantees formulation of a successful strategy. Business strategy draws heavily on management theory and is sometimes criticized for employing 'psycho-babble' or 'management speak'. Good strategies should be simple to understand. Sensible plans and changes can be obscured and discredited by excessive use of terminology which conveys little meaning to employees who do not have management literature as their favourite bedtime reading.

Several distinctive approaches to strategic management have arisen. Ansoff (1968) provided some classic principles:

1　Strategy formation should be a controlled, conscious process of thought. In other words it should not be the result of intuition or accident – it should be as 'deliberate as possible'.

2　Responsibility for the process must rest with the chief executive officer. This fits the 'leader is all' mentality that sees the top person as being the major influence on the organization.

3　The model of strategy formation must be kept simple and informal.

4　Strategies should be unique. The best result from a process of creative design. They should build on the particular 'core competencies' of the organization.

5　Strategies must come out of the design process fully developed.

6　Strategies should be made explicit and, therefore, have to be kept simple.

7　Finally, once these unique, full-blown, explicit and simple strategies are fully formulated, they must then be implemented.

More or less at the same time as this approach was developed a significant variant emerged from Harvard. It emphasized strategic planning as a process and played down the role of the chief executive. Its basic premises were that (Mintzberg, 1994: 42):

1　Strategy formation should be controlled and conscious as well as a formalized and elaborated process, decomposed into distinct steps, each delineated by checklists and supported by techniques.

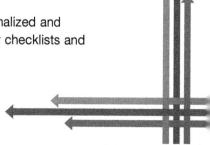

2   Responsibility for the overall process rests with the chief executive in principle; responsibility for its execution rests with the staff planners in practice.

3   Strategies come out of this process fully developed, typically as generic positions, to be explicated so that they can then be implemented through detailed attention to objectives, budgets, programmes and operating plans of various kinds.

Both models view strategy as encompassing all aspects of a business, including its people. Thus strategic thinkers envisaged a major role for human resource planning before HRM was conceived as a separate philosophy of people management. For example, Steiner (1969: 34) wrote:

> The model that may be covered in strategic planning includes every type of activity of concern to an enterprise. Among the areas are profits, capital expenditures, organization, pricing, labour relations, production, marketing, finance, personnel, public relations, advertising, technological capabilities, product improvement, research and development, legal matters, management selection and training, political activities and so on.

Steiner presented strategic planning as an orderly sequence of steps:

1   Objectives-setting develops and quantifies the organization's purposes and goals. This takes a variety of forms, the most sophisticated of which is the Delphi technique. Integral to this step is a determination of the enterprise's fundamental values.

2   External audit for gaining information about the firm's position in the environment. Intricate techniques have been developed to provide exhaustive measures of virtually every external factor that has ever been thought of. Similarly, elaborate forecasting techniques can be employed including scenario building, exploring alternative views of the enterprise's future.

3   A similar internal audit examines the internal, organizational and functional factors that produce the 'competence profile' of the firm.

4   Strategy evaluation taking the above into account within a framework such as SWOT, outlining strengths, weaknesses, opportunities and threats and comparing the consequences of a variety of strategic options.

5   The strategy operationalization phase that produces a hierarchy of objectives and actions, cascaded down throughout the organization.

The orthodox view of strategy is that it is a deliberate, conscious process coming from the top of the organization (Ansoff, 1968). Figure 11.1 outlines a sequence of activities from this perspective.

However, this model cannot explain organizational strategies and the means of evaluating their relative usefulness. A business can choose between recruiting and training its own direct sales people or subcontracting the function to outside agents. It has to be recognized that all options may not be apparent and that trial and error may be the only practical method of evaluation. Other factors such as competition, organizational politics or the absence of resources may limit the choice. As we saw earlier, in order to reduce costs and improve quality Ford outlined plans in 2002 to reduce its workforce worldwide, partly by outsourcing component manufacture to subcontractors located alongside its car assembly plants.

Moreover, this model cannot explain the strategic process entirely. As the future is not perfectly predictable, a feedback mechanism must be built into the process to correct for

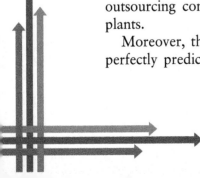

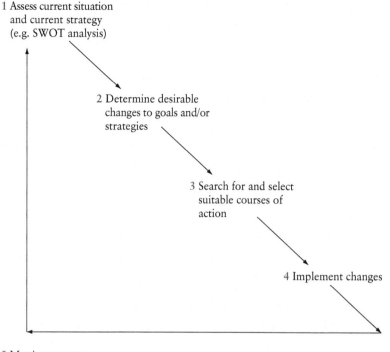

1 Assess current situation
and current strategy
(e.g. SWOT analysis)

2 Determine desirable
changes to goals and/or
strategies

3 Search for and select
suitable courses of
action

4 Implement changes

5 Monitor progress:
ongoing appraisal

**FIGURE 11.1**

The strategy process

Source: Adapted from Thompson (1993, p.32)
*Strategic Management: Awareness and Change*
© Cengage Learning EMEA Ltd. Reproduced
with permission.

unexpected developments. An alternative approach is that of Johnson and Scholes (1984), which divides the process into three components:

*Strategic analysis.* A successful organization is one that understands its market and is sensitive to changes in the business environment. It must be able to analyze its current position, the strengths and weaknesses of its current resources – for example, the skill and flexibility of its human resources – and assess the opportunities and threats present (and likely) to its continuing success.

*Strategic choice.* Determining all the courses of action open to the organization, and the means of evaluating their relative usefulness.

*Strategic implementation.* Senior managers may believe that by determining strategy they have decided the future of the organization. In fact, as we have seen in previous chapters, the structure and culture of the organization and the commitment of lower-level managers can influence or hinder the implementation of strategy. This is particularly evident in de-centralized and loosely controlled organizations that require higher levels of consultation and communication to ensure cooperation. Later in this chapter we will consider these issues in relation to organizational change.

Coherent strategies and integrated practices sound fine in theory but how are they to be translated into action? This 'surface neatness' hides an organizational reality that is far from simple (Blyton and Turnbull, 1992: 2). Mintzberg (1994: 26) argues that the strategies that are actually carried through into practice include an unintended element which he terms 'emergent strategies'. This might result from poor strategic thinking, poor implementation or a sound state of realism. It reflects the view that strategic management should not be confined to the top layers in an organization. Emergent strategy rarely comes from the centre but rather from bright ideas and initiatives at a local level, which were not predicted but were found to work and then adopted more widely: '... big strategies can grow from

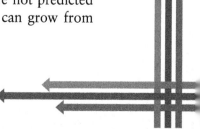

little ideas (initiatives), and in strange places, not to mention at unexpected times, almost anyone in the organization can prove to be a strategist. All he or she needs is a good idea and the freedom and resources required to pursue it' (Mintzberg, 1994: 26).

Further complications arise from the way firms are structured. In Chapter 8 we noted that divisional organizations have decision-making capabilities at a number of levels. It is possible to distinguish between corporate strategies (global, company-wide initiatives) that come from head office and business strategies developed by business units or operating subsidiaries (Purcell, 1995: 67). The latter are concerned with product and marketing decisions but also have human resource implications since business units have a closer involvement with employment markets and working procedures. There are no recognized rules on the relation between corporate and business strategies, but it has been argued that strategic HRM should be focused at the business unit level. Nevertheless, business units cannot operate in isolation from the rest of the firm. Overriding issues such as succession planning and media comment on industrial relations demand corporate people strategies.

However, it is a deadly serious game with people's careers and livelihoods at stake. The reality is that faced with a choice between profit and the well-being of employees, most commercial organizations will select the former. 'Softer' human resource issues continue to be secondary and subordinate to financial matters. Regardless of well-meaning statements to the contrary, within the free market capitalist model there is an emphasis on short-term improvement in financial performance. In Western organizations, financially knowledgeable managers have taken the lead as the 'bottom line' of profit or loss drives business. Strategic actions derived from technological or financial considerations can have direct and relatively immediate effect on an organization's people. Human resource initiatives are accommodated within a broad financial picture in which benefits or changes to people management compete with other resources. In reality, long-term HRM goals such as training and developing skills for the future are rarely considered. If employee commitment, flexibility and product quality are valued, they are sought for profit and not pursued as beneficial for workers.

## TRANSLATING STRATEGY INTO ACTION

At this point we turn to the issue of implementing human resource strategies. The classic approach follows the 'matching' process described in the Michigan model of HRM outlined in Chapter 1. The goal is a realization of the organization's strategic human resource requirements in terms of numbers and, more importantly; attitudes, behaviour and commitment. According to Miller (1989), the key lies with 'the concept of "fit": the fit of human resource management with the thrust of the organization'.

Truss (1999: 44), reviewing a number of authors, finds that 'there is no evidence that a tight fit leads to positive outcomes and the concept of fit implies inflexibility and rigidity which could, in themselves, be detrimental to organizational outcomes.'

She also notes the underlying assumption of some 'matching models' of hard HRM which contend that every business strategy has one appropriate human resource strategy. This implies a 'simple, linear relationship between strategy and human resource strategy' that does not exist. Such models fail to acknowledge the complex relationship between strategy and HRM and they ignore issues of power politics and culture. She concludes: 'The matching model is based on a narrow classical view of strategy formulation which assumes that formulation and implementation are separate activities and, consequently, that strategies in the HR area can simply be "matched" to business strategies at the formulation stage'.

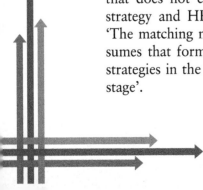

Khilji and Wang (2006) argue that much of the apparent confusion about the effectiveness of strategic HRM results from a failure by researchers to distinguish between 'intended' and 'implemented' strategies. They contend that researchers often depend on single respondents from each organization in industry-wide surveys. Khilji and Wang questioned managers and non-managers from inside and outside HR departments to highlight the differences between the HR practices intended by their company's strategies and those that actually were implemented. They found that the two may be substantially different while consistent implementation leads to higher employee satisfaction with HRM, which is positively related to organizational performance.

Armstrong (1992: 53) argues that the significant issue in HR strategy is that of integration with overall business strategy. In practice, this integration is difficult to achieve. Armstrong outlines some crucial difficulties that continue to be important:

*Diversity of strategic processes, levels and styles.* As we have seen, many organizations do not use neat, traditional approaches to business strategy based on rational planning. In line with the criticisms of Mintzberg and others, it may be more sensible to be open-minded and intuitive. However, from the perspective of people management it becomes difficult to discern appropriate HR strategies and the corporate strategies they are supposed to match. Further, in a diversified organization composed of strategic business units (SBUs), each unit may have its own idiosyncratic strategies. Consequently it becomes difficult to provide corporate HR strategies – such as management development – that can be reconciled with the different needs of individual SBUs.

*The evolutionary nature of business strategy.* It is not possible to provide a rational HR strategy if corporate strategy is evolving quickly and in a piecemeal way. In fact, the concept of 'rational' strategic planning is culture-bound: it is a product of free market economies. Other cultures naturally employ a more diffuse, emergent or evolving method of business planning (Legge, 1995: 104).

*The absence of written business strategies.* This is particularly the case in smaller companies and overwhelmingly in cultural contexts where evolutionary planning is the rule. This does not help to clarify those corporate strategic issues with which HR strategy is expected to fit.

*The qualitative nature of HR issues.* Business plans have tended to be expressed in numerical terms, such as financial data, sales forecasts and competitive position. As we shall see later, traditional 'manpower planning' fitted this mould. Equally, human resource strategy has been identified with the 'hard' rationalist model of HRM. However, 'soft' or qualitative issues such as culture, motivation and employee relations have become increasingly important – even in free market countries.

Armstrong's solution to these problems is to emphasize the need for human resource practitioners to achieve an understanding of how business strategies are formed. They should adopt a wider point of view and an understanding of key business issues such as:

→ Corporate intentions for growth or retrenchment, including strategic alliances (mergers, acquisitions, joint ventures, discussed earlier), product and market development, disposals.

→ Methods of increasing competitiveness such as improvements in productivity, quality and service, reducing costs.

→ A perceived need for a more positive, performance culture.

→ Other cultural consequences of the organization's mission such as 'commitment, mutuality, communications, involvement, devolution and teamworking'.

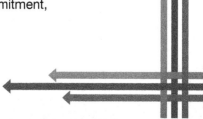

Organizations vary considerably in the formality of their strategic planning, ranging from detailed 200-page documents to unwritten 'orientations'. Neat theoretical approaches with successive stages of analysis, choice and implementation are rarely seen in practice. The organizational characteristics of a firm, and the environmental constraints upon it, affect and sometimes transform the process. As Whipp (1992: 33) explains:

> Seldom is there an easily isolated logic to strategic change. Instead that process may derive its motive force from an amalgam of economic, personal and political imperatives. ... The application of over-rational, linear programmes of HRM as a means of securing competitive success is shown to be at odds with experience both in the UK and elsewhere.

Whipp concludes that control of the environmental, organizational and strategic aspects of both competition and human resources is so problematic that the relationship between the two can only be indirect and fragile. Another critical factor is that the human resource is but one of the resources of the firm. Strengths and weaknesses in other areas, such as marketing and finance, may obscure the best people management.

Whipp also points to the environmental context within which HR strategy is implemented. We have discussed cultural influences already. Individual companies also have their own control and industrial relations traditions. Attempts to import HRM into companies outside North America and link it to business strategy have foundered because many organizations have no tradition of strategy.

The greatest difficulties are experienced in large, diversified organizations with a wide range of interests. They are highlighted in recession when the business needs do not fit with 'soft' HR values. HR strategies may focus on redundancies and sacking employees inevitably damages or destroys a caring corporate image. Legge (1995) outlines a strategy described as 'tough love' – being cruel to be kind – in which employees are expected to be both dedicated and disposable. In fact, human resource strategy may only be unproblematic in the ideal circumstances described by Guest (1987):

1   It should take place within a purpose-built modern location, a greenfield site employing carefully selected 'green' labour. Such staff would have no previous experience of the industry in which the company operates and therefore would be untarnished by an 'undesirable' industrial sub-culture. They would not be hidebound by traditional but outmoded ways of doing things.

2   The organization requires highly professional management, preferably Japanese or American.

3   Employees should be given intrinsically rewarding work rather than uninteresting functions for which pay is the sole motivation.

4   Workers should have security of employment and not be constantly in fear of losing their jobs.

Guest acknowledges that these conditions are difficult to achieve in practice since most organizations – Japanese transplant factories excepted – have pre-existing staff, buildings and equipment that cannot be discarded. They bring with them patterns of power and behaviour that may be contrary to the HR philosophy.

More positively, human resource strategies can be aimed at improving an organization's competitiveness by increasing its 'knowledge base' or competence. This includes shedding old values and techniques in favour of new ones. It requires a collective change of the organization's shared world view – including perceptions of the company and the market. Proactive SHRM is particularly important in highly competitive conditions where decisions

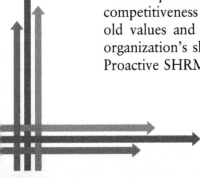

about outsourcing parts of the organization, such as the HR function itself, are key elements of strategic decision-making. In an Australian study, Sheehan (2009) identified training and development, recruitment and selection, and HRIS as the major areas for HR outsourcing. She found that large organizations tended to use consultants to initiate outsourcing. The private sector was more concerned with recruitment and selection and performance-related pay while public sector organizations were most likely to outsource HRIS.

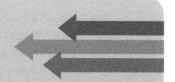

# HRM IN REALITY HR OUTSOURCING

Outsourcing basic human resource services can be the key to achieving a more influential and strategic role for the HR function. However, an executive briefing from the Chartered Institute of Personnel and Development (CIPD) also concludes that:

→ the decision to outsource needs to be carefully considered

→ it will not be right for all, and

→ considerable effort needs to be devoted to ensuring a smooth transfer of responsibilities.

Written by Professor William Scott-Jackson, Tim Newham and Melanie Gurney of the Centre for Applied HR Research, Oxford Brookes University, the report – *HR Outsourcing: the key decisions* – draws on the experiences of 17 organizations that are either outsourcing HR services or have considered the possibility and rejected it. The report is intended to offer practical guidance to HR and non-HR professionals responsible for developing and improving the delivery of HR services in their organizations.

Vanessa Robinson, organization and resourcing adviser at the CIPD, said:

People management plays a crucial role in delivering organizational performance. In today's modern, knowledge economy this is more true than ever before. The decision to outsource HR services is therefore not to be taken lightly.

However, there are many circumstances in which outsourcing HR services can deliver tangible benefits to the organization, for example freeing HR professionals to devote more time to a strategic role in supporting organizational performance.

*Advantages and disadvantages of outsourcing*
The report identifies a number of 'strategic drivers' for outsourcing HR services:

→ *Reducing costs:* Key determinator in many outsourcing decisions, but should not be considered in isolation from other costs/benefits.

→ *Increasing effectiveness of HR delivery:* Experienced outsourcing providers can often deal with HR processes more effectively. For example, recruitment may be undertaken more quickly, reducing employee turnover costs and speeding up the pace of growth.

→ *Providing greater expertise:* External providers may offer greater levels of specialist knowledge or experience than affordably available in-house.

→ *Moving HR up the value chain:* Outsourcing human resource administration can lead to a shift in HR focus towards policy and decision-making.

→ *To aid organizational growth:* Fast-growing organizations can lack the HR capacity to deliver business objectives, making HR outsourcing an attractive solution.

The report warns against regarding HR outsourcing as a panacea for organizational problems. The potential pitfalls include:

→ According to the report, handing over unnecessarily complex or badly understood systems to an external provider can be like 'picking up spaghetti'. This limits potential benefits from outsourcing. If processes cannot be improved before a move, the organization may have to

accept off-the-shelf replacements that are not specifically geared to their needs.

→ The greatest financial benefits of outsourcing often come from using sophisticated software. If effective IT systems already exist in-house, cost savings may not be achieved from an external provider.

→ Good employee management practices remain essential, and the key relationship between staff and their line managers remains in-house, leaving plenty of work on manager/staff relationships that still has to be handled despite the outsourcing relationship.

→ Local knowledge and ownership of human resource processes could be lost.

Vanessa Robinson continued:

The decision to outsource HR services is a complicated one. Cost reasons alone are not sufficient to drive the decision. Decisionmakers need to ask whether there is a need to change the

way the HR department operates and review existing provision. This review needs to consider cost, administrative efficiency and HR policy strategy and expertise. Where gaps are identified, organizations need to consider whether these are best solved by minor tinkering or major transformation.

It must also not be forgotten that a transition from in-house HR provision to the use of an outsourced provider is a significant change for the organization, and must be managed accordingly. If significant time is not devoted to the process of change, with unequivocal top-level support, there is a danger that staff/line manager relationships and other aspects of people management policy may be neglected.

*Overall, is outsourcing the HR function likely to benefit an organization?*

*Source: Reprinted with permission from HRM Guide UK (http://www.hrmguide.co.uk).*

## SUMMARY

Strategic thinking has its basis in rational thinking. In practice, strategists have accepted that there must be a place for the unexpected. Strategy and planning provide a framework for human resource requirements over a defined period but traditional personnel managers have experienced difficulty in understanding and implementing strategy. Human resource strategies tend to focus on numbers and also attitudes, behaviour and commitment in line with harder 'matching' models of HRM but their implementation is problematic. Recent thinking has accommodated the notion that HR strategy is not as simple as some rationalist accounts imply and that strategy itself has the same emotional, irrational and intuitive components as any other form of thinking or decision-making.

Organizational competencies are the sum product of the competencies of the workforce. This suggests that people management should drive rather than follow business strategy, by building employee competencies through selection, assessment, reward and development. In the next chapter, we elaborate further on the building of organizational competence with an examination of a fundamental aspect of people management – resourcing.

## FURTHER READING

1 Mintzberg, Ahlsrand and Lampel (1998), *Strategy Safari: A Guided Tour Through the Wilds of Strategic Management,* published by The Free Press provides an interesting excursion through the different types or 'schools' of strategic management.

2 Mintzberg's *Strategy Bites Back* (*Financial Times,* 2004) provides a newer treatment of a range of strategic approaches.

3 Good reviews of strategic human resource management are found in the articles by Purcell and by Schuler *et al.* in J. Storey (ed.) *Human Resource Management: A Critical Text, 2nd* edition, published by Cengage Learning (2001).

4 *Strategic Human Resource Management: Theory and Practice* (2nd edition, Sage, 2005) edited by Graeme Salaman, John Storey and Jon Billsberry is a useful reader.

 ## REVIEW QUESTIONS

1 What is a strategy? What is meant by first, second and third-order strategies?

2 Is HRM really 'strategic'? How does human resource strategy fit into the business planning process?

3 What is 'strategic human resource management'? Summarize the main goals of strategic human resource management and identify some of the key differences between strategic and operational HRM.

4 When is outsourcing a suitable strategy for the HR function?

5 To what extent is it possible to demonstrate that human resource strategies are vital for business success?

6 Within any organization, how are management styles and corporate culture likely to influence human resource strategy?

7 What are the ideal conditions for the implementation of a human resource strategy? What deficiencies are commonly found in strategic human resource plans?

8 Is strategic human resource management more important in some countries/industries than others?

9 What do you see as the main barriers to successful implementation of strategic HRM?

 ## CASE STUDY FOR DISCUSSION AND ANALYSIS

 ### Supreme Sportscars

Supreme Sportscars makes high-powered luxury cars. With a deliberately limited manufacturing capacity, sales have been steady at 190 vehicles a month, with a two-year waiting list. The factory is poorly equipped with a large proportion of the work being done by traditional hand methods. However, the company has always been profitable at this level. The employees are loyal but modestly paid. They take pride in their craftsmanship and the reputation of the cars. They have close relationships with the lower-level managers, most of whom were promoted from the ranks.

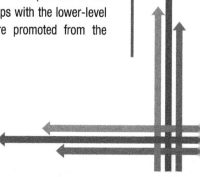

Five years ago, the company was acquired by a major US manufacturer. Initially, the American company had significant expansion plans based on a small and cheaper sports car but nothing came of those plans. Under a new chief executive, the corporate strategy has changed and now the parent company is looking to dispose of Supreme Sportscars, possibly in the form of a management buy-out. Design of the new car is virtually complete but nothing has been done to increase production capacity. There are two key executives in the current company.

The managing director is Arnold Davies, a 45-year-old marketing man. He was recruited by the parent company last year after a career spent mainly in promoting and advertising washing machines and refrigerators. He has few academic or technical qualifications but is an intelligent, decisive man with a reputation for getting things done. A flamboyant character, he drives a bright red Supreme car from the top-end of the range. The workforce have accepted him but have no great respect for his managerial qualities. He believes in leading from the front and has asked your management consultancy to advise him on the merits of a management buy-out.

You are aware that a large multinational car manufacturer is interested in acquiring Supreme Sportscars and badging its own cars under this name. They would establish a new production facility. They would not consider a joint venture but might be prepared to take some of the management team and the design unit. The parent company is wary of selling to the multinational in case this encourages further competition for their other products.

The divisional accountant, Jeff Mathias, is an important figure in any decision. He is a long-term staff member of the US company, well qualified and experienced. He is a quiet but firm person, known to be open to new ideas but also very loyal to his employers. He is respected by the other managers, although the nature of his work isolates him from the day-to-day running of the factory. He is well paid but is conscious that he will never become rich working for the US company. Mathias is also aware that the parent company is about to announce major job cuts worldwide because of heavy losses in the USA and declining sales in Europe.

*This is your first impression of the problem. How would you proceed with collecting relevant information, determining the crucial issues and devising the decision strategy?*

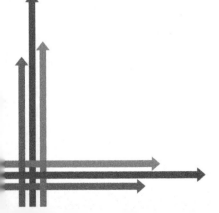

# CHAPTER 12
## Change strategies

## LEARNING OBJECTIVES

The purpose of this chapter is to:

→ Introduce the concept of transformational human resource strategies.

→ Compare incremental and packaged change programmes.

→ Discuss the HR role in mergers and acquisitions.

→ Consider the issue of behavioural transformation and negative change.

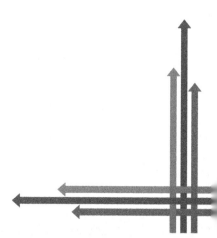

# TRANSFORMATIONAL HR STRATEGIES

Enthusiasts have seen a transformational power in HRM and transformation, or change, is an inevitable consequence of many human resource strategies (Bourne and Haddon, 2010). In this chapter we will consider various kinds of change initiatives from both a strategic and implementational perspective.

Change strategies fall into one of two categories: turnaround change and organizational transformation (Bertsch and Williams, 1994):

1   *Turnaround change.* This is financially driven, often to ensure corporate survival by cutting unprofitable products and services. It involves the redesign of organizational structures, disposal of non-core activities and large-scale redundancies. This kind of change is painful but straightforward since existing hierarchical control systems can administer the process.

2   *Behavioural transformations.* This involves changing behaviour patterns throughout the company. Hierarchical control is inadequate because different power centres are likely to conflict and differences between business units make behavioural consistency a difficult objective to achieve.

Whatever the strategic purpose and product of change, its organization is likely to take the form of one of three models (Buchanan and Boddy, 1992):

*Project management.* This adopts a rational, linear problem-solving approach, very much in the tradition of classical business strategy. Decisions are generated at the top and orchestrated by a project manager who assigns objectives, allocates budgets and responsibilities and sets deadlines. The project management model embodies a control mechanism which monitors progress in the determined direction.

*Participative management.* This model takes more account of the skills and concerns of people affected by the change at lower levels of the organization. It involves a degree of emergent strategy. This approach is more time-consuming for managers and runs the risk of deviating into side issues. Participative management may lead to changes being blocked by inflexible interest groups. In general, however, it is more compatible with concepts of empowerment, commitment and team management.

*A political perspective.* This framework goes further in accepting and dealing with interpersonal and cultural aspects of change. It reflects awareness of power distribution within an organization and reasons for resistance. It is most useful when there is a lack of clarity or agreement over the objectives of the firm, or the need for strategic change. This approach has particular relevance in comprehending the effects of mergers and takeovers. It requires front stage political 'performances' from senior managers, together with Machiavellian intrigue in building behind-the-scenes power blocks and undermining resistance.

Each model has its merits and disadvantages. Individual organizations may also employ combinations of more than one approach.

## Restructuring

Restructuring is the most common form of major organizational change (Key concept 12.1). According to its protagonists, restructuring should not be a defensive cost-cutting process but rather a proactive attempt to achieve innovative products and services by achieving synergy (Key concept 12.2).

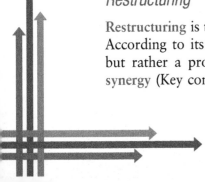

**KEY CONCEPT 12.1** RESTRUCTURING

Breaking up and recombining organizational structures. Advantages include reduced costs, eliminating duplication and greater efficiency. Disadvantages include disorder; interfering with normal activities; destruction of long-term commitment; loss of direction, especially in careers and overwork from excessive cost-cutting. Recent strategic thinking has also emphasized the importance of relating business objectives to core organizational competencies. In other words, organizations should do what they are good at, leading to a new trend for companies to demerge, splitting into focused activity areas on which separate management teams can concentrate.

**KEY CONCEPT 12.2** SYNERGY

Making the new whole worth more than its old parts, sometimes described as '2 + 2 = 5'. Synergies involve economies from integrating activities, horizontally or vertically; but also unrealized potential for new ideas, products or processes by melding expertise from the different sources into centres of excellence.

Restructuring usually involves reorganization – a move from one form of organization to another. For example, a business may change from a divisional to a network structure. This requires breaking up the previous hierarchy or departmental structure. Some organizations are notoriously prone to reorganizations at intervals of two to three years or less, with the consequences of the last restructuring not being fully absorbed and analyzed before being swept up in the next.

Restructuring can affect the HR function directly. Pollitt (2005b) describes how pharmaceutical giant AstraZeneca changed from site and functionally based human resources teams offering a full range of generalist support, to a 'one team' approach. Use of HR metrics helped to demonstrate the value of HR to the AstraZeneca businesses. The rationale was to create a more efficient and customer-oriented delivery of HR services and to ensure smooth implementation by communicating the new mindset to HR staff, combined with specific skills training to manage customer interactions both at strategic and transformational levels. The 'one team' approach has brought together everyone involved in HR delivery and it is claimed that there is a greater sense of team working, improved communication, a much more consultative approach and a customer-focused culture. HR is now in line with organizational strategy and is a value-adding part of the business.

## CHANGE AND ORGANIZATION STRUCTURES

Melé (2005) studied the conversion of a medium-sized bureaucratic organization with highly specialized jobs into one in which employees were much more autonomous in managing their own work. Bureaucratic rules were reduced, but not eliminated completely, and

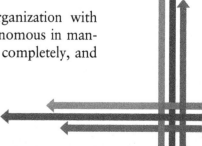

management became less authoritarian. Employees could therefore apply greater entrepreneurial spirit, developing their talents in pursuit of company goals. It is argued that the new organizational form is ethically superior and reflects the basic requirements of the principle of subsidiarity. This holds that a larger and higher-ranking body should not exercise functions which could be efficiently carried out by a smaller and lesser body. The former should support the latter by aiding it in the coordination of its activities with those of the greater community. While usually applied in a political context, Melé explores the principle as a moral base for organizational forms within business, arguing that it would help to mitigate the effects of those bureaucracies in which individuals are often not fully appreciated.

Labovitz and Rosansky (1997: 7) consider that senior managers can achieve alignment to ensure advancement through:

→ Carefully crafting and articulating the essence of their business and determining the 'main thing'.

→ Defining a few critical strategic goals and imperatives and deploying them throughout their organizations.

→ Tying performance measures and metrics to those goals.

→ Linking those measures to a system of rewards and recognition.

→ Personally reviewing the performance of their people to ensure the goals are met.

Labovitz and Rosansky criticize older ideas about organizational structure that are based on the notion of breaking up a managerial problem into pieces: departments and divisions. As they point out (1997: 8):

> Psychologists have long recognized that human beings like people who are like themselves and tend to reject people who are different from them. Yet organizations continue to create differences between people in the interest of efficiency. Line versus staff, management versus labour, field versus corporate, international versus domestic, East versus West, accounting versus sales – the list goes on. No wonder it's so hard to focus people around common goals when they are so different from each other simply by virtue of what they do and where they do it. Specialization and expertise can be a wedge that drives people further apart and makes it difficult for them to work together.

The difficulty for corporate management comes in the attempt to achieve both synergy and workable new diversified or decentralized structures at one and the same time (Marginson *et al.*, 1993a: 7). Public statements through the media and shareholder information normally present such changes as deliberate and thought-through, the implication being that restructuring would be dealt with by means of a project management approach. However, the notion that restructuring is usually decided at the most senior level on the grounds of balance sheet rationality is often illusory (Purcell, 1995: 70). As we observed in earlier discussions on strategy and management, when faced with uncertainty, complex situations and conflict within the organization, managers typically resort to 'political' decision making. Ficery *et al.* (2007) attribute a failure of synergy to six main causes: defining a synergy too narrowly or broadly; missing a window of opportunity; using incentives incorrectly or insufficiently; not involving the right people in synergy capture; mismatch between systems and culture systems; and (bluntly) using the wrong process. Estimating synergy benefits during the process of agreeing a merger is difficult and there is a tendency towards overoptimism among senior managers often leading to over-payment, which cancels out much of the benefit (Chaterjee, 2007).

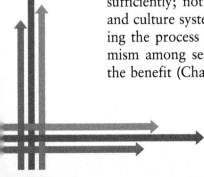

Unfortunately, as we concluded earlier, employees are a secondary consideration of change in free market organizations (Willmott, 1995: 313). Participative management is squeezed out in favour of the project management or political approach. Developing Willmott's remark that 'the turkeys are unlikely to vote for Christmas', it is evident that they are generally kept in the dark until it is too late. Hence, little account is taken of the people who will be disrupted by the process and those who have to maintain quality and value during a period of major upheaval. Often the principal role of people managers is to sort out the resulting mess and smooth ruffled feathers.

## Shrinkage

As we observed earlier, focusing on core activities and disposing of others has become particularly fashionable. In some cases, businesses have decided that management control and shareholder value are best served by a demerger. More commonly, shrinkage involves reducing the number of employees or downsizing – a term coined by journalists according to Baumol *et al.* (2003) – although this has largely been confined to the manufacturing sector. In either case, HR managers are involved with communicating the change, conducting union negotiations and arranging redundancies or redeployment. For example, faced with a dramatic change in the nature of the music industry, EMI was forced to slim its workforce, but attempt to retain key employees and its quality employer brand.

A particular concern is the cost-effectiveness of individual employees and departments. The more expensive, the greater the degree of justification required to retain them. For example, the 'de-layering' initiatives of the 1980s and 1990s focused on expensive middle-managers. Kanter (1989: 94) suggests that 'overhead' functions such as divisional headquarters have a duty to justify themselves to the business units they are meant to support. Approval and checking may delay decision-making, hindering the ability to compete. Wherever

## HRM IN REALITY SURVEYING EMPLOYEE OPINIONS

A 2008 survey by Opinion Research Corporation found that many US businesses are missing out on vital feedback and ideas from their own workforces.

Opinion Research Corporation's annual employee research survey shows that 44 per cent of the 1437 respondents do not carry out employee surveys and almost a half (46 per cent) of businesses that conducted surveys did not make any organizational changes as a result of employee feedback.

Employee surveys were most popular in the South (57 per cent of companies questioned) while those in the North Central region (Ohio, Indiana, Illinois, Michigan, Wisconsin, Minnesota, Iowa, Missouri, North Dakota, South Dakota, Nebraska, Kansas) were the least likely (52 per cent) to take any action following employee surveys, compared with 42 per cent in the West.

Terry Reilly, Director of the Employee Engagement practice at Opinion Research Corporation US said:

> Your employees hold the key to your success. An employee survey gives them the opportunity to let their feedback be heard and become part of the ongoing strategy of the organization.

The research shows a strong correlation between positive employee perception and the responsiveness of an organization to employee survey feedback. Eighty-four per cent of workers in businesses that acted on survey feedback felt that the changes positively affected them personally. However, nearly one quarter (23 per cent) of these did not think that the change was communicated well in the workplace.

US results were much better than those from a similar study in the UK where only 32 per cent of

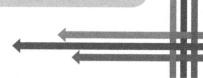

respondents thought that change was managed effectively in their organizations - compared to 63 per cent in the US. And only 43 per cent of British respondents said they had the opportunity to contribute their views before changes were made to their jobs. This compared to 62 per cent in the US.

Terry Reilly commented:

> Ineffective management of change within an organization can lead to increased uncertainty in the workforce. Offering employees the opportunity to voice their opinions before change is implemented can significantly improve employee engagement, and, in turn – the success of the organization.

*Top themes in employee surveys*

An analysis of employee responses to opinion surveys in 2006 found a number of recurrent themes. HR Solutions, Inc., a Chicago-based management consulting firm specializing in Employee Engagement Surveys, compiled a top ten list of the issues that concern employees the most:

1 **Higher salaries**. Pay is the number one topic for employee dissatisfaction.

2 **Internal pay equity**. Employees are particularly concerned about 'pay compression' (defined as the differential in pay between new and more tenured employees).

3 **Benefits programs**. Particularly health/dental, retirement, and paid time off/vacation days. Many employees are unhappy about the cost of health insurance, especially prescription drug programs.

4 **Over-management**. 'Too many chiefs, not enough Indians' is a typical comment.

5 **Pay increase guidelines**. There should be a greater emphasis on merit.

6 **The HR department**. They need to be more responsive to employees' questions and/or concerns.

7 **Favouritism**.

8 **Improved communication and availability**. This applies to both supervisors and upper management.

9 **Over-work**. Workloads are too heavy and/or departments are understaffed.

10 **Facility cleanliness**.

Responses from written feedback can be different than verbal employee feedback sessions, according to Jennifer Rand, Principal Consultant with HR Solutions. 'Most of what the consultants hear during the feedback sessions supports in great detail the themes of the written comments. The comments most prevalent are usually those things that have changed, whether negative or positive, i.e. benefits, since it is human nature to resist change', she said.

HR Solutions say that organizations should not overlook the write-in comment section of their employee survey as Quick Wins oftentimes originate from it. Quick Wins are easily implemented, actionable improvements to workplace setting or environment involving little resource investment. They can lead to immediate improvements in employee engagement and reassure employees that managers are acting on the survey findings.

*How might employee surveys assist in providing a favourable climate for change?*

*Source: Reprinted with permission from HRM Guide USA (http://www.hrmguide.com/).*

---

possible, these should be eliminated completely or transferred to the business units whose activities are involved. Decentralization is a dominant force, leaving small, slimmed-down central functions. Restructuring can be dangerous when companies treat people purely as costs rather than as assets. Kanter points to the inevitable 'discontinuity, disorder and distraction' that interfere with people's normal activities. She concludes that 'top management typically *overestimates* the degree of cooperation it will get and *underestimates* the integration costs'.

Cowboy management in these circumstances can destroy long-term commitment since restructuring removes many of life's certainties. Most of us try to create a state of order and predictability around our jobs. Restructuring can destroy this. No longer can we count on a job for life with any one company, but some sense of direction is essential to preserve motivation and obtain the best performance. Neither can people be expected to cope with

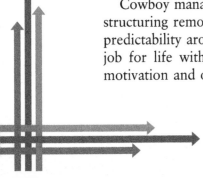

**TABLE 12.1**

Themes of
organization
development

Source: Adapted from
French and Bell (1990).

**293**

CHAPTER 12 Change strategies

| Theme | Features |
|---|---|
| **1** Top management support | Initiatives will not succeed unless higher management levels are fully committed to the change process and its maintenance |
| **2** Problem-solving and renewal process | Allows adaptability and viability to be generated in an organization that may be living in the past. This should allow the organization continually to redefine its purpose |
| **3** Collaborative diagnosis and management of culture | The process of change must involve all levels within the organization in a search for ideas that will lead to improvement. This is a non-hierarchical, shared evaluation of the culture and long-term goals of the organization |
| **4** Formal work team | Focusing on work groups, group dynamics and team development |
| **5** Consultant facilitator | Bringing in an external change agent or catalyst, experienced in the mechanics of change, able to spot resistance and unbiased by any prevailing agenda |
| **6** Action research | A primary feature of classic organization development that is absent in many modern packaged initiatives |

overwork caused by excessive cost-cutting. According to American experience, much downsizing is really 'dumb-sizing', since two-thirds of the companies who have slashed workforces in recent years report no increase in efficiency. Often the principal role of human resource specialists is in rescuing the situation after the change has happened. Motivation and commitment must be rebuilt and skills training made available for staff involved in new tasks.

### *Incremental change*

In the 1960s and 1970s, change often came under the label of organizational development (OD). This is an undramatic – but effective – long-term change process based on incremental improvements, essentially a continuous flow of emergent strategies. With the advent of modern change programmes such as 'business process re-engineering', this low-risk and long-term approach has gone out of fashion to a considerable extent. As we can see from Table 12.1, its underlying principles are similar to Japanese methods of continuous improvement and the methodology has considerable parallels with radical change initiatives described later in this chapter.

## ACTION LEARNING

What is action learning? Rothwell (1999: 5) states that it is a 'real-time learning experience that is carried out with two equally important purposes in mind: meeting an organizational

need and developing individuals or groups'. Rothwell notes that Reg Revans, the originator of action learning, avoided defining the term, preferring to say what it was not. But there are many definitions including the following by Pedler (2008: 1): 'an approach to problem solving and learning in groups to bring about change in individuals, teams, organizations and systems'.

Marquardt and Revans (1999: 4) feel that 'Perhaps action learning's greatest value is its capacity for equipping individuals, teams and organizations to more effectively respond to change'. They go on to contend that action learning has a 'unique and inherent capacity' to deal simultaneously with five pressing organizational needs:

1   *Problem solving.* The more difficult the problem, the better suited is action learning to meet the challenge.

2   *Organizational learning.* Action learning provides a valuable focus for company-wide learning.

3   *Team building.* Helps build teams and team skills for future team building.

4   *Leadership development.* Prepares leaders to deal with future problems.

5   *Professional growth and career development.* Action learning facilitates high levels of self-awareness, self-development and continuous learning.

The whole process revolves around a real-life problem that needs to be important to the organization. Marquardt and Revans (1999: 5) state:

> The problem should be significant, be within the responsibility of the team, and provide opportunity for learning. Selection of the problem is fundamental to action learning because we learn best when undertaking some action, which can then be reflected upon. The problem gives the group something to focus on that is real and important, that is relevant and that means something to them.

This democratic – or, at least, participatory – process may follow a sequence such as (Rothwell, 1999: 5):

→   pinpoint the cause(s) of problems

→   solve the problems

→   formulate goals

→   work toward achieving goals

→   establish a shared vision of the future.

People are chosen for an action learning team (composed of four to eight members) for their experience and ability to contribute to the learning process – and also for the developmental benefit to them. So they must already possess relevant knowledge or skills for the particular issue they are working on. It is beneficial to have participants from a wide range of departments or functions, representing a number of views. They need to be positive and open-minded about the issue and possible solutions. It is also customary to appoint a team facilitator who is not a leader but helps the team work together effectively. Stark (2006) gives examples of effective action learning for different professional groups in the UK (nurses and educators) but argues that there are tensions and challenges in organizations such as political agendas that discourage learning and favour the status quo.

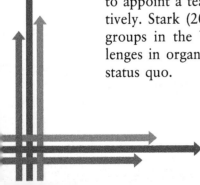

There are times when action learning is not appropriate according to Rothwell (*ibid.*: 18):

→ When the issue or need to be addressed is simple or straightforward.

→ It is pressing or urgent, such as an emergency or catastrophe.

→ The organization does not have the expertise to deal with the problem.

→ Managers do not value their employees or see merit in the developmental benefits.

Competitive pressures often demand a faster, more dramatic process than that provided by organizational development or action learning. Many modern managers would question whether their organization had the time required. More pertinently, we can ask if ambitious executives on short-term contracts have enough time to make their mark with such a slow methodology. It is likely that a glossier and more public method will be better appreciated. This is provided by 'packaged', or 'off-the-shelf' approaches, which begin with top management and are cascaded down the organization. They are normally dramatized with considerable emphasis on communication and a spotlight placed on the lead personality.

In the 1980s most large organizations engaged in 'total quality management' (TQM) programmes, focusing on continuous improvement, quality assurance and zero faults. TQM programmes are geared to organizational processes such as production. HR involvement includes the selection of flexible people who are amenable to increasingly demanding levels of quality.

## BUSINESS PROCESS RE-ENGINEERING

Re-engineering is a methodology of the late 20th century (see Key concept 12.3) that inspired many change strategies. The technique was first publicized by Hammer (1990) in a *Harvard Business Review* article with the somewhat dramatic title of 'Re-engineering Work: Don't Automate, Obliterate'. In typical guru fashion he outlined amazing benefits in a range of companies, proclaiming the existence of seven fundamental principles of re-engineering:

→ Organize around outcomes, not tasks.

→ Those who use the output should perform the process.

→ Information processing work should be subsumed into the real work that produces the information.

→ Geographically dispersed resources should be used as though they were centralized.

→ Link parallel activities instead of integrating tasks.

→ Decisions should be taken where work is performed and control built into the process.

→ Information should only be captured once – at source.

### KEY CONCEPT 12.3 BUSINESS PROCESS RE-ENGINEERING

A 'fundamental rethinking and radical redesign of business processes to achieve dramatic improvements in critical contemporary measures of performance, such as cost, quality, service and speed' (Hammer and Champy, 1993).

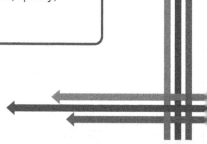

# HRM IN REALITY OFFSHORING COULD SAVE US$58 BILLION A YEAR

Research from The Hackett Group, a strategic advisory firm and an Answerthink company, estimates that Fortune 500 companies could potentially save US$58 billion annually, or over US$116 million on average, by offshoring many of their back office activities. Advances in technology, along with increasingly educated global workforces, enable the portability of business support activities across information technology (IT), finance, human resources (HR) and procurement, to take advantage of labour arbitrage. Increased use of offshore resources may impact up to 1.47 million general and administrative jobs, or nearly 3000 at a typical Fortune 500 company.

The report published in 2006 concludes that globalization has created an environment where executives must constantly re-evaluate their cost structures for general and administrative operations against a host of emerging global resources. The best companies are strategically improving performance in finance, IT, HR, procurement, working capital and other areas in ways that help them respond to the pressures of globalization.

However, the report argues that many companies are relying on outdated sourcing analysis techniques resulting in an underestimation of potential benefits of offshoring back office operations. With labour arbitrage savings approaching 60 per cent, executives should analyze their process optimization opportunities to capture the potential value of centralization. Failure to do so risks allowing activities that provide no competitive advantage to remain decentralized in industrialized countries with associated higher costs. Distributed activities are generally not portable, and therefore not included within the scope of a globalization initiative. The education base and skill sets available in India, China, the Philippines, Pakistan, Eastern Europe, Brazil and other emerging countries continue to expand, offering a new level of savings combined with improved quality and talent, significantly strengthening the business case for globalization.

Hackett director, Julio Ramirez, said:

Companies have long been aware that they can take out cost and improve back office efficiency by streamlining businesses processes, improving the way they use technology and centralizing operations, either in a shared service centre or with an outsourcer. But over the past few years, the resources available offshore have matured rapidly, creating immediate opportunities to materially reduce companies' cost structures.

Hackett director, Michel Janssen, added:

Today, companies can turn to established offshore resources that deliver labour costs reductions while maintaining or even improving the skill level of staff. The potential savings of up to US$116 million annually for a company are simply too compelling to ignore. Yet most executives will miss the potential impact of service globalization due to the under-scoping of initiatives. Taking full advantage of service globalization requires a deep understanding of the nature of business processes and how they can be optimally organized and delivered.

The report recommends use of a well-balanced assessment methodology that fully considers the business' strategy, culture, transactional characteristics and readiness for change. By taking the broadest logical view of relevant processes, combined with a holistic evaluation methodology, firms can ensure that they are maximizing the benefit opportunities available through global markets while managing the risk associated with these progressive transformation initiatives.

Current analysis of the Fortune 500 draws upon ongoing benchmark studies that have captured outsourcing costs since 1992. While information technology represents the largest functional opportunity, significant savings can be generated in other general and administrative areas, including finance, human resources and procurement.

*Annual savings (millions)*

→ Information technology US$58.5

→ Finance US$32.1

→ Human resources US$15.6

→ Procurement US$9.9.

Analysis of the savings opportunity breakdown for a typical Fortune 500 company is based upon the median number of full-time employees (FTEs) per process group, labour arbitrage cost differential and the potential degree for offshoring by process group.

*What are the human resource management advantages and disadvantages of offshoring back office activities?*

*Source: Reprinted with permission from* HRM Guide USA *(http://www.hrmguide.com).*

Business process re-engineering (BPR) appears under the guise of a number of similar terms and a variety of definitions. Depending on the definition used, re-engineering can involve change in individual work tasks; in interpersonal work processes within a department; between sections of a business; or beyond the boundaries of a firm in a networked or virtual organization. Critics argue that perhaps it is no more than organization and methods (O&M), TQM and just-in-time 'dusted down and repackaged' (Burke and Peppard, 1995: 28).

Nevertheless, BPR swept the Western business world. Companies such as AT&T, BT, Ford, Mercury and Rank Xerox have used the methodology. Why was it apparently so popular? Instead of 5–10 per cent improvements from other methods, the proponents of re-engineering promised 30 per cent, 50 per cent or even more. But BPR requires total rethinking of the organization from the bottom up, rather than tinkering with an existing situation.

Hammer and Champy presented a process perspective in contrast to the functional basis of most businesses. Hence, organizations and departments are not re-engineered but processes are. For instance the process of order fulfilment is everything from an order request to its delivery to the customer, regardless of department or level. Hammer and Champy argue that traditional hierarchical structures 'stifle innovation and creativity'. Instead, new technology should be introduced to cut out stages and people in a process. Moreover, a multi-skilled team should be employed, able to deal with a process as a whole. In all, they describe ten interrelated changes that Grint (1995: 83) traces to much earlier origins (see Table 12.2). In fact, an examination of these change principles reveals some strong links between BPR and concepts, such as empowerment and facilitatory management, associated with HRM elsewhere in this book.

Business process re-engineering also has close parallels with the notion of a 'learning organization' discussed in Chapter 18. BPR works on the principle that an organization cannot learn before it has first unlearned. BPR does this by starting with a 'blank piece of paper' approach using techniques such as cognitive mapping and soft systems methodology. These are diagrammatic methods aimed at tapping creativity and ensuring that a holistic approach is taken. Four stages are identified:

1   Have a vision.

2   Identify and understand the current processes.

3   Redesign the processes.

4   Implement the redesigned processes.

Shim and Kumar (2010) describe how such an approach, using computer simulation, can improve emergency care provision in a hospital situation.

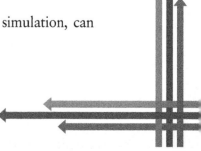

**TABLE 12.2**
Origins of change
principles in
business process
re-engineering

Source: Adapted from Grint
(1995: 85).

| Principle | Origins |
|---|---|
| **1** Switch from functional departments to processes | Principle of 1950s socio-technical systems and Volvo Kalmar experiment |
| **2** Move from simple tasks to multidimensional work | 1970s quality of working life and job enrichment |
| **3** Reversal of power relationship from superordinate to subordinate empowerment | Seen in both above |
| **4** Shift from training to education | A criticism of British 'education' since the 19th century |
| **5** From payment for attendance to payment for value added | Common in Ancient Greece |
| **6** Bifurcation of link between reward for current performance and advancement through assessment of ability | The 'Peter Principle' – every employee tends to rise to his (or her) level of incompetence |
| **7** From concern for boss to concern for customer | See modern Japan |
| **8** Managers become coaches rather than supervisors | Hawthorne experiments – USA 1930s |
| **9** Flattening of hierarchies | Kalmar experiments |
| **10** Executives move from scorekeepers to leaders | Human relations |

Generally, BPR is simultaneously presented as an empowering programme, with fine rhetoric about teamworking, multi-skilling and flattened hierarchies, and as a top-down exercise demanding (as ever) commitment from senior executives! In a study of post-BPR work in the Singapore Internal Revenue Service it was found that processes had been so tightly prescribed that there was there was no room for employees to exercise the empowerment they had been granted (Sia and Neo, 2008).

Of course, consultants have to remember who pays the bill. Perhaps the true emphasis is reflected in the key roles required for re-engineering as presented by Hammer and Champy (1993):

→ Leader – a visionary and motivator.

→ Process owner – sufficiently senior to oversee the entire process to be re-engineered.

→ Re-engineering team – composed of insiders who understand present activities; and outsiders to question assumptions.

→ An optional steering committee to oversee the organization's re-engineering as a whole.

→ 'Re-engineering czar' – the operational head of the organization's re-engineering activities.

Clearly, this is a directed process. Employees may be 'permitted and required to think, interact, use judgement and make decisions' but this only applies to the workers who are allocated jobs after the process has been re-engineered – eliminating one or two departments along the way. The attractiveness to senior executives is evident in the promise of redundancy; the benefits to employees are somewhat less obvious.

Burke and Peppard (1995: 34) identify a number of further barriers to implementing BPR:

→ There is a paradox in that people with knowledge of a particular process are unlikely to have the authority to redesign it, and vice versa.

→ Redesign disturbs existing patterns of power in an organization. The power base may not coincide with senior management but with a 'dominant coalition' with a vested interest in frustrating BPR.

→ The firm's culture may work against a process-based organization and consequent changes in work practices, job content and relationships.

→ Within multinational companies, processes may cross national boundaries, bringing in further difficulties.

Given the importance of employees in implementing BPR, and the embodiment of strong ideas about people management in its basic texts, it is surprising to find that human resource issues have scarcely been addressed (Willmott, 1995: 306). Tinaikar, Hartman and Nath (1995: 109) in a survey of 248 articles on BPR found:

> Almost all of the articles (95.9 per cent) portray BPR as being concerned with only technical issues. The few articles discussing social issues such as empowerment of the lower levels, resistance to change, etc, focused primarily on the managerially relevant benefits of BPR. Cost-cutting through technology and downsizing, or the politically correct 'rightsizing', were some of the most common themes. However, the implications of this potential job loss through BPR were singularly neglected.

They conclude that the human aspect has been trivialized in the BPR literature. However, it is not unreasonable to wonder if this lack of concern for people may be partly responsible for the high failure rate of re-engineering initiatives. An online search in 2010 by this author through indexes of recent academic papers for discussion of HR issues in the context of BPR found a similar dearth of material. Generally, the bestselling texts on BPR have few references to human resources.

Pink (2001: 108) considers that: 'In the beginning [of the new economy] there was re-engineering. And it was good. Then it was big. Then it got scary'. Pink goes on:

> Re-engineering corporations quickly became a $50 billion industry. The craze turned Hammer, a former MIT computer-science professor, into a rock star of the then-fledgling new economy. His bearded face began appearing at corporate conferences, inside boardrooms and on lists of America's most influential people. He scolded CEOs for not zeroing in on first principles. He exhorted them to repent. Some of his warnings verged on the apocalyptic: 'Re-engineering,' he wrote, 'is the only thing that stands between many US corporations – indeed, the US economy – and disaster'.

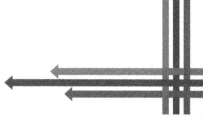

It seemed at one stage that BPR could be regarded as the answer to everything. But business process re-engineering is just one more set of practices in a long list of methodologies that have been in and out of fashion over recent decades. Perhaps it is not too surprising to read in Hammer (2001: 5), a decade further on from his seminal paper:

> It is told that Albert Einstein once handed his secretary an exam to be distributed to his graduate students. The secretary scanned the paper and objected, 'But Professor Einstein, these are the same questions you used last year. Won't the students already know the answers?' 'It's all right, you see', replied Einstein, 'the questions are the same, but the answers are different'. What is true of physics is true of business. Today's business world is not that of Drucker or of Peters and Waterman, and it calls for a new edition of the management agenda.

Of course, Hammer argues that a new agenda is required because circumstances have changed. 'Executives of the most powerful companies now tremble before their independent and demanding customers.' This implies that customers were somehow not independent or demanding in the past. An alternative explanation is that the last agenda (for which you can read 'fashion') did not work all that well. Amongst the recent innovations, he lists:

→ just-in-time inventory management.

→ total quality management and its avatar 'six sigma quality'.

→ cross-functional teams.

→ portfolio management and stage gates (in product development).

→ supply chain integration, including vendor-managed inventories and collaborative planning and forecasting.

→ performance-linked compensation.

→ competency profiling in human resources.

→ measurement systems based on EVA (economic value added) or balanced scorecards.

→ customer–supplier relationships.

→ business process re-engineering.

But Hammer (2001: 8) regards these as being no more than the first phase in dealing with customer expectations. In fact, innovative as they were, 'yesterday's innovation is baseline today and obsolete tomorrow'.

## STRATEGIC ALLIANCES

Redesign or restructuring may take place within one organization, or go beyond its boundaries, perhaps resulting from the combination of one firm with another. There are several relevant variables to consider at the strategic stage:

*Strategic intent.* Regardless of negotiated positions and public positions of the partner companies, what are their long-term intentions? Are they committed to a joint venture? Does one partner intend to achieve control? Managers will be wary of losing their power.

*Consolidation.* How much autonomy and organizational independence is to be allowed? Mergers and acquisitions tend towards much greater consolidation than joint ventures and consortia. Employees feel threatened by obvious opportunities for staff reduction.

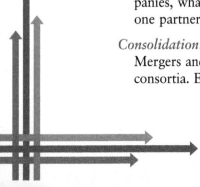

*Cultural integration.* Is cultural plurality to be respected? Does the alliance intend a common culture? If so, will it be based on the culture of the dominant partner or a negotiated hybrid? Being forced to change familiar ways is threatening.

---

**KEY CONCEPT 12.4** MERGERS AND ACQUISITIONS

'A merger occurs when one corporation is combined with and disappears into another corporation. For instance, the Missouri Corporation, just like the river, merges and disappears corporately into the Mississippi Corporation. Missouri Corporation stock certificates are turned in and exchanged for Mississippi Corporation stock certificates. Holes are punched in the Missouri certificates, and they are all stuck in the vault. The Missouri Corporation has ceased to exist. Missouri is referred to as the *decedent,* while the Mississippi Corporation is referred to as the *survivor'* (Reed and Lajoux, 1998: 7). Acquisition, on the other hand is a generic term used to describe a transfer of ownership. Here, the two parties in the transaction may continue as entities in some form or other after the acquisition.

---

Alliances and mergers draw on the capacity and potential of participants but they have a poor history of success. Surveys show that over 50 per cent of mergers and acquisitions fail to achieve strategic objectives – often disastrously. An often-quoted McKinsey and Company study of mergers between 1972 and 1982 (involving 200 of the largest US corporations) found increased value to shareholders in just 23 per cent. The greatest proportion, 33 per cent, was seen in relatively small takeovers of closely related businesses. The explanation seems to have attracted yet another analogy with poultry, although the meaning is quite different: 'You don't put two turkeys together and make an eagle!' (unnamed economist quoted in Peters, 1987). Often the advantages are outweighed by (Porter, 1990; Buono, 1991):

→ Restructuring costs: including redundancy payments, consultancy and legal fees, accommodation transfer.

→ Strategic difficulties: harmonization of goals and objectives.

→ Organizational problems: difficulties in coordinating two different structures; overloading the parent organization's management systems; reorganization taking attention away from day-to-day activities.

→ Behavioural problems and barriers: managers fight to preserve their territories or take over others; motivation falls when staff feel they have been taken over by remote managers.

Tampakoudis (2010) concludes that apparently irrational takeovers are driven by personal managerial objectives in the face of negative empirical information. Moreover, takeovers take place in surges with the best bargains to be had at the beginning of an economic cycle, while later acquisitions require hefty premiums that cannot be covered by any synergy (Mauboussin, 2010).

From a HR perspective, according to Mackay (1992, p.10):

Most of the evidence suggests that a failure to acknowledge the human dimension undermines many potentially successful ventures. ... There is a feeling that if 'the figures are right' all else

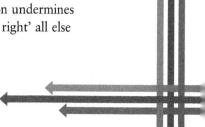

will follow smoothly. Wrong! It is precisely 'all else' that can frustrate the best laid plans of marketing men and accountants as cultures fail to gel and key executives engage in destructive battles for dominance.

D'Annunzio-Green and Francis (2005) studied pressures faced by managers in a contract catering firm involved in an organizational change initiative that encouraged them to become self-sufficient and display entrepreneurial behaviours in an environment where they were also expected to comply with new operating procedures aimed at strengthening central control and cutting costs. They highlight the duality between the quantitative need for discipline in managerial procedures, while at the same time paying attention to the qualitative need for investment in human resources.

The nature of the power relationship is particularly significant. Many studies show that acquisitions are notoriously unsuccessful because of the manner of the takeover. Specifically, the benefits of an acquisition or merger can be destroyed by the way in which the merger process is handled. Staff who are working for new owners tend to feel defensive and threatened. It is almost as if they have been colonized. Similar feelings are experienced when internal restructuring results in merged departments or the absorption of one section by another. Frequently, takeovers are handled insensitively. Acquisitions and mergers bring power differences into sharp and highly visible focus. There is a temptation to charge into the acquired firm or department or to take a condescending attitude. Many takeovers have parallels with the sacking of Rome. The new managers are inclined to feel superior and to regard methods which are different from their own as inefficient or second-rate. Arrogance and organizational chauvinism on the 'conqueror's' part lead to defensiveness and concern on the other side. People sense a loss of power to determine their own fate (Kanter, 1989: 65):

> Arrogance can destroy the essence of the company. Strangers in suits wander about the organization, misunderstanding what they see. Observation is accompanied by sniggers and sneering comments, serving to boost the acquiring management team's egos and sense of superiority. Mackay describes this as 'tribal warfare' – one culture trying to assert pre-eminence over the other.

The consequences are serious. This is not simply a matter of upsetting workers, important though that may be in terms of its consequences on morale and cooperation. There is a considerable risk of throwing the baby out with the bathwater by obliterating the victim's processes before their consequences and rationale are fully understood.

Employee fears and anxieties can be minimized but research shows that people who have been 'taken over' continue to be suspicious and uncomfortable in the new organization for some time. Maurer (1996: 11) notes:

> Change is unsettling. It disrupts our world. Some fear they will lose status, control, even their jobs. The larger the change, the stronger the resistance. Successful change requires vision, persistence, courage, an ability to thrive on ambiguity and a willingness to engage those who have a stake in the outcome.

Kavanagh and Ashkanasy (2006) examined mergers between three large public sector organizations and found that resulting changes are often imposed on the leaders themselves. Pace of change frequently inhibits successful re-engineering of the culture. A successful merger hinges on individual perceptions about the manner in which the process is handled and the direction of change. Communication and a transparent change process are important, as this will often determine who is regarded as a leader post-merger. Leaders need to be competent and trained in the process of transformation to ensure that individuals within the organization accept changes prompted by a merger.

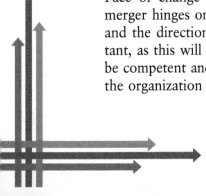

## HRM IN REALITY — MERGERS AND ACQUISITIONS FAILING TO ACHIEVE VALUE

Mergers and acquisitions (M&As) continue apace but many deals fail to create expected value, according to a recent survey by Accenture and the Economist Intelligence Unit. The survey of 420 corporate executives from the United States of America, Germany, the United Kingdom, Sweden, Norway and Finland conducted in March 2006 also found that over half of recent deals in which respondents had been involved were cross-border transactions.

Less than half (45 per cent) of respondents thought that their most recent M&As achieved expected cost-saving synergies, while even fewer (30 per cent) said they had been able to successfully integrate IT systems in their most recent cross-border deal. Also, almost a half (49 per cent) said their deals did not achieve expected revenue synergies.

'Missing synergy goals by even a small percentage can mean losing hundreds of millions of dollars of shareholder value', said Art Bert, a senior executive in Accenture's strategy practice. 'The most successful deals are approached with a comprehensive integration plan, with core team continuity through most of the transaction life cycle, from target identification, valuation, due diligence, deal execution, pre-close planning and post-closing integration.'

Fifty-eight per cent of executives involved in a recent deal said their company's latest acquisition was a cross-border transaction. Around one half of respondents to the survey expected businesses in their industries to make cross-border acquisitions over the next five years. The following reasons were given:

→ to guarantee profitability (55 per cent)

→ to hit strategic corporate targets (49 per cent)

→ just to survive (26 per cent).

Almost three-quarters (70 per cent +) of senior executives considered that the identification and execution of cross-border M&As was more difficult than domestic transactions.

According to Art Bert:

There is a growing body of evidence that most large transactions fail to create shareholder value for acquirers. But what makes M&A so alluring is the less common, successfully executed deal that allows an acquirer to create shareholder value far beyond what its peers and competitors can achieve. This is why we see most high-performing companies undertaking a disproportionate number of deals relative to their industry peers.

Almost a third (31 per cent) of respondents attributed 20 per cent or more of their companies' total revenue growth over the previous three years to acquisitions and 83 per cent thought that at least some growth came from deals. Similar responses were given for anticipated revenue over the next three years with 30 per cent expecting M&As to fuel growth of 20 per cent or more and 88 per cent expecting at least some growth from acquisitions.

'M&A remains a vital strategic tool for corporate executives worldwide', Bert said. 'Yet management teams must not be misled into thinking that deal closing is a prize, in and of itself. Rather, evaluating and integrating an acquired business in a manner that delivers a superior return on investment, demonstrating that a transaction is really the best use of shareholders' money, is what sets a good deal apart from a bad one.'

Respondents identified the following as some of the critical factors for M&A success:

→ Orchestrating and executing the integration process (56 per cent for domestic and 47 per cent for cross-border deals).

→ Conducting due diligence (42 per cent for domestic and 43 per cent for cross-border deals).

→ Achieving an optimal price for a deal (20 per cent for domestic and 19 per cent for cross-border deals).

Most corporate executives thought that their firms were successful at retaining valuable employees from both the target business (72 per cent) and the acquiring company (77 per cent). Similarly, most also agreed or strongly agreed that their transactions did not have a negative impact on customers of the target business (67 per cent) or the acquirer (73 per cent).

*What factors make cross-border M&As more difficult than domestic transactions?*

Source: Reprinted from HRM Guide USA (http://www.hrmguide.com).

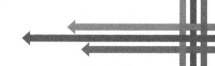

## MERGERS AND THE HR FUNCTION

Clemente and Greenspan (1999: 1) point out that:

> There are literally hundreds of reasons why the M&A failure rate is so high. But many can be traced to the exclusion of human resource professionals in the pre-deal planning phase and the function's last-minute inclusion after the transaction has closed. It's a classic case of 'too little, too late'.

Clemente and Greenspan (1999) present a description of the typical merger or acquisition. The focus is on 'making the numbers work' and the sequence begins with an investment banker or equivalent presenting an apparently suitable candidate company to management. If this makes 'financial sense' the process is launched.

The 'due diligence' phase then begins, involving a detailed examination of financial, legal and regulatory, accounting and tax issues. If these check out, the merger partners 'plunge forward', assuming that all the strategic aspects will somehow fall in line. As the authors point out, the statistics on failure suggest that this is often highly erroneous thinking. Clearly, the 'ledgers and liability' aspects of the process are extremely important but the all-consuming focus on these matters ignores people issues. Clemente and Greenspan ask: 'If people issues are so important to the success of the deal, how can such little focus be paid to those issues in the strategy development, target company screening and due diligence phases?'

They answer their own question by stating that in most cases the merger partners have not looked closely enough at the 'people component' – strategic variables at the very heart of the deal. Most mergers and acquisitions are driven by apparent cost-cutting synergies and stock prices. But if they were driven by true strategic vision instead, HR professionals would need to be involved from the beginning to assess the people implications that do not feature in balance sheets or income statements. The authors conclude:

> … identifying key human assets in a target company and quickly taking steps to prevent them from walking out the door on announcement of the deal is an HR-related imperative every company must take. Yet, historically, HR comes into the M&A process too late to make this vital contribution.

In most cases, the deal-making is more or less complete by the time that HR gets involved. HR specialists are left with the difficult role of developing communication strategies; aligning payroll, benefits and compensation systems; and melding different and possibly incompatible processes and cultures. But by this time a number of key personnel may have gone and those remaining may be confused or hostile.

Instead, Clemente and Greenspan argue, HR professionals should be involved in the earliest stage of any acquisition involving people. HR managers have the demanding task of integrating HR practices and performing two other roles simultaneously: a strategic role for company-wide integration and also a support role for business unit transactions (Antila, 2006). This means that human resource specialists must be familiar with the organization's strategic objectives, and its business and marketing plans. HR professionals must contribute to 'target screening' to identify and evaluate the worth and 'integrate-ability' of the proposed merger partner's human assets. This includes an evaluation of the two cultures and their potential compatibility.

Hanson (2001) observes that early coordination between HR specialists in both companies is ideal but due to the 'sensitive nature of many organization transactions, it is possible that the HR team on the receiving side of the transaction will be notified before the team on

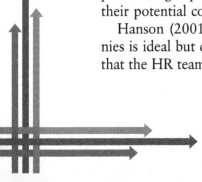

the sending side, or vice versa'. Tellingly, as someone writing from experience, she concurs with Clemente and Greenspan, noting that: 'The deal negotiators and attorneys will usually dictate when the intercompany communications can begin in the HR planning process'. Antila (*ibid.*) concludes that HR is important in the merger and acquisition process but is not always self-evident.

## Mergers and acquisitions: project planning

Hanson (2001) advocates the use of a project plan as an organizational tool to schedule necessary actions and set deadlines. A simple plan document would have columns for the following:

1   major steps in the process.

2   a breakdown of specific tasks within each step.

3   ownership of each step/task, i.e. who is responsible.

4   completion date for each task.

5   comments/state of progress.

A wide variety of project and spreadsheet software can be used with the updated project plan being made available to the integration team through web technology. In Hanson's opinion the project plan is a mechanism for communication and control of the integration process. But the project manager, she argues, must be tenacious in the following respects:

→   documenting necessary actions as they surface.

→   assigning them to a reliable owner.

→   determining appropriate deadlines that are compatible with other deliverables communicating with applicable parties.

→   following up to ensure that progress is on track.

→   escalating problems.

→   closing actions as they are completed.

## HR due diligence

Hanson highlights the importance of HR due diligence as an early stage in the project plan. A due diligence investigation is designed to establish liabilities and vulnerabilities *before* signing the final agreement. According to Hanson the HR review offers the following possibilities:

1   Discovery of liabilities that could impact on the financial viability of the transaction.

2   Discovery of discrepancies that might be addressable in the agreement to both parties' satisfaction.

3   Discovery of variations in policy and practice that will be essential when integrating and communicating with employees.

The investigation may have to take place in two stages: a preliminary overview before the letter of intent is signed; and a more thorough investigation thereafter when confidentiality

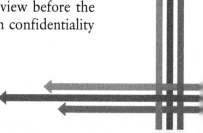

Research published in *Psychological Science* in 2008 reported differences in attitudes to men and women who lose their temper in the workplace. In three separate studies, psychologists Victoria Brescoll from Yale University and Eric Uhlmann from Northwestern University found that while such outbursts tend to be accepted or even rewarded in men, women are judged less competent as a result.

Hillary Clinton's recent presidential campaign raised the question of whether anger was damaging to a female candidate. Researchers found this to be unequivocally the case unless the anger was in response to treatment of a family member.

Victoria Brescoll commented: 'An angry woman loses status, no matter what her position'.

Researchers showed participants videos of actors applying for a job. They were asked to rate them on their perceived competence and whether they should be hired, the degree of responsibility they should be given, and how much they should get paid. Both men and women assigned higher status, salary and competence to men expressing anger. However, when actors expressed sadness, women applicants were ranked equally to men in status and competence but not in salary.

The second study focused on lower-status jobs and compared angry applicants to those not displaying any emotion. Once again, angry men were valued more highly than angry women. However, these differences were not apparent in the emotionally neutral group. The third study allowed women actors to explain why they were angry, resulting in improved ratings. However, when men gave an explanation it tended to be interpreted as a sign of weakness.

Victoria Brescoll concluded: 'Whether you are running for president or looking for a clerical job, you cannot afford to get angry if you are a woman'.

### 'Bad Apples' at work

A study from the University of Washington Business School published in *Research in Organizational Behavior* in 2007 examined how negative behaviour by one person in an organization can impact on teams and groups. Researchers describe these individuals as 'bad apples'

acting like a virus within teams, with the capacity to 'upset or spoil the whole apple cart'.

Together with Terence Mitchell, a professor of management and organization and UW psychology professor, William Felps, a doctoral student and lead author, decided to investigate the effect of a negative co-worker on workplace atmosphere after his wife experienced the phenomenon. She characterized her work environment as cold and unfriendly but this changed when a co-worker described as 'particularly caustic' and 'always making fun of other people' was away ill for several days.

William Felps explained:

> And when he was gone, my wife said that the atmosphere of the office changed dramatically. People started helping each other, playing classical music on their radios and going out for drinks after work. But when he returned to the office, things returned to the unpleasant way they were. She hadn't noticed this employee as being a very important person in the office before he came down with this illness but, upon observing the social atmosphere when he was gone, she came to believe that he had a profound and negative impact. He truly was the 'bad apple' that spoiled the barrel.

The researchers analyzed about two dozen studies focusing on workplace team and group interaction, with specific reference to the impact of individuals whose negativity may be expressed in various ways: not doing their fair share of work, being 'chronically unhappy and emotionally unstable', or being aggressive and bullying. They found that it only takes one such 'toxic' team member to provide the catalyst for organizational dysfunction. In a follow-up survey, they found most people they could identify at least one 'bad apple' from their own workplace experience.

The researchers reviewed various working environments (including manufacturing, fast food and universities) where tasks and assignments were performed by groups of approximately 5–15 individuals with interdependent jobs or where significant interaction was necessary. They explain that employees in such circumstances tend to be less tolerant and are more likely to challenge negative behaviours.

In one study of about 50 manufacturing teams, they found those with a disagreeable or irresponsible member were significantly more likely to perform poorly, experiencing conflict, poor communication and lack of cooperation between team members.

Terence Mitchell commented:

> Most organizations do not have very effective ways to handle the problem. This is especially true when the problem employee has longevity, experience or power. Companies need to move quickly to deal with such problems because the negativity of just one individual is pervasive and destructive and can spread quickly.

The study identified three ways in which group members may react to a negative member. Motivational intervention, where concerns are expressed and the person asked to change; if this proves unsuccessful rejection may follow where the individual is removed from the situation. These strategies require team members to have sufficient power; lack of power leads people to become frustrated and distracted. This leads to the third strategy, being defensive – common coping mechanisms include denial, social withdrawal, anger, anxiety and fear. Researchers explain that as trust weakens along with the positive culture, members physically and psychologically disengage themselves from the team. The study concluded that negative behaviour has a greater impact than positive behaviour.

Terence Mitchell said:

> People do not expect negative events and behaviours, so when we see them we pay attention to them, ruminate over them and generally attempt to marshal all our resources to cope with the negativity in some way. Good behaviour is not put into the spotlight as much as negative behaviour is.

The researchers differentiate between the negativity of 'bad apples' and innovative challenging employees 'who think outside the box' and may not always be appreciated as a result. If negative individuals emerge after selection screening, researchers suggest that organizations should allocate them to independent work positions where possible; or the only option may be to let them go.

William Felps commented:

> Managers at companies, particularly those in which employees often work in teams, should take special care when hiring new employees. This would include checking references and administering personality tests so that those who are really low on agreeableness, emotional stability or conscientiousness are screened out.

*What can be done about negative behaviour when it impacts on the need for change in a workplace?*

Source: Reprinted with permission from HRM Guide USA (http://www.hrmguide.com/).

can be guaranteed, but before the final agreement. According to Hanson, the investigation involves a number of data-gathering components that divide into hard and soft. Hard facts are those that can be found in written records, reports, surveys, documented policies and statistics. They include information on pay, benefits, bonuses, employment regulations, third-party claims, employee relations, safety and so on. Soft data are less easily established but can be critical, including key employee losses, management style, CEO reputation and senior management integrity. Hanson points to the particular importance of compensation and benefits plan information, not only in the due diligence stage but also later when close comparison is required. Issues of long-term liability are critical as regards pension plans and medical benefits.

In later stages of the integration plan, pay and other benefits have implications for the cost of 'golden parachutes' for people no longer required. Serious differences between salary structures, overtime and 'perks' may also have significant consequences on morale and retention. Inevitably the question arises as to whether the more generous schemes are to be pushed down or the less generous increased in the future.

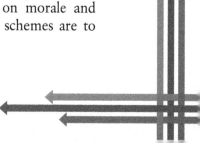

# BEHAVIOURAL TRANSFORMATION

> If you ask people to brainstorm words to describe change, they come up with a mixture of negative and positive terms. On the one side, *fear, anxiety, loss, danger, panic;* on the other, *exhilaration, risk-taking, excitement, improvements; energizing.* For better or worse, change arouses emotions, and when emotions intensify, leadership is key. (Fullan, 2001: 1, original emphases)

We noted earlier that the most difficult form of change involves modifying employees' attitudes, behaviour and commitment. Initiatives may come about as a result of deliberate strategic planning. Frequently, however, the process begins with a vague feeling among board members that there is 'something wrong' within the organization even though they are uncertain as to what it might be. The feeling may be fuelled by customer dissatisfaction, failure of innovation, conflict between departments or financial difficulties. The popularity of guru ideas and the spread of HRM have encouraged many senior executives to look to their people in order to improve overall organizational performance, quality of service and productivity. Black and Gregerson (2002: 20) describe the realization of a need for change in the following way:

> Clearly, if you do not see a truck racing toward you, you are unlikely to jump out of the way. Likewise, if you do not realize that you are standing on a treasure of gold, you are unlikely to bend down and pick it up. It is no brilliant observation to say that if people fail to see the need for change (whether threat or opportunity driving it), they will not change.

It is impossible to plan an effective change programme without first defining what cultural change aims to achieve and how this differs from the existing situation. The objective of many organizations in managing cultural change is to move from a static or rigid culture to one that is flexible and adaptable (Fowler, 1993).

Fowler suggests that the process could begin with a theoretical comparison of static and adaptable cultures. Such a scale might include 30 items and would focus on the nature of the initiative – for example, quality or customer care. The current organization is then scored on this scale. Frequently, detailed and accurate information does not exist in a form that allows this to be done. This can be gathered from a 'where are we now' exercise, normally taking the form of survey research and feedback. Typically this involves the use of questionnaires and structured interviews at all levels of the organization. Research can focus on employee attitudes towards:

→ the organization

→ its methods

→ communication channels company culture

→ customers

→ mechanisms for initiating and sustaining innovation and change.

Data are collated and a preliminary analysis fed back to the 'top team' and other interested parties, such as trade unions. After discussion – possibly involving a reappraisal of the company's mission and core values – action is agreed with the consultancy. To gain full cooperation it is best to discuss and agree the programme with employees and their representatives. Conventionally, the purpose and manner of any change is introduced to staff through presentations, discussions, videos, staff magazines and newspapers.

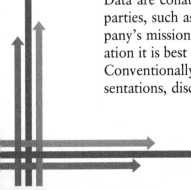

# HRM IN REALITY    THE HR ROLE IN PUBLIC SECTOR REFORM

Successive governments have seen public sector HR as either a cost to be managed or a means of dealing with redundancies, but not as a crucial strategic function, according to a recent CIPD report.

The report, *Boosting HR performance in the public sector*, prepared jointly with the the Public Sector People Managers' Association (PPMA), points to the risk of failure for the Government's public service reform plans to deliver lasting improvements because they under-emphasise people and HR management issues. According to Stephanie Bird, CIPD Director of HR Capability:

"Public service transformation is critically dependent on developing new skills, changing engrained behaviours and managing the uncertainty and conflict that can arise as a result. Unless HR is involved at the heart of this process to ensure the key people management issues are addressed, public service reform plans will remain frustrated."

"Unfortunately, HR in the public sector has been seen by successive governments as a cost to be managed, or a way of making redundancies. It is no coincidence that attempts by previous administrations to create a step-change in the quality of public service delivery have failed. This government cannot afford to make the same mistakes."

Widespread reporting of cuts in public sector staff, including government departments and local authorities, have led to fears of job losses among the people who are crucial to delivering reforms. John Philpott, the CIPD's Chief Economist has estimated that the scale of the cuts introduced by the UK's Conservative/Liberal democrat coalition, totalling £81 billion over the next four years, will mean that public sector job losses will reach 725,000 by 2015–16. The report argues that effective leadership and people management, careful change management and organizational development are crucial to maintaining employee morale and engagement and encouraging staff to accept new ways of working. Managers need the ability to manage across organizational boundaries if radical plans to improve co-ordination and collaboration between different public services and deliver more cost-effective services are to succeed. According to the report, public sector organizations will need:

→ more effective collaboration, with each other and with the voluntary and private sectors, to prevent

overlapping and duplicated services and to be more cost-effective

→ to identify more efficient ways of working and foster innovation

→ to identify potential costs savings by means of greater use of shared services and outsourcing

→ a more effective focus on meeting the changing needs of the public through enhanced front-line autonomy

→ to negotiate new/local terms and conditions of employment

→ to manage and communicate change effectively, involving employees through effective consultation to ensure employee/union buy-in.

Prime Minister David Cameron emphasized the need to change the nature of public services:

"We know instinctively that the state is often too inhuman, monolithic and clumsy to tackle our deepest social problems. We know that the best ideas come from the ground up, not the top down. We know that when you give people and communities more power over their lives, more power to come together and work together to make life better – great things happen."

The Government plans to do this by supporting mutuals, co-operatives, charities and social enterprises and giving them greater involvement in running public services.

The report discusses the fundamental importance of the way changes are managed, the extent to which employees feel they are consulted and have a voice and their acceptance and 'buy in' to new ways of working. The critical people management issues underpinning major change programmes highlight HR's role. The Human Resource function should provide the organizational development strategies supporting the business needs of transforming public services. If HR is not accepted as a transactional function by policy-makers and HR specialists are not allowed a significant role in engaging with or influencing the Government's reform agenda, the process of transforming public services will fail.

Dean Shoesmith, PPMA President, argues that HR is at a crossroads:

"The public service reform agenda provides both an opportunity and a challenge. HR can build and establish its reputation as a key strategic function if it is at the heart of managing change, helping to facilitate service delivery redesign and building the necessary leadership and management skills for sustained public service transformation. However, if HR is preoccupied by its traditional activities, such as hand-holding line managers, then it will be left behind and its reputation as a transactional function will be reinforced. The case studies profiled in our collaboration with the CIPD show how HR is already underpinning successful public sector transformation – we hope this report provides useful guidance to support the adoption of best practice across the sector."

According to the report, the entire public sector is facing renewed pressure to use shared services or outsourcing for more cost-effective HR services delivery. This results in an additional emphasis on a need for public service front-line managers to become better people managers because the HR function will no longer have the same resources to hand-hold managers on issues such as managing conflict, stress and absence, and wider aspects of performance management. There will be a need for major parts of the public sector to renegotiate (at a national or local level) revised terms and conditions of employment to improve efficiency and offer a more locally appropriate range of services. The change agenda will have to be communicated clearly and positively, with effective internal communication channels providing a clear narrative as to why change is needed and also offering opportunities for meaningful consultation.

The scale of the proposed changes may appear daunting but they play to the strengths of HR specialists if they choose to use them. Without HR being at the heart of the change initiatives, there is a risk of piecemeal efforts that miss key components of people management that are crucial to employee engagement and bringing strategies, visions and values to life at the front line.

*Source: Reprinted with permission from HRM Guide UK (http://www.hrmguide.co.uk).*

Action to improve such a situation could involve a cascading process in which groups of interested employees are asked to consider the data in relation to the company's core values. Staff could then be encouraged to suggest improvements and innovations and to take responsibility for seeing them through. There are instances of successful behavioural transformations of existing businesses, using a culture-change approach.

## NEGATIVE CHANGE

To quote Maurer (1996: 11):

> If the cost of failed change is high for organizations, the cost is equally dear for people. The first casualty is trust: people start to blame one another. Too many botched plans, and people become afraid to try again. Even so-called 'successful' efforts often leave a bitter taste in the mouths of those who were forced to change. The toll on individuals is enormous.

Implicitly, anyone opposing change is viewed as negative. Often, however, change is a destructive process and the end-product inferior to the original. For example, devolution of human resource management to middle managers in part of the Irish health service resulted in increased bureaucracy and worse decision making by both HR and middle managers, with HR simultaneously devolving activities and attempting to keep control of information systems (Conway and Monks, 2010).

In some cases the negative effects of change may be disguised by redefining quality requirements so that the lowering of standards becomes invisible or obscured. Newcomers to the situation know no better. Many may be involved in the change process and have a commitment to perceiving it as being necessary.

A redefinition of quality coincides inevitably with a change in the nature and flow of information, making a true 'before and after' comparison impossible. The proponents of change are unlikely to present their initiatives as failures; antagonists will never be happy with modifications in methods they have cherished. In the absence of objective evidence, debate is reduced to political confrontation with opponents of organizational change labelling new approaches as 'change for change's sake'. In fact, this is rarely the case. Change is difficult and disruptive and is not lightly entered into, but the true reasons for change may differ from its public justifications.

For example, we noted earlier that change is commonly associated with new management. This is not a coincidence. New managers have to work hard if the status quo is left alone. They are forever at the mercy of old networks and power balances. Far easier to highlight deficiencies in the current situation, pronounce it to be lacking in quality, and sweep it away to be replaced with another of their own making. Power-holders in the old networks can be eliminated or sidelined; there are always ambitious replacements available who are willing to become loyalists of the new regime. Young, or formerly disaffected, staff will show a naive enthusiasm for their new-found opportunities. Even better – from this somewhat cynical perspective – people can be imported from outside the organization who will be anxious to perform as required.

 ## SUMMARY

In this chapter we investigated transformational or change management. Nowadays, change initiatives are common elements of human resource strategies as companies and public sector organizations struggle to achieve their objectives in a competitive environment. Frequently these involve some form of organizational restructuring using a change programme such as business process re-engineering. Change programmes are fashion-driven and quickly become obsolete, to be replaced by the next heavily touted set of magic solutions. Some of the most difficult aspects of change management for human resource practitioners come from mergers and acquisitions where their involvement is often late – if not too late to rescue a disastrous situation. Finally we looked at behavioural transformation, involving attempts to change corporate culture and recognized that negative attitudes to change are to be expected and are not necessarily unhealthy.

## FURTHER READING

1 Bernard Burnes's *Managing Change: A Strategic Approach to Organisational Dynamics* (FT Prentice Hall, 2009) 5th edition places change in a broader context of management theory.

2 John Hayes provides a practical guide for students and managers in *The Theory and Practice of Change Management* (Palgrave Macmillan, 2010).

3 Hammer and Champy's *Re-engineering the Corporation: A Manifesto for Business Revolution* (Harper Business, 1993) was probably the best-selling business book of the 1990s.

4 Black and Gregersen's *Leading Strategic Change,* FT Prentice Hall (2002) is focused on the leadership of change but pays particular attention to resistance and harnessing negative attitudes.

# REVIEW QUESTIONS

1 List as many possible organizational changes you can think of that would involve human resource specialists in their planning or implementation.

2 How important is leadership in achieving permanent change within an organization?

3 What is a transformational HR strategy?

4 Define: (a) synergy; (b) restructuring; (c) business process re-engineering. Has business process re-engineering been no more than a passing fad or is it a significant breakthrough in change management practice?

5 How would you distinguish between incremental and programmed methods of change management?

6 What is action learning? Is action learning most effective for change management or developing employees?

7 Why do people resist change? Is it possible for negative attitudes towards change to have positive benefits for an organization?

8 What role should human resource practitioners play ideally in a merger or acquisition? How does this differ from reality?

9 Why do so many mergers and acquisitions fail?

10 Summarize the concept of HR due diligence in your own words. Why is it important in increasing the probability of successful mergers and acquisitions?

# CASE STUDY FOR DISCUSSION AND ANALYSIS

## West Five Care Trust

The West Five Care Trust controls four hospitals in a suburban area. Two of the hospitals are modern and have extra accommodation space. The other two are old but prestigious specialist units located in expensive areas. The Trust considers that it would make considerable financial sense to close the older hospitals and transfer their functions to the modern sites. Several senior physicians are extremely unhappy about the consequences and have launched a public campaign to save the specialist units. This has angered the general manager who has only just presented the plan as a proposal to the management committee. He considers the physicians to be disloyal as they have taken a confidential business matter to the press. He is also baffled since the new hospitals would offer them far better facilities.

The general manager was recently recruited from industry and has been keen to exercise his right to manage. In his first six months, he successfully outsourced cleaning and catering, brushing aside union opposition. He has also instituted stringent cost-control measures and now vets all budget requests personally, including expenses for attending conferences.

*As human resources manager how would you analyze the situation and how could you help?*

# CHAPTER 13
# Resourcing strategies

## LEARNING OBJECTIVES

The purpose of this chapter is to:

→ Provide an overview of employee resourcing strategies.

→ Discuss the purposes and methods of human resource planning.

→ Outline the process of job analysis.

→ Debate resourcing strategy in the context of staff retention and redundancy.

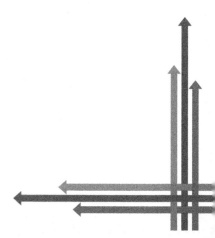

# RESOURCING

This chapter acts as a bridge between strategy and some of the core areas of HRM: recruitment and selection. The topic has traditionally been labelled as 'staffing'. The basis of people management lies in how work gets done and who does it. Therefore, the rationale behind *why* we should decide on one solution rather than another is fundamental to HRM. There are important issues involved at all levels of analysis. At the environmental level, employee resourcing takes place against a background of:

→ fluctuating economic conditions and global competition

→ choice and availability within the local job market

→ competition for scarce skills.

At the organizational level, the structure and functions of an enterprise are composed of the tasks that people perform. Allocating work to unsuitable or inadequately skilled people reduces the effectiveness of the whole organization. The consequences can be significant and – particularly with high-level or specialized work – may be critical to its future performance. Employee resourcing is no longer a matter of recruiting and selecting new people to fit existing posts. As we saw in earlier chapters, organizations have a range of 'flexible' alternatives.

At the strategic level, employee resourcing involves decisions on:

→ subcontracting or creating vacancies

→ allocating tasks

→ choice of selection methods.

As an activity, it is a major element of the work of human resource specialists, involving considerable technical expertise. Employee resourcing can involve sophisticated methods intended to realize long-term objectives and balancing considerations such as: (a) satisfying the immediate need to minimize employee costs while maximizing worker contribution to the organization; and (b) fulfilling a longer-term aim of obtaining the optimal mix of skills and commitment in the workforce (Price, 2000). In the context of ageing populations and changes in retirement legislation, there is a need for proactive planning throughout the developed world (McKinnon, 2010).

Employee resourcing is also a subject of vital importance at a personal level because most of us have to apply for a job: probably the first practical aspect of human resource management we encounter. In many cases it is a frustrating and sometimes baffling process of rejection. Readers in employment may well participate on both sides of the issue – as selectors or as applicants. Inevitably, therefore, resourcing deserves serious discussion. In this chapter we focus initially on *why* resourcing decisions are taken.

The first section of the chapter begins with a consideration of the environmental constraints on resourcing and discusses the implications of the move towards flexible organizations. Next we determine the nature of resourcing strategy and consider various types.

In the second section we discuss human resource planning, examining the hard or 'people as numbers' approach – involving forecasting methods – and soft planning which takes commitment and culture into account.

Next we consider the use made of information gained from job analyses. We discuss the role of the job description and person specification in resourcing decisions. The chapter moves on to a debate on the merits of the 'best practice' approach in flexible organizations. Finally we discuss strategy and planning in relation to redundancies.

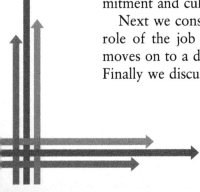

Employee resourcing is a fundamental aspect of people management (see Key concept 13.1). We can define four key stages:

*Strategy and planning.* Determining future human resources needs in terms of availability, expertise and location. We observed in Part One that HRM literature stresses the integration of resourcing activities with other people processes, such as performance management and human resource development, as well as the overall objectives of the enterprise.

*Research and data collection.* Determining the nature of work to be done and the criteria or competencies necessary to perform them. Additionally, obtaining adequate information about the people who possess these competencies, whether as employees, consultants or subcontractors.

*Marketing.* Making the work known – and attractive – to potential applicants in the internal and external job markets. Conventionally this function is contained within the term 'recruitment'.

*Decision-making.* Selection or allocation: choosing individuals to perform the work.

Marketing and decision-making are discussed in Chapters 14 and 15 on recruitment and selection. In this chapter we will concentrate on strategy and planning and the research necessary to establish the need for particular jobs.

---

### KEY CONCEPT 13.1 EMPLOYEE RESOURCING

Resourcing is the process by which people are identified and allocated to perform necessary work. Resourcing has two strategic imperatives: first, minimizing employee costs and maximizing employee value to the organization; second, obtaining the correct behavioural mix of attitude and commitment in the workforce. Employees are expensive assets. They must be allocated carefully and sparingly. In terms of costs and efficiency, effective resourcing depends on the care taken in deciding which tasks are worthwhile and the levels of skill and ability required to perform them.

---

## ENVIRONMENTAL CONSTRAINTS ON RESOURCING

Unlike many other aspects of people management, employee resourcing involves direct interaction between organizations and their environment. In Part Two we observed that, ultimately, businesses are dependent on the external job market for the supply of suitable staff. It is the source of school-leavers and university graduates for junior posts and experienced people for senior or specialized positions. Even in conditions of high unemployment there are shortages of people with skills that are in demand.

Countries such as Australia and Britain, for example, have a long record of failure in providing their young people with appropriate vocational training. If companies are unable to find staff or subcontractors with appropriate skills, their growth prospects and competitiveness are constrained. This may be so severe that companies are forced to relocate. Some multinationals have been forced to transfer operations from low-cost economies to high-wage countries, such as Germany, where skilled workers are available. Alternatively,

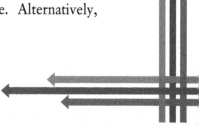

businesses may compete for scarce skills through increased remuneration packages and benefits. Purcell (1989), for instance, sees star companies identified by the Boston Consulting matrix (discussed later in this chapter) as being prepared to pay above market rates to recruit and retain the best employees. In the public sector, the sheer scale and complexity of services such as the UK's National Health Services make it difficult to balance supply and demand for staff (Parsons, 2010).

Economic changes over the last two decades have led to systematic responses in the attitudes and practices of employers. In his discussion of the flexible firm, Atkinson (1984) identifies a number of themes which underpin the employment plans of businesses in free market countries:

*Market stagnation.* Prolonged periods of recession and the increased competitiveness of world markets have produced a managerial obsession with the permanent reduction of unit employee costs.

*Job loss.* Most large firms have undergone dramatic reductions in levels of employment. These reductions have been expensive in redundancy costs and have had significant negative effects on relations with remaining employees.

*Uncertainty.* Despite continuous announcements of recovery, firms have been cautious about preparing for growth. In particular, they have been wary of a commitment to more full-time employees.

*Technological change.* This is happening at increasing pace and reducing cost, requiring organizations, and their employees, to respond quickly by changing products, manufacturing methods and ways of working.

*Working time.* Employers have maximized the value of employee time through restructuring work patterns to match periods of demand. This has led to a preference for part-time workers.

These factors have encouraged a move towards flexible jobs in flexible organizations.

**HRM IN REALITY** UNDERSTANDING GENERATIONAL DIFFERENCES IN THE WORKPLACE

Organizations that only consider age when addressing generational divisions in the workforce risk losing knowledge to retirements and higher staff turnover according to research from the University of Illinois published in the *Academy of Management Review* in 2010.

Lead author Aparna Joshi, a professor of labour and employment relations explained:

The challenges are complex, but the solutions being offered are too simplistic. Our aim should be to match the complexity of the problem with more

nuanced solutions. The payoffs could be huge in terms of benefits, such as mining the knowledge base of older workers.

The study found that businesses tend to rely on stereotypes associated with Baby Boomers or Generation X'ers, ignoring other relevant factors.

Aparna Joshi commented:

Our message is the problem isn't that simple and there are no one-size-fits-all solutions. Just as we

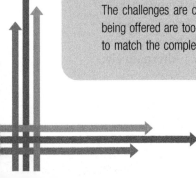

don't want to take simplistic approaches to race and gender issues, we shouldn't automatically assume that a grey-haired man isn't on Facebook or good at technology. Assumptions based solely on age can lead to some very faulty conclusions and missteps.

Researchers analyzed data from previous decades and identified three primary factors that could contribute to generational factions in the workplace preventing employees from interacting and sharing knowledge. Age is one such factor, but goes beyond broad labels. For example, individuals are further defined by their common experience of significant external events (such as World War II, the assassination of President Kennedy or the 9/11 terrorist attacks). This can give rise to subgroups within generations.

Other factions are multi-generational. They can be based on when employees started work with a firm (comparable to lifelong bonds formed by soldiers during deployment) or their position in the workforce (such as a top management team facing replacement by a new generation of leaders or supervisors working with subordinates who could ultimately take over their jobs).

Aparna Joshi said:

What we are headed toward is creating a better understanding of the complexities of generations in the workplace and, we hope, more realistic solutions. Businesses need to make targeted diagnosis like a doctor diagnoses an illness, rather than just prescribing penicillin for every ailment.

Researchers suggest that reducing divisions between workers can enhance productivity and efficiency. Institutional knowledge is passed on, rather than being lost through retirement; new recruits are more engaged, reducing costly turnover.

Aparna Joshi concluded:

It's human nature that workers interact with their cohorts, seeking out their own. Figuring out ways to bring them together will allow companies to tap into all of those knowledge silos and reach full potential.

*What changes should businesses make in their resourcing strategies to attract and retain older workers?*

Source: Reprinted with permission from HRM Guide USA (http://www.hrmguide.com/).

# RESOURCING AND THE FLEXIBLE ORGANIZATION

During periods of relatively high unemployment in the 1980s and 1990s, and again in the period after the economic crisis of 2008–2009, organizations in many countries felt able to dictate the terms of employment they were prepared to offer new recruits, often moving away from traditional nine-to-five working days. As we have previously observed, there is a pronounced trend away from full-time work towards other job patterns particularly part-time jobs. Equally, some groups of workers – such as older employees – find part-time employment attractive as a prelude to eventual retirement. We also noted earlier that many businesses have outsourced non-core activities – such as catering and cleaning – allocating them to external contractors. Similarly, technically specialized functions, such as the management of computer and telecommunications networks, have been subcontracted to specialist firms.

A modern flexible organization may adopt a structure along the lines of Handy's three-leaf 'shamrock' model (Handy, 1989: 70):

→ A professional core made up of managers, technicians, and qualified specialists.

→ Contractors providing non-core activities, who are not direct employees of the organization.

→ The flexible labour force composed of part-timers, temporary staff, consultants and contract staff performing tasks as and when required.

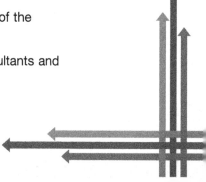

The allocation of work between the 'leaves' of the shamrock organization is generally decided upon at a senior level. The implications are considerable, often requiring main board approval, particularly for the employment of subcontractors. The decision to 'outsource' activities is usually taken on purely financial grounds, leaving people managers to clear up the resulting employee relations mess.

# RESOURCING STRATEGIES

Most large organizations employ human resource or personnel specialists to conduct or, at least, coordinate employee resourcing. This is a role that has long been regarded as part of the domain of personnel management (Iles and Mabey, 1992: 255) and personnel textbooks conventionally described resourcing as a passive, technical procedure – a matching of available candidates to the requirements of the organization. In fact, successful recruitment must be proactive and is more likely to be a response to stakeholder-driven policies than numerical analysis (Harness, 2009). Organizations can take one of three actions to fulfil their employee resourcing needs:

1   *Re-allocate tasks* between employees, so that existing staff take on more or different work. This may be part of an organizational change programme, such as restructuring or reorganization. The emphasis is on flexible working practices, requiring multi-skilled workers and sophisticated assessment and development programmes.

2   *Re-allocate people* from the internal employment market, through promotion or transfer between different departments. Traditionally, German and Japanese organizations have filled their supervisory and management posts from existing staff. Large Japanese organizations expect their potential managers to move between different functions during their careers. Japanese human resource managers, for instance, are likely to have worked in finance, production and marketing rather than specializing in 'personnel'.

3   *Recruit* new staff from the external job market. Countries in the free market tradition have focused most of their resourcing activities on bringing in people from outside the organization. Employers have a choice between:
    – *Recruiting anybody and everybody.* Until comparatively recently, many workers in heavy industry were employed casually at the factory gate. In many parts of the world construction labourers and seasonal agricultural workers continue to be taken on in a casual fashion. With no commitment on either side, a rigid chain of command then rules. This approach predominates for employment at low skill and wage levels. It is especially common in small low-technology companies.
    – *Recruiting selectively.* Skilled and motivated workers are selected. These employees can be allowed to get on with the job with only broad guidelines or a policy framework to observe. This approach predominates in large organizations. The result has been the creation of an internal and external recruitment industry, including selection experts, recruitment consultants and headhunters.

External recruitment has the virtue of bringing in a wider range of experience but limits career opportunities for existing employees. It is predominantly a free market approach to resourcing but even Japanese businesses are now recruiting externally, particularly for scarce technological skills such as software engineering.

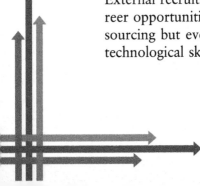

## Types of resourcing strategy

Resourcing is a dynamic process: the movement of human resources through an organization. In terms of systems theory this can be represented as input; throughput; and output.

Businesses can assign people largely from existing staff or from the external job market. Companies that focus on internal supply are likely to view people as assets, carrying long-term value, rather than as costs. This is in line with practice in social market and Japanese organizations. It also reflects the spirit of the Harvard model of HRM discussed in Chapter 2. In essence the choice is between 'growing' or 'buying' (see Key concept 13.2). 'Growing' is the central theme of human resource development discussed in Chapter 20. Needless to say, firms in free markets such as the UK and the USA have a tendency to 'buy' – and dispose – of employees as required.

---

**KEY CONCEPT 13.2**   GROW OR BUY?

Organizations can focus on internal or external job markets, or draw from both. Firms with an internal focus recruit at junior levels and 'grow' their employees into valuable assets through training, development and experience in the organization. Alternatively, companies can buy talent at a variety of levels from the external employment market. A mixed strategy offers a balance of continuity and commitment from long-term staff together with fresh ideas from imported 'new blood'.

---

Choices between 'growing' or 'buying' can be related to environmental conditions and organizational culture. In an early discussion of human resource strategy, Miles and Snow (1978) devised a typology based on the degree of risk taken by businesses in stable or unstable environments. They classified organizations as defenders, prospectors, analysers and reactors. A similar typology by Sonnenfeld, Peiperl and Kotter (1988) shown in Table 13.1 uses slightly more dramatic terminology: clubs, baseball teams, fortresses and academies.

*Defenders.* These are firms with small niche markets or narrow product ranges. As organizations they have an equally narrow focus, requiring stability and reliability. They need loyal employees with a long-term commitment. Staff enter at junior levels and are 'made' into worthwhile employees through extensive training and career development along largely functional routes. Incremental growth allows for new career opportunities within an internal job market grounded in a strong culture. Loyalty and commitment are encouraged through performance assessment based on behavioural compliance characteristics. Staff turnover is low, partly because employees are chained by organization-specific skills and a degree of institutionalization. This strategy is employed by 'clubs' in the classification of Sonnenfeld *et al.* (1988).

*Prospectors.* Innovative firms, moving in and out of markets to capitalize on opportunities and avoid competition. Top management consider themselves to be dynamic. Equating to 'baseball teams' of Sonnenfeld *et al.*, they are typical of sports and entertainment businesses. The instability of their marketplace requires constant flexibility and environmental scanning – a feature that Jackson *et al.* (2008: 78) consider as the first stage of any human resource planning exercise. In the eyes of 1970s and 1980s theorists, locked into the 'right person' recruitment models that we will discuss shortly, this could only be met by buying rather than making talent. Uncertainty does not allow for career systems, the focus being on recruitment from the external job market. New recruits have to be able to 'hit the

**TABLE 13.1**
Resourcing
strategies

Source: Based on
Sonnenfeld *et al.* (1988).

| Type | Characteristics | Key HR function | Sectors |
|------|----------------|-----------------|---------|
| **1** Academies | Active growers<br>Low staff turnover<br>Long-term service | Development | Office products<br>Pharmaceuticals<br>Electronics |
| **2** Clubs | Passive growers<br>Seniority<br>Commitment<br>Status<br>Equal treatment | Retention or 'maintenance' | Public utilities<br>Government<br>Insurance<br>Military |
| **3** Baseball teams | Active buyers<br>Staff identify with profession more than firm | Recruitment of star performers | Accounting<br>Law<br>Consulting<br>Software<br>Advertising |
| **4** Fortresses | Cautious buyers<br>Survival<br>Cost-cutting | Recruitment of generalists<br>Redundancies | Publishing<br>Textiles<br>Retailing hotels |

ground running' (Rousseau, 1995: 188). Rewards are high and geared to immediate results. However, commitment is low on both sides of the employment relationship: recruits are seen as 'passing through'. Learning is personal rather than organizational and knowledge leaves with the employee.

*Analyzers.* These firms are cautious innovators, waiting for prospectors to open up new markets before entering themselves. Analyzer organizations are structured into stable and efficient production units with highly flexible and responsive marketing or service units. They emphasize quality and skill and equate to Sonnenfeld *et al.'s* 'academies'. As hybrids they take a mixed approach to making and buying employees: stable business units rely on internal promotion and development; flexible units buy in expertise as and when required.

*Reactors.* These are 'fortresses' in the classification of Sonnenfeld *et al.*: failed defenders, analyzers or prospectors, desperately attempting to survive. Their strategies are often incoherent, unable to 'make' employees but often 'buying' and selling. In their attempts to recover or instigate the 'turnaround' changes discussed in Chapter 12, the emphasis is likely to be on redundancies.

## HUMAN RESOURCE PLANNING

For resourcing strategies to be implemented they must be translated into practical action. The strategic process can be organized logically – for example, following the decision

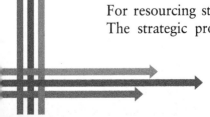

## FIGURE 13.1

A resourcing decision sequence

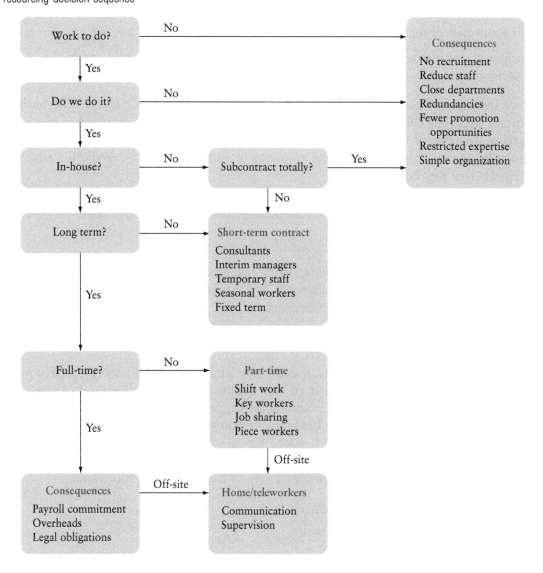

sequence shown in Figure 13.1. For these decisions to be taken, information must be obtained, consequences gauged, political soundings taken and preferences assessed.

It is clear that many of these decisions are fundamental to an organization. If the implications are major, strategic decisions are taken at the centre of the business. The role of the human resource function is two-fold:

To participate in the decision process by providing information and opinion on each option, including:

→ redundancy or recruitment costs

→ consequences on morale

→ redeployment/outplacement opportunities

→ availability of skilled staff within the organization

→ availability of suitable people in the job market

→ time constraints

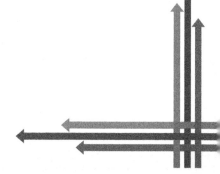

→ development/training needs/schedules

→ management requirements.

This forms part of the information collated from the organization as a whole.

To support line managers dealing with the people consequences of implementing the decision. Information already gathered provides the basis for a human resource plan.

In other instances, decision making has consequences of lesser significance to the business. Resourcing decisions taken at an operational level may lead from departmental expansion or cost-saving, transfer of activities, new product ranges and comparatively small changes in function. In practice, therefore, human resource planning has short-, medium-, and long-term aspects (see Key concept 13.3).

**KEY CONCEPT 13.3** HUMAN RESOURCE PLANNING

A process that anticipates and maps out the consequences of business strategy on an organization's human resource requirements. This is reflected in planning of skill and competence needs as well as total headcounts.

Older texts refer to this topic as 'manpower planning'. (Presumably 'womanpower planning' was not much different!) Use of this quaint term has declined – but not disappeared – in favour of human resource planning (HRP) or workforce planning, or even talent planning. Some authors distinguish between manpower planning and HRP as distinct approaches (Hendry, 1995: 190).

Primarily a 'numbers game', manpower planning emphasized accurate personnel records and forecasting techniques (see Key concept 13.4). It focused on questions such as:

→ How many staff do we have/need?

→ How are they distributed?

→ What is the age profile?

→ How many will leave in each of the next five years?

→ How many will be required in one, five, ten years?

**KEY CONCEPT 13.4** MANPOWER PLANNING

'A strategy for the acquisition, utilization, improvement and retention of an enterprise's human resources.' Anonymous government publication cited in Pratt and Bennett (1989: 101).

O'Doherty (1997) argues that although simple workforce headcount predictions may have been undertaken by most companies, the use of detailed manpower forecasts was confined to large-scale organizations such as the public services, the armed forces, postal services and major banking groups. Corbridge and Pilbeam (1998) note that specialist

planners in such organizations devised complex mathematical models but this was often an unreal process that attracted criticism.

Some authors see little difference between HRP and manpower planning. For example Graham and Bennett (1992: 172) define human resource planning as:

> … an attempt to forecast how many and what kind of employees will be required in the future, and to what extent this demand is likely to be met. It involves the comparison of an organization's current human resources with likely future needs and, consequently, the establishment of programmes for hiring, training, redeploying and possibly discarding employees. Effective HRP should result in the right people doing the right things in the right place at precisely the right time.

The manpower planning approach regards the human resource manager as a personnel technician. Within this framework, the function of the human resource planner is to provide 'management' with the necessary advice to make decisions on issues such as:

→ recruitment

→ avoiding redundancies

→ training – numbers and categories

→ management development

→ estimates of 'labour' costs

→ productivity bargaining

→ accommodation requirements.

In this tradition, Graham and Bennett (1992: 175) envisage a long-term human resource plan as a detailed specification, by location, function and job category of the number of employees 'it is practicable to employ at various stages in the future' (see Table 13.2). A plan should include:

→ jobs that will come into being, be ceased, or changed.

→ possibilities for redeployment and retraining.

→ changes in management and supervision.

→ training requirements.

→ programmes for recruitment, redundancy and early retirement.

→ implications for employee relations.

→ a feedback mechanism to company objectives.

→ methods for dealing with HR problems such as inability to obtain sufficient technically skilled workers.

Such a plan requires organization, belief in the process and detailed information. Not surprisingly, many organizations cannot meet these criteria. Tyson (1995: 77), reporting on a study of 30 large UK-based organizations, found that most had plans of three to five years' duration. Shorter-term plans were used by some retail firms that kept detail down to a year or so, whereas capital-intensive firms were more likely to favour long-term planning. Generally, managers were unhappy about five-year plans, regarding them as 'a constraint on business'.

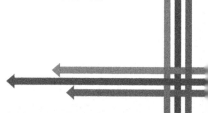

**TABLE 13.2**
Steps for long-term
human resource
planning

Source: Based on Graham
and Bennett (1992: 174).

| Step | Aspects |
| --- | --- |
| **1** Create a company HRP group | This should include the main functional managers of the company, together with human resource specialists. |
| **2** State the organization's human resource objectives | Within the context of the overall business objectives and considering:<br><br>→ capital equipment plans<br><br>→ reorganization such as centralization or decentralization<br><br>→ changes in products or in output<br><br>→ marketing plans<br><br>→ financial limitations |
| **3** Audit present utilization of human resources | Sometimes described as the 'internal manpower audit', detailing:<br><br>→ number of employees in various categories<br><br>→ an estimate of employee turnover for each grade, analyzing the effects of high or low turnover on performance<br><br>→ amount of overtime worked<br><br>→ assessment of performance and potential of current employees<br><br>→ comparison of payment levels with local firms. |
| **4** Assess the external environment | Placing the organization in its business context in terms of:<br><br>→ the recruitment position<br><br>→ population trends<br><br>→ local housing and transport plans<br><br>→ national agreements dealing with conditions of work<br><br>→ government policies in education, retirement, regional subsidies and so on. |
| **5** Assess potential supply of labour | Including:<br><br>→ local population movements (emigration and immigration)<br><br>→ recruitment and redundancy by other firms<br><br>→ employing new work categories – e.g. part-time workers<br><br>→ productivity improvements, working hours and practices. |

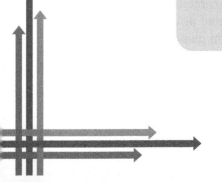

Rothwell and Kazanas (2003: 2) reclassify the two approaches as 'technical' (concerned with numerical and behavioural measurements) and managerial. Tyson (1995: 80) identifies three distinct approaches to planning:

*Formal, long-range planning.* Creating a planning framework, usually expressed in financial terms with verbal commentaries. Notably, all the companies studied that used this approach consulted widely with interest groups.

*Flexible strategies.* Covering most of the organizations studied. Plans changed frequently in response to market changes. Plans were intentionally short-term, often with minimal written detail.

*Attributional strategies.* 'One step at a time'. Previous actions can be rationalized but, in truth, organizations using this approach are cautious and are not really committed to any specific strategy. This can be compared with Mintzberg's concept of 'emergent strategies' discussed in the previous chapter.

In general it is worth observing (Price, 2000) that:

> Modern human resource planners have tended to move away from predicting headcounts towards building 'what if' models or scenarios which allow the implications of different strategies to be debated. However, traditional HR planning techniques have become considerably easier to implement with the spread of Human Resource Information Systems which trap key employee information and generate reports and analyses as a matter of course.

## People as numbers

Generally, it is accepted that modern workforce or human resource planning should have a wider perspective, in tune with the philosophy of HRM, including 'softer' issues such as competence, commitment and career development. Modern human resource planning continues to use the 'hard' techniques of manpower planning but also includes a new focus on shaping values, beliefs and culture, anticipating strategy, market conditions and demographic change.

Nevertheless, in line with the tradition of formal, observable and 'objective' planning, numerical measurement and forecasting have been favoured over qualitative studies of opinion, attitude and motivation. 'Hard' data allow managers and planners to sit in their offices and wait for information. 'No need to go out and meet the troops, or the customers, to find out how the products get bought ... all that just wastes valuable time' (Mintzberg, 1994: 258). The growth of information technology and management information systems has made numerical data readily available and possibly further discouraged collection of qualitative information. Numbers give a comforting feeling of unarguable objectivity and allow managers to detach themselves from shopfloor emotions. It is much easier to sack a number than a real human being.

## Forecasting methods

Human resource planners have a choice of techniques available to them that have become increasingly easier to use as HR technology improves. For example:

*Extrapolation.* This method assumes that the past is a reliable guide to the future. Various techniques are suitable for short- and medium-term forecasting, such as time series, trend analysis and measures of cyclical requirements. Since they rely on present knowledge and cannot take the unpredictable into account, forecasts are best in a stable environment.

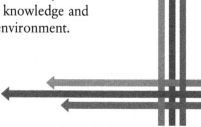

## HRM IN REALITY   HALF FULL-TIMERS WOULD LIKE FLEXIBLE WORKING

A survey of full-time employees across 29 industry sectors by Brisbane-based HR and Change Management consultants Astor Levin in 2008 found that almost a half (49 per cent would favour flexible working arrangements). Thirty-one per cent indicated they would use it now and 18 per cent said they would use flexible working at a future time. In fact, 39 per cent of the workforce already use flexible work arrangements.

Recent projections indicate that over the next five years Australian employers will face a deficit of around 195 000 workers. Astor Levin consider that employers offering flexible work arrangements will be more attractive to job seekers than those who do not. Yet, according to the consultancy firm, many business owners think that seeing every member of staff busily working away (or appearing to busily work away) at their desks every day of the working week indicates productivity or commitment. There is also the issue of controlling the activities of employees who are not sitting in the same building. Astor Levin senior consultant Elissa Faint recommends the following actions for employers that are still stuck in this 'old way' of thinking:

→ work out if there is an advantage to offering flexible work arrangements (through e.g., staff surveys/exit interviews)

→ determine the organization's goals and whether offering flexibility would have a positive or negative effect

→ evaluate the cost impact (including health and safety and legal/insurance implications)

→ get 'buy-in' to the concept from the management team.

When organizations have adopted flexible work arrangements they must ensure that appropriate policies and procedures are in place. They should choose who goes on to flexible arrangements on the basis of their work and productivity records and the program should be run (at least initially) on a trial basis.

According to Elissa Faint:

> The current scarcity of employees in many industry sectors means that employers must take a close look at what they are offering their workforce – if flexible working arrangements would allow them to attract and retain the best candidates they should certainly be considering introducing this to maintain their competitive advantage.

*Are there any disadvantages to employers flexible in offering employment arrangements?*

*Source: Reprinted with permission from HRM Guide Australia (http://www.hrmguide.net/australia/).*

---

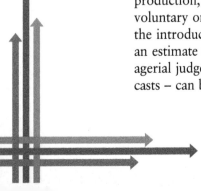

They tend to do little harm if kept pessimistic, but enthusiasm and political considerations often lead to overestimation. This can have expensive consequences.

*Projected throughput/production/sales information.* As a normal part of the planning process, production, sales and marketing departments and their equivalents in the public services or voluntary organizations will prepare their own forecasts. Intelligent use of this data, taking the introduction of new technology and quality improvements into account, will provide an estimate of the quantity and nature of the human resources needed. Work study, managerial judgement and a certain amount of scepticism – particularly regarding sales forecasts – can be used to transform this information into employee requirements.

*Employee analysis.* Modern HRIS products offer extensive possibilities for employee analysis; modelling the total profile of an organization's human resources. Employees can be classified in a variety of ways, such as function, department or grade. Age and length of service are important predictors of future availability. Skills levels and training or development needs can be compared with annual performance assessments.

*Scenario building.* Scenarios are not strictly forecasts but speculations on the future. It is impossible to predict what will happen in 20 – or even five – years' time, but it is possible to describe some alternatives. Working through a variety of possible states can identify the uncertainties, help us gain an understanding of the main driving factors and produce a range of options. Given the dramatic changes and discontinuities experienced today, scenario building seems to be one of the most realistic and useful forms of planning. Instead of prescribing detailed plans, the process allows strategists to simulate events and their consequences for resources and costs of different courses of action.

## Employee turnover

In recent years managers have been preoccupied with reducing the size of the workforce, closing plants and encouraging people to leave. In times of economic growth the emphasis changes to retaining the people with required skills. Human resource planning has a role in anticipating wastage. For example, the London Metropolitan Police had experienced difficulty in maintaining the requirement for police constables with the retirement of experienced officers. One way was to extend working life by offering flexible working hours, mentoring roles and pension incentives as alternatives to retirement. However, the consequences of blocking the careers of younger officers had also to be considered (Flynn, 2010). Turnover covers the whole input–output process from recruitment to dismissal or retirement and takes the consequences of promotion and transfer into account. Wastage deals only with leavers. Its importance lies in the freedom of employees to leave when they choose and hence its relatively uncontrollable nature for employers.

Control of staff turnover or wastage is critical when there is a general skills shortage. Ahlrichs (2000: 2) comments that:

> Employers have not ignored the hiring and retention crisis, but their choice of responses has been inadequate at best and off-target at worst. Misled by memories of applicants lined up outside the door, they have focused on the recruiting portion of the problem and largely ignored retention.
>
> They have regarded employees as mere lists of hard skills, as plug-in parts who are interchangeable as long as the resumé matches the job description. They continue to hound their HR departments for more and better candidates while ignoring the cost of turnover and HR's strategies to bond with, develop and retain existing employees.

Early work by Rice, Hull and Trist (1950) identified three main phases of turnover:

1  *Induction crisis.* Individuals who leave shortly after joining an organization: uncommitted employees tend to leave in the first few months. Recent research appears to show that there are several kinds of induction crisis experienced in different ways in different organizations.

2  *Differential transit.* During the first year or so, when some employees conclude that the organization is an unsuitable career vehicle or source of income.

3  *Settled connection.* Becoming a long-term 'stayer'.

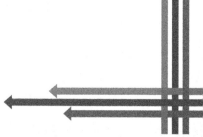

Despite the increase in flexible approaches to employment and the demise of the 'job for life' this pattern remains common. Dibble (1999: 19) suggests a working assumption that a company's employee population follows a normal distribution:

→ Crucial to the organization's success, so we want to do everything we can to keep them (three per cent).

→ Very important and we are willing to do a lot to keep them (15 per cent).

→ Employees we are happy to have and whose requests we will try hard to accommodate (68 per cent).

→ Need to improve or leave (13 per cent).

→ In a process leading to termination of employment (three per cent).

## HRM IN REALITY — INTEGRATING HR TECHNOLOGY

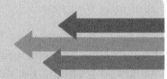

HR technology is a major growth market with increasingly sophisticated HR information systems (HRIS), HR management systems (HRMS), applicant tracking software and other IT products become available. Web-based HRIS is fast becoming a basic element of people management. Large corporations use HRIS extensively and more and more providers are addressing the potential of web-based HRMS solutions for medium and smaller businesses.

The 13th Annual HR Technology® Conference and Expo that took place in Chicago from September 29 to October 1 2010 saw a number of new and award-winning products on show. Among this year's developments is *Aquire InSight*, selected by *Human Resource Executive* magazine as one of its 2010 Top HR Products. Developed by workforce planning and analytics specialists Aquire, it is aimed to fill a void in the business analytics marketplace. It is claimed to improve HR planning decisions by delivering workforce analytics related to talent management initiatives and workforce trends directly to top managers. Aquire hosts a secure reporting engine enabling users to provide managers with access to workforce-performance metrics specific to their particular departments. The deal includes dedicated access to a certified workforce analyst, who can hypothesis test business drivers and link workforce trends to business trends.

*Aquire InSight* can integrate information from HRIS and talent management systems, presenting disparate data in a comprehensive format directly to decision makers when they need it. The Talent Pipeline shows the movement of talent throughout the organization and can focus on each individual manager's staff development results. *Aquire InSight* also lets users match business events with workforce trends on a timeline.

Meanwhile, HumanConcepts has launched Workforce Monitor™ described as an intuitive, analytical dashboard that allows managers to analyze their organization based on measures such as organizational unit, headcount or span of control and dimensions including age, gender, tenure, salary and ethnic origin. As an example, users can look at the overall headcount of the organization and then analyze this by department to identify units which are out of alignment. The system can provide a visual representation of headcounts across departments, by ethnic origin, by salary ranges and a host of other dimensions.

In a survey of 200 global enterprises and medium-sized businesses, SumTotal® Systems conclude that integrating 'talent functions' within one software platform can eliminate the need for separate data silos and make cross-functional reporting easier. This allows significant benefits as organizations can obtain more holistic views of workforce productivity and growth potential without time-consuming manual abstraction and collation of information. They identified the top five HR benefits of integration as:

→ Reduced voluntary turnover

→ Higher workforce productivity

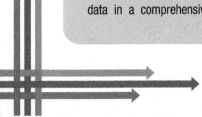

→ Better workforce alignment to overall business strategy

→ Improved internal talent mobility

→ Faster on-boarding (time-to-productivity).

SumTotal also looked at 15 possible HR process integrations and concluded that the top five were:

→ Employee Development and Succession Planning: Enable employee development planning for future roles

→ Employee Development and Learning Management: Enable employee development plans to be executed via learning and training

→ Learning Management and Performance Management: Enable learning and training activities as a key component of goal completion

→ Reporting and Core HR: Enable a single, centralized reporting repository across all HR functions

→ Performance Management and Compensation Management: Enable merit-based pay-for-performance.

Christopher Faust, vice president of global marketing at SumTotal Systems, said:

> Seamlessly linking HR processes and technologies to facilitate real-time business intelligence for improved decision making is a critical priority for HR leaders today. More and more global enterprises are experiencing firsthand the business benefits that a single, complete talent platform can deliver. Our research continues to validate the top strategies that drive tangible business value which help organizations to accelerate their growth, retain their top performers and improve overall workforce productivity.

*How has HR technology transformed the process of workforce planning in recent years?*

*Source: Reprinted with permission from HRM Guide USA (http://www.hrmguide.com/).*

The degree of wastage can be determined by a variety of turnover indices of varying sophistication. Three examples are:

1 The British Institute of Management (BIM) Index (annual labour turnover)

$$\frac{\text{Leavers in year}}{\text{Average number of staff in post that year}} \times 100 = \% \text{wastage}$$

2 Cohort analysis – a survival curve is drawn of employees taken on at the same time to determine what happens to a group.

3 Census method – for example, providing a histogram of the length of employee service.

## 'Soft' planning

HRM implies that planning has to go beyond the 'numbers game' into the softer areas of employee attitudes, behaviour and commitment. These aspects are critical to HR development, performance assessment and the management of change. At this point, we can consider an outline of the 'soft' planning process:

1 *Where are we now?* Information needs to be gathered through some form of human resource audit. This can be linked to a conventional SWOT analysis of the organization's human capital:
   – *strengths*, such as existing skills, individual expertise and unused talents
   – *weaknesses,* including inadequate skills, talents that are missing in the workforce because they are too expensive, inflexible people and 'dead wood'

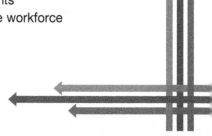

– *opportunities,* such as experience that can be developed in existing staff and talent that can be bought from the external job market.

– *threats,* including the risk of talent being lost to competitors.

2   *Where do we want to be?* Essentially, a clear strategic vision and a set of objectives.

3   *What do we need to do?* For example, following the logical sequence in Figure 13.1 decisions must be made on the use of in-house or external staff (see Table 13.3).

4   *Devise an action plan.* Some kind of resource planning is used by as many as 60 per cent of large organizations but it has to be conceded that it is often done poorly. Ideally, it should be linked to corporate strategy but corporate planners tend to ignore the human dimension.

**TABLE 13.3**
In-house and external human resources

| In-house resources | Outsourcing |
| --- | --- |
| Management control | Legal contract |
| Long-term people (can be developed; build experience; understand organization) | Focus on paying only for work you need |
| People are hassle | No extra pay/commitment |
| Contractual arrangements (talent expensive; overheads; large structure; hierarchy; support systems) | Range of options, e.g. consultants (variable expertise; expensive) or contingent workers (usually ex-managers; best for operational work) or home-workers (lower level/specialist; low overheads; supervision issues) or subcontracting |
| People are ambitious (require advancement; can go elsewhere – taking knowledge) | |

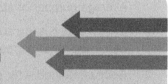

# HRM IN REALITY   STRATEGIC WORKFORCE PLANNING

A study from The Conference Board in 2006 reports that the ageing workforce and an emerging retirement wave among 'baby boomers' are driving more businesses toward 'strategic workforce planning'.

Strategic workforce planning is a new approach to traditional human resource planning that involves analyzing and forecasting the talent required by organizations to meet the objectives of their business strategies. It helps:

→   control employee costs

→   assess talent needs

→   make informed business decisions such as whether it's more cost effective to outsource an activity or add full-time employees

→   assess human-capital needs and risks.

In short, according to the study, *Strategic Workforce Planning: Forecasting Human Capital Needs to Execute Business Strategy,* strategic workforce planning is aimed at helping businesses ensure they have the right people in the right place at the right time and at the right price.

'In many companies, traditional workforce planning was an onerous process that HR imposed on management', said Mary B. Young, senior research

associate, The Conference Board and author of the report. 'Too often, the net result was a humongous report, blinding spreadsheets and a dizzying amount of data that provided very little value to the business.'

Methodology has moved on to meet changing business needs, new tools and technology. The study shows that some businesses have enhanced the simple gap analysis (workforce demand versus supply) used for traditional 'manpower' planning by adopting the logic and analytical tools of other management functions, including finance, strategic planning, risk management and marketing.

Rather than focusing on spreadsheets, the planning process needs to concentrate on the business plan and its implications for the workforce. Consistent, organization-wide data is essential. Other critical areas identified in the study include:

→ making the process and tools simple and efficient

→ developing HR's capabilities and comfort level

→ establishing a common language to describe jobs and required competencies

→ integrating workforce planning with business and budget planning

→ driving the plan deep into the organization.

While most companies in the study are finding their way in the process, strategic human resource planning can deliver value already through:

→ generating insights and knowledge to help managers make business decisions

→ providing a deeper and more subtle understanding of workforce dynamics than was previously available

→ enabling more efficient human capital management, for example by evaluating different staffing options for their long-term impacts or creating a stronger internal job market

→ enabling the HR function to achieve a long-held desire to become a player and a valued contributor at a higher level of strategic management.

'Strategic workforce planning enables the organization to slice-and-dice its workforce data to discover critical issues, compare different groups, understand patterns and trends, home in on critical segments of the workforce such as mature workers and top performers and customize its approach to managing different segments of its workforce', said Mary Young. 'By enabling leaders to see

across lines of business, workforce planning can leverage talent within a company. Ultimately, the same workforce planning database tools will enable employees to shop for new jobs, assess their own developmental needs and prepare for career moves inside the organization.'

Some of the techniques adopted by companies exampled in the study include:

A workforce analytics approach: mining both current and historical workforce data to identify the key relationships among the variables and between employee and business data. Dow Chemical has used this approach throughout a ten-year evolution of its workforce planning process.

Forecasting and scenario modelling: using data to create forecasts that incorporate multiple 'what-if' scenarios. These enable executives to evaluate strategic options. The study describes how a 'major bank' decides where to locate a new call centre based partly on this approach.

Human capital planning: used by Corning and others to segment jobs on a basis of their 'mission-criticality', making different levels of workforce investment in each segment. This approach focuses on broad three- to four-year trends, rather than precise headcounts and short-term plans.

Hewlett-Packard and IBM are cited as being committed to strategic workforce planning, customizing the process to address each company's specific conditions and needs. IBM's HR and finance departments help senior business leaders prepare realistic plans to execute their business strategy and manage drivers of employee costs. At HP, the study states that high-level discussions and a two-way educational process between business leaders and HR emphasizes qualitative over quantitative factors.

'While no organization claims to have achieved it yet, many believe that the ultimate payoff from strategic workforce planning will be a vibrant, internal job market that transcends the boundaries between business units and geographies', concluded Young. 'The company will be able to mine employee data to locate talent anywhere in the organization, woo passive job candidates and find the best use for each employee.'

*How would you distinguish strategic workforce planning from traditional HR planning?*

*Source: Reprinted with permission from* HRM Guide USA *(http://www.hrmguide.com).*

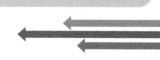

Iles (2001: 139) argues that the extension of human resource planning to include 'soft' issues such as motivation, commitment and culture has its dangers since it:

> … tends to conflate HRP with HRM as a whole, and takes the specificity away from HRP as a discrete dimension of employee resourcing concerned with forecasting and assessing the extent to which the organization will meet its labour requirements (or perhaps increasingly its knowledge requirements, which may take the focus of HRP away from labour supply concerns to an interest in knowledge supply, and away from focusing on employees alone to emphasizing knowledge resources, chains and intermediaries).

## RESOURCING INFORMATION

Effective in-house resourcing requires accurate and comprehensive information. Strategies and human resource plans must be translated into actual jobs and people found or developed to perform them. Some basic questions can be asked:

→ What tasks are involved?

→ What skills or competencies are required to do the work?

→ Are they to be found within the organization?

→ If not, should extra people be recruited?

### Researching the job

Conventionally, the first question is answered by a job analysis (Key concept 13.5). It is a more-or-less detailed examination of the sub-tasks within an identified job. Jobs vary between the 'crystallized', such as manufacturing assembly where the job is precisely defined, to managerial and professional jobs in which individuals have considerable freedom to vary their work (McCormick and Ilgen, 1987: 38). The degree of freedom is determined partly by technology or personal expertise and partly by the organization. Job analysis is geared towards tasks that are already being done in some form or can be easily extrapolated from current activities.

---

**KEY CONCEPT 13.5**  JOB ANALYSIS

The process of job analysis is that of gathering and analyzing job-related information. This includes details about tasks to be performed as part of a job and the personal qualities required to do them. Job analysis can provide information for a variety of purposes including: determining training needs, development criteria and appropriate pay and productivity improvements. For resourcing purposes, job analysis can generate job and personnel specifications.

---

Job analysis techniques vary from the rudimentary to the sophisticated. Long-regarded as a somewhat tedious aspect of the HR function, job analysis has been highlighted as a valuable technique in ensuring compliance with anti-discrimination legislation in the USA. Conversely, the move towards flexible working has deterred many organizations in other countries from closely defining jobs.

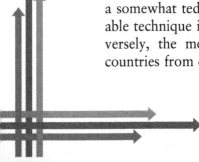

The simplest forms of job analysis are conducted by observing or interviewing existing jobholders and supervisors. Alternatively, the same people can produce a self-report according to an agreed format. Information is also available from records, 'experts', training materials, equipment descriptions and manuals. A basic six-step approach could be conducted as follows (Smith and Robertson, 1993: 15):

1 Make use of relevant existing documents such as training manuals.

2 Ask the line manager responsible about the main purposes of the job, the tasks involved and the links with other people.

3 Ask the same questions of jobholders, preferably backed by a detailed activity record over a week or two.

4 Where possible, sit in and observe jobholders at work – preferably on more than one day and at different times.

5 Try to do the job yourself. (This is not possible if specialist machinery or training are required.)

6 Write the job description.

The job-related information produced by job analysis can be arranged according to a number of headings (see Table 13.4) to ensure that all relevant details are covered. This method is cheap and relatively easy. However, more complex methods may be justified, such as questionnaires, generally purchased 'off-the-shelf' from specialist companies. Questionnaire

| Heading | Subject matter |
| --- | --- |
| Job identification | Job title, department, grade or level |
| Relationships | Name or title of immediate boss; number and type(s) of staff jobholder is responsible for; links with other departments |
| Outputs | What are the end-products or results of the job |
| Activities | The behaviours or actions of the worker in achieving these outputs |
| Performance | Required standards, agreed objectives |
| Individual requirements | Abilities, skills, experience, temperament, training, languages, etc. |
| Working conditions | The physical and social surroundings of the job such as workspace, working hours, leave entitlement |
| Equipment | Computers, machine tools, vehicles, etc. used as an essential part of the job |
| Other information | Promotion outlets, training available, transfer opportunities |

**TABLE 13.4**
A basic job analysis checklist

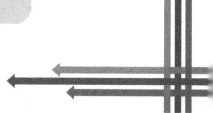

techniques can provide a wealth of information but are often expensive and time-consuming.

The critical incidents technique can also provide a rich, qualitative perspective on a job. Incumbents are asked to describe a number of specific real-life incidents in which they participated. The most effective incidents are those which detail qualities required to do the job well.

Job analysis is not a value-free source of information. Employees are prone to:

*Exaggeration.* Making jobs seem more demanding or complex than they really are.

*Omission.* Humdrum tasks are forgotten in favour of less frequent but more interesting activities.

In contrast, information given by supervisors may lead to:

*Understatement.* Jobs are portrayed as being easier and less complex than they are in reality.

*Misunderstanding.* Frequently bosses do not know workers' jobs in any detail.

The various systems of job analysis also differ in the kind of information collected:

*Job-oriented methods.* Detailed specifications of the tasks involved in specific jobs, for example 'spray chassis with anti-corrosive'. This approach produces accurate descriptions of individual tasks but it is difficult to extrapolate these to other jobs.

*Worker-oriented methods.* More generalized accounts of required behaviour that can be compared with those employed in other jobs.

*Competence-oriented methods.* Sometimes termed 'attribute' or 'trait'-oriented approaches. Highly descriptive in terms of the skills, experience and personal qualities required. Require considerable skill on the part of the analyst in translating job content into competencies.

### The job description

Whatever the degree of sophistication, the common outcome of job analysis is the job definition or description. In the past, job descriptions have been used as quasi-legal documents, with employees declaring their contents to be a definitive list of the tasks they were expected to perform. Uncooperative employees would refuse to do anything that was not on the list and unions and employers would enter into trench warfare over any changes. Today, in a climate of change and flexibility, employers are reluctant to agree to a rigid list of tasks, preferring the employee to be ready to take on any required function. Job descriptions are out of date almost as soon as they are written and cannot be seen as documents to be adhered to rigidly.

Conventionally, job descriptions detail information such as job titles, summaries of main functions and more detailed lists of activities within each job. The 'flexible job description' has a significant role in modern resourcing strategies allowing greater latitude in career development and succession planning (Pennell, 2010).

### Researching people

Depending on the method used, job analysis provides a detailed description of the work to be performed but may not indicate the knowledge, skills or abilities needed to do so. The 'right person' model of resourcing advocates a personnel specification for this purpose.

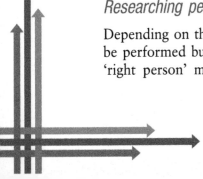

Personnel specifications translate the requirements of the job into the human attributes necessary to do that job.

Personnel specifications list 'essential' criteria that must be satisfied, and other criteria that rule out certain people from being able to do the job. Competence analyses and sophisticated forms of worker-oriented job analysis generate personnel specifications as part of the package. The step from job to person specification is never entirely objective, requiring inference or intuition. In fact, there is a risk of introducing discriminatory criteria which rule out particular groups. Personnel specifications may be no more than blueprints for 'clones', a matter that will be explored further later in this chapter.

Checklists such as Rodger's Seven-Point Plan (Rodger, 1952) have been commonly used for preparing personnel specifications. The desired qualities are categorized under seven headings:

1    physical qualities, including speech and appearance

2    attainments – qualifications, membership of professional associations

3    general intelligence

4    specific aptitudes, such as numerical ability

5    interests and hobbies

6    personality

7    domestic circumstances.

Slavish use of such a plan leads to evident danger. Items 1 and 7 could easily cause discriminatory choices and require rigorous and critical examination. As we shall see in the next chapter, further information is obtained by using selection techniques including formal interviews, psychometric tests, assessment centres and biodata.

## STRATEGIES FOR REDUNDANCY

Most of the discussion so far in this chapter has addressed human resource strategies relating to successful, growing companies. As we noted with reactor strategies, managers are also expected to implement redundancies and closures as a result of strategic decisions. Sir John Harvey Jones once observed that most companies refer to their workers as 'our greatest resource' but, in practice, do little to make them feel that way. We have observed in earlier chapters that the workforce is one group of stakeholders among many and within the free market model of capitalism they are probably the weakest. Presenting a caring image to staff and the consuming public may have advantages but greater attention is paid to more powerful voices when action is required. Directors and financiers ensure that their interests are satisfied first – well before those of the employees. This reflects a 'people as objects' rather than 'people as people' approach.

Most job losses are due to age-old causes: business failures, organizational restructuring and cutting back on capacity in response to lower sales or funding levels. Generally, the terms 'redundancy' and 'retrenchment' have lost much of their old stigma.

### Planning for redundancies

There are some new features to job-cutting which are indicative of systematic changes in the way that human resource strategists view the process. Despite the emphasis on job security

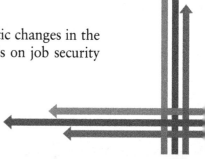

as a prerequisite for an effective human resource strategy, reality in free market economies demands planning for redundancies. These may result from company failure, funding cuts, rationalization or reduction in demand for products and people. There are several terms for the process of losing a job, all with different connotations and nuances: being made redundant, 'letting you go', 'getting the sack' and so on. One euphemism is 'deselection', implying that some form of systematic or thought-out procedure has been used to decide who will lose their jobs.

Hendry (1995: 202) details a number of key issues:

→ To what extent can over-staffing be corrected through natural wastage or redeployment?

→ What agreements constrain the redundancy process. For example, 'last in, first out'?

→ When should a redundancy programme be announced? How much consultation is required?

→ How are redundancy entitlements to be calculated?

→ Is it possible to have an entirely voluntary process? What restrictions should be placed on key staff leaving?

→ Should the organization play an active role in outplacement?

→ When will savings in salary and related items pay for the redundancy costs?

Large companies often employ portfolio management systems that view business units as growth, closure or disposal prospects. A classic, if simple, portfolio planning model is based on the Boston Consulting matrix shown in Figure 13.2. This offers a further typology for resourcing strategy:

*Stars.* Profitable business units with a dominant market position. Good prospects for employees with promotion opportunities and competitive salaries.

*Cash cows.* Mature companies with a high market share but low growth rate. They produce a cash surplus as investment costs are low but profits are good. Secure but unchallenging for employees – promotions are only possible when staff leave or retire. The focus may be on managing a steady decline, squeezing as much profit out of the enterprise as possible. Comfortable salaries until later stages when hard cost-cutting is required.

*Wild cats.* New ventures with low market share but high growth rates. A risky environment for employees. If lucky, the group will invest and there will be considerable career opportunities and rapid promotion – provided they work for potential stars. Employees are expected to be flexible and the work can be exciting and fast-moving. If unlucky, they face closure or disposal to another organization. This type closely parallels the 'prospector' strategy discussed earlier.

**FIGURE 13.2**

Boston Consulting Group portfolio planning matrix

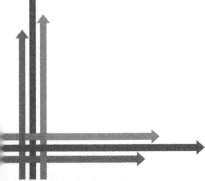

|  | Competitive position (e.g. market share) | |
|  | High | Low |
| High (Growth rate) | Star | Wild cat |
| Low | Cash cow | Dog |

*Dogs.* Certain failures. Low growth, low share of market and no strategic potential. The only hope for employees is sale to a more positive owner. Essentially, these are 'reactor' companies.

Companies using portfolio planning are likely to take decisions on purely financial criteria without regard to the welfare of employees. HRM in such organizations tends to be tough-minded, favouring employees in profitable business units. Those in less successful areas are likely to be disposed of unceremoniously.

## Redundancy and retention

Managers in charge of redundancy programmes typically focus on target numbers, with little or no thought about the quality of the staff leaving the business. Retention strategies for key staff are even more important during periods of redundancy. As Thomson and Mabey (1994, p.11) point out:

> It is the quality of the staff … not the quantity, which is the essential factor in downsizing. As we all know from experience, where there are programmes of voluntary redundancy, it is often the most skilled employees who go first because they are more marketable outside.
>
> An obsession with numbers leads to a haemorrhaging of valuable skills: years of work on building a strong competence base can be undone in a matter of weeks.

'Last in, first out', remains a common rule. Lee (2004) investigated the reasons why seniority rules are applied so widely to layoffs and promotion decisions in the USA. Under certain circumstances, he acknowledges, there may be economic benefits from the use of seniority rules but the evidence shows a greater popularity than economic explanations would account for. Lee notes that they have often arisen from employees' demands for fair and objective decisions. Lee concludes that seniority rules have procedural merits as they can reduce the likelihood of conflicts and help coordination among workers and employers, particularly when employees consider that selection procedures and results might be lacking objectivity or be unfair.

## International organizations and redundancies

Businesses with operations in different countries must take their respective severance rules into account.

**HRM IN REALITY**   TIPS FOR HANDLING LAY-OFFS

Consulting firm Drake Beam Morin (DBM) warned employers against short-sighted workforce decisions and badly handled employee terminations. Lay-offs may be necessary at times, but they can have a negative impact on an organization's productivity levels and affect their ability to retain and attract talented employees in the future.

'From a company's standpoint, the decision to terminate a group of employees is fraught with potential legal, financial and public relations consequences', said Thomas Silveri, president and chief executive officer of DBM. 'It is critical that managers communicate the news of lay-offs in a professional, legal and humane way in order to treat the departing employees with

sensitivity and to maintain a respectful corporate image.'

DBM conducted a global study revealing that one out of every ten individuals who lost their jobs involuntarily told a colleague first of their job loss. So the manner in which employees are laid off can have a direct impact on the morale, commitment and retention of remaining staff.

Based on extensive experience, DBM recommends a five-step process for managers involved in laying off staff:

1 *Prepare the materials.* Explain the rationale and prepare all severance information in writing (notification letter; salary continuation/severance period; benefits; outplacement, etc.).

2 *Prepare the message.* Write the script you will use during the meeting and the key information you will convey to remaining employees. Keep it short and to the point.

3 *Arrange the next steps.* Schedule meetings with your organization's human resources and outplacement professionals. Review what should be done with the departing employees' personal belongings and specify when the employees should leave the organization.

4 *Prepare yourself emotionally.* Don't assume personal responsibility for the termination. Remember it is a business decision based on business needs. Acknowledge your anxiety, prepare your approach and talk about your feelings with the human resource and outplacement professionals.

5 *Anticipate employee reactions.* There are typically five reactions to termination: anticipation, disbelief, escape, euphoria or violence. By acknowledging these various reactions and learning to recognize them, you will ensure that no matter what the reaction, you will be prepared to handle it in the best way.

DBM recommends that the following 'Dos and Dont's' should be followed when conducting a termination meeting:

**Do**

→ invite the employee in to sit down

→ get right to the point

→ explain the actions taken and the reasons for them

→ listen to the employee and wait for a response

→ restate the message if necessary

→ use your prepared notes/guidelines

→ clarify the separation date

→ give an overview of the separation package

→ explain the logistics for leaving the company

→ provide appropriate written materials

→ close the meeting within 15 minutes

→ escort the employee to the next appointment.

**Don't**

→ say 'Good morning,' 'Good to see you', or 'How are you?'

→ engage in small talk

→ use humour

→ be apologetic

→ defend, justify or argue

→ threaten

→ discuss other employees

→ sympathize

→ try to minimize the situation

→ make promises

→ personalize the anger

→ use platitudes like 'I know how you feel', or 'You will be just fine', etc.

'Managers need to learn how to manage this process in a way that preserves the current productivity levels and the company's ability to attract top talent in the future', said Silveri.

*What are the consequences of bad feeling when employees leave an organization?*

*Source: Reprinted with permission from HRM Guide USA (http://www.hrmguide.net/usa/).*

Since the late 1990s, critics have argued that the cutting process has gone too far: as we have noted before, de-layering or downsizing have led to 'dumbsizing'. Organizations have slimmed down to the point where they are denuded of the skills needed to grasp new opportunities and remaining staff are demoralized and overworked. With skilled staff in demand and often difficult to find, there is a greater focus on active retention. Moore, Cruickshank and Haas (2006) investigated the role of occupational therapy managers in influencing the job satisfaction of their staff. Those who showed care and support, while at the same time demonstrating strong advocacy and the ability to make decisions for the good of the department rather than for the benefit of the individual, influenced job satisfaction positively. Job dissatisfaction was strongest when managers were seen to treat staff differently, construed as a demonstration of favouritism. Results suggest that access to benefits, such as flexible working conditions and educational funding, should be transparent and guided by clear policies.

 ## SUMMARY

Employee resourcing is a wider issue than recruitment and selection. In this chapter we discussed strategies for determining resourcing from either the internal or external employment markets. We considered a variety of models for resourcing strategies. We also discussed some approaches to human resource planning and the use made of information collected during the resourcing process. We reviewed the issue of retention, staff turnover and wastage in terms of measurement, forecasting and action. Some of the limitations of job descriptions and personnel specifications were identified. Finally, we considered redundancies as an aspect of resourcing strategy.

 ## FURTHER READING

1 Stephen Taylor's (2008) *People Resourcing,* 4th edition, published by the CIPD, examines the topic of employee resourcing in a practitioner context.

2 *People Resourcing and Talent Planning: HRM in Action* (2010) 4th edition, FT/Prentice Hall by Stephen Pilbeam and Marjorie Corbridge analyzes contemporary practice.

3 The planning process is discussed in *Strategic Human Resource Management: Theory and Practice* (2nd edition, Sage, 2005) edited by Graeme Salaman, John Storey and Jon Billsberry Rothwell.

 ## REVIEW QUESTIONS

1 Why is employee resourcing a core activity for human resource staff?

2 How does employee resourcing relate to organizational strategy? Summarize the main resourcing strategy options open to modern organizations.

3 Consider an organization of your choice.

   (a) Does it obtain its human resource requirements from existing staff where possible?

   (b) At what levels are people brought in from the external employment market?

   (c) Would it be beneficial to change these practices?

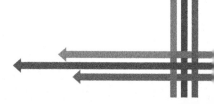

4   Distinguish between 'hard' and 'soft' human resource planning. Which is of greatest value to modern businesses?

5   Are resourcing decisions normally taken on a short-term operational basis or at a strategic level?

6   Are long-term resourcing strategies realistic?

7   To what degree are resourcing strategies constrained by the nature of the external employment market?

8   How has the concept of flexibility affected resource decisions?

9   What is the relationship between resourcing strategy, HR planning and job analysis? Compare and contrast the classification systems proposed by Miles and Snow and Sonnenfeld, Peiperl and Kotter.

10   Is human resource planning a worthwhile activity?

11   Why is it important to measure and forecast staff turnover? Is there merit in the claim that resourcing strategies should focus on employee retention rather than recruitment?

12   When and why would you conduct a job analysis? What is the difference between a job description and personnel specification?

13   Are redundancies inevitably a matter of cynical expediency?

 **CASE STUDY FOR DISCUSSION AND ANALYSIS**

## Pribake

Pribake manufactures biscuits ('cookies'). The company requires a steady stream of new product ideas, a small proportion of which will form a permanent element of its range. The board are considering a new appointment but cannot agree on the nature of the post. The production director feels that there is a need for an operational manager to look after chocolate-coated products. Conversely, the marketing director wants an 'ideas' person to devise new products and enliven the company's range. The two cannot agree and the managing director has imposed a compromise. She has asked the human resource manager to find an individual who can meet both requirements. After some dispute they have produced a basic job definition along the following lines:

Job title. **New products production manager.**

Job summary. **Reporting at a high level with responsibility for development team and – possibly – maintenance staff. Overseeing manufacture of chocolate-coated range. Developing new product ideas and progressing through from trial to production stages.**

Desirable qualities. **General management skills. Able to manipulate technology effectively and realistically. If the successful candidate does not have direct knowledge of the actual machinery and techniques used in the company's factories, then he/she must have the ability to appraise systems and technology quickly.**

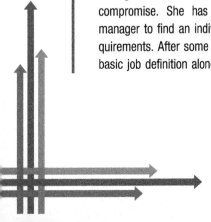

After much discussion the HR manager has produced a list of additional competencies which seem to meet the requirements of the post:

→ Creativity – to develop marketable products which can be produced at a reasonable cost.

→ Experience of, or familiarity with market research techniques and able to formulate research programmes and evaluate results.

→ Ability to design and test product manufacturing processes.

→ Familiarity with the properties and possibilities of available materials: for example what can and cannot be done with different kinds of chocolate.

→ Familiarity with production line equipment including ability to appraise production line speeds, error factors and quality improvements. New products must not pose insurmountable problems for production machinery or workforce.

→ Versatility – the fewest development problems arise when products can be manufactured on existing equipment and made from simple and easily obtainable raw ingredients.

→ Managerial skills to motivate and control the development team and ensure its effectiveness. A solitary genius will not work well in this environment.

→ Ability to communicate persuasively with management and workforce, especially when products are trialled and inevitable teething problems occur. Also to communicate with senior management and marketing staff in promoting products within the company and in the marketplace.

The directors have also agreed on the following criteria:

→ Academic qualifications: likely to be a graduate with a production or engineering speciality.

→ Ability: above average. Strong in mechanical aptitude. High on creativity scores. High on verbal fluency. A flair for design.

→ Personality: neither highly introverted nor extroverted. Good leadership and persuasion skills.

→ Experience: there are significant elements of the job which seem to demand familiarity with this particular industry.

*What deficiencies are apparent in the job description, competence list and additional selection criteria?*

*How would you conduct the recruitment and selection exercise for this vacancy?*

*What is the likelihood of finding a suitable candidate?*

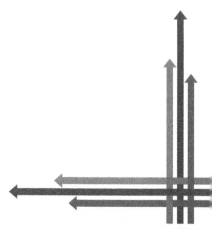

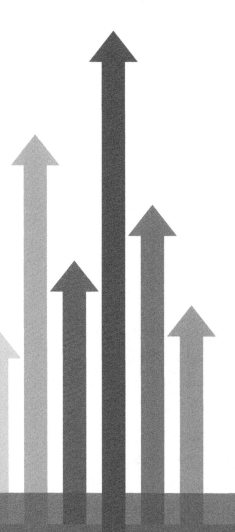

# PART FIVE
## TALENT MANAGEMENT

This part of the book addresses some of the core areas of human resource practice: recruitment and selection, performance and reward management and human resource development. These areas are extensively covered in critical academic literature and prescriptive ('how to') books for specialists in people management. Our discussion attempts to strike a balance between these two approaches, allowing you to gain an understanding of the wide range of practical techniques in use as well as an appreciation of some of the weaknesses and inconsistencies in the methodology and underlying theory.

### The chapters in Part Five address some key issues, including:

→ **Why are some recruitment channels more popular than others?**

→ **What are the most cost-effective recruitment and selection methods?**

→ **How are new recruits integrated with the organization?**

→ **What is performance management?**

→ **What is the relationship between performance management reward management?**

→ **How do we integrate performance, reward and human resource development into a meaningful talent management process.**

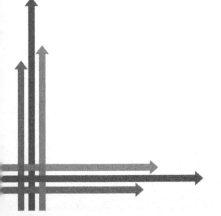

# CHAPTER 14
## Recruitment

## LEARNING OBJECTIVES

The purpose of this chapter is to:

→ Discuss the meaning and significance of recruitment in its organizational context.

→ Provide a typology of recruitment strategies.

→ Critically review preliminary information-gathering techniques.

→ Discuss the merits of references and biodata.

# RECRUITMENT AS A TEXTBOOK SUBJECT

In Chapter 13 we discussed the 'why' of resourcing, evaluating strategies and plans that guide the process. We considered also the initial information gathering from job analysis and the sometimes unwise strategies employed by selectors. This chapter and the next follow on with an examination of the operational elements of resourcing, commonly termed recruitment and selection.

Recruitment and selection are major issues for human resource specialists. HRM and other management literature puts great emphasis on the process of selecting and orienting new recruits. There is no shortage of material on these topics and, together with performance assessment, they are critical elements of effective people management. Not surprisingly, therefore, these aspects of employee resourcing have attracted a great deal of attention from human resource practitioners and occupational psychologists. As we will see in Chapter 15, the topic range has a well rehearsed familiarity because selection methods are regarded as basic tools for human resource managers. Indeed, the underlying 'best practice' model has achieved the status of holy writ in certain quarters, with any deviation regarded as heresy.

Iles and Salaman (1995: 203) argue: 'The limitation of the psychological and personnel-driven approaches to selection is that they are entirely, if understandably, concerned with improving the efficiency of the processes, and not with understanding their wider provenance and significance'. And again (Iles, 2001: 134): '... despite the need for a fuller understanding of these processes, the bulk of existing social science and HR literature is concerned primarily and solely with assessing the efficiency of these processes, often in rather descriptive, prescriptive and atheoretical ways'.

As we noted in the last chapter, we cannot discuss how recruitment and selection take place without asking why certain techniques are used in preference to others. Iles (2001) sees much deeper consequences, meaning and significance in the exercise and justification of recruitment and selection processes. Within the HRM paradigm, they are not simply mechanisms for filling vacancies. Recruitment and redundancy can be viewed as key 'push' and 'pull' levers for organizational change. Recruitment and selection allow management to determine and gradually modify the behavioural characteristics and competencies of the workforce with a trend towards increasing sophistication in choice of methods in countries as disparate as the UK (Branine, 2008), where management fads are favoured, and Egypt (El-Kot and Leat, 2008), where there is considerable resistance to western notions of selection.

# MATCHING PEOPLE AND JOBS

Focusing on in-house resourcing, how can we make the best use of people? In practice, it is rarely possible to match perfectly the requirements of an individual job with the skills and abilities of the people available. Square pegs in round holes are not only bad for the organization: wrongly placed workers are often unhappy and bored, or anxious about being out of their depth. In line with the three basic recruitment strategies outlined in Table 14.1, any mismatch between person and job can be resolved in one of the following ways (Drenth and Algera, 1987):

→ Select the best qualified person for the job ('right person' approach).

→ Change job characteristics to fit the abilities of the people employed ('culture-fit' model).

→ Train people to perform more effectively (flexible person approach).

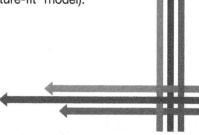

**TABLE 14.1**
Recruitment
strategies

| Approach | Objective | Organization | HR emphasis |
| --- | --- | --- | --- |
| **1** *Suitability – right person for the job* | Get the job done | Traditional<br>Hierarchical<br>Fixed job categories | Job analysis<br>HR planning<br>Selection |
| **2** *Malleability – fit the culture* | Fit in with today's organization | Small core<br>Strong culture<br>Variable periphery | Appraisal<br>Job training<br>Development |
| **3** *Flexibility – employee for tomorrow* | Build a competitive organization | Flexible<br>Lean<br>Virtual | Performance<br>Skills training<br>Talent management |

An organization may choose any one or a combination of these methods. However, all depend on the ability to identify and measure the characteristics necessary for successful job performance. At first sight this seems simple and obvious but a close examination reveals how complex it can be. People can perform a particular job successfully for varied

## HRM IN REALITY NEW TRENDS IN HIRING

Organizations are planning to increase hiring as the economy recovers but are making significant changes to their recruitment strategies according to research from *Job Search Television Network* (JSTN), a leading video and social media based recruiting company. Cuts to recruiting staffs and budgets during the recession have resulted in a greater emphasis on lower cost, efficient technological solutions. The report notes increasingly targeted use of social media in the recruitment process.

Roger Stanton, CEO of Job Search Television Network, commented:

> LinkedIn and Facebook with links to video has been hot for a while, but now we're seeing clients 'micro-target' employees using niche blogs and LinkedIn groups. For example, one of our clients successfully uses niche blogs to locate workers

with very specific types of financial service backgrounds. They started doing this when a new blog showed up on JSTN's client metric report. When they posted a video to the blog, it quickly became a 'home run'. Clients are finding sites they weren't aware of because JSTN's video provides highly detailed traffic metrics and they can make changes on the fly.

The study also considered the proportion of viewers who go on to apply for the position advertised.

Roger Stanton explained:

> We will usually see an enormous spike in viewership for a position right after a video is placed on websites and social media. With clients hitting average conversion rates of viewers to applicants around 18.8 per cent, the video is far

exceeding other sources. In some cases, the conversion rate is as high 45 per cent! That can mean thousands of people have seen the video for a job, at very little cost to the employer and it provides very powerful employment branding. The candidates who do apply are more likely to be a more qualified fit for the job, since they've seen the video and have responded based on the compelling information they have viewed.

**The study found renewed interest in Employment Referral Programs (ERP) in the recruitment process, but again with a different emphasis.**

Roger Stanton said:

The idea of ERP programs is coming back in a big way, because it is so much faster and cheaper if you can get a referral from your current employees. The difference this time is that since email readership is going down, particularly among younger employees who prefer social media, companies are using video messaging. The video can be placed on a company's Facebook page, blogs, etc. and is far more likely to get watched and sent to friends via mobile phones. And again, the traffic results can be closely tracked for ROI [return on investment] purposes.

**The study identified mobile phones as the third major trend in hiring for 2010.**

Roger Stanton explained:

We knew when payment systems started being developed for cell phones that mobile would replace computers as the centre of our digital lives.

This is why JSTN was created with the ability to TEXT ID videos to mobile phones. Now with smart phones penetrating the market at exponential rates, we're seeing this really take off. Looking forward, research states that by 2014, over 66 per cent of all mobile data traffic will be video [Cisco Visual Networking Index: Forecast and Methodology, 2009–2014]. One of our clients regularly sends job videos to prospects on cell phones with amazing results. Not only does the receiver actually view the video, they also usually forward it to numerous contacts in their network. The video quickly goes viral.

Roger Stanton concluded:

What these trends point to is that we are truly becoming a video-centric society, with much of that centreing on mobile phones. Companies are recognizing that if they want to reach prospective hires, this is where they need to be. And with tight budgets, its not surprising they would turn to these technologies now to reach new candidate pools at low cost while maintaining professional identity. As we come into the fall hiring season, which will ramp up in earnest right after Labour Day, you'll really see these trends as play out in the workplace.

*Will the use of social media and mobile videos appeal to all candidates?*

*Source: Reprinted with permission from* HRM Guide USA *(http://www.hrmguide.com).*

and sometimes contrasting reasons. For example, a good manager may be personally well-organized and able to clear mountains of paperwork quickly. Another manager may deal with similar tasks equally efficiently through skilful delegation. As such, it is the *totality of effectiveness* of the individual that matters rather than specific skills and abilities. Effectiveness also depends on context. Most jobs require an individual to work within a team where required skills or qualities can be spread between its members. In such a case it may not be necessary for every team member to possess all qualities needed for effective performance.

## The right person?

Resourcing strategies should maintain the required number and quality of staff within an organization. They should also ensure suitability for its future development. There are two

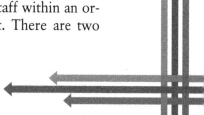

underlying and apparently contradictory approaches in common use (Haire, 1959). The first methodology emphasizes the right (or best) person for the job. The individual is the variable element in the search; the job is fixed. This approach is associated with traditional Western personnel management. People are sought with appropriate abilities and experience to perform the job with minimal training. It implies that individual jobs are relatively long term and unchanging and that people can be 'bought in' at any stage in their careers. Vacancies are filled from the internal or external employment market. When the job is no longer required, the incumbent is disposed of.

This model is conventionally described as 'best practice' in the UK and other free market countries. Accordingly, most texts on recruitment and selection traditionally outline a 'prescriptive approach to recruitment based on a systematic analysis of the requirements of an individual job' (Wright and Storey, 1994: 192). Almost invariably the account focuses on a series of selection techniques with limited discussion of the logic behind the resourcing process. There is rarely a suggestion that any other approach may be worth considering. Wright and Storey also rightly point out that 'best practice' only takes place in the largest organizations. Small and medium-sized enterprises generally recruit in an informal manner and rarely use sophisticated selection methods.

The 'right person' approach attempts to be 'objective'. It requires clear answers to questions such as:

→ Is there a job to fill?

→ If so, what tasks and responsibilities are involved?

→ What qualities, skills or experience are required to perform the tasks?

→ What process will best identify these criteria?

In essence, it is an attempt to find a seven-sided object to fit a seven-sided hole. It is a *discrimination* rather than a selection process: a matching technique that attempts to pin down the 'right' or 'best' applicant. By definition it excludes those people who are believed not to fit – a view of people as objects (Townley, 1994: 94). Townley perceives an underlying belief that 'employees who are carefully and appropriately matched to their jobs are satisfied and productive'. Matching involves generating a taxonomy of qualities and skills (criteria) that are believed to be essential or desirable – including qualifications and experience. In turn a matrix is constructed that ranks candidates in relation to the job criteria and imposes a decision point at which some people are accepted and others rejected. In the simplest case, this process can take place inside a selector's head. In the most complex, it involves elaborate selection techniques, multiple dimensions and rating scales and requires a computer to calculate the resulting matrix. The 'right person' approach functions well when:

→ It is possible to define a job tightly.

→ The job is discrete and separable from other functions.

→ The job is best done by an individual with a specific range of skills.

Frequently, however, these criteria do not apply and jobs are identified for less rational reasons such as:

→ we have *always* had a 'major accounts manager'

→ department 'x' *must* handle the task

→ people *like* it done in a particular way.

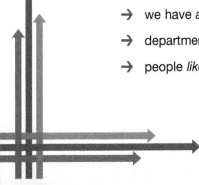

The 'right person' model is geared to static, self-satisfied organizations. It meets the needs of the 'job box' model of organizational structure discussed in Chapter 8, where people come and go but the job continues indefinitely. It leads to positions being offered to people who match traditional criteria – the kind of people we have always had. It closes the appointments process to people who traditionally have been unsuccessful. In terms of equal opportunities this approach continues to disadvantage people from 'different' backgrounds and alternative outlooks. In essence it is a cloning process: resourcing a firm with more of the same people (see Key concept 14.1). It eliminates any opportunity for the organization to be creative or experimental.

> ### KEY CONCEPT 14.1 CLONING
>
> Cloning, or 'elective homogeneity' is the tendency for selectors to pick people like themselves, thereby reducing the breadth of skills and personalities in an organization. Simply matching the set of characteristics possessed by previous successful post holders, it is a safe, conservative way to fill jobs. As a low-risk, but backward-looking approach, it is unlikely to meet the future needs of the organization.

### Fit with the organization

The second approach described by Haire focuses on fitting the person to the organization. Jobs are changed and reshaped to make the best use of individuals' skills within the organization. People are permanent but jobs can be varied. If more employees are required, a search is made for individuals who appear to have the personal qualities necessary to 'fit in' with the organization's culture. Personality is more important than technical skills in this context.

Culture fit predominates in the traditional large Japanese company. The emphasis is on matching individuals to organizational culture rather than to organizational structure. Recruitment focuses on young people who can be socialized into the company's way of working. Western managers have taken an interest in this approach in recent decades. It has been justified in terms of attracting creative and innovative employees. However, there is a distinction between creative and plastic minds. In reality, it is a means of hiring more potential clones who have the further 'advantages' of being young, cheap and easy to manage.

### Flexibility

A third, more demanding, approach can provide a significant competitive advantage for organizations: recruiting 'flexible employees', prepared for future change and able to contribute rather than conform. Rather than aiming for rigid skills and ability profiles or malleable and gullible personalities, recruit people who are versatile and adaptable. This reflects a long-term strategy, geared towards realizing talent for tomorrow's requirements. It is not simply meeting current needs or filling the organization with compliant clones. The emphasis is on diversity. Organizations should identify a range of individuals required for the future – including 'mavericks to buck the system' and not just 'conformist clones' (Armstrong, 1992: 135).

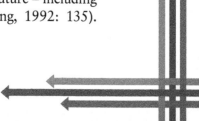

They will require training and development; they will not be docile and managing them may be difficult; but their potential is massively greater than any clone.

Taking this approach, some of the rhetoric of HRM can become reality. Instead of viewing resourcing simply as a matter of recruiting individuals to meet immediate needs, it also widens the long-term pool of skills and abilities. There is a genuine need for integration and coordination between resourcing strategies and other aspects of talent management such as assessment, development and reward. Creative people must be freed from overbearing control. They cannot be managed through compliance: engagement and commitment form the 'glue' that can bind individual talents and innovation to organizational objectives.

All options, including subcontracting, must be considered carefully before hiring new people. This form of flexibility offers long-term benefits but needs people ready for new demands and hence a need for a detailed knowledge of individual jobs, people's capabilities and the range of work to be performed now and in the future.

## SELECTORS AND STRATEGIES

The 'right person' approach is entirely concerned with the individual, whereas the 'cultural fit' model is consistent with a focus on teamworking. In practice, the models are easily confused with each other and many selectors apply a mixture of both. Frequently, selectors believe they are using 'best practice' to find the person who meets the specified criteria when, in fact, the person chosen is the one whose face fits. All too often resourcing emphasizes the selection of people who fit existing culture and practice at the expense of future needs.

Why does this occur? Employee resourcing involves risk and uncertainty. Above all, assessors want to avoid the consequences of picking the 'wrong' person. This may be for the valid reason that an unsuitable person will not perform to required standards. However, selectors are also aware of the consequences of an unfortunate choice rebounding directly on themselves (and their reputations). This encourages selectors to take 'safe' decisions minimizing risk of error. The individual clearly identified as a 'good bloke' by the organization and its senior managers becomes an attractive choice.

The in-breeding found at higher levels of management has been described as 'organizational dry rot' (Smith, 1991: 29). Poverty of ideas, stultified thinking and blinkered behaviour can be due to a narrow range of experience. It is imperative, therefore, that resourcing activities should increase the breadth of experience within an organization. To do this the interests of the organization should be divorced from those of any specific stakeholders, including those of its senior managers. However, resourcing costs money directly (e.g. advertising) and indirectly (the time occupied by comparatively well-paid people). As a consequence many organizations avoid the hassle and expense by taking a casual approach to one of the most critical aspects of people management.

Geerlings and van Veen (2006) argue that there is little material in the HR literature on the long–term consequences of selection policies. They simulated job-mobility patterns over time to show how different policies affected different situations. There is a common tendency to take on less capable recruits when there is a shortage of well-qualified people in order to deal with short-term problems. Geerlings and van Veen found that this was counterproductive in the long-term with even a brief deviation from a resourcing strategy inhibiting the achievement of organizational goals for many years thereafter.

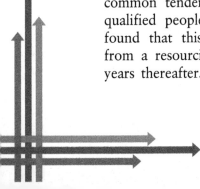

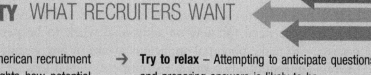

# HRM IN REALITY WHAT RECRUITERS WANT

A 2010 study from leading North American recruitment firm Rosenzweig & Company highlights how potential employees can best respond to increased use of recruiters as the economy recovers.

Jay Rosenzweig, managing partner said:

> It's been a long while since many people have been in these interviewing situations making it even more important than ever to have a firm grasp of the process well before the interview begins.

The report offers key advice for individuals recruited for a job opportunity:

→ **The headhunter works for the employer, but can also be your friend** – The report points out that recruiters can provide general advice and be used as a sounding board. The recruiter can act as an intermediary between candidates and potential employers, responding to comments or concerns before direct contact takes place.

→ **Retainer v. contingency** – Clarify the basis on which recruiters are being employed. Retainer-based contracts where payment is assured tend to be less focused on quick results and commission, reducing the risk of inappropriate placements.

→ **Sell yourself** – Convey your skills, experience and career plans without overstating your accomplishments. Provide recruiters with sufficient information to promote your candidacy to a potential employer.

→ **Be yourself** – Recruiters and potential employers can detect insincerity. Trying to redefine your background or personality in an attempt to fit a specific role is unlikely to be successful.

→ **Do your homework** – Research your prospective employers including recent financial and operational developments. However, do not present yourself as an expert on the organization.

→ **Try to relax** – Attempting to anticipate questions and preparing answers is likely to be counterproductive. Candidates may be unsuccessful if overeagerness is interpreted as desperation.

→ **Be honest about any other opportunities you are considering** – Both recruiters and potential employers will understand that you may be considering other options but will not appreciate being misled.

→ **Come clean** – Be honest with the recruiter about any past issues that could affect the attitude of a prospective employer. It is better to volunteer potentially negative information than risk it emerging at a later date.

→ **Accept constructive criticism** – If recruiters or potential employers provide constructive criticism, use it as a learning opportunity.

Jay Rosenzweig commented:

> Job seekers have had lean years and very little movement on the jobs front, including at the higher levels. Some people who've survived the recession with their job intact may think they hold all the cards if a company or recruiter calls. But now, more than ever, the best advice is to check your ego at the door and understand the 'buy and sell' process when presented with dream job opportunities. One of the most fundamental rules in this business is to know when to talk and know when to listen.

*How important is it for a job applicant to understand the recruiting process?*

*Source: Reprinted with permission from HRM Guide USA (http://www.hrmguide.com).*

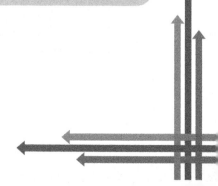

# MARKETING THE JOB

Following on from our discussion in Chapter 13, if resourcing strategy and planning have identified the need for new or additional work to be performed in-house, it is obviously necessary to make potential applicants aware of any vacancy. Essentially, this is a marketing process conventionally termed 'recruitment' which Lewis (1985: 29) defines as: 'the activity that generates a pool of applicants, who have the desire to be employed by an organization, from which those suitable can be selected.'

Potential candidates may come from an internal trawl of the organization, or from the external job market. The latter are reached through channels such as recruitment advertising, employment agencies, professional associations or word of mouth. We saw in Chapter 9 that organizations with a strong culture are likely to seek malleable new employees at school leaving or graduate levels. More senior jobs are filled from the internal job market. When companies look for the 'right person', however, detailed personnel specifications may rule out internal candidates. In each case, the recruitment phase is critical because it determines the range of choice available to the selectors: 'The more effectively this stage is carried out the less important the actual selection of candidates becomes: if a firm can attract 20 high flyers for a job it hardly matters whether they choose amongst these high flyers with a pin, an interview or tests' (Smith, Gregg and Andrews, 1989: 24).

## HRM IN REALITY  USING SOCIAL MEDIA TO IMPROVE JOB CHANCES

Until recently, the rules of the game were simple: post your resume or CV on a host of jobsites and recruiters would come looking for you. But the game has changed and is continuing to evolve, according to recruiters at MRINetwork, one of the world's largest search and recruitment organizations.

Tony McKinnon, president of MRINetwork said:

> Social media sites have become increasingly important platforms for finding jobs by facilitating connections and demonstrating the achievements and interests of job seekers. But capturing the attention of prospective employers and recruiters – who have made the sites a routine part of their searches – has also become more difficult because of the overwhelming amount of information available.

He offers several useful tips to adapt job seekers' messages so they are more likely to 'go viral':

**1 Keep it simple.** Text should be pruned to a core message and always stick to the point. Don't leave room for misinterpretation. McKinnon advises that any superfluous or flowery language and clever

wordplay should be removed. 'Remember, too, that your audience may include many for whom English is a second language.' But, he cautions, brevity should not come at the expense of clarity. People should be able to tell:

→ what your message is

→ why it is important

→ why it affects them personally, and

→ what they should do about it.

**2 Tailor the message to your audience's needs.** The people you want to reach need to see what's in it for them. McKinnon says 'Relate to them by tying your story to what drives them. Make it about them and what they should do about it'. He suggests the use of pronouns such as 'you', 'your', 'our' and 'ours'.

**3 Consider your timing.** Your message could be drowned out if you post at a time when many others do the same. You may get noticed more if

you post at an earlier or later time, even if there are fewer people reading their online sources then. Experiment with different timeslots.

4 **Be selective in choosing your channels**. The three most popular channels are Facebook, Twitter and LinkedIn but influential people may be looking at other channels as well such as:

→ Blogs: try blogsearch.google.com, technorati.com twingly.com, and make friends with key bloggers and try some cross-posting.

→ Groups: with millions of groups a little browsing should locate the most popular ones to join. McKinnon also suggest joining suitable groups on Facebook and LinkedIn where you can post messages and develop a following.

5 **Craft an interesting story**. McKinnon says that, fundamentally, people care about people. 'We all seek connections, so don't just push a bunch of isolated facts. Craft a story and keep spinning it as you send out your messages. Not all your content has to be tied to one single thread, but weaving it into many of your posts will give readers continuity and help keep them coming back for more.'

6 **Push to get the word out**. McKinnon observes that it is hard to predict what might go viral and get noticed. He recommends enlist the help of friends, colleagues and other people in your network. Use every method you can think of, for example: turning your message into a blog post on your own blog, or asking other bloggers to post it or publish a link to it on their blogs. Ask your Twitter followers to re-tweet it. Post it on friends' Facebook walls and ask them to share it with their friends. Post on LinkedIn Groups and send a message to your LinkedIn network to post it as a status update.

McKinnon concludes:

As recruiters, we know how difficult it is for job seekers to capture the attention of the people who can help them the most. But if you plan your approach, focus your content, pick your medium and involve your friends, you can significantly increase your chances of getting through the noise.

*To what extent is the process of job hunting/recruitment a game played between applicants and recruiters?*

*Source: Reprinted with permission from Job Skills Information (http://www.jobskills.info/).*

Internal recruitment marketing can take place by word of mouth, staff notices, newsletters, blogs, webcasts, or social networking through media such as Twitter and Facebook. Recruiting may be on a 'one-off' basis or linked to a development programme as discussed in Chapter 18. External recruitment marketing can be done similarly through the web, other media advertisements, various public and private employment agencies and headhunting. The role of the state varies, with some countries such as Italy requiring official notification to state employment agencies. As with other marketing campaigns the selection of appropriate channels, creativity of vacancy presentation and size of budget will determine success.

## INFORMAL RECRUITING

Cultural factors are important in determining the orientation between internal and external job markets. They also influence the nature of recruitment. People may appear to have found their job or career by chance, but this apparent serendipity obscures non-random factors such as personal relationships, social networks and cultural background (McDonald, 2010). In fact, nepotism and cronyism remains the norm in many countries. Arasli and Tumer (2010) point to job stress caused by such practices in the North Cyprus banking sector. Two decades ago Papalexandris (1991) compared multinational corporations operating

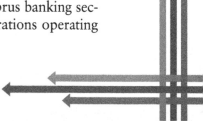

in Greece and Greek-owned companies. She found that Greek employers preferred to recruit from among relatives, and friends of the owners or existing employees. Advertisements and agencies were used only when this failed to produce suitable candidates. Greek employers paid more attention to recommendations and previous experience than to qualifications such as degrees (Eleftheriou and Robertson, 1999). In contrast, foreign-owned companies followed 'best practice' and focused on younger, inexperienced graduates attracted through agencies and advertisements. Drydakis and Vlassis (2010) studied the consequences of partial attitudes towards applicants in the case of Albanian immigrants to Greece who were 21.4 per cent less likely to be invited for interview than native Greeks.

Formalized introduction schemes along similar lines occur in other countries, serving to perpetuate recruitment from pools of like-minded people. However, they have the benefit of supplying candidates who have a more realistic view of the organization, than people attracted by recruitment advertising. The former have gained their knowledge from the informal network, the latter from PR information. As a result, word-of-mouth applicants are likely to stay longer and be more suitable than recruits obtained by advertising. Word of mouth is discriminatory since it restricts applications to established communities and excludes minority groups who are not part of informal networks (Smith, 1991: 31). Inevitably, people will recommend others from their own in-group even if they have no intention of discriminating.

Informal recruitment is common. More widely, Table 14.2 shows a comparison of UK recruitment methods in 2000 and 2006 (CIPD, 2000, 2006).

At a senior level, headhunting has become a common, if not predominant, method of recruitment. Otherwise known as executive search, consultancies are used to locate supposedly 'outstanding' people. The marked absence of women and ethnic minorities in senior positions reveals this to be a further mechanism for cloning.

**TABLE 14.2**

Percentage of firms using selected recruitment methods

| Recruitment method | 2000 | 2006 |
| --- | --- | --- |
| Ads in specialist/trade press | 86 | 66 |
| Local newspaper ads | 81 | 79 |
| National newspaper ads | 68 | 45 |
| Jobcentre Plus | 68 | 51 |
| Employment agencies | 66 | 76 |
| Speculative/word of mouth | 53+ | 49 |
| Internet | 47 | |
| Company website | – | 75 |
| Commercial job board | – | 16 |
| Links with education | 44 | 37 |
| Radio/TV | 12 | 7 |

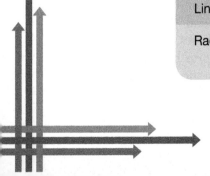

## HRM IN REALITY — ANY JOBS GOING FOR ASTRONAUTS?

Superhero, trapeze artist, goddess, astronaut and slave are just some of the jobs people have looked for online, according to an analysis of six million career searches made on Fish4-jobs.

'The vast majority of searches done on our site every month are serious ones', says Fish4jobs publisher Ian Sprackling. However, he continues:

A lot of workers seem to fantasize about a completely new career as a 'superhero' for example, or hope to see a position open as an 'astronaut'. Though we unfortunately can't claim to hold current vacancies for 'billionaires', we do have an enormous range of dream jobs available. For example, the people who thought it would be a laugh to type in 'tree surgeon', 'tarot card reader', 'wine taster' and 'lap dancer' will have been in for a surprise as positions for all four were advertised on the Fish4jobs website over the past month!

The research found that more than 1000 people could not spell common job titles correctly, including 15 different misspellings for 'secretary':

| sercretary | sacratary | secreatarie |
| secrretary | scretary | secutery |
| secetary | secretie | secitery |
| sectary | secraterie | secreatire |
| sacretery | secritarie | secrectree |

Apart from 110 people spelling 'secretary' wrongly, 51 people replaced receptionist with anything from 'recepshionist' to 'receiptionist'. Manager became 'meneger', 'managar' and 'manger' for 34 applicants. According to Ian Sprackling:

Though it's easy to miss out the odd letter here or there when doing a search on a PC, attention to detail is one of the most important things employers look for. Therefore let's hope that the person wanting to become a 'manger' hasn't made the same mistake on his/her CV. However, the people who got it completely wrong and decided they want to become a 'recepshionists' or 'secreties' should maybe consider a career change!

Top ten searches for jobs that don't exist comprised:

1 mover and shaker
2 billionaire
3 superhero
4 nun
5 busy bee
6 slave
7 astronaut
8 layabout
9 male porn star
10 trapeze artist.

Top ten unusual searches, where there have been vacancies on Fish4-jobs—comprised:

1 lap dancer (posted for a club in Blackpool)
2 'car jockey' (an excusive hotel in Scotland wanted 'car jockeys' to park guests' cars)
3 tarot card reader (two vacancies available, one working from a call centre)
4 trainee forensic psychiatrist (postgraduate post in Newcastle)
5 tree surgeon (several vacancies)
6 footwear designer (design company in West Yorkshire)
7 drag racer (company in Basingstoke has sought professional drag car drivers)
8 rectal surgeon (a vacancy was posted for a health professional specializing in 'colorectal surgery')
9 reporter for the local paper (several positions nationwide)
10 'lollipop' lady (over the summer, several councils were seeking school road-crossing attendants).

*How would you recruit an astronaut?*

Source: Reprinted with permission from HRM Guide UK (http://www.hrmguide.co.uk).

# WEB-BASED RECRUITMENT

The internet has become the dominant recruitment medium in recent years. It has become normal for jobseekers to scan employment sites on the web for opportunities; so much so that many organizations block access to job sites from their workstations to prevent employees from job hunting during working hours.

Most large organizations, and many smaller ones, make extensive use of corporate websites in their recruitment programmes. Typically, general career information is presented in an engaging manner to promote the employer brand and gain interest from prospective applicants. It has become common for the early stages of the selection process to be made accessible online, allowing résumés and CVs to be uploaded, application forms to be completed and preselection tests to be conducted.

**HRM IN REALITY** RECRUITERS WARY OF SOCIAL MEDIA

Sixty-five per cent of graduate recruiters are wary of using social media and one in seven perceives it as 'dangerous' according to research by recruitment and marketing communications specialists Penna Barkers conducted in 2010. However, nearly half (44 per cent) have some kind of presence on Facebook and one-third have uploaded graduate recruitment videos to YouTube.

Phill Lane, head of planning commented:

> We've found that graduate recruiters generally fall into two camps – those that are reticent about using social media to reach out to students, and those that actively embrace these channels. A common concern is that social media allows potential and unsuccessful candidates to post comments that are detrimental to employers' reputations. Such comments are available for all to see, even when they are unfounded or incorrect.

The latest Social Media Audit of 84 graduate recruiters found that 95 per cent acknowledged the importance of keeping up to date with online chatter to assess the impact on organizational image. However 60 per cent felt they did not have sufficient time to do this. More than half (56 per cent) felt unable to monitor their reputation well and more than one-fifth (21 per cent) undertook no monitoring.

The study found that when describing their knowledge and use of social media, nearly a quarter (23 per cent) described themselves as novices and 23 per cent as confident. No respondents considered themselves expert.

Phill Lane said:

> Graduate recruiters are often being asked to use social media as part of their day jobs in a way that is very different to their private use of the same channels. They are nearly twice as likely to blog on behalf of their employer as they are to blog on their own behalf and almost three times more likely to Tweet professionally, so it's no surprise that some of this usage is outside of their comfort zone.
>
> It's also clear that graduate recruiters attach different values to information they view online. We found that they are far more comfortable using traditional recruitment channels to review candidates. Despite the fact that there has been a number of concerns over how much people lie on their CVs, graduate recruiters believe a CV is two and a half times more reliable than information posted on LinkedIn in allowing them to form an opinion of a candidate and eight times as reliable as a Facebook profile.

Other significant findings include:

→ Seven per cent of graduate recruiters are 'evangelical' about the use of social media, 27 per cent 'try not to be too bureaucratic' towards it

→ Ninety per cent think it is important to use social media to manage their reputation

→ Twenty-seven per cent maintain a blog as part of their graduate recruitment strategy

→ Seventy-five per cent are concerned that line managers might be using Facebook to screen candidates

→ Thirty per cent don't know whose responsibility it is to monitor their reputation.

Phill Lane concluded:

What we are trying to do is work with recruiters to develop coherent plans, both for monitoring their reputation online, and also for managing it alongside the rest of their communications channels. By treating social media as part of the channel strategy, offering guidance and training, we are helping employers navigate these challenges and taking away the feeling that getting involved in social media is a risky business.

*What are the advantages and disadvantages of online information sources in comparison to more traditional methods?*

*Source: Reprinted with permission from HRM Guide UK (http://www.hrmguide.co.uk/).*

# FORMAL RECRUITING

The effectiveness of recruitment is usually measured in terms of expediency – attracting enough minimally qualified applicants. Rarely are the long-term consequences to the organization of cloned and barely adequate employees or the costs of recruitment taken into account. Doubts have also been expressed about the quality of people who are engaged in recruiting. Remarkably, the advertisements placed by recruitment agencies for their own staffing vacancies rarely ask for any knowledge of people management or selection techniques. Almost invariably they emphasize selling skills such as communication, dynamism and youth.

The likelihood of attracting 'suitable' applicants depends on the detail and specificity of the recruitment advertisement or literature. Key factors such as salary, job title, career and travel opportunities obviously influence response rates along with the 'personality' of the organization projected by the advertisement (Nolan and Harold, 2010). Not surprisingly, experienced and inexperienced job seekers show different reactions to advertisements because the experienced 'read between the lines' (Walker *et al.*, 2008). As examples of marketing, considerable effort and money can be invested in the effectiveness of recruitment

**HRM IN REALITY** JOBSEEKERS WANT TRADITIONAL EMPLOYER CHARACTERISTICS

Interesting work, recognition and reward for good performance and opportunities for promotion attract jobseekers the most, according to an Accenture global recruitment survey conducted in 2006.

The survey also shows that fashionable offerings such as corporate citizenship and diversity programmes are not as attractive to jobseekers as 'traditional' benefits such as robust rewards programmes and personal development opportunities.

A total of 4100 entry-level and experienced jobseekers in 21 countries in the Asia-Pacific region, North and South America, and Europe were surveyed online to identify the career goals they valued most. Accenture carried out the research between November 2005 and

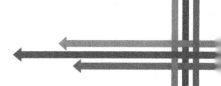

March 2006 as part of the company's efforts to make sure that it remains competitive, relevant and attractive to the most talented applicants.

'Challenging and interesting work' was selected as a priority employer characteristic by 60 per cent of all respondents with the potential for accomplishments to be recognized and rewarded coming a close second (58 per cent of respondents).

The others in the top five characteristics of greatest interest to jobseekers were:

→ opportunities for fast career growth (44 per cent);

→ indications that an employer was well-established and likely to prosper in the long term (42 per cent); and

→ indications that an organization has a particular focus on its employees (42 per cent).

Main findings of the survey:

*Percentage of jobseekers selecting priority employer characteristic*

1 Challenging and interesting work (60 per cent)

2 Recognizes and rewards accomplishments (58 per cent)

3 Provides an opportunity for fast career growth and advancement (44 per cent)

4 Financially strong/will prosper in the long run (42 per cent)

5 People-oriented (42 per cent)

6 Offers flexible work arrangements (41 per cent)

7 Innovative (33 per cent)

8 Approachable (27 per cent)

9 Team-oriented environment (27 per cent)

10 Global company (26 per cent)

11 Offers a variety of work (26 per cent)

12 Smart (21 per cent)

13 Collaborative environment (17 per cent)

14 Committed to the community/corporate citizenship (16 per cent)

15 Diverse workforce (16 per cent)

'Interestingly, we found that what is considered important to potential recruits was remarkably consistent across geographies', said John Campagnino, Accenture's global director of recruitment. 'Also notable was the fact that while we know from our own employees that corporate social responsibility and diversity are important employer characteristics – things our employees demand and place high value in – the research also validated what many of us intuitively know: namely, that more tangible benefits such as rewards and recognition are most important from an external recruit's perspective.'

*Would you place the employer characteristics in the same order of priority?*

Source: Reprinted with permission from HRM Guide (http://www.hrmguide.com/).

advertisements. However, employers do not wish to be swamped with applications from clearly unsuitable people. In some instances, honest job descriptions are designed to put off unwelcome applicants.

## TARGETING AND DIVERSITY

In the UK, the recent massive increase in higher education has produced a consequent increase in the number of new graduates. British employers are copying US organizations in targeting specific universities, courses and even lecturers. As we observed in Chapter 2, the pecking order favours 'old' universities, reflecting the prejudices of employers. This tendency is as old as the new generation of (ex-poly) universities as we can see from five 'insights' into targeting

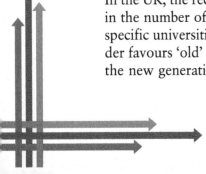

from indicated by a Glasgow consultancy, *Yellowbrick Training and Development* at the time (*Financial Times,* 25 October, 1995; *Guardian,* 26 October, 1995):

→ Competition for the 'best' graduates requires employers to have a clear idea of what they mean by 'best'. Recruitment needs to send a strong, distinctive message to these people.

→ There must be a move away from junior staff indiscriminately attracting as many applicants as possible to a more selective process involving senior management.

→ Target key institutions and specific courses.

→ Recruit whenever the needs of the business dictate, rather than to a fixed 'milkround' calendar.

→ There will be a diminished role for glossy brochures. Instead, vacation and placement jobs will be used to provide 'two-way interviews'.

It is clear that many employers are likely to use this form of targeting to ring-fence jobs so that only specific groups are considered. Essentially, they discriminate against institutions where ethnic minorities and working-class people are more heavily represented.

The choice and variety of new graduates has extended considerably in the UK during recent years as the result of government initiatives to widen access to higher education. A number of institutions have achieved university status, largely catering for students with a lower economic status, ethnic minorities and adult learners. But the people who were intended to gain the most benefit of this expansion in higher education actually 'gain somewhat less than their middle-class peers from achievement of a degree' (Purcell, 2002). And they earn less, on average, than people with similar qualifications who enter the job market with a 'traditional' graduate background.

The UK has moved from an elite to a mass-market system of university education but recruiters have not changed their practices in line with this development. On the contrary, a significant number have introduced or emphasized recruitment practices that act against graduates from non-traditional backgrounds. This is a matter of critical concern to people considering an investment in time and money in order to gain a degree.

Purcell (2002) points to a situation where:

→ graduates with non-traditional backgrounds complain that they are finding it difficult to access jobs that offer them the fullest range of opportunities and make the most of their skills; while

→ companies appear to find difficulty in understanding the diversity of higher education courses and say that they cannot fill jobs with the right *calibre* of graduates.

Purcell (2002) contends that many of these problems result from the conservative recruitment strategies adopted by many organizations. Additionally, there is evidence to show that such strategies impact more on some groups of 'non-traditional' graduates than others – specifically those in older age groups. They appear to show the highest degree of dissatisfaction with the quality of their subsequent jobs and the value of having a degree. Also, the social background of graduates, regardless of age has a correlation with their levels of pay and job satisfaction after graduation. The lower their economic status before they embarked on higher education, the lower the consequent pay and job satisfaction.

Recruitment can be used to present a more positive, welcoming image to groups which are underrepresented but, to be successful, this must be reinforced by similar initiatives further on in selection, induction and development mechanisms. Purcell (2002) identifies a

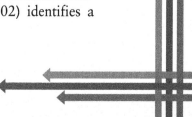

number of key characteristics of 'leading practice employers', a similar concept to that of 'employers of choice' in North America:

→ In line with the concept of employer branding, they understand that recruitment is intimately connected with marketing. This means that they have to actively sell their organizations as equal opportunity employers.

→ They are clear about the skills and competencies they need for specific jobs and do not confuse these with (irrelevant) attributes. They target sources of these skills and competencies and design their recruitment and selection processes to identify them.

---

**HRM IN REALITY** JOB SEEKERS WITH NON-ANGLO NAMES FACE DISCRIMINATION

University of British Columbia research published in 2010 has found that job seekers with typical Anglophone names are more likely to be invited for interview than applicants with Chinese, Indian or Pakistani names.

Thousands of resumés were sent to Canadian employers and the study found that applications using Anglophone names such as Jill Wilson or John Martin attracted invitations for interviews 40 per cent more often than those with names like Sana Khan or Lei Li. This suggests that Canadians and recent immigrants with non-'English' names are facing discrimination from employers. The findings help to explain why skilled immigrants with university degrees and significant work experience still do badly in today's job market.

In a working paper released by Metropolis BC, part of an international immigration and diversity research network, UBC Economics Professor Philip Oreopoulos states: 'The findings suggest that a distinct foreign-sounding name may be a significant disadvantage on the job market – even if you are a second- or third-generation citizen'.

Six thousand mock resumés were prepared for the study. They were intended to represent recent immigrants and Canadians with and without Anglophone names. The resumés were tailored to meet job requirements and sent to 2000 online job postings advertised by employers covering 20 occupational categories in the Greater Toronto Area – the largest and most multicultural city in Canada. Each resumé listed a bachelor's degree and four to six years experience. Names and Canadian or foreign education and work experience were randomly assigned.

Philip Oreopoulos said: 'If employers are engaging in name-based discrimination, they may be contravening the Human Rights Act', adding that more research is required to determine whether the behaviour is intentional. 'They may also be missing out on hiring the best person for the job.'

The study also found that apparent work experience in Canada seemed to make a huge difference in employer attitudes. Interview invites were almost doubled when mock resumés with foreign names and education listed just one previous job in Canada.

'This suggests policies that prioritize Canadian experience or help new immigrants find initial domestic work experience might significantly increase their employment chances', said Philip Oreopoulos, hoping that the study findings will help to improve current immigration and diversity practices.

*How can blatant discrimination be identified and countered in the recruitment process?*

*Source: Reprinted with permission from HRM Guide Canada (http://www.hrmguide.net/canada/).*

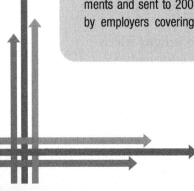

→ Where skills shortages exist they work with regional bodies and higher education institutes to draw attention to vacancies and opportunities, so that under-represented groups are positively encouraged to apply.

→ Expectations of recruits (internal and external) are managed to ensure that they understand the nature of the work, the culture of the organization and the career opportunities available.

→ Work experience and placement opportunities are offered through higher education institutes, to encourage students to gain employment skills and experience and to allow them to make sensible career choices.

→ They provide training and development programmes, plus assessment of progress, making internal progression possible.

→ They recognize the diversity and changing needs of their staff through work–life balance, flexibility and people-friendly working policies.

Ming Chia (2005) looked at the effects of academic performance, extracurricular activities and emotional intelligence (EI) on initial and subsequent interviews and on job offers. The applications of graduates with accounting majors to major public accounting firms were investigated. Ming Chia found that academic performance and extracurricular activities influenced the number of initial interviews offered. The number of subsequent interviews depended on the number of initial job interviews and also the applicant's level of emotional intelligence. Job offers were again affected by the candidate's level of emotional intelligence and the numbers of initial and subsequent job interviews.

## RESEARCHING CANDIDATES

Recruitment attracts a pool of applicants from whom successful candidates may be chosen. We now move on to the selection stages of the employee resourcing process. If a job analysis has been conducted, the criteria or competencies that are deemed necessary have been identified. These may be well-defined and focused on experience and skills, as in the 'right person' approach; or general and related to education, intellect and personality for the 'cultural fit' and 'flexible person' models. Since decision-making is based on these criteria, relevant information must be obtained from applicants. The initial response to a vacancy announcement can take a number of forms but each offers the opportunity for: (a) recruiters to obtain information on applicants; and (b) applicants to gain an understanding of the job and the organization.

The commonest responses requested are by telephone or letter. Telephone responses may be used for an exchange of information or as a means of eliciting an application form and literature describing the job and organization.

## APPLICATIONS

### Application letters, CVs and résumés

Application or cover letters and résumés or CVs (*curriculum vitae*) are typically used initially. There is some variation between cultures. North American résumés are intended to present career objectives and history (usually in reverse chronological order, starting with the present) on one tightly written typed page. CVs in the British tradition are typically

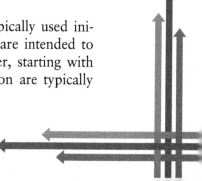

# HRM IN REALITY ATTRACTIVE WOMEN CAN BE DISADVANTAGED

Attractive women may experience discrimination when applying for jobs traditionally considered 'masculine' and where appearance is not considered important, according to research led by the University of Colorado Denver Business School published in the *Journal of Social Psychology* in 2010. This includes positions like manager of research and development, director of finance, mechanical engineer and construction supervisor. No such discrimination was experienced by attractive men.

Lead author Stefanie Johnson, assistant professor of management, said:

> In these professions being attractive was highly detrimental to women. In every other kind of job, attractive women were preferred.
>
> This wasn't the case with men which shows that there is still a double standard when it comes to gender.

The researchers reviewed numerous studies that conclude physically attractive individuals enjoy considerable advantages such as:

→ higher salaries

→ better performance evaluations

→ higher levels of college admissions

→ better responses from voters when running for public office

→ more favourable trial outcomes.

They cite a Newsweek survey of 202 hiring managers and 964 members of the public that concluded that looks are important in all aspects of the workplace, especially for women employees. Looks ranked third out of nine 'character' attributes above education and sense of humour.

Researchers identified two studies that found that being attractive made applicants for most jobs seem more suitable irrespective of gender. However, women experienced greater benefit when applying for feminine sex-typed jobs compared with less traditional roles.

In one experiment, volunteers were asked to assign photographs of 55 male and 55 female applicants according to their suitability for a variety of jobs. Appearance was considered unimportant for jobs like director of security, hardware salesperson, prison guard and tow truck driver. Attractive women tended to be overlooked in these categories, but were linked with positions like receptionist or secretary.

Researchers caution against allowing stereotypes about physical appearance to influence hiring decisions at the expense of the overall characteristics of the applicant.

Stefanie Johnson commented:

> One could argue that, under certain conditions, physical appearance may be a legitimate basis for hiring. In jobs involving face-to-face client contact, such as sales, more physically attractive applicants could conceivably perform better than those who are less attractive. However it is important that physical attractiveness is weighed equally for men and women to avoid discrimination against women.

*Can appearance have any valid bearing on recruitment?*

*Source: Reprinted with permission from PsyArticles.com (http://www.psyarticles.com).*

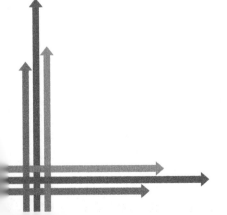

more detailed, running into two and sometimes more typed pages. The latter approach is also used by professionals in North America. In France, by contrast, advertisements often request a handwritten application letter, CV and photograph. (Many French companies use graphologists in the selection process.) French CVs are shorter and more factual than the British model and include little or no personal information such as hobbies or sporting interests. Japanese recruiters expect an official family registry record, a physical examination report and letters of recommendation in addition to CV and photographs. The use of photographs arouses disquiet in countries where equal opportunities are a major issue since they imply that selection will be influenced by appearance and colour.

Watkins and Johnston (2000) investigated the effect of physical attractiveness and résumé quality on how job applicants were evaluated during the screening phase of the selection process. A total of 180 participants read a job advertisement and one of two differing quality versions of a *curriculum vitae*. Each CV had a passport-sized head-and-shoulders photograph of either an average or an attractive female attached. A control study was also conducted where a photograph was not attached. Participants were asked to state how likely they were to offer an interview to the applicant, rate the quality of the application and state the likely starting salary to be offered to the applicant. Overall, attractiveness had no impact with high-quality applications but was an advantage when the application was mediocre. For example, average quality résumés were evaluated more positively when a photograph was attached and attractive photographs increased the rating of a mediocre application.

Job clubs and career advisers spend a great deal of time coaching jobseekers on the preparation of polished application letters, résumés and *curriculum vitae*. Paradoxically, however, coaching often results in a bland, standardized application that does not stand out among hundreds of others.

The privacy and data protection issues arising from this practice are complex. The European Union has attempted to control the use of automated selection processes through a directive that forms the basis, for example, of the UK's Data Protection Act 1998 (PPRU, 1999). The code of practice for this act states in respect of shortlisting:

1  Be consistent in the way personal data are used in the process of shortlisting candidates for a particular position.

2  Inform applicants if an automated shortlisting system will be used as the sole basis for making a decision. Make provisions to consider representations from applicants about this and to take these into account before making the final decision.

3  Ensure that tests based on the interpretation of scientific evidence, such as psychological tests and handwriting analysis, are only used and interpreted by those who have received appropriate training.

## Application forms/blanks

Both letters and CVs/résumés present a problem in a large recruitment programme: applicants may not provide all the relevant information and what there is will be presented in different ways. Comparison of applicants is easier if data is supplied in a standard form. Therefore, applicants replying to a job advertisement typically receive an application form (usually termed an application blank in North America), often asking for information already supplied. Stone-Romero, Stone and Hyatt (2003) found that completing an application blank was regarded as the least invasive of privacy out of 12 selection procedures.

Candidates face a paradox with application forms. Because information is regimented into a particular order and restricted space, jobseekers may present very similar applications.

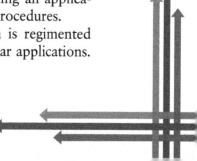

# HRM IN REALITY  DISCREPANCIES IN APPLICATIONS

A 2006 survey checked 2487 job applications for the financial services industry for discrepancies, embellishments and false information. Conducted by Powerchex, a pre-employment screening firm, the research looked at applications from a total of 1029 women and 1458 men over a six-month period. Employment histories, dates, university degrees, professional qualifications and criminal records were verified and checked against information provided by job applicants. With results compiled by the Shell Technology and Enterprise Program, the research was undertaken to discover any trends in discrepancies and the most common embellishments in job applications.

The survey found that 25 per cent of applications had at least one major discrepancy. While the majority of applicants falsifying information did so only once, some submitted forms with up to four major discrepancies. There is no significant difference between men and women in this respect.

The most common discrepancies overall relate to:

→ employment titles or duties (12 per cent)

→ employment dates

→ bankruptcy or county court judgments

→ academic qualifications

→ reasons for leaving previous employment

→ compensation received

→ directorships held

→ criminal record (less than one per cent).

The authors found that 37 per cent of applicants had gaps in their employment history and suggest that giving false information about dates (9.5 per cent of discrepancies) is probably intended to conceal this. The least common discrepancy identified related to criminal records which the authors link to applicants being aware that this can easily be checked against an existing database.

The survey found that the tendency to have discrepancies on applications increased with age, possibly suggesting that older workers feel the need to embellish in order to compete. Discrepancies were found in 28 per cent of applications from those aged 51–60, compared with 22 per cent of those aged 21–30. An alternative explanation might be difficulty in remembering the details of a complex employment history. British applicants gave false information in 32 per cent of cases overall (38 per cent of men and 26 per cent of women), compared with 25 per cent of their non-British counterparts.

The trend towards jobhopping is reflected in the survey, with 72.5 per cent having held at least two jobs in the last five years. Income had an interesting effect with people earning between £80001 and £90000 most likely to give false information (40 per cent) and those earning between £60001 and £70000 least likely to do so (nine per cent).

If the authors are correct in the assumption that all discrepancies identified are deliberate – and that is surely questionable – this survey indicates that one in four job applicants to the financial services sector are prepared to falsify information on their job applications in order to gain employment.

*Is it reasonable to assume that all discrepancies are likely to be deliberate falsifications?*

*Source: Reprinted with permission from HRM Guide UK (http://www.hrmguide.co.uk).*

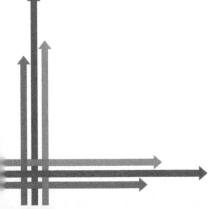

As with application letters, if candidates do not include details that distinguish them from (sometimes hundreds) of others they stand little chance of being shortlisted. Conversely, if their responses are too unorthodox, the form immediately becomes a test of conventionality.

An applicant's heart sinks when a carefully crafted résumé or CV appears to be ignored and a standard form arrives in the post or email inbox. Hours are wasted completing forms that are not read because applicants are rejected on decision criteria, such as qualifications, not mentioned in the marketing process. However, an organization that does not use application forms has a major problem dealing with hundreds of applications. How are they to be analyzed and compared? How is the choice of a shortlist to be made? Applicants will leave out crucial items of information, particularly when they are likely to have a negative impact. When and how is this information to be acquired? Interviews are expensive methods for filling in the gaps in a CV or résumé. Moreover, it is unfair to raise hopes, cause inconvenience and possibly expense for interviewees who are disqualified on the basis of information that could be picked up from an application form.

Provided that they are not devised as mediaeval instruments of torture, short and pertinent application forms will continue to have a major role in recruitment. Purcell (2002) found that employers were increasingly tailoring application forms to identify specific competencies required for individual jobs.

## QUALIFICATIONS

We noted that educational qualifications are of major importance in some cultures, for example France and Japan. In other countries their value varies, depending on the level and nature of the vacancy. Purcell (2002) found that employers tended to use degrees as thresholds for considering applicants in order to guarantee minimum potential and ability. Also, with the massive increase in degree-qualified candidates in the UK, many employers were questioning the need for a degree as a basic qualification for a wide range of jobs. Many had moved, or were in the process of moving away from qualifications as a key element in the selection process. Instead they were looking for evidence of competencies, particularly generic competencies such as communication and teamworking or personal attributes such as resilience and commitment. In particular, they were increasingly valuing experience.

Purcell (2002) noted a clear difference between employers seeking to fill professional and technical jobs and those looking for general management or administration candidates. The former emphasized degrees as a qualification, particularly in subjects that featured numeracy, whereas degrees were often thought unnecessary for entry jobs in more generalized fields. Purcell quotes the instance of one high-street bank that sought to obtain A-level (high-school graduate) candidates for a five-year management programme rather than university graduates. They targeted working-class applicants who might consider the programme more attractive than a debt-incurring degree course.

## BIODATA

Application forms and model CVs invariably include biodata; sections on experience, hobbies and other spare-time activities. Applicants frequently have serious difficulties in providing answers if they have fairly mundane interests. Does a passing interest in stamps and a

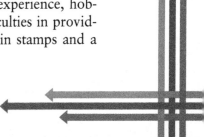

small collection of DVDs allow us to describe our hobbies as philately and music? Do holi-day snapshots justify 'photography'?

---

**KEY CONCEPT 14.2** BIODATA

Roberts (1997, p.10) describes biodata as a 'set of questions framed around "coincidences" in the lives of good performers'. People who are good at a particular job are likely to be more similar to each other than to individuals selected at random from the general population. Such similarities extend beyond work-related factors into hobbies, sports and social activities.

---

Traditionally, little use was made of this type of information. But it can be useful in discriminating (and that word is used advisedly) between applicants who are similar in most other respects. In fact, as we have already mentioned, an increase in coaching, books and professional writers aimed at preparing CVs or résumés and answering conventional forms, has resulted in applications becoming more and more similar. Supposing an employer advertises for trainee customer service assistants. The response is likely to include numerous applications from school-leavers with insufficient qualifications to proceed into higher education. These applicants may seem much the same on paper, but some have greater initiative or people skills than others. Biodata (biographical data) forms have been developed to identify non-academic qualities such as these. Biodata consists of systematic information about hobbies, interests and life history. The underlying rationale is described by Smith, Gregg and Andrews (1989: 54):

> Biodata methods are based on the assumption that *either* our characteristics are formed by the experiences we are subjected to in the course of our lives *or* our abilities cause us to select or become involved in certain types of life event. In either case, it follows that if we can accurately assess the events of a person's life, we can deduce something about their skills and abilities.

Biodata forms request detailed information of this kind, normally in the form of a multiple-choice questionnaire, covering:

→ age, sex, place of birth, residence.

→ family background, number of brothers and sisters, parental history.

→ education, work experience.

→ marital status, number of children.

→ physical characteristics (weight, height) and medical history.

→ hobbies and leisure interests.

→ reading habits: newspapers, magazines, type and frequency of books read.

Question items are largely factual or 'hard' and could be checked with other sources if necessary. Other items are 'soft' and include opinions, attitudes and feelings. It is also possible to collect the same data in a structured interview. Biodata is an expensive procedure to set up but cheap to administer, especially if the data can be entered on computer by optical scanning.

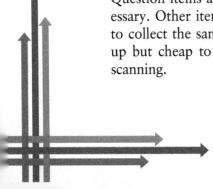

A typical biodata exercise follows an established sequence (Smith, Gregg and Andrews, 1989):

1   Job analysis identifies criteria for good performance.

2   A 'brainstorming' exercise generates relevant biodata items, such as 'interest in people', 'stability', 'imagination'.

3   Draft questionnaires are given to a large number – ideally over 300 – existing employees.

4   Replies are correlated with job performance. Items which correlate poorly or discriminate against particular groups should be discarded.

5   The revised questionnaire is then given to applicants.

6   Biodata items become out of date quickly. They should be rechecked every two years.

Biodata cannot be used in small organizations or for a 'one-off job. A simplified version could be provided as a decision aid in such circumstances. This would entail interviewers collecting narrative personal histories and scoring the information against a previously determined scale. The main use of biodata is in pre-selection of basic or entry-level jobs such as apprenticeships or posts for trainees. The logic is that if candidates are matched with existing staff, people with similar interests can be found who are likely to be suitable for the job. The greatest value of the technique is its ability to reduce staff turnover.

Biodata is specifically used to select people who are similar to those already employed. Although designed to eliminate unfairness, in a less obvious way it consolidates and makes 'scientific' an embedded practice that is prejudicial to the disadvantaged. Furnham (1992: 231) reviews a number of studies comparing biodata with job performance and finds strong supporting evidence for its usefulness. He instances Russell *et al.* (1990) who examined the life details of 900 naval recruits and measured five biographical features:

→   life problems and difficulties

→   aspects of task performance

→   work ethic/self-discipline

→   assistance from others

→   extraordinary goals or effort.

These were found to relate to other measures such as military performance rating. Furnham notes that factor analyses of biodata information relate to well-attested personality dimensions. Biodata correlate well with later supervisor ratings and can be useful in predicting turnover (Bret *et al.*, 2009).

Roberts (1997) observes that we do not need to know why biodata items are significant in order to use them. In many respects it is similar to the actuarial techniques used by insurance companies to quote for car insurance cover. Clearly, however, there are distinct implications for equal opportunities in a technique which, it could be argued, is designed not to promote diversity and that raises a possibility of breaching anti-discrimination laws unless the biodata items are carefully assessed. There is also the issue of faking to consider (Lautenschlager, 1994; Levashina *et al.*, 2009). The 'correct' (expected) answers to questions on non-cognitive tests such as biodata questionnaires are often easy to guess. In fact present-day biodata questions may be indistinguishable from items on personality tests and may attract the same problems of impression management and dishonesty. The consequent uncertainty about the effect of distorted responses on selection decisions and validity is a matter for

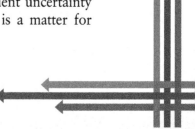

concern (Snell, Sydell and Lueke, 1999). However, Anderson *et al.* (2010) found that applicants tended to have positive views towards biodata as a fair method of collecting information.

## REFERENCES

Virtually all employers request references as a matter of course, usually without any thought as to their purpose and value. Where a purpose is expressed, they tend to serve one or both of the following functions: (a) a factual check to maximize the probability of a truthful application; and (b) to provide evidence of character or ability.

The latter assumes that the referee is disinterested and capable of making a valid judgement and is frequently misused. Candidates are most unlikely to offer referees who will write unfavourably. A classic study is frequently quoted to demonstrate the dubious value

**HRM IN REALITY**  REFERENCES CAN BE DECISIVE

Despite the emphasis placed on strong resumes and interview performance, the results of a reference check can be decisive in determining the outcome of a job application, according to a 2010 survey conducted by OfficeTeam, a leading staffing service specializing in the placement of skilled administrative professionals.

The survey was based on telephone interviews with more than 300 Canadian senior managers at companies with 20 or more employees. Respondents reported removing 26 per cent of candidates from consideration after checking their references.

When speaking to reference providers, 29 per cent said they were most interested in information about the applicant's strengths and weaknesses; 27 per cent wanted a description of their past job duties and experience. Other areas of interest included:

→ workplace accomplishments (14 per cent)

→ confirmation of job title and dates of employment (nine per cent)

→ insight into the applicant's preferred work culture (seven per cent).

The report offers advice for job seekers when selecting reference providers:

→ **Choose wisely** – Identify individuals able to discuss your abilities and experience directly relevant to the position, not just those with the most impressive job titles. Offer a mixture who can address different aspects of your background; for example, a previous co-worker to describe your interpersonal skills, a past direct report to comment on your management style.

→ **Check in beforehand** – Always ask permission in advance. Give all reference providers a copy of your resume, the job description and the name of the person likely to contact them.

→ **Be prepared** – Provide detailed contact information for your references (including name, title, daytime phone number and email address). Give a brief explanation of the nature of your relationship with each individual. Consider supplying additional references in case the hiring manager is unable to contact one of those on the list.

→ **Think outside the box** – Employers may seek out additional contacts (for example, online or using their own networks) to gain a broader view. Try to remain on good terms with past supervisors and colleagues. Be selective about who is represented in your online network on sites such as LinkedIn.

→ **Give thanks** – Express gratitude to those who agree to give references, even if they are not contacted ultimately. Update them on your progress and offer to reciprocate.

Robert Hosking, OfficeTeam executive director said:

When hiring managers narrow the field to a few potential candidates, the reference check often becomes the deciding factor. To distinguish themselves from the competition, job seekers should assemble a solid list of contacts who can persuasively communicate their qualifications and professional attributes.

*Are good references essential?*

*Source: Reprinted with permission from HRM Guide Canada (http://www.hrmguide.net/canada/).*

of the reference (Mosel and Goheen, 1958). In the study 1000 applications for the US civil service were examined and it was found that:

→ fewer than one per cent had poor references for ability or character.

→ approximately 50 per cent were described as outstanding by the referees.

→ the remaining references were at least satisfactory.

Moreover, when the work performance of successful candidates described by referees as being particularly suitable for the job were compared with those that were not, no difference was found between the two groups.

There is a growing and welcome trend for references to be simple factual checks rather than a source of 'evidence' for the selection process. There is also an issue regarding a referee's liability for the consequences of their comments. This is dependent upon employment law within specific countries.

 **SUMMARY**

Recruitment and selection are core areas of human resource management but are frequently discussed in a prescriptive manner. They are not simply techniques for filling jobs – they are also levers for organizational change, sustaining employee commitment and achieving high performance. In free market countries, the personnel profession has adopted a 'best practice' model which fits the prevailing business ideology. This model prescribes a quest for the 'right (best) person for the job'. The 'best-person' or psychometric model has achieved the status of orthodoxy in free market countries. But different models of resourcing have been developed with a greater concern for personality and attitude than presumed ability. Recruits may be sought who will 'fit in' with the culture of the corporation; who will be content to build a career within the organization; who will absorb the goals of the organization.

 **FURTHER READING**

There are many titles available covering the topic of recruitment, usually in conjunction with selection. Some of the best include:

1 *Competency-Based Recruitment and Selection* by Robert Wood and Tim Payne (John Wiley and Sons, 1998)

2 *Recruitment and Selection* by Gareth Roberts (CIPD, 2005)

3 *A Manager's Guide to Recruitment and Selection* by Margaret Dale (Kogan Page, 2003).

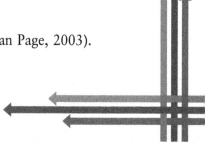

**REVIEW QUESTIONS**

1 Distinguish between recruitment and selection. What is the purpose of recruitment?

2 Why is employee resourcing more than a matter of filling jobs?

3 What do you see as the main advantages and disadvantages of the 'right-person', 'culture fit' and 'flexibility' models of recruitment?

4 What are the critical characteristics of leading practice employers or employers of choice?

5 Write a covering letter and a résumé or CV that would be suitable for an application to a HR department in a large multinational company.

6 What are the best ways of obtaining basic candidate information? What types of information can be gleaned from application forms?

7 Review the positive and negative aspects of using biodata questionnaires.

8 What roles do the internet and company websites have in recruitment? How do they compare with other recruitment marketing channels?

9 Evaluate the role of the line manager in resourcing.

10 What are the legal pitfalls in the recruitment process?

**CASE STUDY FOR DISCUSSION AND ANALYSIS**

### Saveplenty stores/Recruiting in Paris

1 The general manager of Saveplenty Stores has been interviewing applicants for sales and management jobs for 23 years. She believes that she can identify good and bad candidates by chatting to them for ten minutes. You have been placed in her department as a graduate trainee and have been given the task of organizing recruitment for a new superstore.

*How would you do this and what role should the general manager play?*

2 You are a human resource specialist with Online Solutions, a large software company. The company has agreed to set up a joint venture in Paris with a major French computer manufacturer. The venture will adapt and distribute software in French-speaking countries. Being fluent in French, you have been chosen as HR manager. Most of the other senior staff are longstanding managers from the French company. Your first task is to recruit approximately 60 junior managers and technical staff. The procedures and choices have to involve your French colleagues.

*How would you conduct the exercise and what difficulties would you expect?*

# CHAPTER 15
## Employee selection

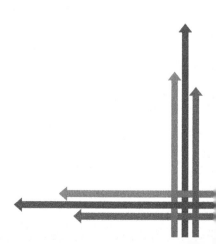

# RESOURCING DECISIONS

According to *The Dictionary of Daily Wants* (1859):

> In seeking employment, much depends upon the applicant's manner and dress; if he is rude and ungainly, and expresses himself in an awkward manner, an employer will at once conceive a prejudice against him, and curtly decline the proffer of his services. But if, on the other hand, he is pleasing in his manners and dress, he will not only be engaged to fill a vacancy, but will sometimes be taken into the establishment, although no vacancy exists. Applicants for employment should also be scrupulously neat in their attire, and clean in their persons; for an employer naturally argues that a person who is careless of himself will be equally so about about his business.

Selection is a decision-making activity: 'the psychological calculation of suitability' (Townley, 1994: 94). If the recruitment process is open, selection decision-making normally takes place in a series of stages. Recruitment marketing may attract hundreds – sometimes thousands – of responses. The first decision stage is termed pre-selection. Its purpose is to reduce applications to a manageable number with the emphasis on rejection rather than selection. Evidence is gathered from letters, résumés/CVs, application forms and possibly bio-data or screening tests. Preselection increasingly involves telephone screening interviews, ranging from basic checking of information supplied in the application process to a 20-minute question and answer sequence not unlike the formal interview. Regardless of the methods used, the intention is to arrive at a comparatively small number – the shortlist of apparently well-suited applicants.

Pre-selection is open to considerable abuse and plays a major role in the cloning process. Frequently decisions are made on arbitrary grounds, ranging from the absurd – use of the 'wrong' colour of ink, for example – to the discriminatory, excluding particular groups such as women, ethnic minorities and graduates from other than specific schools or universities. Pre-selection offers those so inclined an ideal opportunity to reject unwanted candidates without having to give detailed reasons. Unless the organization has an applicant tracking system, with each application logged, categorized and tracked throughout the selection procedure, pre-selection can be a glaring loophole, allowing hidden and illegal discrimination to take place. It is common for two identical applications to be treated differently if one is sent with an obvious ethnic minority name and the other is evidently from the majority population. Herriot and Fletcher (1990) note the irony that pre-selection and initial interview result in rejection of the largest proportion of candidates and yet these stages are the least valid and reliable.

After pre-selection screening, surviving applicants meet the formal decision-making procedure termed 'selection'. Biased selection processes can result in hiring unsuitable people (false positives); or may lead to a failure to hire applicants who would have been suitable for the job (false negatives). In the 'best person' model, selection is a matching process, where:

→ an applicant's qualities are compared with criteria deemed necessary for the job;

→ when the measurement of the former is extremely difficult; and

→ evidence for the latter is a matter of opinion.

In contrast, 'culture fit' focuses on personality and compatibility with existing staff. In Japan, the traditional approach paid attention to such matters as political views, family background and personal finances – irrelevant to the average Western company (Whitehill,

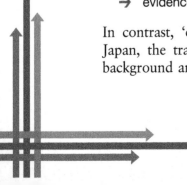

1991). We have noted that these two models are frequently confused and decision-making is a matter of identifying the 'ideal' or clone candidate, a process rationalized by talk of 'fitting in'.

An alternative explanation comes from the cognitive process interpretation of selection (Vandenberghe, 1999). For whatever reason, selectors develop a cognitive schema (mental picture) of the 'ideal' candidate for a specific job or more generally as a recruit for their particular organization. The cognitive schema may be a complicated mental network of beliefs and attitudes shared by a group of selectors against which prospective candidates are assessed.

How consistent are selectors when it comes to looking for the qualities they consider important? In a study of selection decisions in Hong Kong, Moy (2006) compared recruiters' judgement on the qualities deemed to be necessary for effective performance and the qualities they actually looked for in their selection processes. She found that conscientiousness was thought to be the most important quality for effective performance whereas the quality that they spent most time assessing during interviews was extroversion.

Sophisticated selection methods are not common in small companies, most of which continue to depend on informal methods for selection decisions – typically references and one or two interviews – although more sophisticated methods such as work samples can be effective (Wyatt *et al.*, 2010). In contrast, large organizations have adopted a range of methods to aid decision-making. Regardless of the resourcing model employed, procedures have become more elaborate. At Mazda in Michigan, USA, for example, the process involved several weeks' assessment and included application forms, aptitude tests, personal interviews, group problem-solving and simulated work exercises. These were designed to weed out 'druggies, rowdies, unionists'. Selection emphasized team-working behavioural traits rather than technical skills and successful candidates had an average age of 31, little or no factory experience and were overwhelmingly (70 per cent) male. Guest (1992) observes that the 'excellence literature', authored by Tom Peters and others, together with accounts of Japanese management methods focused the minds of many Western managers on the importance of recruitment, selection and socialization of employees. This leads to an interest in factors that can be assessed by a range of technical methods such as psychometric tests. In recent years their use has increased in Europe, particularly in the UK, whereas equal opportunities legislation has forced a different approach in the USA.

So, confining our discussion to 'best-person' and 'culture-fit' models for the moment, is selection best conducted subjectively or objectively? Smith and Robertson (1993: 255) compare the two approaches:

*Clinical,* or subjective. Just as a doctor diagnoses a medical condition on the basis of perceived sympoms, an 'expert' or experienced person reviews information on candidates. Choice is based on the expert's experience and expertise.

*Actuarial.* Comparable to calculating an insurance premium. Various factors are quantified and put into a weighted equation. For example, experience may be given twice the value of educational qualifications. The candidate scoring the highest number of points is selected.

They conclude that the actuarial approach is better than the clinical method, but not to a very major extent. But what happens in practice? Nowicki and Rosse (2002) note that the state of practice in employee selection differs markedly from the state of research. They conducted interviews with 166 line managers and asked them to describe their own successes and failures in hiring. The managers attributed successful hiring largely to luck and

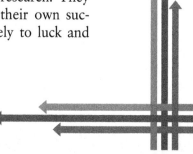

intuition, but they also acknowledged the value of more systematic and rigorous approaches to selection. From their comments it seemed that they simply lacked awareness of research on selection such as comparative validities, rather than choosing to ignore this information. There is also evidence for a strong belief among many selectors in the importance of personal experience, intuition and the ability to spot good performers (Highhouse, 2010) – to the point where, in the case of executive selection, decisions may be more often wrong than right (Hollenbeck, 2009).

From a diversity perspective, Peppas (2006) compared Hispanic and non-Hispanic hirers in the USA on the importance they attached to 26 different selection criteria. Peppas found that there were significant differences on 13 of the criteria with Hispanics tending to favour more subjective criteria while non-Hispanics preferred objective criteria.

## PSYCHOMETRIC TESTS

Psychological tests have become commonplace. Psychometric means 'measurement of the mind'. Psychometric tests purport to measure psychological characteristics including personality (see Key concept 15.1), motivation, career interests, competencies and intellectual abilities. Traditionally they take the form of pen and paper multiple-choice questionnaires but modern forms can also be presented on computer screens. Most tests require applicants to work through a large number of items in a given amount of time. Some ask candidates to choose between various alternatives, as in the following example:

*'Which of the following best describes you?'*

1    I never take time off from work because of illness.

2    Sometimes I take time off work if I am very ill.

3    I believe in taking care of myself. If I am ill, I stay at home.

This kind of item is typical of personality and motivation tests. Other tests use pictures and geometrical shapes. Tests of number ability might offer a series of numbers and ask for the next two:

2 4 8 16 ? ?

This is a simple illustration – tests normally include items of increasing difficulty. The limited amount of time allowed ensures that few people can complete all items correctly.

### KEY CONCEPT 15.1  PERSONALITY

Many lay people and psychologists believe that personality is a definite 'something' with a continuing existence at all stages of an individual's life, manifesting itself in every situation that person encounters. Generally expressed in terms of types or traits, the latter form the basis of most personality tests used for resourcing and the documentation employed for many performance appraisal systems. An alternative approach is to regard personality as an artefact of a particular set of circumstances. In other words, apparent personality depends on the meaning individuals give to a particular situation.

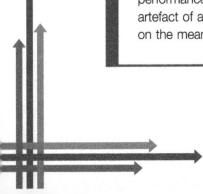

Users argue that they provide valuable evidence that is not revealed by other methods. Additionally, there is a widespread belief that they are somehow objective, contrasting strongly with the subjectivity of interviewing. Candidates often feel that they may justifiably 'sell' themselves in an interview, creating an excessively favourable impression, whereas tests will magically reveal the truth. They give resourcing the semblance of scientific professionalism (Townley, 1989).

Tests are based on the psychometric model (Key concept 15.2) which '... assumes that there is an optimal set ... of psychological characteristics for success at any human activity (in this instance, success at a particular job)' (Kline, 1993: 374). However, in our discussion of human resource planning we have seen that identifying such optimal sets is extremely difficult in practice. Specifically, job or personal specifications derived from traditional job analysis are backward-looking: they do not describe requirements for the future, as many tightly prescribed 'jobs' disappear in favour of more fluid, flexible roles. Older notions of psychological 'dimensions' by which jobs and people are matched are being replaced by the more complex multi-dimensional concept of competencies.

---

**KEY CONCEPT 15.2** THE PSYCHOMETRIC MODEL

The dominant approach to selection in British and US textbooks. In its traditional form, it grounds the 'best-person' model in psychological theory and testing. It embodies the use of refined techniques to achieve the best 'match' between job characteristics identified by formal job analysis and individual characteristics measured by psychological tests, structured interviews and other assessment methods.

---

Psychological testing has been used for different purposes in mainland Europe and North America, with the UK taking an intermediate view. The reasons for this are complex and reflect different traditions. The 'softer' European approach has relied on more descriptive, observational methods such as projective techniques and qualitative performance tests that draw on psychoanalytic theory. Conversely, the American approach has been dominated by behaviourist attitudes, emphasizing 'objectivity' and the quantitative use of data. This led to the development of a massive range of 'paper and pencil' tests, suitable for individual or group use. Many European selection theorists have never been convinced of their merits. However, in recent years, growth of a more systematic methodology has meant that the two approaches have converged to a considerable extent. Table 15.1 shows some of the advantages and disadvantages of using tests.

Jenkins (2001) reviewed 17 surveys of psychometric test usage published between the early 1970s and 2000. The wide variation in methodology, sampling sizes and sample frames made it difficult to provide precise estimates of test usage for specific periods. However, a clear growth in use was seen from the 1980s onwards, with evidence of widespread adoption by large organizations in particular. Wolf and Jenkins (2006) used case studies of organizations to identify the factors behind this and checked their consistency with Workplace Employee Relations Survey (WERS) data to see if these were national trends in the UK. The regulatory environment was found to be the most important factor: organizations were using tests as a precaution to protect their selection decisions from any challenge.

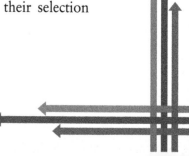

**TABLE 15.1**

Advantages and disadvantages of tests

Source: Adapted from Furnham (1992, p.39).

| Advantages | Disadvantages |
|---|---|
| → Test results are numerical – allowing direct comparison of applicants on the same criteria. | → Responses can be faked on many tests to give a 'desirable' score. Some include 'lie detectors' to overcome this. |
| → Tests provide 'hard' data that can be evaluated for their predictive usefulness in later years – i.e. compare predicted with actual performance. | → Some people lack sufficient self-insight to give accurate responses. |
| → Tests provide explicit and specific results unlike interviews and references that can be vague or 'coded'. | → Tests are unreliable – temporary factors such as anxiety, headaches, illness can lead to variable results. |
| → Tests measure substance rather than image. | → Tests are invalid – many tests do not measure what they say they measure. |
| → A battery of tests can cover a comprehensive range of abilities and personal qualities. | → Tests are irrelevant – many tests do not measure qualities that are relevant to a specific organization, such as honesty and punctuality. |
| → Tests are 'scientific' – empirically based with a grounding in theory. They are reliable, valid and discriminate between good, average and mediocre. | → Tests require minimum literacy and a grasp of American jargon. |
| → Tests provide a conceptual language to users, enhancing understanding of behaviour. | → Good norms do not exist for most populations – comparison with white, middle-class, male US students has little practical value. |
| → Empirical data from tests provide objective evidence to justify decisions. | → Tests are unfair to anyone who is not a white, middle-class, male American because most have been constructed using them as a reference population. |
| → Tests provide insights and explanations for behaviour. They can be used to justify individual rejections. | → Freedom of information legislation opens 'objective' data to greater scope for challenge than vague, unrecorded interview data. |
| | → Firms tend to use the same tests so that practice effects and knowledge of desirable answers can destroy their value. |

Jenkins (2001) considers that large organizations are more likely to use tests because they have a greater number of vacancies across which to spread the fixed costs associated with testing, and they are more likely to have specialized human resource specialists who are familiar with and trained for psychometric testing. Wolf and Jenkins (2006) also found the growing formal professionalization of HR departments to be a significant factor.

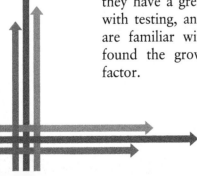

## HRM IN REALITY    MAKING THE MOST OF PSYCHOMETRICS

Change management and training consultancy, cda, believes that too many companies are failing to maximize on the benefits of using psychometrics as an integral part of their recruitment policy. This is restricting return on investment and development of staff potential.

They quote the CIPD Recruitment, Retention and Development Survey 2006 indicating that 60 per cent of organizations are now using psychometrics as part of the recruitment process. Costs are significant, typically averaging up to several thousand pounds including training and licences. Nevertheless, it is said to represent a worthwhile investment. Comprehensive use of psychometrics is thought to result in a 'better-fit' recruit who is more likely to meet an employer's requirements, stay longer, contribute more and generally provide a better return on investment.

However, a significant percentage of firms using psychometrics only do so in the initial recruitment process and are not continuing to apply the approach as part of ongoing development.

Lisa Michelangeli, psychologist at cda said:

> We encounter too many instances of what we call 'Silver Bullet' mentality. While there has been an increased recognition of the value of psychometrics, there can be an assumption that its integration into the recruitment process is a guarantee that it will result in a calibre of recruit who will have a long-term positive impact on the organization.

Some firms are not achieving full-value realization of their investment because they do not use the outputs of the psychometrics to inform development beyond the recruitment stage. For example, if a group of individuals is recruited, the outputs of the personality assessment can inform the development of the team and how they interact with each other. This is an example of the invaluable opportunities that we encounter organizations not always making the most of. Psychometrics are not a one-fix cure-all but have to be an integral part of the ongoing development process.

Consultants with cda report that this situation can be exacerbated by discontinuity between HR and line management. Often the HR function is involved only in the hiring (and firing) process and not in employee development, which can be regarded by line managers as their territory.

Lisa Michelangeli continues:

> Given the sums of money companies are investing, we believe that it is essential for business leaders to ensure that their HR experts are educating and then supporting line management in incorporating the output of psychometrics into the various stages of the employee lifecycle.
>
> For example, when line managers are trained in benefits such as the objective basis for performance management that psychometrics can provide, they embrace the practice wholeheartedly. However, it does need the business leaders to instigate clear policy to ensure that the essential instruction and ongoing support is properly implemented by HR and incorporated by line management. Leaving it to chance is not good enough.

*Why do many organizations fail to make use of psychometric results after recruitment and selection?*

*Source: Reprinted with permission from HRM Guide UK (http://www.hrmguide.co.uk).*

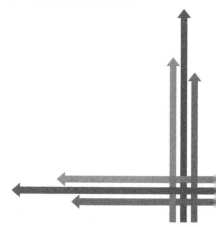

# CRITICISM OF PSYCHOLOGICAL TESTING

Increasing use of psychological testing has caused disquiet among psychologists for at least twenty years, particularly the proliferation of personality assessments. There are many available on the market promoted by people without adequate training and making extravagant claims about their value and effectiveness. Many employers, including those with human resource specialists, do not have the ability to identify good and bad products. In an attempt to distinguish the trained from the untrained, the British Psychological Society has introduced a Certificate in Occupation Testing Competence. Some of the most important criticisms are:

1 **Justification.** Furnham (1992: 5) criticizes the underlying research which 'justifies' specific personality measures on a number of grounds:

   → The personality characteristics chosen are often arbitrary and uninformed. Often they are historical relics, long-abandoned and condemned by psychologists but still exploited as commercial products.

   → Statistical analyses tend to be simple and naive, leading to more findings of significant differences than there are in reality (type II errors). Usually, simple correlations are used – rather than 'robust and sensitive' multivariate statistics – when all the variables involved are multi-factorial.

   → Most studies are exploratory, with no theoretical basis and are not part of systematic programmes. As a result, they tend to be 'one-off, sometimes with interesting implications but no particular consequence.

   → Organizational and social factors are often ignored – personality may not be the only relevant factor.

2 **Validity.** Blinkhorn and Johnson (1990) criticize personality tests as predictors of job performance when compared with ability and aptitude tests. They argue that their validity coefficients are often no better than chance. However, other specialists consider that personality tests are still valuable if they are used carefully and are not taken to be the main predictors. For example, 'conscientiousness' is linked to job performance and 'extroversion' scores are useful predictors for sales ability. Ironically, projective tests, with the lowest predictive value, have higher 'face' validities – looking as if they do what they are supposed to do – than psychometric tests, especially to younger and less educated people (Sartori, 2010).

The greatest difficulty with personality tests is that candidates can lie. Moreover, they can fake results in different ways and to a varying extent (Zickar, Gibby and Robie, 2004). Individuals may score highly on extroversion because they are extroverts. Alternatively they can present themselves as outgoing because it is clear from the job description that selectors are seeking extroverts. There is also some evidence of a small to medium practice effect when internal candidates take repeated tests for vacancies (Hausknecht, 2010). In a meta-analysis, Li and Bagger (2006) looked at the effects of impression management and self-deception on the criterion validity of personality constructs. They used the balanced inventory of desirable responding (BIDR) and failed to find any evidence that impression management and self-deception created spurious effects on the relationship between personality measures and performance. They also found that removing the influence of these two dimensions from measures of personality did not significantly attenuate the criterion validity of personality variables.

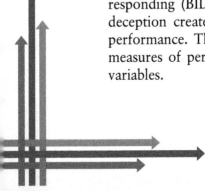

It has also been argued that, since tests are based on personality theory, they cannot be interpreted without knowledge of the theory in which most selectors are untrained. Another contentious issue is the effect of practice. If applicants are exposed to the same test on more than one occasion, they gain from the previous experience, often remembering answers. The doubts about personality tests have become well-known. Lievens, Highhouse and De Corte (2005) asked experienced retail store supervisors to rate job applicant profiles described on two dimensions including General Mental Ability (GMA). Unlike previous research, supervisors were also informed about the method of assessment used. The importance attached to extroversion and GMA decreased when store supervisors knew that scores were derived from a paper-and-pencil test rather than an unstructured interview. Store supervisors with more selection-related experience also attached more importance to GMA.

Wood and Baron (1992: 34) consider the effect of psychological tests in terms of 'adverse impact' on ethnic minority groups: "Adverse impact" occurs when there is a significant disparity in test scores between ethnic groups, resulting in one group being disproportionately preferred over the other. The test is then said to have an adverse impact on the lower-scoring group'. They argue that the greater the degree of adverse impact, the more this has to be justified. Employers must be careful to test strictly for qualities that can be proven to be required for the job. Even when this can be demonstrated it remains important to find the method of measurement with the least adverse impact. A common problem is the effect of language proficiency on test performance. Typically, ethnic minority candidates are undergoing a selection procedure in the dominant community language, such as English, when they are stronger linguistically in another, such as Hindi or Italian. Their performance is masked by their comprehension of the questions and their ability to express their answers in a manner that is meaningful to the testers. Often, tests are time-limited. This is a reasonable gauge of mental speed for native speakers because their use of language is automatic. However, it is detrimental to people answering out of their native languages, since they need to translate at a conscious mental level. In effect the test becomes an assessment of 'proficiency in English' rather than a measure of its true objectives such as 'problem-solving ability' or 'motivation'. The test has become unfair for anyone whose first language is not English.

A classic case involving British Rail (BR) showed that, in an analysis of 4000 tests taken by potential drivers, white people were twice as successful as ethnic minority candidates. Eight guards of Asian origin took BR to an industrial tribunal on the grounds that the tests were discriminatory. The verbal reasoning tests employed were not directly related to the job and were particularly difficult for people who spoke English as a second language. BR admitted that the tests had adverse impact on Asian workers and undertook to seek the advice of the Commission for Racial Equality in developing revised selection techniques.

Similarly, the Council for Legal Education (CLE) introduced a critical reasoning test for around 2300 applicants to the English Bar's training school. The CLE had attempted to provide a test that was as fair as possible, involving two firms of occupational psychologists and Birkbeck College of the University of London. However, the test was trialled on a group of existing students that included very few from ethnic minority groups. According to Makbool Javaid, chair of the Society of Black Lawyers, it was felt that 'some of the questions would be difficult to answer for anyone who was not from a middle-class public school kind of background' (*Times Higher Education*, 18 March, 1994). The results produced a storm of protest and the tests were soon reconsidered. These reservations are widely known among human resource specialists and may explain Storey's (1994a) report of a reduction in use of personality tests around that time.

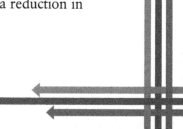

# INTERVIEWING

The interview is a social ritual which is expected by all participants, including applicants. It is such a 'normal' feature of filling vacancies that candidates for a job would be extremely surprised not to be interviewed at least once.

## Informal interviews

Many employers invite applicants for informal interviews prior to the main selection procedure. These interviews are useful for information exchange, particularly in the case of professionals (Breakwell, 1990: 10). They provide the opportunity to discuss the full nature of the job, the working environment, prospects for further development and promotion. Candidates who decide that the job is not for them can elect to go no further. To avoid interviews degenerating into pointless chats, Breakwell emphasizes that both interviewer and applicant need to have checklists of essential points to cover. Interviewers should:

→ Give a balanced picture of the job, including an honest account of its disadvantages together with a (larger) number of positive aspects. Honesty might seem dangerous but is best in the long run.

→ A description of the organization in the same terms.

→ Introduce the interviewee to other people in the department. This also allows interested parties to vet the applicant.

Blackman (2002a) investigated the common practice of informal telephone interviews. The study was aimed at determining if impoverished personality judgements of job applicants would come from telephone interviews in comparison to face-to-face interviews, given the lack of crucial non-verbal communication. Mock job interviews were used in both face-to-face format and telephone format. A significantly higher correlation was found between personality ratings of face-to-face interviewers and other sources of an applicant's personality ratings. Not surprisingly, face-to-face interviewers also rated applicants significantly higher or more favourably on personality traits that are normally best-revealed by non-verbal communication.

There seems to be some ambiguity as to whether informal interviews should be used as part of the pre-selection process by the employer rather than self-selection by the candidate. The crux of the issue depends on what interviewees have been told. If they have been led to believe that it is a truly informal information session they will not consider the process to be fair if they are subsequently told that they have not been shortlisted as a result.

## Formal interviews

A selection interview can be defined neatly as 'a conversation with a purpose' but not infrequently the purpose is obscure to the point of invisibility. More often than not 'purposeless chat' would be nearer the mark. It is a form of social interaction in which the interviewer is engaged in active person perception of the interviewee (see Key concept 15.3). From the interviewee's perspective 'one is managing a demonstration of knowledge or ability through a social vehicle, and one inevitably needs to attend to the social as well as the cognitive aspect of the interview' (Sternberg, 1994: 181). In other words, the impression created depends as much on social factors as any demonstration of experience or expertise.

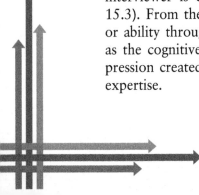

### KEY CONCEPT 15.3   PERSON PERCEPTION

The perception of other people. Cues such as facial expression, posture, gesture, body movement, tone of voice, etc., are used to evaluate their current mood and overall personalities (McKenna, 1994: 144). Each one of us has an 'implicit personality theory' based on our experience, assumptions about people, beliefs and prejudices. The evidence of our senses is used to collect data about the perceived person and attribute characteristics to them according to our implicit theory. This is a simplification process and leads to a number of well-known errors of judgement, including:

→ *Logical error:* assuming that certain traits are always found together, e.g. if a person is described as 'objective' we tend to perceive them as 'cold'.

→ *Halo effect:* the tendency to perceive people as all 'good' or all 'bad'.

→ *Stereotyping:* seeing all members of a particular group, e.g. Africans, Scots, to have the same characteristics. Stereotyping leads to prejudice.

For many unskilled or semi-skilled jobs, the formal interview tends to be perfunctory and can be over in a few sentences. This is not necessarily a bad thing. For decades, the evidence has been that the more sophisticated and lengthy proceedings entered into by major organizations often have been no better in terms of outcome. According to Sternberg (1994: 182):

> Interviewers tend to prefer interviewees who are relaxed, who put the interviewers at ease, who are socially as well as verbally facile, and who have some degree of interpersonal sparkle.

In fact, the interview has attracted severe criticism for a very long time. W.D. Scott is quoted as having said in 1915 that the selection interview is not a dependable selection method (Lewis, 1985: 150). Since then the interview has been attacked on the grounds of its subjective nature, questionable validity and unreliability. Webster (1964) noted some significant findings:

→ First impressions count. Interviewers make their minds up in the first few minutes, then seek evidence to support their opinion.

→ The candidate's appearance is the most significant factor, followed by information on the application form.

→ Unfavourable evidence is valued more strongly than favourable evidence.

→ The interviewer's opinion 'comes over' to the candidate during the interview and influences the candidate's further performance in an unfavourable or favourable direction.

A study of medical students in Canada (Razack *et al.*, 2009) found that sequential 'mini-interviews' were preferred to traditional unstructured interviews. Candidates felt they were enjoyable and allowed them to be competitive.

Hebl and Skorinko (2005) investigated the significance of acknowledgments made by physically disabled individuals in an interview setting, and looked at timing of an acknowledgment in relation to impressions formed by evaluators. 137 participants observed interviews of disabled applicants who acknowledged their disability at the beginning, middle, or

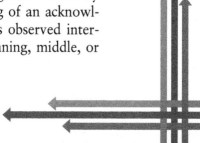

## HRM IN REALITY  SNAP JUDGEMENTS ABOUT FACES

Recent research indicates that when we see an unfamiliar face, our brains decide intuitively whether a person is attractive and trustworthy within a tenth of a second – so quickly that reason may play no part in the process.

The study by Princeton University assistant professor of psychology, Alex Todorov, and research student, Janine Willis, published in the July 2006 issue of *Psychological Science* asked about 200 observers to look at 66 different faces flashed onto a screen for one of three time durations: 100 milliseconds, 500 milliseconds or a full second.

The observers recorded whether they found the face to be trustworthy or not, and also how confident they were in their analysis. Similar experiments tested for other traits, such as likeability, competence and aggressiveness. Judgements made after the shortest exposure time correlated highly with those made without time constraints. With more time to decide, observers' judgements did not change, but their confidence in them increased.

Alex Todorov said:

> The link between facial features and character may be tenuous at best, but that doesn't stop our minds from sizing other people up at a glance. We decide very quickly whether a person possesses many of the traits we feel are important, such as likeability and competence, even though we have not exchanged a single word with them. It appears that we are hardwired to draw these inferences in a fast, unreflective way.

Todorov said that it is not yet clear why the brain makes such snap judgements. However, functional magnetic resonance imaging of brain activity suggests that the part of the brain that responds directly to fear may be involved in judgements of trustworthiness.

> 'The fear response involves the amygdala, a part of the brain that existed in animals for millions of years before the development of the prefrontal cortex, where rational thoughts come from. We imagine trust to be a rather sophisticated response, but our observations indicate that trust might be a case of a high-level judgement being made by a low-level brain structure. Perhaps the signal bypasses the cortex altogether', Alex Todorov continued.

He cautioned that the findings do not imply that quick first impressions cannot be overcome by the rational mind:

> As time passes and you get to know people, you, of course, develop a more rounded conception of them. But because we make these judgements without conscious thought, we should be aware of what is happening when we look at a person's face.

*If our brains are 'hard-wired' to make snap judgements on faces, what are the likely consequences for fair selection?*

*Source: Reprinted with permission from HRM Guide USA (http://www.hrmguide.com).*

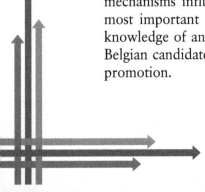

end of a job interview or made no acknowledgement at all. Applicants who acknowledged their disability early in the interview were perceived more favourably than those who acknowledged at the end of the interview or not at all.

In a Canadian study, Chapman and Webster (2006) also found that signal and expectancy mechanisms influenced candidate intentions and job choice. These effects appeared to be most important for applicants who had multiple job opportunities and less pre-interview knowledge of an organization. Comparing two impression management techniques used by Belgian candidates Proost *et al.* (2010) found that ingratiation was more effective than self-promotion.

# HRM IN REALITY JOB HUNTING ADVICE

Today's competitive market requires considerably more effort than in recent years according to a survey conducted in 2010 by Canadian specialized staffing service *The Creative Group.*

The survey, based on over 500 telephone interviews with advertising and marketing executives, found that an average of six applicants are interviewed before a vacancy is filled.

The report offers advice to improve the chances of job seekers meeting with potential employers:

1 **Do your prep work** – Applicants with more than basic knowledge of the job and company are better able to comment on their potential contribution. The researchers suggest visiting the organization's website, Facebook page or Twitter feed; searching online and using your personal network for additional information.

2 **Put your best foot forward from the start** – Be polite to reception staff, smile and behave warmly with everyone you meet. Resist the temptation to contact friends while waiting; you'll make a better impression by remaining focused.

3 **Be aware of body language** – Factors such as eye contact, facial expression and posture will affect the impression you make on hiring managers. When practising for an interview, ask friends or family for feedback on any off-putting mannerisms.

4 **Have a good story to tell** – Prepare appropriate examples of how you have helped solve business problems. Outline the challenge faced, your actions and the outcome achieved.

5 **Come with interesting questions** – This isn't the time to inquire about salary or paid vacation. Asking about aspects of the job you might not have anticipated or the process for collaborating on projects confirms your interest while providing information to help determine if the job and company is right for you.

6 **Be yourself** – A hiring manager wants to experience a genuine person who is right for the position. Avoid rehearsed or contrived responses.

7 **Remain positive** – If you are unsuccessful use it as a learning experience. If you have developed good rapport with the interviewer, request feedback on how you might improve. Accepting rejection graciously will leave a positive impression.

Lara Dodo, a vice president for The Creative Group's Canadian operations commented:

> Given the high calibre of talent currently available, employers are being prudent in their hiring and are weighing their options before extending an offer. By taking the time to thoughtfully prepare for the interview, including researching the company and substantiating previous accomplishments, job seekers can impress hiring managers and land the job.

*Can you suggest ways in which prejudice based on names may be avoided?*

*Source: Reprinted with permission from HRM Guide Canada (http://www.hrmguide.net/canada/).*

# EVALUATING METHODS

How do we judge the value or effectiveness of interviewing – or any other method of selection? Before going further it is useful to consider the four basic requirements (Smith, 1991: 32):

1 *Practicality.* Selection methods must be practical in a given situation – for example, cost, convenience and time available. Attitudes of employers and candidates to the methods are also relevant.

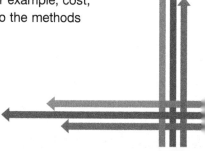

2  *Sensitivity.* The ability of a method to distinguish one candidate from another. Interviews may rank a number of candidates fairly closely, whereas tests may give a wide range of scores.

3  *Reliability.* How consistent are the results? Conventionally, there are three forms of reliability measure:
   – Comparison over time. If a method is used on the same group of candidates on different days, are the scores likely to be similar? This is sometimes called test – retest or intra-rater reliability.
   – Inter-rater reliability. If two or more assessors are involved, how much agreement is there between them?
   – Internal consistency. If several items in a test or procedure are meant to measure the same characteristic, such as sociability, how close are the ratings?

4  *Validity.* Does the method achieve its purpose in distinguishing the most suitable applicants from the others? Three measures of validity are available:
   – Face validity. Does the method appear to be measuring what it is supposed to measure? This is important because it is essential that candidates believe that they have been fairly treated. Disappointed applicants frequently complain about apparently irrelevant interview questions or test items. For example, one selection test includes the question: 'Do you like tall women?' Whether or not this has deep psychological significance, its appearance is enough to bring derision on the test.
   – Construct validity. To what extent does the method measure a particular construct or human quality such as commitment?
   – Predictive validity. How well does the method predict the suitability of a successful candidate?

Reliability and validity are expressed as correlational coefficients where perfection is represented by 1.0 and pure chance is shown by zero. Table 15.2 shows the estimated validities of different selection methods. Establishing the validity of a particular procedure logically requires the employer to take on a large number of applicants, good and bad, and then compare their job performance with that predicted by the selection method. This kind of predictive validity study is impractical in most circumstances. Sometimes termed 'the one that got away' problem, we never know how the people we did not select might have performed.

**TABLE 15.2**
Comparative validities

Source: Based on Bertua *et al.* (2005) Smith (1991) and Roth *et al.* (2005).

| Validity range | Methods | Rating |
|---|---|---|
| 0.5 to 0.6 | Cognitive ability tests | Good to excellent |
| 0.3 to 0.39 | Work sample tests | Acceptable |
| | Biodata | |
| | Assessment centres | |
| | Structured interviews | |
| Less than 0.3 | Personality tests | Poor |
| | Typical interviews | |
| | References | |
| | Graphology | |
| Chance (0) | Astrology | |

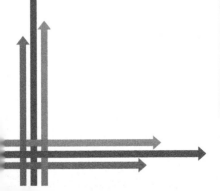

Research shows that similar results can be obtained by a method termed 'concurrent study' where selection methods are employed on existing employees at the same time as the selection procedure is taking place. Performance of existing employees is then correlated with prediction scores of the selection method. Again, however, this is rarely done, partly because accurate performance measures are difficult to obtain for many jobs.

In a meta-analysis on the validity of over 500 tests of general mental ability and specific cognitive abilities, Bertua, Anderson and Salgado (2005) found that both types of tests are valid predictors of job performance and training success. They calculated that operational validities were in the magnitude of 0.5 to 0.6, in line with previous meta-analyses in the USA.

Fairness is a further requirement: specifically, candidates' perceptions of the equity of the process. Good candidates are more likely to accept an offer if they consider that the procedure has been fair, effective and considerate while rejected applicants will continue to have a positive view of an organization's employer brand if they feel they have been fairly treated. Schleicher *et al.* (2006) looked at a sample of 754 applicants to a US government agency. They found evidence that candidates' perception of their 'opportunity to perform' was an important predictor of their overall feelings about the fairness of the selection process, and was the single most important procedural rule after receiving negative feedback. Intriguingly, in a simulated exercise, Schinkel, van Dierendonck and Anderson (2004) found that rejected candidates who were given performance feedback were more likely to show negative effects on core self-evaluations and affective well-being than those who were simply given rejection messages.

People have different perceptions of fairness. Truxillo *et al.* (2006) related the 'Big Five' personality measures (neuroticism, extroversion, agreeableness, conscientiousness and openness to experience) to candidates' perceptions of post-test fairness, themselves and the hiring organization. After controlling for gender and test score, they found that personality accounted for significant variance in all three, although the relationship with fairness was weakest. Neuroticism and agreeableness were the personality factors that most consistently predicted candidate perceptions. In a later study (Truxillo *et al.*, 2009) candidates showed more favourable attitudes towards the selection process when they were provided with explanations of various procedures.

Moscoso and Salgado (2004) examined students' reactions to selection methods in Spain and Portugal. They found similar results in both countries with interviews, résumés and work sample tests being rated most highly and contacts, integrity tests and graphology being judged least favourably. Face validity and opportunity to perform were the most important bases for a favourable judgment. In a meta-analysis including samples from 17 countries, Anderson *et al.* (2010) found three clusters of perceived favourability among candidates:

→ *most preferred* – work samples, interviews.

→ *favourably evaluated* – résumés, cognitive tests, references, biodata, personality inventories.

→ *least preferred* – honesty tests, personal contacts, graphology.

In a study of 255 HR professionals involved with selection, assessment and training, Furnham (2008) found that assessment centres, cognitive ability tests and work samples were considered to be the most valid techniques. However, interviews came first in terms of practicality. The professionals had positive views about personality and ability tests but were only familiar with a limited range of tests, particularly those related to personality and motivation. Table 15.3 shows the relative usage of different selection methods in the UK.

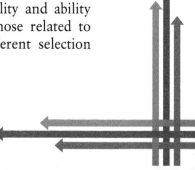

**TABLE 15.3**
Selection methods
used by large orga-
nizations in the UK,
2006

Source: Based on CIPD
(2006).

| Method | % |
|---|---|
| Interviews | |
| Structured panel | 88 |
| Structured one-to-one | 81 |
| Biographical | 85 |
| Competency-based | 85 |
| Telephone | 56 |
| Tests | |
| Specific skills | 82 |
| General ability | 75 |
| Literacy/numeracy | 72 |
| Personality/aptitude | 60 |
| Online selection | 25 |
| References (pre-interview) | |
| Employment | 50 |
| Academic | 37 |
| Assessment centres | 48 |
| Group exercises | 48 |
| Other | 6 |

## INTERVIEWS REVISITED

Since the late 1980s there has been a revision of opinion concerning the value of interviews (Smith, 1991; Eder and Harris, 1999). Earlier research findings were based on small samples. The use of meta-analytic techniques allows the combination of statistics from a number of small studies to give much larger samples. For example, Weisner and Cronshaw (1988) combined validity coefficients from 150 studies and conclude that interviews can be more valid than suspected. In fact, their validity depends on the type of interview. Traditional, or unstructured interviews comprise the vast majority and are generally no more than cosy chats. Their validity was found to be 0.2 (very poor) whereas structured interviews, especially those based on job analysis, were found to be significantly better with a validity of 0.63.

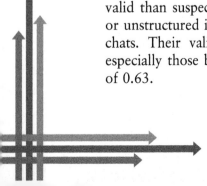

## HRM IN REALITY    SUPPORT FOR SITUATIONAL INTERVIEWS

Research from the Richard Ivey School of Business at the University of Western Ontario published in *Applied Psychology: An International Review* found that employers using situational interviews (a structured format in which all candidates are scored on the same job-related questions) introduce less bias and are fairer when recruiting women and visible minorities, irrespective of the strength of any associated employment equity programme.

The researchers explain that these programmes, a legal requirement for some larger Canadian organizations, are intended to increase the recruitment of under-represented groups. However, they are subject to criticism for encouraging reverse discrimination and contributing to low workplace morale.

The current findings suggest that the qualifications of visible minorities recruited under an employment equity programme are less likely to be questioned if situational interviews are used. This affects a significant minority of the Canadian population (currently 10 per cent rising to 20 per cent by 2017, according to Statistics Canada).

Situational interviews present job applicants with potential workplace dilemmas. Candidates' responses to the same predetermined questions are scored as 'outstanding', 'minimally acceptable' or 'unacceptable'. The researchers contrast this with the free-flowing nature of an unstructured interview that may result in the hiring process appearing inconsistent and subjective, especially when used by organizations with employment equity programs.

Lead author Gerard Seijts, associate professor of organizational behaviour said: 'The situational interview encourages organizations to treat job applicants consistently. It allows job candidates to be hired on the basis of merit'.

*Are situational interviews likely to be as enjoyable for a candidate as unstructured interviews?*

*Source: Reprinted with permission from HRM Guide Canada (http://www.hrmguide.net/canada/).*

---

Structured interviews are conducted to a format, rather than a script, and focus questioning on the job rather than irrelevant incidentals such as holidays and golf. Two standard methods are:

→ Criterion referenced interviews, based on job analysis with a set of questions geared to experience and skill for interviewers to choose from.

→ Situational interviews, based on the 'critical incidents' technique. A reasonable number (typically 20) of real-life work incidents are obtained from jobholders or their supervisors. Possible ways of dealing with these situations are outlined and rated as suitable or unsuitable, frequently on a points system. These situations are presented to candidates as hypothetical problems and responses evaluated against predetermined ratings.

Peeters and Lievens (2006) investigated how structured interview formats, instructions to convey favourable impressions and applicants' individual differences influenced the use and effectiveness of verbal and non-verbal impression management (IM) tactics. They found that interview format affected the kind of tactics used, which in turn positively influenced interviewer evaluations. Behaviour description interviews triggered self-focused defensive tactics, whereas situational interviews triggered other-focused tactics. Instructions to convey a desirable impression also enhanced the use of specific tactics (self-focused and other-focused verbal

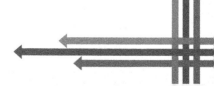

IM) and moderated the effects of individual differences on IM use. They suggest that non-verbal behaviour might be less intentionally controllable in selection situations.

Moscoso (2000) reviewed evidence on the criterion and construct validity of the interview. Based on the content of questions included in selection interviews, Moscoso identified two types of structured interview: the conventional structured interview and the behavioural structured interview. Criterion validity studies generally support the view that behavioural structured interviews show the highest validity coefficients. Moscoso found a lower level of investigation into construct validity but concluded from studies available that conventional structured interviews and behavioural structured interviews were clearly measuring different constructs. Also, behavioural structured interviews seemed to produce more frequent negative applicant reactions than conventional structured interviews.

A further study by Salgado and Moscoso (2002) included a series of meta-analyses on the construct validity of conventional interviews and behavioural interviews. Conventional interviews typically include questions aimed at checking credentials, description of experience and self-evaluative information. Behavioural interviews consist mainly of questions regarding job knowledge, job experience and behaviour descriptions. They found that conventional interviews assessed general mental ability, job experience, the 'Big Five' personality dimensions and social skills. Behavioural interviews, on the other hand, mainly assessed job knowledge, job experience, situational judgement and social skills. Although there was some overlap, the two main forms of interview seemed to be different.

In a more recent study, Krajewski et al. (2006) analyzed data from 157 applicants to managerial positions and found a significant correlation between predictions from past-behaviour structured interviews and subsequent job performance. Situational interview formats did not produce a significant correlation. They also found a closer relationship between past-behaviour structured interviews and relevant cognitive ability measures, assessment centre exercises and personality traits.

Van Iddekinge et al. (2006) examined differences in criterion-related validity estimates among ratings from individual interviewers and interview panels in the US army. They found considerable variation in interviewer validity coefficients in relation to multiple performance criteria. Results also indicated the importance of adopting a multivariate perspective when evaluating interviewer validity differences. Similar findings emerged for ratings averaged within interview panels. However, most or all of the variance for some interview-criterion combinations appeared to be due to statistical artefacts.

To be effective, an interview must be more than a friendly chat. The greater the degree of planning beforehand, the greater the likelihood of a higher degree of validity as a selection tool. The function of the interview is to obtain predictive evidence regarding a candidate's likely performance on specific criteria. The questioning style can be linked to the kind of evidence required and may take one of three principal routes:

*(Hypothetical) problem-solving questioning* in which the candidate is presented with situations to evaluate or solve and which can be expected to test the candidate's abilities in a number of respects, e.g. intellect, grasp of information, problem-solving ability, lateral thinking, practicality, creativity, etc. Situational interviews have been found to increase candidates perceptions of fair selection (Seijts and Kyei-Poku, 2010).

*Behavioural (past) event questioning,* which assumes that previous handling of situations and problems predicts an individual's future performance in similar circumstances.

*Patterned behavioural event (life) questioning,* which attempts to identify an individual's career or life strategy, establishing how rational and sensible changes in that person's life have been and drawing conclusions about stability, seriousness of application and likely motivation. The 'culture fit' approach emphasizes this perspective. For example, Japanese

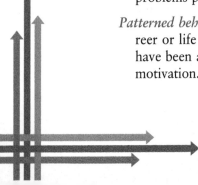

companies such as Toyota are more interested in personality than technical skill. They look for a personal philosophy that fits the corporate culture. Modern call centres similarly seek a range of competencies from customer care through to commitment-related qualities (Callaghan and Thompson, 2002).

Kutcher and Bragger (2004) investigated the potential of structured interviews for mitigating biases. They asked 133 participants to observe videotaped interviews, varying between structured or unstructured interview scripts and average weight or overweight job applicants. The results confirmed a bias against overweight interviewees which was moderated by the use of structured interviews. A further study with a greater level of structure in the interviews appeared to increase the moderating effect.

Blackman (2002b) investigated structured and unstructured employment interviews in relation to the assessment of applicants' job-related personality traits. The hypothesis was that unstructured interviews would lead to more accurate personality assessments since interviewees would feel less constrained by a script and more readily manifest their true selves. Behaviour in mock job interviews (structured and unstructured) was coded by an independent rater. Self-ratings of job-related personality traits on the California Q-set were obtained for each interviewee, together with ratings of their personality from the interviewer and a peer of the interviewee. A correlation analysis supported the original hypothesis, showing that average self–interviewer and peer–interviewer agreement was significantly greater when interviews had used the unstructured method.

Barclay (2001), however, comes out in favour of the behavioural structured interview. A survey of the use of behavioural interviewing in selection for UK organizations showed that both interviewers and applicants were positive about the method. Barclay identifies the following as key benefits:

→ better quality information-gathering leading to improved selection decisions.

→ more consistency and improved skills of interviewers.

→ better opportunities for applicants to explain their skills.

But Barclay also recognizes limitations in respect to training, practice and time required and scoring.

Other approaches that have ethical considerations to take into account include stress interviewing and 'sweet and sour'. Stress interviewing, where the candidate is pressurized, sometimes aggressively, is justified on the basis that the job is pressurized and, therefore, it is important to establish how the candidate is likely to perform under stressful circumstances. 'Sweet and sour' interviews are those where interviewers take completely different approaches, one pleasant, one unpleasant in an attempt to gain a wider range of responses from the candidate.

## Preparation for interviews

Training for interviewers stresses a number of factors conducive to making a good impression on the candidate. The interviewer should ensure that relevant information (application form, etc.) is read beforehand – it is surprising how many interviewers are found to be reading such material for the first time *during* the interview. The interview should take place in an appropriate environment – a quiet room without interruptions, with comfortable but business-like furniture and so on. The candidate should be put at ease as much as possible.

A major change in recent years has been the improvement in applicants' interview techniques. Redundant staff are commonly given the opportunity of outplacement counselling, which normally includes advice on CV preparation and coaching in interview technique.

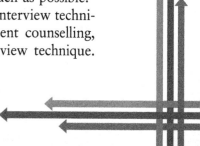

## HRM IN REALITY   CANDIDATES WHO PERFORM LAST FINISH FIRST

It isn't surprising when singers who advance to the next round in competitions such as 'American Idol' each week are those who performed at the end of the previous week's episode. Researcher Wändi Bruine De Bruin of Carnegie Mellon University has found that participants appearing towards the end of juried competitions seem to do better than those performing at the beginning – and this finding has implications for recruitment and selection.

Bruine De Bruin's latest paper, published in the journal *Acta Psychologica* (2005), describes her studies on European figure-skating competitions and the Eurovision Song Contest, a pop song competition that has taken place in Europe since 1956 (and which, like American Idol, includes voting by fans watching at home). Bruine De Bruin found that participants appearing near the end of the contests received higher marks from judges than those who performed earlier. This phenomenon, known as the serial position effect, doesn't just affect would-be pop idols; it is possible that the effect may occur in other situations such as job interviews and student exams.

Bruine De Bruin found that the effect was progressive, with scores increasing throughout the competitions, not just when judges evaluated all candidates at the end of each contest, but also when they were asked to rate each individual performance after it had been completed. Bruine De Bruin conducted some of her research at Eindhoven University of Technology in The Netherlands.

'A friend of mine asked to go last in a series of job interviews, after hearing about my research. She got the job. I like to think that she got the job because she has great skills, but order effects may have tipped the balance for her', Bruine De Bruin said.

*Can you suggest any ways to minimize order effects in selection procedures?*

*Source: Reprinted with permission from HRM Guide USA (http://www.hrmguide.com).*

---

Managers who are rarely involved in selection, perhaps only conducting interviews once or twice a year, are at a disadvantage against trained applicants. Interview coaching is similar in principle to training politicians for television appearances. Astute trainees can learn how to mask insincerity and to promise the earth with apparent conviction.

Against trained interviewers, the most useful tactic for applicants is to become familiar with the company they are applying to join. This requires research on the company's history, products or services and its reported strategy. Knowledge of the industry or sector in which it operates is also valuable. This information should not be acquired by pestering the recruitment section on the telephone. Given the number of applications to advertised vacancies at present, this is likely to be unwise. Whether or not any direct questions are asked on these subjects, applicants who have researched the territory will be able to form their responses in a way which makes it clear that they have done so.

### Interviewing techniques

There are significant variations in the way employers conduct interviews. The most common method is the 'singleton' interview when the candidate's fate is determined by one session with a single interviewer. For obvious reasons, this method is likely to be regarded as

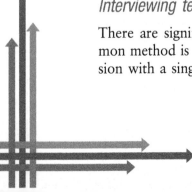

unfair by interviewees who are not selected. There is no check or record of bias on the part of the interviewer who may have made a judgement on a complete whim.

A long-standing method which attempts to overcome this problem is the panel or board interview, involving a number of interviewers. The use of interviewers with particular experience of the job being filled has been identified as a strength of the European Union staffing model – although many other aspects of the EU's selection procedure have been castigated (Ban, 2010). Typically in a panel interview, two or three people ask questions in turn. A classic format involves an 'operational' interviewer, usually a line manager from the department offering the job and a personnel interviewer, normally from the HR department. There may be an additional chairperson. Each asks questions appropriate to their areas of expertise, the operational assessor asking task-related questions and the personnel assessor investigating career aspiration and motivation. The board is sometimes much larger: there are instances of seven or nine interviewers.

Superficially, the panel interview is judged to be fairer since all questioning takes place in a public arena and candidates' responses are heard by all parties. It also offers the candidate a more varied range of questions, expanding the evidence available to the assessors. As a consequence, personal bias should have less effect. However, the situation is likely to be more stressful for candidates. There are also opportunities for organizational politics to enter the situation, especially when the procedure is an internal selection.

Dipboye *et al.* (2001) looked at unstructured panel interviews for corrections officers and found a weak aggregate level of validity in the prediction of job performance and training success. Aggregate analyses also showed only a small incremental contribution to the prediction of job performance from panel judgements relative to paper credentials, and found the two sources of information to be only weakly related. But there was a considerable variation in simple and incremental validity at the level of individual panel members and among sub-groups of panels. They conclude that aggregate analyses underestimate the validity of the typical unstructured panel interview.

A further variant is the 'sequential' method, with two or more interviews but with the candidate only being expected to face one interviewer at a time. This method carries most of the advantages of singleton and panel interviews with fewer of the disadvantages.

It is possible to use group interviews in certain circumstances. We will see later in this chapter that they are useful within assessment centre programmes as information sessions.

As with many other aspects of selection, interviewing has been formalized and packaged into training programmes available for both selectors and candidates. Untrained assessors are likely to conduct interviews in an unstructured way. Interview training is a useful component of management training. The best training programmes encourage people to become aware of their body language and questioning styles, helping them to develop interview techniques that open up fresh areas of evidence. Many junior managers and job club participants have had the opportunity to see themselves 'in action' on video, taking part in mock interviews. Initially demoralizing (for most), it is an invaluable method of feedback.

Packaged training methods have led to a certain sameness, however, and seasoned job applicants and interviewers now enter into formalized duals where each participant is aware of the underlying dynamics. Typically, interviewers are taught to:

→ Ask open, not closed, questions to elicit the maximum information. Questions beginning with how, what, why, when, reduce the frequency of yes/no answers and force candidates to think about their replies.

→ Provide supportive body language that suggests interest in what the candidate is saying without indicating approval or disapproval.

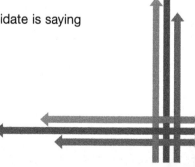

→ Employ questioning styles such as the use of funnelling. Here the interviewer asks a succession of how, what, why, questions on the same subject in an attempt to achieve a depth of evidence.

→ Consider factual or hypothetical questions, such as 'How would you go about setting up a telephone system for a remote island in the Pacific?' Provided that the interviewee is not a qualified telecommunications engineer, an applicant for a totally unconnected job will have to think hard to provide a full, imaginative but practical answer.

## WORK SAMPLES

Interviews suffer from a basic problem: they obtain answers from candidates which, in effect, are unverifiable claims. When asked what they would do in a particular situation it is only natural for candidates to give the answer which they feel the interviewer wants to hear. There is no guarantee that a candidate would actually behave in that way in a real situation. In addition, it is common for candidates to exaggerate their abilities or experience and play down their inadequacies.

The work sample technique attempts to overcome this problem by asking candidates to take on 'mini jobs' in a selection situation. Properly designed work samples capture key elements of a real job. As such, they are realistic rather than hypothetical or abstract and should include features of the context in which the job functions. Work samples have shown some of the highest validity scores compared with other selection methods (Smith, Gregg and Andrews, 1989: 70). Roth, Bobko and Mcfarland (2005) re-examined classic literature supporting work sample tests as among the most valid predictors of job performance and suggest that the level of the validity may be approximately one-third less than previously thought. They also found that work sample tests were associated with an observed correlation of 0.32 with tests of general cognitive ability.

Work samples are comparatively easy to organize and even the smallest of companies could employ the simpler forms such as:

→ a typing test for jobs requiring keyboard skills

→ bricklaying

→ role playing

→ group decisions

→ presentations

→ reports.

The most sophisticated of work sample procedures include in-basket tests, sometimes called in-tray exercises. Normally used for managerial jobs, candidates are given a typical in-tray containing a selection of material such as letters to be answered, reports to be analyzed, items to be prioritized, etc. They are given instructions on what to do and a time limit. Standard scoring methods are available. Work samples are often used as part of an assessment centre programme. Wyatt *et al.* (2010) found that high and low performers in a medium-sized recruitment company could be distinguished using two work sample tests that had been constructed using the critical incident technique. In fact, there was a high correlation between test results and individual performance.

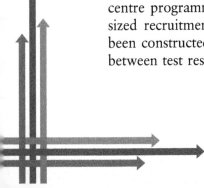

# ASSESSMENT CENTRES

Recent surveys indicate increasing use of assessment centres, especially by large companies. They have been heavily researched in recent years, with the emphasis on their reliability and predictive validity. They show up well in comparison with most other forms of selection or assessment such as interviews and psychometric tests (e.g. Krause *et al.*, 2006) Meta-analyses indicate respectable validity coefficients for assessment centres in predicting managerial success (Hermelin *et al.*, 2007). However, as we will discuss shortly, their use is not entirely without difficulties.

Assessment centres are procedures and not necessarily places. They function on the principle that no individual method of selection is particularly good and no individual assessor is infallible although overall assessment centre ratings correlate well with preliminary interviews and cognitive tests (Dayan, 2008). Accordingly, they use multiple methods and several assessors in structured programmes that attempt to minimize the inadequacies of each method and cancel out the prejudices of individual selectors. Inevitably, assessment centres are very expensive methods of selection. However, cheaper methods are focused towards past or present performance. This may be adequate where applicants are being assessed for jobs that are broadly similar to their current or previous work. When this is not the case, and applicants are being considered for more stretching tasks, they fail to provide the evidence as to how candidates are likely to perform. Most management promotions come into this category. Good managers need to demonstrate knowledge, skills and abilities that may not have been required at lower levels. How can we identify these characteristics? Assessment centres are particularly useful in this respect because they are focused on potential. They bring taxing problems and challenges to candidates in a situation that allows systematic observation and measurement of their performance.

The origins of the assessment centre lie in the violent history of the 20th century and the need for officer selection. Originally devised by the German army in the 1930s, assessment centre techniques were soon taken up in other countries. The British War Office Selection Board subjected candidates to a three- to four-day assessment, geared to evaluate leadership and organizational abilities. This included exercises in which intending officers had to negotiate obstacles such as rivers with a motley collection of squaddies and an assortment of ropes, planks and oil drums. They also included lengthy interviews and long written reports.

Some modern assessment centres with an 'outward bound' inclination continue to include such exercises, but most consist of group discussions, psychometric tests, interviews and exercises such as 'in-basket' work samples and presentations. The underlying intention is to measure applicants on the competencies deemed to be appropriate to the job. Simulations in the assessment centre are designed to bring out the behaviour which demonstrates possession of these competencies. The intention is not to estimate current ability but to predict future performance, possibly at higher management levels.

After World War II the method spread to the public sector and then to industry. The first industrial application was at the American Telephone and Telegraph Company (AT&T). Their experience had a major influence on subsequent use elsewhere, following a number of studies in which employees were compared with initial assessment centre evaluations. These studies showed a significant correlation between the evaluations and subsequent work performance (Smith, Gregg and Andrews, 1989).

The model form of assessment centre is an expensive process (Byham, 1984). A typical assessment centre involves six participants and lasts from one to three days. As participants go through the simulations they are observed by assessors (usually three) who are specially trained in observing and evaluating behaviour. Assessors observe different participants in

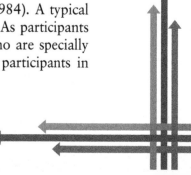

each simulation and take notes on special observation forms. Then, after the simulations are completed, assessors spend one or more days sharing their observations and reaching agreement on evaluations of participants. Their final assessment, contained in a summary report for each participant, gives a detailed account of participants' strengths and development needs as well as an evaluation of overall potential for success in the 'target' position. Based on Blanksby and Iles (1990), the following list sets out the seven conditions that classically characterize assessment centres.

1   A number of assessment techniques must be used, of which at least one must be a simulation. Simulations could take the form of work samples, group exercises and in-baskets. Simulations are designed to bring out behaviours that are related to dimensions of performance on the actual job in question.

2   There must be multiple trained assessors.

3   Ratings must be pooled between assessors and assessment techniques in order to provide a judgement on selection, training or development programme.

4   Overall assessment of behaviour has to take place at a different time from the observation of behaviour.

5   Simulation exercises must be pre-developed to elicit a number of desired behaviours. They must be tested in advance to ensure that the results are relevant to the organization and that they are reliable and objective.

6   All dimensions, qualities, attributes or characteristics to be measured by the assessment centre must be determined by some form of job analysis.

7   The assessment techniques used must be designed to provide evidence for the evaluation of these dimensions.

## Problems with assessment centres

Whether or not it is costed in financial terms, the impact of assessment centres on management time is considerable. Managers may appreciate the value of high-quality selection procedures, but will be reluctant to devote so much time unless all other parts of the selection process have been thorough. For example, Hilton Hotels International conducted a one-day assessment centre as a final stage in a selection process for general managers. They contracted an outside provider to conduct exhaustive online tests to ensure that candidates who got that far deserved their place (Beal, 2004).

The effectiveness of an assessment centre depends upon its design and the anticipation of problems. Additionally, the traditional process is group-based and is unusable in situations where only one or two candidates are being considered. Common design faults have been well documented (Dulewicz, 1991):

→  The criteria for measurement are too woolly. Often, the competencies on which candidates are being assessed are very poorly defined and not expressed in behavioural terms that can be measured.

→  The competencies are not mutually exclusive and overlap each other. Candidates are rewarded or penalized twice, depending on their strength in a particular area. Moreover, if candidates become aware of the criteria on which they are being assessed they can skew their behaviour accordingly (König et al., 2007).

→  Criteria are tied to the past, rather than being forward-looking.

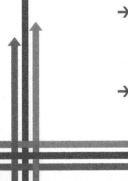

→ Exercises are badly designed and do not relate to experiences that are likely to occur within the organization. Alternatively, and perhaps because of this, they do not relate to the assessment criteria.

→ Assessment centres contain a wide range of procedures, from group exercises to psychometric tests. Results from these procedures take a variety of forms. Integrating the results is complex, particularly when combining evidence on single competencies from a number of procedures. Poor technical design at this stage will lead to misleading findings.

→ Poor assessor training. Line managers are unlikely to be good assessors unless they have been trained to avoid pitfalls such as 'halos and horns'. Also they require guidance on the range and skew of their assessments. Assessors need to be consistent in how they pitch their ratings, avoiding over-leniency or severity. For example, in a study of the rating of ethnic minority candidates for the Dutch police, de Meijer *et al.* (2007) found that assessors were using more (and irrelevant) cues to judge minority candidates than those from the ethnic majority. Having to assess too many candidates at the same time can also lead to poor rating quality (Melchers *et al.*, 2010).

→ Poor pre-selection and briefing of candidates. The consequence is that some candidates flounder from the beginning of the programme. Others become hostile towards a procedure that appears to them to be unfair or disorganized.

→ Poor programming, leaving both assessors and candidates unsure of what they are supposed to be doing. They may be allotted too little or too much time at different points in the assessment.

→ Inadequate handling of the programme events due to lack of coordination or commitment.

→ Inadequate (or non-existent) follow-up. This may occur in the form of badly handled feedback counselling or inaction on assessors' recommendations.

→ Poor evaluation of candidates' experience and assessors' performance on the programme.

Dulewicz (*ibid.*) considered that there were three broad phases that accounted for most of these difficulties:

1 programme design
2 selection and training of assessors
3 effective follow-up action.

He attributed many of the shortcomings to inexperience. Assessment centres are involved and complex. Good design is dependent on the knowledge and skills to design and develop what is a 'highly precise and sophisticated tool'.

## Graphology

Graphology, or handwriting analysis, has a long history on the mainland of Europe dating back to the Ancient Greeks and Romans (Thomas and Vaught, 2001). Its modern form originated in Italy in the 17th century and was further refined in France and Germany where it is used widely. The essence of graphology is that analysts claim to be able to describe an individual's personality from a sample of their handwriting. Their theoretical base is that of trait psychology which holds that personality has a number of fixed dimensions that are relatively unchangeable and do not depend on the situation. This is not to say that people do not change, indeed many graphologists believe their strongest asset to be the identification

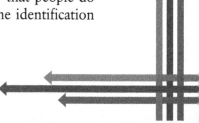

of neurotic or stress-related conditions that may be transient. Some graphologists also claim to be able to detect such characteristics as alcohol problems, homosexuality and dishonesty.

For example, the following excerpt from a press report stated that the British company S.G. Warburg accepted a graphologist's opinion that 'cramped' handwriting indicated drug addiction:

> The recent candidate interviewed for a junior job in Warburg's computer department provided an excellent CV, and seemed able and confident in the course of two interviews. His handwriting sample, however, was abnormally cramped. The lines were crooked and the letters spidery and badly squashed. At best, it seemed the writing of an ill-educated child. But Mrs Nezos [graphologist] thought otherwise. For an employer like Warburg, the prospect of hiring a drug addict is too frightening to contemplate. The man was turned down for the job. (*Independent on Sunday,* 20 October, 1991)

It is commonly believed that handwriting analysis is routine and highly respected in many continental European countries whereas it is generally regarded with disdain in most English-speaking countries. However, there are signs of increasing acceptability in countries such as the USA: In the trade journal *Pest Control,* a contributor lauded the services of a handwriting analyst (Tennenbaum, 2005):

> Heidi mentioned that she could do analysis for potential employees. 'I can tell you everything about them, whether they'd be better in sales, for example', she said. All she would need is a page-long essay from each candidate ... the content doesn't matter as much as the handwriting itself.

The contributor was so impressed, it seems, that he no longer takes on new employees for his US$2 million company without her verbal approval (at less than US$75 a time) or a more expensive typed report. 'With that report in hand, I can decide whether I still want the person based on résumé, references and overall "gut feeling". ... Nothing else work[s] this consistently well. It's amazing.'

In a similar pitch at a trade audience in New Zealand (Hogenesch, 2004: 10) another graphologist acknowledged that handwriting analysis has not yet caught on in that country, but that it is 'a science' and 'recognized as an authentic tool': 'Handwriting ... is like body language. It is virtually impossible to hide or disguise personality characteristics by altering one's handwriting. In the eyes of a skilled handwriting analyst the true personality is unfailingly revealed'.

The evidence is not so flattering. Cox and Tapsell (1991) compared analyses by graphologists and non-graphologists of 50 handwriting samples provided by managers on a training course. When assessment centre results were compared with the handwriting analyses, they found that the graphologists did slightly worse than the non-graphologists in rating the candidates. Moreover, the two graphologists failed to agree with each other! Thomas and Vaught (2001: 35) surveyed the available literature on graphology and concluded that there was no evidence that handwriting analysis was a valid method of predicting job performance:

> ... there is virtually no research that supports the use of graphology as an effective selection technique. At its best, it has only moderate reliability. There is little evidence that graphology is accurate in predicting personality traits, or that the narrow traits that many analysts infer from handwriting samples correlate with job performance. Finally, there is no evidence of a direct link between handwriting analysis and various measures of job performance.

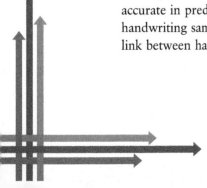

Some critics are even more damning, for example Dr Barry Beyerstein, professor of biological psychology at Simon Fraser University in British Columbia (Ellin, 2004: 10). Dr Beyerstein said:

> Graphology is a pseudoscience that claims to be a quick and easy way of saying how someone's wired, but there's no evidence that this is encoded in handwriting.
>
> In these litigious times, you can't ask people about their sexual orientation or previous run-ins with the law or their home life or marital status. But graphologists make statements that no legitimate personnel person could make with such a degree of certainty and you can find a lot of gullible people who'll sign on. You'd think hard-nosed business people would be the last to be taken in, but they lap it up.

Why is graphology apparently so popular in continental Europe and supposed to be increasingly used in the USA and the UK (Ellin, 2004)? Thomas and Vaught (2001) speculate that one reason may be that it has an apparent face validity that people can relate to: it looks like it 'should' work as a method. However, in studies on selection techniques in a number of countries (Anderson and Witvliet, 2008, Anderson *et al.*, 2010), graphology was one of the least favoured by candidates. Finally, Bangerter *et al.* (2009) found that graphology is not as popular in continental Europe as claimed, that few job advertisements asked for handwritten letters and the handwritten letters that were received by employers were rarely analyzed by graphologists. They concluded that the popularity of graphology is a self-perpetuating myth.

 ## SUMMARY

In free market countries, the personnel profession has adopted a 'best practice' model that fits the prevailing business ideology. This model prescribes a quest for the 'right (best) person for the job'. To achieve this goal, criteria are used to rate prospective applicants by means of selection techniques, including biographical data, interviews, psychometric tests, group exercises, simulated work samples and even handwriting analysis. The most definitive form of selection is likely to take place within the context of assessment centres, involving several assessors and a variety of selection techniques. The 'best-person' or psychometric model has achieved the status of orthodoxy in free market countries. Elsewhere different models of resourcing apply. For example, in Japan there is a greater concern with personality and background than presumed ability. Recruits are sought who will 'fit in' with the culture of the corporation; who will be content to build a career within the organization; who will absorb the goals of the organization.

 ## FURTHER READING

1  *The Professional Recruiter's Handbook: Delivering Excellence in Recruitment Practice* by Jane Newell Brown and Ann Swayne (2009), published by Kogan Page is based on techniques used by successful companies.

2  *The Assessment and Selection Handbook: Tools, Techniques and Exercises for Effective Recruitment and Development* by Ian Taylor (Kogan Page, 2008) is a 'how to' on the assessment centre approach.
Books on interviewing include:

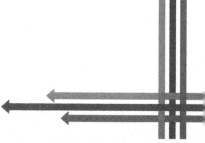

3 *The Interview Book: Your Definitive Guide to the Perfect Interview Technique* by James Innes (Prentice Hall, 2009); and

4 *Effective Interviewing* by Robert Edenborough, (Kogan Page, 2002).

5 Robert Edenborough has also written *Assessment Methods in Recruitment, Selection and Performance: A Manager's Guide to Psychometric Testing, Interviews and Assessment Centres* (Kogan Page, 2005).

# REVIEW QUESTIONS

1 Are selection methods objective?

2 When and why would you conduct an informal interview?

3 Discuss the merits and disadvantages of unstructured, structured and behaviourally structured interview methods. Evaluate Peters' approach against our discussion on the various types of interview.

4 Review the advantages and disadvantages of using psychometric tests for small and large organizations. Are psychometric tests fair?

5 What criteria can be used to judge the effectiveness of selection methods?

6 Define 'validity' and 'reliability' in your own words.

7 Why are some selection methods used more often than others?

8 What are the arguments for and against the use of assessment centres for employee selection?

9 Explain why hiring managers do not necessarily use the best decision-making practices in employee selection.

10 Is it possible to guarantee equality of opportunity in a resourcing process?

# CASE STUDY FOR DISCUSSION AND ANALYSIS

## Everylang

Everylang is a small, fast-growing translation bureau. It needs to keep tight control of its costs in a very competitive market. The owner considers that its success depends on quality, presentation, speed of work and the ability to provide translations to and from any language. Most of the work is from the main European languages and into English. The company employs 12 staff, while the remaining work (over half) is farmed out to freelance translators who are only paid for the work they do. They communicate with the office by a variety of means, including courier, post, fax and email. It is sometimes difficult to get and maintain relationships with top-quality freelancers.

*Situation*

Everylang has now grown to the point where the owner-manager is too busy with marketing, finance and developing new customers to be able to cope with the day-to-day operations. You have been invited as an external consultant to advise on selecting an office manager for Everylang. It is apparent that the owner knows a great deal about the translation market but is inexpert in managing people. The owner is keen to promote a member of the existing staff, partly in order to improve motivation but mainly in order to keep costs down. Five have applied and you have been provided with the following job summary on which to base your initial thoughts.

| | |
|---|---|
| *Title*: | Office manager. |
| *Pay*: | Translator salary + 30 per cent + profit-related bonus and benefits. |
| *Main purpose of job*: | Day-to-day running of Everylang office, ensuring that incoming work is dealt with and returned to agreed standard of quality and delivery time. |
| *Functions*: | Providing quotations for customers; dealing with enquiries; allocating work to full-time staff or freelancers; recording and progressing all incoming work, delivery on time and to the agreed quality; dealing with complaints; finding and monitoring new freelancers; completing computer records for billing and administration; and dealing with any personal problems among staff. |
| *Personnel specification*: | None existing. |

## Applicants

*Helen.* Age 42. Five years with Everylang. No formal qualifications. Translates French and Spanish. Ex-secretary. Has been translating for almost 20 years and knows a large number of other translators. Very efficient, quick and accurate. She is keen on long legal translations and has developed a considerable knowledge of business law in French-speaking countries. Pleasant personality but a little short-tempered. She has a good working relationship with other staff members but tends to keep her distance and does not socialize with them. Likes to take a six-week holiday at her parents' home in France every summer. She has an arrangement with the owner to take this partly as unpaid leave.

*John.* Age 36. Has been 12 years with Everylang. High school qualifications in French and Italian. Also has a diploma in translating and interpreting in the same languages. A great language enthusiast, he is proud of his standard of work. He translates mostly from French, specializing in letters and product information. Takes a keen interest in the welfare of the other staff. They have a considerable regard for him, respecting his professionalism and his interest in them. Over the last year he has had arguments with the owner over policy and thinks the company is growing too fast. He believes that the ever-increasing pressure of work is leading to inadequate checking of translations. Personally, he is quite efficient but pays too much attention to small details. Has been thinking of going self-employed.

*Jill.* Age 32. Three years with Everylang. Left school at 16. Took evening classes in French for several years. Cheerful, chatty person who gets on well with customers. Not a particularly good translator but useful for short French translations needed quickly. Can understand Scandinavian languages quite well, particularly Norwegian – she worked in Norway as a managing director's personal secretary for two years. The other staff do not respect her as a translator and often patronize her. She copes well, brushing off their remarks and getting on with her job. She has applied for a number of other jobs recently – without success.

*Francesca.* Age 26. Graduate in Spanish and Italian. Diploma in Translating. Also speaks Portuguese. Has 18 months' service. Undoubtedly the best translator in the office. She had considered becoming a language teacher but dropped out of the training programme after a year and joined Everylang. She is younger than the other staff and relations are not particularly good. Gets on extremely well with major clients who find her vivacious personality attractive to deal with. She gives customers a feeling of confidence in her abilities. Francesca sees Everylang as a long-term career job, is ambitious and enthusiastic about major expansion. At the moment, she is having major problems with her

pre-school age child who suffers from asthma. Sometimes she takes time off with little notice. She has promised the boss that her difficulties will be sorted out soon.

*David.* Age 55. Three years with company. BA and MA in German Literature. Former export manager, made redundant from a major company. He translated on a freelance basis before joining Everylang. He is the only full-time German translator. A workaholic – he never seems to leave the office and is always ready to work overtime to complete a piece of work. He is regarded as bookish by the other staff. Sometimes David is extremely critical of other people's standard of work.

He considers the qualifications of some of the other translators to be inadequate for the jobs they are doing. In general, he thinks that the owner is unimaginative and has failed to capitalize on non-European languages. He is very unhappy about his salary which is much lower than his pay as export manager. However, he knows that he cannot cope with the uncertainties of being a freelancer.

The company does not have a performance assessment system.

*What criteria would you apply in seeking the most suitable applicant?*

*What methods would you use to obtain further information about these candidates?*

*What are the likely advantages and disadvantages of promoting any one of these individuals?*

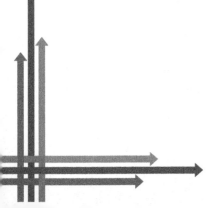

# CHAPTER 16
# Performance management

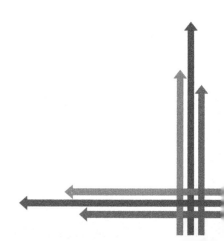

# PERFORMANCE ASSESSMENT

In the last chapter we looked at how the performance of potential recruits can be predicted from evidence collected during selection procedures. In this chapter we extend our debate to the evaluation of current employee performance.

Performance assessment has a long history based on comparative judgements of human worth. In the early part of the 19th century, for example, Robert Owen used coloured wooden cubes, hung above workstations, to indicate the performance of individual employees at his New Lanark cotton mills in Scotland. Various merit ratings were represented by different coloured cubes, which were changed to indicate improvement or decline in employee performance (Heilbroner, 1953, cited in Murphy and Cleveland, 1995, p.3). As with the employee selection techniques described in Chapter 15, modern performance assessment developed from sophisticated rating systems designed by work psychologists for military use during the two world wars. By the 1950s, such methods had been adopted by most large US business organizations, spreading worldwide thereafter. Initially, performance assessment was used to provide information for promotions, salary increases and discipline. More recently, performance measurement has had wider purposes:

→ To identify and enhance desirable or effective work behaviour.

→ Reinforcing this behaviour by linking rewards to measured performance.

→ Developing desired competencies and building human capital within organizations.

Enthusiasts for performance assessment argue that it serves a key integrating role within an organization's human resource processes. Firstly, it provides a checking mechanism for resourcing policies and procedures, evaluating the quality of recruits and hence the underlying decision-making process. Secondly, it monitors employee commitment and the relevance of their working behaviour to business objectives. Thirdly, it provides a rationale for an organization's pay policies. Taken at face value, these intentions seem entirely compatible with an integrated and strategic approach to human resource management. In reality, however, the definition and measurement of good performance is a controversial matter, involving fundamental issues of motivation, assessment and reward.

All aspects of performance management (see Key concept 16.1) arouse controversy, especially appraisals and performance-related pay. Critics point to weaknesses in their methodology and basic philosophy. There is also some debate about the use made of performance information, particularly in public services (Moynihan and Pandey, 2010; Al-Raisi et al., 2010). Employees are often dissatisfied with the methods of performance management systems and managers are frequently reluctant to engage in the process because of its confrontational nature. At a deeper level, it can be argued that if true commitment exists, performance management is superfluous. In too many organizations it enforces the compliance of an unhappy workforce. However, Pettijohn et al. (2001) demonstrated that a positive attitude towards appraisal – from employees and managers – is possible if managers are provided with information designed to increase the benefits of engaging in the evaluation process and more thought is given to the appropriateness of measurement criteria.

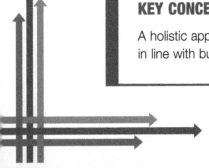

**KEY CONCEPT 16.1** PERFORMANCE MANAGEMENT

A holistic approach to assessing and improving the performance of an organization's people in line with business objectives.

Despite its problematic reputation, the use of performance assessment has been reinforced through the increasing prevalence of performance-related pay (PRP). As we will see in Chapter 17 this is based frequently on an oversimplified view of work motivation. Employers, consultants and neo-liberal politicians remain wedded to PRP schemes despite considerable evidence against their effectiveness as motivators. Fletcher (2001) argues that performance assessment has widened both as a concept and as a set of practices, becoming more obviously a part of HRM's strategic integration of human resource activities and business policies. Consequently, research and discussion of the topic has moved beyond measurement issues and criticisms of the accuracy of performance ratings to encompass the social and motivational aspects of assessment. Fletcher divides current concerns into two thematic groups:

→ The content of appraisal: contextual performance, goal orientation and self-awareness.

→ The process of appraisal: appraiser-appraisee interaction, and multi-source feedback that have cross-cultural implications and are open to technological change.

We begin with a discussion of the environmental factors that have led to the widespread use of performance assessment techniques. These include legislation, the demands of technological change, increasing flexibility and diversification, and changes in workforce composition. We proceed to look at the way in which organizations favour certain stereotypes of good performance. The next section evaluates decision making underlying the adoption of performance assessment strategies. Finally we discuss the activities involved in assessment such as appraisal and counselling.

# THE ENVIRONMENTAL CONTEXT

The business environment exercises both a direct and an indirect influence on the conduct of performance assessment. Whereas legislation has specific consequences, particularly in the USA, most environmental factors have a diffuse and often unrealized effect on assessment and pay structures. It is likely that different individuals – and organizations – will respond in varying ways to these factors. Some will be highly sensitive to possible legal implications, practice elsewhere and the state of the job market; others will be virtually immune to these influences. The main environmental factors identified as having a contextual influence on performance management are examined in the following sub-sections.

## Business culture

At a national level, culture affects performance management through socio-political traditions and attitudes that determine whether assessment is acceptable, and to what degree. Cultural norms dictate 'acceptable' standards of performance and the management methods by which they are assured. For example, in a number of Asian societies, the employment relationship is a matter of honour, and obligations are regarded as morally, rather than contractually, binding between the two parties. In a situation where people are automatically expected to do the job as agreed, the role of performance assessment is questionable. Entrekin and Chung (2001) and Hempel (2001) conducted studies of Hong Kong Chinese and Western managers in Hong Kong. Both studies found considerable differences in attitudes towards appraisal and the attribution of good performance between Hong Kong Chinese managers and their counterparts from the UK or the USA. Entrekin and Chung (2001) concluded that Western managers and Chinese managers in Western-owned firms regarded performance assessment more highly than Hong Kong Chinese managers in Hong Kong-owned firms. And, given a choice,

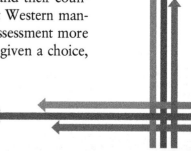

supervisory (top-down) appraisal was preferred by Chinese managers over other approaches such as subordinate or peer evaluation. However, Paik, Vance and Stage (2000) examined the characteristics of performance assessment systems in four South-East Asian countries – Indonesia, Malaysia, the Philippines and Thailand – and found significant differences in managerial practices and behaviours relevant to the design and conduct of performance appraisal. They suggest that the cultural context of performance assessment is complex and that the familiar clustering of cultures is too simplistic to explain the differences that exist. Similarly, in a comparison of public sector performance management in Ontario (Canada) and Ghana, Ohemeng (2010) concludes that a 'one size fits all' approach is ineffective.

### Legislation

In free market economies, the employment relationship between workers and employing organizations is seen as a contractual matter. This relationship is expressed in formal or legalistic statements of obligation between the two, such as written employment contracts, job descriptions and performance objectives. Performance measurement has the purpose of ensuring that the employee fulfils the contract. Commitment in Western organizations is rarely a 'hearts and minds' phenomenon and this is exemplified in the policing nature of performance management. It is a modern version of scientific management in which the detail of work is supervised in a sometimes overbearing way. Within English-speaking countries, performance-related pay encapsulates a fusion of the work ethic (Key concept 16.2) and free market ideology: work is virtuous and virtue should be rewarded generously – bearing in mind that there are generational differences in attitudes (Meriac *et al.*, 2010).

---

**KEY CONCEPT 16.2**  THE WORK ETHIC

The belief that work is virtuous in itself. Hard work is to be admired and leisure is equated with laziness. Spare time is perceived as evil: 'the devil makes work for idle hands'. In some societies the work ethic became a fundamental religious principle, the Puritans and Calvinists holding it to be such a virtue that Max Weber termed it 'the Protestant work ethic'.

---

Performance measurement has become a sensitive legal issue in the USA because of possible consequences for equal opportunities (Murphy and Cleveland, 1995: 11). Since the 1970s, assessments have been regarded as tests and are subject to guidelines enforced by the Equal Employment Opportunities Commission. Employers taking personnel decisions on the basis of performance assessment have to be mindful of possible legal action on one of two grounds: (a) the validity or accuracy of assessment ratings as predictors of future performance and promotion potential; or (b) the validity or accuracy of ratings as measures of past behaviour. This legislation is specific to the USA, but all human resource managers have to be mindful of possible breaches of equal opportunities legislation in their own countries.

### General economic conditions

Prevailing attitudes towards employees and, in turn, their response to performance assessment are considerably affected by issues such as unemployment. In line with our discussion in Chapter 5, growth and shrinkage in the job market is conventionally believed to be followed by changes in the behaviour of workers and employers. At times of high unemployment, workers are thought to be concerned about losing their jobs and hence are more

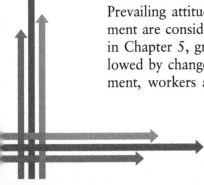

conscientious and tolerant of strict management. When suitable employees are scarce, managers must be cautious – unflattering assessments can trigger an employee's move to another organization. With fluctuating levels of organizational commitment, managers may attempt to increase levels of support for employees who have low levels of commitment (Perryer et al., 2010).

The relationship between the economy and assessment is circular and complex. Performance management is justified by organizational efficiency, and the overall efficiency of organizations in a country is crucial for its economic well-being. Income generated by effective, as opposed to inefficient, performance encourages economic wealth. Performance management has become the chosen Western instrument to drive out ineffective activity. It incorporates both stick and carrot: the first in terms of sanction, criticism or discipline; the second in the form of praise or cash.

### Industry sector

Methods of performance management vary considerably between different industrial sectors, partly as a function of the nature of the work involved, tradition and fashion. Sales-dominated industries, such as financial services, tend to have clear individual or team objectives that can be translated readily into performance targets. Performance-related pay is common in this sector and commission-only contracts are not unusual. In other sectors, objectives are more diffuse and difficult to measure so that PRP is not easily justified.

### Technological change

The advent of technological advances such as wi-fi and mobile broadband have made work outside conventional offices much easier to perform but, in some respects, more difficult to manage. This raises intriguing issues for performance management. For instance, how does a manager assess the performance of a homeworker when there is little or no personal contact between the two? Technology has the power to provide extensive statistics such as the the time an individual spends logged on to a system, number of key strokes and volume of output; but does this information provide a meaningful measure of job performance? If the employee's task involves elements of creativity, accuracy and thoroughness, how can these be assessed? Being at the work location, and even being busy, is not the same as being effective. Performance management hinges inevitably on results.

### Flexibility and diversification

As we have already seen, in the 1980s and early 1990s, the traditional nature of the employment relationship in free market countries changed, moving the balance of power firmly in favour of employers. We noted that job descriptions have disappeared or, at least, have been diluted, so that employees can be asked to do virtually anything required by the organization. Conversely, performance criteria have been more tightly defined, typically expressed in the form of demanding objectives: forever-moving goalposts. Performance assessment has become the crucial means of monitoring this relationship.

### Employee relations

Performance management is a means of enhancing managerial control, particularly through individual performance-related pay schemes. In Chapter 20 we will see that the individualization of pay diminishes or neutralizes the role of collective bargaining. The purpose and influence of trade unions is undermined, reducing both their effectiveness and attractiveness

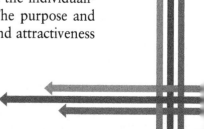

as an alternative focus for employee commitment. Brown and Heywood (2005) used data from the Australian Workplace Industrial Relations Survey to estimate the determinants of performance appraisal systems. As we might expect, complementary human resource management practices, such as formal training and incentive pay, are associated with an increased likelihood of performance appraisal, but union density is associated with a reduced likelihood of performance appraisal.

### Workforce composition

Largely forgotten in the controversy over PRP, the other main function of performance assessment is the identification of individual strengths and weaknesses. As we will see in Chapter 18, the latter can be targeted for improvement through training and development. Strengths may indicate a potential star performer, worthy of a management career route and promotion. Assessment employed to determine development needs ultimately serves to increase a nation's human capital.

Less positively, demographics and a history of unequal opportunities affect the conduct of assessment, since they largely determine who assesses whom.

## THE ORGANIZATION AND EFFECTIVE PERFORMANCE

How do organizations decide which performance criteria should be measured? How do they differentiate between a good, average or indifferent employee? Two central propositions can be used to justify performance assessment (Armstrong and Baron, 1998):

1   People, either as individuals or teams, put the greatest effort into performing well if they know and understand what is expected of them and have had an involvement in specifying those expectations.

2   Employees' ability to meet performance expectations is based on:
    – individual levels of capability
    – the degree of support provided by management
    – the processes, systems and resources made available to them by the organization.

Noblet *et al.* (2005) suggest that wide-ranging changes that have occurred in the public sector over recent years have placed increasing demands on employees. They found that the presence of support at work, the amount of control employees had over their job, perceptions of pay and the perception of a lack of human resources were found to predict employee outcome variables. They emphasize the impact that middle managers and HR managers can have in reducing detrimental effects caused by introduction of new public management. Public sector managers can use design of jobs and development of social support mechanisms, such as employee assistance programmes, to sustain the quality of working life for their employees.

In practice, according to Armstrong and Barron (1998), performance management has the following aims:

→   Assisting in achieving sustainable improvements in an organization's overall performance.

→   Serving as a lever for change in developing a more performance-oriented culture.

→   Increasing employee motivation and commitment.

→   Giving individual employees the means to develop competencies, improve job satisfaction and reach their full potential to their own benefit and that of the organization.

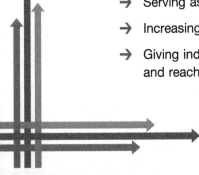

→ Improving team spirit and performance.

→ Offering a mechanism for regular dialogue and improved communication between individual employees and their managers.

→ Providing an outlet for employees to express their aspirations and concerns.

What is the reality? DeNisi and Pritchard (2006) argue that almost a century of research on performance appraisal has resulted in very few specific recommendations about designing and implementing appraisal and performance management systems whose goal is performance improvement. They suggest that there has been too great a focus on measurement issues and not enough attention has been paid to the outcome of the performance management exercise.

In our discussion of organizational HRM in Part Three we observed that organizations take many forms. No matter how an organization is structured, its output is the product of an interaction between different employees, departments, divisions and so on. Frequently, it is difficult to determine whose performance has been critical, or most significant, to the completion of a particular task. Current trends towards networking and team-based projects make individual performance even harder to gauge. Claus Offe once stated that identifying an individual's contribution to meeting an organization's goals is like listening to the sound of one hand clapping. Yet some people are singled out as key performers. On what basis? It is arguable that they may not be outstandingly good performers in an absolute sense but, simply, the people who conform most closely to the organization's norms.

Each organization defines effective performance in its own terms: being a 'good' manager in one organization is not the same as being good in another (Gunz, 1990). Company cultures and management styles vary and effective performance often translates as conformity to the house-style. According to Gunz, organizations differ greatly so that:

1   The contexts in which managers operate vary considerably.

2   This leads to different ideas about effective management so that some companies, for example, emphasize engineering quality, others financial performance or market dominance.

3   In each case people find it comparatively easy to recognize good management but may find it hard to say why. This leads to certain types of people being promoted. As these people are seen to succeed everyone else draws their own conclusions about what it takes to get ahead.

4   This closes the loop, reinforcing the dominant image of effectiveness.

As Gunz concludes:

… promotion patterns in a firm will be resistant to change because of the model's closed loop. The system is remaking itself in its own image, something organizational managers are usually aware of even if they do not always admit it openly.

This is consistent with evidence from a large number of studies reviewed by Campbell *et al.* (1970) who found that judgements of managerial effectiveness or *good*ness are actually measures of personal success. When people are asked to identify a good manager, they do so on the basis of an individual's promotion record, salary, global ranking of success and so on. Often the identification of promotable staff is devolved to individual managers. They tend to favour subordinates who are reliable – that is, they do things in the way the managers would – or who have skills the manager does not possess.

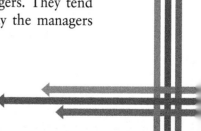

Most of all, as we have noted already in previous discussions of the cloning process, they favour employees who are similar to themselves. Bates (2002) investigated 'liking' and two types of rater–ratee similarity to predict ratings of managerial competencies. The study showed that technical proficiency, rater–ratee liking, demographic and attitudinal similarity about work were all significant predictors of proficiency ratings. Technical proficiency was the strongest predictor of ratings, followed by attitudinal similarity. A combination of liking, attitudinal and demographic similarity seemed to have a significant influence on ratings, over and above technical performance.

Morgan (1986: 144) draws parallels between organizations and political systems in that both vary from autocracy to the democratic decision-making seen in some voluntary organizations. He attributes a major role in determining successful performance to political processes such as conflict, power-play and intrigue. Following this line of logic, it is clear that any performance assessment system is vulnerable to the cloning process. Without thought, performance management can drive out diversity. It is also open to manipulation by employees who can identify the qualities necessary to 'get on' in a particular organization.

Behaviour can be fine-tuned to meet the organization's expectations. The latter can be termed 'impression management' (see Key concept 16.3).

---

**KEY CONCEPT 16.3** IMPRESSION MANAGEMENT

Image is created as part of one's self-identity. It is a product of individual and social elements, constantly shaped and reshaped to fit the expected behaviours of the current role. In other words, people act. An image can be learned or acquired through training – a deliberate process called impression management.

---

### Impression management

Every organization has its cultural symbols and rites: standards of dress and personal appearance, time-keeping, participating in semi-social activities, etc. We choose to conform or not. We may pretend to be enthusiastic, agree with management opinions, or even take up golf for networking rather than sporting reasons. Such behaviour can be described as 'manipulating the impression others gain about us' (Hinton, 1993: 23). The archetypal example is the selection or promotion interview where most of us make a special effort with appearance and manner to achieve a favourable impression. This is easy to sustain for 20–40 minutes, but not necessarily convincing. Long-term success requires a consistent and believable image sustained over a considerable period.

The most significant quality required for selection to top jobs is the ability to create a good impression (Miller and Hanson, 1991). The key feature of a well-honed image is that it gives the impression that applicants have qualities they do not possess: a false portrayal of abilities, disguising the lack of true competencies behind socially valued characteristics.

Control of one's public image depends on self-awareness. Degrees of self-awareness vary. Some people are invariably 'themselves' whereas others are acutely sensitive to the impression they convey and modify their behaviour constantly. For example, salespeople are much more likely to succeed if they can 'fine-tune' the impression made on customers. Snyder (1974) attributed this to 'self-monitoring'. Good salespeople are high self-monitors, responding quickly to customers' reactions. Low self-monitors make little effort to modify

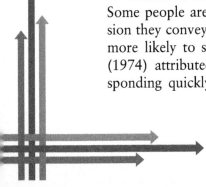

their behaviour, even in an employment interview. Day and Schleicher (2006) reviewed empirical and theoretical evidence on the importance of self-monitoring and concluded that high self-monitors are particularly good at 'getting along', for example in meeting others' social expectations, and 'getting ahead', instancing job performance and leadership emergence. Hinton (1993) points to skilled politicians who change their message depending on the audience, and are thereby perceived as being 'in-touch with the people'. They may make contradictory statements to different audiences and portray themselves as liberal or conservative as required.

Some images derive from the role models around us: successful people in the company or media stars. In the UK – particularly in England – the class structure, education system and institutions such as the civil service and the City serve to create and promote specific images. Picking people like ourselves to join our in-group is symptomatic of this condition at a national or institutional level. Too many organizations are dominated by identikit clones with similar images and ideas, whose concept of talent-spotting is finding more of the same. Women, in particular are disadvantaged in their stock of relationships (social capital) and impression management may be one approach to compensate for this (Kumra and Vinnicombe, 2010).

## Influencers

Miller and Hanson (1991) note that our ability to recognize real ability 'is contaminated by what we have come to call *the smile factor*' – closely related to the halo effect. The one-to-one interview is the most susceptible but at assessment centres 'the fish-bowl setting gives influencers/impressers space to perform'. A classic example is the excellent salesman who fails to perform well after promotion to sales manager. Time and time again the different requirements of the two jobs are ignored. Miller and Hanson studied four groups of widely different US executives and people deemed to have 'high potential' by their organizations. They describe their results as: '… to put it mildly, alarming. These organizations seeking leaders for major responsibilities were apparently confusing demonstrated leadership with some of the behavioural characteristics which some leaders exhibit.'

They found that all the people studied were particularly good at influencing others. They communicated well and were able to get other people to accept their ideas. They were generally sensitive and articulate, able to listen as well as talk. However, few had the motivation and the ability to manage or exercise leadership. They termed the majority 'influencers', people who wanted 'to have an impact on others but who did not want continuing or complete responsibility for the performance of others'. They were natural coaches and facilitators but reluctant to confront staff over missed deadlines or other forms of poor performance.

Admitting that influencers are likely to be bright and analytical, Miller and Hanson consider them to be too aware of the complexities inherent in any situation. They lack the confidence to take one direction as opposed to any other and, therefore, cannot be proactive or take risks. Further, because they are not aware in detail of the activities of their staff, they are unable to monitor changes effectively. Leaders are able to take tough decisions, can handle ambiguity and give direction. Miller and Hanson concluded that 'as many as eight out of ten people promoted into executive positions are influencers rather than leaders: most of the people running these organizations are not leaders; they only look as though they are'. Mount, Ilies and Johnson (2006) explored the hypothesis that personality traits will differentially predict counterproductive work behaviours. They found that direct relationships between traits such as 'agreeableness' and interpersonal behaviour, and 'conscientiousness' and organizational behaviour at work are partly explained by an employee's level of job satisfaction.

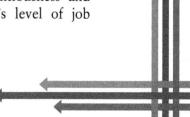

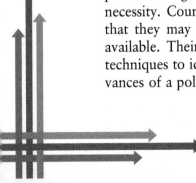

> ### KEY CONCEPT 16.4  CHARISMA
>
> Weber (1947) regarded charisma as one of three sources of authority (the other two being 'rational-legal' and 'traditional'), portraying it as a magical and hypnotic force based on direct personal contact. In modern life charisma is often fake – a product of carefully orchestrated mass communications.

There is nothing new in saying that 'real self' and 'outward image' are different constructions and that success is probably more dependent on the latter than the former. However, it is worth stressing that organizations do not benefit from this process. Images are distracting and misleading. Promotion on the basis of image does not produce employees capable of doing the job to an internationally competitive standard. Performance assessments tend to value image qualities: apparent self-confidence, the ability to talk charismatically, etc. Indeed, 'charisma' – the essential characteristic of the successful double-glazing salesman – is much admired and respected in a leader (see Key concept 16.4). According to Bryman (1992: 22):

> In business and management periodicals the term is employed a great deal in the context of discussions of certain prominent figures. In such discussions, the term is often employed to describe someone who is flamboyant, who is a powerful speaker and who can persuade others of the importance of his or her message. The non-charismatic leader, by contrast, is often depicted as a lacklustre, ineffectual individual.

Charismatics are perceived as having the power to transform organizations; as having a mission; able to inspire awe and obedience. For example, in a study of large French organizations, Bacha (2010) found that employees' perception of energetic, charismatic CEOs was associated with firm performance. They can also be lethal: a poison-pill for the ultimate well-being of any organization. Yet, like particularly dim lemmings, people managers – from personnel officers to boards of directors – will opt for the charismatic in preference to the non-charismatic.

It can be argued that at senior levels managers need to be figureheads and spokespersons for their organizations. For these roles, the required fluency, credibility and general communicating skills are those of a charismatic person. Indeed there may be a case for such a role to be entirely that of figurehead, not requiring any substantive abilities beyond those required for that role. A monarch or president, for example, can serve as a figurehead without executive power, allowing a prime minister to administer and direct. However, the tendency to overvalue charismatic skills has repeatedly led to foolish choices for 'number one' in large and small organizations. A further danger for performance assessment lies in the tendency to use cloning criteria at junior levels that are only relevant for people at the top of the organization.

Image can be construed as a decorative edifice built on the foundation of substance. An image which satisfies an audience does not necessarily preclude ability. Curiously, failure does not seem to dent common belief in the value of charisma. Similarly, the success of people with image and substance is commonly attributed to charisma – reinforcing belief in its necessity. Countering this process is difficult. It requires a recognition by senior managers that they may have succeeded by cultivating successful images rather than being the best available. Their organizations need assessment methods that are immune to this process: techniques to identify substance or necessary competencies, rather than the obscuring irrelevances of a polished image (Key concept 16.5).

> **KEY CONCEPT 16.5** SUBSTANCE VERSUS IMAGE
>
> 'Substance' can be defined as that body of competencies, knowledge and experience required to fulfil a particular function. Image' is the *apparent* totality of such knowledge and abilities as outwardly presented by an individual or group.

Langtry and Langtry (1991) compare two extreme management types which are oversimplified but identifiable within most organizations. '*I*' stands for image or 'me', '*O*' equals objective or 'others':

→ *I* managers maintain a high profile, speak well at meetings and are particularly effective at interviews. They are good networkers and make a point of getting to know the right people. They develop a good 'veneer', deliberately projecting a positive and confident image. Effective self-publicists, they make sure that everyone knows how hard they work and how successful they are. They are skilled careerists, and with sufficient emphasis and repetition they ensure that myth becomes reality.

→ *O* managers do not indulge in such elaborate charades. Innovative and supportive, they are quietly hard-working, getting on with the job as efficiently as possible. They only come to the attention of senior management when they challenge simplistic ideas which the *I* manager enthusiastically adopts. The tendency is for their work to be ignored in favour of the *I* manager's claims and their criticism to be interpreted as negative. Their fatal mistake is to assume that recognition will follow a job well done. Usually, however, the *I* manager goes streaking past them up the career ladder.

Obviously, this delightful typology divides managers too sharply into two simple categories but it captures the essence of the problem.

## Assessment and organizational change

The conduct of performance management is affected also by the success of the organization. Assessors and assessed may vary their standards depending on their perception of the organization's overall performance, career prospects and, consequently, their feelings of security and optimism. The emotional background to assessment can be directly affected by the prevailing culture of the organization. Attempts to develop a strong, cohesive culture encourage closer agreement between raters on the standards they expect.

As we observed in the early chapters of this book, de-layering and downsizing have had the effect of increasing the ratio of staff to managers throughout the Western business world. As a consequence, managers have a greater number of assessments to conduct on people they know less about. Widespread structural changes in large organizations also bring new combinations of people together with little knowledge of each other – but, perhaps, fewer longstanding prejudices.

Intriguingly, managers' routes to power appear to have a direct effect on the way they assess subordinates (Murphy and Cleveland, 1995: 415):

Attribution theory suggests that raters who have risen through the ranks will have a distorted perception of how well they performed in the job (they will readily recall good performance and will discount poor performance), which may lead to unrealistically high standards.

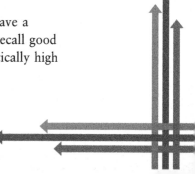

On the other hand, managers look after their own and assess their own staff generously. It is well known that performance ratings tend to the positive, with more people being judged as good performers than one would expect from a normal population. This is termed 'rater inflation'. It happens generally, but is particularly evident when assessors rate employees they have themselves previously promoted or selected. Rater inflation is common also when the process involves an element of self-assessment. Dunning, Heath and Suls (2004) argue that several psychological processes conspire to produce inaccurate self-assessments. People's self-views hold only a 'tenuous to modest' relationship with actual behaviour and performance.

The correlation between self-ratings of skill and actual performance in many domains is only 'moderate to meagre'. At times, other people's predictions prove more accurate.

Dunning *et al.* suggest that there is a tendency for individuals to overrate themselves:

> People say that they are 'above average' in skill (a conclusion that defies statistical possibility), overestimate the likelihood that they will engage in desirable behaviours and achieve favourable outcomes, furnish overly optimistic estimates of when they will complete future projects and reach judgments with too much confidence.

In the workplace, flawed self-assessments occur at all levels. Employees tend to overestimate their skill, making it difficult to give meaningful feedback. CEOs can be overconfident in their judgements, particularly when developing new markets or projects. Dunning *et al.* suggest that possible solutions include training in routine correction for bias in self-assessments and requiring people to justify decisions in front of their peers. They conclude that self-assessment of skill, expertise and knowledge is intrinsically difficult, and should be approached with caution.

Most explanations of rater inflation are couched in terms of organizational politics:

*Preserving morale.* A positive performance assessment – whether or not it is deserved – is an act of praise. It offers an opportunity for a manager to say 'thank you' and 'well done', boosting morale and commitment. It engenders good working relationships between managers and subordinates. It maintains a cosy atmosphere.

*Avoiding confrontation.* Conversely, a critical assessment is likely to have the opposite effects.

*Management image.* If managers rate staff poorly there is an implication that they make bad selection decisions and run poor-quality departments. This can have unfortunate consequences on their own performance ratings.

From a psychological perspective, it can be argued that managers develop a bonding, or personal working relationship with their favoured staff that inevitably leads to biased assessments of their performance. The organization's human resource strategies should be focused, in part at least, on overcoming this problem. In the next section we consider the strategic choices that are open to us.

## PERFORMANCE STRATEGIES

'Organizations face a critical paradox. No other management tool is more critical to productivity than effective performance appraisals, yet they can actually impair employees' performance' (English, 1991: 56).

As we observed at the beginning of this chapter, performance assessment or appraisal has been in use for a considerable period, particularly for management and sub-management grades in large corporations. The range of jobs covered by performance assessment is

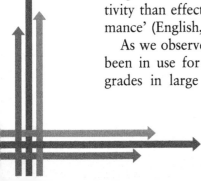

steadily increasing but there remain areas of employment where performance measurement does not yet feature and there is a great deal of conflict over its introduction.

From a strategic perspective, the process of assessment is an exercise in management power and control. It is a method by which an enterprise can evaluate its employees and feed back the organization's views to them. Furthermore, evaluation can be linked to 'stick and carrot' measures in the form of critical comment indicating the firm's disapproval, and incentives to reward and encourage 'good' performance in the form of enhanced pay and promotion prospects.

We saw in Part One of this book that 'behavioural consistency' is a major focus for models of HRM which hold that business competitiveness is improved by enhancing employee attitudes, behaviour and commitment. To do so, it is imperative that the organization has effective methods of communicating its standards or norms of behaviour. Assessors and assessed may have entirely different perceptions of both the reasons for performance appraisal and the criteria for judgement. Proponents argue that performance management should be: 'a process or set of processes for establishing shared understanding about what *is* to be achieved, and of managing and developing people in a way which increases the probability that it *will* be achieved in the short and longer term' (Armstrong, 1992: 163).

Performance management strategies are particularly concerned with workforce motivation or, more accurately, management belief in the factors that lead to employee effort and commitment.

## Motivation and performance

A considerable body of literature exists on the relationship between motivation and work performance. Theories range from the simplistic rational 'economic man' concepts underlying scientific management – implying that workers are only interested in money – to complex 'expectancy' theories which explain motivation in terms of a calculus of conflicting needs. Morgan (1986: 149) points to the diverse range of interests that people bring to the workplace:

→ *Task interests:* focused on the job being performed so that, for example, someone in sales is committed to selling, enjoys dealing with customers and takes pride in being able to clinch a sale.

→ *Career interests:* aspirations and visions of one's future – which may or may not include the current job.

These are complemented by extramural interests which incorporate leisure pursuits and domestic relationships. They cannot be divorced from work, since they compete for an individual's time and psychological or physical effort. Performance management strategies must take account of people as whole beings, with work forming just a part of their lives.

Gazioglu and Tansel (2006) analyzed job satisfaction with respect to a variety of personal and job characteristics using data from 28 240 British employees in the 1997 Workplace Employee Relations Survey. Four measures of job satisfaction were considered: influence over job; amount of pay; sense of achievement; and respect from supervisors. They found that those in education and health were less satisfied with their pay but more satisfied with their sense of achievement. Employees who received job training were more satisfied than those who had not. Women are more satisfied than men, and there is a U-shaped relationship between satisfaction and age. Unlike previous studies, they found that married individuals have lower job satisfaction levels than the unmarried.

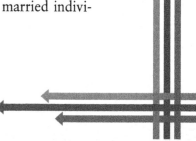

## *Achievers and non-achievers*

A number of researchers have attempted to identify the important factors leading to successful performance by comparing recognized high achievers with average performers. This method focuses on distinguishing key psychological differences between people in the two groups. However, as Furnham (1990: 30) notes: 'it cannot be assumed that these factors *caused* the success, indeed they may have been a *consequence* of success'. Factors such as confidence and knowledge of a particular area may have been present at an early stage in a person's career or, alternatively, developed as that career became successful. For example, Charles Handy uses the term 'helicopter view' to describe the broad strategic grasp of business expected from senior managers. They are unlikely to have achieved this perspective without wide experience at lower levels.

Reviewing some of the vast selection of books on the rich and famous, Furnham finds consistent themes such as:

→ *Perseverance:* tenacity, single-minded determination and concentration.

→ *Ability:* especially in creating and exploiting opportunities.

→ *Contacts:* knowing the right people.

→ *Self-reliance:* striving for independence.

→ *Thinking big:* but taking modest risks.

→ *Time management:* making the best use of time and planning progress.

The weakness in these studies lies in their essentially retrospective and descriptive nature. They do not set out to test the hypothesis that individuals setting out on a career with a particular set of personality characteristics will be more successful than average. Nevertheless, Furnham (*ibid.*: 31) finds that certain values that he describes as PWE (the Protestant work ethic) recur, providing: 'some evidence for the fact that specific PWE values – namely tenacity, perseverance, autonomy, independence, and hard work – are to be found in financially successful individuals and companies alike'.

## HRM IN REALITY OVERACHIEVING EXECUTIVES

Business executives are showing a dramatic boost in their achievement drives, according to a new study by Hay Group's McClelland Center for Research and Innovation. In fact, they are overachieving to the point of harming not only their own careers, but also the organizations they lead.

The study, 'Leadership Run Amok: The Destructive Potential of Overachievers' by Scott W. Spreier, Mary H. Fontaine and Ruth L. Malloy in the *Harvard Business Review* (June, 2006), shows that executives' achievement motives – defined as 'an innate drive to continually

improve performance or meet or exceed a standard of excellence' – have risen sharply in the last ten years. This has happened at a time of innovation and rapid business growth, but also in a period of business scandals and public loss of confidence in senior managers.

The authors of the study argue that this is not a coincidence. Overachievement often leads to ineffective and sometimes unethical leadership. They cite Enron's Jeff Skilling as an extreme but classic example of an organizational overachiever driven to continually improve results – without regard to the ways in which

they were achieved. They also note that the desire to continually do better and to be the best remains a growing problem in other organizations.

According to Scott Spreier, one of the study's authors: 'Achievement has long been an important ingredient in the recipe for individual, organizational, even national success. And in today's uber-competitive environment, it is fast becoming the performance enhancer of choice as more organizations hire, promote and reward achievement-driven leaders.'

Spreier observes that, like most stimulants, it's easy to overdose on achievement. 'Be careful what you ask for', cautions Spreier. 'It can backfire big-time. We've seen highly ethical, well-meaning executives transformed into vicious louts who behave very badly. They focus on the end to the exclusion of the means and become coercive and demanding, destroying morale and motivation. The really hard cases cut corners, lie, even cheat, all in the name of outstanding results.'

*The dark side of achievement*

The authors say that the key to avoiding this is to become aware of how easily our achievement drive can become aroused, and then learning how to better manage it.

'The most effective executives acknowledge their strong need for achievement and its importance in driving organizational performance', says co-author Mary Fontaine, who directs the McClelland Centre. She argues that they also recognize their own drive can often diminish their impact as leaders. So they adopt styles of leadership that more effectively drive performance through others.

'The best leaders aren't out there blindly setting a blistering pace themselves and demanding the same from others', Fontaine says. 'Instead they take a step back, create the vision, set the direction and standards and then coach and engage others. In the process, they create energizing work climates in which people feel they have the flexibility, autonomy and clarity they need to continually perform at the top of their game.'

However, even savvy and self-aware executives find it hard to take such an approach in today's competitive climate. They may realize that chanelling their achievement drive through others by collaborating and coaching is the best approach but they can lose control in the heat of battle and resort to coercion and control.

Balance is the key, says Ruth Malloy, also a co-author of the study. 'Good leaders know when to draw from their achievement drive and when to control it so that it doesn't get in the way of their effectiveness.'

*What are the likely consequences of having over-achieving managers assessing employee performance?*

*Source: Reprinted with permission from HRM Guide USA (http://www.hrmguide.com).*

## Locus of control

Performance management is based on the underlying belief that managers can influence behaviour and, therefore, that rationality is the basis of human action. Unfortunately, the available psychological evidence suggests that this is not the case. Research shows that people vary significantly in their reactions to the persuasion or coercion of others, depending on their perception of the ability they have to control their own lives. At one extreme, some individuals will believe that what happens in their lives is the consequence of their own decisions, abilities and behaviour. These people are judged to have an 'expectancy of internal control'. There is evidence that individuals who have an expectancy of internal control ('internals') are better performers and tend to occupy most of the higher level jobs (Andrisani and Nestel, 1976). Internals take more notice of the feedback provided by performance mangement but do so according to their own agenda. If good performance produces appropriate rewards, they will deliver more of the same. If it does not, they are likely to devote their internal strengths to finding another job. Such individuals have core

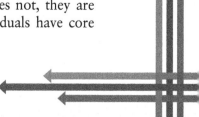

self-evaluations, considered to be 'a broad, integrative trait indicated by self-esteem, locus of control, generalized self-efficacy, and (low) neuroticism (high emotional stability)' (Judge, 2009).

At the other extreme are individuals who attribute events to fate, to God, luck or to more powerful people. They consider life to be outside their personal remit and are permanent victims of chance or the wishes of others. They are said to have an 'expectancy of external control' (Furnham, 1990: 42). People with an expectancy of external control ('externals') will be more compliant at the surface level, following instructions from supervisors and fitting social expectations. 'Following orders' they will fit neatly into bureaucratic structures but will demonstrate little initiative. Externals see little connection between their own performance and eventual success. When criticized for below-average work they will attribute their failure to causes outside themselves and the disapproval of the appraiser to personal dislike.

Are you in charge of life, or is life in charge of you? Most people have times when the former is true, and other times when the progress of life is firmly out of their hands. Some are permanently in one camp or the other. It is clear that being in charge of one's own life, career and circumstances leads to feelings of well-being and confidence and equates with successful and happy times. This is true 'empowerment'. However, it is doubtful whether performance management is entirely compatible with this state. In the next section we elaborate on how organizations can place performance assessment within a wider framework of human resource management.

# PERFORMANCE MANAGEMENT SYSTEMS

Among the 10-Cs checklist criteria for HRM discussed in Chapter 3 and elsewhere we placed consistency, coordination and control. These strategic aspects of performance assessment are exemplified in the integration of appraisal and performance-related pay processes within performance management systems and for those systems to be computerized, even in developing countries, for example in Ugandan universities (Kagaari *et al.*, 2010). Armstrong (1992: 162) sees the functions of such systems as:

→ Reinforcement of the organization's values and norms.

→ Integration of individual objectives with those of the organization.

→ Allowing individuals to express their views on the job.

→ Providing the means for managers and staff to share their expectations of performance.

## *Management by objectives*

The origins of strategic performance management can be traced to the concept of management by objectives (Raia, 1974). This is a technique to establish individual performance objectives that are tangible, measurable and verifiable. Individual objectives are derived or cascaded from organizational goals. Top managers agree their own specific objectives compatible with the organization's goals but restricted to their own areas of responsibility. Subordinates do the same at each lower level, forming an interlocked and coherent hierarchy of performance targets. Hence management by objectives lies within the strategic way of thinking that forms a key element in HRM (see Table 16.1). Management by objectives (MBO) encompasses four main stages as detailed in the following sub-sections.

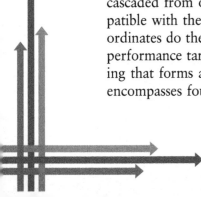

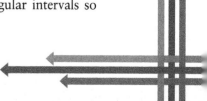

| Essential elements | Key stages |
|---|---|
| Goal-setting | **1** Establish long-range strategic objectives |
| | **2** Formulate specific overall organizational goals |
| | **3** Agree departmental objectives |
| | **4** Set individual performance targets |
| Action planning | **5** Draw up action plans |
| Self-control | **6** Implement and take corrective action |
| Periodic reviews | **7** Review performance against objectives |
| | **8** Appraise overall performance, reinforce appropriate behaviour and strengthen motivation through:<br>→ *management development*<br>→ *reward*<br>→ *career and HR planning* |

**TABLE 16.1**

The management by objectives process

Source: Adapted from Raia (1974).

**Goal-setting** This is the heart of the MBO process. Goals are specific and desired results are to be achieved within an agreed period of time. They must represent real progress. They should be:

→ *Challenging:* stretching the individual beyond comfortable performance.

→ *Attainable:* realistic within cost and resource constraints.

→ *Measurable:* specific, quantifiable and verifiable. Objectives are best set in numerical terms such as 'increased sales by $x$ thousand', 'reduced staff by $y$ per cent'.

→ *Relevant:* directly related to the person's job and consistent with overall organizational objectives.

Alternatively, goals are sometimes set against the acronym SMART, linked to: Specific or stretching; Measurable; Agreed or Achievable; Realistic; Time-bounded.

**Action planning** Goals or performance targets are the 'ends' of the MBO process, action plans are the 'means'. They require individual employees to ask themselves what, who, when, where and how an objective can be achieved.

**Self-control** MBO is a self-driven process with each person participating in setting their own goals and action plans. This results in greater commitment to their own objectives and an improved understanding of the process. They are expected to control their own behaviour in order to achieve performance targets. In return it is essential that they are given sufficient information and feedback to gauge their progress.

**Periodic reviews** It is not sufficient to review progress at the end of the MBO process. Individuals must be provided with an opportunity to check their performance at regular intervals so that obstacles can be identified. Reviews should take a positive, coaching approach rather than a critical approach.

MBO pre-dates human resource management and derives from a period when strategic thinking and the integration of organizational objectives were being emphasized by management writers. Since then, the development of HRM has preserved the focus on strategy and integration. This has been reinforced by the fashion for performance-related pay, fostered by the prevalent belief that reward should be firmly tied to results. Whereas MBO concentrated on individual management of one's own performance, the spread of PRP is underpinned by the use of assessment systems to manage the individual. MBO has gone out of fashion to a considerable extent although its basic techniques have been absorbed into newer approaches. It has been criticized for the paperwork involved, the administrative burden it creates and the realization that goals set for individuals are actually dependent on a team, a department or even a substantial part of the organization (Armstrong and Baron, 1998).

## Prescriptions for performance management systems

Bevan and Thompson (1992) describe a model performance management system:

→ The organization has a shared vision of its objectives or a mission statement that is communicated to its employees.

→ There are individual performance management targets, related to unit and wider organizational objectives.

→ There is a regular formal review of progress towards achieving the targets.

→ There is a review process that identifies training, development and reward outcomes.

→ The whole process is itself evaluated – feeding back through changes and improvements.

Rather similar to the MBO approach, the central features of such a system are an objective-setting process and a formal appraisal system. Typically, the performance management system is owned and implemented by line managers. The role of human resource specialists is to aid and advise line managers on the development of the system. In a slightly different approach, English (1991) argues for a 'rational' system of performance management which should have the following characteristics:

→ A clear statement of what is to be achieved by the organization.

→ Individual and group responsibilities support the organization's goals.

→ All performance is measured and assessed in terms of those responsibilities and goals.

→ All rewards are based on employee performance.

→ Organizational structure, processes, resources, and authority systems are designed to optimize the performance of all employees.

→ There is an ongoing effort to create and guide appropriate organizational goals and to seek newer, more appropriate goals.

Many organizations consider that they have a performance management system along these lines. Often they do not because one or more of the following conditions are missing:

→ Agreement among all critical parties on what is to be performed.

→ An effective way to measure desired performance.

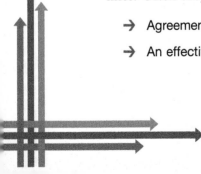

→ A reward system tied directly to performance.

→ An environment conducive to successful performance.

→ A communication programme to gain understanding, acceptance and commitment to the system.

→ A performance-based organizational culture.

# THE ASSESSMENT PROCESS

In this section we consider performance assessment as an activity. Traditionally, performance assessment uses a rating system known as appraisal (Key concept 16.6). In most companies it is a matter of something being done to the employee rather than a process in which the employee plays a valued and important part. Assessments are generally an annual exercise, although some organizations may undertake them more frequently, perhaps every six months, especially with new entrants or recent promotees. For lower-grade employees, some companies are content with an assessment every two years.

---

**KEY CONCEPT 16.6** APPRAISALS

Performance assessment is one of the many people management techniques that 'classify and order individuals hierarchically' (Townley, 1994: 33). Appraisals rate individuals on quasi-objective criteria or standards deemed to be relevant to performance. Traditional appraisals rated individuals on a list of qualities – primarily work-related attitudes and personality traits. Modern assessment is often focused on competencies.

---

## *Appraisal and conformity*

Appraisals tend to be formalized. In many organizations they take the shape of pre-printed forms or web input screens and instructions prepared for the appraising manager or supervisor. Dates of completion and return are fixed and the whole process monitored and administered by the personnel or HR department. Theoretically, appraisals can be completed in a number of ways:

→ *Self-assessment.* Individuals assess themselves against rating criteria, or targeted objectives.

→ *Peer assessment.* Fellow team members, departmental colleagues, or selected individuals with whom an employee has working interaction, provide assessments.

→ *Line management.* The employee's immediate supervisor(s) provide the assessment. Alternatively, other line managers may be involved.

→ *Upward appraisal.* Managers are appraised by their staff.

→ *360-degree or multi-rater feedback.* Raters may include anyone with a direct knowledge of an individual's performance, including colleagues, direct reports, managers and internal customers.

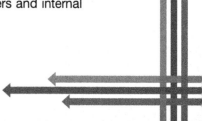

The traditional performance appraisal was completed by the immediate supervisor or line manager with, usually, further comments or countersignature provided by the supervisor's own manager. This has been described as the 'father and grandfather' system – appropriate terms, given the essentially paternalistic nature of the process.

Appraisal normally requires rating on a series of categories. Management and lower-level appraisals are commonly conducted in different ways. Management assessments tend to feature results-oriented criteria, typically against objectives agreed at the beginning of the year. Non-managerial appraisals are more likely to be 'trait-ratings' – no matter what the questions may ask overtly, they are actually rating the employee on behavioural or personality criteria. In essence, they are no more than crude personality questionnaires. This remains the case if the criteria are couched in terms of job-related qualities.

## HRM IN REALITY — PERFORMANCE MANAGEMENT SYSTEMS FAIL TO MOTIVATE

'Most organizations have lost sight of the fact that performance management systems should aim to enhance performance by motivating staff.' This is the conclusion of recent research by The Work Foundation in six case study organizations. The report suggests that 'HR professionals are too concerned with "tweaking" PM forms and software rather than focusing on what should result from the process – improved performance.'

The report, 'What Makes for Effective Performance Management', by Kathy Armstrong and Adrian Ward, published in 2006, identifies 'profound confusion' about what PM is for. It is treated as a reward mechanism, a learning and development experience, or an exercise in control. Motivation appears to be less of a priority. The report argues that while the task of managing performance was universally held to be a 'good thing' by the organizations concerned, they were unable to identify any concrete organizational benefits to justify this opinion.

Marianne Huggett, a consultant with The Work Foundation, said:

An awful lot of organizations appear to be perpetually tweaking the process of performance management while ignoring the bigger picture of what it is supposed to be about in the first place – improving an organization's performance. In too many organizations, performance management is a matter of elegant bureaucracy – a tiresome form-filling exercise staff and managers could cheerfully live without. Meanwhile, there is a reluctance to

ask hard questions about what really comes out of it. In some cases, organizations might be well advised not to worry so much about the forms and bureaucracy, and simply try and encourage ongoing dialogue and quality conversations between line managers and employees instead.

Armstrong and Ward say that 'process can take up the most time and resources, but add only a small amount of value. This can be particularly dangerous where there is little or no attention paid to improving management's skills in managing performance – where the system itself is hoped to solve all the performance management issues, rather than the managers.'

The report cautions against crude use of measurement in PM. The case study organizations use various techniques including 360-degree feedback to 'vast amounts' of quantitative data. Often, this data is synthesized into a single rating that is intended to represent an individual's net contribution and determine their remuneration. This frequently describes an individual's performance as 'satisfactory' or 'average' – which the authors suggest is 'not an overly motivating message'. Furthermore, some managers use performance-related pay mechanisms to compensate staff they regard as being poorly paid.

'The real danger of becoming embroiled in the technical debates about rating, ranking and quotas is that it can drain the capacity of performance management to be a powerful vehicle for feedback, motivation and, yes, performance improvement' the authors say.

The report identifies seven critical issues of process and people management capability that organizations should debate when setting the parameters of performance management:

*Process*: the means by which individual performance is directed, assessed and rewarded.

*People management capability*: the skills, attitudes, behaviours and knowledge that line managers need in order to raise performance.

Armstrong and Ward argue that successful PM depends on the interplay of all of these factors.

*Why is a rating of 'satisfactory' unlikely to motivate an employee?*

*Source: Reprinted with permission from HRM Guide UK (http://www.hrmguide.co.uk/).*

According to Philp (1990):

The disadvantages of this approach are numerous. For instance, the terms themselves are extremely ambiguous and it is unlikely that any group of managers would share exactly the same interpretation of any of them. Any appraisal using such words would be extremely subjective and, as a result, totally unfair. Also, because assessment in these terms deals with the individual rather than with the results they produce for the organization, it is very difficult to communicate with the individual involved. The person being appraised is likely to see any critical assessment of this type as a personal attack. The factors deal with the emotive areas closely concerned with personality, and the majority of people will tend to react defensively.

Nurse (2005) studied workers' perceptions of performance appraisal to determine whether they experienced fair outcomes, and whether it was seen to contribute towards career advancement. Non-union respondents expressed fewer unfavourable perceptions about the interaction than did their trade union counterparts. Workers who believed that performers were not treated fairly as a result of performance appraisal similarly agreed that their expectations regarding development and advancement were not being met. The study found moderate relationships between perceptions about treatment of performers and their expectations about career advancement, as expressed through opportunities for training and development, pay for performance and promotions. Brown *et al.* (2010) point to the need for organizations to evaluate the cost of improving the quality of appraisals against the potential consequences on job satisfaction, commitment and intention to quit.

Appraisals are generally disliked by employees and employers alike. Human resource practitioners are often made responsible for the paper-distribution and then for policing the process, coercing unwilling participants into completing the paperwork and holding one-to-one confrontations with appraisees.

Despite the fact that most assessors are completely unqualified to make judgements on anyone's personality, even in the most general of terms, the traditional appraisal form asks for a numerical rating on a scale of 1–4 or 1–7 (from excellent to appalling). More detail is asked for as supplementary verbal comments, which could range from one word such as 'good' to a paragraph or more of detailed criticism or praise. Moreover, there is usually an overall rating that may be tied to promotability and a section to indicate areas for development or training. Finally, there are normally sections for comments by the person being appraised, possibly in the form of notes of a counselling interview and comments by the appraising manager's own supervisor.

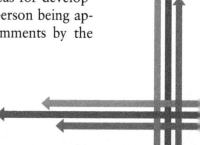

## HRM IN REALITY  PERFORMANCE REVIEWS STILL VALUABLE

A 2010 survey of human resource managers found that performance reviews are still considered a valuable element in staff assessment. Conducted on behalf of *OfficeTeam*, a leading Canadian staffing service specializing in temporary placement of office and administrative support personnel, the survey was based on telephone interviews with more than 150 managers in organizations with at least 20 employees.

Over three-quarters of respondents (78 per cent) felt that formal evaluations are effective in improving job performance. Half said they conduct appraisals once a year; one in five (20 per cent) hold them at least quarterly.

Asked to rate their organization's performance appraisal process in improving employee performance over one-quarter of respondents (27 per cent) felt it was very effective and 51 per cent that it was somewhat effective. The responses of a further 15 per cent were less positive.

Respondents were asked about the frequency of formal performance appraisals. The majority conducted them annually (50 per cent) with 22 per cent conducted 'as necessary', 15 per cent twice a year, 5 per cent quarterly and 9 per cent 'never'.

The report suggests five ways in which employees can achieve the best outcome from performance appraisals:

→ **Sort out the details**. Preparation is important. Ask your supervisor for a copy of the assessment form and clarify any additional expectations (such as bringing information about specific projects to the meeting or completing a self-evaluation).

→ **Showcase your accomplishments**. Highlight any praise or awards received since your last formal

review. Keep an ongoing list of achievements to remind you and your supervisor of how the company has benefited from your work.

→ **Make it a two-way conversation**. Your manager will identify areas where you are excelling and where improvement is needed. In turn, ask questions about the assessment and request support or guidance.

→ **Share your ideas**. Discuss what you hope to achieve in the future and ensure these goals are compatible with your long-term professional objectives.

→ **Follow through**. Regularly review agreed goals and keep your supervisor informed about your progress.

Robert Hosking, executive director, commented:

Despite their bad rap, performance reviews benefit both managers and employees, provided adequate preparation goes into them. It's understood that supervisors must take the time to provide constructive feedback to team members, but workers also should play an active role in the process. This is their chance to highlight key accomplishments and discuss career aspirations.

*What do you consider to be the ideal period between assessments?*

*Source: Reprinted with permission from* HRM Guide Canada *(http://www.hrmguide.net/canada/).*

---

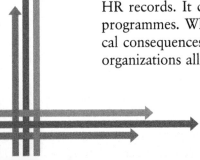

    The document is usually signed by all the contributors and forms part of the company's HR records. It can be used for promotion boards, training and management development programmes. What happens if an employee disagrees with the assessment? Despite its critical consequences for promotion prospects and, perhaps, remuneration, only one half of all organizations allow any form of appeal.

## Upward feedback

The emphasis of performance management has been on top-down assessments open to a degree of power play by managers and senior executives. Over the last decade or so there has been a trend towards constructive, developmental approaches and moving away from a fixation with ratings. It has also become increasingly acceptable to take views of individual performance from a wide range of perspectives. Upward feedback is a process whereby managers receive comments and criticisms from their subordinates. This may be facilitated by an intermediary to organize the process and maintain a positive and non-acrimonious climate.

Upward feedback is not an appraisal as such and is not linked to standardized competencies. Instead (Forbes, 1996):

→ It is intended to deliver candid, accurate feedback from a team to its manager.

→ The basis lies in the team's perception of the actions of its manager.

→ Upward feedback is not a system of judgement 'but only asks him or her for more, less, or the same of a broad series of behaviours'.

→ Leadership, management, task and people factors are given equal weight.

→ The facilitator gives confidential feedback, initially to the manager, then between the team and its manager.

→ Team members and the manager – and that person's manager – can compare their views on what is required, bringing areas of misunderstanding or disagreement out into the open.

Because upward feedback is not formal appraisal, managers do not need to fear being judged. Conventionally, upward feedback begins with the most senior executive and cascades downwards, with each level in turn receiving feedback.

Based on Forbes *(ibid.)*, the benefits of upward feedback can be summarized as follows:

1   Individual/team action plans can improve cooperation between team and manager.

2   Supervisors are encouraged to vary their management style and emphasis.

3   Ideas, problems and suggestions can be collected across a range of individuals or teams. In turn these can be used to set up new cross-functional teams or aid in the management of change.

4   Training requirements can be pinpointed and linked to specific outcomes for the team.

5   It facilitates empowerment and self-management.

6   A benchmark is gradually developed taking the form of an organizational map and data on how employees, managers and senior executives view requirements in 20 defined behavioural areas in up to 100 practices. An annual comparison can be made from this.

7   It opens up a more communicative culture where different forms of performance assessment can be introduced.

Dierendonck *et al.* (2007) concluded that managers tended to have low awareness of the effect of their behaviour on subordinates and that upward feedback did not lead to much long-term improvement in this respect. Upward feedback also has its disadvantages. Managers may receive negative comments from assertive and ambitious employees intent on

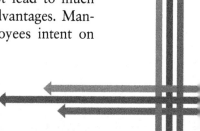

undermining their confidence and authority. No one likes to be rated as a poor performer and some managers may be less firm or directive, even when appropriate, in order to avoid criticism. Similarly, managers may be less critical or demanding of their subordinates in order to reduce the probability of unfavourable feedback.

Waldman and Atwater (2001), in a study of upward feedback in a large telecommunications firm, found that managers who receive poor formal appraisal scores from their bosses are more likely to value the usefulness of upward feedback. Managers who receive lower subordinate ratings are more likely to ask for additional feedback. In general, subordinates are more likely than managers to believe that upward feedback scores should be incorporated into formal performance assessments. Waldman and Atwater also found that subordinate ratings were correlated with formal appraisal scores. Kilburn and Cates (2010) observed that leaders who emphasized relationships with followers were more likely to receive voluntary upward feedback.

### 360-degree or multi-rater assessments

Multi-rater assessments have been used by large US corporations for some time and have gradually become more common in other countries. The evolution of business organizations into flatter, team-based structures has led to multiple reporting lines and wider spans of command for managers, so that assessments by single line managers are not as appropriate as they were in the past (Kettley, 1996). A multi-source rating system such as 360-degree performance profiling typically involves information collected from the people working with the person being appraised, managers, staff reporting to that individual and internal (or, exceptionally) external customers. The process follows a sequence such as the following:

1   A skill model or competence framework is devised that lists essential job skills and behaviours.

2   A performance management survey is defined on the basis of the skill model.

3   Individual employees are each asked to recommend eight to 12 raters for their personal reviews. Immediate supervisors choose six to ten of these to complete performance surveys, rating the employee on each skill area, typically on a scale of 1–10. Raters need to have direct knowledge of the employee's performance but supervisors need to ensure that they are not all friends of the appraisee.

4   The reports are collected together and a summary is given to the appraisee, highlighting both strengths and development needs.

This method of performance assessment has its advantages and disadvantages over more traditional methods. It is clear that the number of people involved, and the amount of form-filling required, can lead to a considerable expenditure of time and effort, even when online forms, data-scanning and report-producing software are used. The anonymity of the process may also allow malicious and undefended negative ratings to be given.

Morgan, Cannan and Cullinane (2005) examined the introduction of 360-degree feedback in the civil service as it underwent modernization. They found that at an organizational level it failed to develop the self-awareness anticipated. It was not aligned with other development plans or the organization's core competencies. At an individual level some participants believed that they achieved little from the process overall. The authors suggest this may be related to an expectation that the HRM system would be more proactive in planning development action on their behalf.

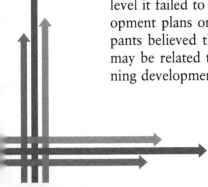

# LIMITATIONS OF PERFORMANCE MANAGEMENT

Performance appraisal has become one of the most widely used management tools despite widespread criticism of its effectiveness. To add to the controversy, Strebler, Robinson and Bevan (2001) from the UK's Institute of Employment Studies (IES) argue from research on over 1000 British managers that many performance appraisal systems have a limited impact on overall business performance and fail both employees and organizations.

Many organizations try to use performance appraisal and review as a 'strategic lever', not just for the performance of individuals, but also the performance of the whole business. However, according to Strebler and her colleagues:

> This assumes that managers have the ability and motivation to make performance review work, by translating strategic goals into operational practice. Ideally, they should use the appraisal to help the employee see how their contribution adds value to the business as a whole. Too often, however, they are rushed discussions where performance ratings are handed out, where petty lapses in performances are picked upon, or where performance-related pay is awarded.

Additionally, Strebler *et al. (ibid.)* contend that performance review is rapidly becoming an 'over-burdened management tool'. Along with its appraisal and objective-setting aspects, line managers are expected to pinpoint staff training requirements, provide career counselling, identify future star performers and do something about poor performers. These are all important elements of people management but the attempt to do so much at the same time often leads to poor results from appraisal schemes.

Performance review systems are frequently rooted in the hierarchical organizations of the past, and often still drive pay or promotion decisions. Organizations are flatter today and there may be limited opportunities for upward progression. Rewards can also take forms other than pay increases. So, according to Strebler *et al. (ibid.),* new systems are needed that meet the requirements of individual organizations: textbook models might not be suitable for particular strategies or structures.

They advise a transformation of the performance review 'from a beast of burden into a thoroughbred', starting with business strategy, then being clear about the roles, skills and behaviours required for delivering that strategy. There are some simple rules:

→  Clear aims and measurable criteria for success.

→  Involving employees in design and implementation of the system.

→  Keeping it simple to understand and operate.

→  Making its effective use one of managers' core performance goals.

→  Ensuring that employees are always able to see the link between their performance goals and those of the organization.

→  Using it to keep roles clear and focus on performance improvement.

→  Backing up the system with adequate training and development.

→  Making any direct link with reward crystal clear, and providing proper safeguards to guarantee equity.

→  Reviewing the system regularly and openly to make sure it's working.

Strebler *et al. (ibid.)* conclude that human resources functions that can deliver this will be making a real and visible strategic contribution to their organizations.

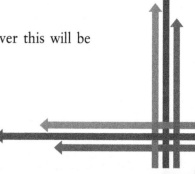

# COUNSELLING INTERVIEWS

Having tested the manager's talents as untrained psychologist, the next part of the process expects the manager to be a qualified counsellor! This counselling interview takes the form of a face-to-face dialogue between (normally) the appraising manager and the appraisee, although it is sometimes done by the countersigning manager. The whole process is designed to focus the power of the organization on a direct and individual basis. However, it is also clear that the scope for conflict and its avoidance are considerable.

Many, perhaps most, managers are reluctant to engage in the appraisal process. First, because it is difficult to criticize someone's performance honestly, knowing that the appraisee will read the comments. Potentially, the whole exercise is confrontational and many counselling interviews have turned sour because of carelessly worded appraisals. Most people find criticism difficult to accept and registering a point with an employee without causing offence requires diplomatic skills.

The process is dependent on the personality and management style of the appraising manager. Some managers will be blunt and, perhaps, brutal in their approach. As a consequence, they may not produce any improvement in behaviour but, rather, sullen resentment and a reduction in quality of performance. Others will regard the whole exercise as something to be avoided. As we noted earlier, the result will be rater-inflation: an assessment that is over-generous or, at best, neutral in order to avoid conflict. The process also depends to a great extent on the quality of the appraising manager. If that individual is not particularly capable, the evaluation of the subordinate may well be inaccurate or misleading and may blight the person's career.

## HRM IN REALITY CEO PERFORMANCE AND EDUCATION

CEOs with top college degrees do no better at improving their organization's long-term performance than average and are as liable to be blamed for poor results according to 2010 research led by the Whittemore School of Business and Economics at the University of New Hampshire.

Lead researcher Brian Bolton, assistant professor of finance said:

> These findings suggest that both boards and researchers should use caution in placing too much emphasis on an individual's education when trying to assess their ability to lead the company and maximize shareholder value.

The study reviewed data covering nearly 15000 years of CEO experience and more than 2600 turnovers between 1992 and 2007. Researchers analyzed the role educational attainment played in decisions to remove a current CEO, selection of a replacement, and organizational performance. Six main measures were used: whether or not the individual had attended a top 20 undergraduate school; had an MBA, law or master's degree; and whether or not the higher degree was from a top 20 programme.

The study found that poor performance is the most significant factor in a decision to replace a CEO, regardless of education. However, researchers found a significant positive correlation between the education levels of new CEOs and those they replace. For example, a board will seek to replace a poorly performing CEO with an MBA degree with someone similarly qualified.

Researchers found that hiring new CEOs with MBA degrees tends to produce short-term improvements in operating performance that may not be maintained. They conclude that CEO education does not necessarily equate with talent and ability.

Brian Bolton commented:

Even though CEO education does not lead to superior performance by firms, firms may rely on CEO education in hiring decisions because they have few other identifiable and measurable criteria to use. All else being equal, they rely on what they believe to be the observable pedigrees of the executive. Of course, all else is rarely equal, especially when dealing with something as nebulous and potentially unobservable as managerial talent. Interpersonal skills, leadership ability and strategic vision are among the traits that CEOs should possess; these can be difficult to identify and even more difficult to measure. As a result, boards rely on those characteristics which they may be able to observe: work experience, track record and education.

*Why is it that good leaders do not necessarily need a good education?*

Source: Reprinted with permission from HRM Guide USA (http://www.hrmguide.com).

It can be argued that there is an increasing tendency to focus on marginal performers in the light of harsh economic conditions. Companies consider that they are unable to carry inefficient employees and the assessment procedure offers a source of data that will support dismissals. In theory, performance appraisal provides documentary evidence of inefficiency that would be hard to refute. In practice, rater-inflation often undermines the process, providing generous appraisals for questionable performances.

# OBJECTIVITY AND SUBJECTIVITY IN ASSESSMENT

As we have seen, some of the key issues of performance management revolve around questions of fairness, judgement and interpretation of both results and behaviour. Serious attempts have been made to address these areas. Performance assessment focuses on one or more of the following criteria:

*Results*. In line with MBO and similar objectives-based systems, employees are rated on their achievements, expressed as well-defined, personal or organizational targets. For example, a salesperson may be given the objective of US$x thousand worth of sales in the year. How this is achieved is not the subject of assessment. As we have already observed, objectives are easier to define for some jobs than others. This approach can be complicated by the use of a 'moving target'.

*Processes*. In this case the emphasis is not on measurable results but on *how* the outcomes are achieved. It can be argued that compliance with quality procedures or, alternatively, provision of a particular level of service are examples of process assessments. However, if these are measurable in some way, they can be translated into results – for example, proportion of defective items or number of complaints.

*Behaviour*. Weaker and less objective assessments – but probably the most common – focus on employee behaviour which is only tangentially connected with either achieved results or work processes. A favourite approach for managers incapable of seeing the 'wood from the trees', they allow ample opportunity to dwell on personal prejudices over appearance, dress and manner. Such assessments provide a direct feeder mechanism into culture-bound and organizationally unhealthy practices designed to increase conformity and eliminate diversity.

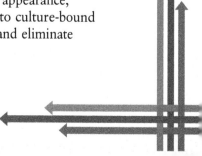

A number of large organizations have countered this tendency by using behaviourally anchored scales.

> *Behaviourally anchored scales (BARS).* These are relatively expensive techniques to maintain, requiring 'experts' to develop rating scales anchored to real-life behaviour through critical incidents. However, they force appraisers to make comparatively objective judgements, placing individual behaviour in the context of the organization as a whole, rather than on inadequate personality categorizations. They are less usable in situations where new technology or procedural changes require frequent updating of scales.

> *Behavioural observation scales (BOS).* These are constructed in a similar way to BARS but assessors are required to list the frequency of occurrence of particular behaviours within a particular period, rather than make comparative judgements of better or worse performance.

Different behaviour-oriented rating formats may enhance or inhibit the value of performance appraisal as a development tool. Tziner, Joanis and Murphy (2000) compared the effects of rating scale formats on a number of indices of the usefulness of performance appraisal for employee development. Using simple graphic scales, behaviourally anchored rating scales or behaviour observation scales, ratings were made of the job performance of 96 police officers. The BOS ratings produced both the highest ratee satisfaction with the performance appraisal process and the most favourable perceptions of performance goals. Additionally, experts judged the performance improvement goals for officers appraised with BOS to be the most observable and specific.

### Competence ratings

In recent years the trend in performance management has been towards assessing people on 'dimensions' of suitable attributes or 'competencies'. These may be derived from job analyses and describe a limited number of core skills or behaviours necessary to do a certain job. In fact, such competencies aggregate to form a key strategic element of business competitiveness – the overall competencies of the firm. There is some ambiguity about the meaning of the term at the level of the individual – it is sometimes used as an equivalent for a psychological trait (perseverance) and, at other times, as a complex hybrid of learning and skill (ability to use computers).

Armstrong and Baron (1998) suggest that competencies should address the following points:

1  What are the 'elements' of the job – its main tasks or key areas?

2  What is an acceptable standard of performance for each element?

3  Which skills and what knowledge does a jobholder need to have in order to be fully capable in each of these job elements – and at what level?

4  How will employees or their managers know that they have achieved the required levels of competence?

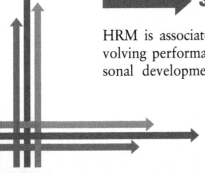

## SUMMARY

HRM is associated with sophisticated and intensive performance assessment, typically involving performance-related pay. The assessment of performance can be beneficial to personal development. We considered performance management as an integrated system.

Theoretical descriptions of such systems emphasize their value to the link between individual employee performance and the achievement of strategic goals. However, there are philosophical issues of what precisely represents 'good' performance, and further technical problems of measurement. We completed the chapter with a critique of appraisal methods and a discussion of recent attempts to objectify their use.

 ## FURTHER READING

1 *Armstrong's Handbook of Performance Management: An Evidence-Based Guide to Delivering High Performance*, 4th edition, by Michael Armstrong (Kogan Page, 2009) is a wide-ranging text that conveys the full flavour of the subject.

2 *Managing Performance* by Michael Armstrong and Angela Baron (CIPD, 2004) is another example.

3 *The Manager's Guide to Performance Management* by Robert Bacal (McGraw-Hill Education, 2003) is particularly reader-friendly.

4 Clive Fletcher's *Appraisal and Feedback: Making Performance Review Work* (CIPD, 2007) is written by a major researcher in the field of assessment.

5 *Abolishing Performance Appraisals: Why They Backfire and What to Do Instead* by Tom Coens and Mary Jenkins (Berrett-Koehler Publishers, 2002) takes an original but positive approach to the process of assessment.

 ## REVIEW QUESTIONS

1 Why is performance assessment important? What factors determine individual success in an organization?

2 Summarize the external factors that can affect the process of performance assessment within an organization. Do they help or hinder that process?

3 Do organizations prefer conformists? What are the implications of the personal relationship between manager and employee on performance assessment?

4 Should males and females be assessed differently?

5 Discuss the view that performance appraisals are unnecessary.

6 Explain the following terms: (a) behavioural consistency; and (b) competencies.

7 Compare and contrast Bevan and Thompson's textbook model of performance management with English's rational model.

8 Evaluate a significant business (or political) leader. How much of that person's success is due to charisma or impression management?

9 Discuss the ways in which externals and internals react to performance assessment. Would an objective-setting method such as MBO produce the same effects on performance for a person with an internal locus of control as it would for someone with an external locus of control?

10 Is management by objectives discredited as a performance management technique?

11  How would you conduct a 360-degree performance assessment? Compare and contrast the processes of upward feedback and 360-degree profiling.

12  Define 'rater-inflation'. What are its causes and implications? Is it possible for appraisals to be objective?

 **CASE STUDIES FOR DISCUSSION AND ANALYSIS**

## The consumer relations department/ International Holidays

1  As general manager, the consumer relations department has been the source of considerable difficulties for you this year. The manager, Jean Davis, her assistant Lyndon Greaves, and the six staff are involved in a constant battle with the sales department. First, they say that the number of complaints has gone up substantially. Jean says that customers seem far more ready to find fault with deliveries than ever before. She blames the salesforce for errors in order-taking. She has become aggressive in the way she deals with sales and has accused you of ignoring the problem. Lyndon is more reasonable but says that his people are grossly overworked. They have developed a backlog in clearing customers' emails and phone calls and sick leave has increased.

Conversely, the sales department is working better than ever before. They have a new PRP system in place, based on targets for orders taken by each person. The field sales force have embraced PRP enthusiastically with orders 20 per cent up on last year. Most have received generous bonuses. The board are very pleased with this and have asked you to extend PRP to other departments, including consumer relations. However, Jean and Lyndon are very negative about the idea, demanding to know how they are likely to be assessed when they are behind on their targets.

*What is your analysis of the situation and how would you deal with it?*

2  International Holidays is a travel agency group. The company has 43 shop units, each employing between four and eight front-office staff. Each unit has a manager. The company has been suffering from low trading levels in recent years. The situation has not been helped by the trend towards internet booking which has reduced the number of people coming to the company's retail units and threatens the viability of several locations. The managing director has asked you to set up a performance management system to improve the motivation of the staff.

*How would you do this?*

*What difficulties would you expect in ensuring that the system achieves its objectives?*

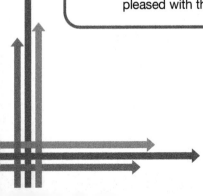

# CHAPTER 17
# Reward management

## LEARNING OBJECTIVES

The purpose of this chapter is to:

→ Investigate the relationship between the human resource function and payroll administration.

→ Outline the rationale behind different compensation packages.

→ Evaluate the link between pay and performance.

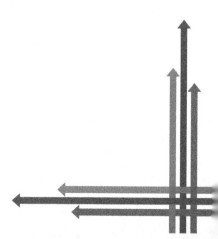

# PAY AND COMPENSATION

Pay is an important feature of human resource management – after all, it is the main reason why people work. It is a sensitive and controversial area that has been extensively debated at both practical and theoretical levels. In the USA the term 'compensation' is used to encompass everything received by an employed individual in return for work. For example, Milcovich, Newman and Milcovich (2001: 6) state: 'Employees may see compensation as a *return in exchange* between their employer and themselves, as an *entitlement* for being an employee of the company, or as a *reward* for a job well done' (original emphases).

The reward or compensation that people receive for their contribution to an organization includes monetary and non-monetary components. Remuneration does not simply compensate employees for their efforts – it also has an impact on the recruitment and retention of talented people.

The term 'reward management' covers both the strategy and the practice of pay systems. Traditionally, human resource or personnel sections have been concerned with levels and schemes of payment whereas the process of paying employees – the payroll function – has been the responsibility of finance departments. There is a trend towards integrating the two, driven by computerized packages offering a range of facilities.

There are two basic types of pay schemes, although many organizations have systems that include elements of both:

*Fixed levels of pay.* Wages or salaries that do not vary from one period to the next except by defined pay increases, generally on an annual basis. There may be scales of payments determined by age, responsibility or seniority. Most 'white-collar' jobs were paid in this way until recently.

*Reward linked to performance.* The link may be daily, weekly, monthly or annualized. Payment for any one period varies from that for any other period, depending on quantity or quality of work. Sales functions are commonly paid on the basis of turnover; manual and production workers may be paid according to work completed or items produced. Catering staff typically rely on direct payment from satisfied customers in the form of service charges or tips (gratuities).

Both methods work smoothly, provided that scales are easy to understand and the methods of measuring completed work are overt, accurate and fair. However, there has been considerable dissatisfaction with the management of pay on both sides of the employment relationship. In recent years, attempts have been made to remedy the situation through new systems and a greater reliance on performance-related pay.

## KEY CONCEPT 17.1 REWARD MANAGEMENT

Reward or compensation management is an aspect of HRM that focuses pay and other benefits on the achievement of objectives. Typically, it incorporates other changes in pay administration and policy, including: decentralization of responsibility for setting pay levels; uniform appraisal schemes; flexible working practices; and performance-related pay.

Within HRM literature there is some ambiguity as to whether reward should play a supporting role, a view implicit in the Harvard model of HRM, or, conversely, that it should *drive* organizational performance – an opinion which finds greater favour among exponents

of 'hard' HRM (Kessler, 1995: 10). Milcovich *et al.* (2001: 5) take a broad perspective, arguing that:

> In addition to treating pay as an expense, a manager also uses it to influence employee behaviours and improve organization performance. The way people are paid affects the quality of their work; their attitude towards customers; their willingness to be flexible or learn new skills or suggest innovations; and even their interest in unions or legal action against their employer. This potential to influence employees' behaviours, and subsequently the productivity and effectiveness of the organization, is another reason it is important to be clear about the meaning of compensation.

Wolf (1999: 41) contends that compensation programmes have been structured to meet three primary design criteria. They must be:

1  *Internally equitable* and pay people in proportion to the relative value of the job.

2  *Externally competitive* and pay people in proportion to the market price of the job.

3  *Personally motivating* to employees.

Wolf adds a fourth objective, which is often kept from line managers: ease of administration for staff. Wolf comments on these objectives:

> Unfortunately, the first two are almost always at cross purposes with each other, forcing an organization to sacrifice one to achieve the other, and achievement of the third means a high degree of individualization, which complicates the fourth, administration.

Many countries have minimum wage rates in place which set the base rate for pay across the job market.

## HR AND PAYROLL ADMINISTRATION

Traditionally, payroll sections and the human resource sections that interface with them have suffered from too much administration. Every transaction triggered 'a paper-intensive, repetitive, and inconsistent process' (Hitzeman, 1997). Today, businesses want their pay functions to do more than just administration. They demand efficient payroll processes together with expertise and service. According to Hitzeman such changes in delivery and expectations are forcing pay-related departments to sharpen their focus on key issues.

Hitzeman argues that the pay function is becoming increasingly complex because:

→  legal aspects have become more involved.

→  staff expect higher standards of service.

→  pay staffing levels have been kept steady or even reduced.

To provide the desired level of service to staff and other 'customers', pay departments need to reorganize both tasks and resources around two central themes: transactions and consulting.

Payroll sections typically deal with issues which go beyond simple pay calculations. They can include:

→  health benefit schemes

→  pension contributions

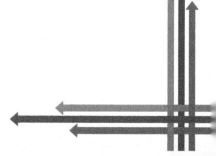

## HRM IN REALITY — TOP TEN EXCUSES FOR NOT PAYING MINIMUM WAGE

HM Revenue & Customs published the top ten excuses used by employers to avoid paying the national minimum wage in 2006. These excuses were to its 16 minimum wage enforcement teams around the UK. The enforcement teams identified nearly £3.3 million in underpaid salaries across the UK between August 2005 and July 2006.

The top ten unusual or outlandish excuses for not paying the minimum wage were:

1 He doesn't deserve it – he's a total waste of space

2 But she only wanted £3 an hour

3 I didn't think the workers were worth NMW

4 I didn't think it applied to small employers

5 He's disabled

6 They can't cope on their own and it's more than they would get in their own country

7 She's on benefits – if you add those to her pay, it totals the NMW

8 He's over 65, so the national minimum wage doesn't apply

9 The workers can't speak English

10 I only took him on as a favour.

*Do these excuses have any justification?*

*Source: Reprinted with permission from HRM Guide UK (http://www.hrmguide.co.uk).*

---

→ savings

→ company share option purchases

→ sickness and other forms of paid time off

→ expenses.

As a result, payroll staff are involved with the following transactions:

→ dealing with routine queries

→ filling in forms

→ issuing forms for staff to complete

→ explaining company policies and procedures.

Traditionally, payroll departments handled a great deal of repetitive work and generated mountains of paper. At the same time they tended to be inconsistent in the responses they provided – similar queries often receiving different answers, depending on the staff member involved. Basically, traditional pay sections were too clerical in focus. A solution has been to split information away from administrative functions into specialist areas. This allows consolidation and standardization of transaction-handling, leading to a degree of efficiency not possible in a traditional, unspecialized department. In large organizations, such a function can become a centre of excellence, taking advantage of professional techniques and up-to-date information technology. This offers the possibility of: more efficient processes and better customer service; consistent handling of queries and situations; better information; and a recognized 'one-stop shop' for pay-related queries.

As another step in this process, organizations may choose to outsource some of the more routine 'number-crunching' functions to specialist companies. Pension administration is a long-standing example. The most obvious justification for outsourcing is to cut costs by:

→ benefiting from the economies of scale open to a specialist provider.

→ reducing the number of internal pay administrators.

→ minimizing capital investment in equipment.

→ reducing overhead costs such as accommodation, heating and lighting.

**HRM IN REALITY** RECESSION IMPACTS ON JOBS, INCOMES AND EMPLOYEE ENGAGEMENT

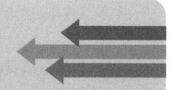

Most European businesses are finding it difficult to attract and motivate the skilled individuals needed to recover from the economic crisis, according to research from global professional services company Towers Watson. Cost-cutting has also had a negative impact on existing employees and organizations are looking afresh at how they attract, motivate and engage their workforces.

In fact, the Towers Watson Global Talent Management and Rewards Survey, prepared in conjunction with WorldatWork, the international association of HR professionals, shows that businesses worldwide are finding that attracting critical-skill employees is a major issue. Sixty-five per cent of organizations surveyed around the globe reported problems attracting critical-skill employees. In Europe, 58 per cent of respondents were experiencing these problems to a great or moderate extent and 61 per cent also said they had similar difficulties attracting top performers.

Globally, the economic crisis had forced businesses to cut costs. In Europe the top three actions were:

→ hiring freezes (75 per cent)

→ salary freezes (63 per cent)

→ layoffs/redundancies (57 per cent).

Respondents acknowledged that these cost-cutting measures have been tough on employees.

→ Sixty-one per cent of European respondents said that employees' workload had increased as a result

→ Forty-seven per cent felt they had adversely impacted on employees' ability to manage workplace stress

→ Forty-four per cent said the measures had a negative effect on employees' healthy work-life balance

→ Fifty-one per cent believed that there had been an adverse impact on overall employee engagement.

Carole Hathaway, senior consultant at Towers Watson, said:

> Employers need to address the adverse issues amongst employees caused by cost-cutting. It is critical that companies re-motivate and re-engage their employees as there is a clear link between increased employee engagement and improved business performance. Business leaders therefore need to show their employees how they intend to build trust and demonstrate interest in their employees' well-being – whilst also doing so in as cost-effective ways as possible.

Many companies are re-evaluating reward and talent management programmes because of the impact of cost-cutting on employee:

→ Fifty-eight per cent of businesses surveyed are ensuring readiness of skilled people for critical roles

→ Fifty-six per cent are creating more movement, rotation and development opportunities for skilled people

→ Fifty-three per cent are investing more in building internal pipelines of talent.

Carole Hathaway added:

> The business climate has clearly affected companies' ability to attract and re-motivate

top-performing employees. At least in part because these key people simply are in no rush to seek employment elsewhere given the uncertainty over economic recovery and the future of their current pay and benefits package. But these are the very people most likely to leave should a better offer come along. Many employers have also underestimated the impact of pensions, job security and flexible working arrangements on employees' decisions whether or not to leave their organization.

*What should organizations do to optimize their reward management strategies in times of economic crisis?*

Source: Reprinted with permission from HRM Guide (http://www.hrmguide.net).

## PAY EVALUATION

What criteria should be used to determine levels of pay? Dickinson (2006) found evidence for widespread social norms about the most appropriate bases for pay differentials with 'responsibility', 'qualifications' and 'performance' being the most commonly cited by employees. However, large organizations have traditionally resorted to job evaluation to provide the justification for different levels of pay. According to the International Labour Organization, 'job evaluation is directed towards rating the job, not the person'. Job evaluation is particularly concerned with:

→ tasks involved in fulfilling a job

→ duties that have to be completed

→ responsibilities attached.

It is not concerned with elements of job analysis required for the recruitment process such as qualifications, experience, proficiency, or the key considerations of performance management – job behaviour, proficiency and attendance.

The outcome of a traditional job evaluation process is a set of job classifications, perhaps expressed as a formal hierarchy of jobs. The next stage, job pricing, results in a pay scale. Therefore, job pricing determines the remuneration or compensation for each job.

Traditional job evaluation involves the comparison of jobs in a formal, systematic way to identify their relative value to an organization. It has an underlying premise: that some jobs are worth more than others. Job evaluation has its roots in the scientific management movement (Taylorism) of the early 20th century. The methodology has had a particularly strong influence in the USA, where it has focused on position-based job evaluation systems. These systems define the scope and value of jobs by using comparatively narrow job classification grades.

The end of the 20th century saw some radical changes in the nature of work. Increasingly, the concept of flexibility displaced the notion that work should be composed of a rigid set of pre-defined tasks. The job description seems increasingly inappropriate for the way work is organized today since the content of many jobs varies from one day to the next. This makes job rating and pay evaluation more difficult. Traditional job evaluation is focused on unchanging job descriptions and requirements, encouraging staff to take a rigid attitude to their work. If performance assessment and pay are linked to the completion of specific tasks, the need for change and a flexible approach to customers is ignored. Modern organizations have turned to competency profiles instead. Over the last few decades, pay evaluation systems have swung from having an individual focus to being job-based and, more recently, back again to a stress on the individual.

## Market-driven criteria

New skills and occupations are characterized by a greater demand for the right people than the job market can supply. The natural response is to increase pay and benefits on offer to these people. However, this has consequences for other staff in the organization and also for any job evaluation system. Scarcity of skills distorts evaluation systems and raises concerns about fairness. Short-term solutions produce further problems in the future when appropriately skilled staff become plentiful. This situation is common in information technology where, at first, only a few individuals are able to use new applications. Within a matter of months large numbers of trained people become available. A year or two later the applications may be replaced by new products and the once-valued skills are redundant.

## Broadbanding and skill-based pay

Broadbanding has been implemented in a number of different ways, but the basic principle is the same: large numbers of individually rated jobs or job types are clustered into a few, much wider job classifications or 'bands'. Although broadbanding was trumpeted as a panacea in the 1990s, Wolf (1999: 45) criticizes the exaggerated claims for its effectiveness, stating that these are made on questionable data. It is clear from a number of surveys that managers are not implementing broadbanding thoroughly – for example, bands often are not broad at all. Many organizations are not measuring the cost or effectiveness of broadbanding in comparison with more traditional methods, and improvements in career management (cited as one of the main benefits by proponents) are not being achieved.

Wolf (*ibid.:* 48) is equally dismissive of skill or competence-based pay systems:

> Whether one relies on old-fashioned job evaluation and traditional job-pay structures or moves to competencies and broad bands, employers still pay for what you know and what you do. No matter how you get there, these are the key compensable elements! Attempts to dress this up in modern garb abound, but the underlying premise remains as an eternal verity.

Kessler (2001: 221) also concludes that competence (and team) based pay are superficially attractive, but they are difficult to put into practice as competencies are difficult to identify and measure, as are the standards for judging team performance. Kessler considers that:

> It is difficult to avoid the conclusion that while use of pay to encourage the development of employee competencies and a team-based work environment are readily identifiable as business priorities, driving the formulation of new pay strategies, there is precious little evidence to suggest that such priorities are being translated into practice.

Can we be confident that pay evaluations are always objective? Mobius and Rosenblat (2006) conducted an experimental study where participants acting as 'employers' determined wages of other participants ('workers') performing a maze-solving task. The skill required had nothing to do with physical attractiveness but physically attractive 'workers' seemed to get a sizeable premium. Three possible explanations were suggested:

→ physically attractive workers are more confident and higher confidence increases wages.

→ for a given level of confidence, physically attractive workers are wrongly considered more able by employers.

→ controlling for worker confidence, physically attractive workers have oral skills (such as communication and social skills) that raise their wages when they interact with employers.

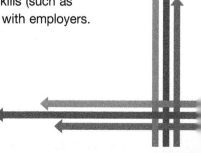

# MOTIVATION, PAY AND BENEFITS

How important is pay as a motivator? Rynes, Gerhart and Minette (2004: 382) observe that 'practitioner journals present claims about pay importance that are inconsistent with research about the actual motivational effects of pay. In general, there appears to be a consistent (but incorrect) message to practitioners that pay is not a very effective motivator – a message that, if believed, could cause practitioners to seriously underestimate the motivational potential of a well-designed compensation system.' They argue that most surveys of motivating factors are misleading because employees tend to give 'socially desirable' responses that place pay well down in the list of motivators. They consider that pay is the most important motivator and cite meta-analytic evidence.

**HRM IN REALITY** POOR LEADERSHIP IN MOTIVATING POORER-PERFORMING STAFF

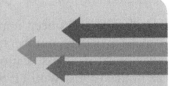

A 2008 European study by consultants Watson Wyatt has found that employers need to be more effective at helping managers to motivate poorer-performing staff.

Carole Hathaway, a senior consultant at Watson Wyatt commented:

> Managers find it easy to manage top-performing employees but are not so adept when it comes to improving poorer performers. Some of the greatest opportunities for improved organizational performance lie in helping managers raise the bar for moderate and poorer performers but it appears from our study that few employers are doing a good job of this.

Watson Wyatt's 2007/2008 Global Strategic Rewards study encompassed 5500 employees and 175 businesses across Europe. The study found that, compared to their poorer-performing colleagues, top performers were 66 per cent more likely to say that their immediate bosses did a good job of communicating organizational and performance management issues.

Watson Wyatt also found that just a third of poor performers could say that their immediate supervisors were good at:

→ communicating expectations for organizational financial performance

→ establishing goals for their individual performance that were linked to business objectives, or

→ providing direct feedback on their individual performance.

Worse, fewer than 30 per cent felt that their immediate manager did a good job of linking organizational performance to rewards or linking individual performance to rewards.

Carole Hathaway said:

> It could be that managers need more support in understanding how to communicate with all their staff, not just the more motivated stronger performers. Employees perform better if they have a clear understanding of their organization's goals and what they can personally do to contribute towards these.
>
> So setting good objectives and getting performance management communication right, especially for the weaker members of a team, is of vital importance.

*Poor leadership affecting business performance*
A survey for RTL in 2007 indicated that UK bosses' lack of leadership skills in setting objectives, motivating employees and dealing with poor performers has an adverse effect on business performance. Commissioned by Ros Taylor Ltd, a leading firm of Chartered Psychologists, the study drew on responses from 1500 people from organizations of varying sizes throughout the UK about leadership in the workplace.

Key findings include:

→ Seventy-seven per cent of respondents said their boss was not interested in them

→ Ninety per cent said their boss did nothing about poor performers

→  Seventy-nine per cent claimed their boss did not set clear objectives

→  Eighty-nine per cent said their boss lacked innovation and was unreceptive to new ideas.

Ros Taylor, managing director of RTL commented:

> That's only 15 per cent of people we asked who thought their boss was any good and 8 per cent who thought they were inspirational. I wish I could say I was shocked – but the truth is it's slightly better than I expected. The fact is that while businesses are quite rightly paying attention to their cost base – squeezing every last ounce of value out of the food chain – they are not so cleverly overlooking a very real business and financial asset.

### Leadership

Let's forget the old clichés about 'soft skills' – bad leadership costs shareholders and stakeholders real money. While companies are spending millions on automation and the new IT architectures they could be spending thousands and saving millions by sharpening up their leadership assets.

Think about it. Many line managers, heads of department and directors are on a minimum £100K+ pa. These people represent something of the order of a £200K+ investment for the company. As a psychologist I am intrigued that companies who bend over backwards to 'think smart' ignore this area. It's the 'one thing' they could do that would deliver tangible results – and yet the vast majority just don't do it. They probably think that, in the old cliché 'leaders are born, not made' and yet in our business we disprove that on an almost daily basis. They can't leave the innovation and blue sky thinking that comes from truly inspirational leadership to chance – or for that matter to a quirk of genetics – it's odd to think that multinational companies who factor the canteen subsidy into the cost of a sausage roll don't have a 'leadership development plan'.

*Why is there a mismatch of perceptions between managers and staff?*

Source: Reprinted with permission from HRM Guide UK (http://www.hrmguide.co.uk).

---

Despite its importance, motivation goes beyond pay. Herpen, Praag and Cools (2005) demonstrated a positive relationship between the perceived characteristics of the complete compensation system and extrinsic motivation. Intrinsic motivation, on the other hand, was not affected by the design of monetary compensation, but by promotion opportunities. They also found that the compensation system significantly affected work satisfaction and turnover intent. Balsam *et al.* (2007) found evidence that stock options reduced employee turnover in the periods when the options could not be exercised.

According to Rosenbloom (2001, p.2):

> Employee benefits constitute a major part of almost any individual's financial and economic security. Such benefits have gone from being considered 'fringe' to the point where they may constitute about 40 per cent of an employee's compensation, and the plans under which they are provided are a major concern of employers.

See Key concept 17.2.

### KEY CONCEPT 17.2  EMPLOYEE BENEFITS

Any form of reward other than regular wages paid to employees.

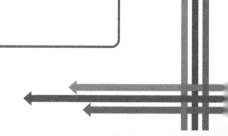

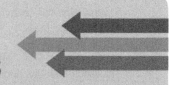

## HRM IN REALITY — INCENTIVE SCHEMES DILUTED BY TOO MANY PERFORMANCE MEASURES

A global study by Watson Wyatt in 2007 concluded that the effectiveness of sales incentive plans can be diluted by too many performance measures and shows significant differences between sectors. For example, the banking sector frequently used multiple measures while the hi-tech sector uses far fewer.

At branch management level, the banking sector uses seven dominant measures:

→ revenue volume

→ number of new accounts

→ number of units sold

→ sales growth

→ profit margin

→ expense control, and

→ customer satisfaction.

Conversely, a role at a similar level in hi-tech companies typically uses a mere three criteria: revenue volume; management by objectives; and profit margin.

Chantal Free, European head of sales effectiveness and compensation consulting at Watson Wyatt commented:

> We believe hi-tech companies are ahead of the curve by moving away from using lots of measures. We are likely to see other sectors following suit in having fewer measures. Companies are finding that having too many measures dilutes their effectiveness and the laudable intentions behind them risk getting lost. Two is ideal for any sales role, and three is the maximum.

Watson Wyatt's survey of over 200 companies in 22 countries, found revenue volume to be the main measure criterion for most industries and job roles. The study also found that team measures were increasingly used because of account management and cross-selling initiatives.

*Why would having too many criteria dilute the effectiveness of incentives?*

*Source: Adapted from HRM Guide UK (http://www.hrmguide.co.uk).*

---

The US Chambers of Commerce survey of employee benefits (cited in Rosenbloom, 2001: 3) includes the following:

1  Employer's share of legally required payments.

2  Employer's share of retirement and savings plan payments.

3  Employer's share of life insurance and death benefit payments.

4  Employer's share of medical and medically related benefit payments.

5  Payment for time not worked (e.g. paid rest periods, paid sick leave, paid vacations, holidays, parental leave, etc.).

6  Miscellaneous benefit payments (including employee discounts, severance pay, educational expenditure and childcare).

Paid time off is still the most common benefit for employees in US private organizations. All US employers in a survey conducted by WorldatWork in 2010 offer paid time off work and three-quarters of respondents find it necessary to offer paid time off programmes in order to compete in the labour market and have 'traditional' and non-traditional ways of doing so. The report, *Paid Time Off Programs and Practices*, was based on 1036 respondents from the

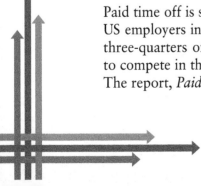

HR, compensation and benefits departments of mostly large US corporations. Lenny Sanicola, benefits practice leader for WorldatWork said:

> With the focus of the Administration and Congress on expanding access to work – life benefits such as paid leave programs, our research report shows that employers recognize the competitive advantage of offering paid time off and believe in continuing these programmes, even through the recession.
>
> Time is the new currency, and employers remain committed to providing paid time off as a key employee benefit and reward.

The report defines three types of programme:

→ **Traditional** – preferred by large organizations and used by 54 per cent of companies. These programs give employees separate allotments for vacation, personal and sick days. A typical programme offers 21 days (12 paid vacation plus nine sick days) on average for one to two years of service.

→ **PTO bank-type** – this model has increased in popularity from 28 per cent in 2002 to 40 per cent in 2010. Employees are given a pooled number of days off to be used as needed, although fixed holidays, jury duty and bereavement are treated separately. PTO bank programs average a total of 19 days.

→ **Unlimited leave** – allowing employees to take as many days as needed. This model is offered by mere one per cent of organizations.

On average, employers offer nine paid statutory holidays each year.

Morris, Bakan and Wood (2006) highlight some of the contradictions and limitations of flexible reward systems in a study of employees in a large retail organization in the UK. They found that participation lengthens the reward cycle; employees are encouraged to remain with the firm to maximize their shareholdings. However, workers may have different agendas according to individual choices made regarding the scale of participation in such schemes. Junior employees are less likely to choose to actively buy into profit sharing and share ownership schemes. Workers in lower job bands achieve less reward from participation but the effects of any undermining of collective solidarities are likely to be particularly pronounced in this group.

## HRM IN REALITY  EXECUTIVE PERKS

A report from Compdata Surveys shows that cell phones are the most popular executive perks. The *Executive Compensation 2008/2009* survey of 5300 organizations found that 60.2 per cent offered cell phones to executives as a perk with 43.8 per cent of employers providing laptops or home PCs in 2008. Fewer than a third of organizations in the survey provided car allowances or company cars.

The report analyzes both national and regional data collected from 5300 organizations across the United States with almost 25000 incumbents. 45 executive and senior management positions were analyzed by base pay and total cash compensation.

The frequency of most executive perks on the revenue size of employing organizations but cell phones were offered by over half of the companies surveyed, regardless of size. Company cars were also offered by 20 to 30 per cent of surveyed organizations across the board. But businesses with revenues over $20 million were the most likely to provide executives with laptops or home PCs.

Perks mentioned in the survey included:

→ mobile phones (60.2 per cent)

→ car allowance (31.3 per cent)

→ company car (26.4 per cent)

→ supplemental life insurance (26.2 per cent)

→ voluntary deferred compensation programs (18.8 per cent)

→ annual physical exam (17.6 per cent)

→ supplemental disability programme (16.9 per cent)

→ club membership(s) (15.7 per cent)

→ supplemental executive retirement plans (10.3 per cent)

→ supplemental medical insurance (6.2 per cent)

→ legal counselling (5.6 per cent)

→ post-retirement insurance (4.6 per cent)

→ supplemental vacations (4.5 per cent)

→ airline VIP lounge membership (3.1 per cent)

→ dependent tuition reimbursement (3.3 per cent).

The number of organizations offering each kind of executive perk has remained consistent over the past four years.

*What perks would motivate you?*

Source: Reprinted with permission from HRM Guide USA (http://www.hrmguide.com).

Rumpel and Medcof (2006) review research on Total Rewards, an approach to reward management adopted by technology-intensive firms such as IBM, Microsoft, AstraZeneca and Johnson & Johnson. Total Rewards takes a holistic approach, going beyond the traditional emphasis on pay and benefits. It considers all the rewards available in the workplace, including opportunities for learning and development, and quality work environment. These factors were found to be a high priority for technical workers and offer an opportunity to tap an organization's unrealized potential. It is argued that effectively managed rewards will ease the critical attraction, retention and motivation challenges faced by high-technology firms.

## PAY AND PERFORMANCE

Many commentators severely criticized the apparently chaotic and disorganized nature of pay management between the 1950s and 1980s. Subsequently there has been an attempt to remedy this situation. The fashion has been towards the development of performance-related pay schemes that are related to assessments of performance through individual employee appraisal. Wolf (1999: 48) sums up a common view:

> Pay for performance is the holy grail of modern compensation administration – widely sought but hard to actually achieve. Pay for performance is the flag, motherhood and apple pie, but it is easier said than done. One primary problem is defining performance properly, so that the organization pays for results and not for effort. Once over that hurdle, there remains the large impediment of finding enough money to make the reward for top performance meaningful.

Pay is a sensitive issue. Most employers have been cautious with the introduction of PRP. Often it is applied to senior managers first, then extended to other employees. Usually, it has been an 'add-on' to normal pay. Rarely does it replace the existing pay scheme completely. More commonly, PRP has:

→ formed part or (rarely) all of the general pay increase.

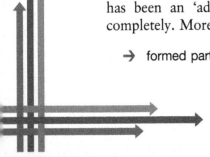

→ been used to extend pay above scale maxima for employees with high levels of performance.

→ replaced increases previously paid on the basis of age, or length of service.

Such caution is due to the complexity and sensitivity of performance-related pay in the context of employee relations. People take pay scales seriously. Negotiating and justifying radical changes to a pay structure can be difficult and time-consuming. It is sensible to do so in a gradual way, commencing with senior managers who are more likely to be committed to demanding performance objectives. Even if they are not, it gives experience of the advantages and disadvantages of performance-related pay. It also gives pay administrators experience of pay schemes that are more complicated to operate than traditional methods.

## The basis of performance-related pay systems

Simplistically, it seems only fair that people should be paid according to their contribution and a number of studies indicate that most people in business agree with this. In a classic experiment, Fossum and Fitch (1985) asked three groups of subjects – students, line managers and compensation managers – to make decisions on pay increases for hypothetical people, taking into account factors such as seniority, budget constraints and cost of living. All three groups gave far more importance to performance and contribution than other factors. Research into the attitudes of corporate boards and chief executive officers, among others, have all produced similar findings.

Theoretically, performance-related pay schemes can benefit both employers and employees. By emphasizing the importance of efficiency and effective job performance, employers can benefit from higher productivity. Higher pay can be targeted at the 'better' performers, encouraging them to stay with the company and continue to perform to a high standard. Good employees benefit from extra pay in return for extra quality of performance. According to this view, properly directed pay can reinforce appropriate behaviour, focusing effort on organizational targets and encouraging a results-based culture. However, these links must be justified and real if they are not to demoralize other members of the workforce. This is particularly important in relation to senior management. Accusations of 'fat cat' behaviour can also seriously affect stock market views of a company's organization. Widespread condemnation followed the payment of massive bonuses to individuals in the financial sector for activities described as 'socially useless' and 'gambling' that were associated with the credit crisis of 2007–2009.

PRP can be related to the performance assessment of the individual, group (team), department or company. There are several systems in common use.

## Appraisal-related pay schemes

**Merit pay** This is paid as part of a person's annual increase on the basis of an overall performance appraisal. The method has a long track record and is commonly regarded as an effective motivator. However, it is frequently undermined by budget restrictions, when the merit element often is set too low to motivate. It is also dependent on line managers whose training to ensure fair appraisals is often questionable (Prowse and Prowse, 2009).

There are also instances when the payment is used as a 'market supplement' to retain individuals who have skills for which there is demand but whose performance is not particularly meritorious. However, it is known that breaking the clear link between appraised performance and payment of PRP reduces the overall effectiveness of PRP as a motivator for other employees.

**Individual incentives** Given as unconsolidated (one-off) payments or gifts such as holidays, golf sets or vouchers.

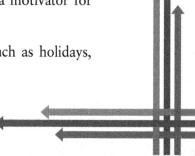

*Collective performance schemes*

**Bonuses** These are paid to all staff in an organization, department or team. In common with all collective performance rewards, they are designed to reinforce corporate identity and performance.

The reward system in Japan is unusual. According to Hart and Kawasaki (1999: 4):

> Most Japanese workers receive the major part of their direct remuneration via two channels. First, and familiar to workers in other countries, they are paid in the form of regular (usually monthly) wages. Secondly, they receive bonus payments which, typically, are paid twice a year. The bonus constitutes around one-fifth to one-quarter of total cash earnings.

Bonuses paid in other countries are much smaller, so why are Japanese bonuses paid at such a level? Hart and Kawasaki offer a range of alternative explanations, including the possibility that bonuses:

> … represent a form of efficiency wage by providing a reward for greater effort. By contrast, and at a general level, wages may reflect more systematic and structural elements of remuneration, such as seniority-based pay scales (the *Nenko* system), while bonuses are used to adjust total compensation to fluctuations in firms' economic experience. In this event, we might expect that the bonus should display more flexibility than the wage. One school of thought in this respect regards bonuses as a form of profit-sharing between the firm and its workforce. Another holds that bonuses reflect shared returns to investments in firm-specific skills and know-how.

Conrad (2010) notes a general trend towards performance-related pay in Japan, with some concerns about the exact mechanism to be used and the risk of demotivational effects.

**Profit-related pay** These are schemes in which employees are allocated a payment equivalent to an agreed proportion of the organization's profits. Profit-related pay has been encouraged in the UK through tax incentives.

**Option schemes** Executive share option schemes are particularly prevalent in the USA but have also become common elsewhere. They allow senior managers to benefit from the continued success of the organization through the purchase of shares at designated dates in the future at a fixed price. The more successful the company, and therefore the greater the likely increase in share value, the higher the reward to the executive. This is seen as an important incentive to motivate people who can dramatically affect the prosperity and even survival of the business.

Employee share option schemes apply to less senior staff and tend to be considerably less generous than executive schemes. Generally, a sum is allocated from company profits and used for share purchase for employees. There may also be save as you earn (SAYE) option schemes registered with the taxation authorities. These allow staff to save a proportion of their salary via the pay administration process and have it accumulated for a fixed period. This may be paid to them at the end of that time, with a bonus equivalent to the interest that could have been earned in a savings account. Alternatively, and more beneficially, the sum plus bonus can be used to purchase shares at the price prevailing at the start of the scheme. Preferential tax arrangements have been made for shares held in trust for a fixed period.

## FLAVOUR OF THE (LAST) MONTH?

Kanter (1989: 233) observes that whenever any US organization comes up with a 'new' pay scheme a merit element is involved. PRP has also been a prominent feature of the attempt to

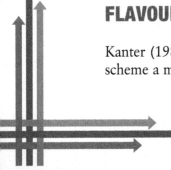

commercialize practices in the public services, intended as a key factor in encouraging businesslike behaviour amongst managers.

In the UK, the earliest use of PRP in the British civil service dates back to an experiment in 1985 affecting a range of senior grades (principal to under-secretary). The scheme involved payment of a minimum £500 unconsolidated bonus paid as a one-off lump sum to no more than a fifth of eligible staff. The exercise drew a range of comments but it was decided to extend the scheme to most other grades including non-management staff. Ironically, the Review Body on Top Salaries that covered judges, permanent secretaries, senior military officers and diplomats, felt that PRP was unsuitable for politically sensitive posts.

Performance-related pay was introduced for the 800 UK National Health Service general managers in 1986 based on annual objectives, individual performance reviews and financial rewards where the achievement of objectives could be clearly demonstrated (Murliss, 1987). For general managers, the process relied on an appraisal procedure called the 'individual performance review' (IPR). The system had the following characteristics:

→ The method was objectives-based, stated wherever possible in quantifiable terms.

→ Appraisals were conducted on the 'parent – grandparent' system. Unit general managers would be assessed by the district general manager, with the chair of the regional health authority acting as 'grandparent'.

→ Managers were rated on one of five bands. 'Grandparents' had final responsibility and were required to ensure that no more than 20 per cent received the highest rating level and 40 per cent the next highest.

→ An individual at the highest level 'consistently exceeds short-term levels of performance and makes excellent progress towards long-term goals' justifying a salary increase of 3-4 per cent a year, up to a maximum of 20 per cent over five years.

→ At the lowest level, an individual 'meets few short-term objectives and makes little or no progress towards long-term goals' receiving no increase at all.

Kauhanen and Piekkola (2006) analyzed how features of performance-related pay schemes affect their perceived motivational effects using a Finnish survey for white-collar employees from 1999. They found that the following features are important for a successful PRP scheme:

1 Employees have to feel they are able to affect the outcomes.

2 The organizational level of performance measurement should be close to the employee – individual and team level performance measurement increase the probability that the scheme is perceived to be motivating.

3 Employees should be familiar with the performance measures.

4 The level of payments should be high enough and rewards frequent enough – levels below the median do not generate positive effects.

5 Employees should participate in the design of the PRP scheme.

Long and Shields (2005) studied the incidence of 13 forms of performance pay in 315 Canadian and Australian firms. Overall, firms in both countries showed similar incidences of most forms of performance pay, with employee profit sharing the notable exception. Firm size and unionization were among the most important predictors of

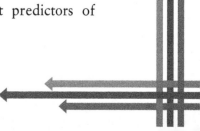

individual and organizational performance pay, but neither factor predicted group performance pay. High involvement firms in both Canada and Australia used more organizational performance pay than other firms, but not more group or individual performance pay. Marsden (2010) concludes that improvement on some performance in the British Civil Service was not due to the motivational effect of PRP, but the linking of personal objectives to organizational goals. Conversely, using a meta-analysis of experimental studies, Weibel *et al.* (2010) consider that motivation is a key element in the public service use of PRP.

## CRITICISMS OF PRP

There is a widespread opinion among senior managers that PRP must be a good thing – but the evidence for its effectiveness is not overwhelming. Indeed, the search for a positive relationship between PRP and good performance has been described as being like 'looking for the Holy Grail' (Fletcher and Williams, 1992). As one variable in a complex situation, it is not surprising that a connection is difficult to prove. A number of major issues can be considered.

### Fairness

The concept of 'fairness' is problematic and open to interpretation, with some people seeing pay as a measure of justice (Milcovich, Newman and Milcovich, 2001: 2). What pay differentials do people consider to be fair? This may vary from country to country. Osberg and Smeeding (2006) compared attitudes in the USA with other countries towards what individuals in specific occupations 'do earn' and what they 'should earn'. Americans showed less awareness of the extent of inequality at the top of income distribution; more polarized attitudes; similar preferences for 'levelling down' at the top of the earnings distribution; but also less concern for reducing differentials at the bottom.

Some employers have gone to elaborate lengths in an attempt to make their system appear fair. This may involve sampling the work of lower-level workers, listening in on phone calls, examining files, or checking through a proportion of completed work. For example, the Bank of America has been cited as spending over a million dollars a year and employing 20 people to monitor 3500 credit card workers for their merit scheme. Not surprisingly, such attempts at 'fairness' have not been entirely popular among employees. The system seems to be distinctly Orwellian: 'Big Brother is watching you'.

### Managerial judgement

The process is dependent on skilled line managers. As we have observed, for various reasons managers feel under pressure to rate their staff as above average. As Kanter (1989) says, 'far from freeing the energies of employees to seek ways to improve their performance, subjectively based merit pay systems throw them back on the merit of their bosses'. Typically such systems are cynically regarded by employees and attacked by unions as being open to abuse and favouritism. They can also result in a rash of high marks by supervisors who feel exposed to the wrath of their employees. Relationships between managers and employees are often uncomfortable, and this process tends to charge that relationship with even more emotion. But line or middle managers are often obliged to implement performance-related systems that they personally do not believe in (Harris, 2000).

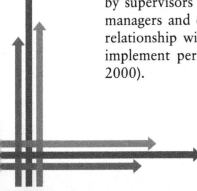

## Value of reward

Many senior managers seem more concerned with managing the pay bill than motivating staff, so that PRP is often budget-led, not performance-led. A frequent complaint is that the merit element is too small as a percentage of the whole – commonly from 3 to 10 per cent. This is not enough to be a motivator for improved performance. The solution is obvious at one level: increase the merit element to a significantly motivating level such as 15–25 per cent. But this only serves to highlight the difficulty in making a judgement on who gets an increase and being seen to be fair about it (Isaac, 2001). Most employers have not felt confident enough about the process to go beyond a token percentage level.

## A demotivator

There may be evidence that people who are rewarded well by PRP are duly motivated, but they are usually a minority in an organization and the effect is outweighed by the demotivation of the majority (Marsden, French and Kobi, 2000). McCausland, Pouliakas and Theodossiou (2005) found that while the predicted job satisfaction of workers receiving PRP is lower on average compared with those on other pay schemes, it has a positive effect on the mean job satisfaction of very highly paid workers. They suggest that lower-paid employees may perceive PRP to be controlling, whereas higher-paid workers derive a utility benefit from what they view as supportive reward schemes. Green and Heywood (2008) on the other hand, conclude that PRP has largely positive effects on worker satisfaction.

## PRP and unions

PRP increases the likelihood of flexibility and management power. Not surprisingly, PRP has attracted hostility from many unions as collective bargaining is side-stepped. Hanley and Nguyen (2005) investigated the impact of performance-related pay at the lower end of the remuneration spectrum in Australia. Their study was based on interviews with union officials and analysis of performance appraisal and performance-related pay clauses in union enterprise bargaining agreements. These clauses ranged from minimal stipulation of existence to detailed processes and principles of design and implementation. Specific clauses in white-collar agreements suggest that they are not totally opposed. However, in blue-collar agreements the lack of such clauses is indicative of their propensity to restrict pay increases to a job classification structure. Clauses that aimed to ensure a performance-oriented culture seemed to be viewed as mere sentiment. Overall, only one union supported the notion of performance-related pay.

## Conflict with the team philosophy

The obsession with individually based, performance pay conflicts with HRM's emphasis on teams where careful thought has to be given to the design of PRP systems, especially when there is an agency perspective (Mitlacher and Paul, 2009). Employee dissatisfaction can result from merit payments being too low to provide any incentive and further criticisms of the operation of the system such as:

→ Upward movement of targets: employees finding themselves on a treadmill that is continually being speeded up.

→ Employees being assessed by managers who do not know them.

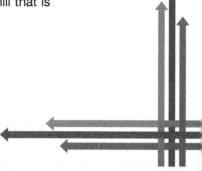

→ Performance pay for junior employees being restricted by 'budgetary constraints' when this limitation does not seem to apply to senior executives.

→ Objectives being imposed rather than negotiated.

→ Subjective criteria leading to disagreements on the quality of performance, leading to a perception of unfairness.

→ Individual targets not being compatible with team performance.

Kellough and Nigro (2002) investigated GeorgiaGain, a compensation system developed for the state of Georgia (USA). Performance-related pay was the centrepiece of the initiative that was intended to include a state-of-the-art performance management system, providing performance measurement and evaluation procedures trusted by supervisors and subordinates. But Kellough and Nigro's survey of state employees found them highly critical of the reform and complaining that it had not produced the intended outcomes in most areas. The reduction of the inflation rate to low single figures has further reduced the perceived effectiveness of incentives. Merit payments of two to three per cent are not seen as much reward for exceptional performance. Indeed such payments may be viewed as insulting. Performance systems established in a high inflation period have proven to be a financial embarrassment to some companies. British Telecom scrapped a system for junior and middle managers on the grounds that managers were being overpaid in comparison with equivalents in other firms. The use of incentives seems to have declined in British manufacturing firms as managers have gained greater control over pay schemes (Arrowsmith and Marginson, 2010).

### Performance and diversity

Fang and Heywood (2006) used the Workplace and Employee Survey to examine the association between payment method and ethnic wage differentials in Canada. Non-Europeans receive lower earnings than Europeans when paid by time rates. However, non-Europeans receive virtually identical earnings to their European counterparts when paid by output. They suggested that tying earnings to productivity made it more difficult for employers to discriminate. Similarly, Heywood and O'Halloran (2005) found no racial wage differential among male workers receiving output-based pay but a significant differential among those paid time rates. The racial wage differential among those receiving bonus pay, usually based on supervisory evaluation, tended to be larger than for those not receiving such bonuses.

## EXECUTIVE PAY

Nowhere has the issue of performance-related pay been more controversial than in the compensation arrangements for senior executives. Bender (2004) found that many companies adopted performance-related pay despite believing that the money did not motivate executives. Instead, the reasons were due to 'best practice' in human resource management. The pay structures were designed to attract and retain executives with the potential of large earnings, focus their efforts in the direction agreed by the board and to demonstrate fairness. Variable pay was seen as a symbol of the director's success, both within and outside the organization. Bender's study suggests that companies may use performance-related pay because their competitors do, and because that legitimizes them in the eyes of the establishment.

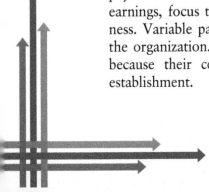

Bebchuk and Fried (2005) studied executive pay practices in the USA and the corporate governance processes that produce them. They suggest that managerial power and influence have come to play a major role in shaping executive pay, and in ways that end up imposing significant costs on investors and the economy. Their main concerns are the distortion of incentives caused by compensation practices that fail to link pay to performance, limit executives' freedom to sell their shares, or restrict benefits paid to departing executives. They call for greater transparency, improvements in pay practices and improvements in board accountability to shareholders.

Gordon (2005) acknowledges the strengths of Bebchuk and Fried's case for managerial power in setting executive pay but expresses three major reservations:

1  Concern about apparent lack of pay for performance does not provide sufficient explanation of the controversy over CEO pay and largely ignores popular disquiet about pay levels.

2  Many of the compensation practices identified as indicative of managerial power may have broader explanations. For example, the vast majority of employee stock options are awarded to people well below executive rank.

3  The best way of improving corporate governance may be not a wholesale expansion of shareholder power, but rather measures to increase the independence of the compensation committee.

Guy (2005) investigated the relationship between earnings differentials and CEO pay in 190 British companies between 1970 and 1990. The study concluded that top executive pay prior to 1984 was a stable function of both firm size and earnings differentials lower on the administrative ladder. The use of share options from 1984 onwards represents a change in the mode of top executive compensation and a de-linking of the pay of top executives and that of lower management. Similarly, Erturk *et al.* (2005) found that CEO pay in the UK and USA in the 1980s and 1990s increased at rates that resulted in ever widening gaps between executive and average pay. These increases, they argue, have significantly outrun any sustained increase in value attributable to management effort.

Girma, Thompson and Wright (2006) examined the impact of mergers and acquisitions on the remuneration of CEOs in the UK from 1981 to 1996. They found that CEO pay was not strongly related to company performance but, as in Guy's (2005) study, increased with firm size. CEOs involved in 'wealth-reducing' acquisitions received significantly lower remuneration than those whose deals met with market approval, suggesting that shareholder-principals had some success in penalizing managers for unwarranted empire-building mergers.

However, Stathopoulos, Espenlaub and Walker (2005) analyzed level and composition of the pay of the top executives of a sample of UK public listed companies and found that remuneration reflected organizational performance. Executives of firms that performed badly experienced cuts in salaries, bonuses and equity-based compensation. The study also revealed increased participation and value in the equity-based schemes provided to CEOs and other executives of poorly performing firms in the longer term. CEOs of poorly performing firms were significantly more likely to be dismissed but emoluments were not directly affected during the year of departure. In the same vein, Merhebi *et al.* (2006) reversed earlier Australian studies that found no link between CEO pay and corporate performance. The study by Merhebi *et al.* suggests that Australian experience is consistent with that of firms from the USA, UK and Canada. In general, however, CEO pay seems to have mushroomed at a considerable rate, particularly in the USA. Venkatasubramanian (2009) calculated that the top Fortune 500 CEOs pay had gone up from a ratio of 40–1 (compared to their lowest paid employee) in the 1970s to 334–1 in recent years.

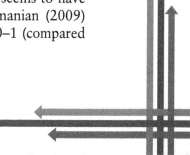

## HRM IN REALITY  WHY CEO PAY KEEPS GOING UP

Regardless of economic conditions, there is one constant in the workplace: CEO salaries keep going UP. A study published in 2010 by Thomas A. DiPrete, Greg Eirich and Matthew Pittinsky puts much of the blame on the practice of compensation benchmarking.

Standard practice in American corporations, benchmarking is a process used by compensation committees to compare peer groups of executives at similar organizations in order to establish a 'fair' market salary for their CEOs. However, it seems that each year a few CEOs 'leapfrog' their peers by getting large increases in compensation that have little to do with the financial performance of their organizations. Their unjustified raises are used by other firms in subsequent benchmarks. Gradually, the study concludes, executive pay is ratcheted up for everyone through a 'contagion effect'. According to DiPrete:

> We show that rising CEO pay is not simply a function of what individual companies do, but is influenced by the behaviour of leapfroggers at other firms.

Using procedures laid out in reward management handbooks the researchers reconstructed likely peer groups for CEOs listed in Standard and Poor's annual compensation surveys. Then they looked for evidence of leapfrogging in those likely peer groups over time. They found that leapfrogging could explain around half the overall increase in CEO pay from 1992 to 2006.

Previously, the debate on the causes of ever-increasing CEO pay had mainly fallen into two groups:

→ CEOs were overpaid because of failures in corporate governance at individual organizations

→ CEOs were paid what they deserved on the basis of profits they delivered to shareholders in a 'superstar' job market.

The researchers say that their findings broaden the debate as unjustified increases for a few CEOs can lead to 'legitimate' salary increases for others. They write that 'the linkages among firms produced by the benchmarking process guarantee that firm-level governance failure becomes a factor in the environment of other firms.'

After the Enron and WorldCom scandals in the early 2000s, the Securities and Exchange Commission changed its rules to require corporations to disclose benchmarking information. The research team state that they are 'now using the new data mandated by the SEC to better understand how the network structure of peer groups affects executive pay setting in American corporations.'

DiPrete added:

> Whether the SEC regulatory change reduces the ratcheting effect of leapfrogging on CEO pay – creating more transparency about who is in the peer group and at what level the company is benchmarking – is an important question for future research.

### Powerful CEOs pay employees more

Research on perceptions of fairness in executive pay and how CEO over- or underpayment cascades down to lower organizational levels was published in the September/October 2006 issue of *Organization Science*. The study looked at data from over 120 firms over a five-year period. Authors James Wade, professor at Rutgers University, Charles O'Reilly, professor at Stanford's Graduate School of Business, and Timothy Pollock at Pennsylvania State University's Smeal College of Business, used techniques of operations research (OR) in their analysis.

Key findings include:

→ **CEO overpayment has higher costs than previously realized**. It has been argued that even if a CEO is overpaid, a large company can easily absorb the cost. However, the study found that CEO pay has direct consequences for compensation at lower employee levels. The effects of CEO overpayment cascade down to subordinates at diminishing degrees. For example,

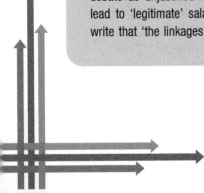

where one CEO was overpaid by 64 per cent, individuals at Level 2 (chief operating officer, chief finance officer, etc.) were overpaid by 26 per cent, while individuals at Level 5 (division general managers) were overpaid by 12 per cent. The cumulative effect of this systemic overpayment impacts on overall organizational performance and shareholder value.

Charles O'Reilly commented:

> Given the large sums paid to some senior executives, the total cost for overpayment could be a big number – and, in some cases, significantly affect shareholder returns.

→ **CEO pay impacts subordinate turnover**. The study found that CEOs serve as a key reference point for employees in determining whether their own pay is fair. If the CEO is overpaid, subordinates are more likely to leave. The turnover effect becomes more pronounced the farther away you get from CEO level. Even if an employee is overpaid relative to the market, they will have a greater propensity to leave if their CEO is overpaid by a larger percentage than they are.

James Wade said:

> CEO compensation impacts employee retention more than we realized. Our research found that CEO overpayment is related to turnover, which can have important long-term consequences. It is quite possible that those most likely to leave because of perceived unfairness are precisely those employees coming up in the organization that would eventually rise to the top management team level.

→ **CEO underpayment also cascades**. The study found that CEO underpayment tends to get cascaded through an organization, with multiplying effects. If the CEO is underpaid more than you are, you are less likely to leave, but if the CEO is underpaid less than you are, you are more likely to leave. As James Wade put it, 'underpaying a CEO could reduce turnover if subordinates are underpaid less than the CEO is underpaid.'

→ **Notions of fairness are powerful**. The study found that CEOs tend to be concerned with the perception of fairness. If the CEO is paid generously, they will typically use their influence to pay others generously as well. And, if they are seen as being underpaid, that will also have an effect.

Timothy Pollock commented:

> Our research shows evidence that CEOs are concerned with fairness, and that they are likelier to share rewards than they are to share burdens. But this can be expensive and has the potential to hurt a firm's bench strength if the rewards aren't fully shared.

→ **Powerful CEOs pay employees more**. CEOs who also serve as chairman of the board tend to pay their employees more. This effect is more pronounced at higher levels, but diminishes at lowers levels. The effect disappeared at Level 5 (division general managers), but was strong at Levels 2–4 (the top management team through the junior vice president ranks).

*What do you consider to be a fair level of pay for a CEO compared to the lowest paid employee?*

*Source: Reprinted with permission from HRM Guide USA (http://www.hrmguide.com).*

Perkins and Hendry (2005) highlighted the important role of non-executive directors in determining executive pay. They studied the nuances of executive pay decision making, including remuneration committee members' reactions to corporate governance reforms. Such initiatives place non-executive directors in the role of intermediaries, explicitly assigned to resolve the conflict of interest inherent in boardroom remuneration systems, while simultaneously expected to play a team role as board members responsible for the overall strategy and operation of the company.

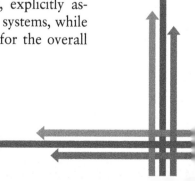

**SUMMARY**

Pay is a key element in the management of people. The importance of pay begins with pay administration that deals accurately and swiftly with payroll-related matters. Much of the information used by pay administrators is shared with the human resource function. Pay evaluation systems also impinge on human resource territory. Free market organizations are particularly concerned with performance-related pay as a motivating factor. However, this trend appears to be ideological rather than rational since practical PRP schemes that deliver the results intended are extremely difficult to construct. Current evidence shows that performance pay is likely to demotivate some people more than it motivates others.

 **FURTHER READING**

1 *Armstrong's Handbook of Reward Management Practice: Improving Performance Through Reward*, 3rd edition, Kogan Page (2010) by Michael Armstrong covers the ground thoroughly.

2 *Strategic Reward: Implementing More Effective Reward Management* by Michael Armstrong and Duncan Brown (Kogan Page, 2009) and

3 *Reward Management*, 2nd edition (CIPD, 2011) by Stephen Perkins and Geoffrey White (Kogan Page, 2005) also cover this topic area well.

**REVIEW QUESTIONS**

1 What is pay for? What effect does the minimum wage have on employer and employee attitudes to rates of pay?

2 What functions should a payroll department fulfil? Is it appropriate to merge the HR function with a payroll department?

3 What are the implications of paying different salaries for the same job?

4 Does job evaluation have a function in a modern pay system?

5 A fair day's work for a fair day's pay'. How can a company's pay system be designed to meet this criterion?

6 Outline the arguments for and against the use of performance-related pay.

7 Should executive directors be paid on a different basis from other employees?

8 What advantages do flexible benefits offer for individual employees and their employers?

9 How large does a merit payment or bonus have to be in order to provide an incentive for effective performance?

10 What are the practical consequences of using employee stock options as a motivator?

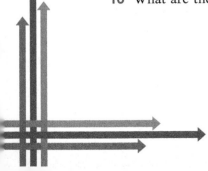

## Fairness

### Scenario 1

A photocopying shop has one employee who has worked in the shop for six months and earns US$9 per hour. Business continues to be satisfactory, but a factory in the area has closed and unemployment has increased. Other small firms have now hired reliable workers working at US$7 an hour to perform jobs similar to those done by the photocopy shop employee. The owner of the shop reduces the employee's wage to US$7.

*Is it fair to cut the worker's wage from US$9 to US$7 an hour? Compare your decision with the second scenario.*

### Scenario 2

A house painter employs two assistants and pays them US$9 per hour. The painter decides to change his business and go into lawn-mowing, where the going wage is lower. He tells the current workers that he will keep them on if they want to work, but will only pay them US$7 per hour.

*Is this employer being fair?*

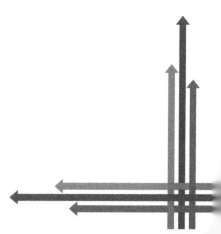

# CHAPTER 18
## Human resource development

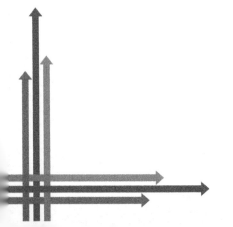

# HRD STRATEGIES

People with appropriate skills, abilities and experience can be bought from outside the organization through recruitment, consultancy and subcontracting, or grown by training and developing existing employees. This chapter focuses on the second approach. The strategic choice between buying and growing is made on the basis of cost-effectiveness, urgency of requirement and the need to motivate staff. Political, cultural and historical elements also influence the decision. Organizations with an internal job market orientation, for example most large German and Japanese companies, have made a practice of growing their own talent whereas the externally-oriented businesses typical of anglophone countries have tended to buy in skilled people.

---

### KEY CONCEPT 18.1   HUMAN RESOURCE DEVELOPMENT

Human resource development (HRD) is a strategic approach to investing in human capital. It draws on other human resource processes, including resourcing and performance assessment, to identify actual and potential talent. HRD provides a framework for self-development, training programmes and career progression to meet an organization's future skill requirements.

---

Learning in the workplace also enhances employee engagement and motivation. For example, Rowden and Conine (2005) found a statistically significant relationship between workplace learning and job satisfaction in small US banks. They highlight the importance of informal and incidental learning and emphasize the need for managers to make learning opportunities available to enhance overall job satisfaction. In an Italian study, Panari *et al.* (2010) also showed that workplace learning opportunities have a role in promoting job satisfaction, reducing stress and improving work–life balance while Alonderiene (2010) found a correlation between informal learning and job satisfaction among SME managers in Lithuania.

Systematic human resource development (see Key concept 18.1) maximizes the human capital of an organization, devoting time, money and thought to improving the pool of essential competencies among its staff. It has a general impact on business performance by enhancing product knowledge and service expertise, motivating staff, drawing on their talents and demonstrating that they are valued by the organization. It is also claimed to empower staff, allowing individuals to take a measure of control over their own careers and develop life patterns that offer increased opportunity and satisfaction. However, Gibb (2002: 138) takes the following view:

> The idea of HRD promises a great deal, and is seductive; but whether there is evidence of organizational examples of this being delivered is questionable. Indeed the 'rhetoric' involved is arguably being used to cover changes which are far removed from the espoused aims; instead of better valuing the human resource, such re-inventions can mask the greater exploitation of people.

According to Sambrook (2001) HRD has its roots in the early organization development interventions of the 1940s, but the term was first used by Nadler in 1972. Nadler (cited in Nadler and Nadler, 1989: 4) described HRD as 'organized learning experiences provided by employers, within a specified period of time, to bring about the possibility of performance improvement and/or personal growth'.

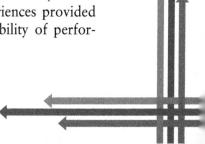

What is the relationship between HRD and training? The two terms are sometimes used to mean the same. However, there is a longstanding tendency to regard training as something done to lower-level workers, whereas development is a process experienced by managers – hence 'management development'. This seems to be incompatible with the central rhetorical principle of HRM that all employees are assets whose competencies need to be developed. It is appropriate, therefore, to regard training as an integral aspect of HRD.

Sambrook (2001) argues that HRD can be thought of as a construct, like 'love' or 'quality'. It is intangible in itself since it cannot be found, touched or seen but it may be investigated through features associated with the concept that might distinguish it from training and development. She argues that training and development was focused on operational issues and took a short-term or reactive approach in which specialists 'did training', delivered it to passive trainees and usually conducted it in classrooms. Sambrook describes this as the 'tell' approach as opposed to 'sell' or 'competent' HRD. Competent HRD focuses on competencies and takes a wider approach, encompassing self-development, employee development, management development and organization development. Probably delivered by facilitators, there is two-way communication and some consultation together with far more diverse training methods. There is an attempt to link HRD to other HR processes and take a wider organizational perspective. Finally, Sambrook identifies strategic HRD or 'gel'. Here the HRD function and the organization are strategically and totally interlinked and there is an emphasis on learning. Individuals are encouraged to take responsibility, to share learning and to be participative and collaborative. Others prefer the label of 'learning and development' while in recent years it has been swept up in the topic of 'talent management'.

Discussion of training and development in the media and management literature tends to become idealistic and evangelical. In reality, many employers take an extremely hard-nosed attitude towards the topic, particularly, as we have seen, in countries such as the UK with a notoriously short-termist view of business. Employer reluctance to embark on training young recruits can be attributed to various factors (Stevens and Walsh, 1991: 37).

**Poaching**  Some employers train while others do not. The non-trainers are likely to poach trained workers from those who train. Whereas Australian and UK firms are afraid of 'free-riders', their German counterparts see themselves as having a responsibility to contribute to the common good. Along with the activities and support of government this attitude maintains a high level of training in Germany. Elsewhere – in France, Japan and the USA, for instance – the poaching problem is less evident since the training of young people takes place largely within the formal education system. Most of the burden and costs are placed upon the trainees.

**Cost**  Young trainees anticipate higher wages in comparison to recruits for semi-skilled jobs. The reduction in numbers of young people coming onto the employment market has increased competition and wages for higher calibre trainees. Also, people are paid when training but do not produce anything and occupy trainers who are not managing or supervising during this period.

**Individual disinterest**  Human capital theory predicts that the young are more likely to choose training than the old because their indirect costs are lower than those of older workers. It also predicts that there should be a direct relationship between additional training and increased income. But the perception of young workers may be that there is no direct link: the skill differential may be small or non-existent. They also see that promotions are not based on qualifications.

**Weak links between training and performance**  Training does not have strategic importance for many companies, partly as we have noted, because of the difficulty of proving the connection between training and improved performance.

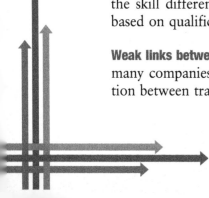

# DEVELOPMENT PROGRAMMES

The fundamental principle of human resource development is that it goes further than piecemeal training and should be part of a planned and systematic process in which:

→ Competencies or capabilities are identified by a performance management system.

→ These are matched with needs specified by the human resource strategy.

→ Gaps are addressed by the development programme.

Within a HRD programme, training is geared towards planned development rather than being an isolated activity unconnected to the organization's objectives. McDowall and Saunders (2010) observed that UK managers favoured the combination of training and development and tended to regard formal training more highly than other forms of learning because its value was easier to assess. In fact, HRD programmes can use a combination of organized patterns of experience as well as formal training. Dechawatanapaisal and Siengthai (2006) studied factors that shape learning behaviour in the workplace and found that psychological discomfort blocks people from acquiring and learning new knowledge during periods of change. However, effective HR practices can help to moderate individuals' inconsistent attitudes, avoid dissonance and facilitate their learning work behaviour. Development programmes that fail to treat employees as individuals may be counterproductive. McDermott, Mangan and O'Connor (2006) examined the perceived progress of graduate recruits and assessed their expectations and corresponding satisfaction levels. Surprisingly, they found that graduates recruited by organizations offering a graduate development programme were less satisfied than their counterparts in organizations with no such programme.

# MANAGEMENT DEVELOPMENT

The main focus of HRD for many organizations lies in management development. In principle, anyone can become a manager and many do so without any formal training or development. However, graduates typically aim for formally designated management trainee positions that promise a structured development programme and steady progression through the management ranks.

The trend has been away from long induction ('onboarding') or orientation periods and work shadowing towards immediate 'real' jobs in which trainees perform useful activities, often with management responsibilities. Traditionally, trainees remain in particular functions for fixed periods of time – perhaps six months, a year, or longer. Of late, competence-driven development programmes have required trainees to achieve a certain standard before moving on.

Storey (2001) justifiably observes that 'the panoply of HRM technology is seen in its fullest form in the management of managers'. General management capabilities are developed in various ways. Companies such as Mars, Proctor & Gamble and Unilever have highly structured programmes. Others are more individually based or informal. Training may also involve academic study. At this point it is useful to consider the role of management education.

Many development programmes involve formal business education, including diplomas, business degrees and, above all, the Masters in Business Administration (MBA). MBA programmes have emphasized rational decision making and a top-down strategic approach to

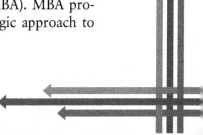

business. In the 1980s, MBA graduates could guarantee substantial salary increases and the likelihood of 'fast-track' careers. More recently, their prospects have become less assured. Nevertheless, academic courses can stretch the boundaries of managers' experience, exposing them to a wide range of concepts, theories and ideas they would never come across otherwise. They also provide students with the means to understand and communicate with people in different business specialisms. Formal education and experiential learning can be used to build a combination of skills, knowledge and abilities – the management competencies necessary for effective managerial performance.

There are two main perspectives on competencies necessary for management:

1   *One best way.* The generic approach assumes that there is a range of competencies or portable techniques that can be learned and used in a variety of organizational settings.

2   *It depends.* The **contingency** view holds that running an organization efficiently requires competencies or methods unique to that enterprise. This approach emphasizes commonsense, experience, rule-of-thumb techniques and wisdom. It acknowledges the complexity of the business environment. It also recognizes that what has worked once in a particular situation is likely to work again.

Taking the former approach, in the 1970s the American Management Associations initiated a major study of management competencies, whereby 2000 successful managers were studied over a five-year period with the intention of identifying generic (common) competencies from actual job performance. The research identified 30 statistically significant competencies of which 18 were generic and could be regarded as essential for all successful managers (Boyatzis, 1982). The remainder were related to organizational requirements or individual management styles. The generic competencies could be placed in four groups: intellectual, entrepreneurial, socio-emotional and interpersonal (the largest group). Nolan *et al.* (2010) looked at the graduate competencies required for entry to hotel management in Ireland and found that interpersonal and product knowledge skills were most important.

The low level of women in management has produced a case for special consideration to be given to the development needs of female managers. For example, the provision of career breaks, refresher training, job-sharing and extended childcare facilities can make a considerable difference in career progress. Specific HRD programmes can be set for women focusing on greater self-awareness, appreciation of career opportunities and encouragement to manage their own careers. This kind of programme boosts confidence and is equally valuable to young trainees and mature returners. However, there are few senior women managers to act as role models. Development programmes involving seminars or attendance on women-only courses allow many female managers to compare notes, discuss issues in common and make sense of advancement in what is primarily a male world. Sharing experiences openly and honestly appears to be easier for women than men.

## COACHING AND MENTORING

Mentor relationships have been found to be highly effective (Key concept 18.2). A 2004 CIPD study showed that coaching is increasingly popular as a means of promoting learning and development. Whereas a mere 16 per cent of respondents thought that training courses were the most effective way for people to learn in the workplace, 96 per cent valued coaching as an effective way to promote learning in organizations. Coaching was also viewed as an important way of reducing 'leakage' from training courses and therefore improved their effectiveness. However, coaching is not viewed entirely through rose-tinted glasses.

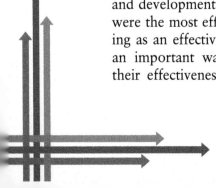

HR professionals are concerned about lack of accreditation and regulation of external providers with only a third of respondents believing that there was sufficient regulation and accreditation of the coaching industry. More than three-quarters of organizations use coaching but a mere 6 per cent have written strategies for coaching all of their employees. The study shows that most coaches are line managers but just 14 per cent of organizations provide compulsory coaching skills for those who manage staff.

> ### KEY CONCEPT 18.2  MENTORING
>
> Mentors are established managers who can provide support, help and advice to more junior members of staff. A mentor should not be a direct line manager, but should have an understanding of the employee's job. Ideally, mentor and junior should have the same gender and ethnic background, so that advice is based on similar life experiences.

Main findings of the survey:

→ More than three-quarters of surveyed organizations used coaching as a training method.

→ Ninety per cent of respondents considered that coaching was a key mechanism for transferring training skills into the workplace.

→ Virtually all respondents (99 per cent) thought that coaching delivered tangible benefits.

→ More than 90 per cent of respondents believed that coaching applied appropriately could positively influence the bottom line.

→ Line managers were most likely to deliver coaching, but fewer than 20 per cent of organizations had 'all' or 'a majority' of their line managers trained to carry it out.

Thomson and Mabey (1994: 60) consider that successful mentors should be seven to ten years (or, perhaps, more) older than the individuals they are mentoring. The age gap should allow the mentor to reflect on their own careers and work experience and be able to give considered responses. Key points (*ibid.:* 61) are:

→ Meeting with a mentor, typically on a monthly basis, encourages an individual to collect his or her thoughts and structure the learning experience by talking those thoughts through with the mentor.

→ Mentors can help to clarify an individual's thinking by questioning and challenging.

→ In order to do so, mentors must have the ability to listen well and to probe into shallow thinking.

→ The primary role of a mentor is not to advise – although this can occur – but to provide feedback and information on recent developments in the organization.

Mentors can help build the individual's self-confidence in what may initially seem an unfriendly and perplexing environment. Coetzer (2006) investigated the role of managers as formal and informal learning facilitators in the workplace environment. Key factors included providing access to a range of workplace activities; promoting communication; facilitating access to direct guidance from workplace models; and designating other learning facilitators. Management practices could also have unintended positive effects on informal

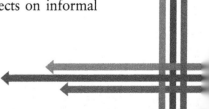

workplace learning. Observing that some individuals appeared to find it easier to receive mentoring than others, Blickle *et al.* (2010) identified a number of predicted perceived barriers to receiving mentoring, including socioeconomic origin, positive affectivity, organizational development culture and previous mentoring experience.

Coaches take a more active role than mentors, appearing in a number of forms, including:

*Career coaching.* According to Chung, Coleman and Gfroerer (2003: 141) career coaches act as 'personal consultants for any work-related concerns such as balancing home and work, learning interviewing skills, developing better managerial skills, executive personal and career development and even managerial training to help managers become career coaches to their employees.'

*Executive coaching.* Coaches are matched with senior executives, providing 'much of the support that more junior employees expect from their managers. Executive coaches may talk through work problems, facilitating decisions, or advise on the executive's own motivation and developing his or her managerial skills' (Price 2005a: 281).

## HRM IN REALITY  PROFESSIONAL SUPPORT FOR COACHES AND MENTORS

Fifteen per cent of UK organizations have no measures in place to assess the impact of coaching or mentoring programmes and 68 per cent do not use this approach to address corporate objectives according to a 2010 study by recruitment specialists, Hays Senior Finance, in association with executive and business leadership trainers, LeaderShape. Most initiatives are directed at individuals, with 72 per cent used for talent development or to address personal issues.

Chris McCarthy, director at Hays Senior Finance, said:

> In far too many cases companies are leaving it to individuals to set the framework for their own coaching or mentoring – with little or no reference to business needs. They then fail to check the standards of their programmes and show little concern for the outcomes. Support can be extremely effective when a professional starts a new role, but it is essential it is carried out in the right manner by people who understand the specific needs of these individuals.

Responding organizations agreed that if a senior recruit leaves within three months there is both a financial cost and an adverse effect on staff morale. The vast majority (96 per cent) felt that such appointments would benefit from confidential support in the early stages. More than half of respondents said they planned to expand their business coaching provision in the next year with

85 per cent expecting their spending on this area to be maintained at current levels or to increase.

The survey identified a lack of ongoing professional development for providers of mentoring or coaching: Nearly three-quarters of organizations (73 per cent) use in-house resources, but no training or support is given to:

→ Sixteen per cent of coaches

→ Twenty-eight per cent of mentors, and

→ Twenty-nine per cent of team or group facilitators.

To help address this issue, LeaderShape has developed a postgraduate qualification accredited by the University of Chester to enable employees to develop and maintain best practice in the workplace.

Chris Gulliver from LeaderShape commented:

> This is a very expensive missed opportunity for UK plc in fast-moving times. Increasing amounts of money are being spent on coaching as a universal panacea but many companies have no comprehensive overview or sense of purpose.
>
> There is a clear lack of framework and training given to those who are delivering many of these programmes with the obvious outcome that they simply don't understand how to use coaching effectively and spend money wisely.

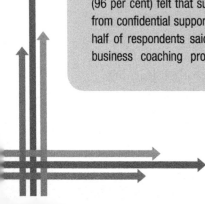

In what other area of business would money be laid out with so little thought to evaluating its impact?

Chris Gulliver added: 'Coaching is not regularly applied where it can often be most effective – within the leadership teams. And it is clear that many services are being given to staff, often in difficult situations, by people who are themselves untrained and unsupported. We believe it is essential to upskill internal providers by training them in a range of coach mentoring and facilitation options. It is equally important to track observed outcomes against business objectives. Otherwise businesses could waste time and money and miss the opportunity to boost success.'

*Source: Reprinted with permission from HRM Guide UK (http://www.hrmguide.co.uk).*

# HRD AND THE ORGANIZATION

Priorities have changed in recent years as the focus has moved from piecemeal training activities to more systematic human resource development with organizations re-orienting themselves away from training individual employees towards becoming 'learning organizations' with the emphasis on continuous learning through a range of delivery methods.

Employees learn continuously but this may take place on an *ad hoc* basis, focused on their own short-term needs rather than long-term development to increase their skills and value to the organization. The declared aim of HRD is to direct learning and development towards objectives that are compatible with business strategy. Competitive advantage can come from the development of an organization's human capital: a learning experience for employees and the organization as a whole (see Key concept 18.3). For some time, this learning experience was encapsulated within a particular model of training: a comparatively straightforward, organized function which depended heavily on planning.

> **KEY CONCEPT 18.3**   LEARNING
>
> A relatively permanent change of behaviour as a result of past experience. Learning is taken to mean more than acquiring knowledge. It encompasses the way in which outmoded values and techniques are shed in favour of new ones. At an organizational level this requires a collective process of change in its shared worldview, including perceptions of the company and its market.

The systematic training model, or textbook approach, tended to be somewhat prescriptive, laying down stages and techniques to be followed. Depending on a series of logical steps it normally involved (Sloman, 1994):

→ a training policy

→ a method for identifying training needs

→ formulation of training objectives

→ development of a training plan

→ implementation of a planned training programme

→ validation, evaluation and review of training.

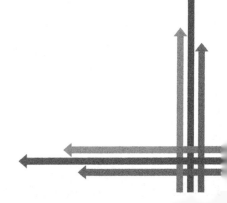

The systematic training model assumed an organizational environment based on slow change, hierarchical lines of authority and clear requirements. It was a logical series of steps centred on the use of an objective training-needs analysis. Normally, this would take the shape of an empirical exercise to identify current needs but bringing in the organization's objectives for consideration. It provided a framework within which the trainer could ensure a thorough and 'professional' job. However, it required a methodical and time-consuming series of activities that do not fit so well with modern organizations.

Today's organizations are constantly changing and have much looser systems of control than the companies of the 1960s. The systematic training model does not incorporate a link with development and other human resource initiatives and, consequently, offers an inadequate framework for modern HRD. For example, structural changes may require the movement of people from activities that are shrinking, or even outsourced, to those which are growing. The skills required are those appropriate to the new work area. It is wasteful in both human and budgetary terms to have to dismiss people in one function while simultaneously hiring new people in another.

Learning in organizations can be approached from either a business or educational perspective. Tight (2000) argues that this is an area in which a variety of 'academic tribes' are operating with only limited contacts with each other, including:

→ adult/continuing/lifelong education

→ organizational behaviour/occupational psychology, and

→ management development/learning/studies.

Each of these 'tribes' has a valuable contribution to make to our understanding. There is a conceptual gap between academic literature on the learning organization and that of organizational learning. Huysman (2000) argues that the two streams of theory and research have operated highly independently of each other. The learning organization stream tends to be mainly prescriptive, linking learning to improvement, while the organizational learning stream analyses learning processes without real interest in the outcome.

Whether or not an organization is growing, there is a need to develop skilled people for the future to replace those who are promoted or leave the company. Consistent with human resource strategy, succession planning links development to career structures and promotion policies. It must also take individual career plans and intentions into account. Typically, such a programme is linked to the human resource plans of the company, reflecting its anticipated needs in the relatively long term. Good employers take this seriously.

## HRM IN REALITY: THE NEW LEARNING EXECUTIVE – STUDY PROFILES CHIEF LEARNING OFFICERS

A study by the American Society for Training & Development (ASTD) and the University of Pennsylvania has produced a picture of a new breed of learning executive – the chief learning officer (CLO) – that has emerged in the past decade. The challenge of running learning like a business and also making learning a critical contributor to organizational success requires a complex skill set. CLOs must run efficient learning functions that are both strategically aligned with and responsive to the needs of their organizations.

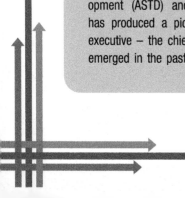

'Profiling a New Breed of Learning Executive', an article in the February 2006 issue of *Training + Development (T+D)* magazine published by ASTD, gives results of the survey of 92 CLOs and identifies the job demands and competencies that are critical for success in this position.

Main findings:

→ *Time.* CLOs spend most of their time on strategy development and communicating with corporate executives.

→ *Biggest challenges.* Communicating and measuring the value of learning, and resource constraints.

→ *Greatest accomplishments.* Expanding the scope and reach of the learning function and gaining the respect of executives and business unit leaders with whom they partner to improve productivity and performance.

Brenda Sugrue, one of the authors of the study and senior director of research for ASTD says:

> The competencies to which these senior learning executives attribute their success emphasize general business skills (leadership, strategic planning and relationship management) rather than specific and deep knowledge of the field of workplace learning and performance.

Additionally, these CLOs recognize the importance of a deeper understanding of the science, technology and measurement of learning and performance.

According to co-author Doug Lynch, vice dean of the Graduate School of Education at the University of Pennsylvania:

> The study results confirm that there are many paths to becoming a CLO and the role requires a combination of business savvy and knowledge of key areas of the learning field. Many CLOs are strong in one but not both of those areas, so the Graduate School of Education and the Wharton School of the University of Pennsylvania is preparing to launch a new curriculum that will prepare professionals specifically for this role.

Daniel Blair, director of ASTD's Learning Executives Network (LXN), added: 'The University of Pennsylvania's initiative to create a targeted curriculum and credential for senior learning executives will help current and aspiring CLOs better prepare to be business partners within their organizations.'

*How does the chief learning officer's role differ from that of a traditional senior trainer?*

*Source: Reprinted with permission from HRM Guide USA (http://www.hrmguide.com).*

# FROM TRAINING TO DEVELOPMENT?

With its incorporation into HRD, training has become a complex topic with a significant shift in both emphasis and importance from the systematic training model. Trainers experience a conflict between, on the one hand, the demand for higher levels of learning to meet the skill needs of new strategic initiatives and an increasingly decentralized approach to the delivery of learning on the other. There have been changes in responsibility in line with the growth of HRM, new forms of organization and outsourcing. Training may be the province of line managers using specialist trainers as an internal or external consultancy resource or, alternatively, responsibility may lie with a centralized learning delivery mechanism that may come from an external supplier.

New approaches require effective communication between strategic decision makers, line managers, specialist trainers and learning providers. Together, such changes have made the traditional model of training management obsolete. Almost two decades ago, Sloman (1994) posed some questions that vexed training managers:

→ It is accepted that training should be closely linked with business strategy. But what does this mean in practice? How should this be done?

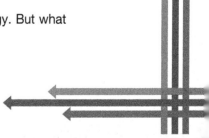

→ How should training relate to corporate culture?

→ How important a breakthrough are competencies?

→ Should the training manager be operating as an internal consultant? If so, what does this mean in practice?

→ Should the company be attempting to become a learning organization, and if so, how?

The strategic link with competitiveness means that HRD has become more important, but there have been pressures on HRD budgets. Critical eyes have looked at development specialists in search of firm evidence of their ability to deliver, in comparison to external providers and new methods of delivering learning. Typically, they are seen more as facilitators and designers of learning programmes than as instructors. Gilley and Gilley (2002: 5) argue that HRD may be sabotaged by trainers who seem more interested in the process of organizing workshops, seminars, meetings and conferences than the organizational purpose of those events. Today's trainers are more involved with strategic decision makers but often have an unclear career path ahead of them. In many cases they have become managers of externally sourced learning materials, providing advice and acting as internal consultants. The idea of regarding a HRD function as an internal consultancy has attracted considerable support. For example, Mitki *et al.* (2007) describe the use of an internal learning exercise in the construction of a corporate identity for a bank. The notion has an obvious appeal for organizations that divide functions into 'buyers' and 'sellers' and provide an internal accounting system which allocates development costs to budget holders. Separate learning centres can be accurately costed and their value established. The role of 'chief learning officer' has also emerged at a strategic level.

There are some debatable aspects to this approach. If an organization employs external providers for learning delivery, it can do so on the basis of single transactions. Should these prove to be unsatisfactory, the purchaser has the option of changing to a different supplier. In other than the largest organizations, the buyer of an internal consultancy's services does not have this freedom. Additionally, the emphasis on 'independence' sits uncomfortably alongside current management thought which places responsibility for all human resource activities with line managers. Some businesses have rationalized these conflicts by regarding themselves as 'learning organizations'.

## THE LEARNING ORGANIZATION

The learning organization 'captured the imagination of trainers and others' in the 1990s (McKenna, 1994: 210). As we can see from Key concept 18.4, it is a view that organizations have to go beyond sporadic training into a permanent state of learning in order to survive in today's business environment. Adapted from Pedler, Boydell and Burgoyne (1989), key characteristics for a learning organization are as follows:

1   The formation of organizational policy and strategy, along with its implementation, evaluation and improvement, is consciously structured as a learning process.

2   There is wide participation and identification in the debate over policy and strategy. Differences are recognized, disagreements aired and conflicts tolerated and worked with in order to reach decisions.

3   Management systems for accounting, budgeting and reporting are organized to assist learning from the consequences of decisions.

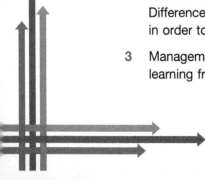

4   Information systems should 'informate' as well as automate. They should allow staff to question operating assumptions and seek information for individual and collective learning about the organization's goals, norms and processes.

5   Information on expectations, and feedback on satisfaction, should be exchanged by individuals and work units at all levels to assist learning.

6   Employees with external links – such as sales representatives and delivery agents – act as environmental scanners, feeding information back to other staff.

7   There is a deliberate attempt to share information and learn jointly with significant others outside the organization such as key customers and suppliers.

8   The organization's culture and management style encourage experimentation, and learning and development from successes and failures.

9   Everyone has access to resources and facilities for self-development.

---

**KEY CONCEPT 18.4**   LEARNING ORGANIZATION

Not simply an organization which carries out extensive training but rather an organization 'which facilitates the learning of all its members and continuously transforms itself (Pedler, Boydell and Burgoyne, 1989). A learning organization is one that lives and breathes knowledge acquisition and skill development – the ultimate extension of 'learning on the job'.

---

The concept of the learning organization remains fairly abstract and, as a senior consultant engagingly described it, 'quite fluffy' (Prothero, 1997, quoted in Walton, 1999). The seminal ideas of the concept come from two main sources: the ideas of Pedler *et al.* (1989) on the 'learning company' and Senge's 'five disciplines'. According to Senge (1990, cited in Price, 2000) learning organizations are organizations in which:

→   the capacity of people to create results they truly desire is continually expanding

→   new and open-minded ways of thinking are fostered

→   people are given freedom to develop their collective aspirations individuals continually learn how to learn together.

This set of goals may seem somewhat ambitious but Senge contends that they can be achieved through the gradual convergence of five 'component technologies', the essential disciplines of which are (Price, 2000):

*Systems thinking.* People in an organization are part of a system. Systems thinking is a discipline which integrates the other disciplines in a business. It allows the 'whole' (organization) to be greater than the 'parts' (people, departments, teams, equipment and so on).

*Personal mastery.* This discipline allows people to clarify and focus their personal visions, focus energy, develop patience and see the world as it really is. Employees who possess a high level of personal mastery can consistently generate results that are important to them through their commitment to lifelong learning.

*Mental models.* These are internalized frameworks that support our views of the world, beliefs in why and how events happen, and our understanding of how things, people

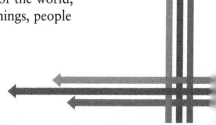

and events are related. Senge advocates bringing these to the surface, discussing them with others in a 'learningful' way and unlearning ways of thinking that are not productive.

*Building shared vision.* Developing 'shared pictures of the future' together so that people are genuinely committed and engaged rather than compliant.

*Team learning.* Senge sees teams as a vital element of a learning organization. Hence there is a great significance in the ability of teams to learn.

It is evident that many of the virtuous aspects of 'learning organizations', such as extensive job rotation, mirror practices commonly found in large Japanese corporations. The concept has been much trumpeted but one can justifiably ask if such idealistic objectives can be met in a harsh, competitive business environment. Critics argue that the concept may be unrealistic and, sometimes, counter-productive. Elkjaer (2001) describes a Danish learning organization that did not last very long and suggests that its short life had been due to the emphasis placed on changing individual employees while the organization itself – its management structures and work practices – had remained fairly constant. This emphasis on individual learning may have arisen because of the general and abstract terms in which learning is discussed in prescriptive accounts of learning organizations.

Organizational learning and its offshoot the 'learning organization' have been criticized as a rhetorical device designed to offer senior managers new mechanisms of control over employees. Huzzard (2001) agrees that the learning organization can be criticized on this basis but considers that it should not be dismissed without an adequate alternative. Parding and Abrahamsson (2010) also find problems in reconciling managerial and professional attitudes within a learning organization. Ellinger *et al.* (2002) investigated the relationship between firms' financial performance and the learning organization concept. They found a positive correlation between seven action imperatives for a learning organization and four objective measures of financial performance. More recently the concept has been linked with knowledge management, emphasizing the complex interrelationships of knowledge sharing, organizational culture and structure necessary for the concept to work (Li *et al*, 2009; Massingham and Diment, 2009). Similarly, in a Korean study Song and Kim (2009) found positive interactions between the learning organizational and workforce commitment.

## EMPOWERMENT AND HRD

The notion of empowerment has a particular relevance in the context of human resource development. There is nothing new in the notion that decision making should be delegated as low down the organization as possible, and that individuals should take responsibility over their own work, but it has significant implications for the career structures and work behaviour of employees. Empowerment is often presented as something provided for the benefit of employees. In fact, its use is often driven by financial considerations deriving from:

*Downsizing.* Slimmer companies typically have fewer management layers. The consequence is that the remaining managers are not available for day-to-day decisions – they *must* be taken by lower-level employees.

*Speed of response.* In an increasingly competitive market, customers expect fast, authoritative decisions on price availability. There is no time for staff to refer to 'the manager'.

In this environment there is a need for confident, speedy decision making based on a high degree of product expertise. Moreover, in return for empowerment, employees must accept

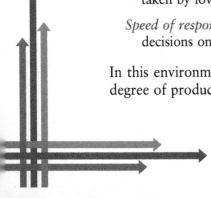

that career opportunities have diminished. As much of the traditional career ladder has disappeared vertical promotion is only available to a few star performers. HRD in this case is focused on building resilient people, able to gain rewards from existing jobs. Their future lies in 'horizontal promotion', regular moves between different jobs on a similar level.

Specifically, development programmes require an emphasis on decision making and customer-handling skills together with in-depth product and service knowledge. In the absence of managerial backup it is necessary that empowered staff have a wide understanding of the organization's functions and goals. They must be able to function well in unclear circumstances, without detailed prescriptive rules and be flexible and proactive enough to make events happen. Ironically, however, Moye and Henkin (2006) found that employees who feel empowered in their work environment tend to have higher levels of trust in their managers.

## SELF-DEVELOPMENT

Development is the responsibility of the individual as well as the organization. Career success requires self-control, self-knowledge, systematic career evaluation and frequent role change. Selecting a career path depends on factors such as:

→ *Self-awareness:* being able to accurately assess one's own skills, abilities and interests.

→ *Ambition:* self-esteem, confidence and motivation.

→ *Opportunity:* education, experience and social contacts.

People develop their lives and become distinctive persons through an interaction of three processes: genetic inheritance, life events and self-creation (Glover, 1988). They are so intertwined that we may be unable to attribute a particular event to any one of them. Genetic inheritance determines much of our physical and mental capabilities. Hence the opportunity to succeed in education or business is constrained, to some extent, by inherited factors outside our control. Even health and the duration of our lives are subject in part to genetic determination.

Our lives also depend heavily on accident or chance since the process of living is predominantly an unsystematic series of incidents. We choose to apply for specific jobs, or particular universities, because they meet our needs at a specific point in time. These decisions produce unanticipated side-effects. For example, later we might find ourselves living in a specific location and engaged in projects we would never have contemplated if we had not taken the job or gone to that university.

However, there are major components of life that are controlled by our own actions, leaving scope for intention and direction. The more we plan and take action, the greater the control we have over our lives. To a degree, we shape our own selves by imagining the kind of person we want to be: perhaps being more successful, being respected, or being seen as kind or helpful. When we take actions that contribute to the achievement of these goals we are involved in a process of self-creation. Few of us have a systematic life plan, but rather a loosely organized collection of sometimes minor aims. Viitala (2005) found that many Finnish managers surveyed had no specific development intentions for themselves. In organizations where management development was well-organized and connected to strategic management, managers were more consciously aware of development needs at a personal as well as at a general level. The study revealed that the managers' development intentions differed from those predicted in studies on management competencies. Technical and business skills were emphasized at the expense of social and intrapersonal skills.

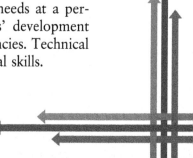

Most people have restricted opportunities, so that self-creation is a matter of taking account of reality and adjusting to what is possible and some commentators question the concept of self-development (Hallier, 2009). However, from a positive perspective, the following independent development checklist (based on Margerison, 1991: 63) may be useful:

→ What is the best way to spend my time?

→ Who else could do my work?

→ What am I improving and why?

→ What do I feel strongly about?

→ What are my special strengths and weaknesses?

→ What am I doing to increase my effectiveness?

→ What are the likely benefits and risks of achieving my objectives?

→ What have I learned in the last month?

→ What motivates me most?

→ How many of my objectives do I achieve on time?

→ What is my action plan for: one month, one year, five years?

## HRM IN REALITY  LEARNING SURVEY

A quarter of British office workers blame their 'David Brent'-style bosses for holding back their development, according to recent research conducted for the online learning specialist, SkillSoft. Sixty-three per cent of the 3000 employees surveyed feel they could be doing better in their career. But many workers say they get no support when it comes to training and career development and bosses fail to recognize and nurture their potential.

The survey also found that public service employees get the most encouragement from their managers with 66 per cent saying their employers are happy for them to develop their skills compared with 56 per cent of people working for private companies. Public sector workers also get more opportunities for on-the-job training – 40 per cent say they get formal training and mentoring. This compares with 31 per cent in private firms who receive the same level of support.

According to Kevin Young, managing director of Skill-Soft: 'It's evident from this study that a large number of people are not being given the opportunity to live up to their potential at work; particularly in the private sector. Just consider the productivity gains that could be achieved if UK businesses stepped up their commitment to developing their employees' skills.'

Sixty-four per cent of those surveyed said their employer allowed them no time in the working day for their professional development. Eighty-nine per cent of employees said they would prefer to be in control of their own learning.

Kevin Young commented: 'This is in line with some research we did last year amongst employees already using e-learning, the majority of whom were taking control of their own professional development by accessing online learning in the office before or after work, or at home in the evenings and at weekends. The effect on their jobs was evident; nearly everyone interviewed could give practical examples of how they had applied their new knowledge at work.' Other key findings:

→ Fifty-three per cent already willingly spend their own free time on professional development. But many more employees said they would spend their spare time studying if bosses allowed them time to learn in the office as well.

→ Forty-three per cent of employees felt that they needed to spend only two to four hours a week on training to achieve their full potential.

→ Asked about the kind of training they needed, 45 per cent said they would like more training in communications and customer relations skills and 50 per cent wanted more management and leadership skills training.

→ Sixty-seven and a half per cent said they deserved higher pay.

→ Most employees enjoy their work – 43 per cent saying that they got some pleasure from their work and 40 per cent go as far as to say they enjoy their jobs 'a lot'. A mere 10 per cent said they don't enjoy their job at all.

*Is it possible for self-development to occur without management support?*

*Source: Reprinted with permission from HRM Guide UK (http://www.hrmguide.co.uk).*

# HRD AS AN ACTIVITY

There is a considerable variation in the way in which HRD is organized and conducted. The difference is greatest between large and small businesses. HRD in small organizations is likely to be unsystematic while large companies may offer sophisticated, highly structured and expensive development programmes. Customer demands are driving training for service and product quality but this is generally focused on 'core' staff with career structures rather than part-time and temporary employees. However, the latter tend to be highly visible to customers, particularly in retailing. In addition we need to distinguish the learning needs of the individual and those of the organization. While individual employees frequently look for wide-ranging courses that will help them in promotion and develop transferable skills which are seen as valuable by other employers, line managers are likely to be more interested in training which improves performance on their present jobs, leading to improved output quality and productivity. In other words, employees seek learning which will make them more marketable whereas organizations prefer training that makes employees more productive.

## *A training needs model*

Nowack (1991) proposes a nine-step model for a training needs exercise.

**1 Prepare a job profile** Jobs for which training is required need to be identified clearly. The job profile is based on 12–15 dimensions, or job requirements, within which groups of behaviours can be classified. The number of dimensions depends on factors such as what the job involves, its complexity and required skills for effective performance.

Information is obtained from subject matter experts: people who have detailed knowledge of the job(s) being considered. This includes workers currently performing that work, their supervisors and others involved with the input or output to and from those jobs. Information comes from individual interviews, focus groups and survey techniques. Focus groups, for example, discuss the skills deemed important to each job and list them in dimensional categories within broad areas of:

→ necessary technical knowledge and experience

→ communication skills

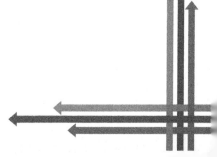

→  decision-making or problem-solving

→  administrative skills

→  management skills.

Each group indicates how important they feel each dimension is to a particular job – from 'very' to 'not' important. They are also asked to estimate the likely frequency of occurrence of each dimension in terms of 'several times a day/week/month/year'. The lists are compared and integrated to form a definitive job profile.

**2 Preparing a learning or training needs questionnaire**  This is a critical part of the process. Targeted towards particular jobs or job levels in the organization, it is addressed to the people performing the jobs and their immediate supervisors. It includes questions aimed at obtaining three categories of information:

→  *Attitudinal:* describing employees' feelings about their work, their perception of organizational procedures and policies, pay, career, management and environment.

→  *Dimensional:* summarizing views on the job dimensions in terms of their importance and employees' proficiency (expressed on a 1–5 scale).

→  *Demographic:* relevant questions on employees' time within the organization.

**3 Administering the questionnaire**  A decision must be taken on the size of sample required to complete the questionnaire. This will depend on the resources available and the number of people involved in target jobs. In a relatively small organization the questionnaire can be directed to all relevant employees; in larger organizations where hundreds of people may be performing similar tasks, a sample will be more appropriate. The target audience should offer alternative perspectives of specific jobs, for example by asking workers and their immediate supervisors to evaluate the workers' jobs.

The questionnaire should be accompanied by a covering letter describing: the purpose of the exercise; details on how and when to return the questionnaire; and its voluntary, anonymous and confidential nature. Standard methods can be adopted to increase the percentage of questionnaires returned, such as offering incentives (prize draw, restaurant vouchers, etc.).

**4 Analyzing responses**  Returned questionnaires are statistically analyzed, preferably by means of a computerized package. A simple mathematical method can indicate the most crucial training needs: each respondent's measure of importance ($I$) is multiplied by the equivalent rating for proficiency (P) for every dimension. The resulting ($I \times P$) scores can be utilized in a variety of ways. For example, mean scores can be compared across dimensions for a specific group or between groups. Alternatively, supervisors' ratings can be compared with employees' judgements of themselves. It is useful also to compare different departments and to check for differences between new and experienced employees.

**5 Interpreting the results**  Nowack suggests that three follow-up questions should be addressed:

→  Is there some commonality between the highest-ranked training needs?

→  What is the explanation for any differences between supervisor and employee assessments?

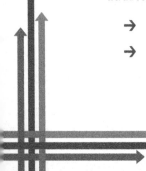

→ Is there a reason for differences between groups of employees, e.g. senior and junior workers?

Different levels of employee will inevitably have different perceptions of the importance of particular development needs. Workers on the shopfloor may be particularly concerned with day-to-day matters such as dealing with complaining customers effectively, or working a particular machine. Managers may be more interested in longer-term, strategic requirements, such as filling in stock returns accurately and understanding the fine differences between product categories in order to identify trends. These differences have to be evaluated logically.

**6 Follow-up focus groups** Interpretation of questionnaire results will identify a need for further clarification. This is best provided by small focus groups which can consist of workers, managers or a mix. They can review $I{\times}P$ scores and offer further explanation. Groups should provide a final executive summary that will be useful for managers and trainees.

**7 Feedback** A feedback of results to managers and respondents is an essential part of the exercise. Planning and presentation of results is crucial for further progress and as a record of the process for future use.

**8 Development objectives** The goal is to produce an objective for each dimension identified from the questionnaire and follow-up exercises. They should be tied to an explicit statement of the competencies required for effective performance of the jobs in question. Each training need must be categorized as:

→ imparting knowledge

→ changing attitudes

→ modifying behaviour.

Having done this, the criteria for successful training can be established. For example, if delegation skills are a training need, what behaviour needs to be established by the trainee?

**9 A pilot training programme** This is a prototype used to test the conclusions of the training needs exercise and provide further information for the final employee development programme.

## LEARNING METHODS

HRD managers are presented with an ever-increasing range of learning methods. Traditionally, they have been divided into:

→ *On-the-job training,* including demonstrations of equipment and procedures, instruction manuals and computer-based training packages.

→ *Off-the-job training,* such as group briefings, projects and formal courses.

Off-the-job training can be in-house, taking place within the organization, or external, for example at a local college or university. Methods of learning can include (Price, 2005a):

→ Traditional lectures – good for imparting factual material and relatively cheap for large numbers of trainees.

→ Case studies – good for problem-solving and simulated experiential learning.

→ Brainstorming – a total contrast to the passivity of the lecture.

→ Critical incident technique – can be more focused and directly relevant than a case study.

→ Discussion and debate – encourages critical thinking.

→ Role plays – another simulated experiential form of learning.

→ Exercises and games – useful for developing team cohesion and skills.

# INDUCTION AND ORIENTATION

Starting a new job ('onboarding') has been compared with one's first day at school. The newcomer is bound to be a little nervous, but hopefully enthusiastic; keen to impress, but not wanting to attract too much attention; anxious to learn quickly, but not wanting to be deluged with names, facts and figures; hoping to fit in, but not look too 'new' and inexperienced. The reception from the employer should ideally anticipate these feelings. After all, the organization has spent good money hiring the newcomer and should treat that person as an investment to be nurtured and encouraged. In reality, however, new recruits are likely to receive an induction or orientation which can be anywhere between two extremes:

*In at the deep end*: expecting the recruit to get on with the job without any real welcome or information.

*Overwhelming*: providing the newcomer with an avalanche of introductions, site tours, information packs, etc.

Most large organizations inflict at least some of the following on new hires:

→ Handing out the employee handbook – the HR department may be proud of it but it is not going to be an easy read.

→ Introducing the new recruit to everybody in the business – embarrassing at best, and likely to be off-putting to a new hire who wants to slide into the job quietly. Besides, no one will remember what they have been told or the names of the people to whom they have been introduced.

→ Dishing out even more facts and figures on day one.

→ Doing so in the form of a lecture or presentation – with slides.

→ Doing it again on day two.

→ Not giving the employee their own 'home' – workspace, desk, phone, computer.

→ Having the immediate supervisor away on holiday, in a continuous series of meetings, or just too busy to be involved.

These activities run the risk of boring and confusing, rather than helping, the new employee. Obviously, there is information that new recruits need and administration (payroll details, social security, etc) that has to be done. Also, there is a degree of ritual – a 'rite of passage' – expected by the new hire, colleagues and the organization. But the process needs to be thought through, especially in relation to timing, quantity and intensity.

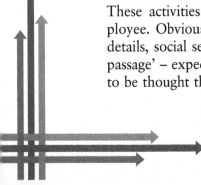

The simple truth is that most people responsible for orienting new employees do not put themselves in the new hire's shoes, i.e. do not take account of just what it is like to start a new job – or think of induction as an adult learning process that has to be designed to take account of the ways in which people learn. Unfortunately, joiners are commonly 'thrown in at the deep end'. Finding themselves in a strange environment and told to get on with it, they are easily forgotten. Raw recruits are left feeling anxious and vulnerable, forced to make sense of new surroundings and learn correct procedures the hard way. Many managers regard this approach with favour: after all, this was how they learned to cope and get to grips with the business. It is regarded as a test of competence, of machismo, of ability to survive in a demanding environment. This can be a valuable 'growth' experience but there is a considerable risk of individuals becoming disillusioned, leaving or developing bad habits.

As we noted in earlier chapters, there is a well known 'induction crisis' in which a proportion of new recruits leave within the first few weeks. Effective recruitment and selection takes time and costs money. Careless handling of new recruits can render this easily into waste. It is a questionable way of dealing with a significant investment. In the same way as young seedlings and transplanted cuttings are the most vulnerable plants a gardener has to look after, newcomers and promotees are the employees at greatest risk of disillusion and failure. They will worry about their ability to fit in, their competence to do the job and the impression they are creating in the eyes of their bosses and colleagues.

## Induction: getting it right

1   Treat each new employee as an individual, i.e. induction must be tailored to orient individual recruits according to their needs. A school-leaver or fresh graduate will require a different approach to a seasoned professional or experienced worker who can 'hit the ground running'. Don't insult the latter – and waste valuable working time – by putting them through the official HR department induction programme! It is not advisable to have an orientation procedure that is applied to everyone regardless.

2   The immediate line manager should be closely involved, even if arrangements are made by the HR department.

3   It is often useful to allocate a 'buddy' or sponsor on the same working level as the new hire. This allows informal learning to take place about unwritten rules of behaviour, location of important services and all kinds of 'how-to's that are obvious to an experienced employee, but not to a newcomer. Pick a positive person for this role.

4   Pace the induction process. It is not necessary to do everything on the first morning. The newcomer will still be learning in six months' time.

5   Give the new recruit a real job to do as soon as possible. There is nothing more demoralizing than feeling oneself to be a 'spare part' or a nuisance in a busy department.

Simulation is a key element in several of these methods. For example, Cowey (2005) describes how simulations can be used to overcome the perception of finance training as being dry, difficult and irrelevant. Adobor and Daneshfar (2006) investigated factors that promote the effective use of simulations in management education. They found that the nature of the simulation and team dynamics affected learning and performance. Positive effects were associated with: the extent to which users perceived the simulation as reflective of real life situations; the ease of use of the simulation; and task conflict, measured by the degree of exchange of ideas. Emotional conflict in the team had a negative association with learning.

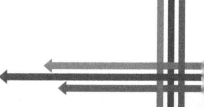

# HRM IN REALITY  E-LEARNING IS GAINING GROUND

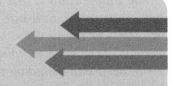

A report from Ambient Insight, *The US Market for Self-paced E-Learning Products and Services: 2009-2014 Forecast and Analysis* shows that demand for online training is growing by 7.4 per cent and predicts that revenues will reach $23.8 billion by 2014.

According to Chief Research Officer, Sam S. Adkins:

> In the past two years, the rate of growth for online learning products has slowed. Yet, despite the recession, and in many cases, because of it, the demand is positive in all the online learning buyer segments. There are distinct revenue opportunities in each of the buyer segments.

E-learning and online training expenditures are estimated for eight buyer segments:

→ consumer

→ corporations

→ federal government

→ state and local government

→ PreK-12 academic

→ higher education

→ non-profits and associations; and

→ healthcare.

The report predicts that corporations will be the top buyers of online training throughout the forecast period, followed by higher education and PreK-12 e-learning buyers.

Ambient CEO Tyson Greer commented:

> We see the highest growth rate in the healthcare segment, followed by PreK-12 and higher education. The healthcare industry has been recession resilient and online training suppliers competing in that segment have been relatively immune from recessionary pressures. The rate of growth in the academic segments is due in part to the success and proliferation of the for-profit online schools.

Ambient Insight forecasts spending on six types of Self-paced E-Learning products for each buyer segment:

→ IT-related packaged courseware

→ non-IT courseware

→ custom online learning content services

→ LMS hosting services

→ course authoring tools, and

→ installed LMS platforms.

They predict that non-IT self-paced courseware will generate the highest revenues throughout the forecast period.

Adkins added:

> The good news is that there are still large untapped revenues for suppliers. For example, the small and medium business (SMB) buyers were slow to adopt online training until the recent recession. There is now a relatively healthy demand for self-paced eLearning products and services in the SMB segments.

*Why is the market for e-learning growing quickly?*

*Source: Reprinted with permission from HRM Guide USA (http://www.hrmguide.com).*

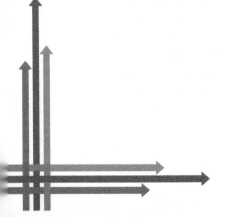

# E-LEARNING

E-learning has followed the pattern of the internet – a journey from unrealistic 'hype' to a more modest but increasingly important reality offering personalized web-based learning (Yalcinalp, S. and Gulbahar, Y., 2010)

In the late 1990s and early 2000s e-learning was discussed in dramatic terms as a revolution in learning technology that would become a massive industry in a few years. But uptake was slow and largely confined to organizations with a strong focus on information technology although there are signs of faster growth. Today, e-learning is increasingly seen as one among many possible elements of open learning and workplace training programmes (Price, 2005b). For example, audio and web-conferencing provider Arkadin created learning academies for global talent management that combined e-learning with mentoring and face-to-face training (Mulin and Reen, 2010). In general, however, attitudes towards e-learning vary across organizational cultures (Conboy *et al.*, 2010).

E-learning is computer-based learning, often using Web2.0 internet technology such as Wikis, to deliver interactive learning materials to any location. Some of the main reasons for using e-learning include (Driscoll, 2002: 8):

*Reducing travel and related costs.* Trainees do not need to travel away from the workplace.

*Enabling learning any time and any place.* Training can be accessed from work, home or anywhere in between.

*Providing just-in-time learning.*

*Leveraging existing infrastructure.* Existing equipment, networks and facilities can be used.

*Enabling delivery independent of a platform.* Accessible from any computer system.

*Providing tools for tracking and record-keeping.* Can be integrated with human resource information systems.

*Making updates easy.*

Waight and Stewart (2005) studied factors influencing companies' efforts to value the adult learner in e-learning. They describe an interdependence between:

1   Championing factors – leadership, learning culture, technology infrastructure, finance.

2   Antecedents – needs assessment, learning analysis, work setting analysis, work analysis, content analysis, task analysis.

3   Moderators – return on investment, learning theory application, technology and creativity.

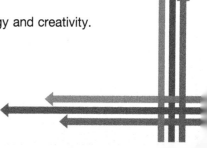

They argue that engagement, learning and transfer can be achieved via e-learning if desirable championing factors, antecedents and moderators are adhered to.

Servage (2005) suggests that the vagueness of e-learning terminology reflects uncritical approaches to e-learning. Servage's review finds North American practitioner literature dominated by concerns about cost and technology in strategizing and implementation to the near exclusion of workers' learning and affective needs. Servage contends that organizational decision makers should seek the input and perspective of multiple stakeholders to ensure that e-learning strategies are appropriate not only in terms of financial and technological feasibility but also in the interests of lasting positive effects on employees and organizational culture. In a higher education context, Kirkwood (2009) finds that outcomes of e-learning can be disappointing as context variables such as learner expectations and teachers' beliefs in the system are significant. Again in higher education, Maltby and Mackie (2009) identify four types of e-learner: model, traditionalist, geek and disengaged.

### Action learning

Many years before the concept of e-learning was thought of, Revans (1972) argued that classroom-based management education is not adequate. He devised a systematic, experiential or 'action learning' programme based on job exchanges that placed managers in unfamiliar situations and asked them to take on challenging tasks. These tasks should have the following characteristics:

1  Based on real work projects.

2  Projects must be owned and defined by senior managers and be important to the future of the organization.

3  The process is an investment requiring a real return on cost.

4  Managers must work in groups, learning from each other and crossing boundaries between functions and departments.

5  Projects must go beyond analysis – they should require real action and change.

6  Content (programmed knowledge) and process (questions/methods) of change should be studied.

7  There must be public commitment from participants to action/report.

Revans' ideas are consistent with the principles of the learning organization discussed earlier in this chapter. The emphasis lies with learning rather than training and with meeting the changing needs of an organization in a competitive world. His approach is also mirrored in many current programmes aimed at developing leaders. Action learning can be integrated with e-learning. Waddill (2006) investigated the impact of the action learning process on the effectiveness of management level web-based instruction (WBI) or e-learning. Converting a leader-led course proved challenging to facilitate, but the action learning online method was found to be effective.

## LEADERSHIP DEVELOPMENT

'I would argue that more leaders have been made by accident, circumstance, sheer grit, or will than have been made by all the leadership courses put together' (Bennis, 1990).

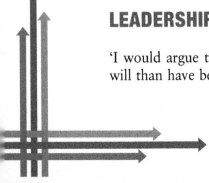

The skills of leadership have attracted management theorists and trainers al_ good leaders are comparatively easy to recognize when they are in positions ( developing people to achieve the necessary qualities is not so easy. Just as the nat ership is not fully understood, the appropriate methods of training and leadership ter of controversy. At the same time leadership training is a lucrative area fo consultants, and management gurus have been ready to produce packaged method.

It is arguable that many supposed 'leadership' courses are actually teaching man skills rather than those of leadership. A typical leadership course concentrates on:

→ Identifying the nature of leadership and the form which the individual trainee wishes to adopt. This incorporates a range of options from being able to give orders (to 'boss') to a more inspirational form.

→ Self-awareness – the identification of those leadership skills which individuals feel themselves to be lacking.

→ A general boost in self-confidence.

The focus in each case depends on factors such as:

→ Participants' level of seniority. It would be counter-productive to encourage a junior manager to adopt the manner and style appropriate to a managing director.

→ The organizational culture in which trainees have to operate. Authoritarian forms of leadership would be disastrous in a participative business.

→ Trainees' personalities. People vary in their degrees of assertiveness and sensitivity and need to develop a leadership style that fits naturally with their personality characteristics. It is easier to develop abilities that already exist in an embryonic form than to attempt to change an individual's whole character. The latter is likely to be impossible.

Part of the programme would involve a team exercise requiring the solution of a hypothetical problem.

Many courses have taken on 'outward bound' elements. These use sport or other outdoor physical activities that require skill as a vehicle for experiential learning. Such programmes claim to develop management skills such as leadership, teamwork, communication, problem solving, managing change and coping with stress. However, much of this learning does not translate naturally to the office. There have also been lasting physical and psychological effects of a negative kind – particularly with older, unfit participants.

## Blended learning

Recently, it has been argued that effective learning needs a combination of methods, an approach described as 'blended learning', integrating best practice in face-to-face and online learning to compensate for the impersonal and isolated nature of e-learning (Sleator, 2010). For example, Collis *et al.* (2005) describe 'putting learning to work', a form of blended learning used at Shell International EP that focuses on learning while in the workplace through work-based activities within technology-supported courses. This has been evolving since 2000.

Graham (2005) looked at IT training of existing employees and argues that it should form an ongoing part of an organization's operations, rather than be reliant on external specialist recruitment and panic reactions to immediate skill shortages. Graham states that a combination of a training needs analysis, psychological, skill-based tests to identify an employee's current ability and willingness to embrace the training, and blended learning, have

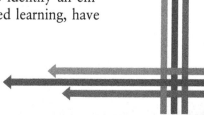

vantages over other training methods. Ausburn (2004) investigated course design elements most valued by adult learners in blended learning environments that combine face-to-face contact with web-based learning. Most valued were course designs containing options, personalization, self-direction, variety and a learning community. Participants benefit when learning relates to real life situations and participants are actively involved with each other, particularly online (Fontanin, 2010), and received adequate tutor support (Sulcic, 2010).

# EVALUATING AND COSTING TRAINING

According to Rosania (2000):

> The fact is that trainers do not inherently lack power; what they lack is the ability to use their power in a way that consistently demonstrates the value of their service to their stakeholders. Trainers do not need fancy titles or affiliation with certain departments to demonstrate their value. What trainers need to change is their thinking about how they can contribute to the success of their organizations.

Of course, one basic issue affecting the credibility of trainers is the need to demonstrate the value of training to the organization. In a review of evaluation methods, Rowden (2001) states: 'The "beancounters" in the organization are likely to know exactly how much training "costs" but they may have little idea of its value. HR must be able to supply that information if it is to truly become a strategic part of the organization.' In general, it seems that the perceived usefulness of the training is a key issue for participants and the sponsoring organization (Giangreco *et al.*, 2009).

What methods are used in practice? The most obvious are 'happy-sheets' or questionnaires handed out to participants on completion of a training course. These are forms that ask trainees to rate the presentation and usefulness of the course and invite comments. The inherent flaws of this approach are well-known (Lewis, 1991):

→ They are usually completed in the euphoric period at the end of the course when trainees are relieved to have survived, when they are looking forward to going home and pressure and stress have lifted. At this point in time the world has taken on a comfortable, rosy glow.

→ A personal relationship has been developed with the trainers, so criticism is toned down to avoid upsetting them.

→ Most of all, the evaluation concentrates on the wrong issues. Often there is cursory attention to the value of the training experience to the trainees, their future job performance and hence the organization. Instead, forms are likely to concentrate on the overall enjoyability of the course and the quality of the environment in which it took place. According to McKenna (1994: 212): 'It is known for trainees to be thoroughly satisfied with a programme merely because the instructor or trainer did a good job entertaining them'. Happy-sheets are excellent for comments on the comfort of hotel accommodation, speed and service in the restaurant and the stuffiness of seminar rooms. Usually they tell us little about the cost-effectiveness of the programme.

The evaluation of training has attracted considerable attention. A number of models exist of which Hamblin's (1974) is, perhaps, one of the best known. Hamblin stratified training into five levels, which could be evaluated independently:

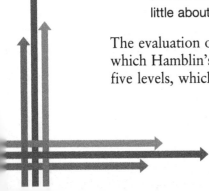

*Level 1.* The reactions of trainees during training to the trainer, other trainees and external factors.

*Level 2.* Learning achieved during training, assuming basic aptitude and receptiveness on the part of the trainee.

*Level 3.* Job behaviour in the work environment at the end of the training period.

*Level 4.* The overall effects on the organization.

*Level 5.* Ultimate values: factors such as business survival, profit, welfare of interested parties and social/political welfare.

Kirkpatrick (1994) split evaluation into four levels:

*Reaction*: is the 'customer' satisfied? If the trainee does not like the programme he or she is unlikely to be motivated to learn.

*Learning*: Brown and Seidner (1998) state that this 'can be described as the extent to which participants change attitudes, improve knowledge and/or increase skill as a result of attending the programme.'

*Behaviour change*: how is actual behaviour changed by training?

*Results*: the return on investment (ROI) or effect of the training on the organization's bottom-line.

Rowden (2001) examines the last two levels in detail. He proposes the following as the most significant for measuring behaviour change: a 360-degree appraisal feedback process and, secondly, a performance-learning-satisfaction evaluation system. In practice, evaluation is seen as a weak link in the learning process. 'It is the step most likely to be neglected or underdone' (Gibb, 2002: 107). Kirkpatrick's model continues to offer promising theoretical and evidence-based value (Steensma and Groeneveld, 2010).

However, the fact that such models exist has not led many organizations to use them! Hendry (1995: 366) echoes some astute criticisms of evaluation:

The whole notion of evaluation is based on training as a discrete event – namely the training course – and justifying the substantial visible costs associated with off-the-job courses and full-time training staff. Take these away, as Hamblin (1974) and Crittan (1993) have observed, and the rationale and pressure for evaluation largely collapses. Evaluation of training events was always a fallacy as long as it ignored the equally important process of practice back on the job which ensures that training transfers.

In practice, Hendry (1995: 364) argues that the most progressive firms use a mixture of:

*'Hard' evaluation criteria.* Short-term improvements in measurable performance, such as in-dividual productivity and quality adherence.

*'Soft' criteria.* Indirect benefits from intermediate human resource goals, including reduction in staff turnover, promotability and flexibility.

Tamkin, Yarnall and Kerrin (2002) and Gibb (2002) concur that although evaluation has grown in priority in recent years, most evaluation activity is unsophisticated. According to Gibb (*ibid.*: 120):

So while L&D evaluation is at least now done more widely than ever before it is stuck at the most basic level possible, with the prevalence and preference in L&D for using the basic recipes of levels of evaluation … In the end the formulas and techniques for evaluation of L&D have

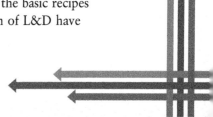

to balance the demands of scientific rigour with those of professional practice, and the theoretical goals of 'truth seeking' with the practical goals of 'pragmatic management'.

 **SUMMARY**

Competitiveness demands a diverse workforce and up-to-date skills. The free market belief in 'buying-in' skill has proven inadequate, even in times of high unemployment. HRD can be a proactive aspect of talent management, focusing on developing employees as investments for the organization and planning for skill availability in advance of need. In the context of learning organizations HRD programmes involve more than training and require mechanisms for accurate assessment, counselling and inbuilt personal challenge using a variety of learning methods in an active, self-directed manner.

**FURTHER READING**

1 Swart, Mann, Brown and Price, *Human Resource Development: Strategy and Tactics* (Butterworth-Heinemann, 2005) is a wide-ranging discussion of HRD and its methods.

2 Stephen Gibb's Human *Resource Development: Processes, Practices and Perspectives*, 2nd edition (Palgrave/ Macmillan, 2007) provides a good practical overview.

3 *Employee Training and Development*, 5th edn, by Raymond A. Noe (McGraw-Hill Higher Education, 2010) has become something of a classic.

4 *Excellence in Coaching: The Industry Guide* edited by Jonathan Passmore (2nd edition, Kogan Page) is a comprehensive text on the subject as is

5 *Coaching and Mentoring* by Robert Garvey, Paul Stokes, and David Megginson (Sage Publications, 2008).

**REVIEW QUESTIONS**

1 What are the limitations of the following concepts in describing learning in the workplace: training, education, human resource development, 'knowledge, skills and abilities'?

2 Consider an organization of your choice: (a) Does this organization offer systematic development? (b) Does it aim to develop employee skills as a long-term strategy?

3 How is human resource development distinguished from training?

4 What additional pressures or incentives could be placed on businesses to take vocational education and training seriously?

5 What are the arguments for and against separate development programmes for women and men?

6 Define the term 'mentoring' and explain its benefits.

7 Why has there been such a strong focus on management development?

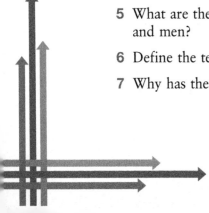

8  How would you distinguish between learning organizations and learning in organizations? Evaluate the view that 'learning organizations are just hype'.

9  What are the most significant links between performance management and learning and development?

10  There has been a trend towards proactive learning and away from passive training. Should the 'training needs analysis' be modified to become more of a 'learning needs analysis'? If so, how?

11  How has the concept of career development changed in recent years? What are the implications of the reduction in management layers in many large organizations on individual career aspirations?

12  Can anyone be a good trainer? Do we still need training specialists if people can learn for themselves?

13  Outline the essential differences between action learning and formal training.

14  What are the most important features of induction and orientation?

15  Is it possible to prove that training is a worthwhile business investment?

16  What are 'e-learning' and 'blended learning'?

## CASE STUDY FOR DISCUSSION AND ANALYSIS

### Lisa

Lisa was a recent recruit. The HR manager was very pleased to have taken her on as her assessment centre results were outstanding. She was a graduate in chemical engineering, apparently keen to apply her university training within the organization, a medium-sized manufacturer of aluminium products.

Previous female graduate recruits had received a brief induction period involving visits to all departments, and then been placed in marketing or personnel jobs. None had risen beyond the junior management grades: higher posts seemed to be reserved for men promoted from production and finance. The board had decided that the company's attitude towards women was old-fashioned and was preventing them from making the best use of their human resources. Lisa was the opportunity to do something positive about the problem. With the support of the MD, the personnel manager set out to offer Lisa a development programme that would give her the opportunity to achieve a senior management post within a reasonable period.

*Situation*

Tina Johnson was a determined and thorough human resource manager. In her late 40s and without much in the way of academic qualifications herself, she was aware that many bright young recruits were going to university before taking their first job. She was also in touch with the greater expectations of young people qualified to this level. She found that they were unhappy with the idea of several years at a junior level before being offered a seriously demanding job.

Lisa did not seem to be any different to the other graduates taken on by the company. Outside the male-dominated production and service areas, there were many female graduates at the lower management levels. Lisa had been with the company for three months and had completed the 'grand tour' which was the company's induction programme.

Tina decided to conduct a development interview with Lisa. She began by asking her how she felt about the company so far.

'It isn't quite what I expected', said Lisa. She seemed ill-at-ease and nervous.

'Oh, in what way?' asked Tina in a friendly but quizzical tone.

'Well, I suppose I was expecting to use my university training from the beginning ... rather than being shown around places like Marketing and Distribution', Lisa answered in a very apologetic way.

Tina decided to persist: 'Yes, but we think it's important for you to have a proper induction programme so that you get a basic understanding of the way the company operates. We invest a lot of time and money in our new recruits ... three months is a long time to spend just on induction, you know'.

Lisa continued to look doubtful, and clearly wasn't convinced: 'I just don't think I learned very much, that's all'.

'Why was that?' said Tina, sensing that she had a problem she had not anticipated.

Lisa took some time composing her answer. It was clear that she was fumbling for words that would allow her to express her opinion without upsetting the HR manager. 'I really wanted to show people that I know a lot about chemical engineering but nobody seems interested. Besides, several people told me that I would probably end up in marketing anyway. Most women do, don't they? Or HR, and I'm definitely not interested in that!' She emphasized 'HR' with a grimace.

After the development interview Lisa wrote a letter to Tina Johnson couched in hostile terms, accusing the company of misleading her and having no idea of how to use graduates. She had been offered a scholarship to study for a PhD at an American university and had accepted it. She would be leaving the company in a month's time.

*How would you have designed Lisa's development programme?*

*What resistance would you have reasonably expected and how would you have overcome it?*

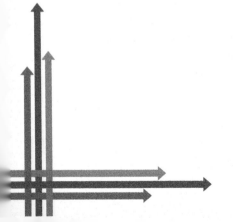

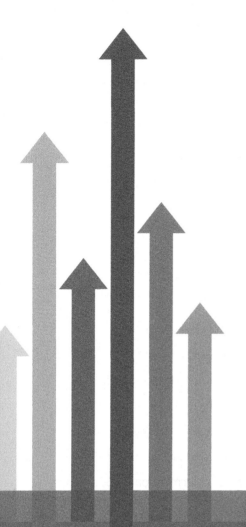

# PART SIX
## EMPLOYEE RELATIONS

This part of the book discusses the promotion of diversity and the management of conflict in the workplace. In Chapter 19 we consider the prevalence of discrimination on a variety of grounds and discuss the use of anti-discriminatory legislation and evaluate the effectiveness of proactive policies and initiatives aimed at the management of diversity within organizations. In Chapter 20 we examine the mechanisms by which organizations and workers communicate and resolve conflict within the employment relationship. In particular, we consider the opportunities for employee voice through collective and individual arrangements, the use of arbitration and mediation and the nature of bargaining.

## The chapters in Part Six address questions such as:

→ **Why should we encourage diversity in human resources?**

→ **What is the purpose of anti-discriminatory legislation and why have some countries adopted different approaches?**

→ **What is the empirical evidence for various types of discrimination?**

→ **Is there any evidence for the effectiveness of legislation or management of diversity initiatives?**

→ **What is the historical and current status of trade unionism?**

→ **How do different cultural and legislative contexts affect the practice of employee relations?**

→ **What formal and informal mechanisms are used for individual and collective workplace bargaining?**

→ **How does negotiation take place?**

→ **What is the role of arbitration?**

# CHAPTER 19
## Promoting diversity

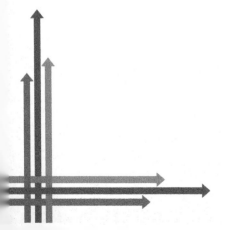

## LEARNING OBJECTIVES

The purpose of this chapter is to:

→ Define and distinguish between the concepts of equal opportunity and the management of diversity.

→ Identify the significant barriers to equality and diversity in employing organizations.

→ Outline the nature and extent of discrimination on the basis of sex and gender.

→ Evaluate the causes and extent of racial discrimination in the employment market.

→ Analyze the basis and effects of institutional racism.

→ Assess the effectiveness of legislation in the reduction of disability discrimination.

→ Consider the increasing significance of anti-age discrimination initiatives.

# THE MEANING OF DIVERSITY

People are different. They vary in gender, culture, race, social, physical and psychological characteristics. But our attitudes towards these differences can be negative or positive, depending upon individual perspectives and prejudices. Bassett-Jones (2005) argues that diversity is a recognizable source of creativity and innovation that can provide a basis for competitive advantage. Diversity is also a cause of misunderstanding, suspicion and conflict in the workplace that can result in absenteeism, poor quality, low morale and loss of competitiveness. Organizations have to manage the resulting paradox.

In earlier chapters we identified the tendency to form like-minded 'in-groups', to favour members of one's own group and for those in authority to recruit people like themselves. This often goes unquestioned – but is unfair. The consequences include a lack of opportunity for women, ethnic minorities, the disabled, older people and other disadvantaged sections of the community as the best jobs are ring-fenced and barriers are placed to prevent their progress.

As members of organizations, it is difficult to challenge the often subconscious actions and elaborately entrenched justifications for unfairness. Not least, because discrimination and prejudice are expressions of power that includes the ability to prevent, inhibit or punish critical comment. Yet, if people are the key assets of a business it is important to realize the maximum benefit from their human capital. True competitive advantage requires the best from everyone – without restrictions; it demands a prejudice-free and inclusive attitude towards actual and potential employees. It requires diversity (see Key concept 19.1).

---

**KEY CONCEPT 19.1** DIVERSITY

'Diversity is the variation of social and cultural identities among people existing together in a defined employment or marketing system' (Cox, O'Neill and Quinn, 2001: 3).

---

In reality, this has to be viewed as an ideal since discriminatory and non-inclusive behaviours have a deep psychological basis. Research shows that prejudice is difficult if not impossible to eliminate. For example, if someone is prejudiced against a particular group, meeting someone with positive qualities from that group does not dispel the prejudice.

Nevertheless, equality of opportunity is an objective worth striving for. It can be addressed at all levels: governments have a role to play through legislation to prevent discrimination; organizations need to focus on the management of diversity, making the most of a wide pool of talent; strategists should consider equal opportunity policies, targeting and positive development of under-represented groups; people managers can monitor their activities and increase awareness to minimize discrimination.

# SOCIETY AND OPPORTUNITY

Effectively, society determines who is given opportunity and who is not through the process of discrimination. Opportunity is also linked to social factors such as economic conditions and educational attainment: access to and success in education can be responsible for discrimination (Tannock, 2008). Overt prejudice is comparatively easy to observe but the true nature of unfairness lies in the way opportunity has been institutionalized within society.

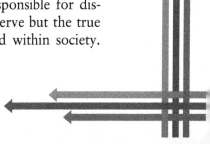

The status quo is constructed to benefit certain types of individual from particular backgrounds or those who are able to adapt most easily to its requirements. Typically this has denied opportunity to women and minority groups.

Most countries have a concentration of particular social groups at the top of their institutions. Others are found further down. As a consequence, skills and abilities are not used to the full – a situation that is detrimental to society as a whole. However, the advantaged are unlikely to admit that their positions come from privilege rather than competence. For them, change is not a priority. This form of 'particularism' (see Key concept 19.2) is still important, although the influence of convergent forces such as globalization and information technology is becoming increasingly prominent (Horwitz *et al.*, 2002; Good and Taylor, 2008).

---

**KEY CONCEPT 19.2** PARTICULARISM

Discrimination favouring particular groups and individuals over others. It derives from a reliance on personal relationships such as ethnic origin, religion or tribal community. It contrasts with 'universalism' in which personal relationships are ignored and emphasis is on other criteria such as qualifications, expertise and ability to do the job.

---

Particularism leads to discrimination. This mechanism can be extended to include a number of forms, including discrimination on the grounds of:

*Age.* Arbitrary age boundaries excluding younger and older workers.

*Appearance.* Preferring people of a certain height or weight, for example.

*Disability.* Discriminating against people with special needs.

*Gender.* Limiting certain types of jobs to either males or females.

*Ethnic origin.* Preference for particular racial or linguistic communities.

*Nationality.*

*Religion.*

*Background.* Often seen as cliques – networks of people from similar backgrounds reserving the best jobs for themselves. In addition, people with socially undesirable backgrounds, such as ex-offenders, are actively discriminated against.

*Nepotism.* Common in small companies that rely heavily on family members.

Marti, Bobier and Baron (2000) found that some forms of discrimination are more easily observed and recognized than others. Participants in their studies were more likely to label actions of gender or racial discrimination as prejudice and also tended to rate such examples as more severe than cases of prejudice on the grounds of age or weight. Harper (2000) reports on a study of longitudinal cohort data covering 11 407 individuals born in Britain in 1958. The results showed that physical appearance had a significant effect on earnings and employment patterns for both men and women. Regardless of gender, people assessed as unattractive or short were penalized. At the extremes, taller men tended to receive higher pay than average, while obese women were paid less than those of average weight. The researchers attributed the bulk of the pay differential for appearance to employer discrimination. In a Swiss study, Krings and Olivares (2007) observed prejudice against a disliked

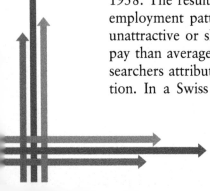

group – but only for jobs requiring interpersonal contact, rather than those needing technical ability.

Discrimination can be direct (Key concept 19.3) or indirect (Key concept 19.4). It can also extend into victimization when employees are treated less favourably as a consequence of asserting their rights. Many countries use legislation to reduce such discrimination, for example, in areas such as equal pay, selection and promotion. The effectiveness of such legislation is reflected in the proportion of disadvantaged groups achieving responsible positions. Often this has been disappointing. In much of the world, the presence of women and people from ethnic minority groups becomes increasingly rare towards the top of most organizations. Some groups, such as the disabled and the over-50s, are conspicuously absent from many firms.

### KEY CONCEPT 19.3   DIRECT DISCRIMINATION

Treating an individual or group less favourably on grounds such as disability, race, religion, age, gender or sexual orientation. An explicit and fairly obvious form of discrimination. The use of different criteria for promoting or paying male or female employees is an example of direct discrimination.

### KEY CONCEPT 19.4   INDIRECT DISCRIMINATION

Less obvious than direct discrimination. Requiring certain criteria that are more easily satisfied by one group than another. One example would be to specify a fixed minimum height requirement for entry into a police force. This is a criterion that would be more easily met by male than female applicants. Another example would be a requirement for an unnecessarily high standard of spoken or written English, that would favour people with a particular educational background.

We turn next to the practical consequences of discrimination on people management at the organizational level.

## DIVERSITY AND THE ORGANIZATION

Why should business organizations and their managers offer equal opportunities to a diverse range of employees? Two fundamental perspectives are identifiable that can be related to different models of HRM (Goss, 1994: 156):

*Human capital.* 'Artificially' blocking the progress of any group results in less than optimal use of an organization's human capital. Discrimination is irrational since it limits the resource value of employees. This view is compatible with 'hard', or free market HRM discussed in Part One of this book.

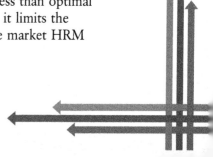

*Social justice.* A moral or ethical interest in social equality, compatible with 'soft' or social market HRM. Economic benefits are secondary to this social duty.

Goss sees the human capital perspective as fluctuating and opportunistic: a shallow commitment '... capable of being adopted or abandoned, in line with legal or economic expediency'. It is also narrow, restricted to legal requirements and short-term employment market conditions. This contrasts with the more principled social justice viewpoint, that embodies a deeper and wider commitment, extending beyond minimum legal requirements.

According to Ross and Schneider (1992) organizations benefit from a deep, principled commitment to equality of opportunity because it leads to:

→ A diverse workforce that enriches ideas and perspectives within an organization.

→ Imaginative ideas to assist total quality management.

→ Recruitment or promotion of the most talented people.

→ An environment that encourages them to stay.

→ Improved motivation and commitment that raises productivity.

→ Reduced wastage and recruitment costs that increase profitability.

Other commentators contend that, whereas this is valid for the economy as a whole, equal opportunity practices may be a significant expense rather than a benefit for individual firms.

All businesses operate within the national or supranational legislation governing equal opportunities in a specific country. For example, the USA and South Africa have required some employers to take measures of positive discrimination, typically requiring them to fill quotas from under-represented sections of the community. Recruitment criteria such as qualification or skill requirements may be relaxed for members of those groups. This represents an attempt to achieve the equal share level of opportunity outlined in Straw's model that also considers equal chance and equal access (detailed in Table 19.1).

**TABLE 19.1**
Levels of opportunity

| Level | Opportunities | Barriers |
|---|---|---|
| **1** Equal chance | Everyone has same chance, e.g. right to apply for vacancies; be considered for a position | Formal or informal barriers, e.g. employers may ignore applications from people living in ethnic minority areas |
| **2** Equal access | Disadvantaged groups not barred from entry into organizations but may be confined to lower levels of work | Institutional barriers, e.g. appraisal methods that favour certain groups, or promotion requirements – such as mobility – that effectively bar many married women |
| **3** Equal share | Access is free. Representation achieved at all levels. Legislation may require quotas for disadvantaged groups, e.g. disabled | Only those lawful, justifiable and necessary, e.g. specific language speakers to work with ethnic groups |

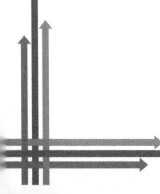

Alternatively, positive action may be required or undertaken voluntarily by governments or employers. Underrepresented groups are assisted and encouraged to participate in training and development initiatives, support groups and mentoring schemes. This requires that organizations are aware of their disadvantaged employees and the jobs they are doing, so that the problem of occupational segregation can be tackled (see Key concept 19.5).

---

**KEY CONCEPT 19.5** OCCUPATIONAL SEGREGATION

Disproportionate representation of particular groups in specific sectors, job types or levels of responsibility. Horizontal segregation places men and women, for example, in different jobs, such as chambermaids (women) and porters (men). Vertical segregation places one group in better-paid positions than another group, so that men are better represented at managerial levels while women are concentrated in lower, administrative jobs.

---

Turnasella (1999) suggests that the employment process is itself responsible for the persistent pay gap between men and women and between ethnic minorities and non-minorities. Employers usually require a salary history from job applicants and frequently ask questions about salary expectations. Applicants with a record of relatively low pay tend to be offered lower offers of remuneration. Intriguingly, in an experimental study involving 100 participants (50 men and 50 women), Blanton, George and Crocker (2001) found that women compared themselves with other women to gauge satisfaction with a pay rate when it was framed as compensation for past work, but compared themselves with the men when framed as part of an offer for future employment. Drawing on police work as an example, Dick and Nadin (2006) argue that personnel selection alone can make little difference to the unequal position of women given the complex causes of social occupational discrimination and segregation along gendered lines.

Corbridge and Pilbeam (1998) also point out that networking and headhunting are inevitably discriminatory because they involve recruitment from a restricted pool of friends, social acquaintances and school or university peers. People from disadvantaged groups, if they are employed at all, tend to be confined to 'boring jobs with no prospects' in the secondary sector (Molander and Winterton, 1994: 96).

The impact of discrimination on equality of pay is less in a unionized environment (Metcalf, Hansen and Charlwood, 2001). The authors attribute this to two factors:

→ Union members and jobs are more homogeneous than their non-union counterparts.

→ Union wage policies narrow the range of pay rates within and across firms and bring up the lowest wage rates.

# STRATEGIES FOR DIVERSITY

Many organizations have adopted equal opportunities policies – statements of commitment to fair human resource management. However, such policies are notoriously ineffective and rarely disturb vested interests. Obstacles to creating a diversified workforce are embedded in

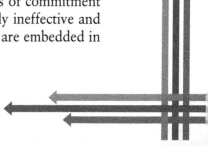

organizational culture – particularly the sub-culture at the top. Can the human resource function steer employers towards an equality perspective? Woodhams and Lupton (2006) found that the presence of an HR professional in small to medium-sized enterprises is associated with greater take-up of gender-based equality policies but not with greater implementation of associated practices.

According to Molander and Winterton (1994:102) serious equal opportunity policies require:

→ Allocation of overall responsibility to a specific senior executive.

→ Agreement of the policy with employee representatives.

→ Effective communication of the policy to all employees. An accurate survey of existing employees in terms of gender, ethnic origin, disability, etc. and the nature and status of their jobs.

→ An audit of human resource practices and their implications for equal opportunities.

→ Setting equal opportunity objectives within the human resource strategy.

→ Resources, such as training and development capabilities, to back up these objectives.

This approach can be incorporated within an integrated framework termed the 'management of diversity' (outlined in Key concept 19.6). The pitfalls in the process are evident.

However, the main difficulties arise from cost and lack of commitment, exemplified by 'tokenism' – the employment or promotion of isolated individuals to represent their gender or colour. 'Paternalism' is a related problem, where discriminatory decisions are taken for the 'benefit' of particular groups.

---

**KEY CONCEPT 19.6** MANAGEMENT OF DIVERSITY

The management of diversity goes beyond equal opportunity. Instead of merely allowing a greater range of people the opportunity to 'fit in', or be an honorary 'large, white male', the concept of diversity embodies the belief that people should be valued for their differences and variety. Diversity is perceived to enrich an organization's human capital. Whereas equal opportunity focuses on various disadvantaged groups, the management of diversity is about individuals. It entails a minimization of cloning in selection and promotion procedures and a model of resourcing aimed at finding flexible employees.

---

Monitoring of potential discrimination is frequently spasmodic, most commonly undertaken when individuals are recruited, than when they are candidates for promotion, and at exit. Training does not seem to be monitored closely for potential discrimination.

The management of diversity is a natural consequence of human resource strategies that focus on flexible working arrangements. Part-time work and, especially, homeworking are particularly attractive to some women and disabled employees. But men also may benefit more flexible working arrangements.

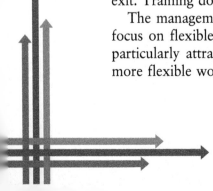

# HRM IN REALITY    GENDER INEQUALITY IN ACADEMIC RESEARCHERS' COMPENSATION

Research from the Mongan Institute for Health Policy at Massachusetts General Hospital published in *Academic Medicine* found that women researchers in the life sciences still receive lower levels of compensation than their male equivalents, including those at higher academic and professional levels. The study also identified gender differences in career advancement paths.

Lead researcher Dr Catherine DesRoches said:

> The gender gap in pay has been well documented, but what was not understood was whether academic accomplishments could overcome the pay gap. Our study found that, across the board, men are being paid substantially more than equally qualified and accomplished women at academic medical centers.

Researchers explain that previous studies documenting gender inequality in compensation and academic rank did not consider differences in professional activities, such as leadership responsibilities. The current study investigated whether such differences exist, whether productivity (reflected by scientific papers published) continues to vary, and whether salary discrepancies persist after these factors are taken into account.

In 2007 researchers randomly selected more than 3000 life science investigators from the top 50 academic medical centres in receipt of funding from the National Institutes of Health in 2003–2004. Respondents completed anonymous questionnaires including details of professional activities; scientific papers published; hours spent on professional, scientific and clinical activities; and total compensation.

The study found that women with the rank of full professor worked significantly more hours than equivalent men. This difference primarily reflected more time spent on administration and other professional tasks rather than patient care, teaching or research. There was no significant gender difference in hours worked by associate professors. Women at the assistant professor level tended to work fewer hours than men, the most common factor being less time expended on research. After controlling for differences in academic ranking, research productivity and other characteristics, researchers found women earned from US$6000 to US$15000 less per year than their male counterparts.

Catherine DesRoches said:

> These differences may seem modest, but over a 30-year career, an average female faculty member with a PhD would earn almost US$215000 less that a comparable male. If that deficit were invested in a retirement account earning 6 per cent per year, the difference would grow to almost US$700000 over a career. For department of medicine faculty, that difference could be almost twice as great.

The researchers did not investigate reasons for differences identified by the survey, but suggest that the greater number of professional responsibilities taken on by female full professors could reflect their organization's attempts to improve diversity at departmental and committee leadership level. Salary discrepancies may reflect on-going discriminatory practices or the specialist areas selected by women.

Principal investigator Eric G. Campbell, associate professor of medicine, concluded:

> Women working in the life sciences should not assume they are being paid as much as equally qualified men, and academic institutions should look hard at their compensation and advancement policies and their cultures. In the end, I suspect major systemic changes will be needed if we ever hope to achieve the ideal of equal pay for equal work in academic medicine.

*Why are male and female academics being paid differently?*

*Source:* HRM Guide USA. *(http://www.hrmguide.com).*

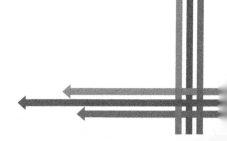

Discussion on women in the workplace tends to focus on family, children and marriage. However, Hamilton, Gordon and Whelan-Berry (2006) found that never-married women without children often experience work–life conflict at similar levels to that experienced by other groups of working women. Work–life benefits typically provided by organizations are frequently regarded as less important and used less often by never-married women without children than by other working women.

## KEY CONCEPT 19.7 THE GLASS CEILING

The term 'glass ceiling' describes the process by which women are barred from promotion by means of an invisible barrier. This involves a number of factors, including attitudes of people in power and the inflexible processes and requirements geared to the cloning process which ensures that 'men of a certain sort' will generally succeed. In the USA, the term is also used to describe the barrier that prevents progress for other disadvantaged groups – for example, ethnic minorities.

## GENDER AND SEXUAL DISCRIMINATION

Women's participation in the employment market has increased rapidly but in most countries their share of senior jobs remains low. The 2009 FTSE Female Index found that women made up 12.2 per cent of directors on the boards of Britain's biggest businesses (Sealy *et al.*, 2009). The report cited a 'discouraging decline' in the number of women executive directors from 16 to 15 and in the number of boards with multiple women directors. A quarter of FTSE boards are exclusively male. Of 14 women appointed who had not previously held FTSE 100 directorships, 13 were not British nationals. The authors contrast the position with that in Norway and Spain. Both countries are actively trying to increase female participation rather than rely on incremental progress. In Norway 30.5 per cent of directors on the top 100 ASA companies are women. In Spain in 2008, 74 per cent of IBEX 35 directors were women.

**HRM IN REALITY** MORE WOMEN FILL CANADA'S TOP BUSINESS JOBS

More women fill top executive jobs in Canada's largest publicly traded businesses than ever before – but this still amounts to a mere 7.2 per cent, according to a report from executive search firm Rosenzweig & Company.

Rosenzweig & Company analyzed the largest hundred publicly traded companies in Canada, based on revenue. Their annual revenues ranged between $41.3 billion and $1.9 billion. Between them, 544 top executive positions were examined.

Jay Rosenzweig, Managing Partner of Rosenzweig & Company said:

The good news is there are more women rising to top jobs and 15 are newly on the list this year, which may indicate turnover and change is in the air. The bad news is that the number remains inexcusably low and Corporate Canada's 'old boys' network' continues to disregard such a diverse talent pool in the workforce for leadership roles.

Unfortunately, the tough economic times could well serve to slow the pace of change. We'd like to see a big jump year-over-year so that women hold more than 10 per cent of all the top jobs soon, but we may be waiting longer now.

This is the fourth annual *Rosenzweig Report on Women at the Top Levels of Corporate Canada*. It shows that 36 women now hold top officer jobs in Canada's 100 largest publicly traded companies, compared with 31 last year. In terms of percentages, women currently hold 7.2 per cent of the top jobs while men have 92.8 per cent. Last year women held 5.8 per cent, with men holding 94.2 per cent.

All these businesses have to name and publicly disclose compensation for their Chief Executive Officer (CEO), Chief Financial Officer (CFO) and at least the next three highest paid executive officers. Some businesses list more than five top executives. But over two-thirds (69 per cent) of Canada's largest public companies do not have women executives in these categories. Canadian banks take the lead in promoting women to top jobs, including RBC, TD, CIBC and BMO. Overall, six corporations listed more than one woman: ATCO, Canadian Utilities, Linamar Corp., BMO, Canadian Pacific Railway and Russel Metals.

'We are hopeful the election of Barack Obama to the top job in the free world will boost diversity in North American boardrooms', said Jay Rosenzweig. 'Clearly, these abysmally low numbers for women – half the population and almost half the workforce – indicate change is needed; and the sooner the better.'

With study after study indicating that increased diversity at leadership levels spreads through organizations and improving financial performance, Jay Rosenzweig concludes: 'This is not simply a social and moral issue, but an issue about maximizing shareholder value'.

*Why are the rates of female participation at the top level so low?*

*Source: Reprinted with permission from HRM Guide Canada (http://www.hrmguide.net/canada/).*

The processes of occupational segregation and 'sex-typing' of jobs continue to be prevalent, so that women are concentrated at the base of most organizational hierarchies in jobs that are less prestigious and lower-paid than those favoured by men. As an example De Graft-Johnson, Manley and Greed (2005) reported on 2003 research indicating that while approximately 37 per cent of architectural students are women, and the percentage is increasing, this is not reflected in the architectural profession. Women represent only 13 per cent of the total and are leaving after qualifying. A multiplicity of factors, such as low pay, poor promotion prospects, discriminatory attitudes and sexist behaviour were found to influence departure.

Fuller, Beck and Unwin (2005) explore the attitudes of young people (aged 14 and 15) and employers to non-traditional occupational choices and recruitment decisions of employers from traditional sectors, such as engineering, construction and childcare. The study finds that organizations with gatekeeping roles between young people and employers are not taking sufficient responsibility for challenging their perceptions and decision-making processes. Occupational stereotypes are deeply entrenched, creating major psychological and social barriers that have to be overcome if a more evenly balanced workforce is to be achieved.

Employer prejudices explain some of the difficulties that women experience. Central to many employers' attitudes is attachment to a family model where the woman stayed at home looking after the children and the man went out to work. This pattern has become uncommon in much of the developed world. Dual-career and one-parent families, equal parenting and the dismantling of life-long career structures have eroded the distinction between male and female roles.

# HRM IN REALITY   GENDER SEGREGATION

A 2010 study from the Institute for Women's Policy Research in Washington, DC analyzes data from the *Current Population Survey* to assess the state of gender segregation in US employment since the early 1970s.

Researchers found that women are making progress in some lucrative male-dominated professions. For example, the percentage of women lawyers has risen from 4.0 per cent in 1972 to 32.2 per cent in 2009. However, according to one frequently used measure, the *Index of Dissimilarity*, overall progress towards equity has stalled since 1996. Women continue to dominate traditional female professions that are usually less well paid. In 2009, they accounted for over 95 per cent of kindergarten teachers, librarians, dental assistants and registered nurses.

Some sectors have seen a significant deterioration, with the percentage of women computer programmers falling from more than one-third in the late 1980s to less than 21 per cent, and from 13 per cent of civil engineers in 2005 to just over seven per cent in 2009. Researchers found that young women experienced more segregation in 2009 than they did ten years previously; wiping out about 20 per cent of the improvement achieved since 1968.

Heidi Hartmann, president of the Institute for Women's Policy Research said: 'It is very likely that the stalled progress in integrating the labour market is contributing to the failure of the wage gap to close'.

Based on 2009 earnings data, the study examines the relationship between median earnings and the gender composition of occupations. It differentiates between those that are predominantly male or female, and those that are relatively gender balanced, considering low, medium and high-skilled fields.

The researchers explain that women are now proportionately more likely than men to have some years of post-secondary education. However, the study found that irrespective of whether a job requires college level education, medium or low level skills, those predominantly held by women typically attract lower median earnings than those with either a more even gender balance or predominantly held by men.

The study acknowledges significant exceptions, particularly among medium-skilled occupations. Dental hygienists, the great majority of whom are women, have higher weekly median earnings (US$956) than occupations almost exclusively held by men such as electricians (US$856) or carpenters (US$665). However, over 80 per cent of dental hygienists have at least an associate degree. Only 20 per cent of electricians, and even fewer carpenters, have attained similar levels of education. Researchers point out that women currently require a higher level of formal education to achieve similar earnings.

Ariane Hegewisch, a study director at the Institute for Women's Policy Research explained:

> All workers are likely to do better if they have at least some post-secondary school qualifications. Yet while it is still possible without college to earn a decent wage in some male-dominated occupations, the same is not true in female-dominated occupations. Almost as important as getting a qualification, however, is the field in which you qualify. A speech language pathologist – an occupation that is predominantly female – on average makes US$1153 per week, compared with a pharmacist – an occupation nearly half female – who receives median earnings of US$1841, a difference of close to US$700 for a week of full-time work.

The study found a less significant difference in median earnings for workers in low-skilled occupations. Researchers explain that the Bureau of Labour Statistics identifies nursing and psychiatric aides; maids, housekeepers and cleaners; and personal and home care aides as the largest categories of female-dominated, low-skilled occupations. They are much more likely to result in wages close to the poverty threshold than male-dominated, low-skilled occupations (such as truck drivers, labourers and ground maintenance workers). Median weekly earnings in 2009 were US$553 for this category of male-dominated occupations compared to US$408 for their female equivalents.

Robert Drago, research director for the Institute for Women's Policy Research, commented:

> Policy makers need to pay attention to the stalled progress in gender desegregation. Occupational

segregation carries costs for the economy and employers by exacerbating skill shortages and causing reduced productivity. It also costs working families. Particularly in low-skilled jobs, working in an occupation predominantly held by women instead of one held by men, may be the difference between earning a poverty wage and earning a family supporting wage.

*What causes gender segregation?*

Source: HRM Guide USA *(http://www.hrmguide.com).*

In other parts of the world, the position of female workers has improved. For example, Hossain and Tisdell (2005) found evidence of growing commercialization of women's work in Bangladesh. Most women are self-employed or employed in low-skill jobs, but participation is increasing in high-skill and entrepreneurial jobs as well as policy-making bodies. Gender wage differentials have been considerably reduced in many industries but women tend to be paid less than men. Remarkable improvements in women's educational attainments are positively correlated with workforce participation.

## Gender differences

A further contributor to the problem is our perception of **gender** differences, real or imagined (see Key concept 19.8). There are differences between men and women, other than the physical, but little agreement as to what they are. The common stereotypes are that men tend to favour and aspire towards qualities that are essentially individualistic and competitive, such as intelligence, dynamism, energy and assertiveness. Women, on the other hand, stress qualities of a more cooperative and consensual nature: thoughtfulness, flexibility, perceptiveness and honesty.

### KEY CONCEPT 19.8    GENDER

All human societies divide themselves into two social categories called 'female' and 'male'. Each category is defined on the basis of varying cultural assumptions about the attributes, beliefs and behaviours expected from males and females. The gender of any individual depends on a complex combination of genetic, body, psychological and social elements, none of which are free from possible ambiguity or anomaly (Helman, 1990). Traditionally, sexual differences have been used to justify male-dominated societies in which women have been given inferior and secondary roles in their working lives.

They concluded that since male managers are prevalent, females are disadvantaged by being evaluated against male standards of behaviour. Given similar jobs and appraisal ratings, men are more likely to be offered training or promotion. Kramer and Lambert (2001) examined a large, random sample of female and male employees using a survival analysis technique to investigate the time taken from being hired to being promoted to supervisor.

## HRM IN REALITY | GENDER STEREOTYPING A KEY BARRIER

A study published in the December 2009 issue of the *Psychology of Women Quarterly* shows that management stereotypes are likely to evolve as more women assume leadership roles in the workforce.

Despite improvements in female participation at management levels, women still fill less than 2 per cent of CEO leadership positions in the Fortune 500. It is not surprising to find, therefore, that leaders continue to be thought of as men with the management levels in most industries considered to be 'male-typed'. But in a few industries women have moved into management positions. These industries have become more 'gender-neutral' and there are indications that stereotypes of leaders as men may be changing.

The study, *The Evolving Manager Stereotype: The Effects of Industry Gender Typing on Performance Expectations for Leaders and Their Teams* by Susan F. Cabrera, Stephen J. Sauer and Melissa C. Thomas-Hunt of the Universities of Cornell, Clarkson and Virginia respectively, investigates how male and female leaders and their teams are evaluated differently according to the gender-typing of the industry in which they work.

The researchers' findings were that people have higher expectations for the performance of teams when the leader's gender is consistent with the gender typing of the industry in which the team works. However, expectations for performance of leaders' own performance were not impacted by their consistency with industry gender typing. According to Susan F. Cabrera:

This research demonstrates the power of stereotypes concerning what kinds of people should lead organizations in what kinds of industries. In addition, it suggests that, as more women move into certain sectors of our economy, stereotypes may be evolving in ways that create a more level playing field for women who aspire to leadership positions.

### Gender stereotyping

A survey published in 2007 found that gender stereotyping was a key barrier to the advancement of women in corporate leadership, leaving women leaders with limited and conflicting options.

*The Double-Bind Dilemma for Women in Leadership: Damned if You Do, Doomed if You Don't* was the third in a series of reports examining the effects of gender stereotyping in the workplace by Catalyst, a non-profit organization working to advance opportunities for women and business. The study surveyed men and women business leaders in the US and Europe. Of 1231 participants, 296 were US senior managers and corporate leaders (168 women and 128 men) and 935 were European managers and senior managers (282 women and 653 men). The second part of the study provided qualitative analysis of in-depth, semi-structured interviews with 13 women leaders in a large US corporation.

The report argued that gender stereotyping results in organizations routinely underestimating and underutilizing women's leadership talent. The 2006 Catalyst Census shows that while women make up over 50 per cent of management, professional and related occupations, only 15.6 per cent of Fortune 500 corporate officers and 14.6 per cent of Fortune 500 board directors were women.

Ilene H. Lang, Catalyst president said:

When companies fail to acknowledge and address the impact of gender stereotypic bias, they lose out on top female talent. Ultimately, it's not women's leadership styles that need to change. Only when organizations take action to address the impact of gender stereotyping will they be able to capitalize on the 'full deck' of talent.

The report highlighted numerous previous studies demonstrating similar leadership styles in men and women. However, earlier research by Catalyst found that women business leaders faced persistent gender stereotyping frequently confronting them with double-bind 'no-win' dilemmas not experienced by men. The current study found that men are still perceived as 'default leaders' while women are considered 'atypical leaders' and as violating accepted norms, irrespective of their leadership style.

The survey identified three common dilemmas currently experienced by women business leaders, supported by comments from participants:

1   **Extreme perceptions**. Women business leaders are perceived as 'never just right'. Those who act in a manner consistent with gender stereotypes are considered too soft, those who go against them are considered too tough.

My observations show senior women to be at either end of the spectrum, drivers that do it themselves (even though they might have given it to someone). This type tends to give little recognition and is a perfectionist. The others are very effective delegators, giving lots of recognition and building loyal teams, but can be perceived as 'not tough enough (US man, age 35–44, level not specified).

2   **High competence threshold/lower rewards**. Women leaders face higher standards than their male counterparts and receive less reward. Often they must work doubly hard to achieve the same level of recognition for the same level of work and 'prove' they can lead.

Men and women are seen differently, and the difference in my experience and observation is that we (women) need to show it more times before they believe it. With a woman, they will want to see the behaviour repeated more frequently before they will say that this is really part of the women (sic) and her capabilities (European woman, high-potential manager).

3   **Competent but disliked**. Women exhibiting traditional leadership skills such as assertiveness tend to be seen as competent but not personable or well-liked. Those who adopt a more stereotypically feminine style are liked but not seen as having valued leadership skills.

…it may just be that people are more sensitive to how women behave in that regard. There does seem to be a little more tolerance for harsh behaviour from men rather than women. Women are quicker to get labelled, and with men, it's easier to brush it off… (High-potential woman, US-based manager).

I have experienced in the past that women can be distrusted in leadership roles, especially when they use a dominant style of communication. On the contrary, if they use a collaborative style serving their organization and empowering people, they get more recognition and sincere appreciation from their male equals (Spanish man, age 31–35, middle management).

The report suggested that organizations need to develop strategies to remove the pervasive and damaging impact of gender stereotyping from the work environment to take advantage of the expanding pool of female leadership talent.

Ilene H. Lang explained: 'While women may address double-bind dilemmas with individual strategies this is clearly about organizations shifting their norms and culture to meet marketplace demands'.

The report argues that education about how stereotyping works and holding individuals accountable can decrease the negative impact of gender bias. Actions that organizations can take include:

→   Providing all employees with tools and resources to increase awareness of women leaders' skills and the effects of stereotypic perceptions.

→   Assessing the work environment to identify ways in which women are at risk of stereotypic bias.

→   Creating and implementing innovative work practices that target stereotypic bias; particularly effective when specific areas of risk, such as performance management procedures, are addressed.

The report suggested ways in which organizations can apply this knowledge:

→   Managerial training and diversity education – educating managers and employees about the origin and consequences of bias, inconsistencies between values and actual behaviour, and causes and effects of gender inequality in the workplace.

→   Performance and evaluation management – employing objective and unambiguous evaluation criteria.

*Where do gender stereotypes come from?*

*Source: Reprinted with permission from HRM Guide USA (http://www.hrmguide.com).*

They found evidence for significant pro-male bias in promotion decisions that could not be attributed to differences in time on the job, education, or parenting responsibilities. Brynin (2006) argues that men have traditionally gained more than women from access to technologies at work that bring prestige, job security, more satisfaction and higher pay. Female jobs associated with technologies tend to involve routine work. Busolt and Kugele (2009) described the low incidence of scientific researchers in Europe and the even lower level of female inventors.

Wilson (2005) examined how women academics in two British universities perceive the assumption that they are receiving different and unequal treatment in appraisal. It has been argued that men and women appear to have learned that women are different and not equal in organizations. Wilson's study found that, while the women did not necessarily perceive themselves as being seen to be different, men saw them as having different and inferior qualities. Women were seen as 'other' when measured against standards and norms set by men.

Hakim (2006) argues that high levels of female employment and family-friendly policies actually reduce gender equality in the workforce and reinforce the glass ceiling. The emphasis placed on equal opportunities by policymakers and feminists assumes that discrimination is the primary source of sex differentials in labour market outcomes – notably the pay gap between men and women. However, some careers and occupations cannot be domesticated and this also poses limits to social engineering. The notion of the glass ceiling is itself challenged by the metaphor of a firewall (Bendl and Schmidt, 2010).

Fortin (2005) concluded that women are more likely to underestimate their own skill levels and, therefore, inhibit their own progress. However, some deal with the situation by playing the game according to male rules. In general, women are more likely to regard themselves as 'enablers' of other people, building up the confidence of their staff and encouraging them to develop and use their skills.

In a study of 176 women managers from a number of industries across Australia, Downey, Papageorgiou and Stough (2006) found that female managers displaying transformational leadership behaviours tended to show higher levels of emotional intelligence and intuition than women managers displaying less transformational leadership behaviours.

Much of the debate about male and female behaviour revolves around sexual stereotyping, which has a significant cultural basis not easily amenable to change. Stereotyping can also influence career aspirations. Harper and Haq (2001) examined British cohort data and found that 16-year-old young men and women showed significant differences in their occupational aspirations, appearing to follow a traditional pattern that influenced their decisions to apply for certain types of job. They found no evidence of hiring bias against women except in manual and craft occupations and that the effect of sex discrimination could be exaggerated if occupational aspirations were not taken into account.

Kraus and Yonay (2000) compared the way in which women and men attained workplace authority in female-dominated, mixed, and male-dominated occupations. They found that women have the greatest chances of being given authority when they work in 'male' occupations, arguing that the competition between men and women is weaker in such occupations so that men have less reason to discriminate against women. They observed that men have similar chances regardless of the type of occupation in which they are employed. By contrast, in a meta-analytic study, Davison and Burke (2000) found that female and male applicants received lower ratings when being considered for an opposite-sex-type job.

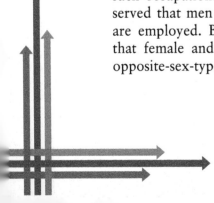

# HRM IN REALITY
# WOMEN PUT OFF COMPUTING CAREERS BY GEEKY ENVIRONMENTS

Recent research led by the University of Washington published in the *Journal of Personality and Social Psychology* in 2010 found that the work environment may be a key factor deterring women from careers in computer science.

Lead author Sapna Cheryan, assistant professor of psychology said:

> When people think of computer science the image that immediately pops into many of their minds is of the computer geek surrounded by such things as computer games, science fiction memorabilia and junk food. That stereotype doesn't appeal to many women who don't like the portrait of masculinity that it evokes.

This helps create what the study refers to as 'ambient belonging' – whether an individual feels comfortable in a particular setting.

Sapna Cheryan explained:

> It is the sense you get right away when you walk into a room. You look at the objects and make an instant appraisal of how you would fit with the objects and the people who are typically found in that environment. You also make a judgment of 'I like it here' or 'I don't belong here'.

Researchers recruited 250 female and male students who were not studying computer science to study why the proportion of women in this speciality is decreasing while the proportion in other sciences such as biology, mathematics and chemistry is increasing.

In the first of a series of experiments, participants spent several moments in a small classroom that either contained objects stereotypically associated with computer science such as Star Trek posters, video game boxes and Coke cans, or non-stereotypical items such as nature posters, art, a dictionary and coffee mugs. The students were told the room was being shared with another class and to ignore the contents.

Participants then completed questionnaires about their attitude toward computer science. Women exposed to the stereotypical setting expressed less interest in computer science than those who saw the non-stereotypical objects. Men did not demonstrate a similar difference.

Other significant findings included:

→ Female participants were given the choice of joining one of two all-female company teams where the only difference was the objects found in the workroom; 82 per cent chose the team with the non-stereotypical setting.

→ Female and male participants were given the choice of similar jobs at one of two companies with equal gender distribution in their workforces. Both groups preferred the non-stereotypical work environment, but women's preferences were significantly stronger. Women also felt less of a sense of ambient belonging in the stereotypical work environment compared to men.

→ Participants were questioned about their attitudes toward a Web design company and were asked to choose between identical job offers from two such companies. Women were more likely to opt for the non-stereotypical company while men had the opposite preference. The more women perceived the stereotypical environment as masculine, the less interested they were in the company concerned.

Sapna Cheryan concluded:

> These studies suggest objects such as science fiction books and Star Trek posters communicate whether or not a person belongs in an environment. Instead of trying to change the women who do not relate to the stereotype, our research suggests that changing the image of computer science so that more women feel they fit in the field will go a long way to recruiting them into computer science.
>
> We want to attract more people to computer science. The stereotype is not as alienating to men as women, but it still affects them as well. A lot of men may also be choosing to not enter the field

because of the stereotype. We need to broaden the image of the field so both women and men feel more welcome. In workplaces and universities we can do this by changing the way offices, hallways and labs look. The media can also play a role by updating the image of computer science. It would be nice for computer scientists in movies and television to be typical people, not only computer geeks.

*What inhibits some women from technological careers?*

*Source: Reprinted with permission from HRM Guide USA (http://www.hrmguide.com).*

## Sexual harassment

Aspects of male culture can be distinctly unattractive both to women and men. From school to shopfloor, locker room to office, the culture of masculinity expresses itself in 'jokes' revolving around three stereotypes of sexuality (Mills and Murgatroyd, 1991: 78):

→ the ideal, or 'real man' syndrome – toughness, football and so on.

→ definitions of males as 'not-females'.

→ the normality of heterosexuality.

Ford (2000) found experimental evidence to suggest that when people who are high in hostile sexism are exposed to sexist jokes they become increasingly tolerant of sex discrimination.

In office and managerial environments **sexual harassment** – ranging from unwelcome comments on appearance to physical advances – remains common. Sexual harassment is a difficult topic for managers to deal with, since it involves personal relationships and the individual interpretations of those involved (see Key concept 19.9). The issue has often been trivialized or ignored in a 'conspiracy of silence'.

---

**KEY CONCEPT 19.9** SEXUAL HARASSMENT

Definitions vary considerably but most are agreed that it is sexual attention which is unwanted, repeated and affects a person's work performance or expectations. However, it is possible for one incident to be sufficiently severe to be regarded as harassment. It differs from sexual banter or flirting since it is one-way; it does not have the involvement and acceptance of both parties. In the USA, the Equal Employment Opportunity Commission has extended the definition of sexual harassment to include a range of actions that lead to a 'hostile work environment'. This definition includes unwelcome touching, joking, teasing, innuendos, slurs and the display of sexually explicit materials.

---

Increasingly, employers can face legal action for sexual harassment by one employee against another. Even in situations that do not proceed to formal complaints or tribunals, the consequences for workplace morale can be significant. At the very least, co-workers are likely to be aware of an awkward atmosphere. Victims may suffer anxiety or depression, adversely affecting concentration and productivity. The likelihood of absenteeism is increased and victims frequently leave to escape harassment. There may also be an impact on non-work relationships.

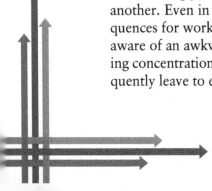

Employers have a moral duty to protect staff from sexual harassment. In general, if employers tolerate sexual harassment they convey the impression that one gender does not deserve respect; they are prepared to sacrifice motivation and commitment; they must accept the consequences for efficiency. Organizations can deal with sexual harassment by (Moynahan, 1993):

→ Surveying the organization to determine the extent of sexual harassment.

→ Writing and circulating a strongly worded policy indicating possible disciplinary action.

→ Providing an effective reporting mechanism, protecting the rights of accusers and the accused.

→ Packaged workshops, which help to define harassment and prevent 'misunderstandings'.

→ Assertiveness training, perhaps particularly appropriate for women working in jobs which have traditionally been regarded as male, which encourages the confidence to provide verbal or even written feedback to unwanted behaviour. The ability to say 'no' firmly and at an early stage is particularly effective.

→ Gender-awareness training to emphasize different perceptions of teasing and 'harmless fun' between men and women.

Some jobs inevitably have greater risk attached from clients and customers, such as social work, nursing and policing. However, in an Australian study of social working, sexual advances were found to be the least prevalent of hostile actions (Koritsas *et al.*, 2010).

Legal definitions of sexual harassment fall into one of two types:

*Quid pro quo.* A narrow, traditional definition of sexual harassment as a demand by a person in power, for example a supervisor, for sexual favours from a subordinate in return for a job, pay increase, promotion, transfer or other benefit.

*Hostile environment.* A wider definition, including unwelcome sexual advances that have the effect of creating a hostile, intimidating, abusive or offensive working environment.

Clarke (2006a) examines concerns raised by employers about consensual sexual relationships occurring at work. The study suggests that the link between sexual relationships and sexual harassment is sometimes used as a justification for regulating relationships, particularly hierarchical ones. There also can be a problem of harassment when relationships end. Clarke comments that the willingness of employers, particularly in the USA, to prohibit or regulate relationships might not be motivated by concern for women's equality at work. Recent changes to the law on sexual harassment in the UK might encourage British employers to consider prohibiting or regulating sexual relationships, but there are countervailing legal principles to be considered, such as anti-discrimination law and privacy rights. The study concludes that sex discrimination law should be directed to ensuring that unacceptable behaviour is not tolerated rather than prohibiting consensual relationships.

# ETHNIC DIVERSITY AND DISCRIMINATION

Most countries have populations of different ethnic origins, typically highlighted by colour or religious differences. Few countries have true equality between these groups.

Racism is commonly equated with hostility and prejudice. The media tends to associate the issue with abuse and violence perpetrated by neo-fascist groups. In general, however,

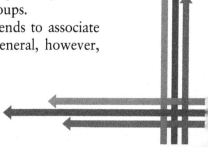

such organizations lack widespread power and influence. The perception of racism as obvious prejudicial opinions and attitudes obscures more insidious forms of discrimination (Sivanandan, 1991). Racism cannot be reduced to 'human nature and individual fallibility' which leave the state, politics and 'major structural aspects of contemporary life out of focus' (Husband, 1991: 50).

Howitt and Owusu-Bempah (1990: 397) conclude that 'seeing racism solely as a form of interpersonal antagonism not only sanitizes it, but prevents us from defining ourselves as racist if we do not *feel* racial hatred'. Hence stereotypes appear that are not seen as 'prejudiced': '...Asian women are seen as 'passive' or 'hysterical' or subject to oppressive practices within the family; there is the stereotype of the strong dominant Afro-Caribbean woman as the head of the household; and the description of the over-aggressive African woman' (Sayal, 1990: 24).

Subeliani and Tsogas (2005) studied the diversity management practices of Rabobank, a major bank in the Netherlands. They found that these were primarily directed at attracting ethnic customers rather than improving the quality of working life and career prospects of ethnic minority employees who remained segregated in lower positions and not allowed openly to express their culture and religion. Indigenous participants in an environmental management programme in Australia were marginalized by the formal governance structure which disguised power imbalances and exploitation (Carter and Hill, 2007). The UK's largest employer, the National Health Service has an extremely diverse workforce but has singularly failed in offering promotion prospects to non-white staff (Kalra *et al.*, 2009).

Foster and Harris (2005) examined the way in which managing diversity was understood and applied in one large, long-established British retailing company. They found that business benefits attributed to diversity management are appealing to employers. However, the concept lacks clarity for line managers both in terms of what it is and how it should be implemented within the framework of anti-discrimination legislation. They suggest that line managers are familiar with the value of demonstrating a common approach in decision making as the key defence against claims of discriminatory treatment. Consequently they tend to regard a diversity management agenda concerned with recognizing and responding to individual differences as more likely to lead to claims of unequal treatment. They argue that, in addition to the operational context, employers need to take account of the tensions facing line managers, their interpretation of diversity management and perceptions of fair treatment.

Stewart and Perlow (2001) looked at applicant race, job status and interviewers' racial attitudes in relation to unfair selection decisions. They found that interviewers with more negative attitudes toward black people showed greater confidence in their decision to hire a black applicant rather than a white applicant for a low-status job and to give a high-status job to a white candidate rather than a black candidate. Frazer and Wiersma (2001) conducted an experiment with 88 white US undergraduates who were asked to look at paper credentials and then interview a high or low-quality black or white applicant. Black and white applicants were 'hired' in equal proportion. But when the interviewers were asked to recall the experience one week later, they rated the answers from black applicants as being significantly less intelligent than the answers given by white applicants. Frazer and Wiersma explain this by postulating that the undergraduates had negative schemas towards black people which they suppressed in the public situation of making a hiring decision, but these negative stereotypes were revealed when unobtrusive measures were used. A study in Austria and Germany suggests that in the case of Muslims race/ethnicity and religion are compounded (Forstenlechner and Al-Waqfi, 2010).

Murji (2006) examines the use of stereotyped images in a series of advertisements that formed part of the 'personal responsibility' campaign by the Commission for Racial Equality (CRE). The aim was to raise awareness of racial stereotyping and, in one case, to provoke members of the public into complaining about the images presented. The CRE was the

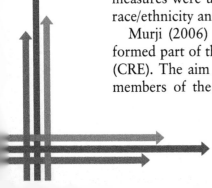

main body charged with implementing and monitoring anti-racism in the UK and the use of racial stereotypes has been controversial, though not always in anticipated ways. It has been argued that the CRE's use of stereotypes is based on questionable evidence, on a problematic conception of positive and negative images, and that it fails to consider how the images can be read in diverse ways. Murji argues that the CRE seemed to rely on a quasi-essentialist view of race and racism and consequently appears unable to engage with racism in its diverse manifestations.

Another significant aspect of the problem is not so much racial discrimination as racial disadvantage. This arises from the inability of the liberal-minded middle classes to perceive the structural advantages that contribute to their own success. Dominelli (1992: 165) argues:

> It is the subtle presence of racism in our normal activities, coupled with our failure to make the connections between the personal, institutional and cultural levels of racism which make it so hard for white people to recognize its existence in their particular behaviour and combat it effectively.

Mason (2000) evaluates the concept of 'pre-labour market inequality' – essentially, the class and cultural background of individuals – and concludes that it has an undoubted impact on individual well-being and intergenerational mobility. But the manner in which class background has its effects is not clear. A higher class position may create an advantage in skill acquisition. Alternatively, higher social status may increase access to people in positions of power and authority. Research and media comment on issues such as choice of school tend to focus on class while ignoring the racial element (Byrne, 2009). Shiner and Modood (2002) observe that young people from ethnic minority backgrounds in Britain are admitted into university in large numbers but class or culturally based institutional biases result in their concentration in the new university sector. Such universities are grossly underfunded in comparison with more established institutions and are less favoured by 'blue chip' recruiters. In the US, faced with disinterest from hiring organizations, career centre staff were found to be favouring white students in comparison to African-American and Latino students (Damaske, 2009). Also in the US black students tend to be particularly isolated when they do attend an elite university (McClintock, 2010).

**HRM IN REALITY** BETTER EDUCATION BUT WORSE JOB PROSPECTS FOR MINORITIES

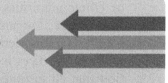

Research by Christian Dustmann and Nikolaos Theodoropoulos from the Centre for Research and Analysis of Migration at University College London, published in *Oxford Economic Papers* in 2010, found that members of Britain's ethnic minority communities, whether born abroad or in the UK, tend to be better educated than their white British-born peers but are less likely to be employed.

The study analyzed data from the British Labour Force Survey from 1979 to 2005. Conducted by the Office for National Statistics, this categorizes ethnic background as white, Indian, Pakistani, black Caribbean, black African, Bangladeshi or Chinese.

Comparing women born in Britain, researchers found that those identifying as Pakistani are 25 per cent less likely to be in employment than their white peers and those as Bangladeshi 47 per cent less likely. In the early 1980s Pakistani and Bangladeshi women born outside Britain had 46 per cent and 60 per cent lower probability of employment respectively than white British-born counterparts.

The study found that British-born members of ethnic minority communities are better educated than their parents' generation born outside the UK and white peers. This improvement is greater for the majority of

British-born ethnic minority groups than for whites. Researchers conclude that this is indicative of the value placed on education but acknowledge differences between communities. The study found that of individuals born in Britain between 1963 and 1975, half of Chinese descent went to university, compared with 15 per cent of black-Caribbeans and 20 per cent of whites.

About 46 per cent of British-born ethnic minorities live in London compared with 10 per cent of their white peers. Consequently the former group tend to earn slightly more, particularly women. However, analysis suggests that if educational attainment and regional distribution were the same in both groups, British-born ethnic minorities would earn less than their white counterparts. This would especially affect men with an estimated discrepancy of 9 per cent.

**Christian Dustmann commented:**

Our research shows that individuals of ethnic-minority descent born in Britain invest considerably into education, and more so than their British-born white peers. However, it is concerning that on average British-born ethnic minorities, and in particular men, would have a wage disadvantage if they had the same education, and lived in the same region, as their white British-born peers.

*How would you explain the differences in attainment between the ethnic groups?*

Source: Reprinted with permission from HRM Guide UK (http://www.hrmguide.co.uk/).

Ben-Tovim *et al.* (1992) criticize the ideology of 'colour blindness' and note other rationalizations for ignoring racism: that raising the question is divisive; that the problems of the ethnic minorities are the same as those of the white population, or the working-class, the inner cities and so on. Awad, Cokley and Ravitch (2005) investigated the relationship between colour-blind attitudes, modern racist attitudes and attitudes toward affirmative action. Detractors of affirmative action maintain that use of race-conscious policies to remedy past discrimination is contra-indicative of a colour-blind society. Supporters maintain that while a colour-blind society may be desirable, acts of past discrimination and current institutional racism make it necessary to use race-conscious policies. The study found that after controlling for race and sex, colour-blind attitudes emerged as the strongest predictor of attitudes toward affirmative action, followed by modern racism.

Braham *et al.* (1992: 106) suggest that widening the definition of discrimination to include indirect or institutional racism provides a better understanding of the barriers faced by ethnic minorities (see Key concept 19.10). Institutional racism is virtually unrecognized in commercial organizations but remains a contentious issue in the public sector – for example the London Metropolitan Police (Shiner, 2010). It is important to acknowledge the wide range of practices involved – some much more obvious than others. Rejecting the proposition that all institutions are uniformly racist, Braham *et al.* argue that 'the kind of procedures ... that disadvantage black people *also* disadvantage other groups'. We noted in Chapter 14 that the process of cloning is focused on replicating the people in power rather than discriminating against any particular group.

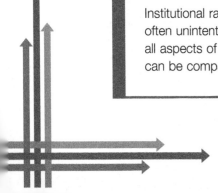

## KEY CONCEPT 19.10 INSTITUTIONAL RACISM

Institutional racism is an indirect and largely invisible process. It is a term encompassing the often unintentional barriers that serve to disadvantage members of ethnic minority groups in all aspects of organizational structure, for example selection and promotion procedures. It can be compared with concepts such as cloning and the glass ceiling.

## HRM IN REALITY — DIVERSITY TRAINING DOESN'T WORK

Diversity training programmes have failed to eliminate bias and increase the number of minorities in management, despite the fact that many corporations have spent increasing amounts of money on this area according to a paper published in the *American Sociological Review* in 2006. Alexandra Kalev of the University of California, Berkeley, Frank Dobbin, professor of sociology in Harvard University's Faculty of Arts and Sciences and Erin Kelly of the University of Minnesota, conclude that such efforts to mitigate managerial bias ultimately fail. In contrast, programmes that establish responsibility for diversity, such as equal opportunity staff positions or diversity task forces, have proved more effective.

Frank Dobbin said:

> For the past 40 years companies have tried to increase diversity, spending millions of dollars a year on any number of programs without actually stopping to determine whether or not their efforts have been worth it. Certainly in the case of diversity training, the answer is no. The only truly effective way to increase the presence of minorities and women in managerial positions is through programs that create organizational responsibility. If no one is specifically charged with the task of increasing diversity, then the buck inevitably gets passed *ad infinitum*. To increase diversity, executives must treat it like any other business goal.

This study is described as the first to examine the efficacy of diversity programmes based on the actual change in minority representation in management positions. The authors examined reports submitted to the Equal Employment Opportunity Commission by private sector establishments and conducted a sample survey on the history of diversity programmes within the companies concerned.

These were categorized into three groups: organizational responsibility programmes such as task forces or staff positions; managerial bias programmes such as diversity training; and programmes that created networking or mentoring opportunities. The data showed that organizational responsibility programmes were the most effective. Diversity task forces yielded the greatest results, increasing the proportion of white women in management positions by 14 per cent, black women by 30 per cent, and black men by 10 per cent.

The study found that diversity training aimed at reducing managerial bias may actually increase it. Programmes in this group were followed by a 6 per cent decline in the proportion of black women in management. White women benefited modestly with a 6 per cent increase. Social networking improved representation of white women, but lowered that of black men. Mentoring programmes showed a strong positive effect for black women. Across the board, diversity programmes benefited white women the most, followed by black women, with black men benefiting the least.

Frank Dobbin commented: 'Although the likelihood of minorities holding management positions has increased, the raw percentages of minorities in management remain quite low.'

*Why doesn't diversity training work?*

Source: Reprinted with permission from HRM Guide USA (http://www.hrmguide.com/).

## OTHER FORMS OF DISCRIMINATION

Disabled people are among the most disadvantaged because barriers to work are not only social and psychological but also physical. Quota systems for the employment of disabled people have largely been ineffective because of inadequate supervision by governments. Also, where social legislation for the disabled is weak, companies have found it comparatively easy to argue that they cannot provide suitable access or facilities to meet their needs.

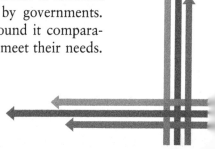

Countries such Canada and the USA have instigated their own legislation. After decades of ineffective quotas, the UK was the first country in the European Union to introduce Disability Discrimination Acts in 1995 and 2005 (subsequently subsumed by the Equality Act that came into force in 2010. These Acts made it illegal for businesses to discriminate against disabled people as employees or customers. Discrimination on the grounds of age is prevalent but often unrecognized. Some countries such as Canada, Australia, New Zealand, and the USA have legislated against ageism and a European Union Directive compelled all member states to introduce legislation against ageism by the year 2006. Prior to the introduction of age discrimination legislation, blatant ageism was common in job advertisements.

## HRM IN REALITY — EQUALITY REPORT: HOW FAIR IS BRITAIN?

The first triennial report from the Equality and Human Rights Commission (EHRC) published in October 2010 concludes that while Britain has made good progress in addressing inequalities and tolerating diversity, significant barriers to a fairer society remain. 'How fair is Britain?' gives insight into opportunities and outcomes for people in Britain according to age, gender, disability, ethnicity, religion or belief, sexual orientation and transgender status. It considers fundamental areas such as life expectancy, health, education and employment as well as security, support and power.

Trevor Phillips, chair of the EHRC said:

Britain is a country which is more tolerant than at any time in living memory, more intolerant of discrimination-but which has yet to live up to its own aspirations. In short, we are a more fair-minded people than previous generations – but we are not yet a fair society.

With supplementary research into the area of employment conducted by the Policy Studies Institute, the report confirms that the percentage of women and black people in work has increased by twice the average between the mid-1990s and 2006–2008. The increase for Bangladeshi and Pakistani people is three times the average. Only 25 per cent of British Muslim women are in paid employment. Indian and Chinese people are twice as likely to be employed in the professions as their white British counterparts.

The economic situation is restricting opportunities for those without qualifications. The employment rate for men who also have disabilities has fallen by 50 per cent since the 1970s.

The Commission highlights continuing occupational segregation in the job market. Examples cited include 25 per cent of Pakistani men whose main work is taxi driving and the gender differential in public service employment (over 40 per cent of women compared to 15 per cent of men).

This contributes to a persistent pay gap. The report finds that, on average, a 40-year old man working in the private or voluntary sector earns 27 per cent more than his female equivalent.

The report cites some evidence that black graduates may earn a quarter less than white counterparts. Men with disabilities earn about 11 per cent less than other male employees. Comparing women with disabilities to men without, the gap increases to 31 per cent. Pay gaps and insecure employment contribute to poverty in later life.

In Britain, women workers continue to predominate in some sectors but are significantly underrepresented in others. Examples include: personal services (83 per cent); secretarial and administrative jobs (77 per cent); architects, planners and surveyors (14 per cent) and engineering (6 per cent).

Lesbian, gay and bisexual employees and those with disabilities are about twice as likely to report discrimination, bullying or harassment in the workplace than other workers.

Trevor Phillips said:

For some, the gateways to opportunity appear permanently closed, no matter how hard they try, whilst others seem to have been issued with an 'access all areas' pass at birth. Recession,

demographic change and new technology all threaten to deepen the fault lines between insiders and outsiders.

In a report for independent think tank Civitas, Peter Saunders, professor emeritus of sociology at the University of Sussex, challenges some of the conclusions in the report, particularly the notion that unequal outcomes are inevitably unfair. For example, he argues that men and women should be free to choose career paths that best utilize their skills and interests. The low representation of Bangladeshi and Pakistani women in the British workforce reflects a cultural emphasis on traditional gender roles, rather than prejudice on the part of employers.

David Green, director of Civitas commented:

[The EHRC's] determination to treat every group disparity as the result of discrimination and it's enthusiasm for using 'corrective measures' to alter the facts on the ground is likely to multiply injustices rather than rectify them.

*Is it fair to accept inequality on the basis of culture?*

*Source: Reprinted with permission from HRM Guide UK (http://www.hrmguide.co.uk).*

## SUMMARY

Equality of opportunity is both a matter of social justice and sound economic sense. Voluntary approaches to minimize discrimination have been largely ineffective and most developed countries have introduced some form of anti-discrimination legislation. There has been a tendency towards all-embracing laws in recent years, increasingly linked to human rights legislation. Granting opportunity is beneficial to organizational effectiveness as well as personal success. The strategic management of diversity leads to a wider range of ideas and abilities, offering greater scope for innovation and competitive performance in the future.

This chapter focused on four areas of workplace discrimination: gender, race/ethnicity, disability and age. We observed that all societies appear to favour certain groups more than others and that most developed societies have attempted to combat prejudice, favouritism and discrimination by introducing relevant laws. Each of the forms of discrimination that we have covered has complex causes that are not easily countered by legislation.

## FURTHER READING

1 *The Dynamics of Managing Diversity: A Critical Approach*, 3rd edition, by Gill Kirton and Anne-Marie Greene (Butterworth-Heinemann, 2010) provides a comprehensive discussion of the subject.

2 *Equality and Discrimination: The New Law* by Brian Doyle, Catherine Casserley, Simon Cheetham, Vivienne Gay and Oliver Hyams (Jordan Publishing, 2010), is a comprehensive, practical analysis of the new anti-discrimination law in the UK.

3 *The Glass Ceiling in the 21st Century: Understanding Barriers to Gender Equality* by Manuela Barreto, Michelle K. Ryan, and Michael T. Schmitt (published by the American Psychological Association, 2009) takes a detailed look on barriers to women's career advancement.

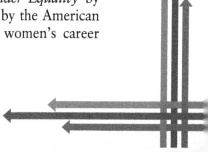

4 *The Spirit Level: Why Equality Is Better For Everyone* by Richard Wilkinson and Kate Pickett, published by Penguin in 2010 covers a wide range of aspects beyond employment.

 **REVIEW QUESTIONS**

1 Distinguish between equal opportunities and the management of diversity. How is it possible to justify either in a commercial organization?

2 Is positive discrimination an effective method of ensuring equal opportunities? Are there any circumstances in which jobs should be reserved for specific individuals or groups without being unfair?

3 Is it true to say that anti-discrimination legislation has had a major effect on equal opportunities in the workplace?

4 Why are women and members of minority groups placed in unfavourable occupational categories?

5 What is occupational segregation and what part does it play in the process of discrimination?

6 Review the evidence for racial discrimination being a more subtle process than overt prejudice.

7 Why does racial discrimination affect some minority groups more than others?

8 Given the reducing proportion of younger people in most developed countries, what could be done to encourage the employment of older workers?

9 What are the limitations on the employment of the disabled? What can be done to improve the situation?

 **CASE STUDY FOR DISCUSSION AND ANALYSIS**

## Frank and Margaret

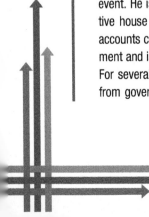

Most people think Frank is a nice guy. He is a good networker, knows everyone in the company and is always the first to buy a round of drinks at any social event. He is married, has three children and an attractive house in a very expensive area. He is the senior accounts controller in the purchasing contracts department and is thought to run a very efficient department. For several years he had a relationship with Margaret from government sales. This broke up in a somewhat

emotional fashion last December when he finally told her that he had no intention of leaving his wife.

Audrey, the government sales coordinator has come to see you regarding some stories that are being told in her department. It seems that Margaret has been telling people that Frank is not entirely honest. She has claimed that he has been taking bribes from contractors, accepting cash, holidays and improvements for his house in return for signing contracts. Margaret has not said this in Audrey's presence because Audrey is a rather straightlaced person who has always made it clear that she disapproved of the relationship. Audrey and Margaret do not get on very well as a result.

*You are the general manager responsible for these departments. How would you proceed?*

### The Black Workers' Support Group

The borough of Kenwood is situated on the outskirts of a large city. It is predominantly populated by white, middle-class people and is considered reasonably affluent by comparison with its inner city neighbours. Just under 20 per cent of residents are over pensionable age, of whom 7 per cent are over 75 years. The vast majority continue to live in their own homes, an increasing proportion living alone. The ageing population has significant resource implications for the local authority.

The Social Services department is responsible for the home care service that comprises three full-time managers and a team of 40 part-time women workers. In addition to providing practical help and social support to their elderly clients, they are often the first people to be alerted to a deterioration in a person's situation. They are a crucial element in enabling people to stay in their own homes, saving the local authority enormous sums of money. However, their status does not reflect their true importance to the community and the section is regularly scrutinized for potential budget cuts.

The local authority has an equal opportunities policy which 'strives towards elimination of discrimination within the workplace'. The Social Services department had noted that the few black staff recruited were in low-paid or insecure posts and tended not to stay long. To try to prevent the policy remaining no more than a piece of paper, it was decided to set up an equal opportunities monitoring committee. This has met quarterly for the last three years and comprises staff representing all grades within Social Services, plus representatives from the main human resources department and two co-opted councillors. It is seen as undesirable to have such a group entirely made up of white representatives so the few black staff available are under constant pressure to volunteer for membership.

One exception to the tendency of black staff to stay no more than a few months is Mary, a middle-aged black woman who has worked for the local authority for 17 years, always as a home carer. She is a tolerant person who likes the flexibility of the work. She has regularly encountered clients whose questions and comments are inadvertently offensive and insensitive but has said little to her managers. However, having been allocated to a couple whose racism is overt and sustained, Mary made a complaint to her harassed line manager, who sympathized and reallocated a white worker to the couple concerned. Mary got on with her job without further comment. Over the next few weeks the manager thought about her own response, felt it had been inadequate, and referred the incident to the equal opportunities monitoring committee. The reaction of group members was diverse:

→ What do you expect? Old people are always unreasonable about everything.

→ They may well be suffering from dementia; if so, they can't be held responsible.

→ Living in this area, they're probably not used to black people and don't know how to react.

→ Would Mary like any further action?

→ We did all we could in practical terms – we can't withdraw the service from them.

→ The line manager should have visited and confronted them.

→ Oh dear, how awful.

→ Has this sort of thing happened before, do we know?

→ Black staff are particularly discriminated against and should receive appropriate support.

The final response came from one of two black members. He proposed a Black Workers' Support Group, open to anybody working for the local authority who defined themselves as black. The group would meet every two months within paid working time. The existence and purpose of the group would be made known to other colleagues who would be asked to demonstrate support by enabling participants to attend. Benefits to the local authority might accrue from being seen to be implementing its own equal opportunities policy and potentially retaining staff who would feel less isolated and marginalized.

The majority of group members had considerable reservations about this proposal although most did not say so openly. While most doubts centred on the impact on overstretched departments and the possible adverse reaction of colleagues asked to cover extra duties, one

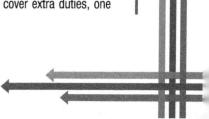

of the councillors was more direct: 'Where exactly will this end? In no time at all we'll be expected to pay for part-time workers' support groups, Irish workers support groups, etc., etc'.

The proposal was referred to the senior managers' meeting for further consideration. There was more support within this forum, but it was felt that the Black Workers' Support Group should be chaired by a senior manager. Black staff pointed out that the group would not operate on such hierarchical terms and, in any event, all managers of the grade proposed were white. Managers' expectation that they would receive copies of the minutes of each meeting met with a similar response. While uneasy with their lack of control, senior managers felt it would be more controversial to refuse permission. The Black Workers' Support Group went ahead and the local authority began to receive enquiries about the scheme from outside the organization and praise for its initiative. With significant cuts proposed to the home help service in the next financial year, and with school-age children to care for, Mary has felt too busy to attend.

*How effective is the equal opportunities policy in Kenwood?*

*Did Mary's supervisor make the right decision?*

*What is the value of the Black Workers' Support Group?*

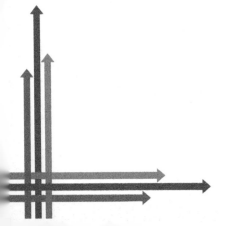

# CHAPTER 20
## Managing conflict

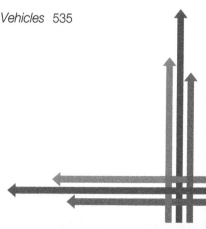

# INTRODUCTION

In earlier chapters we observed that HRM is generally associated with a move from collectivist employee relations – stressing union – employer bargaining arrangements – towards individual-based negotiation, reinforced by personal contracts and performance-based pay systems. The change has not been total in those countries where HRM has been influential and is certainly not universal. In reality, collective negotiation and representation remain common.

In many countries, the trend towards personalized employee relations is being replaced by more formalized models. In the UK and Ireland, for example, European Union legislation is steadily bringing companies into line with the attitudes of the social market, differentiating them from those in the US. This is exemplified by the requirement that all large multinational companies operating in more than one EU country must have Europe-wide works councils, ensuring an enhanced role for collective representation. Ironically, of course, this also means that US multinationals must observe what may be an unfamiliar process of compulsory union consultation within their European operations.

## KEY CONCEPT 20.1 EMPLOYEE RELATIONS

The topic of employee relations is not confined to unionized collective bargaining but encompasses all employment relationships. It goes beyond the negotiation of pay and benefits to include the conduct of the power relationship between individual employees and their employers.

The employment relationship also encapsulates different cultural assumptions about the roles, entitlements and obligations of the stakeholders. Accordingly, national employment systems are heavily influenced by their ideological and cultural traditions. We noted in Part Two that businesses operate within varied legal frameworks, reflecting underlying beliefs about the rights of employers and employees. As an example, we shall see later in this chapter that German companies operate within a social market that places great importance on a balanced relationship between employee and employer. German business culture also emphasizes regulation. Hence the German job market is based on detailed legislation, formalized consultation procedures and protected employee rights. Conversely, legislation in free market countries tends to leave employee consultation to local arrangements and provides little employee protection. Paradoxically, countries such as Canada, the UK and the USA have a history of more advanced equal opportunity legislation than Germany, reflecting their multicultural nature.

We begin this chapter with an evaluation of the role of collective bargaining in different business cultures, ranging from the free market in the USA and UK, through the social market represented by Germany, to Japan as an example of Asia–Pacific approaches. We move on to consider the organizational context and discuss both management and employee strategies.

# COLLECTIVIZATION AND CONFRONTATION

This section considers the problematic concept of the employment relationship. Regarded by neoclassical economists (see Chapter 5) as an exchange of labour for pay, it is also a power relationship in which the employer holds formal authority to direct effort towards specific goals, whereas the employee can – informally – frustrate the achievements of those

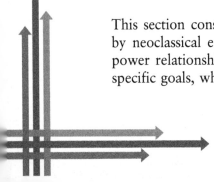

objectives. The employment relationship goes beyond money to include a number of secondary issues, such as working conditions, the length of the working day, holiday time, freedom to arrange one's work and measures of participation.

Through collectivization, workers could band together to protect their mutual interests. From the late 19th century, trade unions have fought for improved conditions for their members. The first unions were formed to defend workers, often in response to cuts in wages. Impeding change without reward, they set the scene for future accusations of intransigence.

Trade unions can be categorized as follows (adapted from McIlwee and Roberts, 1991: 386):

1   *Craft unions:* recruit from distinct trades or occupations, historically linked to apprenticeship systems. Originally aimed to preserve jobs within the craft exclusively for their members. Technological change has blurred and, sometimes, eliminated the craft skills. Unions have survived by broadening their membership criteria.

2   *Industrial unions:* aim to represent all employees in a particular industry regardless of their type of work. The dominant form in Germany but slow to develop in the UK.

3   *General unions:* broad-ranging; represent a variety of industries and job types with little restriction on potential membership. Some are so extensive that they have been termed 'super–unions'.

4   *Occupational unions:* recruit members within a particular occupation or group.

5   *White collar unions:* concentrate on non-manual occupations such as banking.

Unions have been described as a mixture of movement and organization (Flanders, 1970). They address workers' individual needs: protecting them from exploitation; negotiating improved wages and conditions; developing career prospects. However, unions also have a wider, collective purpose, often expressed in a political role. Workers are expected to subordinate personal advantage to the greater interests of the total membership. In this respect, trade unions offer an alternative focus for employee commitment and a power base which may clash with the prerogatives of management. The Australian Bureau of Statistics has a concise definition of a trade union as: 'an organization, consisting predominantly of employees, the principal activities of which include the negotiation of pay and conditions of employment for its members' (cited in Visser, 2006: 40).

The history of trade unionism in different countries varies in a number of respects:

*Business sector.* Focusing on job conditions within an industry or specific company. Initially, unions in most countries were organized around specific crafts; this pattern remained dominant in the UK until the late 20th century. In contrast, since 1945 German trade unions have represented all the workers in a specific industry.

*Ideology.* Extending their role beyond the workplace and influencing social and political change to the advantage of their members. Many unions were instrumental in the creation of political parties. Employee relations have been a battleground for ideology, local disputes being played out as skirmishes in a much larger war.

# EMPLOYEE RELATIONS IN NORTH AMERICA

In the USA the prevailing business culture of scientific management and Fordism created a particular trade union response and an irreconcilable conflict between the interests of 'capital' and 'labour'.

Remarkably, the view from the 1920s (expressed in the box text, Assumptions of confrontational industrial relations) remains typical of many US organizations and business interests

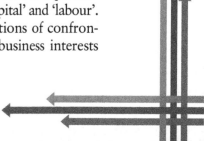

act strongly to prevent union organization (Beachler, 2009). In fact, most American management writers ignore trade unionism, taking a **unitarist** (see Key concept 20.2) rather than the **pluralist** or collective viewpoint common in Europe (Guest, 1992; Ebbinghaus, 2003). Beaumont (1992) argues that this perspective is reflected in a considerable reduction in US union membership and collective bargaining from the mid-20th century onwards. American HRM literature also emphasizes individual relationships and marginalizes trade unions (Blyton and Turnbull, 1994). Unions have been viewed as restricting the nation's competitive position and protecting insiders (those with jobs) at the expense of those without, with prominent attention being paid to corruption and racketeering (Toner, 2009). Indeed Kanter (1989: 117) describes the tradition of American management as being firmly rooted in paranoia:

> One of the lessons America's mythologized cowboys supposedly learned in the rough-and-tumble days of the American frontier was that paranoia was smart psychology. You couldn't trust anybody. They were all out to get you, and they would steal from you as soon as your back was turned.

---

## ASSUMPTIONS OF CONFRONTATIONAL INDUSTRIAL RELATIONS

1 Workers' and employers' interests are generally opposed. Employers: want highest output at least cost; try to lower wages, increase hours, speed up workers; try to remove least efficient workers; maintain worst possible working conditions; discharge workers when possible; replace expensive, skilled workers with cheaper, low-skilled employees; and reduce numbers through automation. Conversely, unions: attempt to obtain continuous employment; seek highest wage rates; and look for the best working conditions.

2 Effort and increased output produce lower wages. Employers prefer reducing prices to increase market share, rather than pass on productivity benefits to workers as higher wages.

3 Wages depend on the relative bargaining strengths of employers and workers.

4 Employers' bargaining strength is always greater than the workers'.

5 Employers' full bargaining strength will be exerted against individuals.

6 Individual bargaining produces competition between workers. This tends to lower wages to the level accepted by the weakest bargaining worker.

7 This applies during employment as well as recruitment. If workers speed up in response to bonuses, there is competition between workers.

*Source: Hoxie (1923).*

---

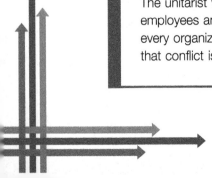

**KEY CONCEPT 20.2**   UNITARISM VERSUS PLURALISM

The unitarist view is implicit in American models of HRM. It holds that the interests of employees and the firm should be the same. Pluralism, on the other hand, recognizes that every organization is composed of different interests that are not balanced. Pluralists accept that conflict is natural and are concerned with the means by which it can be managed.

Unions attempted to counter negative perceptions by introducing ethical training in order to stress their legitimacy, morality and organizational effectiveness (Cohen, 2008).

Geare *et al.* (2006) suggest that HRM theorists appear to believe that unitarism is the norm in employment relationships. At the same time, theorists see HRM as the means to achieving unitarism through the introduction of high commitment management systems in the workplace. But they point out that a number of authors have questioned these assumptions. Van Ruysseveldt *et al.* (1995: 2) contend that '...no modern society has ever accepted a purely individualistic determination of the employment relationship'.

The study by Geare *et al.* attempted to identify current employment values and beliefs of workers and management and examined the extent to which these influence, or are influenced by, the adoption of high commitment practices in the workplace. Curiously, they found that managers considered employment relationships in general to be pluralist, but their own organizations to be unitarist.

'Self-reliance' became the prevailing ethos. Everything outside one's own control was treated as a potential enemy to be dominated. This applied as much to trade unions as it did to competitors. Elsewhere in the democratic world, such an extreme position was unusual. Nevertheless, it cannot be assumed that there is a common agenda between employers and the employed that can be 'managed'. There is an inevitable, if latent, tension between the two (Blyton and Turnbull, 1994: 4).

Historically, unions attempted to replace individual bargaining with collective bargaining (see Key concept 20.3) in order to increase employees' power and counter employers' attempts to create competition between workers. This required solidarity between union members. Union goals were to obtain standardized wages and optimal conditions. Employers tended to prefer dealing with employees on an individual basis.

## KEY CONCEPT 20.3 COLLECTIVE BARGAINING

Collective bargaining takes place between employers and trade unions when employees are members of trade unions that undertake to negotiate on their behalf in matters such as pay, working conditions, other benefits and work allocation; and employers recognize trade unions and their officials as legitimate bargaining agents.

Braverman (1974) regarded the weakness of workers in the employment relationship as an inevitable consequence of the management role, concluding that managers were responsible to the market as well as to shareholders and employees. Businesses would not survive without increasing levels of productivity and efficiency provided by the creativity, imagination and problem-solving abilities of the workforce. However, these same qualities could be used to resist managers' aspirations for change.

Employees had their own objectives that frequently differed from management goals. Under the 19th century craft-based system of production, individual employees held a considerable degree of power through their possession of knowledge. Managers frequently had no idea what workers were doing. Scientific management and Fordism offered the prospect of de-skilling jobs and removing knowledge, and hence bargaining power, from the workforce. Braverman's original analysis has been criticized for oversimplification; most workers were unskilled or semi–skilled. Fordism led to a relative standardization of the employment

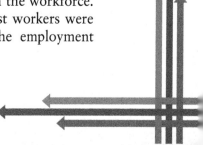

relationship throughout the developed world until around 1980, with the following characteristics (Van Ruysseveldt *et al.*, 1995: 2):

→ Permanent, full-time jobs.

→ Wage increases on the basis of experience and training.

→ Extra payments for inconvenient or anti-social arrangements.

→ Regular working hours and a clearly defined working week.

→ Paid holidays.

→ The right to collective representation and some consultation on changes to working practices.

Trade unions conducted negotiations with employers within this framework. This form of employee relations was associated with vertical and horizontal division of labour, hierarchical management and close supervision. However, this pattern of working life has disintegrated under the pressures of competition from newly-developing countries and the introduction of flexibility. In consequence, the 'traditional' role of trade unions has been undermined.

Union activity traditionally focused on people within the internal employment market. Under newer working practices, the core workforce can be reduced to insignificant numbers and many companies have made a practice of actively discouraging unionization. The use of short-term or part-time contracts has increased. Variable working hours have become a valuable source of flexibility. Extended opening hours have allowed employers to increase profits by maximizing use of equipment and accommodation. The extent of these changes leads Van Ruysseveldt *et al.* (1995: 7) to conclude that pre-1980s analytical and theoretical frameworks for studying employee relations are outdated.

There are significant differences in union density (proportion of the workforce who are trade union members) between Canada and the USA, and also between and within industry sectors. The prevailing explanation for this difference (see Johnson, 2002) is that mandatory voting has discouraged unionization in the USA whereas card-checking (counting the number of existing union members) has encouraged unionization in Canada. There was a marked increase in the proportion of Canadian provinces covered by mandatory voting between 1993 (18 per cent) and 2000 (62 per cent).

In 2008 union density in Canada was 30.4 per cent (Statistics Canada *Labour Force Survey*). According to the US Bureau of Labor Statistics, union density was 12.3 per cent in 2009, representing a 10 per cent fall in membership. Part of an ongoing trend, this also reflects the impact of recession on manufacturing and construction. More than 37 per cent of US government workers were union members in 2009. For the first time, there were more union members in the public sector than the private sector, even though the private sector has five times more jobs.

## EMPLOYEE RELATIONS IN THE UK

The British were once notorious for poor industrial relations that could threaten governments. Weak management and intransigent unions produced industrial chaos, manifested by low productivity, hostility towards change and highly publicized disputes, fundamentally weakening the UK as an economic power in the 1970s and 1980s.

The reputation of British personnel managers was not enhanced during this period, while American-style human resource management was reflected in the increasing influence of

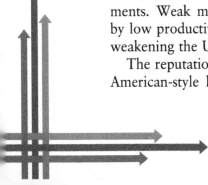

right-wing media commentators and politicians advocating tougher attitudes towards employee relations. By the time HRM emerged in the 1980s, personnel management had become enmeshed in a form of industrial relations characterized by defensive 'fire-fighting' (Hendry, 1995: 12). It had largely abandoned its neutral balancing role between employees and management, undermining any claim to being strategic or proactive. Strikes, pay deals and overtime needs were largely dealt with in an *ad hoc,* piecemeal fashion. In a context of industrial warfare, long-term planning was displaced by short-term coping. Hendry (*ibid.,*: 13) also associates lack of strategic thinking with personnel managers' preference for dealing with industrial relations in an informal manner. Direct knowledge of the personalities involved and willingness to engage in 'off–the–record' discussions resulted in spontaneous compromise deals.

Recessions, 'New Right' politics, restrictive legislation on industrial action (see Part 3) and massive restructuring in many organizations has considerably reduced the power and role of unions and the industrial relations 'industry'. Detailed obligations between employer and employee have been replaced by less formal commitments. Job descriptions have become flexible; demarcations have diminished.

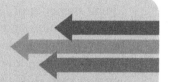

**HRM IN REALITY** UNIONS SUPPORTING ECONOMIC RECOVERY

UK unions are supporting economic recovery by helping to reduce stress and lack of motivation in the workplace according to a 2010 report from the TUC. Examples include working with employers to introduce green initiatives, create redeployment opportunities and negotiate pension scheme changes.

*The Road to Recovery* report argues that providing an opportunity for employees to raise work-related concerns has a number of positive consequences. The report found that unions have a significant role in conflict resolution; employment tribunal claims in unionized workplaces are 1.3 per 1000 employees compared to 2.9 per 1000 in non-unionized workplaces. Union members are less likely to feel de-motivated by changes to working practices. The report cites other research that found union members are less likely to leave their employment, this effect being more pronounced in organizations with higher union membership and active representation.

The report highlights other benefits traditionally associated with union membership: average hourly wages for union members are £13.07 compared to £11.62 for non-members; union-backed legal representation resulted in compensation payments totalling £300million in 2007; and union members tend to have better access to training (eight per cent more likely to receive between two and five days training compared to employees who are not members of a union).

Brendan Barber, TUC general secretary commented:

> Unions are well known for standing up for workers' rights at work and negotiating decent pay deals – and with so many companies trying to cut and freezes wages unnecessarily that's an important task.
>
> But unions' work goes well beyond wages and working conditions. By giving staff a voice at work they can help to resolve conflict and reduce the number of people quitting work.
>
> Conflict between unions and employers will always generate the headlines. But behind the scenes, many employers are working closely with unions to modernize their workplaces and recover from the recession.

*Is this union propaganda or a valid justification for union membership?*

*Source: Reprinted with permission from HRM Guide UK (http://www.hrmguide.co.uk).*

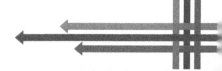

Consequently, the new employee relations extend beyond collective bargaining to include non-unionized organizations with alternative negotiating structures. Hendry (1995: 49) reflects on the perspective of the 'industrial relations orthodoxy' that sees a 'persistent weakening of employee power within organizations through the substitution of individualized systems for collective ones'. HRM is implicated as an anti-union philosophy (Guest, 1989: 44) which:

1   Can be aggressively anti-union, advocating the withdrawal of recognition from existing unions.

2   Can produce more generous rewards through individual pay deals, making unions seem unnecessary.

3   Neutralizes or controls unions through close attention to their activities by means of single-union agreements, no-strike clauses and pendulum arbitration. These can be reinforced with careful recruitment, socialization, communications, teamworking and so on.

In reality, it is difficult to find instances of HRM being responsible for these developments rather than coinciding with them. If anything, it comes into play when dealing with subsequent mending of fences (Hendry, 1995: 51).

Single-union agreements and no-strike deals have further limited the influence of unions and have proved divisive. Unions negotiating for sole recognition have been accused of 'selling out' to employers and 'poaching' members (Goss, 1994: 142).We will see later in this section that, in Germany, single-union arrangements are normal and unions regard them as beneficial.

Intriguingly, Brown (1994) finds that during the 1980s average pay rises were lower in unionized businesses, despite non-unionism being associated with the absence of a bargaining structure. Brown argues that removing trade unions leads to worse people management in areas such as training, health and safety and dismissal practices. By their very existence, unions force managers to manage.

For whatever reason, strikes and other forms of industrial action are considerably more common in larger organizations. This is not necessarily due to the atmosphere being better in small companies; an obvious corollary is that far fewer people in small firms are members of unions. Employers in small companies may actively discourage union organization. Unions are less interested in small groups of staff needing disproportionate amounts of attention accruing limited monetary or political advantage.

Matlay (2002) observes that despite the increasing importance of small and medium-size enterprises (SMEs), most research on employee relations has focused on large organizations. In Matlay's opinion, the few studies involving SMEs have tended to be simplistic, categorizing workplaces as 'small is beautiful' or 'bleak house'. Matlay's own survey of 6000 organizations finds that small business owners or managers tend to use a personalized and informal management style, and that employee relations are widely varied.

Moore (2006) focused on employer perspectives of the bargaining process and found evidence of dynamic relationships following voluntary trade union recognition. In the majority of 213 cases examined, there had been collective bargaining on core issues of pay, hours and holiday entitlement. There was less likely to have been negotiation over pensions, equal opportunities and training. A proportion of voluntary agreements have been formally limited to core issues. Conversely, in the magazine industry the National Union of Journalists (NUJ) regained collective negotiating rights in the face of employer hostility but found it difficult to enforce collective bargaining (Gall, 2007).

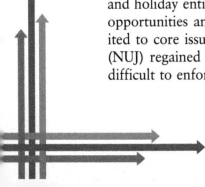

Recent management literature assumes that the balance of power has swung in favour of employers, described by some as the 'new realism'. Fewer than 150000 days a year were lost through industrial action in the UK in 2005, down from a peak of nearly 13 million. However, by 2008, this figure had risen to just over a million working days of which 96 per cent were lost in the public sector.

The private sector has contained industrial action by tactics such as:

→ elaborate communications techniques

→ career development

→ quality circles

→ performance-related pay

→ non-union status.

# THE EUROPEAN UNION

The European Union (EU) has made a number of attempts to develop community-wide initiatives on employee participation, industrial relations and employment conditions. Interpretation and application of EU law by the Commission and the European Court is shaped by their understanding of the 'European social model' (Bercusson, 2002). The EU recognizes employees and their union representatives as 'social partners' within its own institutions but wider progress has been slow, partly reflecting differing perspectives in an ever-increasing number of member states (Cressey, 1993). Free market enthusiasts seek deregulation and decentralization, emphasizing voluntary, non-statutory arrangements. Others, including many members of the European Parliament, favour a regulated, harmonized system. Brewster *et al.* (2007) observe that collective employee voice recognition is prevalent in large organizations throughout Europe. Rizov and Croucher (2009) examined HRM practices and organizational performance in European organizations and found that:

→ Collaborative types of HRM practice are more strongly associated with superior organizational performance than calculative forms.

→ The associations are strongest when they are supported by national institutional and normative settings.

→ Superior organizational performance is also (but less strongly) associated with the existence of employer/employee consultative committees (such as works councils) and collective payment methods.

Works councils are obligatory in companies employing a minimum of 1000 workers in at least two EU countries (provided there are 150 workers or more at at least two sites). Councils are kept informed about the business and consulted on changes to production or working methods, restructuring and planned closures. French and German companies used pre-existing national formats, other organizations reached agreements on widely different bases. The role of employee representatives more recently has been extended to companies employing at least 150 employees, or workplace establishments with at least 100 employees (Bercusson, 2002). In a French study, Fairris and Askenazy (2010) found no evidence of a positive impact of works councils on organizational productivity – and

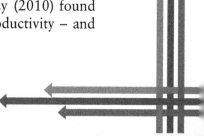

limited evidence of a negative effect in some of their results. However, there was a significant positive effect from worker voice and information-sharing HR practices prevalent in French firms.

People management in Germany is strictly regulated compared to many other countries. Germany has evolved a system that focuses on industrial democracy and harmony although in recent years it has increasingly adopted forms of corporate governance that resemble UK/US forms (Freidank *et al.*, 2010). In practical terms, the main instruments of the German co-determination system are the supervisory boards and works councils that characterize large companies. Supervisory boards include shareholder and worker representatives. In Germany, work councils had three sets of rights (Lawrence, 1993: 34):

→ Co-determination (*Mitbestimmingsrecht*) involves consent on a number of issues: the appointment of an employee to a new position; transfers within the organization; transfers from one wage group to another; determining starting and finishing times for the working day; and the introduction of shift working, overtime, etc.

→ Consultation (*Mitwirkungsrecht*) covers planning issues, including plant closure, new factories, investment decisions and business policy matters.

→ Information (*Informationsrecht*) about company performance and prospects.

The legislation was significantly amended in 2001 (Weiss, 2002) to adapt the traditional organizational structure and improve conditions for SMEs.

## EMPLOYEE RELATIONS IN AUSTRALIA AND NEW ZEALAND

In the 20th century, employee relations in Australia and New Zealand were characterized by industrial conciliation and arbitration (Harbridge and Walsh, 2002). In New Zealand, especially, they were criticized for being highly legalistic and interventionist (Vranken, 1999). But global trends towards greater flexibility led to radically different approaches. The old industrial relations system, essentially multi-employer bargaining, was effectively dismantled in New Zealand and replaced with a system favouring individual contracts. The Australian constitution protected conciliation and arbitration but new legislation considerably weakened the system in the 1990s and again in 2006. Despite the different approaches, the outcome was similar in both countries: a drop in collective bargaining and union density, reductions in benefits and major changes in working time arrangements (Harbridge and Walsh, 2002) to meet the neoliberal objectives of decollectivization and individualization (Bray and Underhill, 2009).

A study by Allan, Brosnan and Walsh (1999) found that New Zealand's decentralized system had encouraged greater employer experimentation (albeit with both positive and negative outcomes), particularly in the private sector. Rasmussen and Lind (2003) associate the Employment Relations Act 2000, based on Canadian experience, with 'a marked shift in New Zealand employment relationships with state interventionism, collective bargaining and employee influence being back in favour.' Barry and May (2004) observe that while this increased protection for trade unions, it resulted in registration of numerous small unions with limited interests.

Briggs (2001) observes that globalization and employers are normally regarded as key agents of change. Paradoxically, however, Briggs argues that unions were responsible for

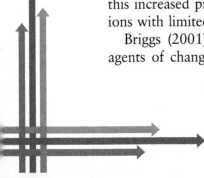

the shift to enterprise bargaining in Australia in the early 1990s. The Australian Industrial Relations Commission (AIRC) had been reluctant to introduce enterprise bargaining but a loss of union solidarity behind centralized wage negotiations and a power struggle between the AIRC and the Australian Council of Trade Unions (ACTU) created a policy vacuum. As a result the Business Council of Australia (BCA), the employers' organization, took the lead in the process of decentralizing pay bargaining. Similarly, Phillimore (2000) attributes some of the changes to union misjudgements and weak workplace bargaining structures.

The Work Choices Act 2006 was designed to reform Australian industrial relations. According to Kevin Andrews, then minister for employment and workplace relations, (www. hrmguide.net/australia/relations/workchoices-andrews.htm, 23 February, 2006) there were a number of 'roadblocks' in the previous system:

→ the paternalistic influence of the AIRC and other third parties.

→ difficulties with bargaining and industrial action that resulted in significant economic loss.

→ the time and red tape involved in agreement making.

→ the absence of a genuine award safety net.

→ the inflexibility of the award system.

→ a confusing and complex web of competing federal and state employment regulation.

The legislation introduced changes including:

→ more rational arrangements for setting minimum wages and conditions.

→ a more streamlined process for the making of workplace agreements.

→ greater award simplification and a more focused role for the Australian Industrial Relations Commission.

→ better balance in unfair dismissal laws which have held back job growth in Australia.

→ introduction of a single national industrial relations system.

The Australian Fair Pay Commission (AFPC) was established to oversee aspects of employment such as minimum wages and conditions of employment including annual leave, personal/carer's leave, parental leave and maximum ordinary hours of work.

Minister Andrews commented:

… it is in Australia's national interest to move towards a single national workplace relations system. Currently, we have six separate workplace relations systems in Australia – one in each state, except Victoria, and a federal system.

Australia has a workforce of around 10 million, and with thousands of different state and federal awards and pieces of legislation, six similar but not identical workplace relations systems creates costs and complexity for all businesses.

The Act exempted organizations with fewer than 100 employees from the federal unfair dismissal laws and strengthened the position of employers in larger organizations. The right to lawful industrial action when negotiating a new collective agreement was protected. Australian unions described the new regulations as harsh and designed to crack down on union activity in the workplace. The overall effect of, essentially anti-union, legislation over this period may have left a permanent legacy of weak collective bargaining in Australia (Cooper and Ellem, 2008).

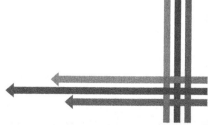

In the event, Work Choices was in operation for about two years, before being substantially amended by the incoming Labor administration under the The Fair Work Act 2009.

**HRM IN REALITY** THE IMPACT OF WORK CHOICES

An online survey conducted by Deakin University on behalf of the Australian Human Resources Institute found that only 3 per cent of respondents thought that the Work Choices Act had made their work easier.

The report *Work Choices: It's Impact within Australian Workplaces* was based on over 1000 responses received from a total membership of about 11000. Researchers found that the work of 5600 HR managers and practitioners was directly impacted by the provisions of the Work Choices Act. About half (49.9 per cent) of respondents came from the private sector with 31 per cent employed by organizations with more than 1000 staff. One third (33.3 per cent) had no union representation. A broad range of industry sectors were represented including: professional, scientific and technical (13.1 per cent); education and training (11.7 per cent) and manufacturing (10.1 per cent).

About half of respondents (49.9 per cent) reported that the Act had had no impact on their job, 33.6 per cent thought it had made it more difficult and 3 per cent that it had made it less difficult. More saw Work Choices as being unlikely to improve fundamental issues such

as: work-family balance (36.5 per cent); productivity (31.5 per cent) and job creation (31.2 per cent) within their organization over the next three years.

Researchers found very limited evidence of changes in procedures (such as managing employment contracts, workplace disputes, and trade unions) or to the status of HR professionals as a consequence of the Act. Respondents reporting change were most likely to focus on increases to: record-keeping (54.5 per cent); number of personal carer days authorized (38.7 per cent); number of sick days (26.7 per cent) and direct communication with employees (26.3 per cent).

Respondents reported decreases in activities such as: state of workplace morale (17.2 per cent); industrial disputes (11.4 per cent) and union involvement in bargaining (11.4 per cent).

*Will Work Choices have a permanent effect on collective bargaining in Australia?*

Source: Reprinted with permission from HRM Guide Australia (http://www.hrmguide.net/australia/).

## TRENDS IN UNION MEMBERSHIP

Over the last 20 years trade union membership has declined over much of Western Europe. According to the European Industrial Relations Observatory (EIRO), union density in the European Union in 2008 varied widely from over 90 per cent in Finland to below 10 per cent in France, Estonia and Lithuania. Other examples include: Belgium, Sweden, Denmark and Norway (70–89 per cent); Bulgaria, the Czech Republic, Germany, Greece, Hungary, the Netherlands, Portugal and the UK (20–29 per cent). The average level of unionization across the EU is likely to be just under 20 per cent in 2010.

Union density in Australia fell from 50.2 per cent in 1970 to 22 per cent of full-time and 15 per cent of part-time workers in 2009. After long-standing decline, membership has risen in the last two years for which figures are available.

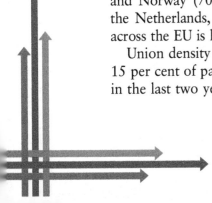

In New Zealand union density fell from 55.2 per cent in 1970 to 17.9 per cent in 2009. Of 159 registered unions, 44.6 per cent have less than 100 members; women make up 59.9 per cent of union members (Household Labour Force Survey).

In 2008 union density in Canada was 30.4 per cent (Statistics Canada *Labour Force Survey*).

According to the US Bureau of Labor Statistics, union density was 12.3 per cent in 2009, representing a 10 per cent fall in membership.

## ORGANIZATIONS AND EMPLOYEE RELATIONS

Earlier in this chapter we observed that traditional industrial relations assumed a formal structure in which management and staff negotiated pay levels and working conditions such as hours of work, grade demarcation, holiday and sick leave entitlement. In some organizations the same structure was used for grievance and disciplinary matters, agreeing levels of performance, attendance requirements – such as shift hours – and work procedures. Within this mechanism, staff were represented by one or more trade unions or staff associations.

In recent years large organizations in free market countries have attempted to emphasize individual rather than collective bargaining through mechanisms such as:

→ Introduction of personal contracts that, for example, allow employers to offer pay increases to those employees, sometimes at the expense of union members.

→ Organizational change methods such as team briefings, that allow managers to disseminate information throughout the organization in meetings (usually monthly), simultaneously collecting ideas and criticisms to be channeled upwards.

→ Quality circles that emphasize direct dialogue between staff and management to improve procedures.

It is not surprising that unions have often resisted the introduction of change methods of this nature because they depend on staff and management talking directly to each other, thereby removing a main source of union power – the filter or gatekeeper of information and innovation. In such situations, collective bargaining has often been restricted to primary issues of pay, holidays and discipline, removing unions from negotiation about procedures.

Individualized systems stress commitment from employees, yet the trend towards downsizing and restructuring imposes a 'fear of commitment' among managers and employees alike (Rousseau, 1995: xii). HR policies that emphasize the individual contribute to this fear since they remove any collective employee defence against the employer. 'Divide and rule.' Hendry (1995: 57) acknowledges a 'more sophisticated pluralist technique which sees the unitary organization as "bad" because the denial of individual and group interests actually makes for a less effective organization'. In other words, there is a valid criticism that the integrating activities of HRM can rub out the healthy diversity that is essential for future development: 'Such paradoxes, discrepancies, and ambiguities highlight the fact that organizational life is beset by paradoxes, and that (mercifully) managers and organizations cannot get a handle completely on human behaviour'.

Peters (1987) distinguishes two contradictory philosophies operating in modern business organizations:

*Minimize human resources.* Workers are pure costs. New methods and equipment are now available globally. Businesses in the developed world can: cut employee costs to match

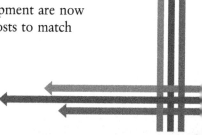

those of poorer countries; or switch to industries that are not labour intensive. This involves actual and threatened redundancies, transferring operations to lower-wage countries and automation.

*Increase the value of the people element.* Employees are assets. This approach emphasizes flexibility and creativity and aims to eliminate unnecessary routine by: the intelligent use of technology; and retraining workers for more complex or varied tasks. According to Peters it should be tied to profit-linked bonuses to ensure commitment.

The first approach leads to industrial conflict. Managers must make cuts and be aggressive towards staff. Workers defend their position and oppose change. The second approach is collaborative. It seeks partnership between workers and employers for mutual benefit. Peters argues that both approaches deliver short-term profits but only the second can maintain competitiveness in the long term.

Other management writers advocate a new form of employee relationship based on cooperation, for example the Major Projects Agreement (MPA) implemented in the construction of London Heathrow Airport's Terminal 5 (Deakin and Koukiadaki, 2009). Kanter (1989: 127) argues that the adversarial model is unsuitable for contemporary business conditions. 'Teaming up' is the route to growth and survival. Corporations need to seek strategic alliances – cooperative arrangements to achieve business goals. Such alliances should be made with unions as well as other businesses. Kanter defines these as 'stakeholder alliances' or 'complementary' coalitions. Stuart and Lucio (2002) found that while some unions were extremely enthusiastic, most companies did not reciprocate. Oxenbridge and Brown (2002) found a dichotomy between production sector firms that nurtured collective bargaining through informal partnership relationships, and service sector businesses that contained collective bargaining tightly through formalized partnership agreements. Haynes and Allen (2001), meanwhile, found equally distinct polarization among unions – some saw partnership as a potentially effective strategy for restoring union influence, others viewed the concept as fatally flawed. For the union representatives and line managers who are engaged in trying to make a social partnership work, the process is one of both accommodation and antagonism (Rittau and Dundon, 2010).

Participation is also a matter of delegation – involving everyone downwards within the organization as well as stakeholder partners. It requires a change in behaviour from managers who have previously exercised power in a clear-cut, overtly decisive fashion. A consensus style requires patience; willingness to discuss ideas at an early stage; and ability to listen. Not all managers can make the transition. Partnerships require managers with team leadership skills.

## EMPLOYEE RELATIONS STRATEGIES

Strategic management styles towards employee relations have been classified to demonstrate a variety of approaches, ranging from authoritarian and anti-unionist to more sophisticated and inclusive strategies (see Table 20-1). In the same way, employees may adopt various styles in response. Trade unions also have varying interpretations of their role, reflecting the cultural, historical and legislative background in which they operate.

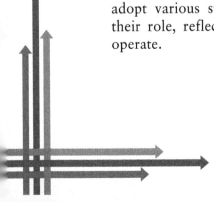

**TABLE 20.1**
Strategic management styles towards employee relations

| Basic | Purcell and Sisson (1983) | Gunnigle *et al.* (1994) |
|---|---|---|
| 1. **Authoritarian.** Typical small company style. Boss rules absolutely – staff have simple 'take it or leave it' choice. Works if employees accept situation, e.g. where there is little or no opportunity to change jobs. Seen in some large organizations. | 1. **Traditional.** Fire-fighting – managers pay little attention to employee relations until trouble arises. Low pay levels. Hostile to unions. Prevails in authoritarian small businesses but seen in larger companies when workers have little choice in their employment. | 1. **Anti-union.** Little or no consideration of employee relations. No collective arrangements such as union representation. Low concern for employee needs. Aggressive opposition to collective bargaining and union recognition. |
| 2. **Individual.** Negotiation between management and individuals. Possible for staff teams to discuss common interests jointly. Non-authoritarian. Emphasis on commitment to company goals. Managers reasonable and approachable. No collective body representing staff. | 2. **Paternalist.** More benevolent, humanistic style; close parallels with HRM approach. Employers consider unions unnecessary because conditions are so generous. Employee relations concentrate on getting employees to identify with the objectives of the business. | 2. **Paternalist.** Concern for employee needs but rejects union recognition and collective bargaining. Little sophistication in human resource policies. |
| 3. **Collective.** Dominant method in western world from 1945 until approx. 1980. Since then, social and free market economies have taken different paths. Social market economies, e.g. Germany, have industry or company-wide trade unions (or staff associations) negotiating with management on behalf of the staff. Free market economies continue to make extensive use of this approach but management literature and HRM emphasize individual bargaining. Many companies utilize both strategies. | 3. **Consultative.** Ideal form of employee relations in some eyes. Emphasis is on informal rather than formal systems of bargaining with continuous dialogue. Unions are fully recognized. | 3. **Sophisticated paternalist.** Emphasizes welfare and well-being of individual staff. Sophisticated HR policies for resourcing, development, reward and communication. Rejects unions and collective bargaining. Equates to 'traditional HRM' – values employees because this is seen to benefit organization. |
|  | 4. **Constitutional.** Similar to consultative approach but emphasis on formal regulatory agreements to control the relationship between powerful parties on either side. Found in social market economies and strongly encouraged by European Union social policy. | 4. **Sophisticated unionized.** Recognizes trade unions but carefully prescribed union role (e.g. single union agreement). Mixed collective and individual arrangements, incorporating HR policies. Neo-pluralist model with HRM-type policies designed to foster consensualism and employee commitment. |
|  | 5. **Opportunistic.** Responsibility for employee relations left to individual divisions/subsidiaries, leaving no common approach and an emphasis on unit profitability. | 5. **Traditional unionized.** Pluralist approach typified by adversarial industrial relations. Collective bargaining but multiple unions complicate matters. |

# EMPLOYEE RELATIONS AS AN ACTIVITY

In many developed countries, dependence on company rules and regulations that clarified what was expected of both employees and employers has been overtaken by the trend towards flexibility and empowerment of staff. This has resulted in 'fuzzier' boundaries between required behaviour and that which is regarded as inappropriate. Employees – particularly managers – have been given greater discretion on decision-making in free market economies. This has been encouraged by 'neo-liberal' governments throughout the world. Within the European Union, however, there has been a countervailing emphasis on formal rules because of the predominance of social market economies. Typically, most large organizations continue to have formal rules on:

1   *Timekeeping*
    – Normally expected times of attendance, often with monitoring ('clocking-in').
    – Sanctions for lateness.

2   *Absence*
    – An approval mechanism for absence.
    – Authorization for taking annual leave.
    – A reporting procedure when people are absent from the workplace.
    – The need for medical self-certification or a doctor's certificate.

3   *Health and safety*
    – Requirements for appearance or cleanliness, e.g. protective clothing, wearing jewellery.
    – Special hazards such as chemicals and dangerous machinery.
    – Prohibition of smoking, alcohol or drugs.

4   *Gross misconduct*
    – Offences regarded as being serious enough to lead to dismissal without notice.
    – Theft, fraud, deliberate falsification of records.
    – Fighting, assault on another person.
    – Deliberate damage to company property.
    – Serious incapability through alcohol or being under the influence of illegal drugs.
    – Serious negligence that causes unacceptable loss, damage or injury.
    – Serious acts of insubordination.
    – Unauthorized entry to computer records.

5   *Use of company facilities*
    – Use of telephone for private calls.
    – Admission to company premises outside working hours.
    – Use of company equipment, e.g. computers, photocopiers, for personal reasons.
    – Abuse of emails and the internet.

6   *Discrimination*
    – Overt discrimination but also sexual harassment and racial abuse.

The enforcement of such rules is a sensitive issue, requiring some kind of formal or informal disciplinary system. Butterfield *et al.* (2005) see disciplinary punishment as an inevitable element of a manager's job. Reviewing literature on the subject, they conclude that although managers typically regard punishment as being justified by deterrence or 'just desserts' (commensurate with the level of offence), the latter is the normal motive for any disciplinary sanction. Impression management plays a significant role: managers are concerned about their reputations to be fair but effective disciplinarians. Actions that are perceived to be

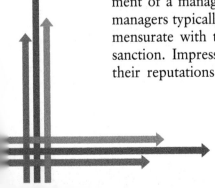

unfair will elicit bad reactions from employees, ranging from sullen lack of cooperation to outright hostility or subversion. Butterfield *et al.* argue that there are specific elements of discipline that are important such as: the timeliness of the punishment; the perceived justice of the punishment; the use of constructive criticism; and keeping the punishment private.

Discipline is not only negative, in the sense of being punitive or preventative, it also makes a positive contribution to organizational performance. An effective organization cannot survive if its members behave in an anarchic way. Order within an organization depends on an appropriate mixture of each of these forms of discipline. Within the context of HRM, however, the emphasis has moved away from managerial discipline towards self and, especially, team discipline. Nevertheless, most organizations continue to have institutionalized disciplinary procedures, largely determined by management. Internet use at work is an interesting and growing disciplinary problem at work.

## HRM IN REALITY INTERNET USE AT WORK

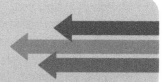

Research by MyJobGroup.co.uk, the operator of the UK's largest network of regional jobsites, found that more than half of British workers access social media websites while at work. Based on a survey of 1000 employees, the study found that of those acknowledging use of sites such as Facebook, Twitter and Myspace, one-third report spending more than 30 minutes a day and nearly 6 per cent more than an hour.

The report suggests that the cost to the UK economy could be as much as £14billion in lost productivity, with SMEs likely to be most adversely affected.

The study found that many respondents were in denial about the negative impact on efficiency. Only 14 per cent admitted to being less productive as a result and 10 per cent claimed social media had made them more productive. There was widespread resistance to banning use of social media during working hours, with over two-thirds of respondents (68 per cent) supporting some form of access.

Lee Fayer, managing director of Myjobgroup.co.uk commented:

> Our results clearly show that UK workers are spending increased time whilst at work on social

media networks, which, left unchecked, could have negative repercussions on the productivity of many companies across the country.

> Whilst we're certainly not kill-joys, people spending over an hour per day in work time on the likes of Facebook and Twitter are seriously hampering companies' efforts to boost productivity, which is more important than ever given the fragile state of our economy.

> Companies would do well to monitor use of social networking sites during work hours and ensure that their employees are not abusing their freedom of access to these sites.

*Has internet misuse become the greatest discipline problem in modern organizations?*

*Source: Reprinted with permission from HRM Guide UK (http://www.hrmguide.co.uk/).*

Dismissal is the ultimate expression of such procedures and also one of the most unpleasant aspects of human resource management. It may arise because of disciplinary issues such as persistent absenteeism, failure of an employee to perform adequately despite support and training, or as a strategic requirement arising from a change in direction by the organization. Most managers regard the 'exiting' process with distaste – often it is more stressful for the sacking manager than the victims. Dismissal inevitably follows some form of conflict.

## HRM IN REALITY CAREER EXITS

According to the 2006 survey on employee exits by career publisher Vault.com, 61 per cent of respondents have exited a job on bad terms with their employer.

Based on 706 responses from American employees in a variety of industries, the survey found the main reasons for leaving were disagreements with management (73 per cent), disagreements with co-workers (12 per cent), or to start employment with a new company immediately (14 per cent).

One respondent commented, 'Owners of the company were liars, cheaters, and didn't treat their employees well'. Another said, 'My manager wanted me to do something that violated FDA regulations, and then he got HR to begin disciplinary steps because I was disobedient'.

Almost half (47 per cent) did not give notice in person, but instead called or emailed their manager. One respondent explained, 'After having it out with my boss's boss, I called my boss and told him I quit. The funny thing was, at the same time I was in his voice-mail, his boss paged him and told him to fire me'.

Types of bad exits included:

→ screaming matches (42 per cent)

→ negative mass emails (24 per cent)

→ negative speeches at company meetings (18 per cent)

→ vandalized or stolen company property (12 per cent)

→ physical scuffles (4 per cent).

About half of respondents (52 per cent) witnessed or took part in a domino effect in which one person's exit caused others to leave the company soon afterwards.

*Source:* HRM Guide USA *(http://www.hrmguide.com).*

## CONFLICT

Where does conflict come from? Conflict has both positive and negative aspects as we can see in Table 20.2. A number of basic psychological causes are apparent, regardless of the overt justification for a dispute (McKenna, 1994: 418):

*Frustration and aggression.* Disagreement often reflects frustration – feelings of being ignored, of being pressurized or of blocked promotion. Any point of difference, no matter how irrelevant, may spark a reaction to frustration. This may appear in the form of verbal aggression, seemingly out of proportion to the importance of the supposed dispute. Clearly, the dispute masks problems that are attributable to poor communication, lack of empowerment and mistrust.

*Different objectives.* The rhetoric of HRM states that organizations should aim for shared goals between management and staff. However, in practice, managers and employees have different priorities. Managers may focus on efficiency and cost-effectiveness, whereas employees want higher pay and longer holidays. Unless there are mechanisms, such as team briefings or quality circles, by which mutual understanding of these goals can be improved, differences are likely to be brought to a head at some stage.

*Different values.* These could be political – a difference in belief about the purpose of business for example – or a disagreement about the manager's right to manage. Many managers believe that they have the authority to issue instructions without being challenged by their staff. On the other hand, some employees consider that managers have this right only if they are prepared to explain their decisions, account for the consequences of their actions, and are prepared to accept questions and criticisms.

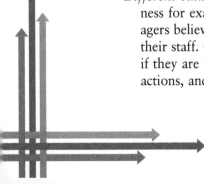

TABLE 20.2
Consequences of
conflict

529

CHAPTER 20   Managing conflict

| Positive | Negative |
|---|---|
| **Clearing the air**. Allowing people to air their grievances can sometimes lead to an improved atmosphere after the disagreement has finished. This serves to bring 'hidden agendas' out into the open. | **Wasting time and energy**. A simple decision can be quick to implement, but negotiation can take an inordinate amount of time. Often participants forget original purpose of negotiation and get caught up with fighting a war. |
| **Understanding each other's position**. When both sides of an agenda are brought out into the open, people must think through their own case in order to express it clearly; and grasp the other point of view in order to challenge it. | **Stress**. Conflicts can become quite personal, abusive and threatening. The postures taken by the two sides can lead to further stress. Mental exhaustion may come from prolonged debate. |
| **Modification of goal**. One side may realize how unpopular or impractical the consequences of their argument may be. | **Worsening the situation**. Conflict may highlight problems, dislikes and grievances better left unstated. Tension may escalate debate into action: strikes, lock-outs, work-to-rule, threatened or implied redundancies. Consequences may be unpleasantness with worse morale and industrial relations after negotiations than before. |

*Jealousy.* Individual employees can be sensitive to other members of staff being paid more than them, or getting extra perks. The conflict arises from jealousy or loss of status.

*Culture.* The tradition of 'us and them' (employees versus management) continues to exist in many organizations, particularly those using an authoritarian style of people management. New staff and management are quickly encouraged to accept the 'normality' of this perspective. In other cases, a change in the management approach disturbs the prevailing employee relations culture.

Conflict is an inevitable feature of negotiating and bargaining. Trained negotiators are taught to deal with conflict, expecting both negative and positive aspects to appear during the process. This will be easier to understand when we consider specific models of negotiation later in this chapter.

Issues of conflict and discipline may not be resolved at local level. Many countries have mechanisms by which disputes may be taken to an outside body, usually in the form of industrial tribunals or arbitration bodies.

# TRIBUNALS AND ARBITRATION SYSTEMS

To what extent can differences between employers and workers be resolved through arbitration or legal tribunals? It is the view in many countries that an impartial, legally based

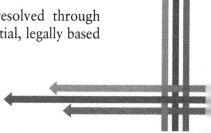

process has a significant role to play in a number of circumstances. Industrial tribunals take many forms, some making legally binding judgements, others not setting a precedent in law. Even in the latter case, however, they have a long-term effect since they establish a set of values and influence the behaviour of others. If there is a judgement on a case of significant racial discrimination, for example, the resulting publicity may lead to a moderation of racist behaviour as people fear the possibility of similar action against themselves.

Chelliah and D'Netto (2006) analyzed 342 decisions in 17 industries by arbitrators in the Australian Industrial Relations Commission to assess whether employees benefited from arbitration. They found that 50.6 per cent of arbitration decisions were in favour of employees but only 10.8 per cent of complainants were reinstated. They suggest that employers need to look at ways of creating a more harmonious workplace. Employees do not benefit much from arbitration and reaching a settlement through mediation may be a better option.

In the UK, the Advisory, Conciliation, and Arbitration Service (Acas) plays a similar role to the Australian Industrial Relations Commission in relation to collective disputes. It provides services including:

*Binding arbitration.* Acas can appoint an arbitrator provided that the two parties agree to accept the arbitrator's decision.

*Voluntary conciliation.* Acas provides a calm environment and help on defining the important issues. Acas conciliation staff act as facilitators and do not make judgements or attempt to impose solutions.

*Mediation.* Intermediate between arbitration and conciliation. Acas mediators make advisory recommendations that are aimed at preventing disputes from degenerating into industrial action. These recommendations are not binding on the parties involved.

Acas also plays a major role in promoting agreed settlements in disputes taken to industrial tribunals.

## HRM IN REALITY   ACAS 2009/2010

In 2009/2010 the Advisory, Conciliation, and Arbitration Service (Acas) dealt with 905 requests for collective conciliation of which 44 per cent involved pay and 14 per cent trade union recognition. The majority (94 per cent) were at least partially resolved.

Some 87 421 individual employment tribunal cases were referred for conciliation; almost all (97 per cent) were successfully resolved. This represents an overall increase of 13 per cent over the previous 12 months.

Nearly 10 000 cases were referred to the pre-claim service introduced in April 2009 that offers prompt conciliation designed to prevent disputes escalating. Results show that tribunal cases have been avoided in about 70 per cent of cases. Acas estimates that simply completing the necessary paperwork for an employment tribunal costs the average employer £2000.

The Acas helpline received over 1 million calls over the period; redundancy, dismissals, discipline and grievance were the most common issues raised. The service is receiving an increasing number of calls about company survival, addressing subjects such as short-time working schemes.

In April 2010 the Acas Model Workplace went online. This interactive assessment tool offers employers ten modules covering different areas of employment relations including performance management and employee representation. Aimed primarily at organizations with 100-300 employees, the Model Workplace is intended to: help employers assess the effectiveness of people management in their organization; give practical guidance on good employee relations; and connect employers to useful resources.

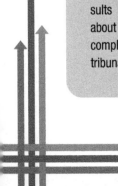

| Ed Sweeney, chair of ACAS said: | John Taylor, chief executive officer of Acas commented: |
|---|---|
| As the country begins to emerge from its longest and deepest recession for more than 60 years businesses have been looking for support and guidance. ACAS has helped thousands of businesses over the past year. We have provided advice in the employment relations field, from short practical courses on issues such as improving attendance and managing change, through to in-depth tailored support. Concern about employment issues and, in particular, redundancies, has remained high. | This has been a very tough year for British business and we have seen demand for our services, especially around dealing with redundancy, increase greatly. As well as continuing to provide conciliation in individual and collective disputes, we have also looked at our other services and the value for money we provide and have identified new ways of improving the British workplace through effective employee relations. |

*Source: Reprinted with permission from* HRM Guide UK *(http://www.hrmguide.co.uk).*

# THE NEGOTIATING PROCESS

Negotiation is an ancient art. It is important in fields as diverse as diplomacy, buying and selling, arranging relationships (marriages, business partnerships), as well as employee relations. Negotiation is a form of decision-making where two or more parties approach a problem or situation wanting to achieve their own objectives – which may or may not turn out to be the same. In the employee relations arena, negotiation usually takes place within the collective bargaining environment.

Participants enter the process with widely different views: some, typically on the employee side, will view it as being fundamental to industrial democracy, fairness and good business conduct; others see it as a barrier to efficiency, a view more prevalent on the management side. The latter view sees negotiation as compromise and second-best to winning: possibly worse than giving in! As can be seen from Table 20.3, the process also has its own jargon.

Negotiation is not simply a matter of 'splitting the difference' so that neither side achieves what it wants. It can produce an outcome that meets both sets of goals. In negotiating, both sides must have some goals in common and some that conflict. For example,

| Statement | Translation |
|---|---|
| We explored all options | Everybody talked a lot |
| A great deal of additional work will be necessary | Nobody understood it |
| The results were inconclusive | Nothing happened |
| While no agreement was reached, definite progress was made | Nobody budged an inch |
| It is hoped that this report will stimulate interest in the problem | Let somebody else do it next time |

**TABLE 20.3**

Communication in collective bargaining

Source: Adapted from *Toctanic* (undated, circa 1989), unofficial staff publication, British Telecom International.

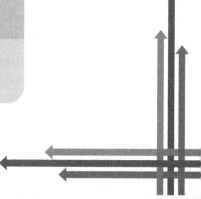

employers and employees will all want the business to survive and expand. However, employers might resist high pay rises to keep costs down, whereas the staff will want increases to boost employee morale. Usually, bargaining takes place because neither side has the power or the authority to force a decision on the other and preserve a harmonious working atmosphere.

Therefore, both sides will open negotiations knowing that they will have to move from the opening position and that there will have to be sacrifices on one item to achieve advantages on another. Even in those ideal circumstances, such as the traditional German model, where deliberate confrontation is not acceptable, there will be an element of conflict between the two sides.

There is also an implicit assumption that the two parties have the same amount of power in the bargaining situation. This is almost certainly not the case and the degree of power will change during the process of negotiation; the location of greatest power may well switch backwards and forwards between the two sides as they achieve positions of advantage. Whatever the actual degree of power, advantages will come from both sides preserving the appearance or illusion of power. There is value, therefore, in playing a game of bluff.

Many texts imply that the methods of bargaining can only be learned through experience and may well suggest that negotiation, like most interpersonal skills, is instinctive rather than learned. Perhaps, the basic requirement is a combination of a competitive, assertive style with a devious and resilient personality. In fact, study of the bargaining process indicates regular patterns and processes that people tend to go through. Gates (2006) provides an overview of skills needed for successful negotiations and seeks to identify the benefits of training key staff in negotiations skills. The study finds that only five per cent of the UK's training budget is spent on negotiations skills development. However, it makes a significant difference to the performance of all staff, both in internal and external negotiations.

Studies of industrial negotiations have indicated that many disputes worsen because of the following factors:

→ lack of clarity of aims or goals by one or both sides

→ poor understanding of the detailed situation

→ the apparent dispute is not the real problem.

## MODELS OF BARGAINING

There are several models of the bargaining process, the clearest of which identifies four main stages (Lyons, 1988: 110):

1 *Initial positioning.* Both parties set out their positions and requirements in an emphatic, firm way aimed at giving the impression that there is no possibility of budging from those positions. The situation can appear hopeless at this stage.

2 *Testing.* The next stage is a less formal probing of the other side's demands, testing out which are really unmovable and which might bend in the right circumstances.

3 *Concession.* Some tentative proposals and concessions are exchanged on which detailed negotiations can take place.

4 *Settlement.* Finally, agreement is reached and the package of new terms is settled and actioned. Lyons argues that successful negotiation requires specific skills, examined in the following subsections.

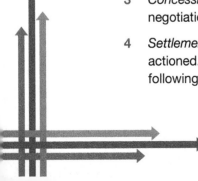

## Analysis

This may be defined as the ability to analyze a situation not only in terms of one's own position and goals but also those of the other side. There should be a long-term perspective – rarely is it clear that one should begin to consider the consequences of the whole process at this basic stage. The analysis must include a decision on which elements can be agreed on an 'I win/you win' basis, as opposed to those which are 'I win/you lose'. It is not worthwhile winning one of the latter if the advantage is trivial in comparison with the longer-term bad feelings that may arise as a consequence.

This phase is frequently glossed over but in fact is possibly the most important. It is the stage at which one should work out what the highest and lowest gains you and your opponent are likely to accept. Additionally, there must be a clear understanding of what the other side really want as opposed to what you think they might want.

## Effective argument

This has to be carefully balanced between being forceful and being reasonable. The whole point of negotiation is to convince the other side of the merits of your argument as against their own. It is a change process. It is important to avoid cheap point-scoring and abuse in order to preserve mutual respect and avoid distraction from irrelevant side issues.

## Signals of cooperation

The skill of sensing and giving signals of cooperation and possible compromise. Kanter (1989: 156) found that the participants in successful 'business partnerships' were 'very adept at "reading" signals that indicated whether partner representatives can be trusted'. On the 'tit-for-tat' principle, maximum opportunity comes from rewarding cooperation or compromise with a compromise of your own. On the other hand, one does not reward the opposition for sticking to an unmovable position: every offer one makes has to be conditional on cooperation in return. It may be necessary to keep communication going in order for this process to happen. In the case of a complete deadlock, it may even be necessary to have 'talks about talks'. All offers and threats must have credibility, remembering that it is not real power that matters but the appearance of it.

## Attention to detail

Lastly, the final conclusion of negotiations requires the ability to attend to detail, making sure that all aspects are taken care of and there is no way for the other side to avoid its agreed obligations.

 **SUMMARY**

'Employee relations' broadens the study of industrial relations to include wider aspects of the employment relationship, including unionized and non-unionized workplaces, personal contracts and socio-emotional, rather than contractual, arrangements. This is an area with diverse ideological underpinnings and political ramifications. Governments have taken an active part in determining its conduct, sometimes disallowing any form of employee voice and framing legislation to encourage individual or collective arrangements. In Europe, harmonization is leading to the establishment of works councils across the EU, giving a new role for collective representation. Australia and New Zealand have seen some of the

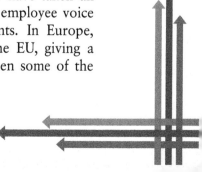

most significant changes in employee relations legislation in recent years. Negotiation, bargaining and mediation are some of the most significant employee relations activities in which human resource specialists are involved.

 **FURTHER READING**

1 *Reassessing the Employment Relationship* edited by Paul Blyton, Edmond Heery and Peter Turnbull (Palgrave Macmillan, 2010) places employee relations in a wide HR context.

2 *Employment Relations* by Ed Rose (FT–Prentice Hall, 3rd edition, 2008) and

3 *Contemporary Employment Relations: A Critical Introduction* by Steve Williams and Derek Adams-Smith (OUP Oxford, 2nd edition, 2009) provide good overviews of the field.

4 *International and Comparative Industrial Relations* edited by Greg Bamber, Russell Lansbury and Nick Wailes (Sage Publications, 5th edition, 2010) compares different countries.

5 *Managing Conflict in the Workplace: How to Develop Trust and Understanding and Manage Disagreements* by Shay and Margaret McConnon (How to Books, 4th edition, 2010) takes a win–win approach to workplace conflict.

6 *The Essential Guide to Mediation and Conflict Resolution* by Norah Doherty and Marcelas Guyler (Kogan Page, 2008) is a comprehensive guide.

7 *The Mind and Heart of the Negotiator* by Leigh L. Thomson (Prentice Hall, 4th edition, 2008) looks at the skills of negotiation and bargaining.

 **REVIEW QUESTIONS**

1 What are the key differences between unitarist and pluralist views of employee relations?

2 What is meant by the employment relationship? To what extent is it reasonable to say that employee relations should encompass all employment relationships?

3 Do trade unions have a role to play in the modern workplace? Discuss the view that employee relations is an outmoded concept that has no place in organizations managed according to the principles of HRM.

4 What are the principal factors responsible for the changes in union power over the last few decades?

5 How central is the German system of employee relations to the European Unions's 'social partnership' model?

6 Are works councils a handicap or a benefit to business efficiency?

7 Is it wise for governments to suppress independent trade unions?

8 What should trade unions do to be 'new realists' in employee relations?

9 What are the key skills of negotiation?

10 Should all disputes be resolved by arbitration?

11 Review the positive and negative aspects of conflict in the workplace. Is conflict healthy?

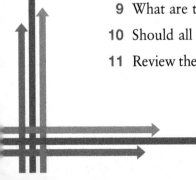

## Middleton Council/Euro Vehicles

1 Middleton Council covers a large urban area bordered by open country. Most of its 300 staff work in the main office complex, Delta House, located in the old town centre. A new shopping mall has opened immediately between the council offices and the old market, transforming a derelict area into a fashionable district. The staff are delighted since they now work in a pleasant and prestigious locality with a massive choice of shops and eating places nearby.

The council has been re-elected after promising a considerable improvement in services. However, all available funds have been devoted to maintaining things as they are. After much debate it has been decided that costs could be cut dramatically by renting out Delta House to a commercial firm and transferring the staff to much cheaper accommodation at the edge of town. The savings could be used to pay for new services promised in the election.

The staff are unionized and have a reputation for resisting changes, no matter how small.

*How would you advise the council to proceed?*

2 Euro Vehicles manufactures vans and other light commercial vehicles. Because of severe competition and a declining market, the workforce has been reduced from 11 300 to 2800 in the last three years and the remaining employees are fearful of further redundancy. There are three unions in the two remaining plants, representing clerical, engineering and supervisory staff. Partly as a result of the recent cuts they are all suspicious of management intentions. Management is authoritarian, based on a rigid departmental structure and values technical competence and seniority over anything else. Most of the managers have been promoted from the engineering and production side of the company and are in their 40s and 50s.

The company's production is largely devoted to basic van models built to a 15-year-old design and sold to large utility companies at a very keen price. Marketing is almost non-existent and the Research and Development department was closed as a cost-cutting measure three years ago. The company is currently owned by a large conglomerate that left the management alone until recently but with strict, detailed financial controls. Consequently, the company has been consistently profitable but with a shrinking level of production and increasingly outdated manufacturing equipment. The conglomerate has decided that this 'hands-off' approach is no longer satisfactory. They are prepared to make a major investment but only if they can be convinced that this will be effectively managed.

*You have been brought in as a consultant to look at the current organization and to recommend changes that would improve the situation.*

*How would you go about this?*

*What are the implications for employee relations?*

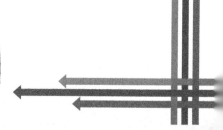

# CONCLUSION

We began this volume with an analysis of the concept of HRM. We found that interpretations of human resource management range from formal models to comparatively loose portrayals of the territory with which HRM should be concerned. There is general agreement on its underlying philosophy, linking people management to business objectives in a strategic, integrated and coherent way. Beyond that, however, commentators and practitioners interpret HRM in different ways, depending on personal agendas and vested interests. As a result HRM ranges from 'soft', humanistic attempts to win over staff and achieve heart-felt commitment, to 'hard'-nosed extraction of maximum effort at minimum cost.

Senior executives do not have a consistent view of HRM – any more than they have a shared understanding of management. Many do not perceive any distinction between general management and managing people. Even less do they wish to be involved with fine academic distinctions between different models of HRM. The actual 'doing' of HRM is passed to middle managers who are responsible for its implementation and can be held (conveniently) accountable for any failures. People policies and practices must be integrated and coherent for HRM to be effective but this division of labour leads to a significant weakness: it offers scope for a dislocation between strategic intentions and the conduct of people management at ground level.

Regardless of the rationale or the nature of its practice, HRM has become a common label for various forms and functions of people management. In English-speaking countries, the term has replaced 'personnel management' in many contexts. Following a South African study by Wood and Els (2000) we can identify four distinct patterns of practice:

1. A simple change in nomenclature of relevant personnel sections where, in a number of cases, staff were not seen as managers but instead were viewed as a distinct, relatively junior category of employee.

2. A broadened personnel function encompassing clearly delineated areas such as training and development.

3. HRM practitioners play an important strategic role as facilitators in the adoption of progressive industrial relations policies, rather than developing a vision for managing human resources across the organization.

4. True strategic HRM.

The adoption of human resource management has been driven by a range of stakeholders with different interests and expectations. It has been interpreted differently around the world but globalization has encouraged an increasing convergence. In the past, new management concepts have generally come from North America. However, the worldwide economy is changing. China, India and Brazil appear destined to be major influences at the beginning of the 21st century and they are not dominated by US-style free market ideas. HR specialists are no longer able to focus solely on their own local employment markets as global competition and outsourcing become dominant factors in the allocation of human resources.

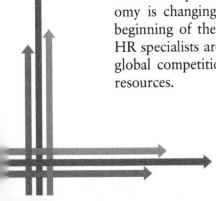

What is clear is that the central tenet of 'soft' HRM – the belief that HRM regards employees as valuable assets and not just costs – is rarely translated into action. The practices associated with HRM are often introduced for reasons of expediency rather than any serious belief in its principles. Indeed, it is arguable that the practice of HRM is rife with hypocrisy and rhetoric. Many organizations in free market countries feel that competitive forces make it impossible to commit themselves to their employees. People management in these firms is firmly focused on cost-cutting. A conflict arises from the inherent contradiction between typical HRM themes such as encouraging long-term employee engagement and short-term cost-effectiveness.

This leads to the question of whether HRM is no more than a matter of fine words. Employees quickly learn to mistrust official rhetoric and instead practise the art of 'sensemaking': looking for cues that indicate the route for success or, at least, survival. Informal messages are transmitted through the choice of people who are rewarded and those whose skills are developed. For example, large-scale redundancies – determined at short notice by senior managers – have followed soothing statements about the importance of human resources to an organization's future.

Is there any evidence that the implementation of HRM has a significant effect on national or organizational economic performance? After all, this is the justification implicit in HRM models for valuing the human resource above all others. Progress has been made in conceptualizing the problem and measuring results. Improvements in HR metrics have resulted in clear evidence for the effectiveness of HRM initiatives, especially when they are delivered in strategic 'bundles'. Fashionable concepts such as 'knowledge management', 'human capital management' and 'talent management' overlap with many features of human resource management and are often delivered as part of the same package of management initiatives. The evidence appears to support the view that 'calculative' practices, such as short-term contracts, lack of employer commitment to job security, low levels of training and unsophisticated human resource practices have been negatively correlated with corporate performance. In contrast, positive correlations have been found between good corporate performance and high-engagement organizations, especially when HR initiatives are introduced as a comprehensive, coherent package, or 'bundle' of practices.

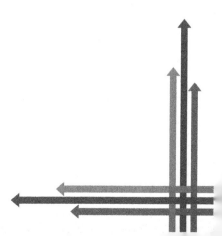

# GLOSSARY

**Action learning** Reg Revans argued that classroom-based management education is not adequate. He devised a systematic, experiential or action learning programme based on job exchanges which place managers in unfamiliar situations and ask them to take on challenging tasks.

**Action research** Organizational development – particularly in its 1960s and 70s form – relied on a methodology described as action research. This was an undramatic but effective long-term change process based on incremental improvements, effectively on a continuous flow of emergent strategies. Action research became relatively unfashionable with the advent of 'packaged' techniques such as business process re-engineering.

**Added-worker hypothesis** A hypothesis that predicts an increase in employment participation rates during periods of high unemployment. The premise is that partners go to work to compensate for the lost income of main wage-earners who are made redundant.

**Adult learning** It has been argued that adult learning is qualitatively different from learning in childhood. The 'andragogy' approach emphasizes the importance of self-directed learning for adults, integrating new material and ideas with current and previous experience.

**Advisory, Conciliation, and Arbitration Service (Acas)** Founded in 1975, this is a UK public body with the ambition to 'improve organizations and working life through better employment relations'. It is run by a council with representatives from business, unions, and the independent sector and has approximately 800 staff in England, Scotland and Wales. There are 11 main regional centres plus a head office in London. ACAS defines its services as follows: *Conciliating:* the act of reconciling or bringing together the parties in a dispute with the aim of moving forward to a settlement acceptable to all sides. *Arbitrating:* an independent arbitrator or arbiter (in Scotland) deciding the outcome of a dispute. The decision may well be binding in law. *Mediating:* acting as an intermediary in talking to both sides. The aim is for the parties to resolve the problem between themselves but the mediator will make suggestions along the way.

**Affective identification** A real intellectual and emotional identification with the organization.

**Affirmative action** (or positive discrimination). A longstanding approach in the USA, designed to advantage the disadvantaged, including women, African-Americans and Hispanics. Laws only applied to the public sector and its suppliers.

**Ageism** Discrimination on the grounds of age is prevalent but often unrecognized. Legislation against ageism is becoming common in developed countries.

**Alienation** A state of estrangement, or a feeling of being an outsider from society. Dull, boring and repetitive work induces a feeling of alienation. Assembly-line workers are involved with a small part of the final product, have little control over the rhythm of their work and may have no idea of the significance of their contribution. Their work can appear to be alien with no relationship or meaning to their lives other than to produce income. As a consequence they may feel little enthusiasm and, often, active hostility towards what seems like forced-labour.

**Alternative dispute resolution (ADR)** The term has been in use for decades but the various forms of ADR have become increasingly used in recent years. The US Federal *Administrative Dispute Resolution Act 1995* states that 'alternative means of dispute resolution' means any procedure that is used to resolve issues in controversy, including, but not limited to, conciliation, facilitation, mediation, factfinding, minitrials, arbitration, and use of ombuds, or any combination thereof.

**American Arbitration Association** The American Arbitration Association makes itself available to resolve a wide range of disputes (including labour/ employment issues) through mediation, arbitration, elections and other out-of-court settlement procedures. A not-for-profit organization, it claims to be the largest provider of ADR (alternative dispute resolution) procedures in the USA. Also provides panels, education and training services.

**Americans with Disabilities Act (ADA)** The Americans with Disabilities Act prohibits discrimination against people with disabilities in employment, transportation, public accommodation, communications, and activities of state and local government. The act was signed into law in 1990 but its various elements came into force on different dates including: state and local government activities, 26 January, 1992;

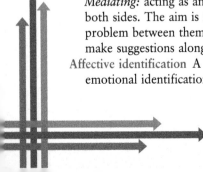

employers with 25 or more workers, 26 July, 1992; employers with 15 or more workers, 26 July, 1994. The Act requires that employers, employment agencies, labour organizations and joint labour-management committees must have non-discriminatory application procedures, qualification standards, and selection criteria and in all other terms and conditions of employment and make reasonable accommodation to the known limitations of a qualified applicant or employee unless to do so would cause an undue hardship. The bill makes exceptions regarding the employment of a person with a contagious disease, a person who illegally uses drugs or alcohol, employment of someone by a religious entity, and private membership clubs. (*Source: US Department of Labor*).

**Application forms (blanks)** Usually sent out to jobseekers who respond to some kind of job advertising. The form or blank is a template for the presentation of personal information that should be relevant to the job applied for. This ensures that all candidates provide the desired range of information in the same order of presentation to facilitate comparison and preparation of a short-list for further selection procedures.

**Application letters** Traditionally used for job applications they have tended to become little more than cover letters in English-speaking countries, generally being discounted in the selection process. However, in a number of continental European countries, especially France and Switzerland, they are requested to be handwritten and may be subject to graphological analysis as one (sometimes the main) selection procedure.

**Appraisals** Appraisals rate individuals on quasi-objective criteria or standards deemed to be relevant to performance. Traditional appraisals rated individuals on a list of qualities, primarily work-related attitudes and personality traits. *See also* 'Performance assessment'.

**Arbitration** Arbitration is a long-standing alternative to court-based litigation. For example, the first institute for arbitration in Denmark was set up in Copenhagen in 1894. The process has a number of variant forms but, in essence, nominated third-parties (arbitrators) can make decisions which are binding on the parties to a dispute. Arbitration procedures can range between the informal and more rule-based systems and are similar to court procedures. Generally, arbitration is seen as providing such benefits as confidentiality, flexibility, speed and relative cheapness.

**Assessment** *See* 'Appraisals', 'Assessment centre', 'Performance assessment'.

**Assessment centre** A concept and not necessarily a place. Normally used for selection or employee development, participants are given a variety of exercises, tests, role plays, interviews, etc. over a period of days. Several rates contribute to the assessment.

**Attitudes** Attitudes are dispositions held by people – towards or against – people, things and ideas. They have individual components based on factors such as personality and understanding, and social elements derived from shared experiences and cultural history. Attitudes are complex systems of belief, evaluation, emotion and behaviour.

**Australian Council of Trade Unions (ACTU)** Formed in 1927, the Australian Council of Trade Unions is the peak council and national centre representing the unionized Australian workforce. The ACTU holds a Congress every three years that sets out a clear set of policies and objectives for unions. The core activity of unions remains the improvement and representation of workers through workplace and industry activity and collective bargaining. The ACTU also has policies on a range of other issues which affect workers, their families and their communities.

**Australian Industrial Relations Commission (AIRC)** The AIRC was a national tribunal dealing with employment issues including dispute settlement and unfair dismissal. Replaced by Fair Work Australia in 2010.

**Balanced scorecard** A conceptual framework used to translate an organization's vision into a set of performance indicators, including measures of: financial performance, customer satisfaction, internal business processes, and learning and growth. Both current performance and efforts to learn and improve can be monitored using these measures.

**Bargaining** *See also* 'Collective bargaining'.

**Behavioural compliance** Simply presenting an appearance of the attitudes and behaviours expected by senior managers. Not a true commitment.

**Behavioural consistency** Maintaining a set of desired behaviours consistently in the workplace. Desired behaviours may be agreed ways of behaving towards customers, team behaviour, etc.

**Benchmarking** Direct comparisons of different measures between an organization and 'best practice' competitors in the same business sector. This indicates the gap in performance, costs, morale, etc., between that organization and industry best practice.

**Best Fit** Matching human resource management and strategy as closely as possible to organizational requirements.

**Best practice** Strategies, activities or techniques that are viewed as being highly effective. Note that what is best practice in one context may not work in another.

**Biodata** Roberts (1997, p.: 10) describes biodata as a 'set of questions framed around "coincidences" in the lives of good performers.' People who are good

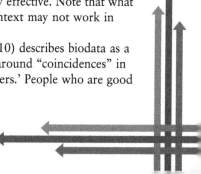

at a particular job are likely to be more similar to each other than to individuals selected at random from the general population. Such similarities extend beyond work-related factors into hobbies, sports and social activities.

**Business culture** *See* 'Corporate culture'.

**Business environment** Everything outside a business organization which interacts with that organization. Traditionally, human resource managers have been closely involved with employment legislation, industrial tribunals, and trade unions at a functional level. HRM's strategic emphasis requires a focus on other environmental variables. Government economic, social security, education and training policies affect the availability, cost and quality of available employees. International competition, strategic alliances and supranational organizations such as the European Union are exercising increasing influence on people management.

**Business goals** The strategic objectives of a business.

**Business process re-engineering (BPR)** A 'fundamental rethinking and radical redesign of business processes to achieve dramatic improvements in critical contemporary measures of performance, such as cost, quality, service and speed' (Hammer and Champy, 1993).

**Centralization** An organizational process in which an activity or function (including control) is concentrated in one place.

**Change** Businesses must change to survive. However, change is a difficult management task. Effective change requires surefooted, considerate people managers who can take employees through the process with minimum anxiety and maximum enthusiasm. It requires the recognition that an organization's people should not be the pawns of strategy but active participants in change.

**Change strategy** An organizational or HR strategy aimed at implementing planned change.

**Charisma** Weber regarded charisma as one of three sources of authority (the other two being 'rational', and 'traditional'), portraying it as a magical and hypnotic force based on direct personal contact. In modern life charisma is often fake – a product of carefully orchestrated mass communications.

**Childcare** In the HR context, a facility that looks after a child during a parent's working hours (including travelling time). Childcare may be provided by an employer as a benefit.

**Cloning** Cloning, or 'elective homogeneity' is the tendency for selectors to pick people like themselves, thereby reducing the breadth of skills and personalities in an organization. Simply matching the set of characteristics possessed by previous successful post holders, it is a safe, conservative way to fill jobs.

As a low risk, but backward-looking approach, it is unlikely to meet the future needs of the organization.

**Co-determination** Cooperation between employees and management in policymaking.

**Coherence** HR strategies and actions must be consistent with each other. For example, if a business has a strategy of increasing sales of high-profit-margin products, rewards in the sales department should be focused on these products rather than less profitable items.

**Collaborative entrepreneurship** Cooperation between two or more individuals in order to found or acquire a business. The degree and nature of collaboration may vary from one company to another in terms of financial input, time devoted, skills and knowledge.

**Collective bargaining** Collective bargaining takes place between employers and trade unions when: employees are members of trade unions which undertake to negotiate on their behalf in matters such as pay, working conditions, other benefits, and work allocation; and employers recognize trade unions and their officials as legitimate bargaining agents.

**Collectivism** The opposite of individualism – a preference for being part of a group. In employment relations, a process of combining into unions or staff associations for the purpose of negotiation with management.

**Collectivization** As individuals, most employees have a limited amount of power in comparison to their employers. But employees can pool the power they have. Through collectivization, workers are able to band together to protect their mutual interests. From the late 19th century onwards, trade unions have fought to improve pay and conditions for their members

**Commitment** Commitment is defined as the degree of identification and involvement which individuals have with their organization's mission, values and goals. This translates into: their desire to stay with the organization; belief in its objectives and values; and the strength of employee effort in the pursuit of business objectives.

**Communication** Good communication is essential to the smooth running of the people management system. It must be a two-way process. This can involve a cascaded flow of information from the top and also feedback from lower levels through surveys, performance measures and open meetings.

**Competence** Organizations must have the capability to meet changing needs. In current parlance this is often expressed in terms of competences – skills, knowledge and abilities. These are qualities possessed by the people who work for those organizations. Competences can be brought into businesses through the recruitment of skilled

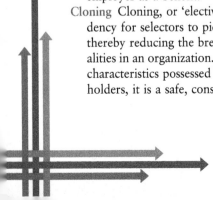

individuals. They can also be developed within existing people by investing in training, education and experiential programmes.

**Competitive advantage** A concept popularized by Michael Porter. A condition which enables an organization to operate in a more efficient or otherwise higher-quality manner than the organizations it competes with.

**Competitiveness** Provision of the best possible value, skills and creativity.

**Comprehensiveness** All people management activities should be part of a single, comprehensive system. This implies that the attitudes, behaviour and culture of every individual in an organization – especially those with people management responsibilities – should be integrated within a deliberate framework.

**Conflict** Disagreement that may result in withdrawal of cooperation or, in an employee relations context, may result in some form of industrial action.

**Conformity** Opposite of creativity. A tendency to obey rules and stick to procedures or conventional ways of doing things.

**Confucian dynamism** Acceptance of the legitimacy of hierarchy and valuing of perseverance and thrift, without undue emphasis on tradition and social obligations that could impede business initiative.

**Congruence** One of the '4 Cs' of the Harvard model. An organization should be regarded as a system whose elements and activities have to fit together.

**Contingency** 'It depends'. Adapting theory to reality.

**Contingency theory** A theory that takes account of the circumstances in one situation at one point in time. Allows for multiple ways of doing things to fit different circumstances.

**Contingent employees** Temporary, intermittent or seasonal workers. The US Bureau of Labor Statistics' definition of contingent worker includes all salary and wage workers who do not expect their employment to last.

**Continuous improvement** Operational philosophy based on the view that performance improvement is the ongoing responsibility of everyone in an organization in order to achieve higher levels of performance, profitability and customer satisfaction.

**Control** HRM is aimed at directing and coordinating employees to meet an organization's objectives and cannot be anarchic nor totally democratic in its approach. Human resource literature mostly advocates a participative approach with a high degree of empowerment and delegation. An autocratic approach is unlikely to encourage good communication and employee commitment.

**Cooperation** Collaborating informally or formally to achieve one or more goals. (*see Cooperatives*).

**Cooperatives** A cooperative is an autonomous association of persons united voluntarily to meet their common economic, social, and cultural needs and aspirations through a jointly owned and democratically-controlled enterprise. (*Source: ICA*).

**Coordination** Tasks divided amongst a group of individuals must be synchronized and integrated in some way so as to achieve the overall objectives of the group. Jobs must fit into a coherent flow of work. Coordination involves the distribution of decisionmaking. This can be formal, with rigid rules and regulations, or informal, giving freedom for local decisions. Coordination may be routine, because of structure and control mechanisms, including a performance management system or direct, by management action.

**Core** In resourcing terms, core staff are crucial to the organization and the last to be outsourced.

**Core and peripheral staff** Core staff are those employees regarded as essential to the organization; peripheral staff are there to meet operational needs but are not regarded as indispensable. Core staff have greater security and may also have better terms and conditions of employment.

**Corporate culture** Defined by Bower (1966) as 'the way we do things around here'. Trice and Beyer (1984) elaborated this as: 'the system of ... publicly and collectively accepted meanings operating for a given group at a given time'. Hofstede (1994) describes corporate culture as 'the psychological assets of an organization, which can be used to predict what will happen to its financial assets in five years time'. *See also* 'Culture'.

**Cost-effectiveness** Expressed in terms of profitability, cost-effectiveness has been used extensively as the justification for large-scale job cuts. But as a reflection of the value of its human assets, an organization has a duty to use its people wisely. In itself, there is nothing wrong with an attention to cost – provided that it does not become the one and only management criterion.

**Counselling interview** In the context of performance and employee development, an interview in which strengths and weaknesses and development actions are discussed. Typically, it follows a performance assessment.

**Cover letters** Introductory letters that accompany CVs or Resumes.

**Creativity** Creativity can lead to new products and services, novel applications and cost savings. A creative environment develops from a trusting, open culture with good communication and a blame-free atmosphere. Conversely, creativity is inhibited by lack of trust or commitment and fear of the consequences of change.

**Credibility** Managers and the organizations they represent must have credibility in the eyes of their employees if they are to expect the best performance. A degree of healthy cynicism is unavoidable,

but in today's downsized workplaces this frequently extends into mistrust of and contempt for senior management. This feeling reflects the way many staff feel they are themselves regarded by management. Regaining trust depends on personal credibility which, in turn, can only come from honesty and sincerity.

**Critical incidents technique** A set of procedures for systematically identifying behaviours which contribute to success or failure of individuals or organizations in specific situations.

**Culture** An all-pervasive system of beliefs and behaviours transmitted socially. Specifically it consists of the set of values – abstract ideals – and norms or rules held by a society, together with its material expressions. *See also* 'Corporate culture'.

**Data** Hard, factual information often in numerical form – it can tell you when, and how often something happened, how much it cost and so on but it does not say why it happened. *See also* 'Knowledge'.

**De-layering** Removing one or more levels in a management hierarchy, thereby creating a flatter organization.

**Demographic trends** Long-term changes in a country's population density, age profile, etc.

**Development** *see Human Resource Development (HRD)*

**Direct** *see Direct Discrimination*

**Direct discrimination** Treating an individual or group less favourably on grounds such as disability, race, religion, age, gender or sexual orientation. Direct discrimination is fairly obvious because of its explicit nature. The use of different criteria for promoting or paying male or female employees is an example of direct discrimination.

**Disability** The Americans with Disabilities Act (1990) defines disability as follows: 'Anyone with a physical or mental impairment substantially limiting one or more major life activities; has a record of such impairment; or is regarded as having such an impairment, is considered a person with a disability.' In terms of employment, the law defines a 'qualified individual with a disability' as a person with a disability who can perform the essential functions of the job with or without reasonable accommodation. (*Source: US Department of Labor*).

**Disability Discrimination Acts** Legislation enabled to deter discrimination against people on the grounds of disability.

**Discouraged worker hypothesis** More people would work if jobs were easy to find – but they do not search when work is scarce. Workers calculate the probability of finding a job in relation to the wage they are likely to get and conclude that the effort is not worthwhile.

**Discrimination** *See* 'Direct discrimination', 'Indirect discrimination'.

**Diversity** 'Diversity is the variation of social and cultural identities among people existing together in defined employment or marketing systems' (Cox, O'Neill and Quinn, 2001).

**Divisional structure** Organizational structure based on semi-autonomous units operating outside the centre.

**Division of labour** The sub-division of work so that specific tasks or jobs are allocated to individuals deemed most suitable on the basis of skill, experience or cultural tradition.

**Divisions** *see Divisional structure*

**Downsizing** Term used to describe sacking, dismissing or otherwise making redundant a substantial proportion of an organization's workforce.

**Economically active** Includes the employed – those in paid work – and the unemployed – those who are looking for paid work but are unable to find it.

**Economic turbulence** Cyclical and non-cyclical changes in the economy that cause periods of high or low demand for goods, services and employees.

**Education** Formal learning outside (and often before entering) the workplace.

**Employee analysis** Modern computer packages offer extensive possibilities for modelling the total profile of an organization's human resources. Employees can be classified in a variety of ways, such as function, department or grade.

**Employee demand** Need for staff.

**Employee engagement** Commitment and emotional involvement in a job or organization.

**Employee involvement** An umbrella term that is inconsistently and imprecisely used to embrace a diverse range of management processes involving participation, communication, decisionmaking, industrial democracy and employee motivation.

**Employee relations** Employee relations is an alternative label for 'industrial relations'. It is not confined to unionized collective bargaining but encompasses all employment relationships. It goes beyond the negotiation of pay and benefits to include the conduct of the power relationship between employee and employer.

**Employee resourcing** Resourcing is the process by which people are identified and allocated to perform necessary work. Resourcing has two strategic imperatives: first, minimizing employee costs and maximizing employee value to the organization; secondly, obtaining the correct behavioural mix of attitude and commitment in the workforce

**Employee self-service** Employees can view company information, change selected personal details, make benefit enquiries (pension plans, sick pay entitlement), book leave and apply for training

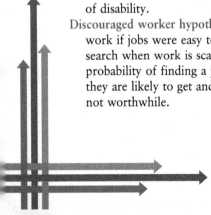

programmes through a company's HR portal or intranet. *See also* 'Manager self-service'.

**Employee supply** Available staff in the employment market.

**Employee turnover** Measurable incidence of people joining and leaving the organization.

**Employee voice** Opportunity for employees to communicate and contribute to organizational policy and decisionmaking.

**Employer branding** The practice of developing, differentiating and leveraging an organization's brand message to its current and future workforce in a manner meaningful to them. Using the methodology of corporate brand-building strategy to attract and keep quality employees. Employer branding is aimed at motivating and securing employees' alignment with the vision and the values of the company.

**Employment market** The employment market comprises all those people who are available for work. Neo-classical economics views this potential workforce as forming a labour market. The market is affected by national or regional supply and demand for appropriately skilled employees. It is constrained by demographic factors such as the number of young people leaving schools and universities and by cultural variables such as expectations for mothers to stay at home looking after children.

**Employment relationship** A formal and informal relationship between the employing organization and an employee. The informal element is sometimes referred to as the psychological contract – an undocumented understanding about the nature of employment within the organization. Regarded by neo-classical economists as an exchange of labour for pay, The employment relationship is also a power relationship in which the employer has the formal authority to direct effort towards specific goals, whereas the employee can – informally – frustrate the achievements of those objectives.

**Empowerment** Being in control of one's own destiny. Enabling someone to take decisions, think, behave and control work in one's own way.

**Entrepreneurship** A classic definition of entrepreneurship is provided by Timmons (1994, p.: 7): 'Entrepreneurship is the process of creating or seizing an opportunity and pursuing it regardless of the resources currently controlled.'

**Equal access** A situation where disadvantaged groups are not barred from entry into organizations but may be confined to lower levels of work.

**Equal chance** A situation where everyone has the same right, for example, to apply for a vacancy or be considered for promotion.

**Equal opportunity policy** A written statement of commitment to fair, non-discriminatory human resource management.

**Equal share** Access is free to any position within an organization and all groups are represented at all levels. May require a quota systems or 'Affirmative action' to achieve this situation.

**Equality** Fair and equitable. (*see Equal access, Equal chance*)

**Equality Act (UK)** Act of 2010 that replaces older legislation such as the Race Relations Act 1976 and the Disability Discrimination Act 1995.

**Ethnic discrimination** *See* 'Race discrimination'.

**Explicit** Open and obvious as opposed to implicit.

**Explicit knowledge** The obvious knowledge found in manuals, documentation, files and other accessible sources. *See also* 'Tacit knowledge'.

**Federation** A loosely-connected arrangement of businesses with a single holding company or separate firms in alliance.

**Flexibility** The concept covers a combination of practices which enable organizations to react quickly and cheaply to environmental changes. In essence, flexibility is demanded from the workforce in terms of pay, contractual rights, hours and conditions, and working practices. This extends to the employment market, requiring jobseekers to show a willingness to move location, change occupation and accept radically different terms of employment. *See also* 'Numerical flexibility', 'Functional flexibility', 'Flexible firm', 'Flexible pay', 'Flexible specialization'.

**Flexible firm** Atkinson's model combining flexibility with Japanese concepts of 'core' and 'peripheral' workforces.

**Flexible pay** Offering different rates of pay for the same work – depending on geographical location and skills availability.

**Flexible specialization** Allocation of time and labour according to consumer demand. Staff receive extra training and resources to widen their specialist skills.

**Fordism** Named after the mass production, assembly-line methods used by Henry Ford for automobile manufacturing.

**Functional** Related to a particular organizational or management function such as marketing, production or HR.

**Functional flexibility** Abolishing demarcation rules and skill barriers so that workers can take on a variety of jobs.

**Functional structure** Form of organization divided into relatively simple parts with defined areas of activity such as production, marketing or personnel.

**Gender** All human societies divide themselves into two social categories called 'female' and 'male' (this does not exclude other categories). Each category is defined on the basis of varying cultural assumptions

about the attributes, beliefs and behaviours expected from males and females. The gender of any individual depends on a complex combination of genetic, body, social, psychological and social elements, none of which is free from possible ambiguity or anomaly. Traditionally, sexual differences have been used to justify male-dominated societies in which women have been given inferior and secondary roles in their working lives.

Gender discrimination Many countries, including all members of the EU, have sex discrimination and equal pay legislation. However, informal psychological and organizational barriers continue to bar the progress of women. The processes of occupational segregation and sex-typing of jobs continue so that women tend to be concentrated at the base of most organizational hierarchies in jobs which are less prestigious and lower paid than those favoured by men.

Gender legislation In December 1975, South Australia became the first state in Australia to have sex discrimination laws.

Glass ceiling The term glass ceiling describes the process which bars women from promotion by means of an invisible barrier. This involves a number of factors, including attitudes of people in power and the inflexible processes and requirements geared to the cloning process which ensures that 'men of a certain type' will generally succeed. In the USA the term is also used to describe the barrier that prevents progress for other disadvantaged groups, for example ethnic minorities.

Globalization A systematic trend towards integration of production and marketing with brand-named goods and virtually identical 'badge-engineered' products such as cars being made available throughout the world. This process has been fostered by 'transnational' or 'multinational' companies operating in more than one country.

Goals In organizational terms these are personal or group objectives.

Graphology Handwriting analysis to identify features of personality – popular as a selection technique in continental Europe.

Hard HRM Storey (1989) distinguished between hard and soft forms of HRM, typified by the Michigan and Harvard models, respectively. 'Hard' HRM focuses on the resource side of human resources. It emphasizes costs in the form of 'headcounts' and places control firmly in the hands of management. Their role is to manage numbers effectively, keeping the workforce closely matched with requirements in terms of both bodies and behaviour. *See also* 'Soft HRM'.

Harvard model The Harvard Business School generated one of the most influential models of HRM.

The Harvard view provides a strategic map of HRM territory which guides all managers in their relations with employees. Beer *et al.* (1984) who devised this approach recognized an element of mutuality in all businesses – that employees are significant stakeholders in an organization.

Headhunting Recruitment method aimed at identifying star performers.

Hierarchy Pattern of responsibility and authority, usually represented by a tree-and-branch organization chart.

High performance work system 'A comprehensive customer-driven system that aligns all of the activities in an organization with the common focus of customer satisfaction through continuous improvement in the quality of goods and services.' (*Source: US Department of Labor*)

HR service centres One of the most widely-used solutions to re-engineered HR in large organizations. Such centres centralize a number of HR processes and may deal with geographically widespread users. Enquiries can be taken by a variety of means including phone, SMS text, or internet.

Human capital Economic growth creates employment, but economic growth partly depends on skilled human resources – a country's human capital. The concept encompasses investment in the skills of the labour force, including education and vocational training to develop specific skills.

Human relations A humanistic approach to management popularized by Elton Mayo and based on the Hawthorne experiments.

Human resource development (HRD) A strategic approach to investing in human capital. It draws on other human resource processes, including resourcing and performance assessment to identify actual and potential talent. HRD provides a framework for self-development, training programmes and career progression to meet an organization's future skill requirements.

Human resource flow Movement of people through an organization commencing with recruitment.

Human resource information systems (HRIS) 'The HRIS system is the primary transaction processor, editor, record-keeper, and functional application system which lies at the heart of all computerized HR work. It maintains employee, organizational and HR plan data sufficient to support most, if not all, of the HR functions depending on the modules installed' (Walker, 2001).

Human resource management A philosophy of people management based on the belief that human resources are uniquely important to sustained business success. An organization gains competitive advantage by using its people effectively, drawing on their expertise and ingenuity to meet clearly defined objectives. HRM is aimed at recruiting

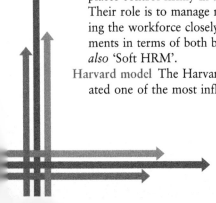

capable, flexible and committed people, managing and rewarding their performance and developing key competencies. *See also* 'Hard HRM', 'Soft HRM'.

**Human resource planning (HRP)** A process which anticipates and maps out the consequences of business strategy on an organization's human resource requirements. This is reflected in planning of skill and competence needs as well as total headcounts.

**Human resource strategy** Overall plan for staffing, developing and rewarding employees and outsourced human resources tied to business objectives.

**Image** The apparent totality of knowledge and abilities as outwardly presented by an individual or group. Can be false. See also 'Impression management'.

**Implicit knowledge** *See* 'Tacit knowledge'.

**Implicit theory** An internal or mental model of how and why a set of events or behaviours takes place. A belief system developed by individuals to explain part of their world or organization based on their own interpretations and experiences.

**Impression management** A deliberate process in which a personal image is learned or acquired through training. *See also* 'Image'.

**Indirect** The opposite of direct or obvious.

**Indirect discrimination** A less obvious form of discrimination than direct discrimination. This may take the form of applying certain conditions or requirements that are more easily satisfied by one group than another. One example would be to specify a fixed minimum height requirement for entry into a police force. This is a requirement that would be more easily met by male than female applicants. Another example would be a requirement for an unnecessarily high standard of spoken or written English which would favour people with a particular educational background. *See also* 'Direct discrimination'.

**Individualism** Opposite of collectivism. Preference to work individually rather than as part of a group.

**Induction** Initial orientation and training of a new recruit.

**Industrial democracy** Egalitarian notion of worker involvement in decisionmaking.

**Informal organization** An organization is both a formal and informal entity. The formal aspect of an organization is its official structure and public image visible in organization charts and annual reports. The informal organization is a more elusive concept, describing the complex network of psychological and social relationships between its people. The informal organization is an unrecognized world of cliques and politics, friendships and enmities, gossip and affairs.

**In-group** Favoured and usually long-standing members of a society, department or organization.

**Insecurity thesis** Heery and Salmon (2000) identify a connection between globalization and the 'insecurity thesis', a belief that: 'Employment in the developed economies has become more insecure or unstable in the sense that both continued employment and the level of remuneration have become less predictable and contingent on factors which lie beyond the employee's control.'

**Institutionalized racism** An indirect and largely invisible process which can be compared with cloning and the glass ceiling. It is a term encompassing the often unintentional barriers and selection/promotion procedures which serve to disadvantage members of ethnic minority groups.

**Japanization** A term that first came into vogue in the mid-1980s. It is used as a label for the attempts of Western firms to make practical use of 'Japanese' ideas and practices and as a description of the presence and impact of Japanese subsidiaries overseas.

**Job analysis** The process of job analysis is that of gathering and analysing job-related information. This includes details about tasks to be performed as part of a job and the personal qualities required to do so. Job analysis can provide information for a variety of purposes including: determining training needs, development criteria, appropriate pay and productivity improvements. For resourcing purposes, job analysis can generate job and personnel specifications.

**Job description** List of essential tasks involved in a particular job.

**Job market** *See* 'Employment market', 'Labour market'.

**Knowledge** 'Knowledge is a fluid mix of framed expertise, values, contextual information and expert insight that provides a framework for evaluating and incorporating new experiences and information. It originates from and is applied in the minds of knowers. In organizations it often becomes embedded not only in documents or repositories but also in organizational routines, processes, practices and norms.' (Davenport and Prusack, 2000).

**Knowledge management** 'Knowledge management caters to the critical issues of organizational adaption, survival and competence in face of increasingly discontinuous environmental change. … Essentially, it embodies organizational processes that seek synergistic combination of data and information processing capacity of information technologies, and the creative and innovative capacity of human beings.' (Malhotra, 1998)

**Labour market** The setting in which people who can provide labour meet those who need labour. Labour

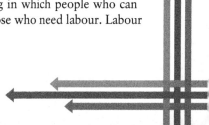

markets can be: internal, within an organization, or external, outside the organization. Labour market is a somewhat old-fashioned term which implies physical labour as opposed to the time, knowledge and intellectual effort required in many modern jobs. 'Job market' or 'employment market' are more meaningful in today's context. *See* 'Employment market'.

**Leadership** Giving direction and authority in decisionmaking and management.

**Learning** A process of acquiring skills and knowledge.

**Learning organization** Organization that 'lives and breathes' learning and knowledge acquisition.

**Management by objectives (MBO)** A technique to establish individual performance objectives which are tangible, measurable and verifiable. Individual objectives are derived or cascaded from organizational goals. Top managers agree their own specific objectives compatible with the organization's goals but restricted to their own areas of responsibility. Subordinates do the same at each lower level, forming an interlocked and coherent hierarchy of performance targets.

**Manager self-service** Managers have direct access to 'front-end' applications in the human resource information system. Typically, they are able to view a range of personal details and aggregate information. They are also allowed to change and input certain details and model the consequences on their budgets of salary increases or bonus payments. *See also* 'Employee self-service'.

**Managing diversity** The management of diversity goes beyond equal opportunity and embodies the belief that people should be valued for their differences and variety. Diversity is perceived to enrich an organization's human capital. Whereas equal opportunity focuses on various disadvantaged groups, the management of diversity is about individuals.

**Manpower planning** (obsolete) 'A strategy for the acquisition, utilization, improvement and retention of an enterprise's human resources' (anonymous government publication cited in Pratt and Bennett (1989, p.: 101). *See also* 'Human resource planning'.

**Matching model** *See* 'Michigan model'.

**Matrix structures** Organizational structures focused on project teams, bringing skilled individuals together from different parts of the organization. Individuals are responsible to their line manager and to the project manager for different aspects of their jobs.

**Mentoring** Individual–individual support in an organization providing guidance on career development, learning and performance.

**Meritocracy** Meritocratic procedures aim to make judgements on the basis of evidence of competence

such as examination results or the achievement of targets.

**Meta-analysis** Statistical technique in which results from a large number of (comparatively) small studies are combined.

**Michigan** Significant in HRM for the matching model developed by its business school.

**Michigan model of HRM** The Michigan model is strongly influenced by strategic management literature. HRM is seen as a strategic process, making the most effective use of an organization's human resources. Hence there must be coherent human resource policies that 'fit' closely with overall business strategies.

**Minimum wage** Lowest allowable level of pay within a state or country.

**Mission statement** A mission statement should convey the essence of what an organization is about: why it exists, what kind of business it intends to be, and who its intended customers are. The mission is translated into objectives or goals within the strategic management process.

**Numerical flexibility** Matching employee numbers to fluctuating production levels or service requirements.

**Occupational segregation** Disproportionate representation of particular groups in specific sectors, job-types or levels of responsibility. Horizontal segregation places men and women, for example, in different jobs, such as chambermaids (women) and porters (men). Vertical segregation places one group in better-paid positions than another group, so that men are better represented at managerial levels while women are concentrated in lower, administrative jobs.

**Offshoring** Transfer of work and/or employment to another country, typically where employment costs and benefits are lower.

**Option scheme** Right to buy shares in an employing organization, often at a favourable price.

**Organization** The means by which human and other resources are deployed so that work gets done.

**Organizational design** The design of an organization patterns its formal structure and culture. It allocates purpose and power to departments and individuals. It lays down guidelines for authoritarian or participative management by its rigidity or flexibility, its hierarchical or non-hierarchical structure.

**Organizational development (OD)** Methodology of change characterized by an ongoing series of relatively small improvements.

**Organizational goals** The logical starting point for human resource management lies in an organization's goals – the reasons for its existence. Most modern businesses express these goals in the form

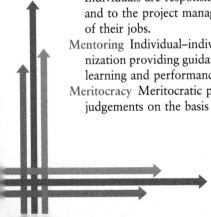

of a mission statement. The allocation and control of human resources serves to assist or constrain the achievement of these objectives.

Organizations The means by which human and other resources are deployed so that work gets done. They are social entities with purposes expressed in the form of common goals and boundaries between themselves and the rest of the world.

Outsourcing Contracting work or an operational function to an external provider.

Particularism A form of discrimination favouring particular groups and individuals over others. It derives from a reliance on personal relationships such as ethnic origin, religion or tribal community. It contrasts with universalism in which personal relationships are ignored and emphasis is on other criteria such as qualifications, expertise and ability to do the job.

Performance A critical element in HRM, the management of which can lead to enhanced competitiveness.

Performance assessment One of the many people management techniques which 'classify and order individuals hierarchically' (Townley, 1994, p.33). Modern assessment is often focused on competences. *See also* 'Appraisals'.

Performance management 'A strategic and integrated approach to increasing the effectiveness of organizations by improving the performance of the people who work in them and by developing the capabilities of teams and individual contributors.' (Armstrong and Baron, 1998)

Performance-related pay (PRP) Pay based on merit as assessed by a performance management process.

Peripheral workforces Secondary or less crucial workers as opposed to core employees.

Personality Generally expressed in terms of types or traits, the latter form the basis of most personality tests used for resourcing and the documentation employed for many performance appraisal systems. An alternative approach is to regard personality as an artefact of a particular set of circumstances. In other words, apparent personality depends on the meaning individuals give to a particular situation.

Personnel specification 'The demands of the job translated into human terms' (Arnold, Robertson and Cooper, 1991, p.: 95). Personnel specifications list 'essential' criteria which must be satisfied, and other criteria which rule out certain people from being able to do the job.

Person perception The perception and evaluation of other people using cues such as facial expression, posture, gesture, tone of voice, etc.

Pluralism The acceptance of several alternative approaches, interests or goals within the same organization or society. A view which recognizes that every organization is composed of different interests which are not balanced. Pluralists accept that conflict is natural and are concerned with the means by which it can be managed.

Positive action Measures to prevent discrimination by insisting, for example, on non-discriminatory recruitment procedures, training programmes and pay rates. This does not include any preferential treatment for disadvantaged groups.

Positive discrimination *See* 'Affirmative action'.

Power distance The perceived status differences between people with high and low degrees of power.

Productivity The amount of output (what is produced) per unit of input used. Labour is one input amongst many. Total productivity is dependent upon a variety of diverse and hard to measure inputs. One simple measure of productivity is the Gross Domestic Product (GDP) per person-hour worked. But it is also a simplistic measure of productivity because it neglects a number of factors such as capital investment.

Psychological contract An informal understanding between the employer and employee. Unlike the formal employment contract, this has no physical existence. It is a set of expectations held by both employers and employees in terms of what they wish to give and receive from their working relationship (Rousseau and Parks, 1993).

Psychometric model The dominant approach to selection in British and US textbooks. In its traditional form, it grounds the 'best-person' model in psychological theory and testing. It embodies the use of refined techniques to achieve the best 'match' between job characteristics identified by formal job analysis and individual characteristics measured by psychological tests, structured interviews and other assessment methods.

Race discrimination Unfavourable treatment on the grounds of race or ethnic origin.

Recruitment Attracting candidates prior to selection.

Reorganization A move from one form of organization to another. For example, a business may change from a divisional to a network structure.

Resourcing *See* 'Employee resourcing'.

Restructuring Breaking up and recombining organizational structures in order to reduce costs, eliminate duplication and achieve greater efficiency.

Retrenchment Downsizing or reducing number of staff on payroll.

Reward management Management of pay, benefits and other forms of compensation.

Rewards Pay, incentives, bonuses and other means of compensating individuals for the effort and time they devote to work.

Scientific management F.W. Taylor devised 'scientific management' as a systematic but controversial programme based on rudimentary time and motion

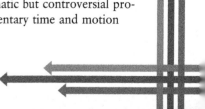

studies, selection of 'first-class men' for the job and premium pay for a 'fair day's work'.

**Selection** A key element of employee resourcing in which successful applicants are evaluated and chosen by means of interviews and tests.

**Sexual discrimination** See 'Gender discrimination'.

**Sexual harassment** Definitions vary considerably but most are agreed that it is sexual attention which is unwanted, repeated, and affects an employee's work performance or expectations from her/his job. However, it is possible for one incident to be sufficiently severe to be regarded as harassment. It differs from sexual banter or flirting since it is one-way; it does not have the involvement and acceptance of both parties. In the USA, the Equal Employment Opportunity Commission has extended the definition of sexual harassment to include a range of actions which lead to a 'hostile work environment'. This definition includes unwelcome touching, joking, teasing, innuendos, slurs, and the display of sexually explicit materials.

**Social dumping** The concept of social dumping describes the practice of switching production from countries with relatively high employee costs to those with cheap labour. It is an accusation made against large multinational corporations. Social dumping has led to long-term structural changes including the closure of older heavy manufacturing industries such as steel and shipbuilding in established industrial countries.

**Social market** A term coined by Alfred Müller-Armack, Secretary of State at the Economics Ministry in Bonn, Federal Republic of Germany between 1958 and 1963. He defined the social market as an economic system that combined market freedom with social equilibrium. In this kind of economic system the government plays a regulating role and creates the framework for market processes, going beyond securing competition to ensure social equity.

**Social protection** According to the World Bank, social protection measures improve or protect human capital, ranging from labour market interventions, unemployment or old-age insurance, to income support, for individuals, households, and communities.

**Soft HRM** Storey (1989) distinguished between hard and soft forms of HRM, typified by the Michigan and Harvard models, respectively. 'Soft' HRM stresses the 'human' aspects of HRM. Its concerns are with communication and motivation. People are led rather than managed. They are involved in determining and realizing strategic objectives.

**Soft planning** Human resource planning based on factors other than numbers of employees.

**Specialization** The division of work between individuals or departments, allocating responsibilities for specific activities or functions to people who can achieve a high standard of work in a relatively narrow range of activities. They may require specific training or expertise. For example, HR managers are concerned with organization of the HR function and resourcing of all other functions.

**Stakeholders** Recognizably separate groups or institutions with a special interest in an organization. These include shareholders, employees, managers, customers, suppliers, lenders and government. Each group has its own priorities and demands and fits into the power structure controlling the organization.

**Strategic choice** Decisionmaking on the basis of meeting strategic requirements.

**Strategic HRM** Directing people, processes and HR systems to achieve strategic objectives so that individual goals are tied to the business needs of the whole organization.

**Strategy** A strategy is the means by which an organization seeks to meet its objectives. It is a deliberate choice, a decision to take a course of action rather than reacting to circumstances. It focuses on significant, long-term goals rather than day-to-day operating matters.

**Substance** The body of competences, knowledge and experience required to fulfil a particular function.

**Synergy** Making the new whole worth more than its old parts, sometimes described as 2 + 2 = 5. Synergies involve economies from integrating activities, horizontally or vertically; but also unrealized potential for new ideas, products or processes by melding expertise from the different sources into centres of excellence.

**Tacit or implicit knowledge** This is found in the heads of an organization's employees. Difficult to access and use – for obvious reasons. Typically, an organization does not even know what this knowledge is. Worse, the knee-jerk reaction of top managers who fire employees at the first sign of any downturn means that the knowledge is often lost.

**Talent management** A strategic and integrated approach to developing a skilled and competent workforce, involving targeted recruitment, development and retention.

**Targeting** Quotas for the employment of particular groups have been enforced in the USA. In Europe quota systems have been applied to the disabled and, in a few countries, other groups such as ex-servicemen but enforcement was not usually strict. See also 'Affirmative action'.

**Taylorism** An approach to management based on the theories of F.W. Taylor. See also 'Scientific management'.

**Tokenism** The employment or promotion of isolated individuals to represent their gender or colour. For example, a 12-member board of directors with

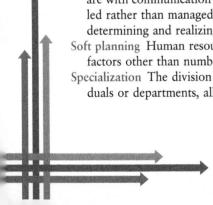

one token woman and one token ethnic minority person.

**Total quality management (TQM)** A methodology focused on continuous improvement, quality assurance and zero faults. TQM programmes are geared to organizational processes such as production. HR involvement includes the selection of flexible people who are amenable to increasingly demanding levels of quality.

**Turnover** *See* 'Employee turnover'.

**Uncertainty avoidance** How people deal with conflict, particularly aggression and the expression of feelings. High uncertainty avoidance favours precise rules, teachers who are always right and superiors who should be obeyed without question. Low uncertainty avoidance favours flexibility, discussion and delegation of decisionmaking.

**Unitarism** A managerialist stance which assumes that everyone in an organization is a member of a team with a common purpose. The unitarist view is implicit in American models of HRM. It embodies a central concern of HRM, that an organization's people, whether managers or lower-level employees, should share the same objectives and work together harmoniously. From this perspective, conflicting objectives are seen as negative and dysfunctional.

**Values** Values are at the heart of corporate culture. They are made up of the key beliefs and concepts shared by an organization's employees. Successful companies are clear about these values and their managers publicly reinforce them. Often values are unwritten and operate at a subconscious level.

**Virtual organizations** Advancing technology allows firms to extend the network concept to form enterprises with no permanent structures. They bring people together for specific projects. Teams dissolve on completion, to reappear in new combinations for other tasks.

**Work ethic** The belief that work is virtuous in itself. Hard work is to be admired and leisure is equated with laziness. In some societies the work ethic became a fundamental religious principle, the Puritans and Calvinists holding it to be such a virtue that Max Weber termed it the protestant work ethic. The concept is sometimes extended to include the virtue of frugality as against waste. It justifies regarding the poor as sinful, since success and ambition are virtuous and wealth is a sign of God's favour.

**World view** A set of values and beliefs held by members of a particular culture. This is meaningful to its members but alien to others.

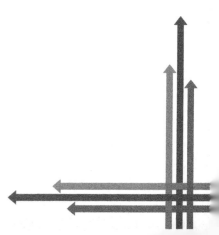

# REFERENCES

Agrawal, R.K. and Sadhana, J. (2010) 'Emotional labour and employee engagement in call centres: a study in Indian context', *International Journal of Work Organisation and Emotion* 3(4) (21 September): 351–67.

Alavi, M.T. and Karami, A. (2009) 'Managers of small and medium enterprises: mission statement and enhanced organisational performance', *The Journal of Management Development* 28(6): 555–62.

Albrecht, S. (2010) 'Understanding employee cynicism toward change in healthcare contexts', *International Journal of Information Systems and Change Management* 4(3) (7 May): 194–09.

Alonderiene, R. (2010) 'Enhancing informal learning to improve job satisfaction: Perspective of SMEs managers in Lithuania', *Baltic Journal of Management* 5(2): 257–87.

Al–Raisi, A., Amin, S. and Tahir, S. (2010) 'Determinants of performance management system in UAE public sector', *International Journal of Trade and Global Markets* 3(3) (26 August): 267–79.

Anaby, D. Jarus, T., Backman, C. and Zumbo, B. (2010) 'The Role of Occupational Characteristics and Occupational Imbalance in Explaining Well–being', *Applied Research in Quality of Life* 5(2) (June): 81–104.

Anderson, D. and Kelliher, C. (2009) 'Flexible working and engagement: the importance of choice', *Strategic HR Review* 8(2): 13–18.

Anderson, N. and Witvliet, C. (2008) 'Fairness Reactions to Personnel Selection Methods: An international comparison between the Netherlands, the United States, France, Spain, Portugal, and Singapore', *International Journal of Selection and Assessment* 16(1) (March): 1–13.

Anderson, N., Salgado, J. F, and Hülsheger, U.R. (2010) 'Applicant Reactions in Selection: Comprehensive meta–analysis into reaction generalization versus situational specificity', *International Journal of Selection and Assessment* 18(3) (September): 291–304.

Anon (2010) 'Clinton Cards Group turns jobs into careers: Retailer launches nationally accredited training program', *Human Resource Management International Digest* 18(4): 24–6.

Arasli, H. and Tumer, M. (2010) 'Nepotism, Favoritism and Cronyism: a study of their effects on job stress and job satisfaction in the banking industry of North Cyprus', Social *Behavior and Personality: an international journal* 36(9): 1237–1250.

Ardichvili, A. and Kuchinke, K.P. (2009) 'International Perspectives on the Meaning of Work and Working: Current Research and Theory', *Advances in Developing Human Resources*, 11, (2): 155–67.

Arrowsmith, J. and Marginson, P. (2010) 'The decline of incentive pay in British manufacturing', *Industrial Relations Journal* 41(4): 289–311.

Atkinson, C. and Hall, Laura (2009) 'The Role of Gender in Varying Forms of Flexible Working', *Gender, Work and Organization* 16(6): 650–666.

Autor, D.H. and Houseman, S.N. (2010) 'Do Temporary–Help Jobs Improve Labor Market Outcomes for Low–Skilled Workers? Evidence from "Work First"', *American Economic Journal: Applied Economics* 2(3): 96–128.

Bach, S. (2005) *Managing Human Resources: Personnel Management in Transition*, Wiley–Blackwell.

Bacha, E. (2010) 'The relationships among organizational performance, environmental uncertainty, and employees' perceptions of CEO charisma', *The Journal of Management Development* 29(1): 28–37.

Bacon, N., Blyton, P. and Dastmalchian, A. (2010) 'The impact of organizational change on steelworkers in craft and production occupational groups' *Human Relations*, Aug, 63: 1223–48.

Balsam, S., Gifford, R. and Kim, S. (2007) 'The effect of stock option grants on voluntary employee turnover', *Review of Accounting and Finance* 6(1): 5–14.

Ban, C. (2010) 'Reforming the staffing process in the European Union institutions: moving the sacred cow out of the road', *International Review of Administrative Sciences*, Mar 2010; 76: 5–24.

Bangerter, A., König, C.J., Blatti, S. and Salvisberg, A. (2009) 'How Widespread is Graphology in Personnel Selection Practice? A case study of a job market myth', *International Journal of Selection and Assessment* 17(2): 219–230(12).

Baumol, W.J., Blinder, A.S. and Wolff, E.N. (2003) *Downsizing in America: Reality, Causes, and Consequences*, Russell Sage Foundation.

Beachler, D.W. (2009) 'Victory and the Promise of Reform: Labor and the 2008 Election', *Working USA* 12(2): 265–77.

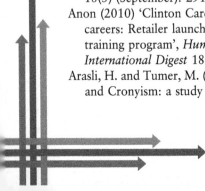

Bendl, R. and Schmidt, A. (2010) 'From 'Glass Ceilings' to 'Firewalls' – Different Metaphors for Describing Discrimination', *Gender, Work and Organization* 17(5): 612–34.

Bennett, A. (2010) 'Employee voice initiatives in the public sector: views from the workplace', *International Journal of Public Sector Management* 23(5): 444–55.

Birdi, K., Clegg, C., Patterson, M., Robinson, A., Stride, C.B., Wall, T.D., and Wood, S.J. (2008) 'The Impact of Human Resource and Operational Management Practices on Company Productivity: A Longitudinal Study', *Personnel Psychology*, 61: 467–501.

Blake–Beard, S., O'Neill, R., Ingols, C., Shapiro, M. (2010) 'Social sustainability, flexible work arrangements, and diverse women', *Gender in Management: An International Journal* 25(5): 408–25.

Blickle, G., Schneider, P.B., Meurs, J.A.. and Perrewé, P.L. (2010) 'Antecedents and Consequences of Perceived Barriers to Obtaining Mentoring: A Longitudinal Investigation', *Journal of Applied Social Psychology* 40(8): 1897–920.

Bloom, N. and Van Reenen, J. (2010) 'New Approaches to Measuring Management and Firm Organization', February 2010, Paper No. CEPDP0969, CEP Discussion Papers, London School of Economics.

Bourne, A. and Haddon, D. (2010) 'An evidence–based approach to developing HR strategy: transformation in Royal Mail', *Strategic HR Review* 9(1): 10–16.

Boxall, P. and Purcell, J. (2003) *Strategy and Human Resource Management*, Palgrave Macmillan.

Boxall, P. and Macky, K. (2009) 'Research and theory on high–performance work systems: progressing the high–involvement stream', *Human Resource Management Journal* 19(1): 3–23.

Bradley, R.T. (2010) 'Passionate attention and the psychophysiology of entrepreneurial intuition: a quantum–holographic theory', *International Journal of Entrepreneurship and Small Business* 9(3): 324–348.

Branine, M. (2008) 'Graduate recruitment and selection in the UK: A study of the recent changes in methods and expectations', *Career Development International* 13(6): 497–513.

Bray, M. and Underhill, E. (2009) 'Industry differences in the neoliberal transformation of Australian industrial relations', *Industrial Relations Journal* 40(5): 372–92.

Bret B.J., Matthews, M.C., Hartley, D.L., and Whitaker, D.H. (2009) 'Using Biodata to Predict Turnover, Organizational Commitment, and Job Performance in Healthcare', *International Journal of Selection and Assessment* 17(2): 189–202.

Brewster, C., Croucher, R., Wood, G. and Brookes, M. (2007) 'Collective and individual voice: convergence in Europe?' (2007) *International Journal of Human Resource Management* 18(7): 1246–62.

Brown, M., Hyatt, D. and Benson, J. (2010) 'Consequences of the performance appraisal experience', *Personnel Review* 39(3): 375–96.

Brown, M., Metz, I., Cregan,C. and Kulik, C.T. (2009) 'Irreconcilable differences? Strategic human resource management and employee well-being', *Asia Pacific Journal of Human Resources*, Dec 2009; 47: 270–294.

Busolt, U. and Kugele, K. (2009) 'The gender innovation and research productivity gap in Europe', *International Journal of Innovation and Sustainable Development* 4, (2–3): 109–122.

Byrne, B. (2009) 'Not just class: towards an understanding of the whiteness of middle–class schooling choice', *Ethnic and Racial Studies* 32(3): 424–441.

Calabrese, F.A. (2010) 'Evolution of twenty–first century knowledge workers', *On The Horizon–The Strategic Planning Resource for Education Professionals* 18(3): 160–170.

Carter, J.L and Hill, G.J E. (2007) 'Critiquing environmental management in indigenous Australia: two case studies', *Area* 39(1): 43–54.

Chakkarath, P. (2010) 'Stereotypes in social psychology: The "West–East" differentiation as a reflection of western traditions of thought', *Psychological Studies* 55(1): 18–25.

Chakravarthy, B. (2010) 'The sharing imperative', *Strategy and Leadership* 38(1): 37–41.

Chatterjee, S. (2007) 'Why is synergy so difficult in mergers of related businesses? *Strategy and Leadership* 35(2): 46–52.

Coffey, M., Dugdill, L. and Tattersall, A. (2009) 'Working in the Public Sector: A Case Study of Social Services', *Journal of Social Work*, Oct 2009; 9: 420–42.

Cohen, M. (2008) 'Union Ethics Training: Building the Legitimacy and Effectiveness of Organized Labor', *WorkingUSA* 11(3): 363–82.

Combs, J., Liu, Y., Hall, A. and Ketchen, D. (2006) 'How much do high–performance work practices matter? A meta–analysis of their effects on organizational performance' *Personnel Psychology*, 59: 501–28.

Conboy, H., Brine, A. and Clarke, J. (2010) 'Emerging technologies as change agent within and across organisational cultures', Source: *International Journal of Web Based Communities* 6(3): 269–83.

Conrad, H. (2010) 'From Seniority to Performance Principle: The Evolution of Pay Practices in Japanese Firms since the 1990s', *Social Science Japan Journal* 2010; 13: 115–35.

Conway, E. and Monks, K. (2010) 'The devolution of HRM to middle managers in the Irish health service', *Personnel Review* 39(3): 361–74.

Cooper, R. and Ellem, B. (2008) 'The Neoliberal State, Trade Unions and Collective Bargaining in Australia', *British Journal of Industrial Relations* 46(3): 532–54.

Costas, J. and Fleming, P. (2009) 'Beyond dis–identification: A discursive approach to self–alienation in contemporary organizations', *Human Relations*, 62; 353.

Craig, E. and Silverstone, Y. (2010) 'Tapping the power of collective engagement', *Strategic HR Review* 9(3): 5–10.

Dahl, M.S. and Sorenson, O. (2009) 'The embedded entrepreneur', *European Management Review* 6(3): 172–81.

Damaske, S. (2009) 'Brown Suits Need Not Apply: The Intersection of Race, Gender, and Class in Institutional Network Building', *Sociological Forum* 24(2): 402–24.

Dayan, K., Fox, S., and Kasten, R. (2008) 'The Preliminary Employment Interview as a Predictor of Assessment Center Outcomes', *International Journal of Selection and Assessment* 16(2): 102–111.

Deakin, S. and Koukiadaki, A. (2009) 'Governance Processes, Labour Management Partnership and Employee Voice in the Construction of Heathrow Terminal 5', *Industrial Law Journal* 38(4): 365–89.

de Meijer, L.A.L., Born, M., van Zielst, J., and van der Molen, H.T. (2007) 'Analyzing Judgments of Ethnically Diverse Applicants During Personnel Selection: A study at the Dutch police', *International Journal of Selection and Assessment* 15(2): 139–52.

Dierendonck, D. van, Haynes, C., Borrill, C. and Stride, C. (2007) 'Effects of upward feedback on leadership behaviour toward subordinates', *The Journal of Management Development* 26(3): 228–38.

Dipboye, R.L. (2007) 'Eight outrageous statements about HR science', *Human Resource Management Review* 17: 96–106.

DiPrete, T.A., Eirich, G. and Pittinsky, M. (2010) "Compensation Benchmarking, Leapfrogs, and the Surge in Executive Pay." *American Journal of Sociology* (May).

Drydakis, N. and Vlassis, M. (2010) 'Ethnic Discrimination in the Greek Labour Market: occupational access, insurance coverage and age offers', *The Manchester School* 78(3): 201–18.

Ebbinghaus B. (2003) 'Ever larger unions: organisational restructuring and its impact on union confederations', *Industrial Relations Journal* 34(5): 446–60.

Edgell, S. (2006) *The sociology of work: continuity and change in paid and unpaid work*, Pine Forge Press.

Edwards, M.R. (2010) 'An integrative review of employer branding and OB theory', *Personnel Review* 39(1): 5–23.

Ehnert, I. (2009) *Sustainable Human resource Management: a Conceptual and Exploratory Analysis From a Paradox Perspective*, Physica–Verlag.

Eleftheriou, A. and Robertson, I. (1999) 'A Survey of Management Selection Practices in Greece', *International Journal of Selection and Assessment* 7(4): 203–208.

El–Kot, G. and Leat, M. (2008) 'A survey of recruitment and selection practices in Egypt', *Education, Business and Society: Contemporary Middle Eastern Issues* 1(3): 200–12.

Fairris, D. and Askenazy, P. (2010) 'Works Councils and Firm Productivity in France', *Journal of Labor Research* 31(3): 209–29.

Fang, A. (2009) 'Workplace responses to vacancies and skill shortages in Canada', *International Journal of Manpower* 30(4): 326–48.

Ficery, K., Herd, T., and Pursche, W. (2007) 'Where has all the synergy gone? The M&A puzzle', *Journal of Business Strategy* 28(5): 29–35.

Fleming, P. (2009) *Authenticity and the cultural politics of work: new forms of informal control*, Oxford University Press.

Flesher, J. (2009) 'The Meaning of Working: A Perspective From Practice', *Advances in Developing Human Resources* 11(2): 253–60.

Fontanin, M. (2010) 'E–learning contribution to the building of a multi–generational workplace learning community in an academic library: observations drawn from practice', *Library Hi Tech News incorporating Online and CD Notes* 27(2): 15–19.

Flynn, M. (2010) 'Mandatory retirement in the police service: the case of the London MPS', *Policing: An International Journal of Police Strategies and Management* 33(2): 376–391.

Fofack, H. (2009) 'Determinants Of Globalization And Growth Prospects For Sub–Saharan African Countries', *Research Working papers*, World Bank, November: 1–34.

Forstenlechner, I. and Al–Waqfi, M.A. (2010) 'A job interview for Mo, but none for Mohammed: Religious discrimination against immigrants in Austria and Germany', *Personnel Review* 39(6): 767–84.

Foster, C., Punjaisri, K. and Cheng, R. (2010) 'Exploring the relationship between corporate, internal and employer branding', *Journal of Product and Brand Management* 19(6): 401–409.

Freidank, C–C, Velte, P. and Weber, S. (2010) 'The changing German corporate governance system–normative implications and empirical evidence', *International Journal of Corporate Governance* 2(1): 42–57.

Fulmer, R., Stumpf, S.A. and Bleak, J. (2009) 'The strategic development of high potential leaders', *Strategy and Leadership* 37(3): 17–22.

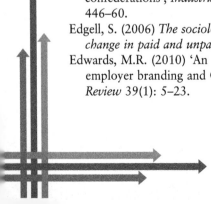

Furnham, A. (2008) 'HR Professionals' Beliefs About, and Knowledge of, Assessment Techniques and Psychometric Tests', *International Journal of Selection and Assessment* 16(3): 300–305.

Gall, G. (2007) 'Turning full circle? Changing industrial relations in the magazine industry in Britain', *Personnel Review* 36(1): 91–108.

Gates, S., and Langevin, P. (2010) 'Human capital measures, strategy, and performance: HR managers' perceptions', *Accounting, Auditing & Accountability Journal* 23(1): 111–132.

Gebauer, H., Edvardsson, B. and Bjurko, M. (2010) 'The impact of service orientation in corporate culture on business performance in manufacturing companies', *Journal of Service Management* 21(2): 237–259.

Georgiadis, A. and Pitelis, C.N. (2010) 'The Interrelationship between HR, Strategy and Profitability in Service SMEs: Empirical Evidence from the UK Tourism Hospitality and Leisure Sector', March, Paper No.' CEPDP0972, CEP Discussion Papers, London School of Economics.

Giangreco, A., Sebastiano, A. and Peccei, R. (2009) 'Trainees' reactions to training: an analysis of the factors affecting overall satisfaction with training', *International Journal of Human Resource Management* 20(1): 96–111.

Godard, J. (2010) "What Is Best for Workers? The Implications of Workplace and Human Resource Management Practices Revisited" *Industrial Relations* 49(3): 466–88.

Golden, A.G. (2009) 'Employee families and organizations as mutually enacted environments: A sensemaking approach to work–life interrelationships.', *Management Communication Quarterly*, 22: 357–84.

Glucksmann, M.A. (2009) 'Formations, Connections and Divisions of Labour', *Sociology*, October, 43: 878–95.

Good, K. and Taylor, I. (2008) 'Botswana: A Minimalist Democracy', *Democratization* 15(4): 750–65.

Gospel, H. and Sako, M. (2010) 'The unbundling of corporate functions: the evolution of shared services and outsourcing in human resource management', *Ind. Corp. Change*, Mar 2010; 10.1093/icc/dtq002.

Green, C. and Heywood, J.S. (2008) 'Does Performance Pay Increase Job Satisfaction?', *Economica* 75(300): 710–28.

Gregg, P. and Wadsworth, J. (2010) *The UK Labour Market and the 2008–2009 Recession*, June 2010, Paper No. CEPOP25: CEP Occasional Papers, London School of Economics.

Guthrie, J.; Flood, P., Liu, W., and MacCurtain, S. (2009) 'High performance work systems in Ireland: human resource and organizational outcomes', *International Journal of Human Resource Management* 20(1): 112–25.

Hallier, J. (2009) 'Rhetoric but whose reality? The influence of employability messages on employee mobility tactics and work group identification', *International Journal of Human Resource Management* 20(4): 846–68.

Harness, T. (2009) 'Research methods for the empirical study of strategic human resource management', *Qualitative Market Research: An International Journal* 12(3): 321–36.

Hatcher, T. (2006) 'An Examination of the Potential of Human Resource Development (HRD) to Improve Organizational Ethics' in *Human Resource Management Ethics*, ed. John R. Deckop, IAP.

Hauscknecht, J.P. (2010) 'Candidate Persistence and Personality Test Practice Effects: Implications for Staffing System Management', *Personnel Psychology* 63(2, Summer): 299–24.

Helpman, E., Itskhoki, O. and Redding, S. (2009) *Inequality and Unemployment in a Global Economy*, July, Paper No. CEPDP0940: CEP Discussion Papers, London School of Economics.

Hermelin, E., Lievens, F., and Robertson, I.T. (2007) 'The Validity of Assessment Centres for the Prediction of Supervisory Performance Ratings: A meta–analysis', International Journal of Selection and Assessment 15(4): 405–11.

Hess, N. and Jepsen, D.M. (2009) 'Career stage and generational differences in psychological contracts', *Career Development International* 14(3): 261–83.

Highhouse, S. (2010) 'Stubborn Reliance on Intuition and Subjectivity in Employee Selection', *Industrial and Organizational Psychology* 1(3): 333–42.

Hills, P. (2009) 'Costs down, talent up', *Strategic HR Review* 8(4): 29–33.

Hirota, S., Kubo, K., Miyajima, H., Hong, P., and Park, Y.W. (2010) 'Corporate mission, corporate policies and business outcomes: evidence from Japan', *Management Decision* 48(7): 1134–53.

Holbeche, L. (2005) *The High Performance Organization: Creating Dynamic Stability and Sustainable Success*, Butterworth–Heinemann.

Hollenbeck, G.P. (2009) 'Executive Selection—What's Right … and What's Wrong', *Industrial and Organizational Psychology* 2(2): 130–43.

Hornung, S., Rousseau, D.M. and Glaser, J. (2009) 'Why supervisors make idiosyncratic deals: antecedents and outcomes of i–deals from a managerial perspective', *Journal of Managerial Psychology* 24(8): 738–64.

ILO (2010) *Global Employment Trends Report 2010*, International Labour Organization.

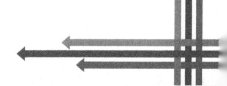

Ingenhoff, D. and Fuhrer, T. (2010) 'Positioning and differentiation by using brand personality attributes: Do mission and vision statements contribute to building a unique corporate identity?' Source: *Corporate Communications: An International Journal* 15(1): 83–101.

Jackson, S.E., Schuler, R.S. and Werner, S. (2008) *Managing Human Resources*, Cengage Learning.

Jones, D.C., Kalmi, P. and Kauhanen, A. (2010) 'How Does Employee Involvement Stack Up? The Effects of Human Resource Management Policies on Performance in a Retail Firm', *Industrial Relations* 49(1): 1–21.

Judge, T.A. (2009) 'Core Self–Evaluations and Work Success', Source: *Current Directions in Psychological Science* 18(1): 58–62.

Kagaari, J.R.K., Munene, J.C. and Ntayi, J.M. (2010) 'Performance management practices, information and communication technology (ICT) adoption and managed performance', *Quality Assurance in Education* 18(2): 106–125.

Kalra, V.S., Abel, P. and Esmail, A. (2009) 'Developing leadership interventions for Black and minority ethnic staff: A case study of the National Health Service (NHS) in the UK', *Journal of Health, Organisation and Management* 23(1): 103–118.

Kaplanis, I. (2010) *Local Human Capital and Its Impact on Local Employment Chances in Britain*, January, Paper No. SERCDP0040: CEP Discussion Papers, London School of Economics.

Kariv, D. (2010) 'The role of management strategies in business performance: men and women entrepreneurs managing creativity and innovation', *International Journal of Entrepreneurship and Small Business* 9(3): 243–263.

Keizer, A. B. (2008) 'Non–regular employment in Japan: continued and renewed dualities', *Work Employment Society*, Sep, 22: 407–25.

Kilburn, B. and Cates, T. (2010) 'Leader behavior: gatekeeper to voluntary upward feedback', *Management Research Review* 33(9): 900–910.

Kirkwood, A. (2009) 'E-learning: you don't always get what you hope for', *Technology, Pedagogy and Education* 18(2): 107–121.

Kirkwood, J. (2009) 'To grow or not? Growing small service firms', *Journal of Small Business and Enterprise Development* 16(3): 485–503.

König, C.J., Melchers, K.G., Kleinmann, M., Richter, G.M., and Klehe, U. (2007) 'Candidates' Ability to Identify Criteria in Nontransparent Selection Procedures: Evidence from an assessment center and a structured interview', International *Journal of Selection and Assessment* 15(3): 283–92.

Koritsas, S., Coles, J. and Boyle, M. (2010) 'Workplace Violence towards Social Workers: The Australian Experience', *British Journal of Social Work* 40(1): 257–71.

Krause, D.E., Kersting, M., Heggestad, E.D., Thornton, and George C. (2006) 'Incremental Validity of Assessment Center Ratings Over Cognitive Ability Tests: A Study at the Executive Management Level ', *International Journal of Selection and Assessment* 14(4): 360–371.

Krings, F. and Olivares, J. (2007) 'At the doorstep to employment: Discrimination against immigrants as a function of applicant ethnicity, job type, and raters' prejudice', *International Journal of Psychology* 42(6): 406–417.

Kuchinke, K.P. (2009) 'Changing Meanings of Work in Germany, Korea, and the United States in Historical Perspectives', *Advances in Developing Human Resources* 11(2): 168–88.

Kumra, S. and Vinnicombe, S. (2010) 'Impressing for Success: A Gendered Analysis of a Key Social Capital Accumulation Strategy', *Gender, Work and Organization* 17(5):521–46.

Levashina, J., Morgeson, F.P., and Campion, M.A. (2009) 'They Don't Do It Often, But They Do It Well: Exploring the relationship between applicant mental abilities and faking', *International Journal of Selection and Assessment* 17(3): 271–81.

Li, J., Brake, G., Champion, A., Fuller, A., Gabel, S. and Hatcher–Busch, L. (2009) 'Workplace learning: the roles of knowledge accessibility and management', *The Journal of Workplace Learning* 21(4): 347–64.

Littunen, H. and Niittykangas, H. (2010) 'The rapid growth of young firms during various stages of entrepreneurship', *Journal of Small Business and Enterprise Development* 17(1): 8–31.

Macey, W.H. and Schneider, B. (2008) 'The Meaning of Employee Engagement', *Industrial and Organizational Psychology* 1(1): 3–30.

Macky, K. and Boxall, P. (2007) 'The relationship between 'high–performance work practices' and employee attitudes: an investigation of additive and interaction effects', *International Journal of Human Resource Management* 18(4): 537–67.

Mahoney–Phillips, J. and Adams, A. (2010) 'Getting the measure of HR', *Strategic HR Review* 9(1): 5–9.

Maltby, A. and Mackie, S. (2009) 'Virtual learning environments–help or hindrance for the 'disengaged' student?' *ALT–J* 17(1): 49–62.

Marsden, D. (2010) 'The Paradox of Performance–Related Pay Systems' in *Paradoxes of Modernization* (June): 185–203.

Marshall, J. and Adamic, M. (2010) 'The story is the message: shaping corporate culture', *Journal of Business Strategy* 31(2): 18–23.

Massingham, P. and Diment, K. (2009) 'Organizational commitment, knowledge management interventions, and learning organization capacity', *The Learning Organization: An International Journal* 16(2): 122–142.

Mathis, R.L. and Jackson, J.H. (2007) *Human Resource Management*, South–Western.

Mattoo, A., Subramanian, A. (2009) 'Criss–Crossing Globalization', *Research Working papers*, World Bank, (November ): 1–36.

Mauboussin, M.J. (2010) 'Surge in the Urge to Merge: M&A Trends and Analysis', *Journal of Applied Corporate Finance* 22(2): 83–93.

Maxwell, R. and Knox, S. (2009) 'Motivating employees to "live the brand": a comparative case study of employer brand attractiveness within the firm', *Journal of Marketing Management* 25(9–10): 893–907.

McCormick, K. (2007) 'Sociologists and "the Japanese model": a passing enthusiasm?' *Work Employment Society*, Dec, 21: 751–71.

McDonald, S. (2010) 'Right place, right time: serendipity and informal job matching', *Socio–Economic Review* 8(2): 307–31.

McDowall, A. and Saunders, M.N.K. (2010) 'UK managers' conceptions of employee training and development', *Journal of European Industrial Training* 34(7): 609–30.

McKinnon, R. (2010) 'An ageing workforce and strategic human resource management: Staffing challenges for social security administrations', *International Social Security Review* 63(3–4): 91–113.

McLaughlin, V. and Mott, C. (2010) 'Leadership brand equity: HR leaders' role in driving economic value', *Strategic HR Review* 9(4): 13–19.

McClintock, E.A. (2010) 'When Does Race Matter? Race, Sex, and Dating at an Elite University', *Journal of Marriage and Family* 72(1): 45–72.

Medlin, R. and Green, K.W. (2009) 'Enhancing performance through goal setting, engagement, and optimism', Source: *Industrial Management & Data Systems* 109(7): 943–56.

Melchers, K.G., Kleinmann, M., and Prinz, M.A. (2010) 'Do Assessors Have Too Much on their Plates? The Effects of Simultaneously Rating Multiple Assessment Center Candidates on Rating Quality', *International Journal of Selection and Assessment* 18(3): 329–41.

Meriac, J., Woehr, D. and Banister, C. (2010) 'Generational Differences in Work Ethic: An Examination of Measurement Equivalence Across Three Cohorts', *Journal of Business and Psychology* 25(2): 315–24.

Mitki, Y., Herstein, R. and Jaffe, E.D. (2007) 'Learning mechanisms for designing corporate identity in the banking industry' , *The International Journal of Bank Marketing* 25(7): 452–68.

Mitlacher, L.W. and Paul, C. (2009) 'Performance–based pay systems for teams: explaining the design of performance–based pay systems for teams from an expanded agency theory perspective', *International Journal of Business Performance Management* 11(3): 171–86.

Montes Rojas, G.V.and Siga, L. (2009) 'On the nature of micro–entrepreneurship: evidence from Argentina', *Applied Economics* 41(21): 2667–80.

Moroko, L. and Uncles, M.D. (2008) 'Characteristics of successful employer brands', *The Journal of Brand Management* 16(3): 160–75.

Moynihan, D.P. and Pandey, S.K. (2010) 'The Big Question for Performance Management: Why Do Managers Use Performance Information?', *Journal of Public Administration Research and Theory* 20(4): 849–866.

Mulin, C. and Reen, H. (2010) 'Arkadin develops employee talent through e-learning', *Strategic HR Review* 9(5): 11–16.

Myrna, J.W. (2009) 'Turning the tables on performance reviews: how to create a better process that empowers, energizes and rewards your employees', *Business Strategy Series* 10(6): 366–73.

Nadler, J.T., Cundiff, Nicole, L., Lowery, M.R. and Jackson, S. (2010) 'Perceptions of organizational attractiveness: The differential relationships of various work schedule flexibility programs', *Management Research Review* 33(9): 865–76.

Navigo (2010) *HR Tech Report 2010: Primary research and analysis of HR technology use in Australia*, Navigo HR Solutions and Information Management.

Nolan, C., Conway, E., Farrell, T. and Monks, K. (2010) 'Competency needs in Irish hotels: employer and graduate perspectives', *Journal of European Industrial Training* 34(5): 432–54.

Nolan, K.P. and Harold, C.M. (2010) 'Fit with what? The influence of multiple self–concept images on organizational attraction', *Journal of Occupational and Organizational Psychology* 83(3): 645–62.

Ohemeng, F. (2010) 'The dangers of internationalization and "one–size–fits–all" in public sector management: Lessons from performance management policies in Ontario and Ghana', *International Journal of Public Sector Management* 23(5): 456–78.

Panari, C., Guglielmi, D., Simbula, S. and Depolo, M. (2010) 'Can an opportunity to learn at work reduce stress?: A revisitation of the job demand–control model', *The Journal of Workplace Learning* 22(3): 166–79.

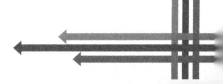

Parding, K. and Abrahamsson, L. (2010) 'Learning gaps in a learning organization: professionals' values versus management values', *The Journal of Workplace Learning* 22(5): 292–305.

Park, R., Appelbaum, E. and Kruse, D. (2010) 'Employee involvement and group incentives in manufacturing companies: a multi–level analysis', *Human Resource Management Journal* 20(3): 227–43.

Parsons, D. (2010) 'Medical–workforce planning: an art or science?: The difficult problem of matching supply and demand', *Human Resource Management International Digest* 18(5): 36–8.

Pearson, G. (2009) *The Rise and Fall of Management: a Brief History of Practice, Theory and Context*, Gower Publishing, Ltd.

Pedler, M. (2008) *Action Learning for Managers*, 2$^{nd}$ revised edition, Gower Publishing.

Pellegrini, E. K. and Scandura, T. A. (2008) 'Paternalistic Leadership: A Review and Agenda for Future Research', *Journal of Management* 34: 566–93.

Pennell, K. (2010) 'The role of flexible job descriptions in succession management', *Library Management* 31(4–5): 279–90.

Perryer, C., Jordan, C., Firns, I. and Travaglione, A. (2010) 'Predicting turnover intentions: The interactive effects of organizational commitment and perceived organizational support', *Management Research Review* 33(9): 911–923.

Preble, J. F. (2010) 'Toward a Framework for Achieving a Sustainable Globalization', *Business and Society Review* 115(3): 329–366.

Proost, K., Schreurs, B., DeWitte, K., and Derous, E. (2010) 'Ingratiation and Self–Promotion in the Selection Interview: The Effects of Using Single Tactics or a Combination of Tactics on Interviewer Judgments', *Journal of Applied Social Psychology* 40(9): 2155–69.

Prowse, P. and Prowse, J. (2009) 'The dilemma of performance appraisal', *Measuring Business Excellence* 13(4): 69–77.

Rafferty, A.E. and Restubog, S.L.D. (2010) 'The Impact of Change Process and Context on Change Reactions and Turnover During a Merger', *Journal of Management* 36: 1309–38.

Rask, M., Korsgaard, S. and Lauring, J. (2010) 'When international management meets diversity management: the case of IKEA', *European J. of International Management* 4(4): 396–416.

Rasmussen, E., Andersen, T. and Haworth, N. (2010) Has the Strategic Role and Professional Status of Human Resource Management peaked in New Zealand?', *Journal of Industrial Relations*, 52: 103–118.

Razack, S., Faremo, S., Drolet, F., Snell, L., Wiseman, J., Pickering, J. (2009) 'Multiple mini–interviews versus traditional interviews: stakeholder acceptability comparison', *Medical Education* 43(10): 993–1000.

Rittau, Y. and Dundon, A. (2010) 'The roles and functions of shop stewards in workplace partnership: Evidence from the Republic of Ireland', *Employee Relations* 32(1): 10–27.

Rizov, M. and Croucher, R. (2009) 'Human resource management and performance in European firms', *Cambridge Journal of Economics* 33(2): 253–72.

Robertson, I.T. and Cooper, C.L. (2010) 'Full engagement: the integration of employee engagement and psychological well–being', *Leadership and Organization Development Journal* 31(4): 324–36.

Robinson, D. and Hayday, S. (2009) *The Engaging Manager*, IES Report 470, November, Institute of Employment Studies.

Rogelberg, S.G., Leach, D.J. and Burnfield, J.L. (2006) '"Not another meeting": Are meeting time demands related to employee wellbeing?' *Journal of Applied Psychology,* 91(2).

Rothwell, P.J and Kazanas, H.C. (2003) *Planning and Managing Human Resources*, 2$^{nd}$ edition, Human Resource Development Press, Inc.

Russell, H., O'Connell, P.J. and McGinnity, F. (2009) 'The Impact of Flexible Working Arrangements on Work–life Conflict and Work Pressure in Ireland', *Gender, Work and Organization* 16(1): 73–97.

Rynes, S.L., Brown, K.G., and Colbert, A.E. (2002) 'Seven common misconceptions about human resource practices: Research findings versus practitioner beliefs,' *Academy of Management Executive* 16(3).

Saba, J. (2010) *The Future of Core HR: Building the Business Case for Automation and Integration*, August, Aberdeen Group.

Samaras, S. A. (2010) 'The measurement of stakeholder salience: a strategy for the exploration of stakeholder theories', International Journal of Data Analysis Techniques and Strategies 2(3): 285–306.

Sartori, R. (2010) 'Face validity in personality tests: psychometric instruments and projective techniques in comparison', *Quality and Quantity* 44(4): 749–759.

Sealy, R., Vinnicombe, S. and Doldor, E. (2009) *The Female FTSE Board Report 2009*, Cranfield School of Management.

Seijts, G.H. and Kyei-Poku, I. (2010) 'The Role of Situational Interviews in Fostering Positive Reactions to Selection Decisions', *Applied Psychology An International Review* 59(3): 431–53.

Shaw, J. (2003) 'Who built the pyramids', *Harvard Magazine*, July–August.

Sheehan, C. (2009) 'Outsourcing HRM activities in Australian organisations', *Asia Pacific Journal of Human Resources*, Aug; 47: 236–53.

Shiner, M. (2010) 'Post–Lawrence Policing in England and Wales: Guilt, Innocence and the Defence of Organizational Ego', *British Journal of Criminology* 50(5): 935–53.

Shim, S.J. and Kumar, A. (2010) 'Simulation for emergency care process reengineering in hospitals', Source: *Business Process Management Journal* 16(5): 795–805.

Sia, S.K. and Neo, B. (2008) 'Business process reengineering, empowerment and work monitoring: An empirical analysis through the Panopticon', *Business Process Management Journal* 14(5): 609–28.

Sleator, R.D. (2010) 'The evolution of eLearning Background, blends and blackboard', *Science Progress* 93(3): 319–34.

Song, J.H. and Kim, H.M. (2009) 'The integrative structure of employee commitment: The influential relations of individuals' characteristics in a supportive learning culture', *Leadership and Organization Development Journal* 30(3): 240–55.

Steensma, H. and Groeneveld, K. (2010) 'Evaluating a training using the "four levels model"', *The Journal of Workplace Learning* 22(5): 319–31.

Sulcic, V. (2010) 'The key factors for acquired knowledge through e–learning', *International Journal of Innovation and Learning* 7(3): 290–302.

Sweet, S., & Meiksins, P. (2008) *Changing contours of work: Jobs and opportunities in the new economy*, Pine Forge Press.

Tamkin, P. (2005) *The Contribution of Skills to Business Performance*, Report RW39, London, Department for Education and Skills.

Tampakoudis, I.A. (2010) 'Visiting the paradox of the upward trends of mergers and acquisitions in the USA in times of poor financial performance', *International Journal of Trade and Global Markets* 3(4): 341–58.

Tannock, S. (2008) 'The problem of education–based discrimination', *British Journal of Sociology of Education* 29(5): 439–49.

Tata, J. and Prasad, S. (2010) 'National cultural values, social capital and micro–enterprise success', *International Journal of Business Environment* 3(1): 95–119.

Thandi, H.S. and Dini, K. (2009) 'Unleashing ethnic entrepreneurship: proactive policy–making in a changing Europe' *International Journal of Business and Globalisation* 4(1):35–54.

Thiel, D. (2009) 'Dynamic modelling of labour assignment flexibility in the French fresh food industry', *Journal of the Operational Research Society* 60(5): 652–62.

Thomson, G. (2010) 'The art and science of experiential leadership: culture at the core of process change success', *Journal of Business Strategy* 31(4): 85–9.

Thomson, P. (2008) 'The business benefits of flexible working', *Strategic HR Review* 7(2): 17–22.

Thornton, W. and Thornton, S. H. (2009) 'India in Search of Itself: The Crisis and Opportunity of Indo–Globalization', *New Political Science* 31(2): 183–200.

Tomlinson, G. (2010) 'Building a culture of high employee engagement', *Strategic HR Review* 9(3): 25–31.

Toner, G.A. (2009) 'New ways of thinking about old crimes: Prosecuting corruption and organized criminal groups engaged in labor–management racketeering', *Journal of Financial Crime* 16(1): 41–59.

Toni, A.F. de and Nonino, F. (2010) 'The key roles in the informal organization: a network analysis perspective', *The Learning Organization: An International Journal* 17(1): 86–103.

Tootell, B., Blackler, M., Toulson, P., and Dewe, P. (2009) 'Metrics: HRM's Holy Grail? A New Zealand case study', *Human Resource Management Journal* 19(4): 375–392.

Truss C. (2001) 'Complexities and Controversies in Linking HRM with Organizational Outcomes', *Journal of Management Studies* 38(8, December): 1121–1149.

Truxillo, D.M., Bodner, T.E, Bertolino, M., Bauer, T.N., and Yonce, C.A. (2009) 'Effects of Explanations on Applicant Reactions: A meta–analytic review', *International Journal of Selection and Assessment* 17(4): 346–61.

Twenge, J.M., Campbell, S.M., Hoffman, B.J. and Lance, C.E. (2010) Generational 'Differences in Work Values: Leisure and Extrinsic Values Increasing, Social and Intrinsic Values Decreasing', *Journal of Management*, Sep, 36: 1117–1142.

Tyson, S. (2006) *Essentials of Human Resource Management*, Butterworth–Heinemann.

Van Ark, B. (2006) 'Europe's Productivity Gap: Catching Up or Getting Stuck?', June, *Conference Board Economic Working Paper*–EPWP #06–02.

Velde, C.R. (2010) 'Intercultural knowledge management: exploring models for repatriation competency transfer in the global workplace', *International Journal of Human Resources Development and Management* 10(4): 297–309.

Venkatasubramanian, V. (2009) 'What is Fair Pay for Executives? An Information Theoretic Analysis of Wage Distributions', *Entropy, 11*(4): 766–81.

Visser, F. and Williams, L. (2007) *Work–life balance in the public sector: rhetoric vs. reality*, Work Foundation.

Wadsworth, J. (2010*) Immigration and the UK Labour Market: The Evidence from Economic Research*, April, Paper No. CEPEA006: CEP Election Analysis, London School of Economics.

Walker, H.J., Feild, H.S.,Giles, W.F.and Bernerth, J.B.(2008) 'The interactive effects of job advertisement characteristics and applicant experience on reactions to recruitment messages', *Journal of Occupational and Organizational Psychology* 81(4): 619–38.

Wang, J., Hutchins, H.M. and Garavan, T.N. (2009) 'Exploring the Strategic Role of Human Resource Development in Organizational Crisis Management', *Human Resource Development Review*, March, 8: 22–53.

Webber, G. and Williams, C. (2008) 'Mothers in "Good" and "Bad" Part–time Jobs: Different Problems, Same Results', *Gender Society*, December, 22: 752–77.

Weibel, A., Rost, K. and Osterloh, M. (2010) 'Pay for Performance in the Public Sector Benefits and (Hidden) Costs', *Journal of Public Administration Research and Theory* 20(2): 387–412.

Whittington, J.L. and Galpin, T.J. (2010) 'The engagement factor: building a high–commitment organization in a low–commitment world', *Journal of Business Strategy* 31(5): 14–24.

Wills, J., May, J., Datta, K., Evans, Y., Herbert, J. and McIlwaine, C. (2009) 'London's Migrant Division of Labour', *European Urban and Regional Studies*, July; 16: 257–71.

Wright, C. (2008) 'Reinventing human resource management: Business partners, internal consultants and the limits to professionalization', *Human Relations*, August, 61: 1063–86.

Wright, P.M., and McMahan, G.C. (1992). 'Theoretical Perspectives for Strategic Human Resource Management', *Journal of Management*, 18, 295–320.

Wyatt, M.R.R., Pathak, S.B. and Zibarras, L.D. (2010) 'Advancing selection in an SME: Is best practice methodology applicable?', *International Small Business Journal*, June; 28: 258–73.

Yalcinalp, S. and Gulbahar, Y. (2010) 'Ontology and taxonomy design and development for personalised web–based learning systems', *British Journal of Educational Technology* 41(6, November): 883–96.

Zemanek, H. (2010) 'Competitiveness Within the Euro Area: The problem that still needs to be solved', *Economic Affairs* 30(3, October): 42–7.

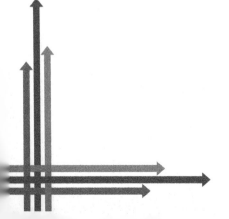

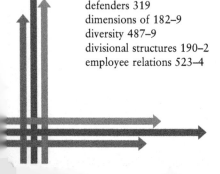

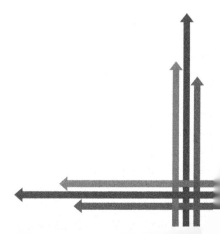

Lightning Source UK Ltd.
Milton Keynes UK
UKOW07f2254300117

293248UK00001B/1/P